Disorders of
Development
&Learning

Disorders of Development &Learning

A Practical Guide to Assessment and Management

Second edition

Mark L. Wolraich, M.D.
Director, Division of Child Development
Professor of Pediatrics
Vanderbilt University
Nashville, Tennessee

 Mosby

St. Louis Baltimore Boston Carlsbad Chicago Naples New York
Philadelphia Portland London Madrid Mexico City Singapore
Sydney Tokyo Toronto Wiesbaden

Vice President and Publisher: Anne S. Patterson
Editor: Laura DeYoung
Senior Developmental Editor: Sandra Clark Brown
Editorial Assistant: Jennifer McCartney
Project Manager: John Rogers
Senior Production Editor: Helen Hudlin
Designer: Amy Buxton
Manufacturing Supervisor: David Graybill

Printed in the United States of America
Composition by the Clarinda Company
Printing/binding by Maple Vail/York

Mosby–Year Book, Inc.
11830 Westline Industrial Drive
St. Louis, MO 63146

Library of Congress Cataloging in Publication Data

Disorders of development and learning: a practical guide to
  assessment and management / [edited by] Mark L. Wolraich. — 2nd ed.
    p.   cm.
    Rev. ed. of : Practical assessment of children with disorders of
  development and learning / [edited by] Mark L. Wolraich. c1987.
    Includes bibliographical references and index.
    ISBN 0-8151-9392-0
    1. Developmental disabilities.   2. Learning disabilities.
  I. Wolraich, Mark.   II. Practical assessment and management of
  children with disorders of development and learning.
    [DNLM: 1. Developmental Disabilities.   2. Learning Disorders.   WS
  350.6 D612 1996]
  RJ135.P73   1996
  618.92'8588—dc20
  DNLM/DLC
  for Library of Congress   96-15337
                                                                 CIP

96   97   98   99   00   /   9   8   7   6   5   4   3   2   1

Contributors

Randell C. Alexander, M.D., Ph.D.
Department of Pediatrics
The University of Iowa
Iowa City, Iowa

Anna Baumgaertel, M.D.
Assistant Professor of Pediatrics
Vanderbilt University Medical
School
Nashville, Tennessee

James A. Blackman, M.D., M.P.H.
Professor of Pediatrics
Kluge Children's Rehabilitation
Center
University of Virginia
Charlottesville, Virginia

Linda Copeland, M.D.
Alta Regional Center
Sacramento, California

Lisa Craft, M.D.
Assistant Professor of Pediatrics
Vanderbilt University Medical
School
Nashville, Tennessee

Christopher W. Fontana, Psy.D.
Clinical Neuropsychology Services
Wheaton, Illinois

Frances P. Glascoe, Ph.D.
Associate Professor of Pediatrics
Vanderbilt University Medical School
Nashville, Tennessee

Edward Goldson, M.D.
Professor, Department of Pediatrics
University of Colorado Health
Sciences Center and
The Children's Hospital
Denver, Colorado

Randi J. Hagerman, M.D.
Professor of Pediatrics
University of Colorado Health
Sciences Center
Child Development Unit
The Children's Hospital
Denver, Colorado

James C. Hardy, Ph.D.
Professor of Pediatrics
Departments of Pediatrics
and Speech Pathology and
Audiology
University of Iowa
Iowa City, Iowa

Robert A. Jacobs, M.D., M.P.H.
Director
USC University Affiliated Program
Children's Hospital Los Angeles
Professor of Pediatrics
USC School of Medicine
Los Angeles, California

Desmond P. Kelly, M.D.
Medical Director, Center for
Developmental Pediatrics
The Children's Hospital of the
Greenville Hospital System
Greenville, South Carolina

Philip J. Mattheis, M.D.
Medical Director, The Rural
Institute on Disabilities
University of Montana
Missoula, Montana

Dianne M. McBrien, M.D.
University Hospital School
University of Iowa
Iowa City, Iowa

Opal Y. Ousley, M.S.
Department of Psychology and
Human Development
Vanderbilt University
Nashville, Tennessee

Craig T. Ramey, Ph.D.
Civitan International Research
Center
The University of Alabama at
Birmingham
Birmingham, Alabama

Sharon L. Ramey, Ph.D.
Civitan International Research
Center
The University of Alabama at
Birmingham
Birmingham, Alabama

Donald K. Routh, Ph.D.
Department of Psychology
University of Miami
Coral Gables, Florida

**David Schor, M.D., M.P.H.,
F.A.A.P.**
Clinical Associate Professor of
Pediatrics
University of Nebraska Medical
Center
Lincoln, Nebraska

Terri L. Shelton, Ph.D.
Department of Psychology
Department of Human
Development and Family Studies
University of North Carolina at
Greensboro
Greensboro, North Carolina

Andrea L. Sherbondy, M.D.
Department of Pediatrics
University of Iowa
Iowa City, Iowa

Abigail B. Sivan, Ph.D.
Rush Presbyterian—St. Luke's
Medical Center
Chicago, Illinois

Wendy L. Stone, Ph.D.
Associate Professor of Pediatrics
Child Development Center
Vanderbilt University Medical
School
Nashville, Tennessee

Stuart W. Teplin, M.D.
Associate Professor of Pediatrics
Clinical Center for the Study of
Development and Learning
University of North Carolina School
of Medicine
Chapel Hill, North Carolina

J. Bruce Tomblin, Ph.D.
Professor
Department of Speech Pathology
and Audiology
University of Iowa
Iowa City, Iowa

Don C. Van Dyke, M.D.
Division of Developmental
Disabilities
Department of Pediatrics
The University of Iowa Hospitals
and Clinics
Iowa City, Iowa

J. Wade White, M.D.
Assistant Director for Clinical
Services
U.S. Naval Hospital
Yokosuka, Japan

Mark L. Wolraich, M.D.
Director, Child Development
Center
Professor of Pediatrics
Vanderbilt University Medical
School
Nashville, Tennessee

This book is dedicated to Debra, Michael, Leanne, and David, from whom I have gained most of my knowledge about normal child development and mother-child interactions.

Preface

Increasing numbers of children with disorders of development and learning constitute a significant component of the primary care clinician's practice. As major catastrophic diseases (e.g., meningitis and polio) become treatable and/or preventable, families and their primary care clinicians find themselves focusing less on life-and-death issues and more on quality of life. Because development and learning are the most important issues in the lives of children, it is not surprising that these issues should become the focus of parents' and providers' attention. Furthermore, programs, such as the Individuals with Disabilities Education Act, that address developmental problems bring these issues into even greater prominence.

Dealing with development and learning disorders in children can be a source of frustration for many primary care clinicians. First, most of the disorders are amenable to management but not to cure. At a time when rapid progress has been made in treating catastrophic illnesses, lack of parallel progress in treating development and learning disorders can lead to frustration for both parents and primary care clinicians. Second, disorders of development and learning involve a number of disciplines, including psychology, speech and language, physical and occupational therapy, and education. Many times the input from these disciplines is greater than the contribution from the medical field. For the primary care clinician, therefore, it can be frustrating not to be the main provider of services and to have to rely on other professionals, particularly if the clinician has not had an opportunity to learn what those other providers are able to do. Third, problems created by developmental and learning disorders are frequently complex. Such problems require input from a number of professionals and sorting out optimal and efficient care plans consumes a good deal of time. In many cases, insurers are not willing to compensate for prolonged care and sometimes it is difficult to determine which services should be reimbursed as medical and which as educational.

While there is little primary care clinicians can do to cure disorders of development and learning or lessen the time demands, there is something that can be done to help in understanding the nature of the problems and the various assessments and management procedures available. Understanding was the intent of the first edition of this book. However, since that edition, the field of developmental pediatrics has grown, and there are now a greater array of services available to children with developmental disabilities and to the primary care clinicians who treat them.

This second edition builds on the first and retains the basic format of that text. The first section provides information about various assessments and general management procedures. The first chapter describes theories of development and learning because any scientific method of management must be based on a theoretical system. The second chapter describes the commonly used assessment procedures of other professionals, such as psychologists and speech and language clinicians. The two other chapters in this section provide information on developmental screening and early intervention and have been significantly revised to include current information available.

The second section of this book provides specific information about the most common developmental and learning disorders likely to be seen by the primary care clinician. Chapters in this section are organized by definitions, etiologies and pathophysiologies, assessments and findings, management, and outcomes. Each of the chapters has been revised to include the most recent information, particularly for attention deficit hyperactivity disorder where new criteria have been developed by DSM-IV. Several chapters have also been added to cover the most common causes of mental retardation (i.e., Down syndrome, fragile X syndrome, and fetal alcohol syndrome). A chapter on the developmental consequences of prematurity and bronchopulmonary dysplasia has also been written.

It is my hope that primary care clinicians will find the book an improved edition from the first and useful in helping them provide better care for their patients with disorders of development and learning.

Mark L. Wolraich

Contents

PART ONE

ASSESSMENT, MANAGEMENT, AND GENERAL INTERVENTIONS

CHAPTER 1

Theories of development and learning

TERRI L. SHELTON

In understanding disorders of development, it is important to review the theories of child development. Researchers and philosophers have posited theories in an effort to understand the acquisition and expression of motor, cognitive, speech, language, and social-emotional abilities. While rarely stated explicitly, categorization and assessment of disorders of development and learning are based on assumptions derived from one or more theoretical models. Therefore a working knowledge of the various theoretical models and their limitations provides an essential framework from which to assess and categorize disorders of development.

This chapter reviews some of the major theoretical models posited to account for various aspects of development. First, the maturational model, exemplified by the developmental theory of Gesell, is presented. Next, the psychodynamic model, detailed by Freud with adaptations by Erikson, is discussed. Then the behavioral perspective or learning model, characterized by the work of Pavlov, Thorndike, Skinner, and the social learning theorists such as Bandura, is outlined. Piaget's theory of cognitive development provides an example of the organismic model, with Kohlberg's extension of this model to moral development. Finally more specific theories of language development, play, and friendships are briefly reviewed because of the importance of these areas to child development. Before presenting these theoretical models, a discussion of the general concept of *theory* itself is offered in an attempt to identify parameters along which the theories may be compared and/or evaluated.

THEORY: DEFINITION AND EVALUATION

A *theory* is a group of logically related statements (e.g., ideas, rules) used to explain past events as well as to predict future occurrences. Thus a theory has both *explanatory* and *predictive* functions. In addition, theories can be evaluated along several parameters. It has been suggested that the value of any theory rests on its ability to be stimulating, parsimonious, inclusive, precise, operational, and empirically valid with respect to both existing and predicted events.[1-4]

One means of evaluating a theory is to examine the amount of research *stimulated* or generated by the theory. In fact, some theories remain viable simply because of their controversial nature. However, in order for a theory to fulfill its explanatory and predictive functions, it needs to meet other criteria. One criterion, that of *parsimony*, implies simplicity in theorizing. Given a set of phenomena to be explained, the explanation that makes the fewest assumptions is the best. This is somewhat difficult to assess in reality, and valid theories certainly would not be discarded simply because of a lack of parsimony. Nevertheless, in an attempt to account for available data, some theories become so complicated that their usefulness is restricted.

Theories can also be compared on the basis of *inclusiveness*, that is according to the number and type of phenomena they encompass.[4] Some theories attempt to explain a great number of different events, while others focus on only a few. Therefore, in addition to inclusiveness, theories can be evaluated or compared on their *precision*. In order to evaluate a theory's precision, one should "try to use it for what it was intended . . . try to apply it to observations of people so as to understand them better . . . Or try to generate predictions concerning the behavior of particular kinds of people that have not been observed directly."[3] The precision or accuracy of any theory also will vary depending on the specific questions being addressed.

In addition to being precise, a theory should be testable or *operational*. That is, there should be a reliable method of measuring the concepts of the theory (e.g., Piaget's object permanence, behavioral concept of reinforcement). In addition, one should be able to test hypotheses generated by the theory.

Finally, a theory should be empirically *valid*. While it is important for a theory to possess the previously discussed qualities, often the crucial test of a theory is its ability to explain and predict available findings. Validity is determined not only by the adequacy of *post hoc* explanations but also by systematic tests of predictions made by the theory.

None of the developmental theories to be discussed in this chapter meets all these criteria. In addition, the relative importance of these criteria varies, depending on the focus of the theory. Nevertheless, these criteria are proposed as a framework for comparing theories. In addition to these general criteria, there are other points of comparison pertinent to a discussion of developmental theories per se. The following issues will be discussed within the context of the various developmental theories. First, what are the basic assumptions of the theory? That is, what is the view of human nature and what is said to develop? Second, what is the relative contribution of heredity vs. environment to development? Third, what are the major components or tenets of the theory? And, finally, what are the theory's strengths and weaknesses?

MATURATIONAL MODEL
Basic assumptions

One of the foremost illustrations of the maturational model is the developmental theory of Arnold Gesell. Trained as a physician, Gesell[5] proposed that the most important determinant in development is biological maturation.

> Environment . . . determines the occasion, the intensity, and the correlation of many aspects of behavior, but it does not engender the basic progressions of behavior development. These are determined by inherent, maturational mechanisms[6,p. 13]

That is, while past evolutionary developments and the present environment are viewed to have some influence, development is thought to progress through an orderly sequence that is primarily determined by biological history. Furthermore, the rate at which one progresses through this sequence is determined by heredity and may be altered only somewhat by experience. Gesell admitted that the environment may exert a more powerful influence during adolescence than during infancy. However, even during this developmental period, environmental influences do not change the basic pattern of development.

In detailing how an individual develops, Gesell did not propose a formal set of hypotheses. However, he did propose five basic principles of development that are largely influenced by Darwin's theory of evolution. These five principles are thought to characterize every child's growth pattern in motor, adaptive, language, and personal-social behavior.

Principle of developmental direction

The principle of developmental direction states that development proceeds in a systematic direction as a function of preprogrammed genetic mechanisms. Both the prenatal development of the embryo as well as other aspects of physical and motor development follow two patterns. In the first pattern, *cephalocaudal*, development proceeds from the head down. Thus arm buds appear before leg buds in the embryo, and the infant shows voluntary motor control of the head and shoulders before control of the lower limbs. In the second pattern, *proximodistal*, development proceeds from the middle of the organism (near) to the periphery (far). In embryonic development, the spinal cord develops before the arm buds. In early motor development, the infant gains control over moving the entire arm before acquiring finer control of the individual fingers.

Principle of reciprocal interweaving

The principle of reciprocal interweaving is modeled after the physiological principle of reciprocal innervations. Inhibition and excitation of different muscles operate in a complementary fashion, resulting in efficient movement. This principle is illustrated in the development of walking and handedness. For example, walking is viewed as series of alternations between flexor (bending) and extensor (extending) dominance of arms and legs in coordination. Although flexor and extensor movements can be seen as contradictory, they result in integration and progression to a greater level of mature movement.

Principle of functional asymmetry

One exception to the previous principle is the principle of functional asymmetry. This principle states that behaviors often go through a period of asymmetric development in the process of achieving maturity later on. An example of this can be found in the asymmetric tonic neck reflex. This reflex evident in early infancy results in the child's head turning in the direction of the outstretched hand, while the other hand bends in a type of fencer's pose. Gesell proposes that this reflex serves as the precursor of later symmetrical reaching. This principle is also thought to lay the groundwork for psychomotor handedness and such actions as throwing a ball.

Principle of individuating maturation

This principle describes development as a process of sequential patterning. That is, certain prerequisite physiological structures must be present in order for other development or learning to occur. For example, it is important for an infant to have a certain degree of trunk stability in order for walking to occur. Providing practice in moving the legs in a stepping fashion will not facilitate walking if the necessary physiological development is absent.

Principle of self-regulatory fluctuation

Similar to the principle of reciprocal interweaving, the principle of self-regulatory fluctuation views development as alternating periods of stability and instability. There is a distinct sequence of stages that occurs and allows the organism to function while accommodating growth.

Critique

One of Gesell's most important contributions is his detailed description of typical child development. Based on data gathered through cinematic records, Gesell and his colleagues authored three books: *The First Five Years of Life*,[6] *The Child from Five to Ten*,[7] and *Youth: Years from Ten to Sixteen*.[8] These volumes detail developmental expectations or norms for motor, personal-social, adaptive, and language behaviors during childhood. This information also forms the basis of one of the first developmental assessments, the *Gesell Developmental Schedule*. This assessment, in turn, serves as the prototype for other infant and child assessments both of typical and abnormal development.

Gesell also contributed to the advancement of research methodology through his introduction of the "co-twin control" research design. In this design, one of a pair of monozygotic twins receives early specific developmental training, while the other twin is not trained until he/she reaches the age when the specific skill in question should develop. The results of these systematic studies were interpreted as indicating that there were few differences in the speed with which skills were acquired between the twins, despite the fact that the control twin received less training. These studies further reinforced Gesell's hypothesis of the relative importance of biological factors and the invariance of the sequence of development.

Gesell's theory is highly content-specific but is fairly comprehensive in its approach. However, Gesell's treatment of all areas of development is not of uniform quality. The greatest impact and application of his approach has been in the area of motor development, with less attention paid to specific applications in the areas of emotional and social development. Nevertheless, Gesell's maturational approach continues to have great impact.

PSYCHOANALYTIC MODEL
Basic assumptions

On the basis of clinical data, Sigmund Freud constructed a general theory of development, which maintained that all biological drives have but a single goal . . . the survival and propagation of the species. Because continuation of the species is accomplished through sexual intercourse, all biological drives must ultimately serve the fundamental sex drive. The need to satisfy or gratify the sex drive influences the basic dynamic, structural, and sequential components of personality.

The *dynamic component* relates to psychic energy. The basic source of this energy is thought to be biologically based. In Freud's final theory, the two basic instincts are *Eros* (i.e., sex, self-preservation, love, life force) and the destructive instinct or *Thanatos* (i.e., aggression, hate, death). Freud assigned the term *libido* to the available energy of Eros. There is no such analogous term for the energy of the destructive instinct. While the form and distribution of this psychic energy may change, the amount of total energy remains the same.

The *structural component* of the theory describes three separate yet interdependent psychological structures—id, ego, and superego—and the way they regulate behavior. The *id* is seen as the source of the instincts and impulses. It is the primary source of psychic energy that exists at birth and uses that energy to satisfy needs through reflexive or reflex-like behaviors. The id operates on the *pleasure principle*. That is, it is not concerned with relative constraints but rather with immediate satisfaction. The energy of the id is invested in any action or is focused on any object that can provide this satisfaction. For example, Freud theorized that an infant may satisfy the hunger drive directly by sucking a nipple and receiving milk and/or indirectly by imagining the nipple or bottle. At this stage there is no distinction between fantasy and reality. This lack of distinction is termed *primary process thinking*.

The id's inability to produce the desired object on a consistent basis leads to the development of the *ego,* which is thought to develop about the age of 6 months as a mediator between the id and reality. The ego operates according to the *reality principle*. For example, the infant soon discovers that thinking something does not make it so. That is, there is a difference between image and reality. The individual then begins to achieve gratification through intention, termed *secondary process thinking.* Thus, the hungry toddler may smile and pull the parent toward food, try to open the refrigerator door, or ask for something to eat. The process by which an individual uses the ego to achieve this gratification is called *identification*.

The constant threat from the id and the environment arouses anxiety. Whenever possible the ego uses reality-oriented problem-solving skills to address this anxiety. However, when the anxiety becomes too great, Freud theorized that various defense mechanisms (e.g., repression, projection) come into play. These mechanisms control and thereby alleviate anxiety by distorting reality in some way.

The third structure, the *superego*, begins to form during early childhood and becomes a major force in personality during middle childhood. It develops as a result of the resolution of conflicts with parents, the demands the world places on the ego, and the child's experiences. The superego represents the internalization of ethical standards of the culture embodied in parental, particularly paternal, authority. The role of the superego is to strive for the ideal and to keep the id from expressing impulses in an inappropriate way. Freud described the psychic energy associated with the superego as being divided between the *ego ideal* and the *conscience*. The ego ideal represents what the child thinks is morally good, while the conscience represents those things the child thinks that the parents view as morally base. The child's personality and behavior are thought to be the result of the conflict among the id, ego, and the superego.

Although Freud believed that the sexual nature of all gratification remains constant throughout life, the forms of the gratification change with age. The *sequential* or *stage component* of the theory details an orderly series of stages in which parts of the body vary that people use to satisfy their drives. Freud believed that the way children experience the conflicts in each of these stages determines their later personality. While Freud emphasized the influence of biological drives, his theory also highlights the importance of the environment in interaction.

> The constitutional factor must await experiences before it can make itself felt; the accidental factor must have a constitutional basis in order to come into operation[9,p. 239]

Thus variations in either the environment or physical development and how well the child negotiates the various psychosexual stages can affect the resulting adult personality structure in some way.

Stages of psychosexual development

Oral stage. The first stage occurs during the first 12 to 18 months of life. The primary focus at this stage is the mouth. The mother's gratifica-

tion of the baby's need to suck and obtain nourishment is critically important. Thus, the id tries to reduce the sexual tension by encouraging the
child to suck, chew, or bite.

Anal stage. In the second and third years of life, the erogenous zone
becomes the anal area and coincides with the need to defecate. Initially,
the child has no control over this process and merely responds to this need.
However, society demands that involuntary expulsion be controlled with
toilet training. How the child handles this initial "conflict" with parents/
caretakers varies according to the age at which training begins and how
strict or relaxed the training is.

Phallic stage. The child's solutions to the conflicts of the oral and anal
stages set the tone for the phallic stage. This stage is thought to last during
the preschool period from 3 or 4 years to 5 or 6 years of age. During this
period, most of the profound psychological changes in the child's personality are thought to take place. Psychic energy becomes invested in the genital area. Stimulation in the genital area creates tension, and, if the tension
is relieved, pleasure results. The problem arises when the child directs these
sexual feelings and the resolution of sexual tension toward the parent of
the opposite sex, yielding the well-known Oedipus or Electra complex.

Freud focused much more on boys than girls in this stage because he
believed the tension and anxiety in this stage was greater for boys. Freud
believed that boys have sexual desires for their mother and do not want to
share her with the father. However, the boy fears that the father will become angry and will retaliate by castrating him. As a way of resolving this
anxiety, the boy begins to identify with the father and strives to be like him.
He is thought to repress his desire for his mother and his hostility for his
father.

Girls are thought to have similar feelings toward fathers. Freud argues
that part of this longing has to do with "penis envy." At the same time,
girls are thought to have hostile feelings toward their mother, blaming her
for bringing the girl into the world, ill equipped without a penis. Like boys,
girls repress the sexual longings and the hostility. However, because the fear
of castration is not a possibility, Freud hypothesized that the anxiety is less
intense. This less intense anxiety results in less identification with the
mother and, according to Freud, girls have a weaker conscience. The ultimate importance of this stage is the resolution of these conflicts that results in the identification with the same-sex parent and the adoption of sex
roles.

Latency. After the particularly stormy phallic stage comes the latency
stage that lasts until puberty. Energy is now devoted to acquiring cognitive

skills, assimilating cultural values, and developing affection for parents and peers of the same sex. Although sexual energy continues, it is channeled into social concerns. This stage is not as important for later personality development or organization as other stages, but it is a period of rest before the conflicts of the next stage.

Genital stage. Sexual energy that was channeled into social concerns reappears during the genital stage. Unlike the phallic stage, this energy is directed toward a peer of the opposite sex. The outcome is mature, adult sexuality with the biological goal of reproduction. Some real or fantasized forms of homosexuality are thought to occur during this stage. However, recent conceptualizations of Freudian theory interpret homosexuality as a more complex development.[10]

Critique

The greatest impact of Freud's theory and the psychoanalytic model on developmental psychology has been the emphasis on the importance of the first few years of life. Freud also highlighted the normalcy of children's sexuality, something of a taboo subject during the Victorian era. Furthermore, although the psychosexual focus is less influential today, the notion of stages of development has greatly influenced other theories.

Another contribution is Freud's impact on the treatment and study of emotional and social disorders. The importance of the unconscious, the role of defense mechanisms, and the development of the now famous technique of free association[9,10] are still present in many conceptualizations and treatment of personality disorders.

Freud's model is quite comprehensive; however, it suffers from methodological inadequacies. The technique of free association carries with it difficulties related to retrospective report and introspection. In addition, many of the terms and central hypotheses about development are untestable because they are imprecise and not directly related to observable behavior. Research that has been done has failed to support some of the basic tenets of the theory. Most notably problematic is Freud's treatment of the development of girls. Research has failed to support his contention of a less developed gender role identity or a less mature conscience among girls. In addition, many developmental theorists have criticized Freud's emphasis on childhood sexuality as the major factor in development and have decried his lack of attention to social influences or other areas of development. Freud's theory remains, however, a rich source of hypotheses for research, and its controversial nature alone has ensured it a place among developmental theories.

PSYCHOSOCIAL DEVELOPMENT MODEL: ERIKSON

An example of the impact of the Freudian or psychoanalytic model is the extension of this model to other areas of development. Most notable of these extensions is the work of Eric Erikson.[11,12] Erikson's theory of psychosocial development borrowed heavily from Freud's theory, conceptualizing the ego in the same manner. Erikson described eight stages of development, with each stage characterized by a psychosocial crisis representing a conflict between the individual and society. However, unlike Freudian theory, Erikson stressed the importance of the ego relative to other structures (e.g., id, superego) as well as the importance of *social* rather than sexual factors in personality development. In addition, Erikson viewed personality development as a process continuing throughout the life span. The various stages, age equivalents, psychosocial conflicts, and outcomes are outlined in Table 1-1.

Critique

In contrast to Freud's psychoanalytic theory, Erikson's interpretation of development has fared better because he recognized the importance of social factors in interaction with the individual. Instead of focusing on particular body parts, Erikson's stages focus on the person's relationship to

Table 1-1   Erikson's eight stages of psychosocial development

Stage (age)	Psychosocial stage	Task/crisis	Outcome
1 (birth-1 yr)	Oral-sensory	Can I trust the world?	Trust vs. distrust
2 (2-3 yr)	Muscular-anal	Can I control my own behavior?	Autonomy vs. doubt
3 (4-5 yr)	Locomotor-genital	Can I become independent of my parents and explore my limits?	Initiative vs. guilt
4 (6-11 yr)	Latency	Can I master the skills necessary to survive and adapt?	Industry vs. inferiority role
5 (12-18 yr)	Puberty	Who am I? What are my beliefs and attitudes?	Identity vs. confusion
6 (young adult)	Young adult	Can I give fully of myself to another?	Intimacy vs. isolation
7 (adult)	Adult	What can I offer future generations?	Generativity vs. stagnation
8 (maturity)	Maturity	Have I found contentment and satisfaction through life's work?	Ego-integrity vs. despair

Modified from Erikson E: *Childhood and society,* New York, 1950, Norton.

the social environment, allowing cultural influences to be incorporated into the theory more easily than into Freud's. However, while more comprehensive and applicable to a wider range of behavior than Freud's theory, Erikson's approach has been criticized as well. For example, his concepts are difficult to operationalize fully and thus difficult to put to an empirical test. This is partly because Erikson, like Freud, based his theorizing on his own experiences with life and his patients as opposed to being more scientifically based in controlled observations or empirical study. In addition, subsequent developmental theorists, such as Carol Gilligan[41a] have criticized Erikson's theory as ignoring the female perspective. Gilligan suggests that personality and social development in women takes place within the context of relationships. For example, in moral decisions, females tend to give greater consideration to the context of moral choices, focusing on human relationships. She also takes exception to Erikson's stages, which stress autonomy and separateness, and suggests that the stage of intimacy vs. isolation may in fact occur before identity vs. role confusion in women. Moreover, even the concept of identity may be based more on relational experiences as opposed to defining one's separateness as described by Erikson's stages.

BEHAVIORAL MODEL: LEARNING THEORY AND SOCIAL LEARNING THEORY

The previous theoretical perspectives of Freud and Gesell emphasize the way in which development results from a complex interaction between biological factors and the environment. While these theories acknowledge the influence of the environment, their emphasis is the underlying innate or biological components that affect the direction and rate of developmental progress. An alternative approach to these theories of development is the behavioral model. Like the psychoanalytic model, the behavioral model can take many forms. However, the basic theoretical approach is that all development adheres to the principles of learning. The theories of Pavlov and Thorndike that highlight classic conditioning, the application of Skinner's operant conditioning, and the social learning approach of Bandura exemplify some of the major applications of the behavioral model. Before presenting these specific variations, the basic assumptions of the behavioral model will be discussed.

Basic assumptions

Behavioral models of development view all development as the cumulative effect of learning. Theorists such as Sidney Bijou define learning as the "relationship in the strengthening and weakening of stimulus and response functions."[13] In addition, the amount and type of experience or developmental opportunities may accelerate or delay development. Certainly behavioral theorists do not deny the influence of biological factors. In fact, biological factors are thought to provide the general limits for the kinds of behaviors that develop. Nor do behavioral theorists ignore universal maturational sequences. For example, a child must have the ability to balance before he or she can walk. However, if basic biological needs are met (e.g., good health, adequate nutrition), development is thought to be most influenced by experience. Unlike the stage theories (e.g., Freud, Erikson, Piaget), behavioral approaches to development do not make a priori claims about the sequence or the presence of stages in development.

Classic conditioning. Pavlov's *Conditioned Reflexes*[14] detailed the behavioral approach to learning. Classic conditioning occurs when two different events occur in such a way that one of the events begins to signal or elicit the other event. This type of paradigm has been used to explain the development of certain behaviors. For example, a young child may begin to connect a frightening experience, such as a nightmare, with darkness. Over time this connection might result in a fear of the dark.

Pavlov identified two factors that may affect the strength of the relationship between the two events: reinforcement and extinction. *Reinforcement* is said to occur when the relationship between the conditioned stimulus (e.g., darkness) and the unconditioned response (e.g., fear) becomes strengthened through repeated association. Conversely, *extinction* is said to occur when the relationship is weakened such that the stimulus no longer elicits the response. For example, if the child does not experience more nightmares in the dark room, the conditioned response (i.e., fear) is likely to disappear or become extinguished.

To account for the complexity of human behaviors, Pavlov described the complementary processes of *generalization* and *differentiation*. Generalization occurs when a conditioned response (e.g., fear) becomes linked to a stimulus that is similar to the initial stimulus (e.g., any dark room). In contrast, differentiation involves the restriction of responses to certain stimuli through systematic reward and punishment. Thus, the child may learn not to be frightened in a dark theater.

Thorndike further elaborated Pavlov's theory by systematically studying how an event that follows a behavior affects the future occurrence of that behavior. This relationship was termed the *law of effect*.[15] Although Thorndike did not propose specific applications of his theory to specific developmental processes, the model has been used to explain the development of certain behaviors. For example, Thorndike addressed the development of intelligence in general. He believed that intelligence reflects the number of S-R (stimulus-response) connections an individual possesses. The number of connections is thought to be related to the provision of as many different types of experiences as possible. The model also has been applied to the development of behavioral problems. For example, aggressive children may find that aggression is satisfying because through it they may receive attention for their behavior.

Operant conditioning. Using the theoretical bases provided by the work of Pavlov, Thorndike, and others, Skinner further refined the rules and conditions that govern a relationship between a response and the events following that response. Thus the basic assumption of Skinner's theory is that behavior is a function of its consequences. The consequences of behavior, not what precedes it, affect learning. Skinner called this *operant conditioning.* Operant behaviors are those that are controlled by what follows them, not by what precedes them. In addition, operant behaviors are not elicited by a stimulus (e.g., the dark room elicits the fear response), but rather they are emitted and under the control of the organism. Thus, attention is directed toward what happens to the child after entering the darkened room (e.g., having a positive experience, such as being entertained in a theater or having a negative experience, such as being frightened by a nightmare).

Skinner's application of the behavioral model also details the factors that influence behavior. For example, a *reinforcement* is any stimulus that follows a behavior that increases the likelihood of it occurring again. A stimulus or event is not designated as a reinforcer a priori but is determined by whether its presence increases the behavior in question. Positive reinforcement is the addition of a positive event that increases the behavior (e.g., parental attention when a child has a tantrum may increase the level and number of tantrums). Negative reinforcement (not to be confused with punishment) is the withdrawal of a negative event that serves to increase behavior. For example, if a parent stops scolding (e.g., cessation of a negative event) when the child complies with a request or command, this may serve to increase the chance that the child will respond to the scolding the next time the parent scolds.

Punishment is the addition or presentation of some behavior or stimulus that decreases the behavior in question. For example, when an adult spanks a child for tantrum behavior, this should serve to decrease the probability of the behavior reoccurring. Although not as widely mentioned as punishment, the withdrawal of a positive reinforcement also serves to decrease behavior. For example, if a child earns points for good behavior but loses points for misbehavior, the *response cost* or loss of points is an example of negative punishment.

Although Pavlov's and, in particular, Skinner's work have been most closely identified with the development and extinction of behavioral problems (e.g., behavior modification), the behavioral perspective has been applied to the specific case of human development. The work of Sidney Bijou and Don Baer[16,17] offers a comprehensive treatment of the role learning plays in the developmental process. This approach puts somewhat less emphasis on the total importance of experience alone. Rather, behavior is viewed as a function of an interaction between environmental and biological factors. According to this approach, all stimuli can be classified into one of four categories. *Physical events* are those produced by humans or those that occur naturally (e.g., automobiles, rain). *Chemical events* include stimuli that act at a distance from the individual (e.g., the smell of fish). *Organismic events* are biological or maturational events (e.g., onset of puberty), and *social events* are the interaction of living organisms (e.g., children playing together). These stimulus events precipitate different behaviors and tend to occur in certain settings as a function of time, repetition, and the reinforcement and punishment principles outlined in other learning theories. When stimulus events become connected to certain responses, this process is called a *setting event*. Setting events are thought to unify a series of stimulus events that are responsible for the development of complex behaviors. Table 1-2 summarizes the relationship between a stimulus or event and the effects on behavior.

Critique

The behavioral model, particularly Skinner's application, has had a great impact on the study of how behaviors develop. Most notably, Skinner has contributed the application of the behavioral model to teaching methods and the modification of behavior. Furthermore, learning theory is perhaps the most testable of the theories presented. Terms are clearly defined and are tied to behavioral anchors, with unobservable, intervening variables kept to a minimum.

However, many have criticized the behavioral model for viewing the individual as passive and not in control of learning experiences. Another criticism raised by developmental theorists is that individuals often develop be-

Table 1-2   Effects of reinforcement and punishment on behavior

Stimulus	Effect on behavior	
	Behavior increases	*Behavior decreases*
Added	Positive reinforcement	Punishment
Withdrawn	Negative reinforcement	Response cost

haviors that were never actually exhibited and thus could not be directly reinforced or punished. In addition, while the behavioral model has been helpful in understanding the development and maintenance of behavior in general, some theorists have criticized the model for not defining how specific behaviors (e.g., motor, cognitive) are developed. Despite these shortcomings, which have been addressed by some extensions of the strict behavioral approach (e.g., Bandura and social earning theorists), the impact of the theory and the research it has generated place the behavioral model as one of the most important theoretical approaches to understanding development.

Social learning theory

Basic assumptions. One extension of the behavioral model that addresses some of its strongest criticisms is the social learning theory of Albert Bandura. Most notably, Bandura and Walters[18] have addressed the important question of how individuals learn so many things without direct or obvious reinforcement. This type of learning is thought to take place through a different process called *vicarious learning*[19] in which significant learning takes place through the process of imitation or modeling. While the concept of imitation or modeling is not defined differently in social learning theory than in other behavioral theories, the relative importance of imitation in learning is different. Social learning theorists hypothesize that vicarious or indirect reinforcement is as effective as direct reinforcement for facilitating and promoting imitation.

Social learning theory differs from other behavioral perspectives in that it places special importance on internal mediational processes. Thus, while the impetus for behavior is still thought to be environmental, the individual actively mediates the experiences with foresight or knowledge as to the consequences of the behavior. Thus there is an interaction between the individual and the environment that Bandura terms *reciprocal determinism*.[20] Applications of social learning theory to development have examined the development of aggression (e.g., effect of television violence on childhood aggression[21,22]) as well as the development of moral judgments, language, and problem-solving behaviors.[23]

Social learning theorists outline four processes that are necessary for imitation or observational learning to occur: attention, retention, motor reproduction, and motivation. An individual first must be capable of paying *attention* to the event before he or she can imitate it. *Retention* involves processes such as rehearsal and recalling the specific sequence of behavior. The third process of *motor reproduction* indicates that the learner must be capable of physically performing the behavior. Finally, the last component is some type of *motivation*. Motivation may be the direct reinforcement process mentioned in the previous theories concerning stimulus and response or it may be vicarious or indirect reinforcement. Punishment also may occur directly or indirectly. For example, a child may learn to imitate or not to imitate an older sibling's behavior, depending on how the sibling's behavior is reinforced or punished.

Critique. An important aspect of the social learning theory is its attention to situational variables and the way an individual's behavior may differ in different situations. Social learning theory also enriches other theories of cognitive development by its consideration of the social context of the development. Similar to learning theory, Bandura's approach is more testable than Freud's or Piaget's theories—even with the addition of cognitive variables. By integrating the areas of operant conditioning, reinforcement, and socialization, social learning theory addresses some of the weaknesses of learning theory while maintaining the advantages of parsimony and clearly defined terminology.

Social learning theory is not without critics, however. Developmentalists have criticized it for not providing a detailed account of cognitive development. While the theory does address simple cognitive organization and abstraction, it does not detail more complicated highly organized cognitive structures such as those found in Piaget. Furthermore, additional observational studies of the theory in operation in natural settings are needed to identify how behaviors may or may not change depending on the social context. Social learning theory has shown that the processes of imitation and modeling as well as vicarious reinforcement can guide development. The next step is to identify how these processes are tied to the specific points in development, the influence of the characteristics of the models, and the effect of the larger social context on the individual.

ORGANISMIC MODEL: PIAGET'S THEORY OF DEVELOPMENT

In examining theories developed to account for a child's acquisition and use of knowledge, researchers typically have adopted one of two approaches. One theoretical camp views variations in cognitive processes as the result of *quantitative* differences in the amount of knowledge acquired. This perspective, as exemplified by the work of Robert Gagne,[24] views development as the "cumulative effects of learning." Thus development results from learning. Learning does not result from the process of development. This type of approach is very similar to the behavioral model.

In contrast, the other theoretical perspective views variations in cognitive abilities as a function of *qualitative* differences in thinking. This family of developmental theories, often termed the *organismic model,* places increased importance on the active role that the individual plays. According to this viewpoint, development occurs in ordered, qualitatively distinct stages and is characterized by an increase in the complexity of cognitive structures acquired.

Basic assumptions

The most influential organismic theory of cognitive development is that proposed by Jean Piaget. Based on clinical observations of his own children and termed the *genetic epistemological approach,*[25] Piaget's theory stresses the active role children take in adapting to their environment. This adaptation involves two complementary processes: assimilation and accommodation. *Assimilation* is the process through which the individual incorporates new knowledge into existing cognitive frameworks or schemas. A *schema* is the primary unit of mental organization and the structure through which individuals adapt to the environment. When assimilation occurs, the schema into which the new event or experience is being assimilated expands but does not qualitatively change. For example, when a young child classifies lions, horses, cats, and other animals into the general class of "doggie," he or she is incorporating new information (e.g., a different type of animal) into a preexisting schema of four-legged furry animals.

In contrast, *accommodation* refers to the adjustment or modification of existing schemas to incorporate new knowledge or information. For example, when seeing a puzzle for the first time, a young child will probably react to it as he or she would react to other toys with which he or she has had an experience. The child may try to hit it, throw it, or mouth it. That is, the child tries to assimilate the puzzle into existing cognitive schemas. However, as the child begins to learn the special characteristics of the puzzle, he or she will display what Piaget terms accommodation. That is, the child will develop a new schema or set of actions specifically for puzzles. Thus, accommodation is the process through which changes in the child's intellectual development correspond to changes in reality. In the previous example, as the child assimilates a cat into the schema of "doggie," the child would have to modify or accommodate the schema, perhaps expanding it to the larger, more inclusive schema of "animal."

This process of assimilation and accommodation occurs continually and allows the child to reach a state of balance or *equilibration*. The term *equilibration* suggests a balance, a harmonious adjustment between at least two factors: the person's existing cognitive structures and the environment. For Piaget, "intelligence" is one particular instance of adapting to the environment and is influential in the process of achieving equilibration. Thus equilibration is the process whereby biological changes/maturation and experience/learning from the environment are integrated with social interaction, thereby allowing the individual to initiate more complex assimilation and accommodation responses.

In the very young child, the functions of assimilation and accommodation are not yet complementary but almost indistinguishable and undifferentiated from one another. This lack of differentiation corresponds to what Piaget refers to as *egocentrism*. Egocentrism is defined as the failure to differentiate between the subject and the object. It may mean difficulty taking the other's perspective in conversation or difficulty in separating reality from fantasy. Characteristic of egocentrism is the child's inability to take the perspective of another person. Thus the child "assimilates experiences from the world at large into schemas derived from his own immediate world, seeing everything in relation to himself."[26]

In the older child and adult, assimilation and accommodation occur simultaneously. While it might appear that an individual would first try to fit a new experience into an already existing structure (assimilation) and, if unsuccessful, would change the existing schema to accommodate the new experience, this is not always the case. Usually there is something familiar enough about the new experience so that it may be assimilated at the same time that the new knowledge is being accommodated.

As mentioned, organismic models emphasize the interaction of *both* biological change and the impact of the environment. While maturation is thought to be controlled by innate mechanisms, with biological factors controlling both neurological changes and sequencing of qualitative changes, the potential outcome of development can be affected by environmental factors.

Stages of development

One of the basic assumptions of Piaget's theory is that development occurs in a series of qualitatively distinct stages that are hierarchically organized such that a later stage subsumes the characteristics of the earlier stages. These stages are thought to form the basis of behavior and to affect a child in a number of ways. For example, Kohlberg[27] applied the theory to moral development. More recently, Bibace and Walsh,[28] and Nagera[29] have found that children's perceptions of illness and hospitalization follow a similar developmental sequence. While these stages are thought to follow the same invariant sequence, they do not necessarily occur at the same age for every individual.

Piaget described four stages of cognitive development: the sensorimotor stage, the preoperational stage, the concrete operational stage, and the formal operational stage. It is important to note that, although Piaget did indicate the age ranges within which each stage generally occurs, the ages listed are approximate as children vary in the ages at which they proceed through the stages.

Sensorimotor stage (birth to 2 years). This stage begins with the simple reflexes of the neonate and ends at approximately 2 years of age with the onset of symbolic thought representing early language. During this stage, the child's interactions with the environment are on an action level and involve sensory and motor movements. Within this stage of development, Piaget noted six substages of qualitatively different developmental behaviors.

Substage 1: early reflex reactions (birth to 1 month). The first substage involves the modification of early reflexes. These initially random reflexes begin to be strengthened, generalized, and differentiated. However, the child cannot differentiate people from objects. During this stage, the child becomes more adaptive in handling the increasing demands of the environment.

Substage 2: primary circular reactions (1 to 4 months). The infant's behavior now becomes characterized by what Piaget calls circular reactions. A circular reaction is the repetition of a sensorimotor behavior (e.g., sucking) with the purpose of modifying existing schemas. These reactions are viewed as "primary" because the infant's focus is on its own body rather than on external objects. While actions are still not goal directed and learning is largely trial-and-error, the child begins to develop some notion of causality. An example of a primary circular reaction would be thumbsucking. Before this stage, thumbsucking was a reflex; now it is a systematic, coordinated behavior. Some pseudo-imitation may be present as when an adult mimicking an infant's facial expression may cause the infant to repeat or intensify the expression. However, the ability to imitate novel behaviors does not occur until substage 4.

Substage 3: secondary circular reactions (4 to 8 months). During this substage, the child's actions are oriented to the external world. Primary circular reactions begin to be generalized, and the infant will repeat an action for the purpose of watching the consequence. Although still not goal-directed behavior, "the accomplishments of this stage . . . constitute the first definite steps toward intentionality or goal orientation."[30] An example of this type of behavior is the infant's interest in using toys or objects for the purpose of sound production (e.g., shaking a rattle). During substage 3, infants will imitate familiar responses if they can see or hear themselves performing the response and if the behavior is within their repertoire.

Another hallmark of this stage is the beginning of coordination between various sensory modalities. For example, the child begins to look, reach for, and obtain an object through eye-hand coordination. The refinement of cross-modality coordination continues throughout the sensorimotor period.

Substage 4: coordination of secondary schemas (8 to 12 months). In contrast to earlier stages, during substage 4 infants are able to apply schemas not only in original contexts but in new situations as well. True intentionality and knowledge of cause-and-effect relationships are also established. The infant knows what he or she wants and can use his or her skills to achieve a goal. Also characteristic of this stage is the infant's realization that objects in the environment are clearly separate from the self. That is, object permanence develops as the child becomes aware that if something is removed from the visual field, it does not cease to exist.

One example of how the child's behavior can be influenced by the acquisition of the concept of object permanence is the development of stranger anxiety. One hypothesis suggests that once the child can keep the caretaker in mind even when the caretaker has disappeared from view, the child is able to detect the discrepancy between the known (e.g., caretaker) and the unknown (e.g., stranger), thus producing a stage of anxiety.

The emergence of the concept of object permanence also influences imitation. The infant is able not only to imitate simple novel responses but also those responses that he or she cannot see or hear himself or herself perform. However, the behavior to be imitated must be similar to the child's spontaneous actions.

Substage 5: tertiary circular reactions (12 to 18 months). The child now uses new means to solve new problems as opposed to implementing old schemas. Whereas primary circular reactions are centered on the child's body and secondary circular reactions are focused on objects, tertiary circular reactions are focused on the relationship between the two. The infant is able to combine actions to imitate behaviors that are more distinct than his or her spontaneous actions. This is also a time of great exploration with children acting almost as "little scientists" through trial-and-error experimentation. Piaget described children at this age as experimenting in order to find out about the nature of objects. Despite these advances, infants of this age are still tied to their immediate physical environment and are not able to imagine actions and probable consequences, a process which comes only with the advent of representational thought in substage 6.

Substage 6: emergence of representational thought (18 to 24 months). The hallmark of this substage is that the child begins to represent events mentally and think about objects that are not present. For this reason Piaget refers to this period as the stage of representational intelligence.[31] Before this stage, the child had to experiment or problem solve overtly on a "present" world. Now external exploration can be completed mentally by the child "re-presenting" the world. For example, when completing a puzzle board, the child before substage 6 would place puzzle pieces in a trial-and-error fashion, sliding the piece over the board until it dropped into place. In contrast, the child in substage 6 is able to look at the puzzle piece and board, construct a mental representation of the piece and of its place in the puzzle, and then place the piece correctly without having touched the board. In addition, the concept of object permanence is now fully developed, as evidenced by the child's ability to search for an object that has been hidden in several places in sequence.

The capacity of mental representation affects the infant's imitative capabilities as well. For example, when confronted with a new model to imitate, the infant no longer needs to perform a series of trials but carries out various movements mentally before overtly carrying out the correct action. This substage also marks the point at which *deferred imitation* evolves. That is, the observed behavior is not imitated immediately but is spontaneously reproduced at some later point. Representational thought also sets the stage for pretend play.

Influence of substages on behavior. An example of how different stages of thought influence the infant's behavior can be traced in the development of object permanence. In substage 1, the infant's reactions are evoked only by immediate sensory events. Infants do not search for objects that are out of sight. Thus, if an infant hears a sound, he or she may stop sucking to listen. However, when the sound ceases, the infant no longer shows awareness. In substage 2, the infant becomes increasingly aware that something produced the sound and, toward the end of this stage, will begin to search for the sound, although in a rudimentary way. In substage 3, the infant demonstrates visual anticipation of future positions of objects. For example, if a toy falls from a child's high chair, the infant is able to look at the floor, anticipating its final resting place. However, the infant attempts to rediscover the object merely by prolonging or repeating the actions that were ongoing when the object disappeared.

By substage 4, the infant tries to find the object by active search. For example, the infant is able to remove a cup to obtain an object hidden underneath. However, if the object was then hidden under one of two cups, the infant would continue to search in the initial hiding place.

In substage 5, the infant now searches for an object in the place where it was last seen, even if the object disappears successively in a number of places. At this stage, however, the infant can understand only visible movements. It is not until substage 6 that the infant can reconstruct correctly a series of invisible displacements. For example, if a pencil is hidden in a hand, and the hand is moved behind three screens, leaving the pencil behind the last screen, the infant in substage 6 looks under the third screen, having formed a mental representation of the pencil.

Preoperational stage (2 to 7 years). The emergence of representational thought at the end of substage 6 provides the basis for the preoperational stage. Whereas the sensorimotor stage is one of direct exploration using the senses and motor abilities, during the preoperational stage, children are concerned with trying to make sense of their world. Unlike the next stage, however, they may make errors in reasoning because they are not yet capable of true mental operations and do not engage in cause-and-effect reasoning like older children and adults.

Piaget subdivides this stage as well. The first two years, from 2 to 4 years of age, has been referred to as the *preconceptual substage*. During this period, the child is now able to engage in *semiotic functions*. Semiotic function is the ability to use one thing to stand for or represent another. Or as Piaget states, a *signifier* evokes a *significate*. Words, gestures, and mental images serve as signifiers. For example, a 4-year-old can pretend that a cardboard box is a car. Because of this ability, children engage in more imaginative play. The later part of the preoperational stage is referred to as the *intuitive substage*, corresponding to 4 to 7 years. During these years, the child begins to reason intuitively but is still tied to the concrete, the here and now that produces errors in reasoning.

While the use of language and symbols represents an advance from sensorimotor thought, children in the preoperational stage continue to make errors in thinking as they begin to try and make sense of their world. The main characteristics of preoperational thought are rigidity, egocentrism, semilogical reasoning, and limited social cognition.

Rigidity of thought. Piaget proposed that thought during the preoperational stage was rigid or lacked flexibility. This aspect is illustrated by centration. *Centration* is the tendency to focus on one salient feature and ignore other features, even when this leads to illogical conclusions. For example, one child may complain bitterly when his friend is given the same amount of juice in a tall, thin glass that he has only a short, wide class. Because of centration, the child focuses only on the dimension of height and ignores the dimension of width, thereby concluding that his friend received more juice. It is not until the concrete operational stage of middle childhood that the child will understand the concept. Thus it is easier to pour the juice into two equally shaped glasses than to try and reason with the child that he or she was not slighted.

Another example of this rigidity is that preschool children are often confused by appearance and reality. They do not realize that an object can change its appearance without changing its basic nature or identity. For example, children act as if a Halloween mask actually changes the identity of the person wearing it. This aspect may explain why a child will become upset if a parent changes a hairstyle or shaves a beard. In the child's mind, the parent may have actually changed.

Egocentrism. Another hallmark of this age according to Piaget is *egocentrism.* The inability to center on more than one aspect of a situation at a time forms the basis of egocentrism. This does not imply that the child is selfish. Rather, it reflects the tendency to consider the world entirely in terms of the child's (or ego's) point of view, that is, to center on oneself. For example, when talking on the phone to an adult, preoperational children may nod or shake their head in answer to questions, not considering that the adult on the other end of the phone cannot see their response. Piaget also thought that egocentrism was reflected in the speech of preschoolers. Children at this age tend to engage in "collective monologues" rather than true dialogues when they play together. The child "feels no desire to influence his hearer nor to tell him anything; not unlike a certain type of drawing room conversation where everyone talks about himself and no one listens."[32]

Semilogical reasoning. Children in this stage tend to try and explain events using semilogical reasoning. This is reflected in what Piaget termed *transductive thinking.* Rather than using inductive (from the specific to the general) or deductive (from the general to the specific) thinking, the child at this stage of thought reasons from the specific or particular to the specific/particular. That is, events that occur at the same time are thought to be causally related. For example, the child may assume that she caused her brother's illness because earlier that day she and her brother had fought and, as a result, she had wished for something bad to happen to him.

Another example of semilogical thinking is *animism.* During the preschool years, children often attribute human characteristics and actions to inanimate objects (e.g., the sidewalk made me fall). They try to explain mysterious events in terms of their own personal experience.

Limited social cognition. The preschooler's egocentrism and use of collective monologue illustrate his or her relatively limited role-taking ability. It is also illustrated in the child's moral judgments. At this age, a child judges the wrongness of an act according to external variables, such as how much damage occurred. The child is less likely to consider internal variables, such as the person's intentions.

Concrete operational stage (7 to 12 years). It is during this stage that the child develops a set of cognitive skills or *operations* that involve the use of symbols to represent concrete objects. In Piaget's terms, operations are internalized mental actions that fit into a logical system. Children in this stage become capable of combining, separating, ordering, and transforming objects in their minds. In describing this stage, one can compare the child's more advanced thinking with the preoperational child's thinking in regard to flexibility of thought, declining egocentrism, logical reasoning, and more advanced social cognition.

Flexibility of thought. Flexibility of thought is illustrated by *decentration* and *reversibility.* Children are now capable of focusing on more than one aspect at a time. They are also able to reverse operations mentally. They realize that certain operations can negate or reverse the effects of others. These two advances enable the child to solve the *conservation* tasks. Children understand that certain properties of an object will remain the same even when other, superficial ones are altered. Thus, the child realizes that the water in the taller, thinner container can be returned in the same amount to the shorter, wider container. This ability also aids in the child beginning to understand subtraction as the reversal of addition and how division is related to multiplication. In addition, unlike the preschool child, children in this age also understand that an object's *identity* remains unchanged despite physical changes as long as nothing has been added or subtracted.

Declining egocentrism. With the advent of decentration comes declining egocentrism. The concrete operational child is now a sociocentric being who is more aware of another's perspective. Children can communicate more effectively about objects a listener cannot see and are better able to adjust their speech to the needs of the listener. Children can think about how others perceive them (social perspective-taking). They also can understand that a person can feel one way and act another.

Logical reasoning. In addition to all the advances in reasoning that come with decentration, children in the concrete operational stage have a better understanding of temporal and spatial relations. They are also less likely to use transductive reasoning and are better able to reason about the causality of events. Another way their logical reasoning is reflected is in their ability to create categories and logically classify objects. This ability is often reflected in children's growing interest in acquiring collections (e.g., baseball cards, rocks, dolls).

Greater social cognition. In addition to growing decentrism, children also are better able to regulate their interaction with each other through rules. They begin to play rule-based games. In moral judgments, they are more able to take intentions into account when making judgments of "good" and "bad" behavior.

Formal operational stage (12 years to adult). Although children in the concrete operational stage show great advances, their thinking is still limited to the here and now—the "concrete." With the advent of the formal operational period, the individual is able to think abstractly and to engage in hypothetico-deductive reasoning (e.g., given a premise, he or she can logically deduce the conclusion). In contrast to the child of the previous stage, the formal operational adolescent/adult is able to think in terms of *what may be* rather than being limited to *what is.* This ability allows the individual to consider many different solutions to a problem before acting on any one.

This stage of thought influences previous conceptions of events and issues. For example, on reaching the formal operational stage, the adolescent begins to adopt a physiologically based conception of illness. There is also an increased understanding of varying degrees of illness as well as personal control over the onset and severity of illness.

Early in this stage, the adolescent demonstrates a renewed egocentrism, resulting from a lack of differentiation between one's own thoughts and what others are thinking. This type of egocentrism is reflected in the self-consciousness and self-criticism that is characteristic of early adolescence. However, as time goes on, the older adolescent and the young adult take into account how others judge them, how they judge the judgment processes of others, and how all this corresponds to social categories in the culture. These newly mastered "operations" are applied to larger issues. Adolescents and adults are able to think about politics and law in terms of abstract principles and are capable of seeing the beneficial, rather than just the punitive, side of laws.

Critique

Strengths. Piagetian theory transformed the field of developmental psychology. Piaget was one of the first to highlight that the child is an *active* participant in learning rather than a passive recipient of experiences. The importance of the child's active participation in conjunction with biological/genetic variables has reconciled many of the arguments of the nature/nurture controversy. In so doing, the integrative role of his theory is evident.

Piaget's early work provided justification for the role of carefully documented observation in research. His detailed descriptions of children's play, their answers to questions, and their attempts to make sense out of the world provided one of the first detailed glimpses into the thought of the child. In describing children's thought processes, Piaget highlighted the central role of cognition in development and in behavior and the inherent capabilities of children's thought, even at young ages.

One has only to examine the index of any developmental text to see the enormous impact Piagetian theory has had on subsequent research. This ongoing research, some of which has highlighted some weaknesses in the original theory, has spawned another group of researchers who call themselves "neoPiagetians." These researchers continue to investigate the basic elements of Piaget's theory (e.g., the active construction of stages, sequences, and structural change) while reconciling some of the research findings that could not be accounted for by the original theory.

Weaknesses. The broad scope of Piaget's theory represents a potential weakness. While Piaget's theory was intended to be applied to development in general, its tenets have been most usefully applied primarily to cognitive development. Its utility in explaining social and emotional development and learning is less apparent.

While the rich description of children's behavior represents a contribution to the field, the theory has been criticized on other methodological grounds. Piaget's clinical method of observing his own children may have contributed to biases in the theory as well as to the lack of systematic control over the environment. In particular, Piaget gave little attention to the influence of sociocultural or historical factors.

Subsequent studies question the validity of Piaget's stages both in terms of whether a stage model is wrong or if his detailing is merely incomplete. Flavell and others[32] have suggested that stagelike, qualitative changes may in fact be related to more gradual, quantitative sorts of developmental changes such as increasing attentional capacity. Concepts within a stage may begin at the same time but complete at different times, having a good deal of or little temporal overlap. In fact, Piaget himself acknowledged this possibility by referring to *horizontal decalages*. This occurs when a general concept emerges earlier on some tasks than others. Another modification suggested has been to look for stagelike changes in a particular content area. Thus, these stages may be domain-specific, a concept that has been more actively explored by neoPiagetians.

Another criticism of Piaget's theory relates to the age ranges thought to accompany the stages. Subsequent research reveals that there is considerable variability in the age at which children acquire certain skills. Earlier experiences, the way in which a question is asked, and the importance of the issue all seem to influence the age at which children acquire certain cognitive structures. For example, preschoolers may be less egocentric than once thought. These young children do adapt their speech when speaking with young children, often employing "motherese" or child-directed language. This is especially true when the child has a younger sibling.

Finally, the original theory has been criticized for not providing enough detail as to how the elaborate system of cognitive structures is translated into behavior. However, neoPiagetians such as Flavell,[33] Case,[34] and others have explored specific ways that performance variables or processing capacities such as memory, attention, and encoding affect behavior.[35-37] However, despite its drawbacks, Piagetian theory, as an example of the organismic model, has provided a productive theory as well as a framework for future study and interpretation of cognitive development.

KOHLBERG'S THEORY OF MORAL DEVELOPMENT
Basic assumptions

Kohlberg,[38] like Piaget, developed a theory of moral reasoning based on the principle of cognitive maturation and qualitatively different stages of development. These stages are thought to occur in an invariant sequence with the successful resolution of one stage necessary for passage to the next, more cognitive complex stage. In order to determine an individual's level of moral development and to assign approximate age ranges to the various levels, Kohlberg designed a research paradigm in which the individual is presented with a moral dilemma and is asked to evaluate and resolve the conflict. As a result of Kohlberg's research, he theorized that there are three basic levels in the development of moral reasoning, with each level containing two substages.

Children at the *preconventional level* of morality depend on the standards of older authority figures. In substage 1 (heteronomous morality), corresponding to the end of the preschool period, children do not consider the interests of others or recognize that these interests differ from their view. Actions are considered in physical terms rather than being based on the psychological interests of others. Avoidance of punishment is the primary motivation, and the rightness or wrongness of an action is based on its objective outcome, or on how authorities respond. In substage 2 (individualism, instrumental purpose, exchange), which usually appears around 7 or 8 years, children become more aware that all people have their own interests to pursue and that these interests may conflict with one another. Following the rules is based on reward, to serve one's own needs, and is determined by what's fair, what's an equal exchange. Kohlberg refers to this stage as "instrumental morality."

During the second level, the *conventional level,* adolescents begin to appreciate the moral codes of society. Shared agreements are more important than individual self-interest. Adolescents live under rules set by adults but adopt the rules as their own. In addition, Kohlberg believed that this level depends in part on the ability to engage in formal operational reasoning because it requires considering several points of view at the same time. In substage 3 (mutual interpersonal expectations, relationships, and interpersonal conformity), adolescents become more aware of shared feelings and that "being good" is important. It includes living up to what is expected by people close to you and a basic belief in the Golden Rule. Substage 4 (social system and conscience) is similar to substage 3 except there is a shift from relationships between individuals to relationships between the individual and the group. Laws are to be upheld to avoid the breakdown of the system. This stage is often referred to as the law-and-order stage.

The final level, *postconventional morality,* requires that persons go beyond social conventions to consider more abstract principles of right and wrong. An individual at this stage recognizes that society's rules may not always be the best in certain instances, and at times one may need to violate them. Morality, thus, is self-generated. Because this level depends on a sophisticated conception of right and wrong, Kohlberg felt that many adults never reached this stage of moral development. In substage 5 (social contract or utility and individual rights), the adult considers moral and legal points of view, recognizing that they sometimes conflict and it may be difficult to integrate them. This substage represents a continuation of earlier substages in terms of decreasing egocentrism and a greater awareness of the individual differences in values and opinions. Laws should be based on the rational consideration of "the greatest good for the greatest number." The last substage, substage 6 (universal ethical principles), is rarely attained by adults. Adults at this substage are thought to follow self-chosen ethical principles. Most laws and social agreements are usually valid because they rest on such principles. However, when laws violate these universal principles (e.g., justice, quality of human rights, respect for the dignity of human beings as individual persons), one acts in accordance with the principle.

Critique

Kohlberg offered one of the first theories of moral development and inspired a great deal of research. While his method has been criticized, his research paradigm of presenting moral dilemmas provided one way of operationalizing an extremely abstract concept of "morality."

Despite its appeal, some of the basic tenets of Kohlberg's theory have not been universally supported by research. Some studies have supported the correspondence between moral reasoning and cognitive development, but others have not.[39,40] Some studies have found that individuals may regress in their development or may skip stages altogether.[41] Another question concerns the degree to which verbal responses about moral dilemmas are related to actual moral behavior. Cultural, situational, and sex differences in moral behavior have yet to be fully understood. Nevertheless, like Piaget's theory, Kohlberg's view of moral development has provided an important starting point for considering this area of child development.

THEORIES OF LANGUAGE DEVELOPMENT

As with the other areas that have been discussed, there has been a good deal of attention directed toward how an individual develops language. Some of the theories involve the application of broader theories (e.g., learning) to explain how children acquire the ability to understand language and to express meanings and thoughts. In contrast, other theories have been developed specifically to explain the process of language development alone. The theories can be roughly divided into three main groups: (1) those that posit that language develops from conditioned learning or imitation (nature), (2) those that highlight the primary role of genetic or biological factors (nurture), and (3) those that emphasize an interactionist approach that recognizes both the role of nature and nurture.

Learning theory

Basic assumptions. Learning theorists[42,43] have attempted to account for language acquisition in terms of the basic tenets of learning theory. Just like the development of other behaviors, language depends on imitation and on learning by association through the mechanisms of classical and operant conditioning.

Classical conditioning assumes that language learning occurs through the pairing of an unknown word with a known concept. With frequent pairings the child begins to learn the meaning of the word. Thus, if the parent always uses the label "bottle" as the child is drinking milk, the child eventually comes to understand that "bottle" is a container for milk or some other liquid. Learning theorists use classical conditioning to account for *understanding* word meanings.

To account for the child's ability to *produce* language, learning theorists use operant conditioning. Skinner's *Verbal Behavior*[42] is one of the most famous descriptions of this type of language acquisition. Skinner hypothesized that language, like any other behavior, is learned through systematic reinforcement and punishment. Infants are thought to utter sound spontaneously, and it is through the reactions of parents and others that language develops. For example, parents may smile or pay more attention to infants when they use sounds resembling words such as "Daddy," "Mommy," or "bottle" and give less attention when infants emit nonsense syllables in the presence of parents or the bottle. Parents are also thought to shape verbal utterances because they are supposedly more attentive to correct sounds and grammatical structures than to incorrect ones. "Thus more and more precise . . . speech responses may be gradually shaped up through successive approximation until the child readily emits the speech units involved in everyday language; in other words, the family acquires a repertoire of correct speech responses."[43]

In addition to learning to emit certain sounds, the child must learn to connect these sounds or words to the proper object or person. Skinner describes this as a process in which the verbal behavior comes under environmental stimulus control. For example, when the child first says "Daddy" or an approximation of the word, he or she is likely to be rewarded, whether or not the child's father is present. However, when the word "Daddy" is uttered in response to any adult, it is not under stimulus control. After a time, the child becomes differentially reinforced to utter "Daddy" only in the presence of the "stimulus," that is, the father.

An extension of the basic learning theory is the social learning theory, which recognizes the role of imitation and vicarious reinforcement. The child's utterances do not have to be directly reinforced. Rather, this approach posits that the child can learn language through the observation and imitation of a model's behavior (e.g., parents, older siblings).

Critique. Learning theories, including classical and operant conditioning and imitation, clearly play a role in the acquisition of word meanings.

These theories, however, do not account for several aspects of a child's language development.

First, learning theory does not explain the development of the more complicated aspects of language, such as syntax. Adults do not necessarily reinforce children specifically for the correctness of grammatical structures.[44] They are more likely to correct errors in the content of their speech. Yet, children do learn the structure of their language.

Second, the rapid rate at which children acquire language is not easily explained by the mechanisms of learning theory. It would be impossible for children to acquire the number of words and structures in the time observed if each acquisition had to follow the process outlined by Skinner and others.

Finally, children often understand and express novel words or sentences. The use of grammatical forms they have never heard to express new ideas does not conform to the basic tenets of imitation. Furthermore, children may use a grammatical morpheme correctly the first time they say it and then go through a period of incorrect usage before returning to the correct form. For example, a 2-year-old may use the correct plural of "hand" as "hands." After months of using the correct form, children may go through a period in which they say "handses" before returning to "hands." Because children would not have heard "handses," it is difficult to explain why this form would appear.

Nativist theories

Basic assumptions. Unlike learning theories, nativist theories hypothesize that innate biological mechanisms account for the acquisition of language. The most influential of these theories of development is that of Noam Chomsky. In 1957, Chomsky published *Syntactic Structures*,[45] in which he proposed that all children have a sense of grammar from birth. This innate sense, which he termed *language acquisition devices (LAD)*, involves hypothetical mental structures thought to allow children to process the language they hear, to internalize the linguistic rules of their culture, and to construct appropriate communications. According to Chomsky, all language has two structures—surface and deep. Surface structure refers to the words that make up a sentence and the organization of the words, while deep structure refers to the underlying meaning of a sentence. Using certain rules, called transformational grammar, the child changes the deep structure (e.g., meaning) into a surface structure or grammatical sentence.

Critique. Several aspects of language development support Chomsky's theory.[46] First, the fact that children are apparently preprogrammed to process language through these transformational rules accounts for the production and understanding of novel structures. In addition, the similarity between the babbling of infants across cultures cannot be accounted for by learning theories and argues for some type of universal innate mechanism for language present from birth. Nevertheless, the theory does not account for why children in the United States grow up speaking English while children in China grow up speaking Chinese. The learning theories are better able to account for why individuals can learn the grammatical structures of whatever language they are exposed to.

Interactionist theories

Basic assumptions. Interactionist theories represent a compromise approach that views children's language development as reflecting the interaction of both nurture or environmental factors as well as innate biological structures. The exact mechanism of this interaction differs among theorists. One example of this approach is the work by Bruner.[47] Bruner used the term *language acquisition support system (LASS)*. He recognized a certain amount of preprogramming related to biological mechanisms. However, he also identified a role for cultural factors where the social environment is organized to incorporate the child (probably through learning mechanisms) as a member of an already existing language-using group. Thus children acquire the syntax and grammatical structures of their particular culture but do not necessarily have to be reinforced or to imitate all language in order to acquire these structures. Interactionist theories, therefore, seem best able to account for the existing research on developmental trends as well as individual differences.

OTHER ASPECTS OF DEVELOPMENT

While the previous theories are extremely broad based and represent milestones in the development of our understanding of children, there are number of recent theories that focus on more narrow aspects of child development. Space prohibits a thorough presentation of these theories, but two important aspects of child development will be discussed briefly. One relates to the development of self; the other, to the development of play and friendships.

Developmental model of self-concept

While many of the theories presented earlier in this chapter address some factors responsible for the development of the concept of self (e.g.,

Erikson's concept of increasing autonomy and initiative), other theories have attempted to examine the child's concept. One of the first aspects in the development of self is the child's ability to recognize himself or herself. Based on inferences drawn from the child's facial expression, most children can recognize their reflection or a picture or themselves around 18 months. The onset of the "terrible twos," coinciding with Erikson's stages of autonomy and individuation, and the increased recognition of adult standards around the ages of 2 and 3 reflect a budding sense of self.

Damon and Hart[48] explored this concept more thoroughly by interviewing children, ranging in age from preschool to adolescence. Damon and Hart report that all children refer to their appearance, their activities, their relations to others, and their psychological characteristics when they describe themselves. However, the relative weight of these characteristics changes over time. As can be seen in Table 1-3, younger children tend to describe themselves primarily in terms of the activities they engage in and to some extent their physical characteristics. This represents a type of *categorical* classification. As children enter into middle childhood, *comparative assessments* take on greater importance. In adolescence, these comparisons take on greater *interpersonal implications,* and descriptions shift from relatively concrete attributes to more inclusive, psychological variables. Another feature of the adolescent's concept of the self is the increased variety of attributes used in self-description. According to Susan Harter[49] and others who study the development of self-concept, younger children

Table 1-3   Developmental model of self-concept

Level	Physical characteristics	Activity-based characteristics	Social characteristics	Psychological characteristics
Categorical identification (4-7 years)	I have brown hair.	I play soccer.	I'm Tyler's sister.	I'm happy.
Comparative assessments (8-11 years)	I'm taller than everyone else in my class.	I'm good at math.	I do well in sports because my Dad practices with me.	I'm shy.
Interpersonal implications (12-15 years)	I am too heavy and because of that people make fun of me.	I play sports and that helps me to meet new friends.	I'm funny so I have a lot of friends.	I understand people, so they like to come to me for support.

From Damon W, Hart D: *Self-understanding in childhood and adolescence,* Cambridge, 1988, Cambridge University Press.

describe themselves in terms of either their cognitive, physical, and social competence or a global notion of self-worth. Adolescents include athletic, scholastic, and job competence but also social acceptance, romantic appeal, conduct, etc. Adolescents also tailor their descriptions of themselves to the particular context, representing what Harter describes as "multiple selves."

Concepts of play

Play can be viewed from at least two different aspects. The first relates to the degree to which play is either social or nonsocial. The second relates to the type of cognitive activity that is involved. While most of the developmental changes in play occur within the relatively narrow age range of early childhood, the importance of play in child development warrants at least a brief mention of these theories of play.

Social play. In one of the earliest studies on play, Parten[50] identified six types of play, ranging from the most nonsocial to the most social. Younger preschoolers were thought to engage more in nonsocial play while older preschoolers spent relatively more time in social interaction.

The first stage Parten described was *nonsocial activity.* In this stage, children might be engaged in what Parten termed *unoccupied behavior,* where the child does not seem to be playing but watches anything of momentary interest. The child may also demonstrate *onlooker behavior,* watching other children play. The child might talk or ask questions about the play but does not enter in. Onlooker behavior is distinguished from unoccupied play in that the child is definitely focused on the play, not just what happens to be exciting. A third type of nonsocial activity described is *solitary independent play.* In this type of play, the child plays alone with toys that are different from those used by nearby children and makes no effort to get close to the children or to interact.

The second stage in the progression to social play is termed *parallel play.* This is a type of limited social participation. Here the child plays near other children with similar materials but does not necessarily play with the children or play with the materials in the same way. He or she plays beside the others rather than with them. Furthermore, there is no attempt to influence the content or style of play of the others.

The most sophisticated play is the third stage or true *social play.* The first form is *associative play,* which is a more advanced type of interaction in behavior. The child truly plays with other children. They talk about their play, borrow and lend toys, and try to control who may play in the group. However, there is no division of labor and no organization around a joint goal. The children are more interested in being around the other children than in the activity itself. The second form is *cooperative play*. Here the children do share an organized goal—to make something, play a formal game, or dramatize a situation. There is a division of labor and roles as children act out a make-believe theme or work on the same project (e.g., building a castle).

While Parten concluded that these stages formed a developmental sequence in which later appearing stages replace earlier ones, recent research suggests that these forms may coexist throughout the preschool years. Nonsocial activity does decline with age but can take up as much as a third of children's free play time even among kindergartners. Solitary and parallel play remain fairly stable from 3 to 6 years, with a slight increase in cooperative play in older kindergartners.

Type of play. What does seem to distinguish the play of older and younger children is the cognitive content of the play. Rubin and colleagues,[51] similar to Piaget and Smilansky[52] identified a developmental progression in this aspect of play. For example, 1- and 2-year-olds are most likely to engage in *functional play*, also called *sensorimotor play*. This is defined as simple, repetitive motor movements with or without objects. For example, the child might run around a room, knead playdough, or bang a Duplo or Lego. In the preschool years, however, ages 3 to 6, children spend more of their time in *constructive play*. Here the goal is to create or construct something. The child becomes more interested in putting together a puzzle or building something out of Duplos rather than simply banging the puzzle or the building pieces. This is sometimes referred to as *practice* or *mastery play* because of the repetition of behavior that enables skills to be coordinated and practiced.

Around the same time (3 to 7 years), children also show an increase in *make-believe play*. Here, children act out everyday and imaginary roles. Playing house or acting out scenes on television with objects that have been built with Legos characterizes this type of play. Finally, in middle childhood (6 to 11 years), children become more interested in *games with rules*.

Friendships

While developmental theories of play certainly impact on the development of friendships, other researchers, such as Selman,[53,54] have specifically examined friendships in greater detail. According to Selman, there is a developmental progression in the child's ability to take the perspective of others and the quality of the friendships developed. This developmental perspective-taking closely corresponds to Piaget's ideas of declining egocentrism as the child grows older.

Selman hypothesizes that children's reasoning in both perspective-taking and friendships develops from (1) egocentric, uncoordinated understanding to (2) an understanding that coordinates two perspectives to, finally, (3) an appreciation of individual perspectives within the larger, more complex, social context.

In stage 0, roughly corresponding to Piaget's preoperational period (ages 3 to 7) children's friendships are classified as *momentary playmates.* Friends are chosen by physical accessibility—something akin to "love the one you're with." In stage 1, or *one-way assistance* (ages 4 to 9), children's friendships are characterized as being determined by whether the friend shares the same interests or will do what the child wants them to do. Stage 2 (ages 6 to 12), called *fair-weather cooperation,* finds children recognizing the reciprocal nature of personal perspectives. Relationships depend on cooperation and compromise and can change very rapidly depending on the children's cooperative abilities. Then in middle childhood to early adolescence (ages 9 to 15), children's friendships develop into stage 3 or what Selman refers to as *intimate and mutually shared relationships.* Friendships are seen as the means to develop intimacy and support. Cliques are likely to form at this age as is possessiveness and jealousy. However, at this stage, children are better able to step outside an interaction and take the perspective of a third party.

The final stage, stage 4, or *autonomous, interdependent friendships,* is thought to begin in adolescence and extend into adulthood. Unlike the previous stage, this stage is characterized by an appreciation and tolerance for the other's need to establish relations with other people while at the same time maintaining an intimate and supportive relationship.

DISCUSSION

As is evident in the previous review, developmental theories vary considerably. Some are broad with less defined terms, while others are more precise. In addition, the various theories focus on different aspects of development, placing different emphasis on the relative contributions of environmental and biological factors. While no one theory can account for all areas of development, knowledge of a number of developmental theories will allow one to adopt an eclectic approach that may be more practical. For example, one may use Gesell's theory in attempting to understand the progression of motor development in an infant but be better helped by choosing another theory when attempting to account for social or cognitive development.

While early theories seemed to have adopted an either/or stance with respect to the nature/nurture question as well as the continuity/discontinuity of development (e.g., does development reflect primarily qualitative or quantitative changes?), more recent research recognizes the folly of this approach. Clearly biological structures and genetic predisposition play a role as well as environmental influences. The relative contribution of each seems to vary, depending on the particular developmental structure and the age of the child.

What many of the earlier theories lacked was a greater understanding of the role of larger social, cultural, and ethnic influences. While Erikson extended Freud's theory by addressing this aspect, most early research on development included a very narrow subject base. Thus, many theories have been based on white, middle class, and middle elementary age children. Furthermore, as is the case with any theory, the prevailing sociocultural factors influence the *theorist's* own interpretation of the research. This is illustrated in Gilligan's reconception of Erikson's theory, highlighting gender differences and requiring that we rethink the relative roles of both establishing intimate relationships as well as identity.

Fortunately, much of the current research does attempt to include these larger sociocultural factors. While research approaches that examine the way the child's biological makeup, immediate social environment, and the larger cultural system interact to affect development are undoubtedly more complicated than those that examine more simplistic influences such as the role of biology or environment alone, developmental theories must be tested and elaborated in order to understand both the progress and the disruption of the developmental process.

REFERENCES
1. Hall CS, Lindzey G: *Theories of personality*, New York, 1970, John Wiley & Sons.
2. Kuhn TS: *The structure of scientific revolutions*, ed 2, Chicago, 1970, University of Chicago Press.
3. Maddi SR: *Personality theories: a comparative analysis*, Homewood, Ill, 1976, Dorsey, p 602.
4. Sidman M: *Tactics of scientific research*, New York, 1960, Basic Books, p 13.
5. Gesell A: *Infancy and human growth*, New York, 1928, Macmillan.
6. Gesell A, Ilg FL, Ames LB: *The first five years of life*, New York, 1940, Harper & Row.
7. Gesell A, Ames LB, Bullis GE: *The child from five to ten*, New York, 1946, Harper & Row.
8. Gesell A: *Youth: years from ten to sixteen*, New York, 1956, Harper & Row.
9. Freud S: Three essays on the theory of sexuality (1905). In Strachey J (translated): *The standard edition of the complete psychological works of Sigmund Freud*, vol 7, London, 1953, Hogarth Press, p 239.

10. Fisher S, Greenberg RP: *The scientific credibility of Freud's theories and therapy,* New York, 1977, Basic Books.
11. Erikson E: *Childhood and society,* New York, 1950, Norton.
12. Erikson E: *Identity, youth and crisis,* 1968, New York, Norton.
13. Bijou S: Ages, stages, and the naturalization of human development, *Am Psychologist* 23:419-427, 1968.
14. Pavlov I: *Conditioned reflexes,* London, 1927, Oxford University Press.
15. Thorndike EL: *Educational psychology,* New York, 1903, Lenicke & Buechner.
16. Bijou SW, Baer DM: *Child development,* vol 1, New York, 1961, Appleton-Century Crofts.
17. Bijou SW, Baer DM: *Behavioral analysis of child development,* Englewood Cliffs, NJ, 1978, Prentice-Hall.
18. Bandura A, Walters RH: *Social learning and personality development,* New York, 1963, Holt.
19. Bandura A: Vicarious and self-reinforcement processes. In Glaser R, editor: *The nature of reinforcement,* New York, 1971, Academic Press, pp 228-278.
20. Bandura A: *Social learning theory,* Englewood Cliffs, NJ, 1977, Prentice-Hall.
21. Bandura A: *Aggression: a social learning analysis,* Englewood Cliffs, NJ, 1973, Prentice-Hall.
22. Bandura A, Ross D, Ross SA: Transmission of aggression through imitation of aggressive models, *J Abnorm Soc Psychol* 63:575-582, 1961.
23. Rosenthal TL, Zimmerman BJ: *Social learning and cognition,* New York, 1978, Academic Press.
24. Gagne R: Contribution of learning to human development, *Psychol Rev* 75:177-191, 1968.
25. Piaget J: *Introduction to genetic epistemology,* Paris, 1950, University Press.
26. Beard R: *An outline of Piaget's developmental psychology,* New York, 1969, Basic Books, p 25.
27. Kohlberg L: The development of children's orientations toward a moral order. I. Sequence in the development of moral thought, *Vita Humana* 6:11-13, 1963.
28. Bibace R, Walsh NE: Development of children's concepts of illness, *Pediatrics* 66:912-917, 1980.
29. Nagera H: Children's reactions to hospitalization and illness, *Child Psychiatry Hum Dev* 9:3-19, 1978.
30. Flavell J: *The developmental psychology of Jean Piaget,* New York, 1963, Van Nostrand, p 102.
31. Piaget J: *The origins of intelligence in children,* New York, 1952, International Universities Press.
32. Piaget J: *The language and thought of the child,* New York, 1923, Harcourt Brace, p 9.
33. Flavell JH: First discussant's comments: what is memory development the development of? *Hum Dev* 14:272-278, 1971.
34. Case R: *Intellectual development: a systematic reinterpretation,* New York, 1985, Academic Press.
35. Trabasso T: The role of memory as a system in making transitive inferences. In Kail RV, Hage JW, editors: *Perspectives on the development of memory and cognition,* Hillsdale, NJ, 1977, Erlbaum.
36. Gelman R: Conservation acquisition: a problem of learning to attend to relevant attributes, *J Experimental Child Psychol* 7:167-187, 1969.
37. Siegler RD, editor: *Children's thinking: what develops?* Hillsdale, NJ, 1978, Erlbaum.
38. Kohlberg L: A cognitive-developmental analysis of children's sex-role concepts and attitudes. In Maccoby EE, editor: *The development of sex differences,* Stanford, Calif, 1966, Stanford University Press, pp 82-173.
39. Kurtines WM, Gewirtz JL, editors: *Handbook of moral behavior and development,* vol 1, Hillsdale, NJ, 1991, Erlbaum.

40. Walker LJ: Sex differences in the development of moral reasoning: a critical review, *Child Dev* 55:677-691, 1977.

41. Gilligan C: In a different voice: women's conceptions of the self and of morality, *Harvard Educ Rev* 47:481-517, 1977.

41a. Gilligan C: *In a different voice: psychological theory and women's development*, Cambridge, MA, 1982, Harvard University.

42. Skinner BF: *Verbal behavior*, New York, 1957, Appleton-Century Crofts.

43. Staats AW, Staats CK: *Complex human behavior: a systematic extension of learning principles*, New York, 1963, Holt Rinehart & Winston, p 121.

44. Brown R, Cazden C, Bellugi U: The child's grammar from 1 to 3. In Hill JP, editor: *Minnesota Symposium on Child Psychology*, vol 2, Minneapolis, 1969, University of Minnesota Press, pp 28-73.

45. Chomsky N: *Syntactic structures*, The Hague, 1957, Mouton.

46. Chomsky N: A review of *Verbal Behavior* by BF Skinner, *Language* 35:26-58, 1959.

47. Bruner JS: *Child's talk*, New York, 1983, Norton.

48. Damon W, Hart D: *Self-understanding in childhood and adolescence*, Cambridge, 1988, Cambridge University Press.

49. Harter S: Issues in the development of the self-concept of children and adolescents. In LaGreca A, editor: *Through the eyes of a child*, Boston, 1990, Allyn and Bacon.

50. Parten M: Social participation among preschool children, *J Abn Soc Psychol* 27:243-269, 1932.

51. Rubin KH, Fein GG, Vanderberg B: Play. In Hetherington EM, editor: *Handbook of child psychology*, vol 4, New York, 1983, Wiley, pp 693-744.

52. Smilansky S: *The effects of sociodramatic play on disadvantaged children: preschool children*, New York, 1968, Wiley.

53. Selman RL: *The growth of interpersonal understanding: developmental and clinical analysis*, New York, 1980, Academic Press.

54. Selman RL, Schultz LH: *Making a friend in youth: developmental theory and pair therapy*, Chicago, 1990, University of Chicago Press.

CHAPTER 2

Measurements of development and learning

In caring for children with developmental disabilities, the primary care physician may have them evaluated by other health, allied health, and mental health professionals. These professionals are likely to employ assessment tools unique to their professional discipline and to provide the physician with a report of their evaluation. It is important, therefore, for the clinician to understand the most commonly used evaluation tools.

This chapter discusses psychological, speech, language, and motor assessment procedures. Because there are a number of available tests, varying with location and time, it is not possible to be comprehensive within the scope of this book. However, the selections discussed reflect the current state of the art for most clinicians.

Commonly Used Measures of Infant and Child Development

CHRISTOPHER W. FONTANA
ABIGAIL B. SIVAN

When clinicians evaluate assessment tests, they employ a variety of statistical parameters that allow them to assess the test instruments. Commonly used parameters include test standardization and norming, reliability, and validity.

Test standardization procedures secure consistency in administration and scoring and establish norms that allow clinicians to compare an examinee's performance to the performance of others. Norms are developed by administering the test to large samples of children with similar characteristics (e.g., age, grade). Clinicians can then compare an individual child's test score to scores obtained by children of the same age or grade.

Reliability refers to the dependability (likelihood that the same score will be obtained at another test administration) and consistency (likelihood that one test item is related to another item) of a test's ability to measure some attribute. Reliability is expressed by a reliability correlation coefficient that ranges in value from 0.0 to 1.0. Coefficients of .80 or higher suggest adequate test reliability. Reliability, however, does not provide any information as to the accuracy (i.e., validity) of a test.

Validity refers to a test's accuracy or whether it actually measures what it purports to measure. While validity may constitute the most important factor in test evaluation, validity by itself has no meaning in the absence of adequate reliability and standardization. Validity coefficients range in value from −1.0 to +1.0. Generally, a validity coefficient of .30 or above is considered adequate. As sample size increases, the strength of the validity coefficient increases. Different types of validity exist. Refer to the chapter on developmental screening for more detail.

Clinicians often report test results in terms of standard scores. Standard scores are transformations that compare the performance of a given person with a group's mean. The most commonly used standard scores are z scores (mean = 0, SD = 1), T scores (mean = 50, SD = 10), and deviation IQs (mean = 100, SD = 15 or 16). These relationships are depicted along with normal curve equivalents in Fig. 2-1.

COMMONLY USED MEASURES OF INTELLECTUAL DEVELOPMENT

Over the years, there have been many definitions of intelligence; some include global functioning/abilities, others stress specific factors. Similarly, test constructors have devised numerous ways to measure intelligence. As a consequence, the precise definition of intelligence depends on what measure of intelligence one uses.[2] The box on p. 43 gives a listing of the more commonly used measures of intelligence.

In 1890, James Cattell introduced the term "mental test." In 1905, Alfred Binet and Theodore Simon in France developed the first practical intelligence test: the Binet-Simon Scale. In 1912, William Stern introduced

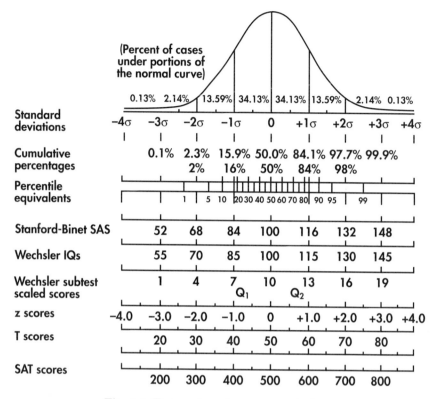

Fig. 2-1 Test results using curve equivalents.

COMMONLY USED MEASURES OF INTELLIGENCE

Columbia Mental Maturity Scale
Detroit Tests of Learning Aptitude—P
Detroit Tests of Learning Aptitude—2
Goodenough-Harris Drawing Test
Kaufman Assessment Battery for Children
Leiter International Performance Scale
McCarthy Scales of Children's Abilities
Pictorial Test of Intelligence
Raven's Progressive Matrices
Slosson Test
Stanford-Binet Intelligence Scale: Fourth Edition
Wechsler Intelligence Scale for Children: Third Edition
Wechsler Preschool and Primary Scale of Intelligence—Revised

the concept of the mental quotient; he devised a formula to determine mental quotients based on an individual's mental age (MA) and chronological age (CA): $IQ = MA/CA \times 100$.[3]

Stanford-Binet Intelligence Scale: Fourth Edition

Since 1905, the original Binet-Simon Scale has undergone several revisions. In 1916, Lewis Terman adapted the Binet-Simon Scale for use in the United States. The American version, the Stanford-Binet Intelligence Scale, continued to use Stern's ratio IQ. By 1960, however, researchers had cast aside Stern's ratio IQ in favor of a standard score, the deviation IQ.

As a standard score, the deviation IQ enabled clinicians to compare scores across age levels. In 1960, researchers combined the most discriminating items from two forms of the Stanford-Binet (Forms L and M) and offered a formal restandardization of the Stanford-Binet in 1972 and again in 1986.[2]

The 1986 standardization group consisted of 5013 individuals weighted for the 1980 census data.[2] Referred to as the Stanford-Binet Intelligence Scale: Fourth Edition (SB:FE), this most recent revision represents a radical departure from its predecessors.

Researchers also based the SB:FE on a theoretically based hierarchical structure of intelligence, one that includes three levels of increasingly specific cognitive functioning.[2] Level 1 represents "g" (general intelligence) and is considered the highest level of interpretation and the best estimate of intellectual functioning. The designation "g" (always in small letters) comes from Spearman's 1927 formulation.[2]

Level 2 divides "g" into three hypothetical constructs: (1) crystallized abilities or the skill and knowledge acquired through cultural exposure and formal and informal education; (2) fluid-analytic abilities or those inherent abilities that are acquired biologically and individualize a person's mental operations and processes; and (3) short-term memory or the subject's ability to retain acquired information.

Level 3 further divides the three constructs just discussed into four hypothetical constructs: verbal reasoning, quantitative reasoning, abstract/visual reasoning, and short-term memory. Each of the level 3's four hypothetical constructs is measured by three or four subtests.

The SB:FE's hierarchical structure of intelligence is based on theory not factor analysis. The box on p. 45 illustrates the SB:FE's three hypothetical constructs.

Subtests are administered and scored with respect to a beginning point (basal) and an ending point (ceiling). To score the SB:FE, the examiner

HYPOTHETICAL CONSTRUCTS OF THE SB:FE

Level 1

"g" or "general intelligence"

Level 2

Crystallized abilities	Fluid-analytic abilities	Short-term memory

Level 3

Verbal reasoning	Quantitative reasoning	Abstract/visual reasoning	Short-term memory

Level 3 subtests

Vocabulary	Quantitative	Pattern analysis	Bead memory
Comprehension	Number series	Copying	Memory for
Absurdities	Equation building	Matrices	sentences
Verbal relations		Paper folding and	Memory for
		cutting	digits
			Memory for
			objects

Table 2-1   Composite SASs and corresponding classification of intelligence

SAS	Classification
>132	Very superior
121-131	Superior
111-120	Above average
89-110	Average
79-89	Below average
68-78	Borderline
<68	Mentally deficient

converts each subtest raw score into a standard age score (SAS). While individual subtests have means of 50 and standard deviations of 8, level 3 constructs (verbal reasoning, quantitative reasoning, abstract/visual reasoning and short-term memory) and a test composite score all have means of 100 and standard deviations of 16.[2] These are interpreted in Table 2-1.

The SB:FE has excellent reliability. The composite score reliabilities range from .95 to .99 across the 17 age groups[7]; individual subtests have a reliability that ranges from as low as .66 to as high as .96.[2] The technical manual provides test-age equivalents for subtest raw scores.[7]

Table 2-2   SB:FE subtest descriptions (grouped according to level 3 theoretical construction)

Level 3 theoretical construct	Subtest	Subtest description
Verbal reasoning	Vocabulary	*Vocabulary* (all ages) assesses both receptive and expressive vocabulary; taps word knowledge and language ability and is used in determining entry levels to other tests.
	Comprehension	*Comprehension* (all ages) taps practical knowledge and judgment and includes questions about basic survival skills as well as complex questions with societal, economic, and political considerations.
	Absurdities	*Absurdities* (ages 2-14) assesses visual perception, attention, concentration, and social awareness, and requires identification of essential incongruities in a series of pictures.
	Verbal relations	*Verbal relations* (ages 12-23) assesses word knowledge, verbal flexibility, concept formation, and reasoning by asking for the similarity among a set of three words and how a fourth word is dissimilar.
Quantitative reasoning	Quantitative	*Quantitative* (all ages) taps attention, concentration, and mental computation ability and requires problem-solving with increasingly complex arithmetic and algebra.
	Number series	*Number series* (ages 7-23) assesses logical reasoning abilities with numbers and requires solving number series problems based on clues from the numbers provided.
	Equation building	*Equation building* (12-23) taps attention, concentration, and mental flexibility when working with numbers by requiring mental computation of number and sign equations of increasing length.
Abstract/ visual reasoning	Pattern analysis	*Pattern analysis* (all ages) taps visual-motor skills and spatial visualization abilities by requiring construction and matching of abstract designs (only timed test on the SB:FE).
	Copying	*Copying* (ages 2-13) taps perceptual organization (input) and fine-motor skills (output) by constructing cube designs and drawing geometric forms of increasing complexity.

Table 2-2   SB:FE subtest descriptions (grouped according to level 3 theoretical construction)—cont'd

Level 3 theoretical construct	Subtest	Subtest description
	Matrices	*Matrices* (ages 7-23) assesses visual perception and reasoning by requiring completion of matrices of increasing complexity.
	Paper folding and cutting	*Paper folding and cutting* (ages 12-23) taps attention, visual, and spatial reasoning by determining the correct design based on observation of various folding and cutting sequences.
Short-term memory	Bead memory	*Bead memory* (all ages) taps fine-motor coordination, visual perception, and short-term memory by requiring construction of bead combinations from memory.
	Memory for sentences	*Memory for sentences* (all ages) taps verbal attention, concentration, comprehension, and processing by requiring correct repetition of sentences.
	Memory for digits	*Memory for digits* (ages 7-23) taps short-term, rote auditory memory by requiring correct repetition of digits forwards and backwards.
	Memory for objects	*Memory for objects* (ages 7-23) taps short-term, visual memory by requiring recall of the correct sequences of shapes.

The SB:FE also has excellent validity. It correlates well with other measures of intelligence and school achievement. Validity coefficients range from .50 to .80. The SB:FE also appears to differentiate exceptional populations (e.g., gifted, learning disabled, mentally retarded) from the standardization sample.[8] Refer to Table 2-2 for a brief description of SB:FE subtests.

Wechsler Preschool and Primary Scale of Intelligence—Revised (WPPSI-R) and Wechsler Intelligence Scale for Children—III (WISC-III)

In 1939, David Wechsler published the Wechsler-Bellevue Intelligence Scale (Wechsler-Bellevue) to assess "global intelligence."[8] Because Wechsler believed that earlier intelligence scales were limited by their emphasis on verbal skills, his tests separated verbal and nonverbal (i.e., performance) intelligence. Wechsler based the Wechsler-Bellevue test on a point-scale format and developed subtests that tapped specific cognitive functions.[2] The Wechsler-Bellevue test served as the template for future Wechsler intelligence tests, which are listed in Table 2-3 and whose subtests are outlined in Table 2-5. The most recent children's revision, the WPPSI-R and WISC-III, retains Wechsler's original format and organization, which included verbal, performance, and full scale IQ scores.

To score the WPPSI-R and WISC-III, the examiner converts individual subtest raw scores into scale scores (mean = 10, standard deviation = 3). The examiner then adds up the five verbal subtest scale scores and refers to the manual to identify the corresponding verbal scale IQ score. The examiner proceeds in same fashion to identify the subject's performance and full scale IQ scores (mean = 100, standard deviation = 15). Table 2-4 shows the deviation IQs and classifications for the WPPSI-R and WISC-III.

In addition to the verbal, performance, and full scale IQs, there are four factor-based index scores on the WISC-III (see the box on p. 49). The four index scores include (1) verbal comprehension, or that knowledge derived from formal education and cultural exposure; (2) perceptual organization, or the ability to perceive and organize visually presented material; (3) freedom from distractibility, or the ability to attend and concentrate; and (4) processing speed, or the ability to quickly process visual material.

Both the WPPSI-R and WISC-III have excellent reliability. The WPPSI-R's reliability for verbal, performance, and full scale IQs generally ranges from .90 to .97[2]; however, the WPPSI-R's reliability for 7-year-olds

Table 2-3   Chronology of Wechsler Intelligence Tests

Adults	Children	Preschoolers
Wechsler-Bellevue Intelligence Scale (W-B) (1935) "template" for subsequent intelligence tests	Wechsler Intelligence Scale for Children (WISC) (1949)	Wechsler Preschool and Primary Scale of Intelligence (WPPSI) (1967)
Wechsler Adult Intelligence Scale (WAIS) (1942)	Wechsler Intelligence Scale for Children, Revised (WISC-R) (1976)	Wechsler Preschool and Primary Scale of Intelligence, Revised (WPPSI-R) (1989)
Wechsler Adult Intelligence Scale, Revised (WAIS-R) (1981)	Wechsler Intelligence Scale for Children, Third Edition (WISC-III) (1990)	
Wechsler Adult Intelligence Scale, Third Edition (WAIS-III) (1996) (expected)		

appears slightly lower. Individual subtest reliability coefficients range from .63 to .86.[2]

The WISC-III's reliability for verbal, performance, and full scale IQs ranges from .89 to .97.[9] Like the WPPSI-R, the WISC-III's individual subtests have lower levels of reliability than the three composite scores and range from .60 to .92.[9]

Recently revised tests, such as the WPPSI-R and WISC-III, have not been available for sufficient time to fully examine their validity. To date, both tests appear to possess adequate validity and correlate well with other intelligence tests. The WISC-III also appears to correlate well with achievement tests. In addition, a recent cross-validation study of WPPSI-R and WISC-III test items revealed strong validity (r = .88).[12]

Overall, critics agree that the WPPSI-R and WISC-III exemplify well-standardized, well-developed intelligence tests. Critics of the WPPSI-R, however, feel the test takes too long (75 minutes) for young children. Crit-

Table 2-4 Deviation IQs and corresponding classification of intelligence

Deviation IQ	Classification
>129	Very superior
120-129	Superior
110-119	High average
90-109	Average
80-89	Low average
70-79	Borderline
<70	Mentally deficient

WISC-III FACTOR-BASED INDEX SCORES AND ACCOMPANYING SUBTESTS

Verbal comprehension

Information
Similarities
Vocabulary
Comprehension

Perceptual organization

Picture completion
Picture arrangement
Block design
Object assembly

Freedom from distractibility

Arithmetic
Digit span

Processing speed

Coding
Symbol search

Table 2-5   WAIS-R, WISC-III, and WPPSI-R subtest descriptions

Subtest	WAIS-R	WISC-III	WPPSI-R	Subtest description	WAIS-R	WISC-III	WPPSI-R
Verbal subtests							
Information	X	X	X	*Information* requires the individual to answer a broad range of questions about basic factors; taps the individual's general fund of information obtained through social, educational, and cultural opportunities.	.89	.85	.84
Digit span	X	(X)	NA	*Digit span* requires the individual to verbally repeat increasingly longer series of digits to the examiner; measures the individual's short-term rote memory.	.83	.73	NA
Vocabulary	X	X	X	*Vocabulary* requires the individual to verbally define words presented by the examiner; provides a good estimate of an individual's educational success.	.96	.89	.84
Arithmetic	X	X	X	*Arithmetic* requires the individual to perform basic arithmetic that becomes increasingly complex; taps the individual's attention, concentration, and mathematical computation.	.84	.74	.80
Comprehension	X	X	X	*Comprehension* requires the individual to answer basic questions concerning personal health and wellness, the environment, and social relations; taps practical knowledge and social judgment.	.84	.73	.83
Similarities	X	X	X	*Similarities* requires the individual to verbally explain the likeness between two things; taps the individual's verbal concept formation and abstract thinking.	.84	.81	.86
Sentences	NA	NA	(X)	*Sentences,* an optional subtest, requires the child to correctly repeat sentences of increasing complexity; measures the child's short-term auditory memory.	NA	NA	.82

Table 2-5   WAIS-R, WISC-III, and WPPSI-R subtest descriptions—cont'd

Subtest	WAIS-R	WISC-III	WPPSI-R	Subtest description	WAIS-R	WISC-III	WPPSI-R
Non-verbal subtests							
Picture completion	X	X	X	*Picture completion* requires the individual to identify the most important missing elements in pictures; the missing element becomes more difficult to identify; taps the individual's ability to differentiate essential from nonessential detail.	.81	.81	.85
Picture arrangement	X	X	NA	*Picture arrangement* requires the individual to generate a meaningful story by placing a series of cards in the correct sequence; taps the individual's ability to size up and comprehend social situations as depicted on a series of cards.	.74	.64	NA
Block design	X	X	X	*Block design* requires the individual to correctly construct designs using two colored cubes within prescribed time limits; taps the child's spatial visualization ability.	.87	.77	.85
Object assembly	X	X	X	*Object assembly* requires the individual to construct jigsaw puzzles of common objects within prescribed time limits; it taps the individual's visuoconstructive skill and ability to synthesize parts into meaningful wholes.	.68	.66	.63
Digit symbol	X	NA	NA	*Digit symbol* requires the adult to draw the correct corresponding symbol to a number according to a key at the top of the page; speed and accuracy increase raw scores; taps psychomotor speed.	.82	NA	NA
Coding	NA	X	NA	*Coding* requires the child to draw the correct corresponding symbol to a number according to a key at the top of the page; speed and accuracy increase raw scores; like WAIS-R's *digit symbol*, it taps psychomotor speed.	NA	.77	NA

Continued

Table 2-5 WAIS-R, WISC-III, and WPPSI-R subtest descriptions—cont'd

Subtest	WAIS-R	WISC-III	WPPSI-R	Subtest description	WAIS-R	WISC-III	WPPSI-R
Symbol search	NA	(X)	NA	*Symbol search*, an optional subtest, requires the child to search for symbols; speed increases the child's score; it measures high-speed visual discrimination.	NA	.74	NA
Mazes	NA	(X)	X	*Mazes* requires the child to correctly draw lines through mazes of increasing complexity within prescribed time limits; this paper-and-pencil task taps visual-motor and planning ability.	NA	.57	.77
Geometric design	NA	NA	X	*Geometric design* requires the child to visually discriminate between different geometric designs and copy designs; it taps the child's visual recognition, perception, and coordination.	NA	NA	.79
Animal pegs	NA	NA	(X)	*Animal pegs*, and optional subtest, requires the child to correctly place colored pegs in their correct holes according to a key; speed counts; taps attention, concentration, memory, and manual dexterity.	NA	NA	.66

(X) = supplementary subtest.

ics of the WISC-III cite the test's limited range of IQs (40 to 160) as a weakness.[2] Table 2-5 offers a brief description of WPPSI-R, WISC-III, and WAIS-R subtests.

The comprehensiveness of the SB:FE and Wechsler tests enables them to stand alone as solid individual mental tests. Each one possesses excellent standardization, reliability, and validity. Occasionally, the SB:FE or Wechsler generates certain patterns that warrant additional follow-up testing. Alternatively, a child's handicapping condition may disallow administration of either the SB:FE or a Wechsler test.

Clinicians, then, can turn to other tests that may provide additional information about a child or a way to test a handicapped child. The box on pp. 53-54 provides information on a number of alternative cognitive measures.

——————— ALTERNATIVE COGNITIVE MEASURES ———————

Columbia Mental Maturity Scale (CMMS)[2,16]

Ages: 3-6 to 9-11 years

Mean and SD: (M = 100, SD = 16)

Advantages: Provides a nonverbal estimate of cognitive functioning; appears less culturally loaded. Good instrument for children with speech/language and/or motor involvement.

Disadvantages: Norms based on 1960 census data; scores not interchangeable with SB:FE or Wechsler tests.

Detroit Tests of Learning Aptitude—P (DTLA-P)[2]

Ages: 3 to 9 years

Mean and SD: (M = 100, SD = 15)

Advantages: Adequate reliability and validity; good screener for general intellectual ability.

Disadvantages: Questionable standardization; no factor analysis.

Detroit Tests of Learning Aptitude—2 (DTLA-2)[2]

Ages: 6-10 to 18 years

Mean and SD: (M = 100, SD = 15)

Advantages: Generates an overall estimate of intellectual functioning.

Disadvantages: No weighting procedures to offset norms that have too many highly educated individuals; no factor analysis.

Goodenough-Harris Drawing Test (Draw-A-Man)[2,17]

Ages: 3-0 to 15-11 years

Mean and SD: (M = 100, SD = 15)

Advantages: Useful screener of nonverbal intellectual ability, especially for culturally diverse, low-functioning children.

Disadvantages: Based on 1960 census data; WISC-III performance scale may provide a better estimate of nonverbal intelligence.

Kaufman Assessment Battery for Children (K-ABC)[2]

Ages: 2-6 to 12-5 years

Mean and SD: (M = 100, SD = 15)

Advantages: Used only to complement SB:FE or Wechsler nonverbal estimates. May have neuropsychological uses.

Disadvantages: Do *not* administer to young (<4) children or children with attention difficulties or high intellectual functioning. Norms show under representation of ethnic minorities.

Continued

ALTERNATIVE COGNITIVE MEASURES—CONT'D

McCarthy Scales of Children's Abilities (McCarthy)[2,18]

Ages: 2-6 to 8-6 years
Mean and SD: (M = 100, SD = 16)
Advantages: May provide additional information on young children with suspected learning disabilities. Manipulatives are appropriate for lower functioning children.
Disadvantages: Standardization based on 1970 census data; no correlation with Wechsler tests; no upward extension (can't track child's progress).

Leiter International Performance Scale (LIPS)[2]

Ages: 2 years to adult
Mean and SD: (Ratio IQ)
Advantages: Often used with autistic children to measure nonverbal intelligence. Useful adjunctive test for children with speech/language, learning disability, sensory, and/or motor involvement.
Disadvantages: Poor norms (LIPS-R standardization in progress); samples a limited range of matching behaviors.

Raven's Progressive Matrices[2]

Ages: (Colored Matrices)   5 to 11 years
(Standard Matrices) 6 to 17 years
(Advanced Matrices) Adults
Mean and SD: (Percentile ranks)
Advantages: Easily administered; good way of measuring nonverbal reasoning, good test for children with severe speech/language, motor, and/or hearing involvement; useful for culturally diverse populations.
Disadvantages: Cannot substitute for the SB:FE or any of the Wechsler tests; expensive.

Slosson Intelligence Test (SIT)[2]

Ages: 2 to 18 years
Mean and SD: (M = 100, SD = 16)
Advantages: Requires minimal training, minimal time to administer; a quick screening device.
Disadvantages: 1981 normative data poorly described; often over-estimates; cannot substitute for SB:FE or Wechsler Tests, especially when assessing children with low or high intelligence.

COMMONLY USED MEASURES OF INFANT DEVELOPMENT

Technological advancements in medicine have dramatically increased the number of infants with medically complex conditions. As a result, many infants and toddlers appear "untestable" using traditional, standardized measures.

Accordingly, psychologists have adjusted their assessment of infants and toddlers to include "convergent assessment" or "integrated strategies." Such strategies provide a combination of norm-based, curriculum-based, judgment-based, and play-based assessment.[19]

Additionally, psychologists use parent or caretaker interviews and behavioral observations in settings both familiar (home) and unfamiliar (clinics and hospitals) to the infant or toddler to obtain the children's actual level of functioning.[15] For infants and toddlers exhibiting less serious developmental and/or medical involvement, psychologists may elect to include a norm-referenced instrument in their assessment repertoire.

Bayley Scales of Infant Development: Second Edition (BSID-II)

The Bayley Scales of Infant Development: Second Edition (BSID-II), a revision of the BSID (1969), is the most widely used method for assessing infants and toddlers who exhibit mild developmental delays. Like its predecessor, the BSID, the BSID-II consists of three scales: the mental scale, motor scale, and behavior rating scale (formerly the infant behavior record). The BSID-II's mental scale now consists of 178 (vs. BSID's 163) items and the motor scale consists of 111 (vs. BSID's 81) items.

The 1993 standardization group consisted of 1700 children stratified across 17 age groups (age 1 month to 42 months) and was based on 1988 census data. The BSID-II has excellent reliability; across the 17 age groups, the mental scale average equals .88 and the motor scale average equals .84.[14]

Similarly, the BSID-II possesses excellent validity. It correlates well with its predecessor (BSID) as well as the General Cognitive Index (GCI) of the McCarthy and the full scale IQ (FSIQ) of the WPPSI-R. Validity coefficients range from .60 to .70. Refer to Table 2-6 for a brief description of the BSID-II scales.

As always, standardized assessment of infants and toddlers may not accurately predict future intellectual abilities in those children with average to above average intelligence. The BSID-II may, however, be more useful as a predictor of future intellectual abilities in children of below or significantly below average intelligence.

Table 2-6 BSID-II scales

Scale	Abilities measured
Mental scale	Sensation, perception; "object constancy;" memory and learning; verbal abilities; higher order thinking; language; and computation
Motor scale	Body control; coordination; recognizing objects by touch
Behavior rating scale	Attention; orientation; emotional control

COMMONLY USED MEASURES OF SOCIAL ADJUSTMENT AND BEHAVIOR

Under most circumstances, either a parent, teacher, or other responsible caretaker asks the pediatrician about a child's development. Usually, the adult is concerned because the child is intrusive, overactive, anxious, or exhibits other behaviors that are bothersome either to the child himself/herself or to others around the child. Adults seldom refer a child who has *not* become bothersome, although the child may be having difficulties. Yet both types of difficulties warrant referral for a social-emotional evaluation.

In doing such an evaluation, the clinician must carefully explore each child's unique environmental background and biological make-up. Each child's developmental history, cultural and ethnic background, family history, socioeconomic status, biological heritage, as well as medical and psychiatric history should be thoroughly reviewed. A careful review of a child's personal history, social adjustment, and behavior problems will also require a multi-method approach to assessment that crosses settings requiring direct observation; parent, teacher, and self-report of psychosocial functioning and behavioral difficulties; projective techniques (e.g. TAT, Rorschach); and interviews.[37,38] Most importantly, the evaluating clinician must design an assessment approach that targets the original reason for referral of the individual child.

Direct observation

Generally, the evaluating clinician will choose a direct observation technique based on the setting, target behaviors exhibited by the child, and the specific reason for referral. The evaluating clinician may choose one or more direct observation methods. These direct observation methods include (1) narrative, (2) interval, (3) event, and (4) ratings recording.[2,39]

Narrative recording works well in group situations. In narrative recording, the observer focuses on generating an objective record of the sequences of behavior exhibited by the child. *Interval* recording uses preselected time intervals to measure specific behaviors exhibited by the child (i.e., target behavior[s]). Interval recording enables observers to zero in on distinct behaviors. In *event* recording, the observer literally "counts" the number of target behaviors exhibited by the child over a specified period of time. *Ratings* recording makes use of a checklist of behaviors. Ratings recording enables observers to follow a number of different behaviors exhibited by one or more children in a group situation.

Parent, teacher, and self-report of psychosocial functioning and behavior difficulties

Clinicians use standardized behavior rating scales to assess a child's psychosocial and behavioral difficulties. These scales assess behaviors as perceived by parents and caretakers, school personnel, and the youth's own self-report. Standardized behavior rating scales may range from comprehensive assessment of a child's overall social-emotional competency and functioning (i.e., broad band scales) to focused assessment of specific behaviors (i.e., narrow band scales).

For example, Achenbach has published behavior rating scales that tap a child's overall psychosocial functioning as perceived by parents/caretakers, school personnel, and the youth's own self-report. Achenbach's rating scales cover a variety of areas, including assessment of a child's social-emotional competence, as well as degree of internalizing (e.g., withdrawn, somatic complaints, anxious/depressed) vs. externalizing (e.g., delinquent and aggressive) behaviors. In contrast, MeriTech, Inc., has published a teacher rating scale that focuses exclusively on four specific behaviors: attention, social skills, hyperactivity, and oppositional.[4]

The boxes on pp. 58-60 list some of the more frequently used behavior rating scales completed by the parent and/or caretaker, scales completed by school personnel, and scales of the child's own self-report.

Projective techniques

Projectives or unstructured tests are designed to draw out information about a child's personality and underlying conflicts. However, a clear drawback to projective testing involves comparing the protocols generated by different clients as well as the absence of clear scoring standards.[8] The box on p. 61 presents some of the more frequently used projective techniques.

BEHAVIOR RATING SCALES (PARENT/CARETAKER)

Achenbach's Child Behavior Checklist (CBCL/4-18)[4,20]

Ages:	4 to 18 years
Mean and SD:	(M = 50, SD = 10)
Description:	Checklist of common behavioral difficulties analyzed with a multiaxial system that allows parents or caretakers to rate a child's social-emotional development.
Content:	Internalizing, externalizing and total T scores. Eight clinical scales: withdrawn, somatic complaints, anxious-depressed, social problems, thought problems, attention problems, delinquent behavior, and aggressive behavior. Total of 113 items.
Advantages:	Well-written manual; comprehensive social-emotional assessment; norms (based on 1989 census data) appear good; excellent reliability and validity; instrument undergoes constant empirical testing.
Disadvantages:	None.

Achenbach's Child Behavior Checklist (CBCL/2-3)[4,36]

Ages:	2 to 3 years
Mean and SD:	(M = 50, SD = 10)
Description:	Provides a downward extension of the CBCL/4-18; allows parents or caretakers to rate a very young child's social-emotional development.
Content:	Internalizing, externalizing, and total T scores. Six clinical scales; 59 items function as counterparts to CBCL/4-18. Total of 99 items.
Advantages:	Same as CBCL/4-18.
Disadvantages:	Same as CBCL/4-18.

Conners' Parent Rating Scale (CPRS-48)[4,23]

Ages:	3 to 17 years
Mean and SD:	(M = 50, SD = 10)
Description:	Four-point rating scale that screens for various childhood behavior disorders.
Content:	Five clinical scales: conduct problem, learning problem, psychosomatic, impulsive-hyperactive, and anxiety; plus a hyperactivity index. Total of 48 items.
Advantages:	Well-written, well-organized manual; numerous studies on drug treatment effects and hyperactivity.
Disadvantages:	No information on test construction, standardization, total score, or basic validity; minimal data on reliability.

_____ **BEHAVIOR RATING SCALES (TEACHER)** _____

Achenbach's Teacher's Report Form (TRF)[4,21]

Ages:	5 to 18 years
Mean and SD:	(M = 50, SD = 10)
Description:	Multiaxial approach that provides clear descriptions of children's social-emotional development at school.
Content:	Same as CBCL/4-18.
Advantages:	Same as CBCL/4-18.
Disadvantages:	Norms, based on 1989 census data, appear fair.

Connor's Teacher Rating Scale (CTRS-28)[4,23]

Ages:	3 to 17 years
Mean and SD:	(M = 50, SD = 10)
Description:	Four-point rating scale that screens for various childhood behavior disorders observed at school.
Content:	Four clinical scales: conduct problem, hyperactivity, inattentive-passive, and hyperactivity index. Total of 28 items.
Advantages:	Same as CPRS-48.
Disadvantages:	No information on test construction, standardization, or norms.

Interview

The interview, a major component in the assessment of children, varies according to the reason for referral and the kind of information the clinician wishes to obtain. Most commonly, the clinician employs a mental status interview to obtain a psychiatric diagnosis. The clinician may also interview the parent(s)/caregiver(s), and/or teacher, and/or child.

When interviewing a child, the clinician begins by observing his/her interactions with the parent(s)/caregiver(s). After that, the clinician may decide to meet informally with the parent(s)/caregiver(s) first or proceed directly to interview the child.

When interviewing the child, the interviewer adjusts his/her language and approach according to the child's developmental level and/or degree of behavioral disturbance. With very young children, the clinician often employs props (such as toys) to facilitate the interview. Like projective techniques, interviews lack clear scoring standards and depend on clinician expertise.

SELF-REPORT RATING SCALES

Achenbach's Youth Self-Report (YSR)[4,22]

Ages: 11 to 18 years
Mean and SD: (M = 50, SD = 10)
Description: Multiaxial approach that provides clear descriptions of chil-
                    dren's view of their self-concept and social-emotional
                    development.
Content: Same as CBCL/4-18; 112 items.
Advantages: Same as CBCL/4-18.
Disadvantages: None.

Minnesota Multiphasic Personality Inventory—Adolescent (MMPI-A)[24]

Ages: 14 to 18 years
Mean and SD: (M = 50, SD = 10)
Description: Broad-band true-false test designed to assess adolescent
                    psychopathology.
Content: Ten original clinical scales; seven validity scales; 15 content
                    scales; six supplementary scales; 28 Harris-Lingoes sub-
                    scales; and three Si subscales; 478 items.
Advantages: Good norms; test based on original MMPI; ongoing reli-
                    ability and validity testing.
Disadvantages: Lack of time to develop stronger validity raises questions
                    concerning the accuracy of measures of adolescent psy-
                    chopathology.

Piers-Harris Self-Concept Scale (Piers-Harris)[25]

Ages: 8 to 18 years
Mean and SD: (M = 50, SD = 10)
Description: Brief self-report measure of children's and adolescent's de-
                    scription of their self-concept.
Content: Six cluster scales: behavior, intellectual and school status,
                    physical appearance and attributes, anxiety, popularity,
                    and happiness and satisfaction; 80 yes-no questions.
Advantages: Easy to read; simple declarative statements; quick screening
                    instrument.
Disadvantages: Poor norms limit generalizability; questionable whether
                    younger children can understand the items.

_____ **PROJECTIVE TECHNIQUES** _____

Children's Apperception Test (animal figures) (CAT) and Children's Apperception Test (human figures) (CAT-H)[26-30]

Ages:	3 to 10 years
Description:	Both CAT and CAT-H function as downward extensions of Murray's TAT; projective tests (CAT uses animal drawings, CAT-H uses human figure drawings) depict various social situations and tap children' relations to important figures and internal drive states.
Content:	Ten pictures (CAT, animals, CAT-H, humans) tap feeding, sibling rivalry, parental relations, aggression, acceptance, loneliness, psychosexual behavior, toilet training, and developmental conflicts.
Advantages:	Story-telling format appeals to young children.
Disadvantages:	No information on norms, reliability, or validity; CAT and CAT-H only as good as the examiner's interpretative skills.

Rorschach Inkblot Test (Rorschach)[29,31-33]

Ages:	5 to adult (using Exner's comprehensive scoring system)
Description:	Projective test uses inkblots that allow a child to elaborate his/her associations; examiner inquiry phase intended to conform child's exact perceptions; designed to tap a child's unconscious.
Content:	Ten symmetrical inkblots; plates 1 to 7 in black and white; plates 8 to 10 in color; inkblots become increasingly complex, abstract, and subject to emotional responses.
Advantages:	Provides a wealth of information concerning a child's underlying personality structure; inkblots nonthreatening; test resistant to faking.
Disadvantages:	Varying estimate of reliability and validity; limited use with children under 14; inquiry phase sometimes difficult with verbally limited children; a complex test for examiners to learn, score, and interpret.

Thematic Apperception Test (TAT)[29,31,34,35]

Ages:	4 to adult
Description:	Upward extension of Bellak's CAT and CAT-H; a projective test that elicits a child's internal drive states, emotions, and conflicts.
Content:	Twenty black and white sketches depicting a variety of personal, social, and conflict situations.
Advantages:	Nonthreatening; allows children to make up stories that provide insight into their fantasy lives.
Disadvantages:	No information on norms, reliability, or validity. TAT as good as the examiner's interpretive skills; requires extensive training and examiner intuition.

COMMONLY USED MEASURES OF ADAPTIVE BEHAVIOR

The clinician uses a standardized measure of adaptive behavior to assess the child's individual strengths and weaknesses relative to the environment. Most commonly, the clinician will assess adaptive behavior of children referred for significant emotional disturbance, developmental disability, and/or mental retardation.

Most adaptive behavior scales use an interview format. Thus the results depend on the rater's familiarity with the child and (to a lesser extent) the examiner's familiarity with the instrument. The box on p. 63 presents some of the more commonly used adaptive behavior scales.

COMMONLY USED MEASURES OF ACADEMIC ACHIEVEMENT

Clinicians use standardized achievement tests to ascertain a child's academic skill levels. These evaluations may screen for additional, in-depth academic attainments; assess a specific academic skill; or generate a comprehensive academic profile. The box on p. 64 presents some of the most commonly used measures of academic achievement.

From kindergarten through twelfth grade, most school districts participate in group-administered achievement tests to determine grade-specific academic strengths and weaknesses. Norm-referenced tests compare the child's obtained score(s) to a standardization group defined by characteristics such as age, gender, and educational level. In contrast, criterion-referenced tests compare the child's performance to a pre-established standard that represents either mastery or a particular level of performance. The box on p. 65 presents a few of the most commonly used measures of group-administered achievement tests.

PROCEDURAL APPLICATION OF COMMONLY USED PSYCHOLOGICAL TESTS

Primary care clinicians actively participate in the assessment and treatment of all facets of a child's life. As such, the primary care clinician may need to become proficient in reviewing the test results of commonly used psychological measures.

For example, suppose a parent(s)/caregiver(s) brings the child in to a primary care clinician to rule out attention deficit/hyperactivity disorder (ADHD). The parent(s)/caregiver(s) gives the primary care clinician a copy of the child's current psychological evaluation. When considering a diag-

AAMD Adaptive Behavior Scale (ABS)[2,29]

Ages:	3 to 69 years
Description:	Assesses adaptive behaviors of mentally deficient, emotionally maladaptive, and developmentally disabled individuals; informants may include parent/caretaker or teacher (the latter using the AAMD ABS School Edition).
Content:	Ten behavior domains assessing survival skills, personal independence, and daily living skills; 14 maladaptive domains assessing personality and behavior disorders.
Advantages:	Useful for measuring adaptive behavior of institutionalized children.
Disadvantages:	Limited standardization and reliability data; insufficient validity information.

Battelle Developmental Inventory[2,29]

Ages:	Newborn to 8 years
Description:	Standardized test that provides comprehensive assessment or developmental skill levels; assists school personnel in developing individualized education plans.
Content:	Five domains: personal-social, adaptive, motor, communication, and cognitive; 341 items (screening version has 96 items).
Advantages:	Useful for assessing developmental levels in very young children.
Disadvantages:	Requires additional reliability and validity data.

Developmental Profile II (DP-II)[43,44]

Ages:	Newborn to 9-6 years
Description:	Quick, standardized inventory that generates an overall profile of a child's functional developmental age.
Content:	Five areas: physical age; self-help age; social age; academic age; and communication age; 186 items.
Advantages:	Does not require extensive training to administer; provides an overall screening of a child's developmental levels.
Disadvantages:	Questionable standardization, reliability, and validity; considered a screening instrument, *not* a comprehensive, individualized instrument for assessing adaptive behavior.

Vineland Adaptive Behavior Scales (VABS)[2,29]

Ages:	Newborn to 18 years
Description:	Assesses adaptive behavior in mentally deficient children.
Content:	Four domains: communication, daily living skills, socialization, and motor skills; adaptive behavior composite score; maladaptive behavior measured on survey and expanded VABS.
Advantages:	Excellent norms; excellent reliability and validity for general composite score.
Disadvantages:	Requires additional research as to its effectiveness in measuring adaptive behavior.

INDIVIDUALLY ADMINISTERED ACHIEVEMENT TESTS

Peabody Individual Achievement Test—Revised (PIAT-R)[29,41]

Ages:	5 to 18 years
Subtests:	General information; reading recognition; reading comprehension; mathematics; spelling; written expression.
Comment:	Comprehensive individually administered achievement test, with content ranging from preschool through post-high school.

Peabody Picture Vocabulary Test—Revised (PPVT-R)[2]

Ages:	2-6 years to adult
Subtest:	Receptive vocabulary.
Comment:	Vocabulary screening instrument for children with expressive language difficulties.

Wechsler Individual Achievement Test (WIAT)[45]

Ages:	5 years to 19-11 years
Subtests:	Screening of basic reading, mathematics reasoning, and spelling. Total test includes screening plus reading comprehension, numerical operations, listening comprehension, oral expression, and written expression.
Comment:	WIAT can function as a screening of gross achievement skills or as a comprehensive, individually administered achievement test. Co-normed with Wechsler Individual Mental tests.

Wide Range Achievement Test 3 (WRAT-3)[42]

Ages:	5 to 75 years
Subtests:	Reading, spelling, and arithmetic.
Comment:	Brief screening test of basic academic skills; comes in two alternate test forms for pre- and post-testing.

Woodcock-Johnson Psycho-Educational Battery—Revised, Part II (WJ-R)[29]

Ages:	3 years to adult
Subtests:	Broad reading, broad mathematics, broad written language, broad knowledge, and skills. Supplemental subtests in reading, mathematics, and written language.
Comment:	Psychometrically sound individual achievement test; supplemental subtests enable clinician to more thoroughly explore academic weaknesses.

GROUP-ADMINISTERED ACHIEVEMENT TESTS

California Achievement Test (CAT)[29]

Grades: Kindergarten through 12th grade
Subjects: Reading, spelling, language, mathematics, and study skills.
Comment: Eleven grade-specific CATs ranging from kindergarten
                (Form E, Level 10) through high school (Forms E and
                F, Level 20).

Iowa Tests of Basic Skills (ITBS)[29]

Ages: Kindergarten through 12th grade
Subjects: Grade-specific.
Comment: Several ITBSs ranging from kindergarten assessment of
                early basic skills to high school assessment of basic skills.

Stanford Achievement Test[29]

Ages: Kindergarten through 9th grade
Subjects: Grade-specific.
Comment: Several tests ranging from kindergarten assessment of
                sounds and letters, word reading, listening to words and
                stories, mathematics, and environment to 9th grade as-
                sessment of reading vocabulary and comprehension,
                English, study skills, spelling, mathematics, science, social
                science, using information, and thinking skills.

---

nosis of ADHD, what would the primary care clinician look for in the psychological report?

First, the primary care clinician may elect to review the reason for referral, history, and behavioral observations from the report. Second, the primary care clinician may wish to review the results of intelligence testing (e.g., the WISC-III).

Using the WISC-III, the primary care clinician knows that this individual mental test (mean = 100, SD = 15) can break down test results into index scores (e.g., verbal comprehension, perceptual organization, freedom from distractibility, and processing speed). As such, the primary care clinician may investigate the child's WISC-III index scores to determine if any significant discrepancies (i.e., >15 points) exist between index scores.

For the sake of illustration, let's say a child's WISC-III index scores revealed average verbal comprehension, perceptual organization, and processing speed in contrast to significantly deficient freedom from distractibility. From here, the primary care clinician could inspect the two subtest scale scores comprising freedom from distractibility (arithmetic and digit span). Finding both subtests significantly lower than the other scaled scores, the primary care clinician may speculate that the child has difficulties with attention and concentration.

From here, the primary care clinician moves on to review achievement test results. Perhaps the child (again) shows significant deficiencies in those academic tasks that demand sustained attention and concentration. The primary care clinician may entertain the idea of a pattern as he/she peruses the psychological test results. From here, the primary care clinician could review the social-emotional test results.

According to the psychological report, the parent(s)/caregiver(s), teacher(s), and student complete the Child Behavior Checklist (CBCL/4-18), Teacher Report Form (TRF) and Youth Self-Report (YSR), respectively. All three behavior rating scales may clearly show that the child exhibits significant difficulties with those symptoms frequently associated with ADHD (e.g., careless mistakes in school work, inability to sustain attention across activities, not being able to listen, easily distracted and forgetful). The results of the Achenbach tests (e.g., CBCL/4-18, TRF, YSR) may support direct observations as well as the developmentally young responses that the child may give during projective testing. A final piece of the puzzle, adaptive testing, may clearly show evidence that the child has experienced neurodevelopmental delays.

In summary, the primary care clinician carefully reviews intelligence testing, achievement testing, behavior rating scales and observations across settings, projectives, adaptive behavior, and sensory-motor skills. The primary care clinician concludes that the child's psychological report appears consistent with those symptoms frequently associated with ADHD.[46,47]

REFERENCES

1. *Standards for educational and psychological testing,* Washington, DC, 1985, American Psychological Association.
2. Sattler JM: *Assessment of children,* ed 3, San Diego, 1992, JM Sattler.
3. Greydanus DE, Wolraich ML, editors: *Behavioral pediatrics,* New York, 1992, Springer-Verlag.
4. Kramer JJ, Close Conoly J, editors: *The Eleventh Mental Measurements Yearbook,* Lincoln, NE, 1994, The University of Nebraska Press.
5. Close Conoly J, Impara JC, editors: *The supplement to the Eleventh Mental Measurements Yearbook,* Lincoln, NE, 1994, The University of Nebraska Press.
6. Thorndike RL, Hagen EP, Sattler JM: *Guide for administering and scoring the Stanford-Binet Intelligence Scale: Fourth Edition,* Chicago, 1986, Riverside Publishing.
7. Thorndike RL, Hagen EP, Sattler JM: *Technical manual, Stanford-Binet Intelligence Scale: Fourth Edition,* Chicago, 1986, Riverside Publishing.
8. Association for Advanced Training in the Behavioral Sciences: *Preparatory course for the psychology written examination,* ed 37, vol 5, *Psychological assessment,* Westlake Village, CA, 1994, The Association.

9. Wechsler D: *Manual for the Wechsler Intelligence Scale for Children: Third Edition*, San Antonio, 1991, The Psychological Corporation.

10. Wechsler D: *Manual for the Wechsler Preschool and Primary Scale of Intelligence—Revised*, San Antonio, 1989, The Psychological Corporation.

11. Kramer JH. Interpretation of individual subtest scores on the WISC-III, *Psychol Assess* 5(2):193-196, 1993.

12. Sattler JM, Atkinson L: Item equivalence across scales: the WPPSI-R and WISC-III, *Psychol Assess* 5(2):203-206, 1993.

13. Sattler JM: *Assessment of children*, ed 2, Boston, 1982, Allyn and Bacon.

14. Bayley N: *Bayley Scales of Infant Development*, ed 2, San Antonio, 1993, The Psychological Corporation.

15. Preator KK, McAllister JR: Best practices, assessing infants and toddlers. In Thomas A, Grimes J, editors: *Best practices in school psychology*, ed 3, Washington, DC, 1995, The National Association of School Psychologists.

16. Burgemeister BB, Hollander Blum L, Large I: *Guide for administering and interpreting the Columbia Mental Maturity Scale*, San Antonio, 1972, Psychological Corp.

17. Goodenough FL, Harris DB: *Manual, Goodenough-Harris Drawing Test*, San Antonio, 1963, The Psychological Corp.

18. McCarthy D: *Manual, McCarthy Scales of Children's Abilities*, San Antonio, 1972, The Psychological Corp.

19. Paget KD: Best practices in the assessment of competence in preschool children. In Thomas A, Grimes J, editors: *Best practices in school psychology*, ed 2, Washington, DC, 1990, The National Association of School Psychologists.

20. Achenbach TM: *Manual for the Child Behavior Checklist/4-18 and 1991 Profile*, Burlington, VT, 1991, University of Vermont Department of Psychiatry.

21. Achenbach TM: *Manual for the Teacher's Report Form and 1991 Profile*, Burlington, VT, 1991, University of Vermont Department of Psychiatry.

22. Achenbach TM: *Manual for the Youth Self-Report and 1991 Profile*, Burlington, VT, 1991, University of Vermont Department of Psychiatry.

23. Conners CK: *Manual for Conners' Rating Scales*, North Tonawanda, NY, 1989, Multi-Health Systems.

24. Archer RP: Minnesota Multiphasic Personality Inventory—Adolescent. In Marvish ME, editor: *The use of psychological testing for treatment planning and outcome assessment*, Hillsdale, NJ, 1994, Lawrence Erlbaum Associates.

25. Piers E: *Piers-Harris Children's Self-Concept Scale*, Los Angeles, 1984, Western Psychological Services.

26. Bellak L, Bellak SS: *A manual for the Children's Apperception Test (animal figures) (CAT)*, ed 8, Larchmont, NY, 1991, CPS Inc.

27. Bellak L, Hurvich MS: *Children's Apperception Test (human figures) (CAT-H)*, Larchmont, NY, 1990, CPS Inc.

28. Bellak, L, Bellak SS: *Manual for supplement to the Children's Apperception Test (CAT-S)*, Larchmont, NY, 1991, CPS Inc.

29. *The ETS Test Collection Catalog*, 6 vols, Phoenix, Oryx Press.

30. Buros OK, editor: *The Sixth Mental Measurements Yearbook*, Highland Park, NJ, 1965, Gryphon Press.

31. Groth-Marnat G: *Handbook of psychological assessment*, ed 2, New York, 1990, John Wiley & Sons.

32. Exner JE: *The Rorschach: a comprehensive system*, vol 1, *Basic foundations*, New York, 1986, John Wiley & Sons.

33. Exner JE: *The Rorschach: a comprehensive system*, vol 2, *Current research and advanced interpretation*, New York, 1978, John Wiley & Sons.

34. Buros OK, editor: *Personality tests and review II,* Highland Park, NJ, 1975, Gryphon Press.
35. Buros OK, editor: *The Seventh Mental Measurements Yearbook,* Highland Park, NJ, 1972, Gryphon Press.
36. Achenbach TM: *Manual for the Child Behavior Checklist/2-3 and 1992 Profile,* Burlington, VT, 1992, University of Vermont Department of Psychiatry.
37. Knoff HM: Best practices in personality assessment. In Thomas A, Grimes J, editors: *Best practices in school psychology,* ed 2, Washington, DC, 1990, The National Association of School Psychologists.
38. Levine MD, Carey WB, Crocker AD, editors: *Developmental-behavioral pediatrics,* ed 2, Philadelphia, 1992, WB Saunders.
39. Hintze JM, Shapiro ES: Best practices in the systematic observation of classroom behavior. In Thomas A, Grimes J, editors: *Best practices in school psychology,* ed 2, Washington, DC, 1990, The National Association of School Psychologists.
40. Lentz FE, Wehmann BA: Best practices in interviewing. In Thomas A, Grimes J, editors: *Best practices in school psychology,* ed 2, Washington, DC, 1990, The National Association of School Psychologists.
41. Markwardt, FC: *Peabody Individual Achievement Test—Revised Manual,* Circle Pines, MN, 1989, American Guidance Service.
42. Wilkinson GS: *The Wide Range Achievement Test—Revision 3, Administration Manual,* Wilmington, DE, 1993, Wide Range.
43. Alpern G, Boll T, Shearer M: *Developmental Profile II Manual,* Los Angeles, 1986, Western Psychological Services.
44. Kramer JJ, Close Conoly J, editors: *The Tenth Mental Measurements Yearbook,* Lincoln, NE, 1989, The University of Nebraska Press.
45. *Manual, Wechsler Individual Achievement Test,* San Antonio, 1992, The Psychological Corporation.
46. Levine MD: Attentional variation and dysfunction. In Levine MD, Carey WB, Crocker AC, editors: *Developmental-behavioral pediatrics,* ed 2, Philadelphia, 1992, WB Saunders.
47. Scheiner AP: Referral processes. In Levine MD, Carey WB, Crocker AC, editors: *Developmental-behavioral pediatrics,* ed 2, Philadelphia, 1992, WB Saunders.

CHAPTER 2B

Assessment of Motor Development

LISA CRAFT

A physician or other health care provider usually refers an infant or child for motor assessment because of delay in achievement of expected milestones or because of abnormal movements or unusual quality of movement. The decision to refer may be based on the physician's clinical judgment or use of a developmental screening instrument. Depending on the nature of the test and the training required, a physical therapist, occupational therapist, or psychologist may then perform the motor evaluation.

The evaluator selects a test to fit the age and needs of the child. The purpose of most tests is to describe a child's current level of motor function using an objective measurement. A test may also be used to program or plan intervention, to monitor a child's progress, and, if appropriate, to predict future outcome. A measure of motor status may assess fine motor, gross motor, and/or perceptual-motor skills and provide a developmental level or age equivalent. Some tests also provide for a description of the quality of a child's skills, considering such factors as speed, timing, and ease or smoothness of movement.

Because most motor tests are descriptive rather than diagnostic, the evaluator and involved physician must determine the significance of the results of the motor assessment. The results must be interpreted in the context of the total child and his/her needs. In fact, a motor assessment may be part of a complete interdisciplinary evaluation that considers other aspects of the child's development, including cognition, communication, personal-social skills, and emotional health. Evaluators must also consider the child's physical development and general health, which may impact his/her achievement of motor skills.

Motor tests do not diagnose motor dysfunction; therefore, the role of the involved physician includes assessment of deep tendon reflexes, primitive and protective reflexes, muscle tone and strength, range of joint motion, quality of movement, and musculoskeletal status as well as the child's physical development and overall health. Medical assessment may determine that the child has an identifiable condition, such as a myopathy or neuropathy, meningomyelocele, congenital anomaly, or cerebral palsy. A child with poor motor skills may also be found to have developmental coordination disorder (clumsiness), which is sometimes associated with conditions such as learning disability or attention deficits. Complete developmental assessment may also determine that a child's motor delay is part of a global developmental problem, such as mental retardation or autism.

TESTS OF MOTOR DEVELOPMENT

Therapists and psychologists use a variety of measures of gross motor and fine motor abilities. Several commonly used tests are described following.

Infants and young children

Bayley Scales of Infant Development: Second Edition (1 month to 42 months of age). The Bayley-II provides a comprehensive assessment that includes a mental scale, motor scale, and behavior rating scale. The motor scale evaluates both fine and gross motor abilities, providing a score expressed as a psychomotor developmental index and as a developmental age. The examiner can also obtain information about the quality of a child's motor movements by using the behavior rating scale. The Bayley-II is typically used to identify developmentally delayed children and is also used as a research tool and to monitor results of intervention. Recent revision of the Bayley has provided extension of the age range and updated normative data. Norms were obtained from a national, stratified random sample of 1700 children, with proportionate representation of demographic groups. The manual presents several studies that support the Bayley-II's construct and content validity. Investigation of predictive validity suggests that specific subscales (rather than the overall scale) and scores obtained in children past 2 years of age are more predictive of future ability. Concurrent validity with two other measures of development was good, with correlations of .63 to .73 and .57 to .77 for the mental scale but only .37 to .41 and .18 to .59 for the motor scale. Reliability coefficients for the motor scale range from .75 to .91, with an average standard error of 6.01. The motor scale shows test-retest reliability of .78 (stability coefficient), with interrater agreement of .75.[1]

Milani-Comparetti Motor Development Screening Test (birth to 2 years). The Milani-Comparetti provides a simple format to assess and follow motor development. This test requires no special equipment and can easily be completed by a physician, nurse, or therapist in a few minutes. It includes assessment of spontaneous movements and developmental reflexes or reactions.[2] The instruction manual was based on the neurodevelopmental examination developed by Milani-Comparetti and Gidoni.[3,4] The Milani-Comparetti functions as a screening tool to provide ages for expected movements and reactions but does not provide normative data.

Movement Assessment of Infants (MAI) (birth to 12 months). The MAI assesses infants' motor abilities by evaluating muscle tone, primitive reflexes, automatic reactions, and volitional movement. The examination provides a risk score that indicates risk of motor delay or abnormal motor function.[5] It provides a description of motor development, but its predictive value has not been fully established.[6-8] Complete normative data have not been provided.

Peabody Developmental Motor Scales (PDMS) and Activity Cards (birth to 83 months). The PDMS, a standardized, norm-referenced and criterion-referenced test, assesses fine and gross motor skills, including abilities that are emerging. It includes a fine motor scale and a gross motor scale, with scores that can be expressed as an age equivalent, percentile rank, standard score, or developmental motor quotient. Uses of the PDMS include identifying children with delayed or abnormal motor skills and monitoring progress. The Activity Cards provide an instructional program to address a child's identified needs. The norming sample for the PDMS included 617 United States children, selected by stratified quota sampling to provide a representative group. Analysis shows content and construct validity to be excellent, including .99 correlation of total score and age. Tests of concurrent validity include correlations ranging from .36 to .62 with two other measures of motor ability. Test-retest reliability was .80 to .95, with interrator reliability of .94 to .97.[9]

The Revised Gesell Developmental Schedules (4 weeks to 36 months). The Gesell includes measurement of gross motor and fine motor skills in young children. It also assesses adaptive, language, and personal-social abilities, thereby providing a comprehensive developmental profile. Evaluation provides a developmental quoteint for each area. Examination of 927 New York children provided norms for the revision of the original Gesell.[10] Further data are needed to determine Gesell's reliability, validity, and adequacy of norms.

Older children

Bruininks-Oseretsky Test of Motor Proficiency (4.5 to 14.5 years). The Bruininks, a standardized test of motor function, contains eight subtests that assess running speed and agility, balance, bilateral coordination, strength, upper-limb coordination, response speed, visual-motor control, and upper-limb speed and dexterity. The complete test provides a gross motor composite, a fine motor composite, and a battery composite. Results can be expressed as a standard score, percentile rank, stanine, or age equivalent. The short form of the Bruininks yields a single score of general motor ability. Norms were obtained on 765 subjects (676 from the United States, 89 from Canada), using a stratified sampling procedure to obtain a representative group. Several studies support the construct and content validity of the Bruininks, which includes most of the abilities that have been identified as important indicators of motor development. Statistical properties that support validity include median correlation of .78 (range of .57 to .86) between subtest scores and chronological age as well as correlation between individual test items and total subtest score ranging from .57 to .86 (internal consistancy). Test-retest reliability coefficients for composite scores ranged from .68 to .88, with coefficients between .29 and .89 for individual subtests. Inter-rater reliability is provided for only 1 of the 8 subtests and reveals a correlation of .98 (for raters who received training) and .90 (for those without formal training).[11] The Bruininks is often used to assess children with mild motor problems or poor coordination and is also useful in evaluating progress.[12]

Developmental Test of Visual-Motor Integration (VMI) (4 years to 17 years, 11 months). The VMI tests a child's ability to integrate visual perception and motor output by requiring the child to copy increasingly complex geometric forms. It endeavors to identify problems that may interfere with learning and behavior in educational settings and other situations. The manual for the VMI provides standard scores and percentile rankings for ages 4-0 through 17-11 and provides age equivalent scores for ages 2-11 through 18-0. A total of 5824 subjects (combined from three U.S. samples) provide the norms for the most recently revised VMI. Samples represent all major sectors of the U.S. population. Reported concurrent validity varies, including correlation of .89 with chronological age, range of .37 to .59 with various tests of intelligence, and average of .50 with academic readiness tests. Studies of interrater reliability reveal a median coefficient of .93 (range .58 to .99). A median of .81 (range .63 to .92) is reported for test-retest reliability.[13]

Peabody Developmental Motor Scales (PDMS) and Activity Cards (birth to 83 months). See previous discussion, p. 70.

Sensory Integration and Praxis Tests (SIPT) (4 years to 8 years, 11 months). The SIPT provides a revision and extension of Ayres' Southern California Sensory Integration Tests.[14] Norms are based on a nationally representative sample of 1997 children (133 from Canada, the remainder from the United States). Construct validity is supported by factor analyses and cluster analyses. Lack of comparable sensory integration and praxis tests makes assessment of concurrent validity difficult. However, evidence is presented to show the SIPT's ability to discriminate between normal and dysfunctional children (p < .01). Test-retest reliability is low (coefficient of approximately .5 or below) for four subtests but acceptable for the others. Interrater reliability is high (.94 to .99) for major parts of the test. The SIPT includes 17 tests of sensory input and motor performance, evaluating processes such as visual perception, visuomotor coordination, kinesthesia, proprioception, tactile perception, vestibular processing, balance, and praxis (motor planning).[15] Sensory integration theory assumes that the ability to process or integrate sensory input has a significant effect on a child's learning skills. Use of these techniques in the assessment and treatment of learning disability has generated controversy.[16] However, the SIPT, interpreted carefully, may yield useful information about sensory and motor difficulties that may be subtle and difficult to define in some children.[17]

Test of Motor Impairment (TOMI). The TOMI[18] contains eight items that test a child's level of motor function in three categories: manual dexterity, ball skills, and balance (static and dynamic). The summation of the scores yields a composite score or impairment score. The TOMI is useful in identifying and evaluating children who have motor coordination problems (clumsiness) that may interfere with daily activities, including school performance. The TOMI has been revised and standardized on a large number of British and North American children.[19-21]

SUMMARY

There is no single, ideal measure of motor development. An assessment should evaluate quality of movement, as well as quantity, and should consider a child's overall development and health. An examiner must rely on experience and clinical judgment in determining the significance of a child's performance on an objective test of motor development.

REFERENCES

1. Bayley N: *Bayley Scales of Infant Development: Second Edition,* San Antonio, 1993, The Psychological Corporation.
2. Meyer Children's Rehabilitation Institute: *The Milani-Comparetti Motor Development Screening Test,* Omaha, 1977, University of Nebraska Medical Center.
3. Milani-Comparetti A, Gidoni EA: Pattern analysis of motor development and its disorders, *Dev Med Child Neurol* 9:625-630, 1967.
4. Milani-Comparetti A, Gidoni EA: Routine developmental examination in normal and retarded children, *Dev Med Child Neurol* 9:631-638, 1967.
5. Chandler LS, Andrews MS, Swanson MW: *Movement Assessment of Infants Screening Test Manual,* Rolling Bay, WA, 1987, University of Washington.
6. Deitz JC, Crowe TK, Harris SR: Relationship between infant neuromotor assessment and preschool motor measures, *Phys Ther* 67(1):14-17, 1987.
7. Piper MC, Darrah J, Byrne P, Watt MJ: Effect of early environmental experience on the motor development of the preterm infant, *Inf Young Child* 3(1):9-24, 1990.
8. Hallam P, Weindling AM, Klenka H, et al: A comparison of three procedures to assess the motor ability of 12-month-old infants with cerebral palsy, *Dev Med Child Neurol* 35:602-607, 1993.
9. Folio MR, Fewell RR: *Peabody Developmental Motor Scales and Activity Cards,* Allen, TX, 1983, DLM Teaching Resources.
10. Knobloch H, Stevens F, Malone AF: *Manual of Developmental Diagnosis—the administration and interpretation of the revised Gesell and Amatruda Developmental and Neurologic Examination,* New York, 1980, Harper & Row.

11. Bruininks RH: *Examiner's Manual—Bruininks-Oseretsky Test of Motor Proficiency,* Circle Pines, MN, 1978, American Guidance Service.
12. Wilson BN, Polatajko HJ, Kaplan BJ, Faris P: Use of the Bruininks-Oseretsky Test of Motor Proficiency in occupational therapy, *Am J Occupa Ther* 49(1):8-17, 1995.
13. Beery KE: *The Developmental Test of Visual-Motor Integration—3rd Revision,* Cleveland, 1989, Modern Curriculum Press.
14. Ayres AJ: *Southern California Sensory Integration Tests,* Los Angeles, 1972, Western Psychological Services.
15. Ayres AJ: *Sensory Integration and Praxis Tests,* Los Angeles, 1989, Western Psychological Services.
16. Humphries T, Wright M, Snider L, McDougall B: A comparison of the effectiveness of sensory integrative therapy and perceptual-motor training in treating children with learning disabilities, *Dev Behav Pediatr* 13(1):31-40, 1992.
17. Henderson SE: The assessment of "clumsy" children: old and new approaches, *J Child Psychol Psychiatr* 28(4):511-527, 1987.
18. Stott DH, Moyes FA, Henderson SE: *The Henderson Revision of the Test of Motor Impairment,* San Antonio, 1984, Psychological Corporation.
19. Maeland AF: Handwriting and perceptual-motor skills in clumsy, dysgraphic, and "normal" children, *Percept Motor Skills* 75:1207-1217, 1992.
20. Levene M, Dowling S, Graham M, et al: Impaired motor function (clumsiness) in 5-year-old children: correlation with neonatal ultrasound scans, *Arch Dis Child* 67:687-690, 1992.
21. Marlow N, Roberts BL, Cooke RWI: Motor skills in extremely low birth weight children at the age of 6 years, *Arch Dis Child* 64:839-847, 1989.

CHAPTER 2C

Assessment of Language and Language Impairment

J. BRUCE TOMBLIN

As children grow they are confronted with increasing demands on their use of language as a tool for communication, learning, and problem-solving. The typical child rapidly acquires an impressive grasp of the complex system of language and also develops considerable facility in its use. The clinical assessment of language in children is intended to examine the child's growth status in language knowledge systems and domains of language use. During the past 20 years numerous instruments have been developed for the purpose of examining children's language growth. This abundance of clinical measures presents a bewildering array of different conceptual schemes for language and models of language assessment. In this chapter, we will attempt to provide a framework for language assessment that accommodates many of these approaches and instruments.

DIMENSIONS OF LANGUAGE AND LANGUAGE USE

Although we often talk about language use as though it is a single unitary cognitive trait, there is considerable evidence that it is comprised of several dimensions or components. Research on certain developmental disorders, such as autism,[1] William's syndrome,[2] specific language impairment,[3] and Down syndrome,[4] has shown that these dimensions can be differentially affected in development and are loosely coupled with regard to development. Table 2-7 is a schematic of the major components of language that are often examined in different language assessment instruments.

LANGUAGE FORM AND MEANING (LANGUAGE CODE)

The language code scheme provides for three major components (see Table 2-7) of any language assessment. The first component pertains to the form and meaning of the message managed by the language code. The language code is concerned with the meaning of messages and the forms that are used to convey these meanings. For the purposes of language assessment, form and meaning in the language code are divided into three areas, each having to do with a structural unit of the message—specifically words, sentences, and sentence complexes referred to as discourse that form stories, explanations etc. At each of these levels, as the child develops, there is an expansion of a meaning system and a form system for conveying this meaning. Thus a child's vocabulary expands as the child acquires new knowledge of things in the world, and, along with this, new word

Table 2-7 Components and subcomponents of language influencing the clinical assessment of children's language

Language components	Subcomponents
Language forms and meanings	Word
	Sentence
	Discourse
Language modalities	Comprehension: listening, reading
	Expression: speaking, writing
Language functions	Social/communicative
	Metalinguistic

forms to refer to this new knowledge. Words alone quickly become insufficient to express the semantic (meaning) relationships of propositions expressing ideas having to do with "who does what to whom, where, why, how, when. . ." This development of more complex propositional meaning is accompanied by the acquisition of grammatical devices to express these meanings. Furthermore, children acquire a facility with meanings that has to do with the complex relationships between propositions found in stories or recounts of past experiences. Along with this meaning development, children learn ways of organizing and expressing these complex relationships.

Traditionally, language assessment has been aimed at examining the child's developmental status with regard to the growth of vocabulary structures. Along with the development of speech sound skills, progress in the acquisition of vocabulary and grammatical skills is viewed as critical to language development during the preschool years. Discourse skills emerge during the preschool years, and in recent years these skills have been found to be very important for success during the early school years. Thus some instruments for language assessment now include measures of discourse development.

MODALITY

Although a principal objective for the assessment of children's language is a determination of the developmental status of the language code, we must always obtain this information in tasks that ask the child to comprehend or produce language. Comprehension requires that the child perceive a particular message and then, by using information-processing skills and a knowledge of the language code, determine a meaning for the message. Production or expression requires that the child conceive a meaning for a message and generate the appropriate word, grammatical form, and discourse organization. The expression of a message also involves the use of knowledge of the language code and information-processing skills as the message is formulated. Both comprehension and expression, therefore, draw upon the child's information-processing abilities and knowledge of the language code. Each of these language usage activities, however, places different demands on these skills, and, therefore, we may find children who have different profiles with regard to their performance as listeners and speakers. Thus language assessment protocols usually involve an examination of both comprehension and expression skills. We will see later that a knowledge of the child's comprehension abilities along with expression abilities is useful for prognostic judgments.

LANGUAGE FUNCTION

The reason we are concerned about children's language development is that language serves as a vital tool for many life activities. Early in the child's life the primary function of language is a social one. For the young child, language is a tool to control others or to be controlled by others, to seek information, and to share experiences. It is within this context of language serving as a social tool that the child acquires a knowledge of the various aspects of the language code. During this time the child has little conscious awareness of the form and content properties of language despite the ability to use the various aspects of the code to accomplish these social acts. The knowledge the child has of language is unconscious or tacit.

As the child approaches school age, he/she begins to consciously discover features of the language that have been learned and used for social functions. The child becomes aware that messages have parts to them such as words and sounds and these parts can be manipulated. This capacity to reflect on language as an object of conscious thought is referred to as metalinguistics. In recent years, it has been found that a child's proficiency with metalinguistic functions has been closely associated with the child's performance in school. The fact that many of the verbal tasks on intelligence tests such as the generation of word definitions involve metalinguistic functions further reinforces this predictive association.

A third function of language is that of a tool for thought, learning, memory, and problem-solving. Language is the principal vehicle through which the child learns in school, and, as the child is confronted with demanding situations, information is coded in language for retention and recall. Furthermore, the child becomes able to use the efficient coding properties of language to engage in problem-solving activities. Successful performance of these functions requires that the child invoke strategic cognitive operations in association with language skills.

APPLICATION OF FRAMEWORK TO LANGUAGE ASSESSMENT

The outline of language function just described provides a framework for the assessment of language in children. The objectives of most clinical examinations of language have to do with establishing the child's ability to use certain forms and content aspects of language within a particular modality and within the context of a particular function. Thus all language assessment procedures examine the child's performance at the intersection of the three primary dimensions of language: function, code, and modality. The specific aspects of language examined are determined by the developmental expectations for the child. Thus, for a 2-year-old, emphasis is placed on the child's speech sound, lexical, and early grammatical comprehension and production within a social/communicative context. In contrast, examination of a 5-year-old is more likely to focus on the comprehension and production of complex sentences and discourse within a social/communicative context, as well as metalingustic functions involving sound elements of words.

Primary objective of language assessment

At this point it should be apparent that our language system is complex and that within the context of the developing child the nature of the system and the demands placed on it change. As a result, there cannot be a single uniform assessment scheme for all children in all clinical circumstances. This means that the clinician must consider the basic objective of the clinical examination and tailor the protocol to fit this objective. The most common assessment objectives are the following.

Screening. There are certain situations in which the clinician wishes to identify those children out of a large client base or school population who may be at risk for language impairment. In this case, only those language behaviors that are highly predictive of language impairment based on a more thorough diagnostic examination need be included in the screening instrument. Such an examination may rely on parental report rather than direct observation of the child's communication performance and may not sample all the dimensions of the language framework described earlier. It is very important that screening instruments provide the clinician with pass-fail criteria that have reasonable diagnostic predictive powers.

Diagnosis. The diagnosis of language impairment is usually concerned with the establishment of the clinical status of the child with respect to language performance. In this context, there has usually been concern voiced about the child's language by the child's parents, teacher, or physician, and the diagnosis then addresses the concerns expressed in this complaint. The objective of the diagnosis, therefore, is to confirm or reject the concerns expressed and, if a problem exists, to provide a characterization of the child's language skills and deficits. This requires that the clinician obtain a more comprehensive sample of the child's communication performance. As noted earlier, the aspects of language that are examined will be determined by the child's age or developmental status. Some of the procedures may be standardized norm-referenced measures of language, whereas other measures may be based on observations of the child's natural communication performance or reports from informants about the child's performance in other settings.

Prognosis. It was noted earlier that the language status of the child is dynamic throughout the developmental period. There is substantial variation among children in the manner in which they progress in language development. Thus the determination that a child has a language problem at a certain point in development does not mean that the child's language difficulties will persist. Of those children who are using very limited language at 2 years of age, 40% will continue to have language difficulties when they are 4 years old.[5] There is also evidence that children who are in the later preschool years may also show sufficient improvement in language to be viewed as adequate language users by 8-years-old.[6] To date the primary prognostic indicator for improvement in language has been the child's receptive language skill. Those children with good language comprehension abilities are more likely to improve than those who have deficits in both comprehension and expression.

Treatment planning. The assessment of language is not only important for the determination of a language problem, it is also important for planning and monitoring treatment programs. Often those assessment instruments designed to be effective in determining the status of the child's language skills are not too helpful in guiding and evaluating a treatment program. Most language intervention programs are designed to promote growth in specific functional language skills. The particular language skills are dictated by the specific language demands placed on the child in the home or at school. Thus assessment procedures used for treatment planning are often direct observations of the child in these settings or simulations of these situations. The clinician must then determine the language skills the child appears to lack to perform these tasks successfully. In the school setting, this approach has been referred to as classroom-based and curriculum-based assessment.

Types of language assessment instruments

In recent years, the practitioner has been provided with a considerable array of language assessment instruments in order to address the clinical objectives mentioned previously. The selection of these instruments depends on the developmental level of the child and the purpose of the examination.

Language assessment of infants and toddlers

Screening. Delays in language development are often the most prominent signs of a broader array of developmental difficulties in children. Likewise, children who have isolated language problems that are persistent are at considerable risk for school and social difficulties. Screening for language delay is, therefore, a common component of Child Find activities whether they are accomplished in a hospital, pediatrician's office, or preschool program. Table 2-8 provides a listing of some of the common instruments used for screening the language skills of infants and toddlers. Many of these instruments sample selected listening and speaking behaviors of children from birth or 12 months to 36 months or more. The examination of language in an infant or toddler is challenging under the best of circumstances, and, when this must be done quickly, the clinician is left with little choice but to obtain information about the child's performance from a parent or other knowledgeable person. Fortunately, several studies[11,13,14] have shown that parental report regarding language development during this period of development is generally accurate and can be used for clinical evaluation purposes. Most of these instruments rely on this report information for most of the information obtained, although in some instances individual items require confirmation based on direct observation.

Diagnosis. Diagnostic evaluation of the language of infants and toddlers has, in the past, relied on three kinds of information, and in most evaluations all three sources of information are obtained. The first type of information is the parental description based on a structured or informal interview. The second type of information derives from standardized elicitation of communication behaviors. This may involve eliciting responses to verbal statements, such as requests to point to "eye," "nose," etc. or requests to name objects that are presented. These activities are most likely

Table 2-8   Language screening measures for infants and toddlers

Measures	Description
Early Language Milestone Scale (ELM; Coplan, 1987): birth to 3 years[7]	Examines listening, speaking, audition, and visual perception.
MacArther Communicative Development Inventory (Fenson et al, 1993)[8]	A parent report inventory of early word and phrase use.
Clinical Linguistic and Auditory Milestone Scale (Capute et al, 1986)[9]	Examines a broad range of communication skills in infants and toddlers.
Receptive-Expressive Emergent Language Scale (Bzoch and League, 1971)[10]	Information concerning prespeech, speech, receptive and expressive language provided by informant.
Language Development Survey (Rescorla, 1989)[11]	A parent checklist emphasizing expressive language. Referral guidelines are provided for toddlers.
Early Screening Profiles (Harrison et al, 1990)[12]	A broad-based screening instrument for children between 2 and 6. Provides information on motor, social, cognitive, and language development.

to be limited to children 18 months or older, and, even then, failure of a child to respond to these activities may reflect the child's discomfort or lack of familiarity with the setting and the task rather than the child's language ability. Several standardized and norm-referenced tests of language development for toddlers and young preschoolers are available and some of these are listed in Table 2-9.

The third method for examining a young child's language use involves play-based assessment. Play-based assessment consists of the examiner, parent, or possibly a sibling engaging the child in unstructured play activities. The clinician then observes the communication behaviors of the child in this setting. Such play activities provide the examiner an opportunity to observe the child using various aspects of the language code in the context of social/communication functions. These observations may be recorded on-

Table 2-9   Diagnostic tests of language development for use with infants and toddlers

Tests	Description
Assessing Prelinguistic and Early Linguistic Behaviors in Developmentally Young Children (Olswang et al, 1987)[15]	Examines cognitive precursors to word development as well as indices of receptive and expressive language and speech development. Provides norms based on 37 typical children.
Communication and Symbolic Behavior Scales (Wetherby and Prizant, 1990)[16]	Employs a combination of parent report, elicited, and naturalistic methods to obtain information on verbal and nonverbal symbolic/communicative behavior in children at developmental levels between 9 months and 2 years.
Preschool Language Scale—3 (Zimmerman, Steiner, and Pond, 1979)[17]	Samples select receptive and expressive language skills to yield receptive, expressive, and total norm-referenced language scores for children from birth to 7 years.
Sequenced Inventory of Communication Development—R (Hedrick, Prather, and Tobin, 1984)[18]	Provides receptive and expressive language age scores for children from 4 months to 4 years based on parent report and direct observation.
Rossetti Infant-Toddler Language Scale (Rosetti, 1990)[19]	A parent report instrument providing information on infant interaction and receptive and expressive speech and language performance. Largely a descriptive tool for children between birth and 4 years.

line and informally interpreted, or the clinician may record the child's behavior and later transcribe the child's utterances for more detailed analysis.
The most common measure obtained from such transcripts is the mean
length of utterance in morphemes (MLU). A morpheme is the smallest unit
of language to convey meaning. Words such as "dogs" or "played" are comprised of two morphemes each, where the stem (dog, play) is counted as one
morpheme and the marker for plurality (s) or past tense serves as a second
morpheme. During early development of grammar, children's grammatical
growth is reflected rather well in the average number of morphemes contained in sentences produced by the child. MLU can be computed rather
easily from a spontaneous speech sample, and norms are available for their
interpretation. Although MLU is a reasonably valid index of the child's
grammatical development until the index reaches a value of 4.5, many clinicians also use MLU as a general index of language development—a practice
that is less well justified particularly in clinical populations.

Naturalistic play-based observations provide a rich and inherently valid
picture of the child's use of language to negotiate play interaction. It is
widely believed that this context provides the most conducive context for
emerging language skills. There are some limitations, however, to play-
based observations. First, the nature and quality of the child's language
depends on the child's communicative partner; therefore, it is difficult to
standardize the setting and to make norm-referenced comparisons. It is also
difficult to obtain systematic information on language comprehension in
these unstructured interactions. As a result we learn more about the child
as a talker than as a listener in this setting.

Treatment planning. Clinical treatment programs for the infant and
toddler usually employ family-based methods in which parents are an integral part of the clinical management program. Much of the focus of these
programs is on parent-child interaction patterns and the general family dynamics and structure. For infants, the clinician may use informal observations or a structured observational tool such as the Parent Behavior Progression.[20] The ECO Scales[21] also provide for characterization of parent-
child communication and social interaction for infants and toddlers. These
assessment instruments provide information on the parent-child interaction patterns that may promote and support language development and
complement assessments of general family functioning that should be performed as a part of a transdisciplinary family treatment program.

Assessment of the preschool and early school age child

By the time the typical child reaches 3 years of age, language and communication skills will have developed to the point that the child can par-

ticipate in short conversational exchanges using basic sentence forms and meanings. By this age the child can also begin to engage in structured language use activities that are often included in standardized norm-referenced tests. It is now possible to obtain much more information on the child's language status directly from the child rather than through parental report. As a result of both the child's ability to participate in structured examinations and the greater complexity of the child's language at this level of development, there are many standardized language screening and diagnostic instruments available for the assessessment of language in children from 3 to 8 years of age.

Screening. Most of the language screening instruments for children in this age group obtain a sample of the child's language behavior within the context of a few elicited behaviors. The tasks included in these measures are similar to those described for language diagnosis, but there are fewer of them. Receptive language skills are examined by asking the child to listen to words and sentences and point to pictures or objects. Expressive language is often tested by asking the child to name pictures or objects and repeat sentences and short stories. In some instances a single score is obtained, cut-off values are provided for pass-fail decisions, and separate scores for comprehension and expression are given. Table 2-10 provides a list of some of the common preschool and early school age language screening tests.

Diagnosis. The diagnosis of language impairment in the preschool and school age child resembles that performed with the toddler in that multiple procedures are employed to obtain a comprehensive view of the child's language development status. With this age group, however, a greater emphasis is placed on direct observation of the child's performance, and parental report is used to supplement these observations. The typical language diagnostic protocol for children of this age will be naturalistic conversational tasks and more structured standardized tasks. The balance between these two approaches will be determined by the orientation of the clinician and the nature of the clinical service site.

The naturalistic observations may be very similar to those performed with the toddler in that the interactions will likely be play based, although the play will need to be age appropriate. Often these interactions will involve conversational talk woven into the play activity. Furthermore, the clinician can, as the co-conversationalist, manipulate the interaction to either facilitate or challenge the child's communication performance. In so doing, the examiner can observe how well the child can initiate and sustain a conversation and respond and repair instances of communication breakdown. In addition to observations of the child's conversational activity, the examiner will also observe the nature of the expressive language used by

Table 2-10   Language screening measures for use with preschool and early school-age children

Measures	Description
Screening Kit of Language Development (Bliss and Allen, 1983)[22]	Can be used with children from 2 to 5 years. Screens performance in receptive vocabulary, comprehension of commands, sentence usage, and story production.
Merrill Language Screening Test (Mumm, Secord, and Dykstra, 1980)	Designed for screening first-grade children for problems involving speech sound production, grammar and sentence complexity, comprehension and production of stories.
Fluharty Preschool Speech and Language Screening Test (Fluharty, 1978)[23]	Can be used to screen children between the ages of 2 and 6 within the areas of speech sound production, sentence production, and language comprehension.
Bankson Language Screening Test (Bankson, 1977)[24]	Designed for children between 4 and 7. Examines receptive vocabulary, expressive grammar, visual perception, and auditory memory/sequencing.
Communication Screen (Striffler and Willig, 1988)[25]	Provides screening information on language comprehension, expressive vocabulary, and sentence usage for 3- to 6-year-old children.

the child at the word and sentence level. A formal analysis of the child's grammatical performance can be accomplished by transcibing the child's utterances and performing one of the analyses described in Table 2-11.

Standardized language assessment tools for children of this age often-involve tasks requiring the comprehension and production of various language forms. Language comprehension tasks typically entail picture identification in response to spoken words or sentences. Common language production tasks involve picture naming for expressive vocabulary and sentence imitation or sentence completion for expressive grammar. Some of the language tests developed for children in this age range are designed to test one specific aspect of language. For example, the most widely used language test, the Peabody Picture Vocabulary Test—R,[26] uses a picture-pointing response to spoken words. This test provides information only about the child's receptive vocabulary development and is limited to ac-quistion of picturable nouns. A somewhat more comprehensive receptive test is the Test for Auditory Comprehension of Language,[28] which asks the child to listen to words, phrases, and sentences and identify the appro-

Table 2-11   Measures of grammatical complexity obtained from analyses of spontaneous speech samples

Measures	Description
Mean Length of Utterance (MLU)	A measure of the average number of morphemes per utterance. MLU is considered a valid index of grammatical development for values ranging from 1.01 to 4.49.
Developmental Sentence Scoring (DSS; Lee, 1974)	A measure of grammatical development found in children's spontaneously produced utterances. The measure is obtained by assigning developmentally weighted values to selected grammatical features of a child's utterances.
Index of Productive Syntax (Scarborough, 1990)[27]	Scores multiple instances of selected grammatical forms. These forms are arranged in development stages for preschool children.

priate picture. Finally, other tests such as the Test of Oral Language Development: 2—P[29] or the Clinical Evaluation of Language Fundamentals—Preschool[30] provide a set of subtests that examine receptive and expressive language at the word, sentence, and, in some instances, discourse levels. In most cases, these tests provide norms so that the clinician can perform a norm-referenced interpretation of the child's performance; however, the user should be careful to determine the adequacy of the norms for the population being examined.

For those children approaching or who are in school, clinicians may choose to include a measure of metalinguistic function. These measures-may involve tasks such as word definition and judgments of sentence acceptablility. However, the most likely measure to be included in testing will be phonological processing, which has been found to be closely associated with early reading success. The Lindamood Auditory Conceptualization Test[31] or the Test of Awareness of Language Segments[32] provides examples of such measures.

Treatment planning. Although standardized norm-referenced tests are useful in determining the existence of a language impairment, these measures are usually inadequate for determining specific treatment objectives. This is due, in large part, to one fact that, while items selected for these norm-referenced tests are chosen because they are effective for measuring individual differences in language performance, they may not be intrinsically functionally important language concepts or structures. As a result, assessment for treatment planning will likely use tests designed to determine skills that have been found to be important for communication performance in such settings as the home or classroom. For example, the Boehm Test of Basic Concepts[33] examines children's ability to comprehend words and phrases that are commonly used in and are important for kindergarten and first-grade classroom performance. Likewise, the Wiig Criterion-Referenced Inventory of Language[30] is designed to test several areas of communication performance that have been judged by the author to be important to communication success in children between the ages of 4 and 13. Naturalistic observation of the child at home or in the classroom is also a method that will provide information concerning the communication skills the child needs for success in a particular setting.

Assessment of the older school age child and adolescent

The provision of clinical speech-language services to the older school age child is becoming more common as we have become aware of the close association between school success and language skill. The methods and goals for this intervention, not surprisingly, are somewhat different than that provided for younger children. Most of those served have persistent and often wide-ranging language problems. Because it is not possible to resolve these difficulties, the treatment objectives are usually directed toward very functional communication skills and, as well, adaptive strategies for successful performance in the classroom and occupational settings.

Screening. Several tests, such as the Adolescent Language Screening Test[34] and the Classroom Communication Screening Procedure for Early Adolescents[35] have been developed for the purpose of screening older children's language problems. At this age level, however, comprehensive screening for language difficulties is not common, and instead most clinicians serving the school student body rely on teacher referral. Instruments such as the Pupil Rating Scale[8] can be used with teachers to aid them in making observations and referrals.

Diagnosis and treatment planning. The language skills examined in the older school age child will be those that are viewed as essential for school, social, and occupational success. Many of these language skills are dictated by the classroom curriculum; therefore, in recent years there has been an emphasis on classroom-based assessment methods both for diagnosis and treatment planning. Cirrin[36] provides a good summary of the approaches that can be used for classroom- and curriculum-based language assessment. This approach involves examining the language skills of the child, the language of the teacher, and the language of the texts and other curricular materials. For those who need more structured and standardized assessments, there are several language tests designed for this age group. The Clinical Evaluation of Language Fundamentals—3[37] is a lengthy battery of language tasks involving language comprehension, production, and metalinguistic tasks. This battery is widely used by clinicians serving the school age population. The Test of Adolescent and Adult Language—3[38] is also often used for the teenager. This test provides norm-referenced information on reading, writing, speaking, and listening. Some of the spoken language tasks involve tasks that place a heavy demand on information-processing skills.

SUMMARY

It should be clear by now that language assessment is a complex endeavor because of the vast range of human functions served by language and the inherent complexity of the system. Language assessment is made even more challenging by the fact that the assessment methods used need to be tailored to the particular clinical setting and purpose as well as the developmental level of the child. However, once the clinician has determined these factors, there are many tools available that can obtain the desired information needed to serve the client.

REFERENCES

1. Tager-Flusberg H: Dissociations in form and function in the acquisition of language by autistic children. In Tager-Flusberg H, editor: *Constraints on language acquisition: studies of atypical children,* Hillsdale, NJ, 1994, Lawrence Erlbaum Associates.
2. Mervis C, Bertrand J: Early lexical development of children with William's syndrome, *Gen Counsel* 6:134-135, 1995.
3. Leonard L: The use of morphology by children with specific language impairment: evidence from three languages. In Chapman R, editor: *Processes in language acquisition and disorders,* St Louis, 1992, Mosby.
4. Fowler A, Gelmanl R, Gleitman L: The course of language learning in children with Down syndrome: longitudinal and language level comparisons with young normally developing children. In Tager-Flusberg H, editor: *Constraints on language acquisition: studies of atypical children,* Hillsdale, NJ, 1994, Lawrence Erlbaum Associates.
5. Paul R: *Language disorders from infancy through adolescence,* St. Louis, 1995, Mosby.
6. Bishop DV, Adams C: A prospective study of the relationship between specific language impairment, phonological disorders, and reading retardation, *J Child Psychol Psychiatr Allied Discipl* 31(7):1027-1050, 1990.
7. Coplan J: *Early Language Milestone Scale,* Austin, TX, 1987, Pro-Ed.
8. Fenson L, Dale P, Resnick S, et al: *The MacArther Communicative Development Inventory,* San Diego, 1993, Singular.
9. Capute A, Shapiro B, Wachtel R, et al: The Clinical Linguistic and Auditory Milestone Scale, *Am J of Dis Child* 40:694-698, 1986.
10. Bzoch K, League R: *Receptive-Expressive Emergent Language Scale,* Gainesville, FL, 1971, Language Education Division, Computer Management Corp.
11. Rescorla L: The Language Development Survey: a screening tool for delayed language in toddlers, *J Speech Hear Disord* 54:587-599, 1989.

12. Harrison P, Kaufman A, Kaufman N, Bruinicks R, Rynders J, Illmer S, Sparrow C, Chicchetti D: *Early Screening Profiles*, Circle Pines, MN, 1990, American Guidance Service.

13. Dale P: The validity of a parent report measures on vocabulary and syntax at 24 months, *J Speech Hearing Res* 34:565-571, 1992.

14. Tomblin JB, Shonrock C, Hardy J: The concurrent validity of the Minnesota Child Development Inventory as a measure of young children's language development, *J Speech Hear Disord* 54:101-105, 1989.

15. Olswang L, Stoel-Gammon C, Coggins T, et al: *Assessing prelinguistic and early linguistic behaviors in the developmentally young*, Seattle, 1987, University of Washington Press.

16. Wetherby A, Prizant B: *Communication and Symbolic Behavior Scales*, Chicago, 1990, Riverside Publisher.

17. Zimmerman I, Steiner V, Pond R: *Preschool Language Scale—3*, San Antonio, 1979, Psychological Corp.

18. Hedrick D, Prather E, Tobin A: *Sequenced Inventory of Communication Development—R*, Seattle, 1984, University of Washington Press.

19. Rosetti L: *The Rossetti Infant-Toddler Language Scale: a measure of communication and interaction*, East Moline, IL, 1990, LinguiSystems.

20. Bromwich R, Khokha E, Fust L, et al: Parent Behavior Progression (PBP) form 1. In Bromwich R, editor: *Working with parents and infants: an interactional approach*, Baltimore, 1981, University Park Press.

21. MacDonald JD, Gillette Y: *ECO Scales*, Chicago, 1989, The Riverside Publishing.

22. Bliss L, Allen DV: *Screening Kit of Language Development*, East Aurora, NY, 1983, Slosson Education Publications.

23. Fluharty NB: *Fluharty Preschool Speech and Language Screening Test*, Chicago, 1971, Riverside Publishing.

24. Bankson NW: *Bankson Language Screening Test*, Baltimore, 1977, University Park Press.

25. Striffler N, Willig S: *The Communicatin Screen*, Tucson, 1981, Communication Skill Builders.

26. Dunn L, Dunn L: *The Peabody Picture Vocabulary Test—Revised*, Circle Pines, MN, 1981, American Guidance Service.

27. Scarborough H: Index of productive syntax, *Appl Psycholinguis* 11:1-22, 1990.

28. Carrow-Wollfolk E: *Test for Auditory Comprehension of Language—Revised*, Allen, TX, 1985, DLM Teaching Resources.

29. Newcomer P, Hammill D: *Test of Oral Language Development—2: Primary*, Austin, 1991, Pro-ed.

30. Wiig E: *Wiig Criterion-Referenced Inventory of Language*, San Antonio, 1990, Psychological Corp.

31. Lindamood C, Lindamood P: *Lindamood Auditory Conceptualization Test*, Allen, TX, 1979, DLM.

32. Sawyer D: *Test of Awareness of Language Segments*, Austin, 1987, Pro-Ed.

33. Boehm A: *Boehm Test of Basic Concepts*, New York, 1969, Psychological Corp.

34. Morgan D, Guilford A: *Adolescent Language Screening Test*, Tulsa, 1984, Modern Educational Corp.

35. Simon C: *Classroom Communication Screening Procedure for Early Adolescents—R*, Tempe, AZ, 1987, Communi-Cog.

36. Cirrin F: Assessing language in the classroom. In Tomblin JB, Morris H, Spriestersbach DC, editors: *Diagnosis in speech-language pathology*, San Diego, 1994, Singular Press.

37. Semel E, Wiig E, Secord W: *Clinical Evaluation of Language Fundamentals—3*, San Antonio, 1995, Psychological Corp.

38. Hammill D, Brown V, Larsen S, et al: *Test of Adolescent and Adult Language—3*, Austin, 1994, Pro-Ed.

CHAPTER 3

Developmental screening

FRANCES PAGE GLASCOE

Pediatricians are often the only professionals with knowledge of development who are in contact with young children. As a consequence, they have the important task of detecting developmental and behavioral problems. This task is challenging because of time constraints, limited reimbursement, refractory patient behavior, at-risk patients who may not often seek well-child care, and difficulties with the accuracy or length of popular screening tests. While 60% of pediatricians use screening tests, only 15% to 25% of pediatricians use these instruments routinely. Most rely instead on clinical judgment.[1-4] Unfortunately, research on clinical judgment suggests it identifies less than half the children with mild mental retardation or serious emotional/behavioral disturbance.[5-7]

How can pediatricians best identify patients with disabilities and monitor carefully those who are at risk for difficulties? How can this be accomplished in a manner that is both time- and cost-effective and workable in pediatric settings? Answers to these questions are the central focus of this chapter. Two somewhat diverse approaches are covered: *developmental screening* and *developmental/school surveillance*. Addressed in this chapter are the following: a rationale for developmental screening, criteria for selecting measures, a comparative review of selected screening tests, and techniques for using measures efficiently in medical settings. The section on developmental surveillance discusses a range of approaches, including the use of primary care classification systems, selection and weighting of clinical information, and techniques for enhancing clinical judgment. This chapter concludes with methods for triaging school-age patients with difficulties.

SCREENING PATIENTS
Rationale for developmental screening

The positive impact of early intervention on children's development, behavior, and subsequent school performance provides strong and compelling justification for pediatricians in their practices to identify children with difficulties. One approach to early detection is to use standardized screening tests. Indeed, the Committee on Disabilities, American Academy of Pediatrics, recommends that pediatricians screen for developmental problems *routinely* at each of the 12 well-child visits scheduled between the ages 0 to 5 years.[8] Why is it necessary to repeatedly screen patients? There are two essential reasons.

Development is malleable. Development is positively influenced by healthy environmental forces; for example, by parents with sufficient social support, education, and mental health whose parenting style is characterized by a high degree of reciprocity (e.g., responsiveness to child-initiated activities and communications).[9-10] Development, however, can be adversely affected by a range of risk factors, such as parental mental health problems, (e.g., substance abuse, depression, or anxiety), parents with less than a high school education, single-parent status, more than three children in the home, numerous stressful events (e.g., job loss, deaths in the family, physical illness, etc.), and minority and low occupational status. Another important risk factor is an authoritarian parenting style, wherein parents' communications with children are characterized by an abundance of commands and minimal mediated learning opportunities, such as expansion on a child-initiated topic of conversation. High-risk children (those with seven or more of the risk factors mentioned) are 24 times more likely than low-risk children to have IQs below 85.[9-10]

Because early environmental risk factors are not static and often change during childhood (e.g., due to divorce or marriage, acquisition or loss of employment, fluctuations in mental health status, addition of new siblings, etc.), developmental progress can be affected. To monitor changes in developmental status, repeated screening is necessary.

Development manifests with age. Children without any early signs of developmental problems may exhibit deficits as they grow older. For example, expressive language disorders cannot be detected until the age at which most peers can combine words. The concept of "age-related developmental manifestations"[11] means that every child has an increasing risk of disabilities as he or she matures. Accordingly, the prevalence of disabilities rises with age: only 1% to 2% of children between 0 to 24 months of age are found to have developmental problems, a figure that increases to 8% when 24- to 72-month-olds are added. For the entire developmental period (0 to 22 years), rates range from 11.8% (when using U.S. Department of Education data)[12] to 16.8% (when assessing consecutive samples of students in public schools).[13] Adding in those with behavioral and emotional problems provides a combined rate 22%.[14] The age-related manifestations of normal and atypical development illustrate the need for careful monitoring over time.

How to select a good screening test

Because of development's malleability and age-related manifestations, there is a clear need not only for screening, but for screening repeatedly. While it may not be practical for clinicians to repeatedly screen (alternative techniques in developmental surveillance are presented later in this chapter), it is still necessary for physicians to employ, occasionally, standardized screening tests. What are the best available tools? Unfortunately, in the United States, test publication is not a regulated industry, in contrast to the Canadian Psychological Association, which requires that publishers and authors report specific indicators of accuracy and attaches criminal penalties to noncompliance. In the absence of such enforceable standards, U.S. clinicians involved in screening must be well-informed about important features in measurement. Derived from *Standards for Educational and Psychological Tests* published by the American Psychological Association[15] and from the recommendations of researchers involved in screening,[16-19] the following screening test standards and related terms are defined.

Screening. Screening is a brief method for sorting those who probably have problems from those who probably do not. The group with probable difficulties are typically referred for more extensive diagnostic work-ups and, if diagnosed, are referred for treatment. Screening is not error-free but should be as accurate as possible in order to minimize the many expenses associated with both over-referrals and underdetection. The *accuracy* of a screening test is defined by its sensitivity, specificity, and positive predictive value.

Sensitivity. The percentage of children with true problems correctly identified by a screening test (e.g., by failing, abnormal, or positive results) is its sensitivity. Ideally, at least 80% of those with difficulties should be identified.

Specificity. The percentage of children without true difficulties correctly identified by a screening test (e.g., by passing, normal, or negative findings) is its specificity. Because there are many more children developing normally than not, specificity should be at least 90%, so as to minimize over-referrals.

Positive predictive value. The percentage of children with failing scores on screening tests who have a true problem is a test's positive predictive value. It is the likelihood that a positive screening test reflects a true problem.

Prescreening. Prescreening tests are extremely brief measures with a high degree of sensitivity but limited specificity. Prescreens are administered routinely to all children and are followed by screening tests only when children fail the prescreen. Although prescreening can simply compound error and lead to under-referrals, accurate prescreening should improve detection rates and save considerable time, because prescreens reduce, often by one half to two thirds, the numbers of children requiring complete screening.

Other characteristics of accurate screening tests

Validity. Accurate tests contain proof of various types of validity. *Content validity* refers to how well a test samples aspects of development. Items should cover a range of realistic behaviors that clearly reflect the domains measured and that are drawn from a wealth of research on developmental sequences. For example, a screening test that measures language should have items measuring both receptive and expressive language skills (and preferably articulation as well). *Concurrent validity* refers to the degree of correlation (preferably .60 or greater) between the screen and diagnostic measures. Concurrent validity should not be limited to correlations with intelligence tests because children can have normal intelligence and still have learning, language, or motor disabilities. Screening tests should be validated against a range of diagnostic measures and should correlate highly with indicators of academic, language, social, and motor skills. *Predictive* or *criterion-related validity* refers to correlations between screening tests and long-term outcome. Although it is not necessary for screening measures to provide evidence of long-term prediction, it is important for screens to sample heavily tasks that are most predictive of school success (i.e., language and preacademic skills such as letter recognition in 4- to 5-year-olds).[21]

Standardization/stratification/sampling. For a test to be valid, sensitive, and specific, it has to be standardized. This means that measures must include a sufficiently clear set of directions so that the testing can be administered in exactly the same way by different examiners working in different settings. Only then can a child's score be interpreted confidently—compared to the test's *norms* (the performance of a large group of children administered the test under similar conditions before test publication). Another question that must be answered before confident score interpretation is—how much was the normative sample like the patient you plan to test? If a child resides in New England and the test was normed in Florida, can scores be compared? If the child is from an impoverished background, is it reasonable to compare his or her performance to a sample that included only children from wealthy, educated families? Ideally, tests should be standardized or normed on a large group of children (e.g., 60 to 100 children per age range [3- to 6-month interval]) and should be stratified geographically and on the basis of ethnicity and socioeconomic status. The absence of appropriate stratification does not mean a test should not be used; it can be used if there is subsequent validation work by the author or by other researchers that supports the application of the measure with different populations.

Reliability. Screening tests should produce roughly the same score even if administered by different examiners or to the same child tested several days to several weeks apart. Reliability is usually expressed as a percentage of agreement (ideally 80% or greater) or as a correlation (ideally .90 or higher). There is, even with the best tests, some variability across domains (motor skills are more inconsistently expressed and hence are less reliable than language, academic, or cognitive skills.)

Miscellaneous. Good screening tests have a number of other features:

1. Materials should be interesting to children but sufficiently minimal in number that examiners can find them easily in the test kit.
2. Directions for item administration should be bold-faced or printed in color so they are easy to locate during testing.
3. Scoring procedures should be clear and simple so that computational errors are minimized.
4. The amount of training required to administer and score the test accurately and training exercises should be included in the manual.
5. Directions for interpreting test results to families should be included (e.g., examiners should be advised to avoid diagnostic labels, offer on-going support, telephone numbers, additional opportunities to discuss the results, etc.) and guidance should be given for the kinds of referrals that may be needed based on various profiles (e.g., failing scores on language domains but average performance in other areas should dictate a referral for speech-language evaluations, while deficits only in motor development areas should suggest neurological, physical, or occupational therapy evaluations).
6. It is helpful to have instruments include a prescreening subtest so as to minimize the time requirements, particularly in medical settings.
7. Alternative methods for administering items is desirable (e.g., parental report, observation, and/or direct elicitation) so that examiners can circumvent child recalcitrance, limited English on the part of parents or children, or parents with minimal knowledge of their child's development (such as when a parent is not the primary caretaker).

Specific screening instruments

There are numerous screening tests on the market. None meet all of the preceding recommendations but some approach the standards. Table 3-1

Text continued on p. 98.

Table 3-1 Screening tests

Test	Age range	Description	Scoring	Accuracy
Developmental screening				
Child Development Inventories (formerly Minnesota Child Development Inventories) Ireton H (1992), Behavior Science Systems, Box 580274, Minneapolis, Minnesota 55458 (612-929-6220) ($41.00)	3-72 months	Three separate instruments of 60 items each, uses parental report. Can be mailed to families, completed in waiting rooms, administered by interview or by direct elicitation. 300-item assessment level version may be used in follow-up studies and subspeciality clinics; produces scores in each domain.	Single cutoff tied to 1.5 standard deviation below the mean	Of seven validation studies, five found good to excellent sensitivity, good specificity. The two critical studies used subjects younger than norms or inappropriate cutoffs[22-27]
First Step (Screening Test for Evaluating Preschoolers) Miller LJ (1993), Psychological Corporation, 555 Academic Court, San Antonio, Texas 78204 (1-800-228-0752) ($139.00)	32-74 months	Uses direct elicitation to measure cognitive/preacademic, communication, motor skills, and observation/parental report to measure social-emotional, attention, behavior, and self-help. Well standardized although higher SES groups predominate. Takes 15 minutes and is easy to administer.	Scaled scores for each domain, classified as acceptable, caution, and at risk	Excellent sensitivity and specificity

Test	Age range	Description	Scoring	Comments
Brigance Screens Brigance AN (1985), Curriculum Associates, Inc., 5 Esquire Road, North Billerica, Massachusetts 01862 (1-800-225-0248) ($248.55)	21-90 months	Seven separate forms, one for each 12-month age range. Taps speech-language, motor, readiness, and general knowledge at younger ages and also reading and math at older ages. Uses direct elicitation and observation. Takes 10-15 minutes; includes 3-5 minute prescreen.	Cutoff and age equivalent scores for motor, language, and readiness and an overall cutoff	Good sensitivity and specificity to giftedness and to developmental and academic problems
Bayley Infant Neurodevelopmental Screen (BINS) Aylward GP (1995), The Psychological Corporation, 555 Academic Court, San Antonio, Texas 78204 (1-800-228-0752) ($195)	3-24 months	Uses 10-13 directly elicited items per 3-6 month age range; assesses neurological processes, neurodevelopmental skills, and developmental accomplishments (object permanence, imitation, and language).	Categorizes performance into low, moderate, or high risk via cut scores; provides subtest cut scores for each domain assessed in order to focus referrals	Excellent specificity and sensitivity
Battelle Developmental Inventory Screening Test (BDIST) Newborg J et al (1984), Riverside Publishing Company, 8420 Bryn Mawr Avenue, Chicago, Illinois 60631 (1-800-767-8378) ($99.00 + $270 if materials kit is purchased but test stimuli can be obtained for about $50 at discount stores)	12-96 months	Items use a combination of direct assessment, observation, and parental interview. The receptive language subtest may serve as a brief prescreen.[28] Difficult to administer and takes 15 to 35 minutes. Well standardized and validated.	Age equivalents (somewhat deflated), cutoffs at 1.0, 1.5, and 2.0 standard deviations below the mean	Good sensitivity and specificity[28]

Continued.

Table 3-1 Screening tests—cont'd

Test	Age range	Description	Scoring	Accuracy
Developmental screening—cont'd				
Ages and Stages Question-naire (formerly Infant Monitoring System) Bricker D, Squires J (1994), Paul H. Brookes Publishers, PO Box 10624, Baltimore, Maryland 21285 (1-800-638-3775) ($130)	0-36 months	Uses parental report and provides clear drawings and simple directions. Separate copyable forms of 10-15 items for each age range (tied to well-child visit schedule). Can be used in mass mailouts for child-find programs. Well standard-ized and validated.	Single pass/fail score	Good sensitivity and excel-lent specificity
Developmental Indicators for Assessment of Learning—Revised (DIAL-R) Mardell-Czudnowski C, Goldenberg D (1990), American Guidance Services, Circle Pines, Minne-sota (1-800-328-2560) ($264.95)	24-72 months	Separate subtests for mo-tor, language, and cogni-tive skills administered by direct elicitation. Easy to give and in-cludes helpful guidelines for interpreting and re-ferring. Does not tap academic skills.[29]	Percentiles for each subtest and total test	Modest sensitivity (57%), excellent specificity[29]
Denver-II (Formerly Denver Developmental Screening Test—Revised) Frankenburg W, Dodds J, Archer P et al (1990), Denver Developmental Materials, Inc., Box 6919, Denver, Colorado 80206 ($53.00)	0-72 months	Samples language, articula-tion, fine motor/adaptive, personal-social, gross motor skills. Easy to ad-minister and score, takes 20 minutes. Although re-liability is excellent, there are no validation studies.	Produces a single score: untestable, normal, ad-vanced, abnormal, or questionable classified as abnormal (which re-quires repeat screening with a 90% chance of identical scores)	Poor sensitivity (if ques-tionables scored as nor-mal) and poor specificity (if questionables scored as abnormal)[30]

Early Screening Profile (ESP) Harrison P, Kaufman A, Kaufman N, Bruininks R, Rynders J, Ilmer S, Sparrow S, Cicchetti D, American Guidance Services, Circle Pines, Minnesota (1-800-328-2560) ($264.95)	24-72 months	Measures language, articulation, cognition, motor, self-help, social, behavioral, home environment, and health. Excellent standardization but often fails to sample typical behaviors.	Age equivalents, percentiles, cutoffs	Poor sensitivity (27% to 61% across subtests and test total), excellent specificity
Behavioral/emotional screening				
Eyberg Child Behavior Inventory Eyberg S (1980), *Journal of Clinical Child Psychology*, 54:587-599 (measure is included in article)	2½-11 years	Presents parents with a 36-item list of common behavior problems, sampling internalization (anxiety, depression) and externalization (acting out, inattention, hyperactivity). Greater than 16 indicates need for referral. Few than 16 problems enables the measure to function as a problem list for use in-office counseling.	Single cutoff score	Excellent sensitivity and specificity[31-35]
Pediatric Symptom Checklist Jellinek MS, Murphy JM, Robinson J, et al (1988), Pediatric Symptom Checklist: screening school age children for psychosocial dysfunction, *Journal of Pediatrics*, 112:201-209 (test is included in article)	4-16 years	Presents parents with 35 common behavior problems, which parents rate as sometimes, never, or often. A value of 0-2 is assigned. Greater than 28 suggests need for referral.	Single cutoff score	Good sensitivity and excellent specificity in six of seven studies[36-42]

provides a critical discussion of several tests. Tests selected for discussion are those that (1) are suitable for a broad age range (four or more years), (2) cover most or all developmental domains (although some emotional/behavioral screens are discussed separately because few tests measure this domain), (3) approach standards, (4) are particularly useful in medical settings, and/or (5) are popular among health care professionals. Sensitivity and specificity were described as excellent if they exceeded 80%, good if exceeding 70%, and modest if less than 70%.

SCREENING HOME ENVIRONMENTS

Despite the known relationship between the psychosocial well-being of parents and their children, only recently have researchers produced measures that help pediatricians systematically and easily detect and address home environment contributors to children's developmental and behavioral status. Use of the screens in Table 3-2 can help identify families in need of referral for substance abuse, domestic violence, parenting skills, and mental health services. Some pediatric clinics use the screens described in Table 3-2 as routine questionnaires required of families when medical and developmental histories are obtained on patients (Fig. 3-1). There are several benefits to this approach: parents are more likely to disclose problems such as depression or history of physical/sexual abuse as a child in paper-pencil questionnaires than in verbal interviews,[43] and use of screening tools in waiting or exam rooms dramatically reduces the amount of professional time required to collect information.

Interpreting screening test results

There are two common pitfalls in explaining positive screening results to families: (1) overstating the results (e.g., making a diagnosis of mental retardation without the availability of I.Q. and adaptive behavior scores) or (2) understating the results (placing excessive emphasis on screening error while minimizing the high probability of a failing score reflecting a true problem). In both cases, the consequences are that parents may fail to follow through on a referral. The realities of limited follow through are reflected in the finding that fewer than 50% of families actually seek mental health and other recommended services.[51] The following suggestions may ensure that families seek recommended services:

1. Avoid diagnostic labels and use euphemistic language instead (e.g., "he seems behind other children and we need to look at this further

Text continued on p. 104.

Table 3-2 Screening home environments

Test	Age range	Description	Scoring
Parenting Behavior Checklist Fox RA (1993), Clinical Psychology Press, 4 Conant Square, Brandon, Vermont (1-800-433-8234) ($34.00).	1-4 years	Administered by parent report. Items are written at the 2nd to 3rd grade level and are descriptions of actual parenting behavior (e.g., "I spank my child for wetting his pants"). Items tap discipline (high scores indicate physical punishment), nurturing (low scores may indicate neglect), and knowledge of development. Well standardized.	Standard deviations above and below mean	Good sensitivity to changes in parenting skills[44-46]
Self-Administered Questionnaire for Psychosocial Screening (see Fig. 3-1)	Parents	A series of validated items measuring psychosocial risk factors including parental history of abuse as a child,[47] substance abuse,[48] and maternal depression.[49] These and other items comprise the clinic intake form used at the University of Washington. Guidelines for administering the screens and referring families are provided.[50]	"Red flag" responses on individual items	Excellent sensitivity and specificity

Circle either the word or the letter in **bold** for your answer where appropriate. Fill in answers where space is provided.

Are you the child's **A** Mother **D** Other Relative **B** Father **E** Foster Parent **C** Grandparent **F** Other	How many people live in your household? _____

How many times have you moved in the last year? _____ Times	Where is the child living now? **A** House or Apartment With Family **C** Shelter **B** House or Apartment With Relative or Friends **D** Other:

Do you feel that you live in a safe place?
                            Yes   **No**

What is your current monthly income, including public assistance?
          $ _____

Besides you, does anyone else take care of the child?
If yes, who?
                            Yes   **No**

Has child received health care elsewhere?
If yes, where?
                            Yes   **No**

Does the child take any medications?
If yes, what?
                            Yes   **No**

Does the child have any allergies to any medications?
If yes, what?
                            Yes   **No**

Has the child received any immunizations?
                            Yes   **No**

Which ones? _____
Where? _____

Has the child ever been hospitalized?
                            Yes   **No**

When? _____
Where? _____
Why? _____
_____

How would you rate this child's health in general?
  A Excellent   **B** Good   **C** Fair   **D** Poor

Do you have any concerns about your child's behavior or development? If yes, what:
                            Yes   **No**

How old are you? _____ Years Old	Are you? **A** Single **C** Separated **B** Married **D** Divorced **E** Other

What is the highest grade you have completed?
1 2 3 4 5 6 7 8 9 10 11 12 **(High School/GED)**
      13   14   15   16   17 18 19
Some College Or Vocational School   **College Graduate**   **Post Graduate**

PT. NO.

NAME

D.O.B.

Fig. 3-1 Routine questionnaire used when obtaining medical and developmental histories on patients.

Child's Name	Today's Date

FAMILY MEDICAL HISTORY

Does the child's mother, father, or grandparents have any of the following? If yes, who?

Yes	No	High Blood Pressure _____
Yes	No	Diabetes _____
Yes	No	Lung Problems _____
Yes	No	Heart Problems _____
Yes	No	Kidney Problems _____
Yes	No	Liver Problems _____
Yes	No	Miscarriages _____
Yes	No	Learning Problems _____
Yes	No	Nerve Problems (including seizures) _____
Yes	No	Mental Illness (Depression) _____
Yes	No	Drinking Problems _____
Yes	No	Drug Problems _____
Yes	No	Other _____

FAMILY HEALTH HABITS

How often does your child use a seatbelt (carseat)?

A Never   B Rarely   C Sometimes   D Often   E Always

Does anyone in your household smoke?

Yes   No

How much do you smoke?

_____ Packs per day   None

Have you ever had a drinking problem?

Yes   No

Have you tried to cut down on alcohol in the past year?

Yes   No

How many drinks does it take for you to feel high or get a buzz?   1   2   3   4   5   6   7 Or More

Do you ever have more than 5 drinks at one time?

Yes   No

Have you ever had a drug problem?

Yes   No

Have you tried to cut down on drugs in the past year?

Yes   No

Have you used any drugs in the last 24 hours? If yes, which ones?

Cocaine   Heroin   Methadone   Speed   Marijuana   Other:

_____

Are you in a drug or alcohol recovery program now? If yes, which one(s)

Yes   No

_____

PLEASE CONTINUE ON REVERSE SIDE OF THIS FORM

Fig. 3-1, cont'd. For legend see opposite page.   *Continued.*

In the past year, have you ever felt threatened in your home?	Yes	No

In the past year, has your partner or other family member pushed you, hit you, or threatened you with a weapon?	Yes	No

WHEN YOU WERE A CHILD

Did either parent have a drug or alcohol problem?	Yes	No

Were you raised part or all of the time by foster parents or relatives (other than your parents)?	Yes	No

How often did your parents ridicule you or criticize you, saying things that made you feel worthless?

A Frequently **B** Often **C** Occasionally **D** Rarely **E** Never

How often were you shaken?

A Frequently **B** Often **C** Occasionally **D** Rarely **E** Never

How often were you hit with an object such as a hairbrush, board, stick, wire, or cord?

A Frequently **B** Often **C** Occasionally **D** Rarely **E** Never

Do you feel you were physically abused?	Yes	No

Do you feel you were neglected?	Yes	No

Do you feel you were hurt in a sexual way?	Yes	No

Did your parents ever hurt you when they were out of control?	Yes	No

Are you ever afraid you might lose control and hurt your child?	Yes	No

Would you like more information about free parenting programs, parent hot lines, or respite care?	Yes	No

Would you like to talk with other parents who are dealing with parenting and alcohol or drug problems?	Yes	No

How often in the last week has this statement been true for you?

I Felt Depressed . . . . 0 1-2 3-4 5-7 days

In the past year, have you had two weeks or more during which you felt sad, blue, or depressed, or lost pleasure in things that you usually cared about or enjoyed?	Yes	No

Have you had two or more years in your life when you felt depressed or sad most days, even if you felt okay sometimes?	Yes	No

Have you felt depressed or sad much of the time in the past year?	Yes	No

What are your main concerns about your child?

_____

_____

_____

_____

_____

_____

_____

Fig. 3-1, cont'd. For legend see p. 100.

HELP AND SUPPORT

Whom can you count on to be dependable when you need help: (just write their initials and their relationship to you)

A No One   **B** _____   **C** _____

D _____   **E** _____   **F** _____

G _____   **H** _____   **I** _____

How satisfied are you with their support?

A Very Satisfied   **B** Fairly Satisfied   **C** A Little Satisfied
D A Little Dissatisfied   **E** Fairly Dissatisfied   **F** Very Dissatisfied

---

Who accepts you totally, including both your best and worst points?

A No One   **B** _____   **C** _____

D _____   **E** _____   **F** _____

G _____   **H** _____   **I** _____

How satisfied are you with their support?

A Very Satisfied   **B** Fairly Satisfied   **C** A Little Satisfied
D A Little Dissatisfied   **E** Fairly Dissatisfied   **F** Very Dissatisfied

---

Whom do you feel truly loves you deeply?

A No One   **B** _____   **C** _____

D _____   **E** _____   **F** _____

G _____   **H** _____   **I** _____

How satisfied are you with their support?

A Very Satisfied   **B** Fairly Satisfied   **C** A Little Satisfied
D A Little Dissatisfied   **E** Fairly Dissatisfied   **F** Very Dissatisfied

Fig. 3-1, cont'd. For legend see p. 100.

to see if we can help him catch up"; "she seems to be having more difficulty than most children at learning to cooperate, adjusting to life . . .," etc.)

2. Give parents telephone numbers and descriptions of programs (this may reduce literacy barriers in seeking services and minimize parents' fears about how other professionals will treat them).

3. Provide ongoing support (let parents know they may have "cold feet" about following through and that family members waiting at home may disagree with the findings; prepare a parent in advance for possible conflict and offer a second interpretation for other family members to strengthen resolve in pursuing services).

4. Use a prescription pad to list needed referrals (this adds an aura of medical credibility to nonmedical recommendations and may be a powerful tool for encouraging parents to follow through).

Efficient use of screening tests in pediatric practice

Can screening tests be used effectively in pediatric settings? Are there time- and cost-efficient ways to administer tests to all patients? Following is a list of ways some pediatricians have addressed this challenge:

1. Ask parents to complete parent-report instruments while in waiting or exam rooms.

2. Mail parent-report tests in advance of well visits so that physicians need only score and interpret tests during the visit. This often improves the quality of the parent report because families may have sufficient time to respond thoughtfully. Advance mailings are also helpful with families whose English is limited because they can usually find someone in the community to help translate items.

3. Tape-record directions and items on parent-report instruments and use simplified answer sheets to circumvent illiteracy.

4. Train office staff to administer, score, and even interpret screening tests.

5. Pool resources with partners so that a practice can hire a developmental specialist to administer screening tests (and perhaps provide parent counseling, training, diagnostic evaluations, and referrals).

6. Train volunteers to administer screening tests on a periodic basis.

7. Maintain a current list of telephone numbers for local service providers (e.g., speech-language centers, school psychologists, mental

health centers, private psychologists and psychiatrists, state/local child-find services through Individuals with Disabilities Education Act, parent training classes, etc.). The availability of brochures describing services may promote parental follow-through on referral suggestions.

8. Encourage professionals involved in hospital-based care (e.g., child-life workers) to screen patients.

9. Use prescreening tools to identify patients in need of a second appointment during which screening measures are administered. This is especially helpful when important developmental concerns are raised at the end of an encounter (e.g., set up a second appointment and send families home with a parent-report screening tool to complete).

10. Collaborate with local service providers (e.g., day care centers, Head Start, public health clinics, Department of Human Services workers, etc.) to establish community-wide child-find programs that use valid, accurate screening instruments.

DEVELOPMENTAL SURVEILLANCE

Despite the availability of reasonably accurate, brief, and flexible screening measures, their routine use in pediatric settings is modest. Perhaps, as a consequence, recent research has focused on detection methods that capitalize on the process, style, strengths, and constraints of pediatric practice. These methods all reflect variations on the concept of developmental surveillance—"a flexible, continuous process whereby knowledgeable professionals perform skilled observations of children during the provision of health care. The components of developmental surveillance include eliciting and attending to parental concerns, obtaining a relevant developmental history, making accurate and informative observations of children, and sharing opinions and concerns with other relevant professionals (e.g., preschool teachers)."[52] Screening tests may be used but need not be the central focus of early detection. The notion of developmental surveillance is clearly imbedded in the recommendations of the American Academy of Pediatrics' Committee on Health Promotion, which suggests that relatively informal developmental monitoring is an alternative to routine dependence on standardized screening tests.[53] There are several methods for developmental surveillance. Although few of the techniques have been as thoroughly studied as most screening tests (because test standardization and

validation typically include hundreds, if not thousands, of children stratified on numerous variables), many are quite promising:

Simultaneous technique for acuity and readiness testing (START)

START is a standardized protocol for systematically eliciting and observing developmental behaviors during the course of routine vision screening, using either the Allen Cards or the Snellen chart. Pediatricians are
prompted to observe direction-following skills, ease of separation from parents, ability to name Snellen letters, stay on the correct line, etc. The ratings produced by START were compared to a range of developmental assessment tools in two separate studies involving more than 1000 children
between the ages of 4 and 6. Sensitivity ranged from 76% to 84% and specificity exceeded 90%.[55-56] It may be that future research with this highly
accurate technique could extend its use to a broader age range of children.

Predictive value of clinical information

Numerous researchers have considered whether the task of early identification can be enhanced if pediatricians are encouraged to attend to
the readily available clinical information that is most predictive of childhood problems. For example, one study showed that gross motor milestones are not as predictive of developmental problems as language milestones, and developmental history is not as predictive as current developmental status[57]—information that could improve the content of informal
screening, such as that conducted during hospital rounds.

Other studies have focused on the value of eliciting and categorizing
parents' concerns about children's developmental and behavioral status by
illustrating the probabilities that various concerns are associated with childhood problems. Dulcan, Costello et al[58] found that when parents raised
concerns, pediatricians were 13 times more likely to notice a problem and
make needed referrals. Parents' concerns, defined as their appraisal or judgment about a child's development, are also known to be accurate indicators of true developmental problems.[59-66] Across studies, greater than 70%
of children with true problems could be identified by certain types of parental concerns while the absence of such concerns identified greater than
70% of children without problems correctly. Parents derive concerns by
comparing their children to others, and, because comparisons are a relatively simple cognitive skill, accurate concerns can be elicited from parents
with limited intellectual ability, education, or parenting experience.[60]

Nevertheless, not all concerns reflect true developmental problems.
Only concerns about speech-language, hearing, fine motor, behavior (in-

cluding attention), or global development (e.g., "she can't do what other kids can"; "He's slow and behind other kids") tend to reflect measurable difficulties. Concerns in other areas (i.e., social, self-help, and gross motor ["He's bossy; "She won't do for herself"; "She's not good at soccer"]) were not found to be sensitive indicators of developmental problems (assuming, in the case of gross motor concerns, that physicians have ruled out neurological problems).[59-63]

Despite helpful evidence about the usefulness of parents' concerns, they are tricky to elicit and interpret. The following discussion provides clarification and direction.

Eliciting parents' concerns. Careful questioning is needed to elicit parental concerns. Ireton noted that parents were reluctant to respond to questions such as "Do you think your child has any problems?" or "Are you worried about your child's development?" perhaps because terms such as "worry" or "problems" sounded overly significant or ominous.[17] Glascoe et al.[59] attempted a variety of wordings before devising the effective stimulus, *"Please tell me any concerns about the way your child is behaving, learning, and developing";* noting that many parents were unfamiliar with the word "development." In response, parents provided statements such as "He can't talk plain" or "She won't play with other kids" although many parents downplayed the strength of their observations in such statements as, "I was worried about his language but I think he's doing better now"— comments that actually tended to reflect true difficulties. Still, many parents do not think about development as a series of domains. Thus it is necessary to ask a second question that prompts parents to consider each developmental area: *"Any concerns about how he or she ... understands what you say? ... talks? ... makes speech sounds? ... uses hands and fingers to do things? ... uses arms and legs? ... behaves? ... gets along with others? ... is learning to do things for himself/herself? ... is learning preschool and school skills?"*

Relationships between types of concerns and type of problem. In early studies, there appeared to be a direct relationship between the type of parental concern and the type of childhood problem (e.g., behavior concerns reflected behavior problems and speech-language concerns reflected speech-language problems). However, two studies found that the domains of parents' concerns were not always associated with problems in that area. One study included a subsample of children with global developmental delays, including mental retardation. Parents most frequent concerns were about behavior and speech-language development.[63] Other studies showed that parents' complaints about attention span were often indicators of learning disabilities or other developmental problems.[65-66] Concerns about fine motor development, a highly predictive although rarely mentioned indicator of developmental problems, were related, in part, to deficits in social interactions with adults: children were reluctant to engage with their parents in the tasks of coloring, drawing, turning pages in books, cutting with scissors, etc., and thus missed critical opportunities to learn preschool and school skills. Perhaps, as a consequence, children, whose parents were concerned about fine motor skills, often failed screening and diagnostic measures including cognitive, language, and academic items.[59,63]

There are several possible explanations for the mismatch between the type of parental concern and the type of childhood problem. Parents may not perceive development in the same manner as professionals, as a series of distinct domains. Parents may not search for causes or contributors to developmental difficulties. For example, a parent who complains that his or her child behaves poorly may not have considered whether the child (1) hears well, (2) has sufficient language skills to comprehend the command, or (3) has the cognitive skills, including memory, to execute the command. Clearly, it is the task of the health care professional to interpret parental concerns by considering a range of alternative explanations for the complaint.

Responding to concerns. Because of the disparity between the type of concern and the type of problem, it may be inadvisable to make referrals on the basis of parents' concerns alone. Furthermore, parents' concerns have limited positive predictive value and result in a high over-referral rate. This means that physicians must confirm or disconfirm concerns with additional data, such as can be elicited by standardized screening tests. Thus parents' concerns are best viewed as a prescreening technique, which reduces substantially the need to screen every patient. Approximately two thirds of patients will be eliminated from the risk pool because of the absence of parental concerns.

None of the preceding considerations implies that a parent with a significant concern, whose child is not found to have a problem on further screening, is not a parent with a meaningful worry. Such parents may be noticing subtle, subclinical manifestations of an emerging problem. For example, in one study, parents with concerns about behavior, whose children passed a behavior screen, had children with a significantly greater number of behavior problems (mean = 10) than did parents who did not raise concerns (mean = 6).[62] Thus concerned parents, whose children pass screening, are prime candidates for developmental promotion and anticipatory guidance (as well as for reassurance from physicians). These parents may benefit from and respond quite well to suggestions about stimulation activities, parenting texts, and classes. They may also profit from increased vigilance or "temporizing" in order to ensure that mild problems do not escalate into more substantial deficits.

Absence of concerns. A second drawback to using parental concerns in early detection is that 20% to 25% of children with difficulties have parents who do not raise concerns. Although this is not an alarmingly high error rate for developmental/behavioral screening, most professionals feel that this degree of insensitivity is too much. It is not clear why some parents do not report concerns despite having children with substantial problems. There are no obvious differences, such as level of education or parenting experience, between parents who raised or did not raise concerns.[59-63] In brief informal interviews with parents who failed to raise concerns, despite having children with significant difficulties, several made such comments as *"I thought if there really were a problem, my child's pediatrician would notice . . . that if I brought it up, his doctor would just start worrying too, even though there might be nothing wrong."* Several pediatricians commented that such parents often burst into tears when told their children might be having difficulties and that the intensity of this reaction probably indicates long-standing worries. Perhaps one way of preventing such problematic reticence is for pediatricians to encourage parents to share even mild worries and to repeat questions eliciting parents' concerns across encounters. A safeguard is to periodically administer screening tests to children whose parents have not raised concerns.

Process of surveillance using parents' concerns. The following steps outline a systematic, empirically derived, and accurate method of surveillance through the use of parents' concerns:

1. *Elicit parents' concerns.* Ask, *"Please tell me any concerns about the way your child is behaving, learning, and developing."*
2. *Probe parents' concerns.* Ask the following question, pausing after each phrase, *"Any concerns about how he or she understands what you say? ... talks? ... makes speech sounds? ... uses hands and fingers to do things? ... uses arms and legs? ... behaves? ... gets along with others? ... is learning to do things for himself/herself? ... is learning preschool and school skills?"*
3. *Categorize concerns.* Determine which developmental areas are of concern to parents. Sometimes a single concern falls into two or more areas (e.g., *"She won't get dressed or do for herself"* may be categorized as both behavioral and self-help concerns).
4. *Assign probabilities to concerns.* By knowing the likelihood of true problems in relation to each concern, physicians can decide when screening is and is not necessary. This will reduce dramatically the

numbers of children requiring screening tests. Table 3-3 illustrates the range of probabilities (averaged across studies) in which developmental concerns reflect measured deficits.

5. *Use broad-band screening tools.* When the type of parental concern has a high association with true problems (i.e., behavior, speech-language, fine motor, global, or school skills [in children 4 years and older]), broad-band, accurate screening tools (meaning those that tap a range of developmental domains) afford the best method for discerning whether the child has specific or broad delays.

6. *Refer children who fail screening tests carefully.* The use of broad-band tools helps ensure that referrals are focused and appropriate. For example, a child failing multiple domains such as language, cognitive, fine motor, and behavior may need referrals for comprehensive evaluations (e.g., intellectual, neurological, educational, social, speech-language, as well as behavioral intervention). In contrast a child failing only the language domain may be best served by a referral to a speech-language pathologist.

7. *Offer developmental promotion.* When there is a nonsignificant concern (i.e., self-help, social, or gross motor) or when the child passes screening although the parent is concerned, the family is ripe for developmental promotion and is motivated to respond. Because parents may be noticing problems that are subclinical, helping them promote and stimulate children's development is critical. Handouts may be especially useful here, particularly if they are presented carefully and their contents described. The Ambulatory Pediatric Association has a handout file, which can be requested from Dr. Jack Pascoe, Department of Pediatrics, University of Wisconsin Medical School, 600 Highland Avenue, Madison, Wisconsin 53792 or downloaded via the Internet (Pascoe@VMS.MACC.Wisc.edu). Another resource

Table 3-3   Positive predictive value of parents' concerns

Concern	Probability of problem
Behavior-emotions	41%
Speech-language	55%
Social skills	Not significant
Gross motor skills	Not significant
Self-help skills	Not significant
Fine motor skills	75%
School skills (4 years and older only)	40%
Global (e.g., "He's behind other kids")	80%
Two or more of any of the above	35%

is the Academy of Child and Adolescent Psychiatry, which has hand-outs available on the World Wide Web (http://psych.med.umich.edu/web/aacap/FactsFam/).

8. *Periodically screen patients with unconcerned parents.* Given that not all parents raise concerns (either because their children are developing normally or because they are afraid or simply fail to notice), it is advisable to administer screening tests at the following three intervals. The 15-month visit is one optimal time because children should be using several words and, if not, can benefit from early stimulation or intervention. Screening at 24 to 36 months may identify children who have limited vocabulary and syntax and who may benefit from formal language or comprehensive interventions. Screening at 48 months can detect children with preacademic deficits in time to enroll them in services and prevent kindergarten failure.

Fig. 3-2 illustrates the recommended surveillance process, which has known efficacy in early detection and a high degree of utility in medical settings.

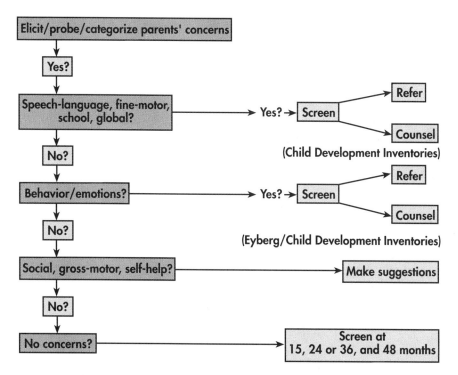

Fig. 3-2 Surveillance with 0- to 5-year-olds.

Improving clinical judgment and judgment heuristics

A final approach to facilitating developmental surveillance is designed to help pediatricians consider theoretical pitfalls in the use of clinical judgment. Because human short-term memory is limited, we rely on heuristics or short-cuts in order to efficiently form clinical impressions. However, because heuristics are influenced by a range of variables including attitudes, beliefs, knowledge, and experiences, the accuracy of impressions varies from physician to physician. In one study, researchers culled from the literature on medical reasoning a number of different judgment heuristics and generated various hypotheses about how these might help or hinder clinical judgments regarding developmental and behavioral problems.[67] Although this topic is too lengthy to cover here, several helpful admonitions should be kept in mind:

1. Disabled children are rarely dysmorphic and most lack a clear medical etiology. Their problems are often subtle, if not invisible, without developmental measurement.
2. Pediatricians may be "primed" to anticipate if not perceive development as typical because of the high frequency of normally developing children in their practices or because a given patient may have been normal at an earlier age, even if not currently. Recognizing and questioning this potential mindset may improve early detection.
3. Knowing that the incidence of developmental problems is at least 8% during the preschool years may help physicians search more often for these relatively common childhood problems.
4. Thinking flexibly about developmental observations or diagnoses may help physicians better explore causes and reconsider current status (e.g., the child who behaves well in the office may still meet criteria for ADHD if supporting information is obtained from parents and teachers).
5. Knowledge of local services and school laws and procedures and a clear plan for developmental detection may improve the ability to identify problems and refer.
6. Time constraints and patient volume may deter early detection. It is wise to have a plan for dealing with "Oh, by the way. . ." complaints raised at the end of an encounter (e.g., sending parents home with parent-report questionnaires in preparation for a subsequent visit). The adverse effects of time constraints are emphasized by a study showing that the accuracy of clinical judgment improves when physicians set aside a specific visit devoted to developmental and behavioral assessment.

Comment. Although the various approaches to developmental surveillance discussed earlier are clearly quick and efficient, exclusive dependence on clinical judgment may be problematic. There is clearly a need for additional validation and research on all current approaches to developmental surveillance.

Future studies should view the predictive value of other types of clinical information (e.g., specific observations about children's sentence length and vocabulary). It would also be helpful to have information about the combined probabilities of observations about children together with environmental variables (e.g., socioeconomic and marital status, parental mental health, education, and parenting behaviors). Given sufficient supporting research on the best combinations of clinical information, pediatricians may be able to accurately and easily detect children with difficulties without administering screening tests.

TRIAGING SCHOOL-AGE PATIENTS

The approach described following is a method of surveillance for children enrolled in formal academic instruction (grades K-12).[68]

Parents often express concerns to pediatricians about deficiencies in their children's school behavior and academic performance (see the box below). Although we know parents' concerns have much merit, it is not always clear how to respond. Further, identical complaints (e.g., short attention span) can have any number of causes: recent family problems, lack of motivation, undiscovered learning disabilities, poor teaching or inappropriate school environment, emotional disturbance, health problems that

---

WARNING SIGNS OF SCHOOL PROBLEMS

Inconsistent performance/does better one-to-one
Poor retention of information that has been retained
Excessive parental involvement in homework/takes too long to complete homework
Loss of self-esteem
Short attention span/hyperactivity
History of speech-language problems, otitis media with fluctuating hearing loss
Frequent school absences
Previously tested but not eligible for special education
Hates school/school phobic/psychosomatic symptoms
Hides school work/lies about assignments
Trouble with letter sounds or letter naming

interfere with school attendance and vitality, poor study skills, lack of motivation, or actual deficits in attending. Uncovering the most likely cause and selecting appropriate evaluations and treatments are the major challenges in managing patients with school problems. An additional challenge is to address such problems within the time constraints of primary care.

It is of dubious value to encourage physicians to measure school performance in office settings. Academic deficits can occur in any subject and several hours of testing are required to provide indicators in all subject areas: reading vocabulary; word attack skills; reading comprehension; math calculations; math concepts; handwriting; spelling, punctuation, capitalization, and usage; science; social studies; humanities; and study skills. Thus it makes more sense to use existing and readily available sources of information: (1) parents and teachers observations and/or (2) the results of group achievement tests administered annually by the schools. These offer a wealth of data (i.e., children's standardized scores for each subtest) that can be very helpful in deciding how best to respond to parents' and teachers' concerns. A further advantage in making use of group achievement tests is that they are thoroughly standardized and validated on thousands of children in the same grade across the country and take 3 to 9 hours to administer, a feat not accomplishable in primary care.

It is reasonable to ask why pediatricians need to view the results of testing administered by the school when the scores are much more accessible to teachers. There are three main reasons: (1) schools use group achievement scores to produce aggregate information on the progress of individual schools, counties, and states, not individual children; (2) diagnostic-prescriptive reasoning is not a typical part of teacher training and teachers do not always know how to identify possible problems and devise treatment plans; (3) similarly, teachers work with large groups of children at the same time (physicians can imagine a comparable situation—a single exam room filled with 25 to 30 children and question how easily the needs of a single child could be identified), and (4) teachers typically work with a child only for a single year and rarely have pediatricians' rich knowledge of developmental, medical, and family histories that are helpful in interpreting test results.

Group achievement tests

The more common group achievement tests include the California Achievement Test, the Iowa Test of Basic Skills, the Metropolitan Achievement Test, and the Stanford Achievement Test. Several states produce their local versions. All such tests reflect national curricular trends. Younger children are measured on prereading skills such as letter naming, while high school students are measured on reference and study skills. Despite their length and scope, group achievement tests are considered screens— designed to identify children who may need further evaluation. See the box below for ways to obtain test scores.

Each test provides a percentile and a stanine per subtest. Stanines are the most helpful statistic for screening because they divide the typical distribution (bell curve) into nine equal parts (Fig. 3-3). A stanine of 1, equivalent to percentiles ≤ 2, includes all scores that are two or more standard deviations below the mean. A stanine of 9, which corresponds to percentiles ≥ 98, includes all scores that are two or more standard deviations

---

———————— HOW TO OBTAIN TEST SCORES ————————

Ask parents to bring their copy to annual well-child visits during the school years
Have parents sign a release and mail this to the school
Have parents go by the school and pick up a copy
With parents' permission, call the school and ask for test results

---

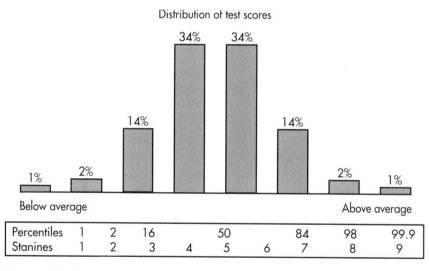

Distribution of test scores

Percentiles	1	2	16		50		84	98	99.9
Stanines	1	2	3	4	5	6	7	8	9

Fig. 3-3 Distribution of student scores from a number of standardized achievement tests. About 70% of children score in the average range on achievement tests, the scores bunching up within one standard deviation on either side of the 50th percentile. *(Modified from Sattler J: Assessment of children's intelligence, Jerome Sattler Publishing, 1988. In Glascoe FP: When parents ask about school problems, Contemp Pediatr 9:107, 1992.)*

above the mean. Stanines 2 through 8 each account for one half of a standard deviation. Any child whose stanines on individual subtests (e.g., reading, language, or math) differ by more than two standard deviations has statistically significant test score scatter. Other important things to remember about stanines are that scores 4 through 6 constitute the average range, 3 begins the below average range and corresponds to a percentile of 16, and 7 begins the above average range and correspond to a percentile rank of 84.

Fig. 3-4 shows actual results from the Stanford Achievement Test on a 6th grader attending a private school. She had been referred to a diagnostic testing center by her pediatrician because of complaints that she took an excessively long time to complete assignments, had failing grades in a foreign language class, and was increasingly despondent about school. By her own admission, she could not "read as fast as other students."

Her achievement test profile shows widely scattered stanines—spanning 2½ standard deviations. The most visible weakness is in word-study

One student's profile

Grade	06	STANFORD ACHIEVEMENT TEST
Level	INT 2	1300
Norm	2	

	GE	NS	NP	NATIONAL PERCENTILE CONFIDENCE BANDS
WORD STUDY SKILLS	4.0	4	23	
READING COMPREHENSION	8.6	6	64	
VOCABULARY	PHS	8	94	
LISTENING COMPREHENSION	8.8	6	70	
SPELLING	8.7	6	69	
LANGUAGE	9.0	6	73	
CONCEPTS OF NUMBER	PHS	8	95	
MATH COMPUTATION	10.2	7	77	
MATH APPLICATIONS	8.7	6	76	
SOCIAL SCIENCE	PHS	9	96	
SCIENCE	6.4	5	48	
USING INFORMATION	12.5	7	85	
TOTAL READING	6.0	5	41	
TOTAL LISTENING	11.7	7	85	
TOTAL LANGUAGE	8.7	6	74	
TOTAL MATH	10.1	7	86	
BASIC BATTERY TOTAL	8.8	6	73	
COMPLETE BATTERY TOTAL	8.8	6	73	
				1 3 5 10 20 30 40 50 60 70 80 90 95 98 99

Fig. 3-4 A sixth-grader's national stanine (NS) scores on the Stanford Achievement Test show significant scatter, from above average in vocabulary, number concepts, and social science to average or below average in word-study skills, science, and reading comprehension. Further testing may reveal underlying learning disabilities. *GE,* grade equivalent; *NP,* national percentile; *NS,* national stanine; *PHS,* post high school. *(From Glascoe FP: When parents ask about school problems,* Contemp Pediatr *9:107, 1992.)*

skills—a measure of phonics (meaning word attack skills, the sounds of letters), syllabification, and recognition of common prefixes, suffixes, and word roots. (In older students the word attack subtest is not often included in the battery, but low scores in spelling may be a similar indicator of word-attack deficits). Although this student performs in the average range, her highest stanine (9) suggests that she may be quite bright and that, overall, a higher performance could be expected. Individualized testing supported these suppositions. On diagnostic testing, she was found to have an IQ of 128 and mild dyslexia—a learning disability in basic reading processes. Unlike many less capable students, she had compensated for her difficulties by guessing at unfamiliar words based on visual appearance (e.g., substituting "curtain" for "curious"). When her guess failed to make sense in context, she had to reread the sentence and guess again. As a consequence, she took 2 to 3 times as long to read a paragraph as her peers. It was recommended that she received tutoring 2 to 3 times per week in word attack skills (had she been in a public school, participation in a resource class, a special education program available in each school, could have been an option). Tutoring was concluded after 4 months when her reading rate and accuracy improved substantially. Subsequent achievement test scores showed marked improvement in all academic areas (group achievement tests are timed and faster readers are able to complete all items). She continued to do well in school and eventually matriculated to a prestigious university.

Problem profiles on group achievement tests

In addition to the profile of a learning disabled reader presented previously, there are five other common problem profiles that appear on group achievement tests:

1. *Below average performance in most areas suggests slow learning.* A referral for psychoeducational and language assessments is warranted. (This can be obtained privately or through the schools and can be facilitated if pediatricians screen vision and hearing and include these results in a letter requesting tutoring sent to the school board's Department of Psychology and the principal). However, slow learners (i.e., IQ between 74 and 84) do not always qualify for special education assistance through the schools because of an omission in federal and state laws. Participation in Chapter I Reading and Math (federally funded remedial programs available in schools where the average family income is low), after school tutoring (often available free from

community centers and volunteer literacy programs), summer school, and vocational training during high school are beneficial. Because these children are often those who were at risk during their preschool years due to family circumstances, earlier identification and referrals to Head Start or other stimulation and parent training programs may prevent subsequent poor school performance, with its attendant risk of dropping out, teen pregnancy, criminality, and unemployment.

2. *Above average performance in most areas (with at least some stanines of 8 and 9) suggests academic talent or giftedness.* Schools usually have a range of services for these students although most require individual psychoeducational testing to determine eligibility. These services include magnet schools, programs for academic acceleration, enrichment programs, parent groups, and community mentors.

3. *Deficits in reading comprehension, math concepts, and general information suggests language impairment.* These children should be referred for psychoeducational and language evaluations. At risk are patients with otitis media with fluctuating or stable monaural or bilateral hearing loss or a history of speech-language difficulties. Those who have been dismissed from speech-language services are also at risk because language skills sometimes plateau when therapy is discontinued.[69] These youngsters may not have visible problems until they reach the third grade or so, when children begin "reading to learn" and not just "learning to read." At this grade level, children are, for the first time, required to read written language commensurate with spoken language. Consequently, deficits appear in all subtests with high-language demands (science, social studies, math concepts, and reading comprehension). Recommended interventions typically include language therapy and resource services with consultation among the language therapist, home, and regular classroom teacher. Private language therapy, if affordable, should further speed progress.

4. *Deficits in math concepts and/or reading comprehension (but not general information) suggests emotional/family difficulties.* Both subtests require concentration and reasoning. The child who is preoccupied with worries or has the ruminant thinking characteristic of depression or anxiety disorders will not be able to sustain attention on lengthy tasks requiring manipulation of ideas. Such a child's history is usually known to the pediatrician and typically includes declining school performance over a period of years and, within the same time frame, a divorce, bereavement, family history of mental health or other psychosocial problems, frequent moves, or exposure to traumatic events.

Appropriate referrals include family and/or individual counseling, as well as psychoeducational and language evaluations to assess needs for academic interventions.

5. *Deficits in language mechanics and/or wide, inconsistent scatter in scores across several school years, suggests ADHD.* These children often have fairly random profiles because of inconsistent attention across subtests. It is not uncommon to see performance in the same subtest over time jump from a stanine of 2 to 8 back to 4, all in the absence of intervention. These children should be referred for psychoeducational testing because of the high concordance between ADHD and learning disabilities. Use of ADHD rating scales (see chapter 10B on ADHD) can help confirm the suspicion and offer direction for other needed interventions such as stimulant medication.

When achievement scores appear adequate but grades are poor

There are times, when despite parents' and teachers' concerns, test results show at least average achievement. In these cases, the chief complaint is usually poor grades. While this may seem paradoxical, grades, unlike achievement tests scores, reflect a student's effort but do not always indicate whether they are learning. For example, a bright student who "goofs off" and fails to complete or turn in assignments or to study for tests, may have an abysmal report card but superior test scores. He or she is learning but is not "performing up to potential." However, poor grades are not benign. They can limit opportunities for extracurricular activities, post-high school options, and above all, they contribute heavily to parent-child conflict, family distress, and poor self-esteem.

To address reasons for poor grades in light of adequate achievement scores, consider each of the following explanations and obtain a thorough description of the nature of student's difficulties. Teachers' observations and appraisals are invaluable.

1. *Are poor study skills and/or lack of motivation a problem?* Children are often not taught how to organize their notebooks or lockers, manage their time, avoid distractions while studying, etc. Ask the student directly how he or she studies for tests; where and when homework is completed; the frequency and timing of extracurricular activities; whether assignments are always completed or sometimes are lost, the correct books brought home, assignment sheets used, study guides created, etc. Equivocal answers should be construed as problematic (e.g., "sometimes I forget" usually means "often"). Brief tutoring in study skills can often rectify the problem.

Undermotivation is more challenging and may reflect habitual "power struggles" in the parent-child relationship between the child's desire for autonomy and the parents' desire for control, accomplishment, and perfection. Parents may provide excessive external structure and thus inadvertently, rather than promote initiative and promptness, reinforce dawdling and incomplete work, both of which diminish children's intrinsic interest in learning. Family counseling and parent training can help parents support their children in taking more responsibility. Additional information on this complex and challenging problem can be found in Lawrence Green's *Kids Who Underachieve* (New York, 1986, Simon & Schuster).

2. *Has the child had frequent school absences?* Children who miss more than 20 school days are at risk for school failure, and those who miss more than 30 are generally nominated for in-grade retention. Patients with chronic illness or trauma may miss a substantial amount of school, but it will take a year or more for their problems to surface as lowered achievement scores. Pediatricians, as generalists on a medical team that may include various subspecialists, may be the only ones to consider the adverse consequences of school absence on school performance. Prompt initiation of homebound services, referrals for tutoring to make up for missed work, and summer school may prevent school problems.

Children who miss school because of chaotic family lives or truancy will benefit from the services of a social worker who may be able to help families provide sufficient structure and consequences. Schools also have attendance officers who are usually skilled in a range of interventions to promote school attendance. Family counseling is also advisable.

3. *Have recent life events adversely affected grades?* Sharp declines in grades may be the only consistent indicator that a child is not coping well with recent life events, such as divorce, a death in the family, psychological trauma, etc. Left unattended, poor grades may result in diminished learning and lowered achievement in subsequent school years. Prompt referrals for mental health services following a difficult life event can prevent a downward spiral. These services may include specialized support groups (e.g., for bereavement or divorce). Short-term tutoring may also be beneficial.

4. *Is the child an average learner in a school that demands above-average performance?* In most private schools and some suburban public schools, the average achievement of enrollees is at the 6th to 7th sta-

nine (65th to 80th percentile). Students in the most rigorous private schools often need to score even higher to be considered average. Thus, a student whose achievement scores hover around a stanine of 5, will be performing near the bottom of the class. Such children can sometimes be successfully maintained in an overly challenging school with some of the following modifications: reduced course load (which may require summer school or an extra senior year), private tutoring, use of a tape recorder or word processor in class, and parental tolerance of Bs and Cs. Even with such modifications, children may spend an inordinate amount of time on homework, be excluded from worthwhile extracurricular activities because of poor grades, and/or develop secondary emotional problems—excessive anxiety or depression or loss of self-esteem. In these cases, a change in placement is needed.

5. *Are test scores misleading because of retention in grade?* Norms for achievement tests are established by grade, not age. Older children who have been held back may have an automatic improvement in test scores (e.g., a rise from the 2nd to the 4th stanine). What appears to be adequate achievement, may be a temporary artifact masking learning or language disabilities, slow learning, etc. Misinterpretation of scores can be avoided by obtaining scores from previous years and a good educational history from parents.

6. *Is the child younger than others in his or her grade?* In the early grades, children whose birthdays occur in summer and early fall and who have not been retained tend to perform near the bottom of their class because they are less mature and experienced. Such children may be recommended for retention in grade or for participation in "transitional classes" through which children are effectively retained but ostensibly without stigma.

This leads to broad questions about in-grade retention, on which pediatricians are often asked to comment. There are several admonitions based on current research:[70] (1) retention in kindergarten or first grade is found in some studies to be helpful because it affords mastery of critical reading and other skills, (2) retention in higher grades is not known to be effective because nominees usually have gaps in learning (e.g., lack of mastery of first grade skills, which will not be readdressed by retention in a higher grade), (3) children nominated for retention are often those with undiagnosed disabilities and referrals for psychoeducational and language evaluations should be recommended, (4) retention is often traumatic for children and parents but this can be dealt with by having the child participate in the decision and by brief counseling for families, (5) retention can be avoided altogether with reduced class sizes (approximately 15 students), teacher training that focuses on techniques for individualized instruction, and availability of a wide range of curricular materials; these observations may best be viewed as the subject of advocacy for pediatricians involved with school board funding decisions; and (6) retention before kindergarten (holding children out because of lack of readiness) is quite problematic because there are no guarantees that "more of the same" will ensure mastery of needed skills. The American Academy of Pediatrics Committees on School Health, Early Childhood, Adoption, and Dependent Care suggest that children who perform poorly on readiness testing (a type of screening test) should not be excluded from programs but rather referred for more thorough evaluations from which appropriate placement decisions can be made.[71]

7. *Is ADHD the cause?* By considering problems with attention and hyperactivity as the last possibility in the algorithm of causes for school problems, pediatricians avoid confusing short attention span as a symptom of other problems with short attention span as the cause for poor grades. This ensures that all other causes for difficulties are either addressed with appropriate interventions or are ruled out. Given the latter case and a description consistent with ADHD, it is wise to ask parents and teachers to complete instruments that confirm this likely diagnosis (see Chapter 10B) and initiate needed interventions. The entire differential for triaging school problems is presented in Fig. 3-5.

Comment. Although the previously described method of school surveillance depends, in part, on well-validated tests, further research is needed on its effectiveness in correctly discriminating the various causes for school problems. Some support is found in studies that show group achievement tests can correctly identify children who are intellectually gifted or reading disabled.[72] Future research should assess other aspects of the method's criterion-related validity, as well as its sensitivity and specificity.

DISCUSSION

Pediatricians, unlike other professionals involved with children, have a unique and longitudinal perspective on patients' lives, health, circumstances, and well-being. This places them in the ideal position to

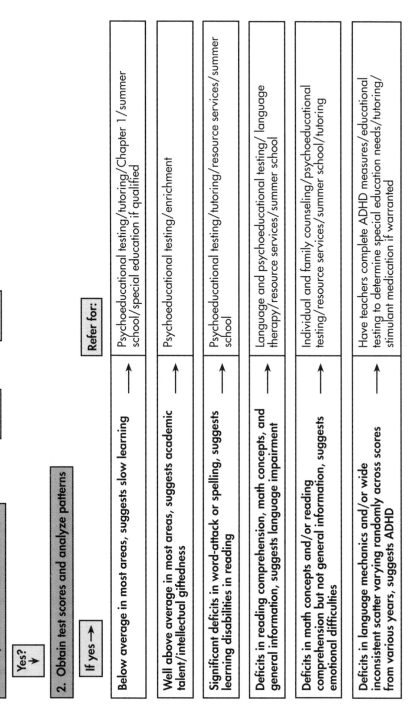

Fig. 3-5 Surveillance of school-aged children.

Continued.

No? →

3. Explore other factors

If yes →   **Refer for:**

Are poor study skills or lack of motivation a problem? ——→ Short-term tutoring/counseling

No? →

Has the child had frequent school absences? ——→ Tutoring/social work services

No? →

Have recent life events adversely affected grades? ——→ Counseling/tutoring if needed

No? →

Is the child average but in an above average school? ——→ Change schools, course load/tutoring/summer school

No? →

Are scores misleading due to retention in grade? ——→ Refer for psychoeducational/language evaluations

No? →

Is child younger than others in grade? ——→ Tutoring to ensure skill mastery and reduce retention risk

No? →

Is child ADHD? ——→ Administer appropriate measures of ADHD/tutoring/stimulant medication if needed

Fig. 3-5, cont'd. Surveillance of school-aged children.

determine the nature and causes of developmental and school problems and to make focused referrals for appropriate assessment and treatment options. The tasks of identifying disabled and at-risk children can fit into the many constraints of primary care by using surveillance methods that depend on available, validated sources of clinical information, such as the concerns of parents, together with easily obtainable standardized data from parent-report screening measures and group achievement tests.

Although developmental and school surveillance are clearly efficient approaches to detection because they are born out of the exigencies of pediatric care, their validity and accuracy depends on the following: (1) the willingness of pediatricians to approach early detection of developmental/ behavioral problems with the same scientific rigor as other common pediatric problems, (2) continued research on clinical information (i.e., which parental concerns, child behaviors, opinions from other professionals, and parenting behaviors are most predictive of true problems), (3) the ability of physicians to select and incorporate clinical information into an accurate opinion and referral, when indicated, (4) the efforts of faculty involved in resident and continuing medical education to effectively train for skills in developmental surveillance, and (5) the involvement of academicians in validation studies comparing developmental surveillance with routine use of standardized measures.

REFERENCES

1. Smith RD: The use of developmental screening tests by primary care pediatricians, *J Pediatr* 93:524-527, 1978.
2. Shonkoff JP, Dworkin PH, Leviton A, et al: Primary care approaches to developmental disabilities, *Pediatrics* 64:506-514, 1979.
3. Scott FG, Lingaraju S, Kilgo J, Kregel J, Lazzari A: A survey of pediatricians on early identification and early intervention services, *J Early Intervent* 17:129-138, 1993.
4. Dobos AE, Dworkin PH, Bernstein B: Pediatricians' approaches to developmental problems: has the gap been narrowed? *J Develop Behavior Pediatr* 15:34-39, 1994.
5. Bierman JM, Connor A, Vaage M, Honzik MP: Pediatricians' assessment of the intelligence of two-year-olds and their mental test scores, *Pediatrics* 43:680-690, 1964.
6. Korsch B, Cobb K, Ashe B: Pediatricians' appraisals of patients' intelligence, *Pediatrics* 29:990-995, 1961.
7. Lavigne JV, Binns JH, Christoffel KK, Rosenbaum D, Arend R, Smith K, Hayford JR, McGuire PA, and the Pediatric Practice Research Group: Behavioral and emotional problems among preschool children in pediatric primary care: prevalence and pediatricians' recognition, *Pediatrics* 91:649-655, 1993.
8. American Academy of Pediatrics: Committee on children with disabilities: screening for developmental disabilities, *Pediatrics* 78:526-528, 1986.
9. Sameroff AJ, Seifer R, Barocas R, Zax M, Greenspan S: Intelligence quotient scores of 4-year-old children: social-environmental risk factors, *Pediatrics* 79:343-350, 1987.
10. Aylward GP: Environmental influences on the developmental outcome of children at risk, *Infants Young Child* 2:1-9, 1990.

11. Bell RQ: Age-specific manifestations in changing psychosocial risk. In Farran DC, McKinney JC, editors: *Risk in intellectual and psychosocial development,* Orlando, Fla, 1986, Academic Press.

12. Algozinne B, Korinek L: Where is special education for students with high prevalence handicaps going? *Exceptional Child* 388-394, 1985.

13. Yeargin-Allsopp M, Murphy CC, Oakley GP, Sikes RK: A multiple-source method for studying the prevalence of developmental disabilities in children: the Metropolitan Atlanta Developmental Disabilities Study, *Pediatrics* 89:624-630, 1992.

14. Zill N, Schoenborn CA: *Developmental, learning, and emotional problems: health of our nation's children, United States, 1988, advance data from vital and health statistics,* No 190, Hyattsville, Md, 1990, National Center for Health Statistics.

15. American Psychological Association: *Standards for educational and psychological tests,* Washington, DC, 1985, American Psychological Association.

16. Barnes KE: *Preschool screening: the measurement and prediction of children at risk,* Springfield, Ill, 1982, Charles C Thomas.

17. Lichtenstein R, Ireton H: *Preschool screening: identifying young children with developmental and educational problems,* Orlando, Fla, 1984, Grune & Stratton.

18. Glascoe FP: Developmental screening: rationale, methods, and application, *Infants Young Child* 4:1-10, 1991.

19. Meisels SJ, Provence S: *Screening and assessment: guidelines for identifying young disabled and developmentally vulnerable children and their families,* Washington, DC, 1989, National Center for Clinical Infant Programs.

20. Frankenburg WK: Selection of diseases and tests in pediatric screening, *Pediatrics* 54:1-5, 1974.

21. Simner ML: The warning signs of school failure: an updated profile of the at-risk kindergarten child, *Topics Early Child Educa* 2:3-11, 1983.

22. Glascoe FP: Letter to the editor on Kopparthi R, McDermott C, Sheftel D: The Minnesota Child Development Inventory: validity and reliability for assessing development in infancy, *J Develop Behavioral Pediatr* 13:142, 1992.

23. Shoemaker OS, Saylor CF, Erickson MT: Concurrent validity of the Minnesota Child Development Inventory with high-risk infants, *J Pediatr Psychol* 18:377-388, 1993.

24. Chaffee CA, Cunningham CE, Secord-Gilber M, Elbard H, Richards J: Screening effectiveness of the Minnesota Child Development Inventory Expressive and Receptive Language Scales: sensitivity, specificity, and predictive value, *Psychol Assess J Consult Clin Psychol* 2:80-85, 1990.

25. Guerin D, Gottfried AW: Minnesota Child Development Inventories: predictors of intelligence, achievement and adaptability, *J Pediatr Psychol* 12:595-609, 1987.

26. Ireton H, Glascoe FP: Assessing children's development using parents' reports: the child development inventory, *Clin Pediatr* (in press).

27. Sturner RA, Funk SG, Thomas PD, Green JA: An adaptation of the Minnesota Child Development Inventory for preschool developmental screening, *J Pediatr Psychol* 7:295-306, 1982.

28. Glascoe FP, Byrne KE, Westbrook AG: The usefulness of the Battelle Developmental Inventory Screening Test, *Clin Pediatr* 32:273-280, 1993.

29. Jacob S, Snider KP, Wilson JF: Validity of the DIAL-R for identifying children with special education needs and predicting early reading achievement, *J Psychoeduca Assess* 6:289-297, 1988.

30. Glascoe FP, Byrne KE, Chang B, Strickland B, Ashford L, Johnson K: The accuracy of the Denver-II in developmental screening, *Pediatrics* 89:1221-1225, 1992.

31. Eyberg SM, Robinson E: Conduct problem behavior: standardization of a behavioral rating scale with adolescents, *J Clin Child Psychol* 12:347-354, 1983.

32. Boggs SR, Eyberg S, Reynolds LA: Concurrent validity of the Eyberg Child Behavior Inventory, *J Clin Child Psychol* 19:75-78, 1990.

33. Eisenstadt TH, McElreath LH, Eyberg SM, McNeil CB: Interparent agreement on the Eyberg Child Behavior Inventory, *Child Fam Behavior Therapy* 16:21-27, 1994.

34. Eisenstadt TH, Eyberg S, McNeil CB, Newcomb K: Parent-child interaction therapy with behavior problem children: relative effectiveness of two stages and overall treatment outcome, *J Clin Child Psychol* 22:42-51, 1993.

35. Funderburk BW, Eyberg SM: Psychometric characteristics of the Sutter-Eyberg Student Behavior Inventory: a school behavior rating scale for use with preschool children, *Behavior Assess* 11:297-313, 1989.

36. Canning EH, Kelleher K: Performance of screening tools for mental health problems in chronically ill children, *Arch Pediatr Adolescent Med* 148:272-278, 1994.

37. Herman-Staab B: Screening, management, and appropriate referral for pediatric behavior problems, *Nurse Prac* 19:40-43, 1994.

38. Murphy JM, Reede J, Jellinek MS, Bishop SJ: Screening for psychosocial dysfunction in inner-city children: further validation of the pediatric symptom checklist, *J Am Acad Child Adolescent Psych* 31:1105-1111, 1992.

39. Murphy JM, Arnett HL, Bishop SJ, Jellinek MS, Reede JY: Screening for psychosocial dysfunction in pediatric practice: a naturalistic study of the Pediatric Symptom Checklist, *Clin Pediatr* 31:660-667, 1992.

40. Rauch PK, Jellinek MS, Murphy JM, Schachner L, Hansen R, Esterly NB, Prendiville J, Bishop SJ, Goshko M: Screening for psychosocial dysfunction in pediatric dermatology practice, *Clin Pediatr* 30:493-497, 1991.

41. Jellinek MS, Bishop SJ, Murphy JM, Biederman J, Rosenbaum JF: Screening for dysfunction in the children of outpatients at a psychopharmacology clinic, *Am J Psych* 148:1031-1036, 1991.

42. Bishop SJ, Murphy JM, Jellinek MS, Dusseault K: Psychosocial screening in pediatric practice: a survey of interested physicians, *Clin Pediatr* 30:142-147, 1991.

43. Kemper KJ: Self-administered questionnaire for structured psychosocial screening in pediatrics, *Pediatrics* 89:433-436, 1992.

44. Peters CL, Fox RA: Parenting inventory: validity and social desirability, *Psychol Reports* 72:683-689, 1993.

45. Fox RA, Bentley KS: Validity of the Parenting Inventory: young children, *Psychol Schools* 29:101-107, 1992.

46. Fox RA: Development of an instrument to measure the behaviors and expectations of parents of young children, *J Pediatr Psychol* 17:231-239, 1992.

47. Kemper KJ, Carlin AS, Buntain-Ricklefs J: Screening for maternal experiences of physical abuse during childhood, *Clin Pediatr* 33:333-339, 1994.

48. Kemper KJ, Greteman A, Bennett E, Babonis TR: Screening mothers of young children for substance abuse, *J Develop Behavior Pediatr* 14:308-312, 1993.

49. Kemper KJ, Babonis TR: Screening for maternal depression in pediatric clinics, *Am J Dis Child* 146:876-898, 1992.

50. Kemper KJ: Psychosocial screening. In Parker S, Zuckerman B, editors: *Behavioral and developmental pediatrics: a handbook for primary care*, Boston, Mass, 1995, Little Brown.

51. Rivara FP: Physical abuse in children under two: a study of therapeutic outcomes, *Child Abuse Neglect* 9(1):81-87, 1985.

52. Dworkin PH: Detection of behavioral, developmental, and psychosocial problems in pediatric primary care practice, *Cur Opin Pediatr* 5:531-536, 1993.

53. American Academy of Pediatrics, Committee on Practice and Ambulatory Medicine: Recommendations for preventative pediatric health care, *Pediatrics* 81:466, 1988.

54. Horwitz SM, Leaf PJ, Leventhal JM, Forsyth BF, Speechly KN: Identification and man-

agement of psychosocial and developmental problems in community-based, primary care pediatric practices, *Pediatrics* 89:480-484, 1992.

55. Sturner RA, Funk SG, Barton J, Sparrow S, Frothingham TE: Simultaneous screening for child health and development: a study of visual/developmental screening of preschool children, *Pediatrics* 65:614-621, 1980.

56. Sturner RA, Funk SG, Green JA: Simultaneous Technique for Acuity and Readiness Testing (START): further concurrent validation of an aid for developmental surveillance, *Pediatrics* 93:82-88, 1994.

57. Kaminer R, Jedrysek E: Early identification of developmental disabilities, *Pediatric Ann* 11:427-437, 1982.

58. Dulcan MK, Costello EJ, Costello AJ, Edelbrock C, Brent D, Janiszewski S: The pediatrician as gatekeeper to mental health care for children: do parents' concerns open the gate? *J Am Acad Child Adolescent Psych* 29:453-458, 1990.

59. Glascoe FP, Altemeier WK, MacLean WE: The importance of parents' concerns about their child's development, *Am J Dis Child* 143:855-958, 1989.

60. Glascoe FP, MacLean WE: How parents appraise their child's development, *Family Relations* 39:280-283, 1990.

61. Glascoe FP: Can clinical judgment detect children with speech-language problems? *Pediatrics* 87:317-322, 1991.

62. Glascoe FP, MacLean WE, Stone WL: The importance of parents' concerns about their child's behavior, *Clin Pediatr* 30:8-11, 1991.

63. Glascoe FP: It's not what it seems: the relationship between parents' concerns and children's global delays, *Clin Pediatr* 1993 (in press).

64. Thompson MD, Thompson G: Early identification of hearing loss: listen to parents, *Clin Pediatr* 30:77-80, 1991.

65. Oberklaid F, Dworkin PH, Levine MD: Developmental-behavioral dysfunction in preschool children, *Am J Dis Child* 133:1126-1131, 1979.

66. Mulhern S, Dworkin PH, Bernstein B: Do parental concerns predict a diagnosis of attention deficit hyperactivity disorder? *Clin Pediatr* (in press).

67. Glascoe FP, Dworkin PH: Obstacles to effective developmental surveillance: errors in clinical reasoning, *J Develop Behavior Pediatr* 14:344-349, 1993.

68. Glascoe FP: Assessment of school problems from a primary care perspective. In Wender EH: *School dysfunction in children and youth: the role of the primary health care provider for children who struggle in school,* Report of the Twenty-Fourth Ross Roundtable on Critical Approaches to Common Pediatric Problems, Columbus, Ohio, 1993, Ross Products Division, Abbott Laboratories, pp 41-52.

69. Scarborough HS, Dobrich W: Development of children with early language delay, *J Speech Hear Res* 30:70-83, 1990.

70. Shepard LA, Smith ML: *Flunking grades: research and policies on retention,* New York, 1989, Falmer Press.

71. Committee on School Health and Committees on Early Childhood, Adoption, and Dependent Care of the American Academy of Pediatrics: The inappropriate use of school "readiness" tests, *Pediatrics* 95:437-438, 1995.

72. Gills JJ, DeFres JC: Validity of school history as a diagnostic criterion for reading disability, *Reading Writing* 2:93-101, 1992.

CHAPTER 4

General management techniques

MARK L. WOLRAICH

Providing services to developmentally disabled children requires interaction with parents and school and community personnel. While this is similar to the situation faced by primary care physicians with patients and families, there are some potential problems or issues unique to this population that are worthy of discussion. The focus of this chapter centers on issues related to parents and other family members. It also focuses on the community and on educational personnel and concludes with a discussion of interdisciplinary management.

PARENTS

Most children with disorders of development or learning have an incurable though nonprogressive condition that can produce a frustrating situation for both their families and the professionals who care for them. The frustrations are heightened in these times of rapid improvement in medical technology because the public has high expectations about what physicians can accomplish. Visits to the physician's office often remind parents of the permanency of their child's disability and increase their frustrations. For this reason, it is important for physicians to be sensitive to these frustrations and to try to accentuate the positive. Parents of developmentally disabled children sometimes report that they have been very excited about some signs of progress, however small, only to be discouraged because this progress seems unimportant to the professional staff providing the service. It is important for physicians and their staff to be as positive as possible and to recognize even minimal progress, particularly if that progress has required great effort on the part of the parents and caregivers. Messages of encouragement help the parents to cope with difficult situations. They are a means by which professionals can support parents in expressing their hope for improvement in a constructive way.

Discussing the diagnosis

The first and most difficult situation that faces physicians is presenting the diagnosis to the parents. A child's disability cannot help but be stressful for parents. The normal reaction of parents, categorized by Drotar et al.[1], progresses through shock, anger, resentment, denial, adaptation, and finally reorganization. While most parents will go through all these reactions, the duration, intensity, and order will vary greatly. Therefore, the physician needs to probe and, most importantly, listen to parents to understand their reactions. Physicians should not assume they understand parental reactions without eliciting information from the parents.

For example, most parents wonder what they did wrong, but these feelings of guilt can vary from parents who quickly put the guilt feelings aside to parents whose guilt feelings are pervasive, affecting how they view and treat their child and the professionals with whom they interact. It is important to try to relieve parental guilt, both by clarifying frequent misconceptions about the cause of the child's condition and by acknowledging that guilt feelings are a normal reaction. Statements to relieve guilt, such as *"You shouldn't feel guilty because . . .,"* are not likely to be effective unless physicians first find out if the parents have specific concerns about something they may have done. It is helpful to allow parents to discuss their concerns and feelings even after they have been reassured.

In addition to providing information, an informative interview with parents needs to include the affective dimension. This means that it is important to discuss parents' reaction to the distressful news. Their reaction can be introduced into the discussion by using empathic statements such as, *"I know this must be difficult for you,"* or *"This is quite a shock."* Acknowledging that most parents normally experience these reactions may also help parents to discuss their feelings. Physicians can further address the affective dimension by acknowledging their own feelings, offering such statements as, *"It is difficult for me to have to tell you. . .,"* to help facilitate the discussion and convey a message about the humanness of the physicians themselves. Part of the affective domain also involves helping parents discuss the reactions of usually supportive people, such as close relatives. An important role clinicians can play is to help parents decide how they will discuss their child's condition with other family members, such as grandparents.

At this initial discussion, it is important that the physician remember that in most cases the parents will not remember much of the information provided. A common mistake is to provide too much information at the initial session. Additional counseling sessions that go over the information are always required. If only one parent can be present at the session or if the parents must learn an extensive amount of information rapidly—for example, to make an informed decision about surgery—tape recording the counseling session on an audiocassette and giving the cassette to the parents can be helpful. This allows the physician to provide more detailed information than the parent or parents will remember, yet this information can be replayed by the parents and for other relatives. Two studies have shown the efficacy of this method in helping parents learn and retain information.[2,3]

Emotionally charged diagnostic terms, such as *cerebral palsy* or *mental retardation*, are frequently misunderstood. It is important to make sure that the parents clearly understand what the terms mean. Many times parents have incorrect and often overly pessimistic views about a condition, more than the reality of the situation warrants. Sometimes the physician will avoid a term, such as *mental retardation,* because of its effect on parents. Unfortunately, this avoidance can also have the undesirable effect of causing miscommunication. For example, *developmental delay* has a considerably different meaning to many parents than *mental retardation.* The undesirable result can be a loss of parental confidence if they feel that the physician has not been entirely honest.

Clinicians may also use complex vocabulary or medical terms that parents do not fully understand. Because parents want to appear knowledgeable, they may not ask for clarification and may actually begin to use the same terms without really understanding them. If visual images are important to the understanding, visual aids can be helpful to clarify descriptions to parents.

Another issue is the strong desire on the part of professionals to have the parents "accept" their child's condition. However, spending a great deal of effort to obtain this goal is not always productive. More important than determining how the parents label their child's condition is determining what services they obtain and what demands they will place on their child and on the professionals treating the child. It is entirely possible for parents to obtain appropriate educational and community services for their child and to have realistic short-term expectations even though they are unable to accept their child's diagnosis or the implications for the long-term prognosis. Parental denial only becomes detrimental when it results in parental refusal to obtain appropriate services or when parents place unrealistic demands on their child or on professionals. In these situations, acceptance is an important issue and parents may need to be encouraged to obtain counseling. Frequently other factors, such as unrealistic guilt feelings, are present, which can be addressed in counseling. Even parents who accept and discuss their child's disability will still express some lasting hope that the diagnosis is mistaken or that some miraculous and unanticipated progress will occur. These reactions are actually constructive because they provide hope for the future. For this reason, it is best to allow parents to hope, even if some of the hopes are unrealistic.

Barriers to communication

A difficult situation occurs when parents disagree about the nature of their child's problem or about the therapy required. In these situations, barriers to good communication frequently exist. In our society the care and management of children usually remains the responsibility of the mother. This means the mother is frequently the person who brings the child in for evaluation and therapy and is the one who becomes involved in the child's program. Therefore, the father may have less opportunity to find out directly about the child's condition. While a mother may understand the child's problems, it may be difficult for her to explain the problem to her husband. Unless the father participates in the child's evaluation and therapy, he will have little opportunity to understand the nature of the child's problem. Also because it is culturally less acceptable for men to express frustration and emotional distress, another barrier to good communication may exist.

Although there is conflicting evidence about whether a child with a disability increases a couple's risk for divorce, caring for such a child clearly is an additional stress factor that can worsen marital relationships when good communication does not exist. It is important for the physician to encourage mothers and fathers to attend evaluations. Physicians should also offer to meet directly with fathers. It is also important to try to identify marital discord in its early stages and to encourage parents to seek marital counseling.

The physician should remain as nonjudgmental as possible. Some parents are willing to sacrifice much of their own comfort, even though they receive minimal response from their severely disabled child. Although most individuals, including physicians, cannot conceive of personally making such a sacrifice, it is a mistake to view this parental behavior as unusual or pathologic. Judgmental behavior on the part of physicians has resulted in some families claiming that they feel alienated by physicians who repeatedly try to convince them that their choice of action is inappropriate. Parents' choices should only become a concern to the physician if other family members, particularly siblings of the disabled child, are being adversely affected by receiving inadequate and negative attention because parental care is focused on the disabled child. Usually, in caring for a disabled child at home, parents are providing a more stimulating and loving environment than can be obtained in any alternative placement and providing it at a lower cost to the state than an out-of-home placement. However, such positive results should not occur to the detriment of other family members.

Alternative resources

Parents may also seek out alternative and unsubstantiated treatments. In most cases, conventional health care cannot offer a cure or dramatic improvement in the child's condition, so alternative forms of care may become attractive, particularly if they make such promises. Unfortunately some of these therapies may lead to significant expense and commitment of the family's time without documented benefit. It is important to educate parents to become informed consumers. They need to know about the concepts of rigorous scientific testing, including the issues of placebo effects, the necessity of "blinding" families and clinicians to the treatment process, the importance of appropriate subject selection, and the need for reliable and valid measures to evaluate effects. However, it is important not to alienate families if they do try alternative treatments. The physician must maintain a close relationship with the family, offer appropriate interventions, and be there if and when the alternative therapy does not prove to be effective.

Although physicians are frequently one of the first professionals involved with a family when the diagnosis of a developmental disability is made, fewer and fewer parents recognize physicians as a major source of information beyond basic medical concerns. If physicians wish to be identified by parents as such a resource, they need to become knowledgeable about what services are available in the community and about what services parents should demand their child receive. Parents need information about school, day care, and therapy services. The physician can also direct parents to other helpful resources (e.g., parental support and advocacy groups, respite care, or financial aid programs, such as Children's Special Services or Shriners' hospitals). Listings of specific agencies are not provided in this book because there is a great deal of variation among localities. Tertiary clinical programs, family resource centers, or advocacy groups in local areas are likely to have the appropriate information.

A common complaint voiced by parents is that professionals frequently fail to recognize the parents themselves as knowledgeable sources of information, observation, and judgment about their child and his or her disability. This situation has been stated eloquently by a group of professionals who are also parents of disabled children.[4] It is important, when possible, to include the parent as an active participant in decisions about the child's therapy. It is also important to encourage parents to share any new information they may uncover about new therapies. This will sometimes help identify new services and will also help parents to avoid spending time and effort on unsubstantiated or harmful therapies.

Anticipatory guidance is also an important service that physicians can provide because physicians are among the few professionals with the opportunity to follow the family and the child as the child develops from birth to adulthood. At certain times stress can be anticipated during the development of a child with a disability. These stressful times are listed in the box below.

Anticipating stressful periods and helping families prepare for them can be an important service provided by the primary care physician. As discussed previously, if there is a need to convey a great deal of complicated information it can be helpful to make use of written and audiovisual materials.

OTHER FAMILY MEMBERS

Because disabled children have complex medical needs, physicians focus their time and interest on the disabled child. However, it is important to identify the emotional needs of siblings. Siblings of disabled children are frequently forgotten by professionals caring for developmentally dis-

---

ANTICIPATED STRESS POINTS

Diagnosis of the condition: This is a time requiring a good deal of study, as well as dealing with emotional responses.

Start of schooling: This is a particularly stressful time if appropriate schooling will not be in a regular class placement.

Reaching the ultimate attainment: This includes, for example, realization that ambulation is not possible for the child or that the child will not learn to read.

Adolescence: Issues such as sexuality may become prominent as well as the issue of independence.

Future placement: Decisions about placement need to be made when the child becomes an adult or when parents can no longer care for the child.

abled patients. Yet they have been found to have a high rate of maladjustment and psychiatric disorders.[4,5] Siblings are frequently in the ambivalent position of feeling jealous of children who, by most measures, are less fortunate than they. Disabled children frequently demand a great deal of parental time, which leaves less time for their normal siblings. Consequently such children may even wish that the disabled child would die or disappear. In communities and families in which a great deal of negative stigma is placed on the disabled child, having a disabled sibling in the same school can also be a source of embarrassment, particularly during adolescence when peer opinion plays such an important role. Worries about peer opinion can result in overprotection of the disabled sibling or, perhaps, denial of any relationship. Parents sometimes require that siblings help with the care of a disabled brother or sister because of the heavy overall burden on the family. This can lead to resentment, which becomes worse during adolescence when a child is trying to assert his or her own independence. Siblings also frequently have misinformation. They may fear that whatever disability their brother or sister has may in some way be transmitted to them. Realistically they may wonder if they are at greater risk of having a disabled child themselves. Because of these mixed emotions, it is not surprising that siblings have adjustment problems.

Because primary care physicians usually provide care for all the children in a family, they are the ones who can most easily identify the emotional needs of siblings. It is important to meet with siblings individually to ascertain how they feel and how they are functioning, so that steps can be taken to encourage counseling if needed. Physicians can also provide advice to parents to sensitize them to the siblings' problems and offer suggestions about actions that can be taken. Physicians are also frequently in an influential position to help parents identify the need for counseling, if it is appropriate.

Grandparents are also important family members who should not be overlooked. Although societal changes have meant that in many cases contact with grandparents is more limited, in some families these individuals play an important role that can be helpful. The better informed they are about their grandchild's condition, the better they will be able to cope and be supportive of the parents. It is also important for physicians to advise parents of their willingness to meet with grandparents or other close family members to provide information. Even if the parents understand the situation, it still may be difficult for them to explain it to their relatives accurately and authoritatively. Tape recording the initial counseling sessions, as stated previously, can also be beneficial.

Making use of parent-support groups can be extremely helpful, particularly when parents take part in early intervention programs. There are also organizations that deal with specific disabilities, such as the Spina Bifida Association or the ARC. Some parent organizations have trained their members to be counselors in order to help other parents who are coping with a child's disability—for example, Pilot Parents. Some aspects of having a disabled child can be better shared with other parents than with professionals. Parents possess the credibility of having experienced the same situations. However, parents may not be ready to talk to other parents, particularly immediately after finding out about their child's disability. Often they initially want some privacy and the opportunity to cope with the information before dealing with others. One must also be cautious because significant mismatches between parents can make for an awkward situation. For instance, if the contacting parents are extremely enthusiastic and dedicated parents, it may be difficult initially for parents with mixed feelings to openly communicate with them. The ideal situation occurs when physicians arrange contacts between parents who have a child with the same disability but who are parents who also have similar personalities and ethnic backgrounds. While this may be difficult to arrange in many primary care settings, it is often possible through tertiary care programs or parental organizations. Finally, it is important, when arranging the contact, to have the experienced parents contact the parents of the new child. Frequently the new parents will not make the contact on their own for fear of imposing on the other family.

SCHOOL PERSONNEL

Management of children with developmental disabilities frequently requires coordination between medical and educational fields. For example, changes in anticonvulsive medication can significantly impact school performance. Teachers may unduly restrict a child's program because they are uninformed about the child's problem and its relationship to activity. It is also extremely difficult for physicians to make accurate decisions about the effects of psychotropic medication, such as methylphenidate (Ritalin), without contact with teachers who are the professionals most likely to observe the medication's effects. The problems in communication between physicians and educators was spotlighted recently in the furor created by children with AIDS who were barred by some school systems. The greater and more complex a child's health needs, the greater is the need for contact with school personnel.

Sometimes teachers may not effectively communicate with parents, and parents may seek help from their physician in deciding what course of action they should take. The physician, independent from both the school and the parents, can be an effective agent in clearing up misinformation. It is important to go over issues of concern with the appropriate school personnel before recommending any course of action to the parents. Physicians who have a constructive relationship with school personnel in their area will be more effective in helping parents to clarify school-related problems.

Physicians also need to be acquainted with services for disabled children provided by school systems. They need to be knowledgeable about the Individuals with Disabilities Education Act (IDEA). This law, originally passed in 1975, mandates educational rights for all developmentally disabled children and also provides funds for states to provide the mandated services. It originally only served children from 5 to 18 years of age but now covers birth through 21 years. (The birth through 2 years of age program [part H] may be separate from the rest of the program and may or may not be run by the educational system.) The specific requirements with which a physician should be familiar are:

1. *Zero reject:* Schools must provide services for all disabled children, regardless of the severity of the disability.
2. *Least restrictive environment:* Schools must provide these services in a setting as close to that of regular school activities as is possible while still meeting the child's educational needs.
3. *Assessment requirements:* Schools cannot assess the child without the prior signed agreement of the parents. Examiners need to use multiple tests, and the tests must avoid bias due to the child's culture or disability. For instance, tests designed for hearing-impaired children should be used to assess a hearing-impaired child because falsely low intelligence scores may be obtained if the child is tested with assessment tools designed for hearing children. In addition, the testing must be completed in a timely fashion (e.g., 40 school days in Tennessee).
4. *Staffing and individual education plan:* Following assessment, the school personnel must then have a staffing to which the parents must be invited. At this staffing, it will first be determined whether a child meets the criteria for having a disability. If the child qualifies, the school personnel must develop an individual education plan (IEP), or in the case of young children (birth through 2 years of age), an individual family service plan (IFSP). The IEP or IFSP must have

short-term and long-term goals, stated in specific behavioral terms, so that progress can be measured. The parents then need to agree in writing to the plan before it can be implemented. If they disagree, school personnel need to come up with an alternative mutually acceptable plan. If school personnel cannot find an alternative plan, the parents can appeal the decision to a district and ultimately to a state hearing board. If the parents are in disagreement with the school or believe there is need for further evaluation, a second opinion can be requested. If the school requests the second opinion or if the results change the school's recommendations, the school usually pays for the evaluation. Otherwise, parents may have to bear the expense.

It is helpful to be familiar with the rules of IDEA in order to advise parents so they can be effective advocates. Many times, problems with school staff result from communication difficulties that the physician, as a third party, can clarify by being the facilitator. In addition, sometimes there is a misunderstanding about the medical aspects of the disability that the physician can also clarify.

It is helpful to advise parents to settle disagreements insofar as possible before demanding a hearing. Hearings are costly to all the parties involved, and families usually must continue to deal with the same personnel following the hearing. Therefore, it is usually better for parents to avoid moving into an adversarial position. There is frequently a fine line between what is effective parental assertiveness in an effort to get the best program for their child, and what is an unrealistic demand that will alienate school staff from the family.

School personnel appreciate having good communication among themselves and physicians in the community. They frequently have questions that physicians can help clarify, although difficulties in gaining access to physicians can be frustrating. Some school personnel have the impression that physicians know little and care less about what goes on in school, but in most cases this is not true. Problems with communication appear to be the major cause for such a negative attitude.

There are several barriers that interfere with appropriate physician-educator communication. One is language. Professional language—jargon—and abbreviations differ. It is important that both groups of professionals provide clear information and avoid technical jargon. Both professions also have different approaches in offering their services. Physicians seek a diagnosis so that treatment plans and prognoses can be developed.

Educators want to know the child's present level of functioning and his or her strengths and weaknesses in order to develop programs and determine appropriate class placement. Both approaches serve a useful purpose and can be interrelated. Physicians need to ensure that educators are aware of how a child's disability and treatment will affect his or her performance. Diagnoses with known outcomes can help school personnel develop realistic programs. On the other hand, physicians can take advantage of the functional information provided by the school in their therapy recommendations.

The difference in professional schedules can also thwart professional communication. Teachers are frequently only accessible before and after school and sometimes in the evenings. These may not be convenient times for physicians. It is important for both parties to be persistent in encouraging and maintaining contacts. Written communication may also facilitate contacts.

INTERDISCIPLINARY MANAGEMENT

Children with developmental disabilities frequently have multiple medical, psychologic, language, and educational needs. These needs require their families to interact with a number of different helping professionals, and such interaction sometimes can be very confusing. Frequently the information provided is contradictory. Furthermore, many of the aspects of care are interrelated, so changes in one area will impact on others. For instance, the child with spina bifida who is catheterizing herself may no longer be able to do so when the orthopedic surgeon prescribes a body shell to lessen a progressive scoliosis, or the cognitive performance of a child with seizures may be worsened when the anticonvulsive medication is changed.

In order to deal with each child as a whole patient and not just a fragmented set of problems, communication is essential. This is difficult and time consuming but necessary. It is even more difficult when professionals represent different service organizations, such as medicine, school, and social service. Developing interdisciplinary services has been the primary thrust of such programs for developmentally disabled children as the University Affiliated Programs (UAP). This approach has been adopted by the educational system under IDEA. It is important for the primary care physician to see that the interdisciplinary approach is utilized with his or her patient. If programs such as the UAP are available and accessible, they may be the best resource.

Taking part in school activities by attending the child's staffings or by providing a written report can also be helpful. Where no coordinated services are available, the physician may need to facilitate the coordination and serve as the professional who pulls everything together to see that coordinated services are provided. This is particularly true for patients requiring input from multiple health personnel, such as children with meningomyelocele. Unfortunately, to date, third-party payers have not recognized the importance of this coordination and frequently are not willing to provide the financial support required to adequately compensate professionals for the time demanded. It is not clear what will happen in managed care situations. However, the importance of this coordination cannot be stressed too strongly. If interdisciplinary coordination is not provided, care will be less than optimal, and both families and patients will be frustrated.

Because most disorders of development and learning are not curable, rewards to physicians must come from the satisfaction of helping families adjust to their child's disability and from helping children achieve their maximum potential, so that the handicap created by the disability is minimized as much as possible. When physicians have attended carefully to the needs of their developmentally disabled patients and have worked to facilitate the development of good communication among family, school personnel, and community personnel, the satisfaction can be great.

REFERENCES

1. Drotar D, Baskiewcz B, Irvin N, et al: The adaptation of parents to the birth of an infant with a congenital malformation: a hypothetical model, *Pediatrics* 56:710-716, 1975.
2. Wolraich ML, Healy A, Henderson M: Audio-cassette recording, an aid to parent counseling, *Spina Bifida Ther* 1:96-99, 1979.
3. Wolraich ML, Lively S, Schultz FR, et al: The effect of intensive initial counseling on the retention of information by mothers of children with meningomyelocele, *J Dev Behav Pediatr* 2:163-165, 1981.
4. Turnbull AP, Turnbull HR: *Parents speak out: views from the other side of the two-way mirror,* Columbus, Ohio, 1978, Charles E Merrill.
5. Trevino F: Siblings of handicapped children: identifying those at risk, *Social Casework* 60:488-493, 1979.
6. Poznanski E: Psychiatric difficulties in siblings of handicapped children, *Pediatrics* 8:232-234, 1969.

CHAPTER 5

Early intervention: optimizing development for children with disabilities and risk conditions

CRAIG T. RAMEY
SHARON L. RAMEY

WHAT IS EARLY INTERVENTION?

Early intervention in human development is, historically, a relatively new concept, emerging in the 1960s and 1970s. It represents a broad array of programs, treatments, and strategies designed to enhance the development of children who are at risk or who have identified developmental disabilities. Ideally, early intervention refers to a systematic and comprehensive process that begins with developmental concerns and extends through the delivery of appropriate supports and services to eligible children and their families. Active monitoring of the effectiveness of early intervention is generally construed as an integral part of the process.

In early intervention, "early" typically refers to the first 5 years of life— the period when brain growth and development is most rapid and when young children acquire language, a sense of self, and the social skills necessary for their everyday self-care and interactions with adults and peers. What is new about early intervention is that professional and societal attitudes have shifted from a predominately care-providing mode to a more active teaching and stimulating orientation. Advocates for early intervention generally agree that the earlier intervention begins, the more likely it is to produce desired results for children and their families. This is in marked contrast to the advice parents of children with developmental dis-

141

abilities typically received from professionals a generation ago. Then parents were frequently advised to wait (to see if their child would catch up or "grow out of" a problem), to be accepting of their child's delays or differences, and to avoid "pushing" their child too soon or too hard to do things that might be beyond their child's abilities. In the past, parents who actively sought additional supports and proceeded to teach their children in a more normative fashion often were viewed by professionals as uncooperative, neurotic, unrealistic, and/or unable to accept their child's "true" limitations. Many of these pioneering parents, however, along with the dedicated professionals who assisted them, became the social activists who sought legislative reform in the 1970s and 1980s to have early intervention become more widely available to all children with disabilities. Currently there is much concern among developmental neurobiologists who study brain growth that if certain kinds of early stimulation are not experienced, the brain may later be unable to compensate for the earlier loss of experience.

The term *early intervention* is used to refer to both the process of planning for and the actual provision of services that are designed to meet each child's individual developmental needs. A central component of many early intervention programs is a child development center and/ or a structured home-visiting program designed to facilitate the intellectual, motoric, communicative, and social development of the infant and young child. Specialized services and therapies (e.g., physical therapy and speech and language therapy), related to a child's individualized needs and to a family's unique knowledge and resources, are frequently delivered within such a center. In most federally funded early intervention programs, each child has an Individualized Education Plan (IEP), and each family has an Individualized Family Service Plan (IFSP). These individualized plans have grown out of an awareness and appreciation of the need to time, pace, and locate resources and services that are tailored to the idiosyncratic nature of the circumstances of particular children and their families if such services are to have maximum positive impact.

Early intervention is *not* simply another label for nonparental child care. Yet many of the questions raised about early intervention are similar to those asked about child care in general. In the remainder of this chapter we discuss the following topics:

1. What are the goals of early intervention?
2. What is a developmental disability?
3. What are the forms or types of early intervention services?

4. How should the content of early intervention be conceptualized?
5. Who is eligible for early intervention services?
6. Is early intervention effective?
7. What are the costs and benefits of early intervention services?
8. Where can more information be obtained about early intervention services?

WHAT ARE THE GOALS OF EARLY INTERVENTION?

Early intervention is designed (1) to prevent developmental disabilities and/or the secondary conditions arising from a disability, (2) to provide early treatment for specific conditions associated with a child's disability so as to maximize a child's likelihood of optimal development gain, and (3) to provide systematic and high-quality support to families (primarily parents) so that families are more knowledgeable about how to meet the developmental needs of their child, have a more positive attitude toward the disability and the child's future opportunities, and become more informed advocates via awareness of the service delivery system and newly emerging treatments as well as their child's legal rights.

WHAT IS A DEVELOPMENTAL DISABILITY?

The U.S. government defines *developmental disability* as a severe, chronic disability of a person that:

1. Is attributable to a mental or physical impairment or a combination of the two
2. Is manifested before the person attains the age of 22
3. Is likely to continue indefinitely
4. Results in substantial limits in the following areas:
   · Cognitive development
   · Physical development
   · Language and speech development
   · Psychosocial development
   · Self-help skills
5. Or is a diagnosed physical or mental condition that has a high probability of resulting in developmental delay
6. Reflects the person's need for a combination and sequence of special interdisciplinary or generic care, treatment, or other services that are of life-long or extended duration and that are individually planned and coordinated

This complex definition is to be operationalized by each state as it deems proper subject to acceptance by federal oversight or approval. A review of state definitions by Shackelford[33] reveals that states express criteria for delay in various ways, such as (1) the difference between chronological age and actual performance level on a developmentally normed examination expressed as a percentage of chronological age, (2) delay expressed as performance at a certain number of months below chronological age, (3) delay as indicated by standard deviations below the mean on a norm-referenced instrument, or (4) delay indicated by atypical development or observed atypical behaviors. The first three of these are quantitative criteria and the fourth provides for clinical judgment. Not only is there wide variability in the type of quantitative criteria used by states to describe developmental delay, but there is also a wide range in the level of delay required for eligibility. Common measurements of level of delay are 25% delay and/or two standard deviations (SD) delay in one or more areas.

States may also, at their discretion, include individuals from birth to age 2 who are at risk of having substantial developmental delays if early intervention services are not provided. In reality, there appears to be wide variation in operationalization and considerable inconsistency in the application of the definition in individual instances.

Before this definition was developed, the following specific conditions or syndromes were considered to define developmental disabilities:

- Mental retardation
- Autism
- Cerebral palsy
- Epilepsy
- Severe learning disorders

Now these conditions are frequently included by either clinical judgment or their past association with poor prognosis.

WHAT ARE THE FORMS OR TYPES OF EARLY INTERVENTION SERVICES?

A wide range of services can be provided under the concept of early intervention. The *Federal Register* specifies the services that may be provided for children birth to age 3 as part of Public Law 99-457, the Amendments to the Education of the Handicapped Act (1986). This legislation is now known as the Individuals with Disabilities Education Act (IDEA). Part H

SERVICES SPECIFIED UNDER PART H (BIRTH TO 3 YEARS) OF THE INDIVIDUALS WITH DISABILITIES EDUCATION ACT (IDEA)*

Services may include but are not limited to the following:

Assistive technology devices and services
Audiology
Family training, counseling, and home visits
Health services
Medical services for diagnosis or evaluation
Nursing services
Nutrition services
Occupational therapy
Physical therapy
Psychological services
Service coordination services
Social work services
Special instruction
Speech-language pathology
Transportation and related costs
Vision services

Note: From 34 Code of Federal Register (CFR) §303.12(d).

SPECIAL EDUCATION AND RELATED SERVICES SPECIFIED UNDER PART B OF THE INDIVIDUALS WITH DISABILITIES ACT (IDEA)*

Services may include but are not limited to the following:

Assistive technology devices and services
Audiology
Counseling services
Early identification and assessment
Medical services for diagnosis or evaluation
Occupational therapy
Parent counseling and training
Physical therapy
Psychological services
Recreation
Rehabilitation counseling services
School health services
Social work services in schools
Special education
Speech pathology
Transportation

Note: From 34 Code of Federal Register (CFR) §§300.5, 300.6, 300.16, and 300.17.

of this act concerns infants and toddlers (birth to 3 years of age) whereas Part B concerns preschoolers from age 3 to 5 years (see boxes above).

These services are intended to be combined and blended in ways that are tailored to the individual needs of children and their families.

HOW SHOULD THE CONTENT OF EARLY INTERVENTION BE CONCEPTUALIZED?

According to Ramey's biosocial systems theory[21] the events that propel development to new levels of accomplishment and sophistication arise from the behavioral interactions or transactions that occur between the infant and young child and the more skillful and purposive adult who has the young child's best interests at heart. The skillfulness of the caregiver(s) and the amount and variety of transactions as well as the child's temperament and other factors condition or regulate the pace and specific content areas of developmental advancement (see Ramey and Blair[23] for an elaborated version of this process). Recently Ramey and Ramey[22] summarized six transactional propensities that seem especially important to include as high-priority, high-frequency characteristics adult caregivers should display, especially in early intervention programs. These characteristics are summarized in the box on p. 147.

WHO IS ELIGIBLE FOR EARLY INTERVENTION SERVICES?

Specifically, the following groups of children are eligible for early intervention services:

- Children of poverty (Comprehensive Child Development Program; Early Head Start)
- Children with multiple risk factors
- Children with diagnosed disabilities

IS EARLY INTERVENTION EFFECTIVE?

During the past four decades a large and remarkably consistent research literature has been developed concerning the efficacy of early intervention. By *efficacy* we mean an affirmative answer to the following question: Can early intervention have a positive influence on children's developmental functioning? The literature is clearest for those children from poverty families who are at risk for developmental delays in cognitive and language performance and for children who are at biological risk due to low birth-weight and premature birth. However, relatively little empirical work using high-quality research designs and extensive interventions has been reported on early interventions developed for children with disabilities diagnosed at birth or shortly thereafter.

WHAT YOUNG CHILDREN NEED IN THEIR EVERYDAY LIVES TO PROMOTE POSITIVE COGNITIVE DEVELOPMENT AND GOOD ATTITUDES TOWARD LEARNING

Encouragement of exploration: To be encouraged by adults to explore and to gather information about their environments.

Mentoring in basic skills: To be mentored (especially by trusted adults) in basic cognitive skills, such as labeling, sorting, sequencing, comparing, and noting means-ends relationships.

Celebration of developmental advances: To have their developmental accomplishments celebrated and reinforced by others, especially those with whom they spend a lot of time.

Guided rehearsal and extension of new skills: To have responsible others help them in rehearsing and then elaborating upon (extending) their newly acquired skills.

Protection from inappropriate disapproval, teasing, or punishment: To avoid negative experiences associated with adults' disapproval, teasing, or punishment for those behaviors that are normative and necessary in children's trial-and-error learning about their environments (e.g., mistakes in trying out a new skill, unintended consequences of curious exploration or information-seeking). *Note:* this does not mean that constructive criticism and negative consequences cannot be used for other child behaviors that children have the ability to understand are socially unacceptable.

Rich and responsive language environment: To have adults provide a predictable and comprehensible communication environment, in which language is used to convey information, provide social rewards, and encourage learning of new materials and skills. *Note:* although language to the child is the most important early intervention, the language environment may be supplemented in valuable ways by the use of written materials or computer-based assistive technology devices.

What is the scientific evidence?

Fortunately, the scientific and programmatic literature about early intervention with biologically and socially at-risk children and their families is extensive, and extensive recent selective reviews are available.[3,4,6,11,12,14,37] Despite some unresolved controversies, discussed following, there are remarkable consistencies in major findings about those early educational interventions that provide intensive, high-quality stimulation to children, that rely on developmental theory to specify the content of the interventions, and that use rigorous scientific designs with adequate controls. Generally, these interventions produce moderate-to-large positive effects on children's cognitive development.

Nevertheless, variation exists in the degree and extensiveness of effects as well as their duration. Listed following are six principles, derived from the scientific literature by Ramey and Ramey,[22] which are believed to be effective on children's cognitive development based on studies of children from economically impoverished families, children with combined environmental and biological risks, and children with disabilities identified during infancy. Evidence supporting these principles is discussed in detail.

The principle of timing. *Generally, interventions that begin earlier and continue longer afford greater benefits to the participants than do those that begin later and do not last as long.*

The age when children experience early educational interventions ranges from birth to 4 years. Typically, children are eligible for early intervention services (e.g., Head Start or Part B programs in the public schools) in their home communities beginning at 3 or 4 years of age. However, many of the more recent programs initiate early intervention when the children are still infants or toddlers. These experimental model programs, including the Abecedarian Project,[24,27,28] the Brookline Early Education Project,[13] the Milwaukee Project,[19] Project CARE,[34] and the Infant Health and Development Program,[26] have been among those demonstrating the largest beneficial effects on children's cognitive and pre-academic performance (see appendix).* Also noteworthy are positive outcomes from historically earlier intensive programs (see the principle of intensity following) that began when children were 3 or 4 years, such as the Perry Preschool Project[32] and the Early Training Project.[10] A consideration of the entire literature supports the notion that high-quality programs for younger children—which usually continue until children enter kindergarten—result in greater benefits than do programs that begin later. There are no compelling data to date, however, to support the notion of an absolute critical period, such that educational intervention provided after a certain age *cannot* be beneficial; rather, this is a principle of *relative* timing effects.

The principle of intensity. *Programs that are more intensive, as indexed by the number of hours per day, days per week, and weeks per year, produce larger positive effects than do interventions that are less intensive. Further, children and parents who participate the most actively and regularly are the ones who show the greatest overall progress.*

---

*The appendix at the end of this chapter contains a somewhat detailed case description of the Infant Health and Development Program to provide a context for examining other programs. It was selected as an example because of the authors' familiarity with it and because it is the largest, successful early intervention program that has been published to date.

There are numerous examples of early intervention programs that did not significantly change children's intellectual or academic performance. A common characteristic of these unsuccessful early intervention programs is that they were not intensive, as indicated by the amount of program provided—in terms of hours per day, days per week, and weeks per year. For example, none of the 16 randomized trials of early intervention programs for handicapped children, conducted by the Utah State Early Intervention Research Institute,[35] provided a full-day, 5-day-per-week program, and no significant effects on children's competencies have been detected so far. Scarr and McCartney[30] provided intervention for only one time per week to economically impoverished families in Bermuda in an effort to replicate the findings of Levenstein's Verbal Interaction Project.[17] They also failed to detect any positive cognitive effects.

Recently, two reports provide experimental evidence that program intensity matters: (1) an early intervention home visit program[20] reported significant cognitive benefits at an intensity level of three visits per week, although no significant cognitive benefits were detected with interventions of lesser intensity, and (2) the Brookline Early Education Project[13] reported that only the most intensive services were sufficient to benefit children at greatest risk for school difficulties (i.e., the children from less well-educated families), while the lowest and intermediate intensities had no measurable consequences.

Only one study addressed the topic of intensity *at the level of the individual child.* Ramey et al.[26] reported that variations in the amount (i.e., intensity) of intervention each child and family received—based on daily, weekly, and monthly monitoring over 3 years—had a strong, linear relationship to the child's intellectual and behavioral development at 36 months. When expressed in terms of prevention of mental retardation, the highest participation group had nearly a 9-fold reduction in the number of low birth weight children who were mentally retarded, compared to children who received only high-quality pediatric follow-up services. For the intermediate participation group, retardation was reduced by a 4.9-fold factor, while for the low participation group the reduction was only 1.3-fold. Especially noteworthy was that this variation in participation did not relate to family and parent variables, such as ethnicity, parental education, family income, or the child's birth weight status. Recently Blair, Ramey, and Hardin,[2] in a year-to-year longitudinal analysis of Infant Health and Development Program participation, found that the intellectual development of children in the intervention group was associated with increased participation in each of the three intervention modalities (the number of home visits received, days attended at child development centers, and the number of parent meetings attended) but not with the children's background characteristics (e.g., maternal education and birth weight). These results further buttress the earlier reported summative relationship between intervention intensity and developmental outcome. Nonetheless, the relationship between individual children's participation—an index of program intensity—and developmental outcomes cannot be ascribed solely to intensity because parental enthusiasm and commitment may also have served to promote children's development.

Principle of direct (vs. intermediary) provision of learning experiences. *Interventions that directly alter children's daily learning experiences produce more positive and lasting results than do those that rely primarily on indirect routes to change children's competencies (e.g., home-based visitations or parent training only).*

Early educational interventions have been presented in many different forms, including those that are center-based with trained staff, those that are home-based and seek to change parents' behavior, and those that combine center- and home-based components. These interventions may be categorized in terms of reliance of *direct* educational contact with the child vs. use of an *intermediary* (usually parent-mediated) contact to provide educational experiences.

The empirical findings regarding the differential effects of these strategies are clear: intermediary techniques have not been as powerful as direct techniques in changing children's intellectual performance.[7,18,30,34] This generalization holds true for economically disadvantaged children, seriously biologically disadvantaged children, and for high-risk children with both environmental and individual risk conditions.

Wasik, Ramey, Bryant, and Sparling[34] conducted the first systematic comparison of direct vs. intermediary forms of early educational intervention. Based on a randomized controlled trial with economically disadvantaged, high-risk children from birth to 5 years of age, they found that combining daily center-based intervention with weekly home visits resulted in cognitive gains for the children, while a weekly home visit (intermediary) program had no discernible effect on children's performance, parental attitudes or behavior, or the home environment itself. That is, children in the intermediary treatment were comparable to the controls who received only nutritional supplements and medical surveillance, even though their parents reported satisfaction with the home visit program. Findings such as these warrant serious consideration and challenge the basis for the popularity of home-based interventions.[29] Nonetheless, the recognition that parents and other family members are natural providers of young children's early learning experiences is important. There are promising findings by Powell and Grantham-McGregor[20] to indicate that three home visits per week—but not less—can produce significant child improvement.

The principle of breadth. *Interventions that provide more comprehensive services and use multiple routes to enhance children's development generally have stronger effects compared to interventions that are narrower in their focus. Interventions that combine direct and indirect routes to improve children's learning and later school adjustment produce the most robust effects.*

The intervention studies that have produced significant effects, such as the Abecedarian Project, Project CARE, the Milwaukee Project, and the Infant Health and Development Program, all have provided a multipronged approach, including provision of ongoing health-related and social services to families—transportation, assistance with meeting urgent needs, and parent supports—as well as a strong educational intervention provided in a child care center. As Schorr and Schorr[31] observe:

> Programs that are successful in reaching and helping the most disadvantaged children and families typically offer a *broad spectrum of services.* They recognize that social and emotional support and concrete help (with food, housing, income, employment, or anything else that seems to the family to be an insurmountable obstacle) may have to be provided before a family can make use of other interventions, from antibiotics to advice on parenting (p. 257).

The principle of individual differences. *Some children appear to benefit more from participation in educational interventions than do other children. Thus far, these individual differences appear to relate to aspects of the children's initial risk condition and the degree to which the program matches the children's style of learning.*

The idea that different individuals respond differently to the same program and its corollary, that different programs may be needed to produce similar outcomes, is an idea that has prevailed in clinical and educational literature. Only recently, however, has this idea been explored systematically in the early educational intervention field. Examples of new findings are described here.

In providing broad-based early educational intervention for premature, low birth weight infants, the Infant Health and Development Program[26] reported that children at greater biological risk (indexed by very low birth weight) did not benefit as much from the program as did less-impaired children—even though both groups showed significant gains. Another study focused on early educational intervention for children with disabilities and considered two influences simultaneously: the degree of the child's impairment and the form of educational intervention provided. Cole, Dale, Mills, and Jenkins[8] found an aptitude-by-treatment effect in a randomized design, comparing Feuerstein's "mediated learning" techniques and more traditional "direct instruction." Contrary to conventional wisdom, relatively higher performing students (as measured on a pretest battery of cognitive, language, and motor tests) gained more from direct instruction, whereas lower performing students showed greater benefits from the mediated learning treatment. Finally, an analysis of findings from the Abecedarian study[27] revealed that the children who showed the greatest relative gains (i.e., compared to controls) were those whose mothers were the most intellectually limited, having IQ scores below 70. In fact, all experimental children whose mothers were mentally retarded performed at least 20 points higher and averaged 32 points higher than did their own mothers (Landesman and Ramey, 1989). These dramatic findings are comparable to the large benefits reported in the Milwaukee Project, which enrolled only economically disadvantaged mothers with IQs below 75.[9] Recently these findings have been substantiated using maternal education as an index of need in the Infant Health and Development Program.[2] There, mothers who had less than a high school education had children who benefitted the most from intensive early intervention.

   The principle of environmental maintenance of development. *Over time, the initial positive effect of early intervention will diminish to the extent that there are not adequate environmental supports to maintain children's positive attitudes and behavior and to encourage continued learning relevant to the children's lives.*

   For many programs, long-lasting and substantial effects on school achievement, grade retention, and special education placement have been detected. In some, but not all studies,[9] however, the long-term effects of early educational intervention on IQ scores are lessened over time. Two important issues are relevant. First, it is not sufficient for disadvantaged children merely to maintain the advantages from effective early educational intervention. Rather, children must continue to develop at normative rates in multiple domains *if* they are to succeed in school settings. Second, no developmental theory is premised on the assumption that positive early learning experiences are sufficient by themselves to ensure that children will perform well throughout their lives. Poor school environments, suboptimal health, a seriously disrupted home environment, and many other conditions are known to influence the behavior of children at all ages. Thus longitudinal inquiry about the long-term effects of early intervention must take into consideration children's subsequent environments and experiences (i.e., after early intervention).

Only one experimental study to date has extended early intervention into the elementary school years to evaluate the importance of environmental supports during the transition to school. The findings are noteworthy: at 8 years of age, children who had received continuous educational intervention for the first 8 years performed the best of any group in reading and mathematics, followed next by those who received early intervention for 5 years, followed next by those who received elementary school education only.[15] Further analysis of IQ scores revealed effects only for the early intervention groups—that is, the supplemental program from kindergarten through age 8 did not result in higher IQ scores.[27] Later, at age 12, children who had received early educational intervention continued to show benefits in terms of both academic achievement and IQ scores as well as a reduction by nearly 50% in their rate of repeating at least one grade during the elementary school year.[27] Fig. 5-1 summarizes these results. Overall, however, the group of children who performed best across all measures were those who had both the preschool and school-age educational interventions.

Reports of early intervention for children with early-diagnosed disabilities have been rare in the literature. To our knowledge there have been no such interventions with children that have also contained a research design featuring random assignment to various treatment or control conditions. The closest approximation to this much-needed research has been the recent publication of a series of 16 randomized studies of typical current interventions—i.e., interventions typically of 1 or 2 or 3½ days per week or less.[36] None of the interventions were reported to positively affect child development or parent involvement. It should be noted, however, that interventions of about this same intensity have also been reported as not effective for socioeconomically defined high-risk children either.[34] Thus there appears to be a threshold of intensity that must be exceeded for early intervention to have a measurable positive effect. How best to quantify that minimal early intervention amount is a topic needing further research.

Conclusions. In summary, early educational intervention can be viewed as a combination of preparatory, preventive, and compensatory efforts. Not all forms of early intervention are effective, and even children within the same intervention programs vary in their response to that intervention. Generally, those who need it the most tend to be the ones who benefit the most if the intervention is comprehensive, coordinated, and intensive. For

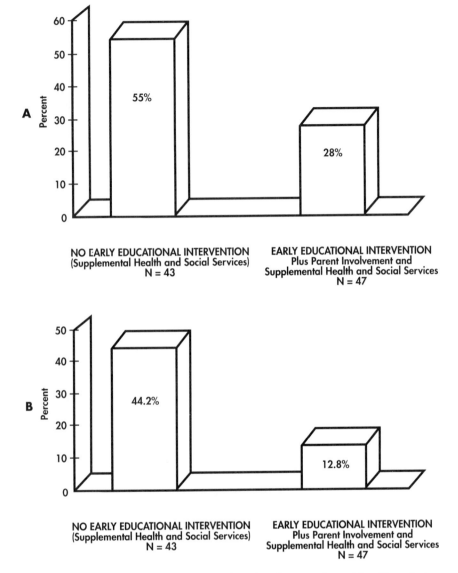

Fig. 5-1 Long-term effects of early education interventions (the Abecedarian Project). **A,** Percentage of high-risk children who repeated at least one grade by age 12. **B,** Percentage of high-risk children with IQs ≤85 (borderline intelligence or mentally retarded) at age 12. *(Modified from Ramey CT, Campbell FA: Poverty, early childhood education, and academic competence: the Abecedarian experiment. In Huston A, editor:* Children in poverty, *New York, 1992, Cambridge University Press, 190-221.*

future research and program development, the goal is to optimize the match between the needs of children and families and the intensity and form of early intervention, thereby maximizing potential benefits to children, families, programs, and communities.

In our opinion early intervention research also needs to address at least four closely related questions that go beyond the issue of efficacy of intervention in affecting children's development. These four questions are:

1. Does the early intervention result in increased parental knowledge about child development and the ways in which parents can support that development?
2. Do parents become more effective advocates for their children with respect to children's rights, entitlements, and developmental opportunities outside the home?
3. Do parents make appropriate use of available relevant services and resources to promote their child's development?
4. Do families who have participated in early intervention cope with childrearing and other aspects of family functioning more positively than comparable families who have not participated?

WHAT ARE THE COSTS AND BENEFITS OF EARLY INTERVENTION?

Economic analyses of early intervention are rare but much needed because such analyses will encourage the search for more cost-effective and cost-efficient interventions. The most frequently cited cost study of early intervention is that by Barnett and Escobar[1] who analyzed data from the Perry Preschool Project—an early childhood education intervention conducted with 3- and 4-year old children from economically poor families. When those early intervention families were followed up shortly after the expected date of high school completion, there were lasting positive effects in terms of reduced special education use, increased high school graduation rates, and reduced teenage delinquency compared to controls. Based on projected lifetime earnings and certain other assumptions, Barnett and Escobar[1] concluded that early intervention not only was cost effective but was projected to return at least a 3 : 1 dollar ratio of benefits for costs invested.

A briefing paper prepared by NEC*TAS[19] also reports some very encouraging recent state-level cost-benefit data:

A number of states have undertaken general and targeted evaluation studies on the benefits of early intervention, including cost benefits and savings. The states are finding evidence to support the cost benefits of early intervention services. The states describe the following benefits:

1. Positive benefit-cost ratios and future savings for every dollar spent in early intervention (e.g., Massachusetts reported a single year's savings of $2705 per child after deducting the cost of early intervention services, Montana reports saving $2 for every $1 spent on early intervention by the time the child is age 7 and projects $4 saved for every $1 spent by age 18, and Florida projects a 20-year cost savings of $20,887 per child).

2. Need for fewer future services such as special education (e.g., Texas reports 20% of children receiving early intervention services need not be referred for special education; Montana reports 36 out of every 100 children need no further special education through at least second grade and another 33 children need only limited services).

3. Reduced need for more costly institutional or group home services (e.g., North Carolina reported a 10-year study of 1000 children showing that children receiving early intervention services were only half as likely to be referred for institutional or group home services as they grew older).

WHERE CAN INFORMATION BE OBTAINED ABOUT EARLY INTERVENTION SERVICES?

Within each state there are several state-level contacts that can provide useful information for parents, professionals, and other interested individuals. These include:

- State's University-Affiliated Program for Developmental Disabilities
- State's Developmental Disability Planning Council
- Interagency Coordinating Council for Early Intervention—the location of this council can be obtained from the lead agency for early intervention in each state (typically a department of education or health or a multiagency department)

At the national level useful information can be obtained from:
The National Early Childhood Technical Assistance System (NEC*TAS)
500 Nations Bank Plaza
137 East Franklin Street
Chapel Hill, NC 27514
Phone: (919) 962-2001 FAX: (919) 966-7463
Internet: NECTASTA.NECTAS@MHS.UNC.EDU

REFERENCES

1. Barnett WS, Escobar CM: Economic costs and benefits of early intervention. In Meisels SJ, Shonkoff JP, editors: *Handbook of early childhood intervention*, New York, 1990, Cambridge University Press.

2. Blair C, Ramey CT, Hardin M: Early intervention for low birth weight premature infants: participation and intellectual development, *Am J Mental Retard* 99(5):542-554, 1995.

3. Blair C, Ramey CT: Early intervention for low birth weight infants: the inferential progress of intervention research. In Guralnick M, editor: *The effectiveness of early intervention: directions for second generation research*, Baltimore, Paul H Brookes (in press).

4. Bryant DM, Ramey CT: Prevention-oriented infant education programs, *J Child Contemp Soc* 7:17-35, 1987.

5. Campbell FA, Ramey CT: Effects of early intervention on intellectual and academic achievement: a follow-up study of children from low-income families, *Child Develop* 65:684-698, 1994.

6. Casto G: Plasticity and the handicapped child: a review of efficacy research. In Gallagher JJ, Ramey CT, editors: *The malleability of children*, Baltimore, 1987, Paul H Brookes, pp 103-113.

7. Casto G, Lewis A: Parent involvement in infant and preschool programs, *Div Early Child* 9:49-56, 1984.

8. Cole KN, Dale PS, Mills PE, Jenkins JR: Interaction between early intervention curricula and student characteristics, *Exceptional Child* (in press).

9. Garber HL: *The Milwaukee Project: preventing mental retardation in children at risk*, Washington, DC, 1988, American Association on Mental Retardation.

10. Gray SW, Ramsey BK, Klaus RA: *From 3 to 20: the early training project*, Baltimore, 1982, University Park Press.

11. Guralnick MJ, Bennett C: *Effectiveness of early intervention*, New York, 1987, Academic Press.

12. Guralnick MJ: *The effectiveness of early intervention: directions for second generation research*, Baltimore, Paul H Brookes (in press).

13. Hauser-Cram P, Pierson DE, Walker DK, Tivnan T: *Early education in the public schools*, San Francisco, 1991, Jossey-Bass.

14. Hibbs ED: *Children and families: studies in prevention and intervention*, Madison, CT, 1988, International Universities Press.

15. Horacek HJ, Ramey CT, Campbell FA, Hoffman KP, Fletcher RH: Predicting school failure and assessing early interventions with high-risk children, *J Am Acad Child Psychiatr* 26(5):758-763, 1987.

16. The Infant Health and Development Program: Enhancing the outcomes of low birth weight, premature infants: a multisite randomized trial, *J Am Med Assoc* 263:3035-3042, 1990.

17. Levenstein P: Cognitive growth in preschoolers through verbal interaction with mothers, *Am J Dis Child* 136:303-309, 1970.

18. Madden J, Levenstein P, Leventsein S: Longitudinal IQ outcomes of the mother-child home program, *Child Develop* 46:1015-1025, 1976.

19. NEC*TAS: *Helping our nation's infants and toddlers with disabilities and their families*, Chapel Hill, NC, 1995.

20. Powell C, Grantham-McGregor S: Home visiting of varying frequency and child development, *Pediatrics* 84:157-164, 1989.

21. Ramey CT, Bryant DM, Sparling JJ, Wasik BH: A biosocial systems perspective on environmental interventions for low birth weight infants, *Clin Obstetr Gynecol* 27(3):672-692, 1984.

22. Ramey SL, Ramey CT: Early educational intervention with disadvantaged children—to what effect? *Appl Prevent Psychol* 1:131-140, 1992.

23. Ramey CT, Blair C: Intellectual development and the role of early experience, *Curr Top Hum Intell* (in press).

24. Ramey CT, Bryant DM, Campbell FA, Sparling JJ, Wasik BH: Early intervention for high-risk children: the Carolina Early Intervention Program. In Price HR, Cowen EL, Lorion RP, Ramos-McCay J, editors: *14 ounces of prevention*, Washington, DC, 1988, American Psychological Association, pp 32-43.

25. Ramey CT, Bryant DM, Sparling JJ, Wasik BH: A biosocial systems perspective on environmental interventions for low birthweight infants, *Clin Obstetr Gynecol* 27:672-692, 1984.

26. Ramey CT, Bryant DM, Wasik BH, Sparling JJ, Fendt KH, LaVange LM: The Infant Health and Development Program for low birthweight, premature infants: program elements, family participation, and child intelligence, *Pediatrics* 89:454-465.

27. Ramey CT, Campbell FA: Poverty, early childhood education, and academic competence: the Abecedarian experiment. In Huston A, editor: *Children in poverty*, New York, 1992, Cambridge University Press, pp 190-221.

28. Ramey CT, Yeates KO, Short EJ: The plasticity of intellectual development: insights from prevention intervention, *Child Develop* 55:1913-1925, 1984.

29. Roberts R, Casto G, Wasik B, Ramey CT: Family support in the home: programs, policy, and social change, *Am Psychol* 46:131-137, 1991.

30. Scarr S, McCartney K: Far from home: an experimental evaluation of the mother-child home program in Bermuda, *Child Develop* 59:531-543, 1988.

31. Schorr LB, Schorr D: *Within our reach: breaking the cycle of disadvantage*, New York, 1988, Anchor Press.

32. Schweinhart LJ, Weikart DP: The effects of the Perry Preschool Program on youths through age 15. In *As the twig is bent . . . lasting effects of preschool programs*, Consortium for Longitudinal Studies, Hillsdale, NJ, 1983, Lawrence Erlbaum, pp 71-101.

33. Shackelford J: State jurisdiction eligibility definitions for part H. In NEC*TAS: *Part H updates*, Chapel Hill, NC, 1995, pp 21-24.

33a. Sparling J, Lewis I: *Partners for learning: birth to 24 months*, Lewisville, NC, 1984, Kaplan Press.

34. Wasik BH, Ramey CT, Bryant DM, Sparling JJ: A longitudinal study of two early intervention strategies: project CARE, *Child Develop* 61:1682-1696, 1990.

35. White KR: Longitudinal studies of the effects of alternative types of early intervention for children with disabilities, *Annual report for project period October 1, 1990-September 30, 1991*, The Early Intervention Research Institute, Logan, 1991, Utah State University.

36. White KR, Boyce GC: Comparative evaluations of early interventions alternatives, *Early Educ Develop* 4(4), 1993.

37. Zigler E, Freedman J: Early experience, malleability, and Head Start. In Gallagher JJ, Ramey CT: *The malleability of children*, Baltimore, 1987, Paul H. Brookes, pp 85-95.

Appendix: the infant health and development program: a case study of a successful early intervention program

The Infant Health and Development Program (IHDP)[26] was an eight-site controlled, randomized trial to test the efficacy of a multi-pronged early intervention program designed to facilitate the social and intellectual development of a targeted population. Families received health surveillance and home visits during year 1 (hospital discharge to 12 months); during years 2 and 3 these services were continued and daily attendance at a child development center was added. The child development center had well-trained teachers, good child-teacher ratios, specialized therapists as needed, and individual education plans (IEP) for children as well as individualized family service plans (IFSP).

TARGETED POPULATION

The target population included all low birth weight (<2500 g) premature (<37 weeks) infants with no major congenital anomalies born in level III hospitals.

PHILOSOPHY AND PRIORITY FOR EACH DEVELOPMENTAL DOMAIN

The IHDP identified three high-priority developmental domains. The three targeted domains were (1) children's health, (2) children's intellectual skills, and (3) children's social development. These priorities were selected based on empirical evidence that the target population was at especially high risk in these three areas during the early years of life. Home visits, child development centers, and parent group meetings were strategies for delivering needed support to families and children in these development domains.

In the area of intellectual skills, home visits concentrated on enhancing parents' decision-making abilities and provided a home education program to promote the children's intellectual development. In the second year of life, the home education program closely paralleled that provided to children in the child development center (on a 5-day-a-week, year-round basis). Social interaction was addressed by providing a curriculum *(Partners for Learning)* that integrated the intellectual and social domains.[33a] Parents' own interactions with children were observed and discussed during each home visit, problems parents identified were addressed, and new suggestions appropriate to the children's changing developmental needs were introduced on a regular basis (e.g., new toys, books, observation sheets). Because working with biologically at-risk children (many of whom came from economically and educationally low resource families) is recognized to be highly demanding, psychological supports via counseling were provided to all home visitors on a frequent and regular basis. Home visitors had opportunities for weekly supervision and weekly (or more frequent) contact with other home visitors engaged in similar activities. Of necessity, an unanticipated component of some home visiting activities concerned seeking help for substance abuse and family violence.

STRATEGY

In the three targeted health and developmental domains, the following strategies were used:

Health

The strategy for addressing health of the children included:

1. Regular high-quality health surveillance (American Academy of Pediatrics recommended schedule of visits and procedures for the first 3 years of life), which included home visitor assistance with scheduling, transportation, referral, and additional care as needed
2. Parent education through home visits that emphasized basic nutrition, hygiene, and the need for specialized care of premature and low birth weight children (adapted for each child)
3. In child development centers, when the children were between 12 and 36 months of corrected age, training of all employees in health care behaviors to meet standards set by American Academy of Pediatrics and the Centers for Disease Control

Intellectual skills

Strategies for promoting intellectual skills included three primary sets of activities:

1. Enhancing the parents' own intellectual competence, particularly related to everyday problems and decision making, by a specially developed Problem Solving Curriculum. This curriculum was implemented and applied to the family's dynamic situation by the home visitors during each home visit. Data were maintained on parents' progress, and use of problem-solving strategies was promoted.
2. Enhancing the parents' intellectual skills and their social interactional skills in the service of promoting their child's intellectual development. A home version of the child development center curriculum, known as *Partners for Learning* was provided to parents in developmental levels appropriate to their child's own progress.[33a] The home visitor helped explain these materials and often demonstrated their use during the home visit.
3. Promoting children's intellectual development directly, via provision of a high-quality, 5-day-a-week, year-round child development center. High standards for the centers were met through the following strategies: the directors had advanced degrees in early childhood education or child development; training was provided to the center directors by experienced educators and psychologists (who had previously enacted the curriculum and established other child development centers); teachers had bachelor's degrees or higher and also received in-service orientation and ongoing training and weekly supervision and feedback on their performance.

INTENSITY

Until the children were 12 months of age, home visits were scheduled weekly (although documentation indicates that this was less frequent for some families because of a variety of reasons). Between 12 months of age and program termination at 36 months, home visits were scheduled every 2 weeks.

COORDINATION ACROSS DOMAINS

The *Partners for Learning* curriculum that was used in both the home visit and the child development centers contains internal guidance algorithms and documentation procedures and associated forms and charts to coordinate developmental activities for children in the domains of social interaction and intellectual skills.[33a] These forms were shared and supplemented by weekly, biweekly, monthly, or as-needed conferences between home visitors and teachers at the Child Development Center.

Home visitors, parents, pediatricians, and nurses had monthly conferences that were summarized and documented.

SENSITIVITY TO CULTURAL AND FAMILY CONTEXT

The IHDP was restricted to families who could receive the program in the English language because the program's development and previous experimental testing was in that language only. No special programmatic features were designed to tailor the program to particular cultural or linguistic groups. Program personnel were encouraged to consider individual families' preferences, and individual tailoring of the program was done explicitly in the areas of health, intellectual development, and social development.

QUALITY AND DEGREE OF DOCUMENTATION

Because IHDP was a controlled randomized test of the efficacy of a multi-pronged early intervention program for low birth weight, premature infants, documentation of all program aspects was extensive. Specifically, all contacts with each family were documented in pre-specified ways, and all personnel were trained in documentation procedures. To ensure that documentation was maintained with rigor throughout the 3 years of program implementation, regular and frequent review of all documentation occurred, with feedback provided to program staff so that they knew their notes and forms had been studied by their supervisors.

OUTCOMES

Assessments by persons unaware of the group assignment (early intervention vs. control) revealed that the early intervention group children:

1. Obtained approximately 7- to 14-point higher developmental scores at 24 and 36 months, depending on their degree of low birth weight
2. Were reported by their parents to have fewer behavioral problems and more positive social skills

3. Were not significantly different with respect to serious illnesses, although early intervention children were reported by lower educated mothers to have one more mild illness per year
4. Had significantly fewer cases of mental retardation

In addition, the early intervention group children:

1. With higher levels of participation scored higher on measures of intellectual performance and social skills
2. With low IQ and/or lesser educated mothers benefitted the most, although almost all children showed demonstratable benefits

CHAPTER 6

Child abuse and developmental disabilities

RANDELL C. ALEXANDER
ANDREA L. SHERBONDY

Society's interest in child abuse was stimulated over three decades ago by the coining of the phrase "the battered child."[1] Since that time, multidisciplinary assessment of child abuse has become the preferred method of evaluation because of the complexity of most abuse situations. Emphasis is now placed on prevention and optimizing family function rather than on a purely punitive approach to the situation. Mandatory reporting has increased early identification of children and families who are in need of special services designed to create a healthy home environment in which children can thrive.

DEFINITIONS OF CHILD ABUSE

Child abuse may be defined in the broadest sense as "any interaction or lack of interaction between a child and his/her caregiver which results in nonaccidental harm to the child's physical or developmental state."[2] It is defined by Congress as the "physical or mental injury, sexual abuse or exploitation, negligent treatment, or maltreatment of a child by a person responsible for the child's welfare under circumstances which indicate that the child's health or welfare is harmed or threatened thereby." Child abuse can be classified into four categories: physical abuse, sexual abuse, emotional maltreatment, and neglect. Although an abusive act is usually classified under one type, it may actually be related to or associated with another type. A pinch injury to the genitalia delivered as part of toilet training is considered to be physical abuse but could easily be considered emotional maltreatment as well. How we define and classify child abuse has implications for disciplinary court actions, for therapeutic services offered to the child and family, and for data collection and research.

The concept of cultural competence (understanding and valuing cultural differences) creates a need for a universal definition of child abuse. If a child is not immunized because of parents' religious beliefs, this inaction, although it can result in harm to the child, is not considered neglect by the legal system. However, if a child's immunizations are delayed because of irresponsibility of the parents, this is considered neglect. Some cultures have rituals that may be associated with physical injury to a child, but usually these acts are not considered abusive unless they are repeated after educational efforts to deter them. For example, bruises may be inflicted on a Vietnamese child by the parent during a cultural process called "coin rubbing"; the bruises are not seen as being harmful but instead are thought to be curative.[3] Professionals must be mindful of cultural differences but must be willing to work together with families for the overall good of the child. This is not to say that suspected abuse should not be reported when cultural differences exist. It is still the professional's and court's job to decide whether abuse has actually occurred.

DEFINITIONS OF DEVELOPMENTAL DISABILITIES (DD)

The Developmental Disabilities Assistance and Bill of Rights Act (1993) defines *developmental disability* as a severe, chronic disability in a person 5 years of age or older [that:]

1. Is attributable to a mental or physical impairment or combination of mental and physical impairments
2. Is manifested before the person attains age 22
3. Is likely to continue indefinitely
4. Results in substantial functional limitations in three or more of the following areas of major life activity: (1) self-care, (2) receptive and expressive language, (3) learning, (4) mobility, (5) self-direction, (6) capacity for independent living, and (7) economic self-sufficiency
5. Reflects the person's need for a combination and sequence of special, interdisciplinary, or generic care, treatment, or other services which are of lifelong or extended duration and are individually planned and coordinated

The term *developmental disability* also applies to individuals from birth to age 5 years who have substantial developmental delay or specific congenital or acquired conditions that may result in a high probability of developmental disabilities if services are not provided.[4,5]

STATISTICS OF CHILD ABUSE AND DEVELOPMENTAL DISABILITIES

The 1995 Report of the U.S. Advisory Board on Child Abuse and Neglect summarizes recent child abuse statistics. Child abuse and neglect is the leading cause of death from trauma in children 4 years of age and under.[6] The annual death toll from abuse and neglect is almost 2000 infants and young children; estimates run as high as 11.6 per 100,000 children under the age of 4 years.[7] The fatality rate for children under 1 year is approximately 2.5 times the rate for children under 5 years of age.[8] Near-fatal abuse and neglect results in 18,000 permanently disabled children per year.[9]

According to the results of the 1993 Annual Fifty-State Survey,[8] an estimated 45 per 1000 U.S. children are reported per year as possible victims of child maltreatment, with about 15 per 1000 being confirmed victims. Child neglect is the most common reported and substantiated form of maltreatment. The breakdown of reported cases according to decreasing frequency is neglect, physical abuse, sexual abuse, and emotional maltreatment.[8] States vary in their classification of child abuse, and this interferes with the ability to draw uniform conclusions from these reports. This variability results in the need for consistent definitions across all states.

The incidence of pre-existing developmental disabilities in certain abused populations may be as high as 70% according to a review by West-cott.[10] In one survey of over 12,000 abused children, deviations in social interaction and functioning were noted in 29% of the children the year before the abuse. Of 37 children with cerebral palsy, 14 developed it after abuse and 23 were abused following the diagnosis.[10] Similar results were obtained in another study of a cerebral palsy clinic.[11] In one study of deaf children at a residential school, 50% reported being sexually abused.[10] These studies, in spite of their shortcomings, raise concerns about the vulnerability of children with disabilities to abuse.[10]

RELATIONSHIP OF CHILD ABUSE AND DEVELOPMENTAL DISABILITIES
High-risk characteristics of parents

The results of the 1993 Annual Fifty-State Survey identify the following parental characteristics that appear to be associated with increased risk of child abuse: substance abuse, need for support services, single parenthood, economic stress, lack of knowledge of child care and development, lack of parenting skills and inappropriate child management techniques, family or domestic violence, and fragmented families.[8] A few studies have estimated that about half of all child abuse and neglect involves substance abuse.[12] Those families with substance abuse problems often are reluctant to accept social and support services and have a higher rate of eventually having the child permanently removed from the home.[12] In general, stress-associated conditions may ultimately jeopardize the safety of children if parental coping is ineffective and social support is lacking.

Increased anger reactivity in mothers and little social support were found to be associated with increased risk of maltreatment of developmentally disabled children with psychiatric disorders.[13] Low coping skills, negative childhood experiences, and strain may lead to high levels of maternal hostility, which is closely associated with psychological child abuse by the mother.[14]

Physical and psychological abuse may be caused by three factors: (1) the parent has high level of hostility, (2) the parent has low level of inhibition of overt aggression, and (3) the parent focuses aggression on the child.[14] Absence of support, lack of insight into own past abuse, substance abuse, a low level of empathy, and cultural influences may all be associated with low levels of inhibition of overt aggression.[14]

Single teenage parents with inadequate support systems appear to be a targeted group for child abuse concerns. The number of single teenage parents is on the rise at a time when the health and welfare systems are in considerable flux. Unless in-school child care is provided, a teenage parent typically terminates his or her formal education in order to care for the child or to pursue work. This group's knowledge of child development and parenting techniques is likely insufficient and may lead to focusing of aggression on the child or neglect of the child's physical and emotional needs. Therefore society is charged with the important duty of educating teenage children regarding child development and reducing other risk factors for abuse, such as poverty, substance abuse, and domestic violence.

On the other hand, parents with physical disabilities typically make any accommodations necessary to ensure care of their children. They are not known to have an increased risk of abusing their children. However, parents with significant cognitive limitations or psychiatric conditions may be at high risk of neglect or physical abuse of their children.

Child risk factors for abuse

Increased risk of physical abuse may be best understood under the "frustration model."[15] This model suggests that a combination of (1) social/

familial stress or crises, (2) parental inadequacy/weakness, and (3) characteristics of the child result in the child being abused.

Developmental disabilities uniformly create additional financial and usually emotional/physical stress on parents and siblings. The burden of care primarily rests on the family's shoulders, and parents may feel inadequate when it comes to caring for the child's special needs. Caring for any child, normal or abnormal, can be difficult for even the most skilled parent at times, resulting in frustration. However, the absolute amount of time spent caring for a special needs child increases the opportunity for physical abuse.

Parents who focus aggression on their child may have had negative experiences with the child that resulted in frustration or may have been disappointed with the child as a result of too high developmental expectations. Child risk factors for these negative parental experiences may be similar to risk factors that are associated with developmental disabilities. These factors include unwanted pregnancy, negative pregnancy and delivery experience, prematurity, parental risk factors, temperamentally difficult child, physically deviant child, and psychologically deviant child.[14]

Children who are disabled are thought to be at greater risk of maltreatment than those who are not disabled.[16] Although it is reasonable to assume that the responsibility of parenting a child with special needs may contribute to increased stress levels, at least one study found no relationship between a history of maltreatment and current stress levels perceived by a family.[17] Very young children and disabled children should also be considered vulnerable to sexual abuse. Child abuse can also occur in institutional settings although it is not clear that there is any increased risk vs. remaining in the home.

Developmental disabilities leading to child abuse

Child abuse and developmental disabilities have a unique relationship in that each is associated with an increased risk of the other. Moreover, certain types of disabilities may be associated with common patterns of abuse. For example, children with Prader-Willi syndrome are often allowed by parents to consume excessive calories although the parents understand that this behavior will lead to increased morbidity and possibly mortality of their child. This may represent denial of critical care or medical neglect. Another type of medical neglect seen in children with spina bifida is parental failure to catheterize the child's neurogenic bladder; this failure could knowingly result in damaged kidneys.

Although identification of child abuse improved considerably following the passage of the Child Abuse Prevention and Treatment Act (P.L. 93-247) in 1974, the effort to identify pre-existing conditions and characteristics has not been uniform. Children with developmental disabilities are at increased risk of maltreatment. However, it is difficult to get an accurate incidence figure because of the large differences in study populations and definitions used by the various investigators.[10] One study of children with developmental disabilities and coexisting psychiatric disorders, reported that severe maltreatment had occurred in 61%.[13] In a study of non-institutionalized females with mental retardation (MR), rape or incest had occurred in one third of the group with mild MR and in one fourth of the group with moderate MR.[18]

Children with disabilities may be more vulnerable to abuse because of several inherent characteristics: (1) dependency on others, (2) lack of choice or control over their own life, (3) need to comply and obey, (4) lack of knowledge about sex and misunderstanding sexual advances, (5) social isolation and rejection, (6) increased responsiveness to attention and affection, (7) increased desire to please, (8) inability to communicate experiences, and (9) inability to distinguish types of touch.[10] A certain "childishness" of learning disabled children may attract abusers, and additional problems with impulsivity and reasoning may increase their vulnerability.[11]

Child neglect often occurs when a parent is mentally retarded; however purposeful abuse may be infrequent.[19] When purposeful abuse does occur by a mother with mental retardation, the abuse is likely to continue if parenting education or supports are not provided.[19] Mentally retarded parents referred to family assessment clinics because of allegations of child maltreatment are likely to have their children removed from the home; those few who keep their children do so with intensive agency support to help their parenting.[20]

Child abuse leading to developmental disabilities

Child abuse can cause selective or global insults to development, depending on the mechanism of injury. A shaken baby may have intracranial hemorrhage and cerebral edema, resulting in severe mental and physical disabilities. A sexually abused child may have little physical injury but massive emotional injury that may have a lifelong impact on social development. A neglected infant with malnutrition may have apparent global delays that improve when the child is placed in a nurturing environment.

Abuse and neglect are likely to be associated with alterations in child development. Neglect may play a stronger role in the development of language problems than abuse and neglect combined.[21] Although research supports the notion that abused and neglected children show poor attachment, which leads to increasingly negative parent-child interactions, it may be that children with pre-existing communication difficulties have poor attachment, which then leads to maltreatment.[21]

ASSESSMENT FOR CHILD ABUSE
Process

As with any medical condition, a history of the patient is usually the key component in arriving at a diagnosis. For example, one study showed that in confirmed cases of sexual abuse, genital abnormalities were seen on physical examination in only 18% of the cases.[22] Therefore it is routine to consider sexual abuse as having occurred based on history alone, without accompanying physical findings. Perhaps an extreme example of this was seen in a Philadelphia study that showed the presence or absence of abnormal genital findings did not matter in whether a case was prosecuted and did not correlate with likelihood of conviction.[23]

In many instances of physical abuse, discrepancies between physical examination findings and the history provided by the caretaker lead to the suspicion of child abuse. The parent of a child with multiple fractures might claim that the child fell off of a couch. However, the magnitude of the injuries is not consistent with the proposed mechanism of injury. Much greater forces must have been applied (and probably not in a single impact). Neglectful parents may say that they are feeding large quantities of formula, yet their child may have failure to thrive. Thus the first step in determining the medical condition of any child (including whether abuse exists or not) is to obtain a thorough history.

When performing any comprehensive evaluation of a child (e.g., a complete physical examination or the first time a child is seen in a practice or clinic), it is important that an extensive family history be obtained. Thus each sibling should be identified, their ages, any physical problems, and their development (e.g., how are they doing in school?). Similarly, the physical condition and development (e.g., What was the last grade you completed in school? Any reading problems? Any speech/language problems?) of each parent, aunt, and uncle should also be individually documented. Questions about grandparents and more extended family members should also be posed. After asking an open-ended question about any conditions that might run in the family, more specific probes are used. After asking about allergies, asthma, cancer, diabetes, etc., questions should be asked in the same tone of voice about the following:

1. Anyone in the family with mental health problems?
2. Anyone in the family with alcohol problems?
3. Anyone in the family with drug problems?
4. Anyone in the family with jail problems?
5. Anyone in the family who has been physically mistreated (children, elderly, dependent adults, any domestic violence)?
6. Anyone in the family who has been sexually mistreated?
7. How were you treated when you grew up?

Hesitation in answering any of these questions frequently is the equivalent of a "yes" response and should be sensitively pursued. Virtually everyone will answer such questions if the examiner maintains a neutral attitude and does not treat one type of question as different from another. The important point is that these questions should be asked in every comprehensive pediatric examination. Experience by the authors over a number of years has shown that such questions are practical and are important regardless of the presenting problem (e.g., child referred for learning problems, developmental disabilities, cardiac problems, etc.).

It is important in asking about substance abuse and child abuse (and probably domestic violence) that the term *abuse* not be directly used. Knutson has shown that over half of undergraduate students will not use the term *physical abuse* even though they describe moderate or severe injuries inflicted by their parents.[24] Similarly, parents may be hesitant to describe their drinking habits as constituting *alcoholism* even if most observers would. When dealing with an abused child, it is not only important to attempt to determine who might be causing the abuse, but the non-abusive parent may be more emotionally vulnerable if he or she suffered abuse also. Sometimes the treatment needs of parents should be aggressively addressed along with any needs of the child.

Key points

Thorough documentation is important in any medical encounter, but it is vital when child abuse concerns are identified. Months or years later, any record may be scrutinized word for word in court. Key points when gathering and documenting such histories are noted in the box on p. 172.

Although one may be uncomfortable months later with how something is written, the most common cause of regret is what was *not* written down.

HISTORY-TAKING AND DOCUMENTATION

Interview each parent/caretaker separately
Interview each child separately
Use open-ended questions as much as possible
Use direct quotes as much as possible
Do not try initially to reconcile conflicting histories, but document each
Empirically, plan on histories that are two to three times longer than for
  other medical conditions
Report any credible suspicions of child abuse to the proper authorities
Be prepared to work with legal authorities and testify in court if necessary

For example, clear documentation of each bruise—stating its color, shape, measurements of size—may seem tedious at the time but will be infinitely preferable to the phrase "multiple bruises" when one is asked to remember events later on the witness stand.

Examination for child abuse begins with a general physical evaluation. Every physical abnormality, the neurological status of the child, and any significant developmental findings should be thoroughly documented. Parent-child interactions may also be important (e.g., failure to thrive). Photographs should be obtained of any suspicious external findings, but these findings must also be documented in the written record. The human eye is still better than photographs in picking up detail, and film has been known to be lost or to fail to develop.

A skeletal survey should be obtained for all children under 2 years of age suspected of having been abused or neglected. Older children should have x-rays if a particular area is painful, or there is an abnormality on examination. Computed tomography (CT) and magnetic resonance imaging (MRI) are useful for intracranial and abdominal injuries. Serial head imaging with MRI is especially useful in conjunction with long-term developmental follow-up.

Laboratory evaluation for serious physical injuries should include measures of liver function to detect possible occult liver fractures. Frequently, hemoglobin and hematocrit will be low with internal bleeding. In the presence of trauma, PT, PTT, and platelets should be obtained. However, slight variations of PT and PTT are common with trauma and do not represent an underlying bleeding tendency.

Passive exposure of children to crack cocaine or methamphetamine (crank) is also a growing problem. However, symptoms are not frequently seen even when the levels are high.[25] Urine for drug analysis should be obtained when there is a family history of drug abuse, anyone in the family tests positive, the child was removed from an environment where such use occurred, or if the child tested positive as a newborn. Positive results constitute neglect.

Sexual abuse evaluations are beyond the scope of this chapter. Physicians should examine the genitalia of every child during complete examinations, not only for the child's health but to learn what normal findings look like. Any suspicions should be referred to a child abuse program where specialized examinations can be conducted as well as appropriate testing for sexually transmitted diseases. Even severely physically impaired children may be victims of sexual abuse, and it is a misconception that physical and/or cognitive impairments somehow protect the child from sexual abuse.

One of the key aids in determining child abuse situations is a good knowledge of child development. While shin bruises may be expected in a normal 3-year-old, they are abnormal in a 3-month-old or some older children with physical impairments. Often children are reported as rolling off a couch onto the floor. When the child is several weeks old, this has a different credibility than when the child is 6 months. Professionals with such knowledge can be of significant help in resolving such cases.

Types of child abuse especially relevant to developmental disabilities

Failure to thrive (FTT) is a common concern for children with significant physical impairments. FTT can be defined as a child who fails to gain weight as expected by a physician. Standardized weight curves are used to determine the rate of weight gain and whether it may be significantly below expectations. Causes of FTT may include parental misunderstanding of necessary infant consumption, problems with breastfeeding or formula preparation, neuromotor swallowing difficulties, neglect, and/or genetic conditions. At a minimum, FTT consists of a physical problem (the child is not growing sufficiently) and a psychosocial problem (concern exists about the poor weight gain). The older concept of "organic" and "non-organic" FTT does not reflect this duality of problems and is not used by most practicing pediatricians.[26]

A child with a swallowing dysfunction that requires 30 minutes to accomplish an adequate caloric intake per meal, will have FTT if the parent is frustrated after 10 minutes and quits. If parents prove resistant to educational efforts, medical neglect can be substantiated. Failure to give regular doses of digoxin to a child with a major heart problem may result in FTT. Both "organic" and "non-organic" components would exist. The issue regarding neglect in cases of FTT is not the degree of impairment of the child, but whether reasonable efforts would allow the child to grow adequately and the caretakers are not making such efforts. Thus hospitalization provides an opportunity for nurses, nutritionists, occupational therapists, and others to assess what it takes to make the child grow; these professionals can then communicate to the caretakers how this care can be accomplished.

Caring for children with physical disabilities is sometimes thought to be easier if the child remains on the small side. This acceptance of a limited FTT likely cheats the child of optimal cognitive potential and may predispose him or her to poorer overall health. Another concern about children with significant feeding problems is one of "perceptual drift." Parents and professionals may become so used to a thin child that they fail to notice slow weight loss. This adaptation can be fatal.[27] It is very important when caring for a child with possible nutritional compromise that compulsive and regular charting be made of growth parameters and that these results be given great attention, sometimes more so than judging the child by appearance alone.

Failure to thrive is more than failure to grow. Deprivation of adequate nutrition, especially during childhood when brain development is most rapid, can lead to lifelong consequences (e.g., microcephaly). However, other processes, such as language development, seem to have an early critical window during which best performance is obtained. Failure to stimulate a child intellectually, emotionally, and through language may cause an insidious deprivation of human potential.

Munchausen syndrome by proxy (MSBP) is a rare form of child abuse that mimics many types of medical conditions. MSBP is defined as the fabrication or production of symptoms by a caregiver in a child, presentation of the child for medical care, and failure of the caregiver to acknowledge the deception.[28] MSBP excludes simple homicide or child abuse. Once a child is removed from the perpetrator, the child's symptoms disappear, or, in cases where damage has been done to the child, the symptoms diminish. The mother is the usual perpetrator, but some fathers have been described.[29]

Some of the conditions that have been fabricated include diabetes mellitus, cystic fibrosis, deafness, immunodeficiency, cerebral palsy, ataxia, gastroesophageal reflux, apnea, seizures, and sleep disorders.[30] Multiple developmental disabilities within a child have also been described.[31] Virtually any symptom can be claimed, and actions can be taken to falsify laboratory tests to fool the physician or induce symptoms. In addition to innumerable blood tests, child victims of MSBP may have intrusive examinations and even surgery based on the convincing lies of the perpetrator. Unnecessary interventions have been known to include medications (e.g., anticonvulsants), apnea monitors, radiological examinations, endoscopies of all possible orifices, pH probes, wheelchairs, catheterizations, hearing aids, and gastrostomy buttons.[32]

The key to diagnosis is recognizing atypical cases (such as the child who does not respond to a generally effective medication), doctor shopping, a parent who seems to want the child to be sick or hospitalized, and/or cases which simply "don't make sense." Unfortunately it usually takes many medical encounters before MSBP is suspected. Once diagnosed, the child should be removed from the perpetrator, and any visits monitored extremely closely (it only takes seconds to inject a child surreptitiously). Other children in the family may have been or will be targeted, so they should all be removed.[28] The prognosis is extremely poor that the perpetrator will admit to the abuse, and no successful treatment has been described to date.

Shaken baby syndrome (SBS) occurs when there is violent shaking of a young child, leading to intracranial injuries. In addition to cerebral edema, intracranial bleeding is nearly always present. About 75% to 90% of the victims will have retinal hemorrhages.[33] Some have other injuries, such as fractured ribs or long bones, abdominal injuries, or bruising. In about half the cases, the child is not only violently shaken but may also have evidence of an impact to the head. However, it is not the intracranial bleeding that is the fundamental problem but rather the cerebral edema. About 20% of the victims die. Many have severe brain injuries, leading to severe developmental disabilities, such as visual impairment, decreased intellect, and neuromotor problems (e.g., spastic quadriplegia). Some have minor problems, and perhaps about 10% to 15% seemingly recover from the less severe form of SBS.

Perpetrators of SBS are very likely to hurt the child again or to violently shake other children.[34] It is not unusual to discover old and new intracranial bleeding in a child. Abusive head trauma is responsible for up to 9% of cerebral palsy cases and is a preventable cause.[11]

Brain imaging has advanced the detection of this condition and allowed the sequential study of its progression. It is routine to obtain CT scans to determine if there is an indication for neurosurgery. MRI is the preferred study for follow-up.[35] Ophthalmological follow-up is also essential. Every child will require comprehensive multi-disciplinary developmental evaluations on an on-going basis to assess the effect of this serious, life-threatening trauma.

Emotional abuse may be overt or may consist of deprivation. Nearly all forms of child abuse result in long-term psychological injury to the child. Thus many adults may long ago have healed from the fractures, bruises, or sexual trauma they received as children, but the emotional scars may linger, fester, and be expressed as somatic or psychological complaints. Because of its long-term effects, child abuse usually resembles a developmental disability more than it does acute trauma.

Consequences of emotional neglect are to kill the spirit, deaden the emotions, and lower the expectations of the child. School performance may suffer. When a parent deliberately inflicts unusual and bizarre punishments, the child may be the victim of torture. It is the responsibility of every professional advocating behavior modification to consider how the technique might be mis-used in the wrong hands. For example, time-out is a very effective tool that is rarely abused. However, one teacher put a physically disabled student in a wheelchair in a corner behind a screen for misbehavior. What started as 5 minutes gradually progressed over the months to hours, while the child sat in her urine-soaked clothing unable to move. Other techniques may also be twisted beyond recognition unless one is careful.

Dental neglect is an under-appreciated phenomenon. Dental neglect is defined by the American Academy of Pediatric Dentistry as failure by a parent or guardian to seek treatment for visually untreated caries, oral infections, and/or oral pain, or a failure of the parent or the guardian to follow through with treatment once informed that such conditions exist.

Because children with physical impairments may have difficulty with fine motor skills, dental hygiene is often suboptimal. Some children may be prone to genetic conditions affecting tooth enamel or saliva production. Others, such as some children with Prader-Willi syndrome, may be prone to rumination and acid etching of the teeth.[36]

As part of regular management, children with developmental disabilities should have particular attention paid to their teeth. For children with self-injury behaviors, a dental examination may reveal a source of occult pain and provide a remedy.

Physical abuse can be exemplified by *fractures*, which normally result only when considerable energy is applied to the bone to overcome the structural integrity of such a strong construction. Simple, short falls are not the cause of intracranial injuries or numerous broken bones. Infants are not developmentally capable of putting themselves in a position to hurt their bones unless they can acquire enough kinetic energy through mechanisms such as falling down stairs. Children with physical impairments may be at the age in which certain accidental fractures occur, but investigation must be made of their individual capabilities before assuming that they were responsible for the injury.

Inactive individuals may not develop the bone density seen in vigorous people. Thus it is common in severe instances of cerebral palsy, spina bifida, and other similar conditions to see radiological evidence of osteopenia. For such individuals, patient care techniques, such as turning the child over in the bed, may occasionally lead to an accidental fracture. Sometimes this occurs in an institutional setting where questions may arise about abuse by staff members, until all the data emerge. Alternatively, sometimes caregivers are abusive and cause fractures. A careful investigation must be conducted, especially if the child suffers repetitive fractures or other children have also been hurt.

MANAGEMENT

Management of child abuse has both legal and therapeutic components. Legal requirements direct professionals to report suspected cases of child abuse so that appropriate social work intervention or prosecution can proceed. Therapeutic interventions by professionals include working with the family and/or child on resolution of identified problems and may not directly relate to the child's placement. Prosecution is one way to protect the child or other children from someone who commits serious abuse. However, courts do not directly heal the tissues, ease the child's torment, or rehabilitate the family. Sometimes the courts do not agree with the professionals. Even if prosecution is achieved, non-offending parents or relatives are unlikely to feel that this is enough. For the injured child, legal response is a poor balm for their wounds.

Child abuse prevention can be divided into three levels: primary, secondary, and tertiary. Primary prevention consists of efforts aimed at the general public, or segments of the public not selected for any particular risk factors. Thus television public service ads may suggest strategies for coping with a difficult situation and should be made available to all viewers. Secondary prevention is aimed at groups felt to be at an increased risk for child abuse. A program directed at teenage parents is an example of secondary prevention. Tertiary prevention is targeted at people who have already committed child abuse, with the hope of preventing its reoccurrence. Management of child abuse can be thought of as a tertiary prevention strategy.

Reporting process

When a reasonable suspicion of child abuse exists, the professional is ethically and legally obligated to report these suspicions. Usually the reports are made to the state Department of Social Services or its equivalent. Many states keep statistics on the number of reported children who have a developmental disability. The exact definition of what constitutes child abuse may vary slightly, but three central components are: (1) there is a child (under 18 years), (2) an action or inaction committed by a caretaker, and (3) some type of injury. When child abuse is considered unsubstantiated, it may be that the professional finds that the definition of caretaker was not met by the individual committing the abuse. Other times, the professional may observe a child being hit but no injury results. Clearly the legal definition may be at variance with the professional's concern.

Child abuse laws are basically reporting laws. The goal is to encourage the increased reporting of child abuse, especially in situations in which the professional might otherwise be reluctant to do so. In all states there are immunity provisions whereby anyone reporting child abuse cannot be successfully sued or prosecuted. In addition, states have mandatory reporters of child abuse who must make reports when they are engaged in their professional practice. This always includes physicians and usually includes other professionals who work with children. In several states, all citizens are considered mandatory reporters. Sanctions for failing to report a suspicious case usually consist of a misdemeanor penalty and the possibility of a civil lawsuit. The purpose of immunity for reporting and sanctions for some individuals if they do not report is to cast a sufficiently wide net to capture cases of abuse. In medical terms, child abuse reporting is a *screening test.*

The *confirmation test* is the child abuse investigation itself. At times the physician is confident that child abuse exists and may know who did it. Other times only a suspicion is present and the goal of the investigation is to either allay those concerns by finding an acceptable explanation or to confirm that child abuse exists so that appropriate action can be taken. Thus the concept of so-called "false" child abuse reports does not make sense when viewed as a screen for suspicious injuries/behaviors/statements.

Most states maintain a central registry for victims and perpetrators of child abuse. This database helps to determine whether a pattern exists. (It also serves the technical function of ensuring that the child/family is not investigated multiple times for the same allegation.) Some states allow day care facilities or other human service employers to check the central registry to determine the suitability of a prospective employee. Such databases can also be used as a research tool when crossed-linked with the birth defects registry or other sources of information.

Child abuse investigations are increasingly using multi-disciplinary teams to help with difficult cases. The field of developmental disabilities has long recognized the value of different professional perspectives, and how these perspectives work in the interest of the child and the family. Team dynamics is a common issue for individuals working in either field. Some child abuse review teams have incorporated developmental disability specialists to learn their unique viewpoint (e.g., the U.S. Advisory Board on Child Abuse and Neglect has a member chosen for expertise in developmental disabilities). Developmental disability teams, however, have yet to explicitly include child abuse specialists, despite the frequency of child abuse and its role in causing some developmental disabilities.

Service delivery

Case plans are constructed by social workers. In more minor cases of child abuse, these suffice. In about 20% of the cases, court involvement is requested. Most court cases are held in juvenile or family court, not for purposes of prosecution of the perpetrator. The goal is to set up a specific case plan and decide on placement of the child. The case plan may require that the child receive a developmental evaluation and developmentally appropriate psychological therapy. The parents may be asked to have a psychological examination. Sometimes they are asked to receive vocational assessment, substance abuse treatment, or individual therapy directed at their area of abusiveness (e.g., domestic violence, sexual offender therapy). By considering the developmental abilities of the adults (e.g. can they read?) and their specific needs, the safety, stability, nurturance, and stimulation of the child may be optimized.

Most children eventually return to the home even if placed in foster care. It should be the goal of the physician and other professionals to maintain a linkage with the family and child. Should the situation change or new instances of child abuse emerge, the process of reporting again affords the opportunity to intervene on behalf of the child and family.

OUTCOMES
Developmental disabilities

It is known that child abuse results in physical, mental, and/or emotional injury, which can be manifested as developmental disabilities. It is also understood that children with disabilities are particularly at risk for maltreatment.

Despite this documented relationship, the incidence and specific types of long-term consequences of maltreatment of children with pre-existing disabilities have not been adequately studied. Westcott's review shows the following ranges of disability, resulting from child abuse and neglect[10]:

Characteristics of children in a study group	Percentage disabled as a result of abuse
Learning disability	3% definitely and 11% possibly
Cerebral palsy and learning disability	9%
Cerebral palsy	38%
Physically abused or neglected	16% (physical or learning disability was the result)
Physically abused and/or neglected	24% (marked retardation was the result)

Psychosocial problems

Concern for welfare of children creates discussion and controversy. Disagreement exists regarding use of mild forms of corporal punishment, such as spanking, and most school personnel and foster parents are advised to refrain from using physical disciplinary methods. A skin mark from spanking, if undetectable after 24 hours, is not considered child abuse in the United States but is in Scandinavia. However, the emotional harm that could result from physically aggressive discipline may not even be considered until it becomes self-evident. A study of the long-term consequences of child abuse may help resolve some of these controversies.

Reports of severely disabled children dying of malnutrition and neglect are common and the physical effects of their abuse are usually quite evident: However the cognitive, emotional, and behavioral effects of abuse and neglect may be more subtle in the severely disabled population and have yet to be quantified systematically.

Psychological long-term effects associated with physical abuse include shyness, fewer friends, disturbed behavior, poor self-esteem, and lower ambitions.[37] Trust may be severely impaired. It is well recognized that there is a strong correlation between individuals with a borderline personality disorder and a childhood history of repeated traumatic experiences, including sexual abuse, physical abuse, and witnessing severe domestic violence: 50% to 80% of such individuals are victims of childhood abuse and trauma.[38] Emotional problems associated with physical abuse in females include somatization, anxiety, depression, dissociation, and psychosis.[39]

Numerous studies have identified a strong association between physical abuse and the long-term consequences of nonfamilial and familial violence.[39] In addition, physical abuse has been associated with self-injury and suicidal behaviors.[39]

Socioeconomic problems

Child abuse results in a great financial burden to society because of the following consequences: medical payments to hospitals and health professionals, cost of maintaining foster care and community interventions (support services and family preservation services), court involvement, and monitoring by social workers (child protective services). The extent to which child protective and family preservation services are provided often directly depends on availability of funding.

Recidivism

Child abusers are likely to repeat their crimes if nothing is done to change their personal characteristics or the circumstances that prompted the abuse. Parents with mental retardation and others with low socioeconomic status who have abused are likely to abuse again if adequate financial and social supports are not provided.

Substance-abusing parents who abuse their children have a high rate of being reported for child abuse.[12] Domestic violence, poverty, lack of social support, and maternal addiction are factors predictive of future abuse in these families.[12]

Certain types of child abuse, such as sexual abuse, have high rates of recidivism because of failure of the sex offender or pedophile to view the action as inappropriate. The sexually abused child must be protected from future abusive acts by proper distancing from the offender.

Neglectful parents rarely acknowledge that they have done anything wrong. Treatment has a poor prognosis unless the parent is able to perceive the wrong and understand how to prevent it.

Children with Munchausen syndrome by proxy must be removed from the abusive parent's care because of high recidivism rates. Recidivism with Munchausen syndrome often proves fatal for the abused child. Other children must also be removed from the parent's care because of the likelihood that another child will assume the role of the abused child if the first is removed.

Once child abuse is substantiated, the likelihood of another substantiated report is about 33%. Undoubtedly cases are missed. Many other cases are never reported in the first place. One study showed that 71% of the victims of shaken baby syndrome had evidence of prior abuse or neglect.[34] About one third of these children had evidence of previous intracranial bleeding from shaking.

PREVENTION

Prevention of child abuse produces a decrease in the incidence of developmental disabilities and prevention of developmental disabilities produces a corresponding decrease in the incidence of child abuse. Not surprisingly there is some correspondence in the strategies for prevention in each area because each area shares many of the same risk factors. Thus teen pregnancy, poverty, parents with limited intelligence, poor social support, and other factors are associated with both child abuse and developmental disabilities. However, two recent advances in child abuse prevention promise to have an impact.

The U.S. Advisory Board on Child Abuse and Neglect was commissioned by Congress to issue a report on child maltreatment–related fatalities. In that 1995 report, a number of specific suggestions were made to manage child fatality cases and to prevent them.[6] One of the recommendations was that every state should have a Child Death Review Team (CDRT). Such teams would review deaths of all children below 18 years of age to determine any patterns and make suggestions about prevention. CDRTs would not be limited to child abuse deaths but would study SIDS, perinatal fatalities, motor vehicle–related deaths, suicide, accidents, and all other causes. Many states have or are in the process of developing such teams. Fatalities represent the tip of the iceberg for many public health agencies. Nevertheless, it is hoped that by pooling data within and between states, important trends may emerge and strategies can be assessed.

A more primary prevention strategy is the *Healthy Families, America Program* developed by the National Committee to Prevent Child Abuse. Efforts are underway in virtually every state to foster this early intervention and support program for all families with newborns. The typical program works as follows. A screening tool is used to decide whether the mother of a newborn falls into a high-risk group. The mother is approached in the hospital to see whether she wishes to participate in this voluntary support service. Thereafter the program aide (nurse or paraprofessional) makes frequent visits to the home for months to years. In addition to serving as support, the program aide usually teaches about child development and helps with care suggestions for the child. In some states, trained volunteers serve the same function for parents felt to be at low risk. Data thus far indicate that children in such programs have much better immunization rates, are enrolled in special needs programs sooner if needed, pregnancies are better spaced, and parent-child interactions are improved. Some preliminary data from several programs seems to show that mental development of the children is enhanced as parents have an increased interest in and understanding of their developmental capabilities.

REFERENCES

1. Kempe CH, Silverman FN, Steel BF, et al: The battered child syndrome, *JAMA* 181:17-24, 1962.
2. Helfer RC, Kempe CH, editors: *The battered child*, ed 4, Chicago, 1987, University of Chicago Press.
3. Korbin JE: Child abuse and neglect: the cultural concept. In Helfer RC, Kempe CH, editors: *The battered child*, ed 4, Chicago, 1987, University of Chicago Press.
4. Koska SB: Legal advocacy for persons with Prader-Willi syndrome. In Greenswag LR, Alexander RC, editors: *Management of Prader-Willi syndrome*, ed 2, New York, 1995, Springer-Verlag.
5. Developmental Disabilities Assistance and Bill of Rights Act, 42 USCA, Section 6000 *et seq*, West Supp, 1993.
6. U.S. Advisory Board on Child Abuse and Neglect: *A nation's shame: fatal child abuse and neglect in the United States*, Washington, DC, 1995, U.S. Government Printing Office.
7. McClain P: *Centers for Disease Control and Prevention*, Atlanta, March 21, 1995.
8. McCurdy K, Daro D: *Current trends in child abuse reporting and fatalities: the results of the 1993 50-state survey*, The National Center on Child Abuse Prevention and Research, Working paper #808, Chicago, 1994, National Committee to Prevent Child Abuse.
9. Baladerian NJ: *Abuse causes disabilities: disability and the family*, Culver City, Calif, 1991, SPECTRUM Institute.
10. Westcott H: The abuse of disabled children: a review of the literature, *Child Care Health Dev* 17(4):243-258, 1991.
11. Diamond LJ, Jaudes PK: Child abuse in a cerebral-palsied population, *Dev Med Child Neurol* 25:169-174, 1983.
12. Chasnoff IJ: Cocaine, pregnancy, and the growing child, *Curr Prob Pediatr* 22(7):302-321, 1992.
13. Ammerman RT, Hersen M, Van Hasselt VB, et al: Maltreatment in psychiatrically hospitalized children and adolescents with developmental disabilities: prevalence and correlates, *J Am Acad Child Adolesc Psychiat* 33(4):567-576, 1994.
14. Lesnik-Oberstein M, Koers AJ, Cohen L: Parental hostility and its sources in psychologically abusive mothers: a test of the three-factor theory, *Child Abuse Neglect* 19(1):33-49, 1995.
15. Birrell R, Birrell J: The maltreatment syndrome in children: a hospital survey, *Med J Austr* 2:1023-1029, 1968.
16. Ammerman RT, Van Hasselt VB, Hersen M: Maltreatment of handicapped children: a review, *J Family Violence* 3:53-72, 1988.
17. Benedict MI, Wulff LM, White RB: Current parental stress in maltreating and nonmaltreating families of children with multiple disabilities, *Child Abuse Neglect* 16:155-163, 1992.
18. Chamberlain A, Rauh J, Passer A, et al: Issues in fertility control for mentally retarded female adolescents and sexual activity, sexual abuse, and contraception, *Pediatrics* 73:445-450, 1984.
19. Tymchuk AJ: Predicting adequacy of parenting by people with mental retardation, *Child Abuse Neglect* 16:165-178, 1992.
20. Dowdney L, Skuse D: Parenting provided by adults with mental retardation, *J Child Psychol Psychiat* 34(1):25-47, 1993.
21. Law J, Conway J: Effect of abuse and neglect on the development of children's speech and language, *Dev Med Child Neurol* 34:943-948, 1992.
22. Adams JA, Ahmad M, Phillips P: Anogenital findings and hymenal diameter in children referred for sexual abuse examination, *Adolesc Pediatr Gynecol* 1:123-127, 1988.

23. De Jong AR, Rose M: Frequency and significance of physical evidence in legally proven cases of child sexual abuse, *Pediatrics* 84(6):1022-1026, 1989.

24. Berger AM, Knutson JF, Mehm JG, et al: The self-support of punitive childhood experiences of young adults and adolescents, *Child Abuse Neglect* 12:251-262, 1988.

25. Moskal MJ, Alexander RC, Mitchell C, et al: *Patterns of cocaine exposure in children* (unpublished).

26. Alexander RC: Failure to thrive, *APSAC Advisor* 5(4):1-13, 1992.

27. Amundson J, Sherbondy A, Van Dyke DC, et al: Early identification and treatment necessary to prevent malnutrition in children and adolescents with severe disabilities, *J Am Diet Assoc* 94:880-883, 1994.

28. Alexander R, Smith W, Stevenson R: Serial Munchausen by proxy, *Pediatrics,* 86(4):581-585, 1990.

29. Makar AF, Squier PJ: Munchausen syndrome by proxy: father as a perpetrator, *Pediatrics* 85:370-373, 1990.

30. Rosenberg DA: Web of deceit: a literature review of Munchausen syndrome by proxy, *Child Abuse Neglect* 11:547-563, 1987.

31. Stevenson R, Alexander R: Munchausen syndrome by proxy, *J Dev Behavior Pediatr* 11(5):262-264, 1990.

32. Levin A, Sheridan M, editors:. *Munchausen syndrome by proxy: issues in diagnosis and treatment,* New York, 1995, Lexington Books.

33. Levitt C, Smith WL, Alexander RC: Abusive head trauma. In Reece R, editor: *Child abuse: medical diagnosis and management,* Philadelphia, 1994, Lea & Febiger.

34. Alexander RC, Crabbe L, Sato Y, et al: Serial abuse in children who are shaken, *Am J Dis Child* 144(1):58-60, 1990.

35. Sato Y, Yuh WTC, Smith WL, et al: MRI evaluation of head injury in child abuse, *Radiology* 173:653-657, 1989.

36. Alexander RC, Greenswag LR, Nowak A: Rumination and vomiting in Prader-Willi syndrome, *Am J Med Gen* 28(4):889-895, 1987.

37. Oates, RK: Personality development after physical abuse, *Arch Dis Child* 59:147-150, 1984.

38. Saunders EA, Arnold F: A critique of conceptual and treatment approaches to borderline psychopathology in light of findings about child abuse, *Psychiatry* 56:188-203, 1993.

39. Malinosky-Rummell R, Hansen DJ: Long-term consequences of childhood physical abuse, *Psycholog Bull* 114(1):68-79, 1993.

PART TWO

SPECIFIC DISORDERS

CHAPTER 7

Disorders of motor development

Cerebral Palsy

JAMES A. BLACKMAN

DEFINITION

Cerebral palsy is a static, nonprogressive disorder of movement and posture due to injuries to the brain sustained during the early developmental period. The term *stable nonprogressive neurological disorder* is sometimes used for this disorder. Terms such as postinfectious or posttraumatic encephalopathy also are used to denote more specific etiological and pathophysiological events occurring after the neonatal period and resulting in problems with motor control.

Little[1] is credited with the first description during the mid-1800s of cerebral palsy. Not long after, Osler[2] and Freud[3] also wrote on the subject. Since that time, as more has become known about cerebral palsy, various definitions and classification systems have been developed. It is important to remember that cerebral palsy is not a single disorder but a group of nonprogressive disorders, with multiple causes and manifestations, that usually result in some degree of permanent impairment of motor function. Disorders that are transient, or due to diseases of the spinal cord, peripheral nerves, or muscles are excluded.[4]

The generally accepted incidence of cerebral palsy is 2/1000. Reports of increased prevalence rates are attributable to the decreased mortality of very low birth weight infants.

Cerebral palsy can affect different parts of the body and can be mani-

186

fested by a wide variety of movement problems. It can result in restricted movement or extraneous, uncontrolled movements. Although many different classifications may be encountered, a simple, clinically useful system describes cerebral palsy by type, distribution, and degree of involvement.

Type

Spasticity occurs in about 60% of all cases of cerebral palsy. It results in reduced movement because of hypertonia and is associated with lesions of the corticospinal (pyramidal) tract, motor cortex, and related areas of the brain, giving rise to hyperexcitable stretch reflexes, clonus, and the presence of the Babinski sign. Spasticity represents increased resistance to fast stretching of muscles that suddenly gives way (the clasp-knife phenomenon). Primitive reflexes such as grasp and startle persist beyond the first few months of life. Tonic reflexes (e.g., the asymmetric tonic neck reflex) are often obligatory and persist as well. When the child is held in vertical suspension, scissoring of the lower extremities is observed because of hypertonia of the hip adductors. Spasticity becomes more evident as the very young child matures.

Dyskinesia (extrapyramidal cerebral palsy), found in 20% of all cases, is caused by injury to the basal ganglia. The involuntary movements of dyskinesia include choreoathetoid and dystonic movements. Although tone may vary in the same individual, dyskinesia is sometimes accompanied by predominantly increased muscle tone or "tension" brought on by certain body positions and heightened emotional states.

Ataxia occurs in about 1% of cases and is characterized by a broad, lurching gait, with balance difficulties. Imbalance may not be apparent until the child is ambulatory.

The remaining cases of cerebral palsy are of the *mixed* type, with a combination of spasticity and dyskinesia or ataxia, or of the *rigid* type in which there is continuous resistance to slow muscle stretch (lead-pipe phenomenon).

Distribution

The distribution of affected body regions is described as follows (usually in the spastic type of cerebral palsy only):

1. *Diplegia:* Involvement of the trunk and all four extremities, *but* the legs more than the arms
2. *Hemiplegia:* Involvement of one side of the body only, with upper extremity frequently more involved

3. *Quadriplegia:* Involvement of both arms, both legs, the head, and the trunk; oral motor function is commonly affected
4. *Paraplegia:* Involvement of the legs only (rarely seen in cerebral palsy)
5. *Monoplegia:* Involvement of one extremity (rarely seen in cerebral palsy)
6. *Triplegia:* Involvement of three extremities (rarely seen in cerebral palsy)

Degree of involvement

There are no adequate, objective measures of degree of severity. An experienced clinician, however, can give subjective estimates of whether neuromuscular involvement is mild, moderate, or severe. *Mild* generally means the manifestations impair function minimally or not at all. *Moderate* generally means that there is some impairment of function, which can be improved significantly with assistive devices. *Severe* means there is significant impairment in function, less effectively improved with assistive devices.

Any label applied to an individual patient (e.g., moderate spastic hemiplegia) should be supplemented with a detailed description of examination findings so that confusion is avoided.

Associated disabilities

Behavior problems. Cerebral palsied children as infants may manifest common problems (e.g., crying, constipation, feeding difficulties) to a greater degree than other children, and these problems tend to persist longer than in normal children. Parents tend to be more concerned about such problems as well.[5]

Children with cerebral palsy will display the typical behaviors appropriate for developmental levels (tantrums, school phobias, independence, adolescent adjustment reactions). While developmentally normal children will manifest these behaviors on schedule, children with delayed development will do so at later chronological ages. A 4-year old with a mental age of 2 years may exhibit tantrum behavior, but parents may be expecting 4-year-old behavior. Another potential difficulty for parents is distinguishing developmentally appropriate behavior from behavior caused by the disability. A spastic child may cry and stiffen when placed in a car seat. Parents can interpret this behavior as discomfort due to cerebral palsy rather than as typical toddler behavior.

Dental disease. Dental caries are no more prevalent among children with cerebral palsy, provided they are exposed to fluorides. However, gum disease is more common, possibly because of poorer oral hygiene. Fifty percent of children on phenytoin for treatment of seizures develop gingival hyperplasia. Malocclusions, dentin irregularities, and fractured teeth can be found as well. Lengthy bottle feedings of milk or juice promote decay of the primary upper front teeth and first molars.[6]

Epilepsy (any form). Incidence averages from 35% to 45%. Seizures usually begin in the first two years of life but may begin much later. They occur most frequently with hemiplegia and quadriplegia.

Feeding and growth problems. Individuals with cerebral palsy, from infancy onward, gain weight poorly. Nutritional deficiencies are frequent. Poor food intake, because of difficulties in effective sucking, chewing, and swallowing, and excessive caloric needs in some types of cerebral palsy (e.g., dyskinesia) account for many cases of poor growth.

Hearing impairment. The prevalence of auditory defects in cerebral palsy is estimated at 12.5%.[7] Deafness with athetoid cerebral palsy has declined with the decrease in kernicterus. Young children with cerebral palsy, possibly because of oral motor involvement or because they are frequently in a recumbent position, are prone to middle ear disease with conductive hearing loss.

Learning disabilities. Disturbances of central processing and movement may lead to learning disabilities. Specific learning problems should be distinguished from mental retardation and limitations in motor performance.

Mental retardation. Accurate estimates of intelligence in physically impaired individuals can be difficult. Approximately one half to two thirds of children with cerebral palsy score within the mentally retarded range on psychometric evaluation. About one half of these score below the mild range. In general, children with dyskinesia tend to score higher than children who are spastic, while quadriplegic cerebral palsy is often associated with severe intellectual deficits.[8] It must be remembered, however, that many persons with cerebral palsy are mentally normal or only mildly retarded. A person with the dyskinetic type of cerebral palsy may appear retarded, and thus may be treated as though he or she were retarded. Physicians should not fall into this trap. Assessment of intellectual status may be difficult and requires assessment by a psychologist familiar with testing children with this disability.

Socioemotional stress. The processes of personality development are often complicated by motor impairment, and this can have a significant impact on the adjustment of an individual. The higher the intelligence of the individual, the more difficult this adjustment may be.

Speech/language impairments. Those children with spastic quadriplegia or a dyskinetic form of cerebral palsy frequently have oral-motor involvement. This manifests itself in difficulties with breathing; laryngeal, pharyngeal, and lingual motor function; and delays in language development. Often children may have better receptive (understanding) than expressive (speech) language skills.

Visual impairment. As many as 50% of all children with spastic cerebral palsy have strabismus. Refractive errors are equally common.[9] As many as 25% of patients with hemiplegia have a homonymous hemianopsia.[10] This is often associated with a sensory deficit and asymmetric undergrowth on the affected side.

ETIOLOGY

In one recent study, 10% of the cases of cerebral palsy were due to perinatal or postnatal factors (infections, toxins, anoxia, trauma); 50% were prenatal, and 33% were mixed.[11] In contrast, previous studies suggested that 60% of cases were due to perinatal factors, while only 30% were accounted for by prenatal events.

Much attention has been given to perinatal predictors of cerebral palsy. While perinatal asphyxia, when severe and prolonged, is associated with a high risk of motor handicap, the majority of infants with low Apgar scores survive neurologically intact.[12]

Of all perinatal factors, intracranial hemorrhage and neonatal seizures are the strongest independent discriminators between neurologically impaired children and controls.[13]

Among 40,000 infants studied prospectively in the Collaborative Perinatal Project, there was a 10-fold to 33-fold increase in the risk of cerebral palsy with the occurrence of any of the following characteristics: birth weight less than 2000 g, head circumference more than 35% above or below the mean, 5-minute Apgar score of three or less, diminished activity or crying lasting for more than 1 day, thermal instability, need for gavage feeding, hypotonia, or hypertonia. Relative risks exceeded 50% with neonatal seizures, or Apgar score of three or less at 10 minutes or later. The risk of cerebral palsy increases 99-fold when hospital nursery staff express having had an "impression" that a newborn functioned as if there were a brain abnormality during the neonatal period.[14]

Kernicterus has become an uncommon cause of cerebral palsy as the prevention and treatment of Rh disease and erythroblastosis fetalis have significantly improved. Most of the recent cases of athetoid cerebral palsy are now due to anoxia instead of kernicterus.

PATHOLOGY

Cerebral palsy is caused by injury to the brain, with the damage varying in location and extent. A few lesions are associated with specific types of cerebral palsy. Kernicterus, a pathological condition associated with a yellow staining of the basal ganglia from neonatal hyperbilirubinemia, produces a syndrome of choreoathetosis, along with difficulty in upward gaze and sensorineural hearing loss.

Periventricular leukomalacia, common in premature infants and characterized by necrosis of white matter adjacent to the lateral ventricles through which descending fibers from the motor cortex pass, is a very strong predictor of disabling cerebral palsy.[15]

Hemorrhages that begin in the subependymal germinal matrix sometimes rupture into the ventricular system leading to hydrocephalus. Large hemorrhages in brain parenchyma cause severe destruction. Most intraperiventricular hemorrhages occur in premature infants less than 32 weeks old, although they can occur in more mature infants. It is sometimes difficult to separate damage caused to the brain by the bleeding itself from that caused by antecedent events, such as hypoxia and ischemia, that may have led to the hemorrhage itself.

Excluding intracranial hemorrhage in premature infants, hypoxic-ischemic injury is the most important cause of neurological morbidity originating in the newborn period. It accounts for more cases of cerebral palsy than any other form of perinatal encephalopathy (e.g., infection or trauma). The majority of cases of hypoxic-ischemic injury appear to be related to intrauterine asphyxia, although subsequent postnatal complications provide additional insults to the brain.[16] Although there are few neuropathic changes in the brain of neonates that are etiologically specific, (kernicterus is an exception), a few general statements can be made. Various types of hypoxic-ischemic injury to the brain result in spastic cerebral palsy in infants of any gestational age. Historically, spastic diplegia was commonly observed in premature infant survivors; but, as more severely ill premature infants survive, quadriplegia is becoming as common.

Neurons of the basal ganglia (caudate, putamen, and globuspallidus) can be injured in the asphyxiated—most commonly term—newborn, resulting in choreoathetosis or dystonia.

It is risky to predict the degree of neuromotor dysfunction in persons based solely on ultrasound or MRI findings. Most clinicians have seen patients with large porencephalic cysts (related to grade 4 intraperiventricular hemorrhage) who have minimal motor involvement. Conversely, a severely affected spastic quadriplegic patient may have little grossly apparent structural abnormality of the brain. There is much about injury, plasticity, and recovery with regard to the nervous system that is not understood.

It is often difficult in a particular case to pinpoint a single event that caused a particular case of cerebral palsy. There is much variation in the type and severity of cerebral palsy (as well as associated problems such as intellectual deficit) among patients with very similar histories. Two children with severe intraventricular hemorrhages or the same Apgar scores may have very different outcomes.

Disturbance in brain development during gestation (due to infection, teratogenic agents, or a cerebral vascular accident) can also result in faulty motor function.

ASSESSMENT AND FINDINGS
History

While no event is an absolute predictor of cerebral palsy, certain situations raise warning flags for a child, warranting closer than usual monitoring. Significant prenatal, perinatal, and postnatal events should prompt special attention, or perhaps additional time for assessment during routine well-child visits. A clinically important behavioral characteristic during infancy is feeding difficulty. If a child continues to need gavage feedings after discharge from the hospital, is difficult to feed, or takes an excessive amount of time to feed, the possibility of cerebral palsy should be considered. The very "easy" child may be of concern as well, such as an infant who needs to be awakened for feedings and rarely cries. In contrast, some infants with central nervous system injury are irritable and difficult to mollify. Constipation is also a typical symptom among infants with cerebral palsy.

At each well-child visit, a developmental history should be obtained. Although particular emphasis may be placed on motor development, other developmental areas should be reviewed as well, such as socialization, attention to visual and auditory stimuli, visual tracking and regard for human faces, manipulation of toys with the hands. General developmental screening instruments for children at-risk are available, such as the Denver II[17] or the Infant Monitoring System[18] but are not adequate if delay is already strongly suspected.

Consideration of parental concern about development can be very useful as well. There is a tendency to put aside such concern because of the variability in the rate of children's development and the feeling that parents may be overly anxious, particularly about a first child. However, parents' observations frequently prove correct. Considerable frustration and loss of confidence in the physician results if concerns are not taken seriously, particularly when the child proves to have a significant disability. One useful clue that parents supply is the observation of hand use in infants. Hand preference is abnormal during the first year of life; if present, its cause should be thoroughly evaluated since it may be a manifestation of hemiplegia.

Physical examination

The routine physical examination may also provide clues to the diagnosis of cerebral palsy. Failure-to-thrive may be one of its first manifestations. Also, a poor rate of head growth may signify previous brain injury. Physical findings such as hip dislocations, lower spinal abnormalities, and cutaneous abnormalities suggest causes other than cerebral palsy for neuromuscular dysfunction or delays in attainment of motor skills.

The diagnosis of cerebral palsy usually can be made with certainty before the child's first birthday, although the exact type and degree of neuromotor involvement may not be clear until later. However, certain neurological findings, such as mild increase or decrease in tone or asymmetries of movement, may be transient and disappear in time, particularly in premature infants.[19]

Systematic assessment of motor function. In assessing infants and young children with possible cerebral palsy, the most useful technique is observation. Experienced clinicians can generally make the diagnosis without ever laying hands on the child. Manipulations often upset the child and make assessment more difficult. The physical examination confirms what one has already observed. There are five useful parameters for assessment of neuromotor function: muscle function, movement, reflexes, structure, and gross motor level.[20]

Muscle function. Two aspects of muscle function should be examined: muscle tone and muscle strength. Muscle tone, the tension in the muscle, is determined by input from the central nervous system. Muscle strength is the intrinsic ability of the muscle to develop tension in response to a load and is determined by several factors, including muscle size and peripheral nerve input.

While sustained hypertonia is present with spasticity, patients with dyskinesia (athetosis) may show fluctuations in muscle tone, with hypertonia sometimes predominating, as in the tension-athetoid type of cerebral palsy. This may not be clearly manifested until after infancy. The history may be helpful if the parents report that their infant's tone is very low when he or she is relaxed or asleep.

Observations of abnormal tone might include poor head control, scissoring of the lower extremities, flexor posturing of the upper extremities, extensor posturing of the lower extremities, floppiness, asymmetry, unsteadiness, poor coordination and balance, difficulty reaching, hypoactivity, or inability to perform age-appropriate motor skills.

In early infancy, hypotonia may be observed in a child who eventually will manifest spasticity or dyskinesia. The child who is hypertonic in the extremities may show hypotonia in the trunk and neck musculature.

The hands-on examination should include passive stretching of the upper extremity flexors, adductors, and pronators, and the lower extremity extensors, adductors, and internal rotators. In spasticity, resistance is felt through the full range of motion on slow stretch, although in mild cases it may be minimal if the stretch is done very slowly. The hallmark of spasticity is the "clasp-knife" response; that is, a catch felt midway through a quick stretch of a muscle followed by release during the remainder of the stretch. Sensors in the muscle spindles detect rapid stretch, and through a monosynaptic pathway cause the muscle being stretched to contract in an attempt to prevent overstretching. In spasticity, the usual dampening of this reflex by the brain is diminished, allowing an exaggerated response. A similar type of response is seen when a muscle's tendon is struck and stretched (e.g., a strong ankle jerk when the Achilles tendon is tapped). Sometimes a repetitive circuit is established with quick stretch, producing clonus. These so-called long track signs, including positive Babinski responses, are indicative of injury to the corticospinal (pyramidal) tract or related motor areas of the brain.

In dyskinesia, variability in muscle tone may be observed and felt. Some dyskinetic children will display "tension," that is, increased muscle tone with excitement, anxiety, or startle. The increased tone may predominate to the point of rigidity. The dyskinetic form of cerebral palsy may present in early infancy as hypotonia. As the injured brain matures, the more typical movements of dyskinesia become evident.

Intrinsic muscle weakness may be difficult to distinguish from hypotonia in infants. Muscle weakness can be caused by muscle or peripheral nerve disease. With these conditions, deep tendon reflexes are generally diminished or absent, whereas they are usually increased in cerebral palsy. Children with cerebral palsy may manifest muscle weakness, however, because of secondary disuse atrophy. Tests such as electromyography, nerve conduction velocities, or muscle enzyme assays can be helpful in distinguishing peripheral nerve and muscle disease from central nervous system disease.

Standardized tests to assess strength are not very useful in children. Instead, in assessing strength, movement against gravity should be observed. A child should be achieving age-appropriate gross motor activities if strength is normal. The clinician should look for abnormal size or asymmetry of muscles and evidence of hypoactivity or decreased endurance. Hands-on examination should include restriction of spontaneous movements, a check for muscle contraction, palpation of the muscle bulk, and observation of the full range of voluntary movement.

Movement. An assessment of movement achieved primarily through observation can provide very useful clues to diagnosis. A child's general activity level should be noted. Some infants with cerebral palsy will display a paucity of movement. Three patterns of movement may be observed: normal movements, abnormal movements (never seen in normal children), and atypical movements (sometimes seen in normal children). With *abnormal movements* a child with high tone may show restricted movements or movements of entire body segments, rather than individual limbs or parts of limbs. For example, a child with spastic diplegia may crawl in a pattern like a mermaid, pulling with the upper extremities and dragging the lower extremities behind in extension. A child with the dyskinetic type of cerebral palsy may show fine, involuntary movements of the extremities, particularly the wrists and fingers, which may be very subtle in the early months of life. Generally, ataxia is not evident until the child is upright, when he may display imbalance and the typical incoordination that results from cerebellar involvement.

Normal children may show *atypical movement* patterns such as unusual methods of mobility. Examples of these are log-rolling, seat-scooting, or bouncing along the floor while supine. Although such atypical movement patterns may be found in normal children, children with neuromuscular involvement commonly manifest such movements. Observing these patterns or hearing of them from parents warrants assessment of the other parameters described here.

Reflexes. Physicians are generally very familiar with the deep tendon reflexes, the Babinski sign, and clonus. Hyperreflexia, the Babinski sign, and clonus may be seen transiently in apparently normal infants although these findings always warrant further follow-up. In the older child in whom long track signs persist, other signs of neuromuscular dysfunction are usually so evident that they simply confirm the obvious. In the pure dyskinetic form of cerebral palsy, the deep tendon reflexes may be normal, and clonus and the Babinski sign may be absent. Diminished or absent deep tendon reflexes in the hypotonic child suggest anterior horn cell disease, peripheral neuropathy, or muscle disease.

Of more significance are the so-called *developmental reflexes.* Nomenclature for these reflexes is somewhat variable, but an understanding of their place in development and how they can be used to detect neurological abnormality is useful. Three groups of developmental reflexes or responses can be identified: primitive, righting, and protective/equilibrium. Primitive reflexes are felt to be mediated at the spinal cord or brain stem level, righting reactions at the mid-brain level, and protective/equilibrium responses at the cortical level. Three aspects of developmental reflexes indicate abnormality: (1) failure of these reflexes to emerge according to schedule; (2) failure to be supressed according to schedule; and (3) obligation, that is, the reflex invariably occurs when the stimulus is presented.

PRIMITIVE REFLEXES. The primitive responses are present at birth or emerge in early infancy. Examples include the asymmetric tonic neck reflex (ATNR), positive support reflex, and the Moro response. The ATNR is elicited by turning the head to one side while the child is in the supine position (Fig. 7-1). In a positive response, the child shows extension of the extremities on the face side and flexion of the upper and lower extremity on the occipital side. If the head is turned to the opposite direction, the reverse response is elicited. In some cases, a complete response will be observed. However, more typically, the response may be transient or evident only by palpation of increased tone rather than by observation of a change in posture.

The ATNR is normally observed in children up to 6 months of age. An early sign of motor disability is the presence of this sign after 6 months of age or an *obligatory* response at any age, that is, the child remains in the ATNR posture as long as the stimulus (head turned to the side) is present.

To check the positive supporting reflex, the child is suspended in the vertical plane in such a way that there is tactile contact of the sole with a table surface and stretching of the toe flexors as if weight bearing were present. In a positive response there is extension of the legs to partially

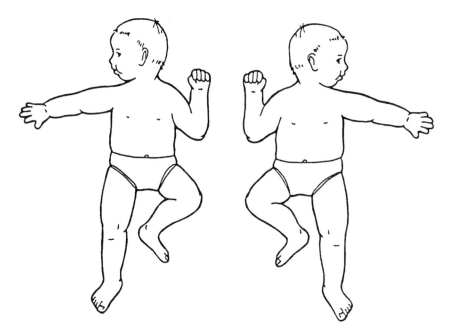

Fig. 7-1 Asymmetric tonic neck reflex (ATNR).

support body weight (Fig. 7-2). This response normally is present in a nonvolitional way at birth, should be suppressed by 3 to 7 months of age, and then is replaced by voluntary standing.

The Moro reflex is elicited by placing the child supine on the examining table, head supported by the examiner's hand. Support is withdrawn suddenly and the head is allowed to fall backward for 10 to 15 degrees. The Moro response includes extension of the trunk; extension and abduction followed by flexion and adduction of the arms.

The Moro reflex is present at birth and is normal up to about 3 months of age. Thereafter, its presence suggests delayed maturation or central nervous system injury. A very exaggerated Moro response is also suspicious, even before 4 months of age. An asymmetric response suggests neuromuscular or skeletal abnormality such as hemiplegia or a fractured clavicle.

RIGHTING REACTIONS. The next group of reflexes are the righting reactions. They help to establish normal head and body relationships in space and to each other. The child is held with the pelvis fixed either in the upright or sitting position. The child is tilted from side to side. A positive (normal) response is the child righting his or her head toward the vertical position (Fig. 7-3).

Fig. 7-2 Positive supporting reflex.

This reflex involves vestibular, optical, and proprioceptor input. There are techniques to distinguish the integrity of these separate inputs, but in the usual examination it is not necessary to make this distinction.

The righting reactions should emerge in the first few months and persist throughout life.

PROTECTIVE/EQUILIBRIUM RESPONSES. The protective extension response (forward parachute) is a useful way to look at asymmetry of the upper extremities and to examine protection responses. This reaction is elicited by suspending the patient in air by the pelvis and moving the head suddenly toward the floor or a chair seat. There should be an immediate outstretching of the arms to protect the head (Fig. 7-4).

Equilibrium reactions are necessary for stability in sitting, standing, and ambulation. To test the equilibrium reaction in sitting or standing, pull or tilt the child *suddenly* to one side. Positive reaction includes righting of the head and thorax, abduction and extension of the arm on the raised side, and protective reaction on the lower side, so that the center of gravity remains centered.

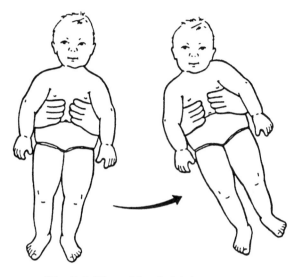

Fig. 7-3 Normal head-righting reaction.

Fig. 7-4 Normal protective extension (forward parachute) response.

The protective/equilibrium responses begin to emerge at about 6 months of age, gradually become stronger, and persist throughout life.

SUMMARY. By 6 months of age, the following reflexes should be suppressed: Moro, involuntary positive supporting, and asymmetric tonic neck reflex. Between 6 and 12 months, the following reflexes or reactions should emerge: righting and equilibrium and protective responses.

An obligatory or very strongly present primitive reflex at any age is abnormal.

There are excellent resources available on the administration and interpretation of developmental reflex tests.[21,22]

Structure. It is important to check for structural or functional defects that explain faulty movement patterns or delays in attainment of motor skills, otherwise suggesting cerebral palsy. Such conditions include congenital dislocation of the hips, spinal cord dysfunction, or other defects of the skeletal system.

There are aspects of the structural examination that are important to check in the child with cerebral palsy. Because of unequal forces on tissues surrounding joints, contractures or dislocations may occur. In the case of spasticity, for example, there is hypertonia of the hip adductors and relative weakness of the hip abductors. As a result of this, there is a tendency for the hips to be held in an adducted position, and the adductor tendons may become shortened with resultant limitation of active or passive abduction. The limited range of hip motion can lead to poor hip joint development and partial or total dislocation of that joint. It should be possible to abduct flexed hips at least 45 degrees. Asymmetry of abduction or limitation in abduction suggests the possibility of partially or completely dislocated hips.

Because of the tendency in spasticity for plantarflexion of the feet, the Achilles tendon may become shortened. Dorsiflexion of the feet should be checked with the knees in extension and in flexion. Greater dorsiflexion may be possible when the knee is flexed, as the gastrocnemius goes somewhat slack since its origin is above the knee. The origin of the soleus (which together with the gastrocnemius ends distally at the Achilles tendon) is below the knee; therefore, resistance to dorsiflexion may continue to be evident even when the knee is flexed. Functionally, ankle range of motion is important with the knee extended, since this is the position the knee will be in with ambulation. Restriction of ankle mobility will impede ambulation. If the feet cannot be passively dorsiflexed beyond the neutral position (toes pointing straight upward with the body in the supine position), bracing or surgical intervention may be indicated. With the older child, contractures of all joints are possible and, therefore, it is important to evaluate each. The physical therapist and orthopedist assist with this evaluation.

Scoliosis secondary to abnormal muscle tone is potentially a problem for all children with cerebral palsy. The child with asymmetry in muscle tone may tend to assume postures that produce a functional scoliosis. Without proper positioning, permanent curvature of the spine may occur. Leg length is a concern in hemiplegias because of the poor growth on the affected side. This can also contribute to the formation of a scoliotic curve.

Gross motor level. It is important to know whether a child's delays in motor skills are due solely to neuromuscular abnormality or whether they are consistent with delays in all areas of development. A mentally retarded child without neuromuscular involvement will generally have developmental skills that are delayed but not deviant; that is, the quality of those skills is appropriate for the developmental level. The child with neuromuscular involvement, on the other hand, is likely to have a scattering of motor skills or depressed motor skill, depending on the degree of severity and the distribution of involvement. In addition, the quality of performance of motor skills will be abnormal or deviant. The child with diplegia, for example, will likely have delays in sitting or ambulation. In addition, the child may crawl using the upper extremities to pull and by dragging the lower extremities along. The pattern of gross motor skills, whether clustered at one age or scattered, may help in determining whether a child's failures to attain motor milestones are due to neuromuscular involvement or mental retardation. A standardized test for gross motor function may be used, such as the Gross Motor Function Measure.[23] Sometimes the primary physician may choose to have this testing performed by other professionals such as physical and occupational therapists. When there are concerns about motor development, it is important to emphasize that the child should have testing in all areas of development, in order to make the diagnosis as well as to detect any secondary problems in children with cerebral palsy.

Differential diagnosis

Degenerative diseases of white matter (e.g., leukodystrophies or demyelinating diseases) and tumors impinging on the descending motor fibers in the brain and spinal cord can produce spasticity. Infections, metabolic disorders, neoplasms, toxins, traumatic injuries, and vascular diseases may cause movement disorders suggesting cerebral palsy. An arteriovenous malformation or a tumor can cause a hemiplegia. In these cases the antecedent history, the rate of attainment of developmental milestones, physical findings, and selected tests should point to the proper diagnosis. A more complete differential diagnosis of cerebral palsy is available.[24]

The key to diagnosis of cerebral palsy is the fact that it is nonprogressive and is caused by a static brain lesion. It is sometimes confusing, especially to parents, that cerebral palsy is called nonprogressive when the manifestations change during infancy. During the early months and years of continued brain growth, neuronal organization and development continue, and for this reason the manifestations of the static lesion can change. A hypotonic infant may become progressively more hypertonic. The elements of dyskinesia become more evident as a child matures. Ataxia may not be evident until a child is ambulatory. Thus, an absolute diagnosis, with the type and severity of cerebral palsy defined, often cannot be firmly fixed until a child is 1 or 2 years of age. It is also not possible to firmly delineate the cerebral palsied child's intellectual skills because of the inherent difficulties in cognitive assessment of individuals whose motor impairment may cause great difficulty with manual dexterity and communication.

A diagnosis other than cerebral palsy should be strongly considered for the child who manifests progressive abnormalities in posture or movement.

The initial assessment of the infant focuses on the accurate diagnosis of cerebral palsy, an interdisciplinary evaluation of the child's overall developmental skills and activities of daily living (especially feeding), and a review of the family's and community's ability to meet the individualized needs of the child.

Subsequent assessments should include general physical examinations, with attention to overall health, sensory function (eyes and ears), and secondary problems of cerebral palsy such as joint contractures or hip dislocations. The focus of ongoing care should not be limited to the disability but should include attention to routine needs appropriate for the developmental level (e.g., toilet training). These needs will be covered under management.

Tests

There are no specific tests for cerebral palsy, but occasionally tests need to be done to rule out other diseases that might mimic cerebral palsy. Although computed tomography (CT) scans often will be abnormal in children with cerebral palsy, they are expensive, expose the child to radiation, and generally do not yield information that is clinically useful in management except, perhaps, to demonstrate the nervous system injury to parents. Magnetic resonance imaging (MRI) is superior to CT diagnostically in that it can identify neuronal migrational abnormalities that occurred in the embryonal stage as well as other subtle abnormalities suggestive of intrauterine infection. MRI is also useful for investigating possible lesions of the brain stem or spinal cord. Other specialized tests, such as evoked response audiometry or electroencephalography, may be indicated for specific related concerns, such as deafness or seizures, rather than for the diagnosis of cerebral palsy itself.

MANAGEMENT

Because of multisystem involvement and multidimensional needs, the key to successful management of the child with cerebral palsy is the inter-disciplinary process (see the box below). No one discipline can assess and manage all aspects in isolation. Furthermore, in order to maximize the benefits of input from various professionals, the integration of findings and coordination of treatment is mandatory. Thus, the physician needs to work with therapists and consultants to support the child with cerebral palsy and the family. When the diagnosis of cerebral palsy is made or suspected, the child should be referred to a center where appropriate subspecialists with experience in conducting interdisciplinary assessments are available. At times, this expertise will be available only at a university-based teaching hospital. In other circumstances, such professionals are available in the child's community through health, educational, mental health, or social agencies. It is important for the primary care physician to communicate closely with the tertiary and community teams. If these services are not available, the primary physician should try to identify appropriate commu-nity and/or school services and may have to function as the coordinator. This is especially critical if a number of the diagnostic and treatment ser-vices are likely to be performed in isolation. The child may need to go to an orthopedist, an ophthalmologist, a physical therapist, and a dietitian, each in a different setting. The more this group of individuals can function as a team, the higher the quality of services will be.

Medical management

Eyes. With the knowledge of the high incidence of ophthalmologic de-fects in children with cerebral palsy, early diagnosis and treatment should occur. A very common finding in children with cerebral palsy is strabis-mus. Early referral is advantageous for a child with cerebral palsy because

---

**DISCIPLINES COMPOSING THE INTERDISCIPLINARY TEAM
IN THE MANAGEMENT OF CEREBRAL PALSY**

Audiology	Dentistry
Medicine	Nutrition
Primary Care	Occupational Therapy
Developmental/Rehabilitation	Physical Therapy
Neurology	Psychology
Orthopedics	Social Work

the problem is unlikely to improve on its own; the earlier treatment is initiated, the better is the chance of maintaining sight in the weak eye. Visual acuity should be reassessed at regular intervals.

Ears. Children with severe cerebral palsy tend to remain in a recumbent position for longer periods of time and may have difficulties with oral motor functioning and swallowing of formula, predisposing them to middle ear dysfunction with consequent conductive hearing loss. Since these children often suffer from the lack of normal opportunities for environmental stimulation because of their restricted mobility and movement, preservation of sensory modalities is important. Thus, middle ear disease should be aggressively treated, especially if accompanied by conductive hearing loss. Technology has greatly improved the ability to test the hearing of very young children. When hearing cannot be tested using standard conditioning techniques, evoked response audiometry may be used to determine whether hearing loss is present and to what degree.

Feeding problems. The child with oral motor involvement or dysphagia may be quite difficult to feed and thus suffer from caloric deprivation. Caretakers become quite frustrated in their efforts, spending many hours of the day in feeding. Therapists (occupational, physical, and speech) can assist by advising about proper positioning (to reduce body tone and effect relaxation); reducing immature, reflexive activity in the mouth (e.g., tongue thrust); and recommending various assistive aids (e.g., special nipples, eating implements) and food textures. Normal food preferences and developmentally appropriate behaviors such as independence and tantrums must be considered in approaching feeding problems. In severe cases, especially when there is mental retardation, a gastrostomy may be indicated to make care more manageable, to ensure adequate nutrition, and to reduce the risk of aspiration. If gastroesophageal reflux is present, a fundoplication procedure should be performed along with the gastrostomy.

Constipation. Constipation is common in patients with cerebral palsy and can be expected to emerge as a problem during the first year of life. If dietary management (adding bulk, fresh fruits and vegetables, Karo syrup) is not adequate, stool softeners with or without mild stimulants (e.g., Maltsupex, Senokot) are almost always effective. Suppositories and enemas on a chronic basis are not usually necessary and are somewhat uncomfortable and embarrassing for older individuals.

Irritability and sleep disturbances. Severely involved infants may be quite irritable and present great difficulty for caretakers. While an overly medicinal approach to disabilities is to be avoided, sometimes mild sedation (e.g., antihistamine) can take the edge off the child's irritability and allow more calm in the household. Given in the evening, the child may fall asleep more readily. Before medications are prescribed, family routine, diet, and health problems should be examined as a possible cause for the irritability.

Drooling. A common concern for caretakers and the cerebral palsied individual who is socially conscious is drooling. Poor oral and pharyngeal motor coordination leads to pooling of oral secretions that spill over from the mouth. Methods to control drooling that have been tried with some success are biofeedback (a frequent signal is given to remind the individual to swallow), anticholinergic medications (e.g., glycopyrrolate), and surgery (parotid and submandibular duct transplantation). In most cases the drooling is annoying but does not cause any health hazards.

Muscle relaxants. Certain drugs are helpful in cases of hypertonia. The three most commonly used are diazepam, dantrolene, and baclofen. Diazepam (Valium) acts on the central nervous system rather than directly on the muscle. This drug is useful for treating spinal cord injury as well as the dyskinetic type of cerebral palsy. Diazepam, however, may cause physical dependency and therefore should not be withdrawn suddenly.

Dantrolene (Dantrium) works directly on the muscle, reducing contraction. It is especially useful with children whose care is made difficult by prolonged muscle contraction and who would not be troubled by a reduction in voluntary muscle power. This drug has potentially serious hepatotoxicity; therefore, risk vs. benefit must be considered and discussed with the patient or parents and liver function must be monitored closely. Severe constipation can also be a troublesome side effect.

Baclofen (Lioresal) acts mainly on the spinal cord to relieve increased muscle tone and muscle spasms. It is used primarily with spinal cord lesions and occasionally for cerebral palsy. The most common side effect is sedation, which tends to disappear a few days after the initial doses. Recently baclofen has been administered on a continuous basis intrathecally with a pump imbedded subcutaneously. This method allows lower overall doses with fewer systemic side effects.[26]

Selective posterior rhizotomy is a neurosurgical procedure designed to reduce spasticity by dividing posterior spinal nerve rootlets. In carefully selected patients, especially those with spastic diplegia, this procedure appears to increase range of motion and improve function.[27]

There has been growing interest in the role of intramuscular botulinum toxin A for temporary muscle relaxation. While the effects of spasticity reduction generally last only 2 to 4 months following injection, in some cases, benefits may persist beyond this time-frame.

Orthopedics

Orthopedics is a major component in the management of cerebral palsy. The child may need various types of braces, splints, or surgical procedures (such as lengthening or transferring of tendons and stabilization of hip joints) to preserve function, assist in ambulation, prevent or treat contracture, or reduce pain. The orthopedist will prescribe treatments, such as daily stretching of muscles or facilitation of normal movement patterns, to be conducted by physical therapists.

Neurology

A neurologist may assist in the early diagnosis of cerebral palsy and help to rule out other neuropathology. Since seizures are common in cerebral palsy, a neurologist can provide consultation on the best possible control with anticonvulsant medications in complicated cases.

Dentistry

An often forgotten aspect of management is dental and general mouth care. A dentist, proficient in serving disabled persons, should become involved early. Consultation with a dentist is recommended within 6 months of the first tooth eruption in order to begin a plan of preventive care to ensure that the child is receiving adequate fluoride and is having the teeth and gums cleansed properly.

Physical therapy

From infancy onward, because of difficulty in motor control, assistance is needed in maintaining correct body posture and alignment. As the child grows, special seating devices may need to be constructed, purchased, or modified to meet specifications of size, degree of disability, and types of orthopedic problems encountered.

Maintaining the best possible position for everyday functioning may include (1) adapting available child-care equipment such as a stroller, car seat, high chair, potty chair, classroom chair; (2) utilizing therapeutic equipment such as adaptable wheelchairs (normally a wheelchair is not considered until the weight of the child exceeds the weight of the wheelchair; or (3) constructing modified seating devices from original designs. Adaptive equipment may have inserts for maintaining specific angles and inclines as well as head and neck supports, appropriate restraining straps, and lap trays.

Orthotics

Orthoses (braces) are generally used to assist a child in standing and walking and to prevent contractures or malalignment of joints.[26] Braces for standing and walking are worn during the day; those for preventing loss of motion or poor alignment of joints are worn at night. Lighter, more cosmetic plastic-molded braces are replacing conventional metal design. Some examples of commonly used braces are listed below.

1. *Ankle-Foot Orthosis (AFO):* Also called short leg brace, the AFO is used to stabilize movement in the distal lower extremity and provide medial or lateral support if needed. Plastic AFOs are light and molded into a fixed position, usually at a 90-degree angle (Fig. 7-5). Occasionally, AFOs are articulated at the ankle joint to allow some mobility. Supramalleolar orthoses (SMOs) are used when only the ankle and foot need support (Fig. 7-6).
2. *Abduction Brace.* This brace stretches the hip adductors (Fig. 7-7). It brings the head of the femur and the acetabulum into proper alignment, thus helping to prevent hip dislocation and subluxations.

Fig. 7-5 Plastic ankle-foot orthosis (AFO).

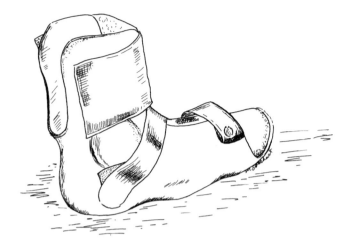

Fig. 7-6 Plastic supramalleolar orthosis (SMO).

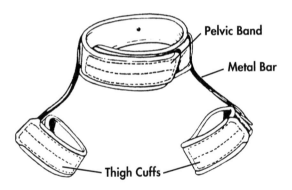

Fig. 7-7 Abduction brace. This particular style is called a Lorenz night splint.

3. *Body Shell.* Used for scoliosis, the body shell is designed to prevent progressive spinal deformity (Fig. 7-8).
4. *Special Shoes.* Special shoe components (Thomas heel, medial wedge) and inserts (cookie or arch insole) are used by some therapists to improve posture and function. The benefits of these shoe modifications have not been proved and orthopedists have mixed opinions of their value.[27]
5. *Tone-Reducing Orthoses.* In patients with spasticity, it has been observed that hyperactive, tonic reflexes of the foot are activated by pressure on certain areas of the sole and produce associated move-

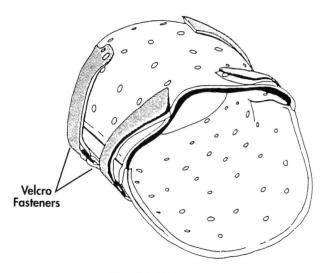

Velcro
Fasteners

Fig. 7-8 Body shell.

ments in other muscles.[28] Special ankle foot orthoses are designed to inhibit overactive tonic reflexes, facilitate underactive ones, and maintain normal position of the foot and ankle to achieve functional improvement.[29] Although these casts are becoming increasingly popular, further evaluation of this treatment modality is needed to determine cost vs. benefits.

Management and the family

During the lifelong process of a child's diagnosis, treatment, complications, and passage through various developmental levels with typical adjustment reactions, support for the family requires considerable input from professionals trained to deal with such issues. Because of the expense involved in evaluations and adaptive equipment, the family's finances are often strained. A social worker can identify resources and services that are unknown to the family and sometimes to the primary physician.

Children of various ages present different sets of problems to consider. In infancy, the problems relate to diagnosis, evaluation of needs, and difficulties with commonly encountered problems such as feeding difficulties, constipation, irritability, and sleep disturbances. While young disabled children apparently do not have such problems at any greater frequency than normal children, it has been shown that these problems may be viewed by the parents as more severe and of longer duration.[5]

Older children with cerebral palsy face difficulties in adapting to school settings where mainstreaming occurs, learning to form satisfying social relationships, developing as much independence as possible, dealing with sexuality, and exploring occupations and long-term living situations. With the more severely disabled child, parents have a greater burden with respect to cost of care, time expended in the care of a very dependent person, and concerns about sharing the responsibility for care, especially as the individual grows older. The primary physician plays an especially important role in providing support to the family, in listening to concerns, and in mobilizing resources.

Early intervention

Many communities have early intervention programs to address therapeutic, developmental, and other needs of the child and family. While the efficacy of physical therapy for cerebral palsy has not been consistently established,[30] there is a theoretical basis of support for facilitating development of normal movement patterns and preventing secondary complications.[31]

During the preschool years, the child often has an opportunity to enter a classroom-based program. This provides additional opportunities for the child to become integrated into a social atmosphere and to receive more intensive therapy if needed, and it also gives the parents some relief from the 24-hour responsibility of caring for a dependent child.

Depending on the severity of intellectual deficit, the child with cerebral palsy will usually be mainstreamed into the regular school environment. The physician can encourage the provision of a nonrestricting atmosphere for a child with a physical disability, while drawing proper attention to any health concerns that will require the cooperation of school personnel, such as the need for medications or exercises. The child should be encouraged to participate as fully as possible in the school routine.

Adolescence is a very difficult period of transition for all children but especially for those with disabilities. Physicians can and should provide a supportive setting in which the adolescent can vent the anger and frustration felt about being disabled. Issues of sexuality must not be ignored. If the physician does not feel comfortable in dealing with these issues, other resources should be found to help the adolescent make a smooth transition into adulthood. As a child passes through high school, the needs for further education, employment, and provision of care for the severely disabled person must be addressed and will require the physician's continued involvement.

PROGNOSIS

The degree of severity with cerebral palsy varies so greatly that it is not possible to make a general prognosis. If a cerebral palsied individual survives infancy, a normal lifespan is likely except in very severely involved children whose immobility makes them more susceptible to possibly fatal respiratory tract infections.

In one follow-up study,[32] children with spasticity tended to have higher IQs, achieved a higher level of schooling, and were more independent socially, economically, and in self-care than individuals who had other types of cerebral palsy (i.e., dyskinetic, ataxic, mixed). Patients with an initial IQ under 50 only achieved an elementary education and were unemployed; IQ had less predictive value in the higher ranges. Levels of self-care correlated highly with degree of employability, school achievement, economic status, and degree of social integration. Sadly, this study also showed that cerebral palsied adults who were potentially employable and capable of social activity were typically unemployed and socially isolated. Appropriate and timely interventions afford much greater opportunities for a pleasant, productive life. The physician can play an important role in the attainment of these goals.

REFERENCES

1. Little WJ: On the influence of abnormal parturition, difficult labour, premature birth, asphyxia neonatorum, on the mental and physical condition of the child, especially in relation to deformities, *Trans Obstet Soc (London)* 3:293, 1862.
2. Osler W: *The cerebral palsies of children,* London, 1889, HK Lewis.
3. Freud S: Die Infantile Cerebrallahmung. In Nothnagel H, editor: *Specielle pathologie und therapie,* Vienna, 1897, A Holder.
4. Mutch L, Alberman E, Hagberg B, et al: Cerebral palsy epidemiology: where are we now and where are we going? *Dev Med Child Neurol* 34:547-551, 1992.
5. Blackman JA, Cobb L: A comparison of parents' perceptions of common behavior problems in developmentally at risk and normal children, *Child Health Care* 18:108-113, 1989.
6. Nowak AJ: Dental disease. In Blackman JA, editor: *Medical aspects of developmental disabilities in children birth to three,* Rockville, MD, 1990, Aspen Systems, pp 101–106.
7. Robinson RO: The frequency of other handicaps in children with cerebral palsy, *Dev Med Child Neurol* 15:305-312, 1973.
8. Cruikshank WM, Holkeban DP, Bice HV: The evaluation of intelligence. In Cruikshank WM, editor: *Cerebral palsy, a developmental disability,* Syracuse, NY, 1976, Syracuse University Press.
9. Black PD: Ocular defects in children with cerebral palsy, *Br Med J* 281:487-488, 1980.
10. Tizard J, Paine R, Crothers B: Disturbances of sensation in children with hemiplegia, *JAMA* 155:628, 1954.
11. Holm VA: The causes of cerebral palsy: a contemporary perspective, *JAMA* 247:1473-1477, 1982.
12. Nelson KB, Ellenberg JH: Apgar scores as predictors of chronic neurological disability, *Pediatrics* 68:36-44, 1981.

13. Nelson KB, Bromcen SH: Perinatal risk factors in children with serious motor and mental handicaps, *Ann Neurol* 2:371-377, 1977.
14. Nelson KB, Ellenberg JH: Neonatal signs as predictors of cerebral palsy, *Pediatrics* 64:225-232, 1979.
15. Pinto-Martini JA, Riolo S, Chaan A, et al: Cranial ultrasound prediction of disabling and non-disabling cerebral palsy at age two in a low birth weight population, *Pediatrics* 95:249-254, 1995.
16. Volpe JJ: *Neurology of the newborn*, ed 3, Philadelphia, 1995, WB Saunders.
17. *Denver II*, Denver, CO, 1989, Denver Developmental Materials.
18. *Ages and Stages Questionnaires (ASQ)*, Baltimore, 1995, Paul Brookes Publishing.
19. Nelson KB, Ellenberg JH: Children who "outgrew" cerebral palsy, *Pediatrics* 69:529-536, 1982.
20. Blackman JA, Lough LK, Huntley JS: *Assessment of neuromotor dysfunction in infants*, Videodisc assisted instruction program, Iowa City, 1989, Cognitive Design Technologies.
21. Capute AJ, Accordo PJ, Vining EPG, et al: *Primitive reflex profiles*, Baltimore, 1978, University Park Press.
22. Blasco PA: Primitive reflexes: their contribution to the early detection of cerebral palsy, *Clin Pediatr* 33:388-397, 1994.
23. *Gross Motor Function Measure (GMFM)*, Hamilton, Ontario, 1990, Gross Motor Measures Group, Chedoke-McMaster Hospitals.
24. Swaiman KF: Cerebral palsy—perinatal motor impairment. In Swaiman KF, Wright FS, editors: *The practice of pediatric neurology*, St Louis, 1982, Mosby.
25. Sugimoto I, Woo M, Nishida N, et al: When do brain abnormalities in cerebral palsy occur? An MRI study, *Dev Med Child Neurol* 37:285-292, 1995.
26. Campbell SK, Almeida GL, Penn RD, et al: The effects of intrathecally administered baclofen on function in patients with spasticity, *Physical Ther* 75:352-362, 1995.
27. Oppenheim WL, Staudt LA, Peacock WJ: The rationale for rhizotomy. In Sussman MD, editor: *The diplegic child*, Rosemont, IL, 1992, American Academy of Orthopaedic Surgeons.
28. Cosgrove AP, Corry IS, Graham HK: Botulinum toxin in the management of the lower limb in cerebral palsy, *Dev Med Child Neurol* 36:379-385, 1994.
29. Jordan R: Therapeutic considerations of the feet and lower extremities in the cerebral palsied child, *Clin Pediatr Med Surg* 1:547-561, 1984.
30. Turnbull JD: Early intervention for children with or at risk of cerebral palsy, *Am J Dis Child* 147:54-59, 1993.
31. Low NL: A hypothesis why "early intervention" in cerebral palsy might be useful, *Brain Dev* 2:133-135, 1980.
32. Klapper ZS, Birch HG: The relation of childhood characteristics to outcome in young adults with cerebral palsy, *Dev Med Child Neurol* 8:645-656, 1966.

CHAPTER 7B _____

Myelodysplasia

ROBERT A. JACOBS

Myelodysplasia is one of the most common and complex birth defects. It occurs at a rate of 0.5 to 1 per 1000 live births. Clinical manifestations are diverse, but the major components are:

- *Spinal cord defect:* Results in weakness, paralysis, and loss of sensation in the lower extremities as well as neurogenic bowel and bladder
- *Arnold-Chiari malformation (ACM), type II:* May lead to hydrocephalus and, in a small number of infants, to symptoms of brainstem dysfunction, including cranial nerve abnormalities, apnea, bradycardia, and/or central hypoventilation

Major orthopedic problems presenting at birth or developing later in association with spinal cord defect include foot deformities, hip dislocation, pathological fractures, and spinal deformities such as kyphosis and scoliosis. Problems associated with hydrocephalus and shunt placement include shunt obstruction and infection, relatively poor visual-spatial perception, hyperverbal behavior, and precocious puberty.

PATTERNS OF CARE

For these complicated and interrelated problems, team care is optimal and is the standard in most communities. The team should be multi- and/or interdisciplinary[1,2] and may involve routine participation by clinicians in pediatrics, orthopedics, urology, neurosurgery, nursing, social work, nutrition, physical and occupational therapy, and orthotics. Consultation from psychology, psychiatry, genetics, ENT, ophthalmology, stomal therapy, radiology, and dental and pulmonary care are also required. It is essential that the care be family-centered (Fig. 7-9).

There are over 200 centers in the United States. They vary in size, membership, location, method of operation, placement in the medical center or community, and funding source. Teams also vary in their degree of centralization, with highly centralized models tending to be tertiary center–

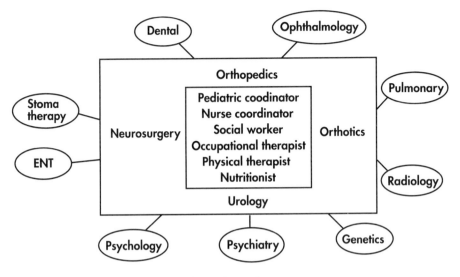

Fig. 7-9 Myelomeningocele team concept.

based. This may lead to problems when the family lives a long distance from the center. Community-based teams are more geographically accessible but have more limited resources, particularly for dealing with highly complex problems.[1] A combination and continuum of care between smaller and more community-based centers and the more technologically sophisticated tertiary center would be optimal, but this is frequently difficult to achieve in a health care environment with a diversity of referral relationships and funding sources.

The situation may be further complicated by major changes in the Medicaid (Title XIX) program and rapid growth of managed care (HMO). These changes have great significance for all individuals with special needs, especially for those with spina bifida who frequently depend on team and center care.[3-5] Failure to provide a multidisciplinary approach with effective case management and care coordination results in a significant decrease in necessary health care and an associated increase in serious morbidity regardless of insurance status.[6] Similar problems of care coordination exist for young adults when they transition to adult care providers who frequently cannot provide team care.[7]

DEFINITION

Spinal cord and spine defects arise from a disturbance in the formation of the neural plate during fetal development. The nomenclature can be confusing because multiple names have been applied to various manifestations of the condition (Table 7-1).

A practical classification for neural tuble defect (NTD) has been proposed based on whether the neural tube is visible (open NTD) or not (closed NTD). Open NTD results embryologically from a failure of primary neurulation, with involvement of the entire central nervous system. Closed NTD represents a failure of canalization and fusion of the end of the primary neural tube. This failure of secondary neurulation affects only the spinal cord and, in general, will not have associated ACM or hydrocephalus.[8] Neurological dysfunction may additionally be categorized by whether the symptomatology is above or below the cele (lesion) level[9] (Fig. 7-10).

ETIOLOGY

NTD are a heterogeneous group of disorders. No single theory or mechanism accounts for all cases. Based on findings from family and epidemiological studies, neural tube defects are felt to be the result of a combination of environmental and genetic factors occurring at a critical point in fetal development. The condition is generally described as having multifactorial causation. Despite this, significant progress has been made over the past decade in prenatal diagnosis and, more importantly, in primary prevention through periconceptual use of folate, which appears to prevent up to 70% of the cases of NTD.[10]

Epidemiology

The reported incidence of NTD varies widely. The highest rate in general has been in parts of the United Kingdom (Wales) and Ireland, among Sikh Hindus in British Columbia, in parts of India and China, and among Hispanics. Low prevalences have been found among African-Americans, Maoris, and in some European countries and Japan. In the United States an East-West gradient of decreasing prevalence has been noted, although in recent years it has not been possible to confirm its continuation. Studies from both the United Kingdom and the United States report major decreases in incidence over the past 20 years.[10-15] These reported decreases appear real and cannot be accounted for solely by abortion of the rising number of affected fetuses identified through prenatal diagnosis or by increased use of periconceptual folic acid and/or multivitamins.

Reports of thoracic level lesions being more common in Sikh Hindus and among whites, particularly white females in North Carolina, support embryological heterogeneity with genetic specificity among some racial groups for certain NTD lesions.[15] This has particular importance because

Table 7-1 Common nomenclature manifestations

Terms	Manifestations
Neural tube defect (NTD)	Anencephaly, encephalocele, and spina bifida, three conditions that appear to be epidemiologically related
Spinal dysraphism and spina bifida	All defects of closure affecting spinal canal/contents
Myelodysplasia	Defects of spinal cord development not necessarily associated with failure of fusion of the arches of the vertebral spine; some forms of myelodysplasia are diplomyelia, hydromyelia, syringomyelia, and diastematomyelia
Spina bifida occulta	Simple failure of fusion of the spinal arches, with no protrusion of the cord or meninges and no disturbance of the soft tissues covering the spinal column
Occult spinal dysraphism	Spina bifida occulta may be "marked" with an overlying angioma, pigmented nevus, dimple, hairy patch, or fistula; these cutaneous markers may indicate the presence of cord tethering with intra- and/or extradural lipoma or dermoid cyst
Spina bifida cystica	Disturbed spine and contents of spinal canal, with an outpouching of meninges with or without spinal cord involvement; includes meningocele, myelomeningocele (meningomyelocele), and lipomyelomeningocele
Meningocele	Lesion not involving neural elements in the cystic outpouching of the meninges and in which the cord is not dysplastic; this may not be entirely obvious from external examination of the cele; it requires surgical and pathological evaluation of the tissue for neural elements as well as clinical evaluation of motor, sensory, and bowel and bladder function
Myelomeningocele or meningomyelocele (MMC)	Dysplastic neural elements protruding through unfused vertebral arches; closed MMC is completely covered with meninges and skin; open MMC implies absence of meninges covering the spinal cord and a connection of spinal fluid to the outside, usually through superiorly placed pore; sac or cele of meningeal and neural tissue may/may not be present and can exhibit varying degrees of epithelialization; following vaginal delivery, determination of whether sac was broken from trauma or was absent in utero is difficult
Lipomeningocele and lipomyelomeningocele	Closed MMC with overgrowth of fatty tissue involving the meninges alone or also including the spinal cord
Myeloschisis	Open defect without a sac but with a malformed cord
Hydrocephalus	Occurs in over 90% of children with myelomeningocele and is usually obstructive in nature; the obstruction is usually at the level of the fourth ventricle, which is posteriorly dislocated or herniated into the cervical spine area
Arnold-Chiari (type II) or Chiari II malformation	Prolongation of the cerebellar vermis and the fourth ventricle into the cervical spine area with a kinked, inferiorly displaced medulla; the posterior fossa of the skull tends to be small, the foramen magnum is larger than usual, and the cervical vertebral canal is funnel shaped; Arnold-Chiari types I and III occur without myelomeningocele or hydrocephalus

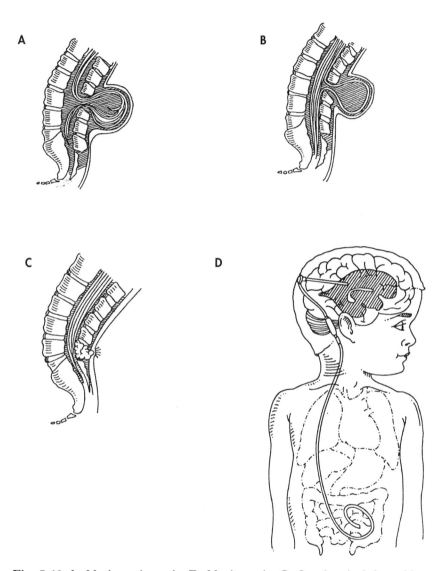

Fig. 7-10 A, Myelomeningocele. **B,** Meningocele. **C,** Occult spinal dysraphism. **D,** Hydrocephalus with ventriculoperitoneal shunt. (From Davoh CT, Kinsman SL: *Medical facts about spina bifida,* Baltimore, 1995, Kennedy Krieger Institute/ Spina Bifida Association of America.)

the beneficial effects of vitamins were not witnessed, and there was decreased protection noted among Hispanic women in California.[16]

Prevalence of NTD in working class families is twice that in upper class families. Seasonal variations occur, with peak incidence of births in November, December, and January. There are peaks in incidence in children born to young (less than 20) and older mothers (over 35). In studies of families, the proportion of siblings affected has been 4% to 5%, or about ten times the incidence of the malformation in the general population. The incidence in offspring of affected parents with spina bifida is 3% to 4%. Among cousins, maternal sisters' children appear to be more often affected, about double the general population.[17]

The changing incidence of neural tube defects over time has suggested a number of causal hypotheses, involving changing environmental factors, such as potato blight as well as many other agents both chemical and infectious. Chemical agents known to affect neurulation are aminopterin, LSD, thalidomide, trimethadione, valproic acid, and carbamazepine.[18-24] In humans, NTD occurs more commonly than expected in conjunction with maternal diabetes and in association with both trisomy 18 and triploidy and with craniosynostosis. In addition, there appears to be an increased incidence of NTD in families in which there have been other "schisis" birth defects, such as cleft palate, omphalocele, extrophy of the bladder, diaphragmatic hernia, and tracheoesophageal fistula.[25-29] Reports of myelomeningocele in association with complex congenital heart disease have been infrequent and are usually associated with other syndromes, including trisomy 18, Kousseff or Ivemark syndromes, DiGeorge sequence, and more recently velo-cardio-facial syndrome with 22g11 deletion.[30,31] An increased incidence of NTD was reported to occur with maternal hyperthermia in the first month of pregnancy,[32] but subsequent reports did not confirm this finding. Studies have explored whether cellular defects of zinc bioavailability may affect NTD pathogenesis in some mothers. Selenium deficiency has been related to increased incidence of NTD, and suggestions of a complex relationship between zinc, selenium, and folic acid support hypotheses of the multifactorial pathogenesis of NTD.[33,34]

Dietary factors have been examined with recent focus on vitamin intake. Postnatal levels of serum vitamin C and red blood cell folate were found to be lower in women who had had infants with neural tube defects.[35] Oral contraceptives decrease many serum vitamin levels, including folic acid and vitamin C. Women who had used oral contraceptives in the 3 months before conception had significantly more infants with NTD.[36,37]

Other birth defects were not seen at an increased rate. Nutritional factors might account for the higher incidence of neural tube defects in infants of mothers from lower socioeconomic classes.[35] In a nonrandomized multicenter prospective trial of vitamin supplementation in pregnant women who had had a previous infant with NTD, there was a significant decrease in risk for those women receiving supplementation.[38] In a randomized control trial of 111 women in Wales who previously had one child with a neural tube defect, the subjects took 4 mg of folic acid or placebo daily before and during early pregnancy. Among the women who were compliant, there were no recurrences of NTD, while 2 of 16 noncompliant women, and 4 in the placebo group had recurrence.[39] Patient self-selection and failure to provide randomized controls to take into account differing incidence between social classes raised methodological concern regarding these studies.

Subsequent studies by the British Medical Research Council (MRC) showed high dose folic acid supplementation (4.0 mg per day) in women with a previous NTD-affected pregnancy reduced the risk by 70%[40]; similar reports come from Hungary and Cuba.[41,42] The Centers for Disease Control and Prevention (CDC) recommended (August, 1991) 4.0 mg of folic acid daily at least 1 month before conception through the first trimester for women with a previous NTD-affected pregnancy when planning future pregnancies.[43] A prospective cohort study of use of folic acid in New England involving women without a history of a previous NTD-affected pregnancy reported a 72% reduction in risk.[44] The United States Public Health Service recommended (1992) that ". . . all women of childbearing age in the United States who are capable of becoming pregnant should consume 0.4 mg of folic acid per day for the purpose of reducing their risk of having a pregnancy affected with spina bifida or other NTDs."[45] This recommendation for low-dose folate is aimed at reducing occurrence of spina bifida and related conditions by 50%.[45] These recommendations may be achieved by daily folate or multivitamin supplementation, fortification of specific foods such as bread or cereal, and/or improved dietary intake.

Women with low-normal plasma vitamin B_{12} may also be at an increased risk for having a NTD-affected pregnancy as those women determined to be folate dependent. An abnormality of homocysteine metabolism in these women suggests an abnormality in methionine synthase function involving its cofactor B_{12}.[46]

Embryology

Several theories have been put forward to explain the pathophysiology and development of the fetus with spina bifida. Two major theories are primary neural tube defect involving failure of closure of the neural tube, which usually occurs during the fourth week of gestation, and secondary neural tube defect, or reopening of the previously closed neural tube.

Neurulation is thought to begin on day 17 post-conception in humans. The neural plate forms through an inductive effect of the paraxial mesoderm on the ectoderm above it, which leads to a folding over and then a fusion of surface glycoproteins followed by cellular fusion to form the neural tube. The "zipper" model is currently thought to account for neural tube closure. It suggests that closure begins at the cervico-medullary junction and proceeds in caudal and cephalic directions until fusion of the anterior and posterior neuropores occurs on day 24 and 26 respectively.[47,48] Recent studies in mice suggest four sites of initial closure, and other authors have suggested a similar mechanism in humans with multiple closure sites.[49-51] This "button" theory has led to postulates that failure of closure at certain sites may account for specific anatomical, ethnic, or environmental differences of expression that have been reported. It also makes a single causation theory difficult to formulate to explain the diverse clinical features of neural tube defects.[50]

Theories have been advanced to address the issue of abnormal neurulation and simultaneous formation of Arnold-Chiari malformation, type II. The traction theory suggests that tethering of the caudal end of the neural tube pulls the cerebellum and brainstem into the spinal canal. Overgrowth of the neural tissue, which causes eversion of the neural plate, is another hypothesis. The hydrodynamic theory suggests that inadequate escape of cerebrospinal fluid during embryogenesis results in bursting of the neural tube, causing spina bifida cystica if this occurs at the caudal end of the neural tube and anencephaly if it occurs at the rostral end. An embryonic neuroschisis theory suggests that the reopening of the neural tube at the midline, with the progression or variable healing of the caudal neural tube and fourth ventricle, results in myelomeningocele (MMC) and Arnold-Chiari malformation. A fifth theory suggests the defect is one of abnormal mesodermal differentiation, which in turn influences neuroectodermal development. The occiput is a mesodermal structure; the Arnold-Chiari malformation and caudal spinal defect could have a common origin in mesodermal malformation.[52] More recently a unified theory depicting "a series of interrelated, time-dependent defects in the development of the ventricular system" has been proposed. It suggests that CSF leakage results in inadequate fetal ventricle distention with resultant small posterior fossa and brain and skull anomaly.[53]

SCREENING: PRENATAL DIAGNOSIS

Alpha-fetoprotein (AFP) is elevated in maternal serum (MSAFP) and amniotic fluid (AFAFP) in NTD[10,54] and other conditions. This has made prenatal diagnosis available through maternal serum screening and amniocentesis for definitive diagnosis. AFP is primarily produced in the fetal liver with release into the fetal serum and amniotic fluid. It becomes measurable in maternal serum at the end of the first trimester. MSAFP is elevated in open NTD, such as encephalocele, spina bifida, and anencephaly; open abdominal wall defects such as gastroschisis and omphalocele; and less common anomalies including sacrococcygeal teratoma, bladder and cloacal exstrophy, cystic hygroma, renal agenesis, obstructive uropathy, congenital nephrosis, fetal skin abnormalities, and upper gastrointestinal tract obstruction. It is decreased in Down syndrome and trisomy 18 pregnancies.[24,55]

In the California AFP Screening Program specimens are taken between 15 to 20 weeks (105 to 140 days) gestation with preference for blood collection between 16 to 18 weeks (112 to 126 days). This timetable is important to provide an adequate timeframe for more definitive diagnostic testing as necessary and to allow sufficient time for decisions regarding continuation or termination of an affected pregnancy. Interpretation of MSAFP results are affected by patient age, gestational age, weight, race, number of fetuses, diabetic status, and medical history with particular attention to the family history for prior NTD and/or maternal use of carbamazepine (Tegretol) or valproic acid (Depakote, Depakene), both of which are reported to produce an increased risk of NTD. The program reports the test as either screen negative or screen positive. The former result does not generally require further screening unless there is a positive family history for NTD or the use of carbamazepine or valproic acid. Screen positive indicates an increased risk for open NTD, abdominal wall defects, or the less common conditions described previously.

The California program currently identifies 97% of fetuses with anencephaly, 80% with open spina bifida, and 85% with gastroschisis and omphalocele. False positives may result from renal abnormalities, fetal demise, fetomaternal hemorrhage, multiple fetuses, underestimation of gestational age, and normal variation. False negatives are an inherent part of any screening procedure, and this program is no different in its inability to identify all fetuses with NTD.[54,55]

Amniocentesis with testing for elevated AFAFP is more definitive than MSAFP, identifying 90% to 95% of affected fetuses with open NTD. The more neural tissue–specific acetylcholinesterase test is 99% to 100% accurate and remains so after 20 weeks gestation when AFAFP has risen and become more difficult to interpret.[56]

Ultrasonography also has been increasingly accurate in prenatal diagnosis of fetal anomalies. Anencephaly can be diagnosed with great accuracy by ultrasonography, while other conditions are less obvious, even in skilled hands. Small, skin-covered, or low sacrum lesions may be difficult to diagnose. Intracranial signs of spina bifida—"lemon" sign deformity of the frontal bone and/or cerebellar compression "banana" sign of the Arnold-Chiari malformation—allow diagnosis by ultrasonography with great specificity. A study to assess the feasibility of ultrasound alone used level 2 ultrasonography and experienced personnel to identify 51 cases of fetuses with spina bifida, encephalocele, gastroschisis, or omphalocele with a sensitivity of 100%. With pregnancy loss due to amniocentesis reported to be as high as 0.5% (1 in 200), it was suggested that some women may choose to rely on the combination of MSAFP and high-definition ultrasound and refuse amniocentesis.[57] The California MSAFP Screening Program (1988 to 1990) identified 161 cases of open spina bifida but noted that 8% of the cases were not identified with initial ultrasonography alone despite level 2 standards of equipment and clearly prescribed requirements for the sonographer.[58] Obesity, prior abdominal surgery, inexperienced personnel, and/or inadequate equipment may all contribute to this or a higher percentage of missed cases in less developed systems for birth defect identification. The researchers, and others, felt ultrasonography alone is inadequate to identify all cases of open spina bifida.[58-60]

Identification of a high-risk pregnancy allows a woman a choice about continuation or termination of the pregnancy. In the California AFP Screening Program of 100 cases of detected anencephaly 71% chose termination, compared to 75% of 72 cases of spina bifida, and 85% of 13 cases of encephalocele. In non-NTD disorders termination of pregnancy was elected in 76% of cases of Down syndrome, 60% of 20 cases of trisomy 18, 13% of 52 cases of gastroschisis, and 56% of 18 cases of omphalocele.[61] Abortion is a controversial topic in the United States and many other countries even when the pregnancy is complicated by a fetus with major congenital anomalies. Many groups including Catholics, Mormons, some Orthodox Jewish groups, and evangelistic faiths categorically reject the option of abortion. However, when pregnancy termination is not an option, identification may frequently be important to allow better management of the pregnancy and delivery.[56,62-65]

ASSESSMENT AND DECISION MAKING

There are moments in the care of those with MMC where difficult decisions must be made. The necessity for many of these decisions reflects advances in technology,[66] which have allowed increased survival and prolonged life but also brought difficult, stressful, and heart-wrenching decisions into the earliest months of pregnancy.

Assessment of the neonate at a specialized center is important to provide accurate and important information to new parents. Questions about future ambulation, cognitive ability, and expectations for survival and life expectancy are frequently asked. Ambulatory potential, based on motor and sensory examination, may be predicted with reasonable accuracy by the orthopedic surgeon and physical therapist (Table 7-2).

Cognitive potential, however, is far more difficult to determine. The presence of massive hydrocephalus as measured by head circumference and radiologic imaging, microcephaly, severe prematurity or very low birth weight, development of meningitis or ventriculitis, intraventricular hemorrhage, other major neonatal complications, and/or other major congenital anomalies are unfavorable risk factors for intellectual prognosis. The presence of adverse factors, however, is not predictive, and this must be appreciated by all who provide counseling and advice to parents.[67,68]

Early provision of accurate information by well-informed practitioners in a caring manner is important to parents,[69,70] even though they may be experiencing significant grief and be overwhelmed to the point where they can absorb very little of the information provided.[66] At the present time most infants born with open NTD in the United States have surgical intervention within the first several days of life. It appears that early closure (within 24 hours) is not necessary, and that delayed (1 to 7 days) or late (after 1 week) closure causes no increase in infection or change in cord function if the lesion is kept clean and in sterile non-adherent dressing. Delay in closure allows time for parents to come to grips with their feelings and grief and to review intervention options with their physician without detriment to their infant.[71] In many countries closure may be significantly delayed due to resource limitations and problems with access to care.[72]

Poor outcome as measured by significant physical disability and impairment of cognitive function in many individuals in whom aggressive early closure was pursued led in the early 1970s to policies of selection and conservative nonsurgical intervention for those thought to have less favorable prognosis.[69,73-75] This policy of selection and nonoperative intervention based on quality of life prognostic criteria became highly controversial and

Table 7-2 Myelomeningocele: correlation between segmental innervation and motor, sensory, and sphincter function and reflexes

Lesion	Major segmental innervation	Cutaneous sensation	Lower limb motor function	Sphincter function	Reflex
Cervical/thoracic	Variable	Variable	None	—	—
Thoracolumbar	T12	Lower abdomen	None	—	—
	L1	Groin	Weak hip flexion	—	—
	L2	Anterior upper thigh	Strong hip flexion	—	—
Lumbar	L3	Anterior distal thigh and knee	Knee extension	—	Knee jerk
	L4	Medial leg	Knee flexion	—	Knee jerk
Lumbrosacral	L5	Lateral leg and medial knee	Foot dorsiflexion and eversion	—	Ankle jerk
	S1	Sole of foot	Foot plantarflexion	—	Ankle jerk
Sacral	S2	Posterior leg and thigh	Toe flexion	Bladder and rectum	Anal wink
	S3	Middle of buttock	—	Bladder and rectum	Anal wink
	S4	Medial buttock	—	Bladder and rectum	Anal wink

From Hatch D, Sumner E, Hellmann J: *The surgical neonate: anesthesia and intensive care*, Boston, 1995, Little, Brown.

in the early 1980s led to issuance of the "Baby Doe" regulations under Section 504 of The Rehabilitation Act of 1975. These federal regulations barred denial of treatment based on the presence of severe disability alone.[69]

Stress on families and their children is high and complicated by the frequent failure to provide accurate information from which families and, later, affected individuals can make their own decisions. Personal problems of low self-esteem and depression in adolescents and young adults with spina bifida develop in response to multiple stressors, which include poor access to public buildings and services, financial difficulties, and school and social continence problems. These adolescents and young adults frequently reside with their parents and depend on them for assistance with bowel programs, skin care, and other routine activities of daily living (ADL). Out-of-school social activities and relationships are frequently limited and many individuals report significant isolation and excessive involvement in sedentary activities.[76] School-age and adolescent youth report themselves to be less competent in academic, athletic, and social activity; physical appearance is particularly detrimental to self-concept in girls with spina bifida.[77] Pursuit of independence for individuals with a disability then depends on development of responsibility for, and compliance with, regimens related to ADL skills, maintenance of skin integrity, bowel and bladder management, and education and vocation planning.

Siblings of those with disabilities may fight more and have higher rates of school failure and delinquent behavior.[78] Concerns about high divorce rates among parents of spina bifida children have been raised, although recent reports suggest no difference in marital quality between couples who have a child with spina bifida and control couples.[79] Professionals must be aware of the importance of the advice and recommendations they give and be sensitive to the strong feelings parents have regarding the importance of their involvement in decision-making in the care and intervention their children receive.[80,81]

NEUROSURGICAL PATHOPHYSIOLOGY AND MANAGEMENT

Most lesions can be closed within the first day or two of life. Delay for up to a week or more may be necessary if significant neonatal complications such as prematurity, respiratory distress, neonatal sepsis and/or meningitis, or acidosis exist; or significant parental stress, grief or indecision requires a delay in operative intervention to allow time for working with a family to develop a successful plan. Delayed closure may be pursued without increased risk of infection or loss of cord function.[71]

Broad-spectrum antibiotic coverage at therapeutic doses is necessary pre- and post-surgery to lower the risk of sepsis, meningitis, and/or urinary tract infection in the perioperative period. Preoperatively, the lesion should be kept moist with saline or betadine dressings. Large lesions may require a delay in closure, two-stage surgical procedure, or skin grafting. It is important that parents recognize that surgical repair of the back lesion will not result in recovery of neurological function. Reflex movements in the lower extremities should not be mistaken for true function and strength necessary for ambulation. Repair does not result in improved cord function in children who lack adequate muscle development at birth.[82]

Recommendation has been made that fetuses diagnosed as having myelomeningocele prenatally be delivered by C-section before the onset of labor to avoid damage to neural elements during vaginal delivery.[62,64,65] Subsequent studies have questioned this recommendation; it appears C-section is justified in selected cases only where there is absence of kyphosis and kyphoscoliosis, other major congenital anomalies, or significant hydrocephalus, and there is the presence of good lower extremity movement on ultrasound after 24 weeks gestation in a fetus with an intact sac and protrusion of neural elements dorsally.[63] However, the significance of this latter recommendation remains unclear because of lack of agreement on the significance and prognostic importance of in utero leg movements in the fetus with myelomeningocele.

Hydrocephalus and shunt placement

Development of hydrocephalus and the need for ventriculoperitoneal shunt (VP) placement occurs in over 90% of infants with open lesions. Placement of the shunt is usually done 5 to 7 days after back closure, once the risk of infection has been minimized. In the face of evident hydrocephalus at birth, some surgeons prefer to place the shunt at the time of initial back closure.[83] Before the ready availability of cranial ultrasound and CT scan, daily head circumference measurements were done to determine the presence or development of hydrocephalus. Since the availability of these imaging studies, diagnosis of hydrocephalus is usually made early in the hospitalization with more timely shunt placement and shorter hospitalization. In children who do not have hydrocephalus in utero or during the initial hospitalization, most who will develop hydrocephalus will do so in the next few months. The potential for late development of hydrocephalus, although small, remains even in the adult. Children with hydrocephalus are shunt dependent and should not be advised or expected to outgrow the need for the shunt. Although frequently stable and asymptomatic with a nonfunctioning shunt, they may at any time develop symptoms and require revision of the shunt.[84]

The peritoneum has been the location of choice for the distal end of the shunt since the early 1970s. Ventriculoatrial (VA) shunts are used if the abdomen is unsuitable for placement of the distal shunt. This may occur because of prior abdominal surgeries, necrotizing enterocolitis (NEC) as a neonate, and recurrent shunt failure or infection risk related to peritonitis or pseudocyst formation. In the 1950s and 1960s, VA shunts led to complications of immunologically mediated glomerulonephritis related to staphylococcal (coagulase negative) shunt infections and/or development of irreversible pulmonary hypertension and cor pulmonale and necessitated selection of an alternate site for distal shunt placement. Complications of pulmonary hypertension and cor pulmonale occur primarily in infants[85,86] but have been reported in older children and adolescents.[31,87] A small, but significant, number of young adults remain with VA shunts placed many years ago. Periodic evaluation with ECG, chest x-ray, and/or cardiac echocardiogram is important as these patients remain at risk despite many years of asymptomatic use.

Shunt malfunction is an expected and not infrequent complication.[88,89] This can be expected to occur 2 to 3 times over the first few years of life, with 70% likelihood of failure by age 10 years.[88] Parents need to be aware of both the inevitability of shunt malfunction as well as the symptomatology. In the young infant, parents and providers must watch for fussiness, irritability, change of sensorium, lethargy, vomiting, or a bulging and tense fontanelle. In older children, headache and vomiting are the predominant symptoms; in adolescents and young adults, atypical symptoms such as neck pain or changes in upper extremity strength or hand function may be the initial or only sign the shunt is not working properly. Other less frequent presentations include changes in behavior or school performance, swelling around the shunt reservoir, valve, or tubing, changes in extraocular muscle function with recent eye deviation or downward gaze ("sunset" sign), apnea, or seizure. Evaluation of the shunt consists of a thorough history and physical examination, and testing, which may include aspiration of the shunt and/or imaging studies using cranial ultrasound, CT scan, or MRI. The onset and duration of symptoms is usually sufficient to allow thorough evaluation. There is, however, an occasional child who presents with cardiovascular instability and/or apnea requiring immediate relief of pressure through shunt aspiration and/or surgical intervention. Seizures are an infrequent presentation of shunt malfunction but require immediate and appropriate evaluation and treatment.

Shunt infections occur following 2% to 4% of shunt surgeries in major medical centers. The rate may be up to 40% in less specialized centers.[56,89,90] Particularly at risk are those with open MMC at birth and/or poorly healing back wounds after initial back closure. The organisms that cause early infection of the open spine are those present in the vaginal and fecal flora with *E. coli* being the most common.[91] In later shunt placement and/or revision *S. epidermidis* is the predominant organism identified and *S. aureus* is also commonly found.[92] Rates of infection with these organisms can be significantly decreased through careful attention to preparation of the skin at the time of surgery, measures to ensure aseptic technique at the time of surgery, and use of prophylactic antibiotics in the perioperative period. The effectiveness of prophylactic antibioties is not, however, uniformly accepted. Most of these infections occur in the first 30 to 60 days after surgery although a small number can occur for many years.

Infections of the CSF with *H. influenzae,* beta-hemolytic streptococcus, meningococcus, or pneumococcus appear to be more common in children with hydrocephalus and shunts than in other children.[56] Routine immunizations are therefore especially important to decrease the risk of *H. influenzae* infection in these children. Additionally, infections with gram-negative organisms occasionally occur through peritoneal contamination, perforation of intra-abdominal organs, development of abdominal pseudo-cyst or other yet unclear mechanisms. VA shunts cause risk of thrombosis and development of septic emboli. SBE prophylaxis for dental and other procedures may be important for those with VA shunts but unnecessary for those with ventriculoperitoneal (VP) shunts although consensus on the issue of antibiotic prophylaxis for those with VP shunts is lacking.[93,94]

Chiari II malformation

Chiari (Arnold Chiari) II malformation (ACM) represents dysgenesis of the hindbrain with downward displacement of the inferior vermis of the cerebellum and an elongated brainstem into the cervical canal. On CT scan the medulla appears kinked at the cervicomedullary junction. ACM is present in over 90% of infants with open myelomeningocele. It is the predominant cause of hydrocephalus in infants with myelomeningocele and less frequently, in about 5% of infants, causes a severe combination of symptoms, which include stridor, apnea, cyanotic spells, bradycardia, opisthotonus and upper extremity weakness, and dysphagia with aspiration. Brainstem and lower cranial nerve abnormalities cause vocal cord paralysis requiring tracheostomy and resultant difficulty with oral feedings and secretions. Poorly coordinated and ineffective swallowing and/or nasal reflux with aspiration represent a significant danger with high morbidity and significant risk of death.[95-98] Differences in symptomatology and outcome have been classified into grades 1, 2, and 3, reflecting varying degrees of anatomical and pathological involvement[99] (Table 7-3).

Significant abnormalities in ventilation, including vocal cord paralysis with obstructive apnea, central apnea and hypoventilation, hypoxia, and breath-holding spells, are common to this syndrome. Abnormalities in control of ventilation during sleep and wakefulness suggest that ACM interferes with central chemosensitivity to both hypoxia and hypercapnia as well as central integration of chemoreceptor output.[100-105] Assessment of respiratory response in the neonate does not have predictive value for which infants with MMC will develop Chiari symptomatology.[106] Brainstem auditory-evoked potentials (BAEP) are commonly abnormal in those with ACM, particularly among those with symptomatic brainstem dysfunction. Although of low specificity, BAEP in neonates with ACM may allow early identification of those at greater risk.[107,108]

Decompression of the posterior fossa and cervical laminectomy is still of uncertain usefulness in alleviating brainstem dysfunction associated with the ACM in the infant, although it has been suggested that recovery occurs more often if the surgery is performed when symptoms first arise. A retrospective review of cases from two major medical centers, one where surgical intervention was routinely done and the other where it was not, does not support the efficacy of posterior fossa decompression in these infants.[97,109] This remains, however, a controversial issue, awaiting a prospective randomized clinical trial with controls. In the older child, surgical de-

Table 7-3   Arnold-Chiari malformation

Types	Clinical	Pathology
Grade 1	Stridor	Brainstem compression
		Traction on vagal nerve
Grade 2	Stridor	Hemorrhage or ischemia
	Apnea	Disruption of neurons/nuclei
Grade 3	Stridor	Necrosis
	Apnea	Dysgenesis
	Cyanotic Spells	
	Dysphagia	

Modified from Charney EB, Norke LB, Sutton LN, et al: Management of Chiari II complication in infants with myelomeningocele, *J Pediatr* 3:364-371, 1987.

compression is often effective in the relief of symptoms of brainstem dysfunction. In these children and young adults, surgery is directed toward relief of specific pressure from syringomyelia, arachnoid or other cysts, and/or cord tethering.

Tethered cord

Tethered cord occurs frequently with closed NTD and between ages 6 to 15 years in 11% to 15% of those with previously operated on open lesions. Operative untethering is indicated for most patients with closed NTD while they are asymptomatic. Surgery for those with previous operative closure should be reserved for those who demonstrate significant clinical symptoms. Neurological deficits of cord tethering are manifested by spasticity, weakness, and decreased sensation in the lower extremities; change in urinary function with increased incontinence, need for bladder catheterization, and frequent UTI; and change in bowel function with constipation and bowel accidents. Back and/or leg pain, progressive scoliosis, and foot deformity are also common presenting symptoms. Symptoms result from traction on the conus medullaris and cauda equina, which causes stretching and ischemia with subsequent loss of neurological function. MRI demonstrates a low-lying conus medullaris adherent to the dorsal dural sac in most, if not all, of those with previously operated on MMC. Improvement after surgery is variable with back pain resolution in most and improvement in gait more likely than relief of urinary symptoms. Urodynamic and somatosensory-evoked potential monitoring may help in identification of those most likely to benefit from an untethering surgery. Use of silastic or lypholized dura during initial repair may create a larger space and reduce the likelihood of scar formation and risk of future tethering.[110-115]

Seizures

Seizures occur in 14% to 29% of patients with MMC and hydrocephalus and, in most reports, 2% to 8% of those without hydrocephalus. They are more common in those with other risk factors such as mental retardation, additional CNS malformation, and/or a history of meningitis, ventriculitis, or intraventricular hemorrhage. In a small percentage of children, shunt malfunction may produce seizures although rarely as the sole symptomatology. As for other children with seizure disorders, discontinuation of therapy may be attempted when the patient has been seizure free for 2 to 4 years.[116-118]

UROLOGICAL PATHOPHYSIOLOGY AND MANAGEMENT

Over 90% of children with MMC will have a significant urological disability. This occurs regardless of the level of lesion, and the clinician is frequently faced with a child with a low sacral lesion with minimal or absent orthopedic involvement but major problems related to neurogenic bladder and/or bowel. Similarly, there is no clear correlation between the level of the child's spinal cord lesion and the type of neurogenic bladder. Some individuals have small capacity bladders with low outlet resistance; others have large capacity, hypotonic bladders with high-outlet resistance. Despite varied forms of neurogenic bladder, physicians should offer patients three goals of therapy:

- Prevention of urinary tract infection
- Preservation of upper urinary tract function to prevent chronic renal failure and end stage renal disease (ESRD)
- Achievement of social continence

Urinary tract infection

Most children with MMC will experience problems with recurrent urinary tract infections although the number and frequency will vary significantly between individuals. Infections result from residual urine and incomplete emptying caused by the neurogenic bladder. Infections are more common in infants because of urethral contamination and their nonambulatory status. Additional factors affecting frequency of UTI are degree of fecal retention and constipation, ambulatory status, dietary habits and the effect on constipation and urine acidity, use of antimicrobial prophylaxis and/or intermittent catheterization regimen, and overall compliance with urinary tract regimens. Recurrent infection leads to and may be aggravated by vesicoureteral reflux or obstruction of the UV junction. This, in turn, causes damage to the upper urinary tract with development of pelviectasis, calycectasis, hydronephrosis, focal scarring, and eventually, if effective intervention does not occur, systemic hypertension and chronic renal failure.

Preservation of renal function

Progression to chronic renal failure and ESRD is usually preventable with appropriate care and compliance on the part of the individual and family. In the 1960s and 1970s ESRD was a common cause of death for individuals with spina bifida. Commonly a complication of the second decade of life, for those over the age of 10 years it was the most common cause of death. Improvements in prevention of UTI and routine surveillance of upper urinary tract function has significantly decreased progression to ESRD. ESRD is now infrequent unless major issues of compliance have arisen. Despite significant improvements in care and outcome, recent reports show renal parenchymal damage in almost 20% of children with spina bifida with prevalence in those over 10 years being twice that of those under 5 years of age[119] (Fig. 7-11).

At birth 85% to 90% of infants with MMC have been found to have normal urinary tracts by radiographic imaging. Approximately 10% have abnormalities, which develop in utero from outlet obstruction and 3% from spinal shock following surgical closure of the back. Urodynamic studies, if available, are recommended in the newborn period. Bladder contractions are present in 57% of neonates and absent in 43% with reflexic bladder where compliance may be good (25%) or poor (18%) during bladder filling. External urethral sphincter assessment by EMG has shown an intact sacral reflex arc in 47% of newborns, partial denervation in 24%, and absent in 29%. Bladder contractility and external sphincter activity are necessary for effective voiding and emptying. Together they result in three patterns of lower urinary tract activity: synergic, dyssynergic (with and without detrusor hypertonicity), and complete denervation. Upper urinary tract changes by age 3 years are reported in 71% of those with dyssynergy on newborn urodynamic evaluation. Only 17% of those who are synergic and 23% of those with complete denervation show these changes.[120]

Outlet obstruction, which is frequently associated with dyssynergy, appears to be a major contributor to upper urinary tract deterioration. The presence of a small, noncompliant, trabeculated bladder represents an additional risk factor for deterioration of renal function.[121] Periodic urodynamic and neurourological surveillance is worthwhile as significant changes may occur over time.[122,123] Identification of risk factors with initiation of clean intermittent catheterization (CIC), anticholinergic medication, and surgery (when necessary) can significantly improve outcome. Nonsurgical management with urodynamic evaluation followed by CIC, anticholinergic medication, fluid restriction, and close follow-up has recently been reported effective in providing satisfactory continence in 80% of cases, preservation of upper urinary tracts in 90%, and relatively low rate of bladder augmentation.[124] Early surgical intervention, however, should be considered when compliance and poor follow-up are of concern. Surgical alternatives to increase capacity and decrease bladder pressure and reflux include ureteral reimplantation, bladder augmentation (enterocystoplasty), and detrusorectomy.

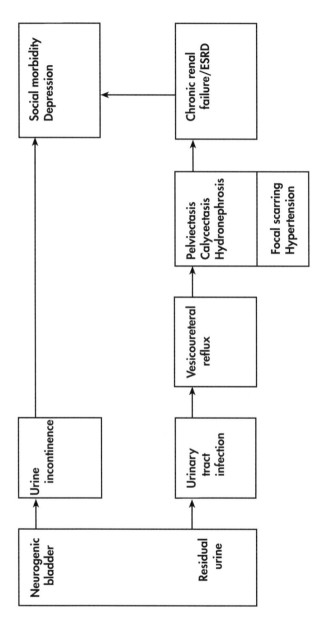

Fig. 7-11 Neurogenic bladder—interrelation of pathological and social morbidity.

Vesicostomy is frequently required in infants to provide decompression and achieve adequate drainage when CIC in combination with antimicrobial and pharmacological management of bladder tonicity are unsuccessful in improving, stabilizing, or preventing further deterioration of upper urinary tract function. Vesicostomy is usually viewed as temporary in the hope that its use will decrease the need for subsequent ureteral reimplantation. It is normally well tolerated although prolapse and stenosis may occur.[125,126] Urine leakage may cause problems with local skin care.

Social continence

Achievement of social continence for both urine and feces is a major therapeutic goal for those with neurogenic bladder and bowel. Incontinence is a significant cause of morbidity and can lead to significant social problems including clinical depression, particularly in the adolescent and young adult. Studies of teenagers with spina bifida emphasize the importance of effective intervention for these problems.[127]

Urine incontinence is the result of reflex emptying, overflow, or an incompetent urinary sphincter. Before CIC the credé maneuver of bladder massage was used to express urine and achieve bladder emptying. This is now only rarely indicated as the pressure generated with manual massage may cause upper urinary tract damage in individuals with ureterovesical reflux and/or infection of the urine. External collecting devices—condom, catheter, or external pubic pressure device—were also used to minimize leakage of urine. Malodor and irritation to the skin with resultant maceration, including ulceration of the insensate skin of the penis, commonly occurred with their use. As a result, they are infrequently used today.

CIC was first recommended in 1971. It is used to remove residual urine, improve urinary drainage, and provide decompression. CIC is superior to indwelling catheters or ileal conduit diversion for decreasing bacteriuria and preventing episodes of pyelonephritis and upper urinary tract deterioration.[128-131] Indwelling catheters are socially unacceptable because of significant malodor and frequent complications of UTI, bladder calculi, incrustation, leakage, urethritis with subsequent stricture, periurethral abscess, and/or fistula formation.[130] The combination of CIC and antibiotic therapy have proved effective in the management and prevention of urinary tract infections and upper urinary tract change and deterioration. Bladder installation of urinary antiseptic agents, either silver nitrate or neomycin, are reported to be effective in decreasing the bacteriuria and infection rate,[132] but they are not widely used and it is unclear whether sufficient benefit is afforded to justify use when adequate drainage is provided.

CIC has provided an important tool to assist in the achievement of urinary continence. In earlier studies CIC alone provided complete continence in only about one-fourth of children. It was not effective in those with small bladder capacity and low-outlet resistance. Anticholinergic medication such as oxybutynin (Ditropan) or propantheline (Probanthine) are used to inhibit bladder contraction and increase capacity and alpha-adrenergic agents such as phenylpropanolamine, ephedrine, or pseudoephedrine (Sudafed) to increase outlet resistance (Table 7-4).

Antimicrobial therapy may be necessary to control and prevent infection and the adverse effects it may have on urinary control. With such medications, in conjunction with CIC, nearly half of such children may become completely continent and almost all show improvement in continence status.[132,133] With clean, nonsterile technique, over 80% can be functionally dry, and self-catheterization can be achieved in a similar number.[129] Considerable success in attaining independence and social continence was also reported in these young adults. Recent interview studies of teenagers and young adults found excellent acceptance of self-catheterization as part of their daily routine at home and school with marked preference for this pro-

Table 7-4 Commonly used urological medications

Drugs	Uses	Side effects
For bladder hyperactivity Propantheline bromide Imipramine hydrochloride Oxybutynin chloride	To reduce detrusor muscle tone or eliminate hyperreflexia, increase bladder capacity, decrease reflux emptying of the bladder	Drying of mucous membranes, blurred vision, tachycardia, palpitations, headache, nausea, vomiting, constipation, drowsiness
For urinary incontinence Pseudoephedrine hydrochloride Ephedrine Imipramine hydrochloride	To increase outflow resistance by increasing the tone at the bladder neck	CNS stimulation, including nervousness, restlessness, insomnia, irritability, dizziness, headache, nausea, and vomiting
For urinary retention Phenoxybenzamine hydrochloride	To decrease bladder outflow resistance at the external striated muscle sphincter	Nasal congestion, miosis, postural hypotension, tachycardia, lethargy, somnolence, nausea, vomiting, diarrhea

Modified from Smith KA: Myelomeningocele: managing bowel and bladder dysfunction in the school-aged child, *Progressions* 3(2):3-11, 1991.

cedure over earlier regimens used.[127,131,134] Self-catheterization increases as age and experience improve. Factors reported to adversely impact self-catheterization potential include poor hand function, blindness, poor cognitive function and/or self-discipline, visual perceptual problems, obesity, severe scoliosis, or poor living conditions with inadequate space or privacy for adequate toileting. Good results have been reported in successfully teaching self-catheterization to individuals with severe physical disability, visual impairment, and mild mental retardation.[131,134] Polyvinyl chloride catheters are available and preferable to rubber catheters because of their greater rigidity and because there is a high rate of latex allergy in persons with spina bifida. Catheters are re-usable but need to be cleaned in tap water and/or antiseptic solution and thoroughly air dried after use. This is important in that use of 4 to 6 catheters daily is costly and usually unnecessary. Re-use of catheters is safe from the standpoint of infection control. Only a small percent of individuals require a new catheter each time to minimize recurrence of UTI. Lubricant may be used and is probably worthwhile as the urethra becomes fibrotic and less compliant after several years. Complications are few but include epididymitis, urethral stricture, perforation with false passage formation, bleeding, and/or loss of catheter into the bladder. CIC and self-catheterization are a lifetime treatment for urine incontinence.[131]

Intravesical transurethral bladder stimulation has been developed as a diagnostic and rehabilitative technique for the neurogenic bladder. This procedure uses direct electrical stimulation of the bladder combined with visual biofeedback and conditioning to achieve control of voiding. It aims at developing the sense of urgency to void through increased sensation and awareness of bladder filling, initiation of detrusor contraction, and increased bladder capacity while maintaining low filling and leak pressures. Initial reports on this technique as an effective nonsurgical approach to continence control have been extremely promising although subsequent studies confirming this are needed.[135,136]

A number of surgical procedures have been developed to provide social continence. These procedures include artifical urinary sphincter, creation of an artifical bladder or Koch pouch with intussuscepted nipple, bladder augmentation (enterocystoplasty), and use of the Mitrofanoff principle in which the appendix with intact vasculature is tunneled submucosally into the bladder. This allows its use as a channel, which may be catheterized from the abdominal wall. CIC is required to effect complete bladder emptying with all these procedures. Catheterization from the abdominal area may be much easier for those with significant bracing, wheelchair use, visual-spatial problems, or upper extremity dysfunction. Post-operative complications include stomal stenosis, bladder calculi, abscess formation, dehydration with metabolic imbalance, and continued incontinence.[137]

BOWEL PATHOPHYSIOLOGY AND MANAGEMENT

Constipation and bowel incontinence are common in individuals with spina bifida.[138] These problems develop in early infancy and effective therapeutic intervention requires awareness by health professionals of the importance of this part of care in the overall management of the child and education of the parents as to how to deal with bowel continence effectively from the earliest years. Bowel management depends on the level and extent of neurological involvement. Continence requires normal external sphincter control, internal sphincter reflex relaxation, rectal sensation, and normal colonic motility. The former three components depend on intact sacral nerve roots; the latter on sympathetic innervation from the thoracic and sacral spinal cord regions. Bowel control is achieved by the coordinated action of the skeletal and smooth muscle of the colon and rectum and their efferent nerves. Fullness in the distal colon and rectum is transmitted via the afferent pelvic nerves to S2-S4. A bowel movement depends on intact sensation at the anorectal junction for evacuation to occur. Tactile sensation of the perianal skin comes from the S2-S4 nerve roots and is critical to awareness and prevention of fecal soiling. Absence of rectal sensation is a key factor in fecal incontinence in those with spina bifida.[139-143]

The goals of a bowel program are (1) avoidance of constipation, (2) regular complete evacuation, and (3) prevention of incontinence with achievement of accident-free days. Maintenance of a regular, soft, formed stool is important to prevent constipation, megacolon, and development of overflow incontinence. Bowel management consists of regularly scheduled toileting, stool softeners to prevent constipation, and dietary measures, including additional fiber when necessary. Regular toileting timed to benefit from the stimulation of the gastrocolic reflex after meals, stable sitting position, the benefits of gravity, valsalva maneuver when adequate abdominal musculature allows, and a soft formed stool allow effective toileting. Those with inability to sit with stability or to use the valsalva maneuver because of the high level of their lesion may frequently require a regular suppository or enema, digital stimulation, or manual removal. The latter technique of manual removal is less frequently used today. It is not preferred because of the drawbacks of chronic constipation on bowel tone and urinary function, risk of serious impaction with need for hospitalization, long-term risk of colon cancer,[127,139,141-143] and personal embarrassment and psychological trauma. Additional problems of an inadequate bowel program include malodor with nasal fatigue[139] (where the child may be unaware of fecal soiling), skin irritation, anal fissures, rectal prolapse, low self-esteem, and depression.

Current bowel management practice in the United States is largely the result of a program initiated by The Spina Bifida Association of America (SBAA). SBAA sought to train at least one nurse in every spina bifida program in the country about bowel management. Their program recognizes that there cannot be a single bowel program for all children with spina bifida. A group of protocols based on age and type of stool pattern were developed and disseminated to spina bifida program nurses and consumers at conferences, site visits, and the annual SBAA meeting. This project appears to have been highly successful in dramatically altering community practices of bowel management and in time should significantly lower the high failure rate of bowel management reported by parents and individuals with spina bifida.[139,144]

Alternative methods of treatment for bowel continence have been reported. These methods include the Willis Home Bowel Washout Program,[145] enema continence catheter,[146] anal closure magnet, anal plug,[147] and biofeedback training with behavior modification.[148,149] None of these techniques has received wide acceptance, and, unlike the SBAA approach of beginning preventive intervention in early infancy, they respond to a chronic problem that has long-established physiological and behavioral patterns. Reports of biofeedback training, although encouraging, have generally involved small numbers of patients with spina bifida and required manometry equipment use in lengthy, costly sessions, making this approach difficult to use in most clinics. Recent reports describe use of the Malone antegrade continence enema with good results. For individuals with intractable constipation and fecal soiling, a cutaneous appendicael conduit to the right colon allows administration of an antegrade enema through an abdominal stoma on a regular basis. A high degree of patient satisfaction is reported with the procedure.[150,151]

ORTHOPEDIC PATHOPHYSIOLOGY AND MANAGEMENT

A variety of orthopedic deformities of the spine, hips, knees, and feet are seen in those with spina bifida. Severity and specifics of the deformities depend on the level of the lesion and the type of paralysis. Paralysis may be flaccid, spastic, or a combination of these.

The goal of orthopedic management is a stable posture and optimal function. Treatment objectives include potentiating ambulation when possible, maintaining joints in the most functional position when paralysis does not allow normal movement, and prevention of decubitus ulcers, infection, and pathological fractures. Knowledge of the level of spinal cord dysfunction allows effective planning of orthopedic management and prevention of deformity and contracture. Effective management depends on a combination of orthotic treatment, physical therapy, and orthopedic surgery. Close collaboration of these disciplines is essential for effective treatment and outcome.

Significant evaluation is necessary to determine whether independent ambulation or use of a wheelchair for mobility, either part or all of the time, is best. Experience has shown that children with functional quadriceps and lesions below L3 will be functional ambulators, although they may require a wheelchair for longer trips. Children with no functional quadriceps or lesions above L3 are unlikely to be community ambulators.[152,153] Children with lesions below S1 are likely to ambulate without bracing. There are exceptions to these generalizations based on factors that include motivation of the child and family, maintenance of normal body weight, good upper extremity function, and level of cognitive function. In the overweight child, walking may be very inefficient and uneconomical of energy expenditure, particularly when extensive bracing is required. Most children will lose the ability to walk if their weight is excessive. Children with upper extremity and truncal spasticity are unlikely to ambulate if more than minimal bracing is required. Approximately 20% of children with myelodysplasia, particularly those with hydrocephalus, will have abnormal tone and strength in their upper extremities, compromising ambulation potential. Intellectual abilities will also affect the ability to use extensive bracing and crutches for ambulation.[154-156]

Foot

Approximately 75% of children with MMC have foot deformities. Two types of foot deformity are common to those with spina bifida. The first group includes equinus, varus, and cavus deformities. These deformities are treated with manipulation (passive range of motion) or immobilization by casting in the infant, with soft tissue releases in the child under 4 years and with osteotomy from age 4 years until skeletal maturity. After skeletal maturity, arthrodesis can be performed if required. If an arthrodesis is performed before skeletal maturity, growth will be compromised. The second group of foot deformities are the calcaneus deformities. These are generally not treated at all until the child begins weight bearing. Tendon transfers and soft tissue releases, including tendon excision and neurectomy, are performed during the "toddler-age" period. An extra-articular arthrodesis, or an inlay fusion of joints, may be performed before skeletal maturity if the foot is compromised by a non-healing, calcaneus decubitus ulcer.[157,158]

Hip and knee

Treatment for the hip and knee depends on the age of the child. Over half of children with MMC will have hip subluxation or dislocation, which may be present at birth or develop later.[157] In the infant and young child, interventions include hip abductor bracing for hip subluxation or dislocation and tenotomy for balancing muscle power around joints. Only rarely have tendon transfers been successful in increasing a child's mobility because unrecognized spasticity may lead to further deformity. Surgery to relocate the hip is performed less frequently than in the past.[159-161]

Older children may require a femoral derotational osteotomy or procedure to relocate a painful or unilateral dislocated hip that interferes with ambulation or accomplishment of stable seating. This is particularly important in those with lower level lesions where ambulation potential exists. Attempts to reduce the hip and correct pelvic obliquity without changing the forces acting on the pelvis will result in redislocation of the hip. Following surgical intervention, it is essential that seating be re-evaluated and modified as necessary to avoid development of decubiti. Additional attention must be given to the length of time in plaster immobilization because prolonged casting results in a higher rate of pathological fractures in the post-operative period.[160]

Knee problems are common among teenagers and young adults with MMC. Characteristics of gait may cause stress on the knee with resultant instability and degenerative change. This has significant importance for those who are community ambulators.[162]

Scoliosis

Scoliosis represents a significant problem for almost 90% of children with T12 or above lesions, 80% with high lumbar lesions, 23% with low lumbar lesions, and infrequently for children with lesions below S1.[161,163] Scoliosis may be either congenital or developmental (paralytic). Once present, it is usually progressive.[164] In lumbar level paralysis, the scoliosis is usually developmental, caused by imbalance of the paraspinal muscles. It may also result from a tethered cord or from bony abnormalities. Scoliosis in a child with an S1 or lower lesion should raise suspicion of a tethered cord.

Scoliosis is treated by use of a custom-made polypropylene thoracolumbosacral orthoses (TLSO) and good position to prevent, slow, or arrest progression of the deformity. A major goal of therapy is to delay surgical intervention for as long as possible. Failure to control the spinal curvature can result in problems with wheelchair seating, decubiti, back pain, and compromise of cardiac and pulmonary function.[164-166] A thoracolumbosacral body jacket, however, may be restrictive and interfere with respiration, making it difficult to continue with non-surgical intervention. Surgical therapy, when decided on, includes anterior, posterior, or combined spinal fusion and instrumentation with or without accompanying fusion.[167,168]

Kyphosis

Kyphosis occurs in 6% of children with MMC. When kyphosis occurs, it is present at birth and is invariably progressive. It may make initial closure of the back lesion difficult, if not impossible. The kyphos or gibbus tends to be unresponsive to bracing, and intervention becomes necessary to relieve pressure on the overlying skin, which frequently breaks down with poor healing and/or infection. A kyphos (or gibbus) will also eventually cause shortening of the trunk, crowding of abdominal and thoracic contents, and resultant respiratory compromise. The goals of treatment are relief of skin pressure, improvement of abdominal and respiratory function, and provision of a stable sitting balance.[164,169]

At the current time the best available treatment for kyphosis involves excision of vertebral bodies and extensive spinal fusion, with accompanying seating orthosis or TLSO as required for additional support. Surgery is difficult, with a high complication rate for failure of fusion, for infection, and/or for skin breakdown.[164,170]

Pathological Fractures

Pathological fractures are common, occurring in 11% to 30% of children with spina bifida. Those with high-level lesions are more frequently affected. Pathological fractures result from osteoporosis and sensory loss in a joint with reduced ability to handle shock. Limited weight bearing and muscle activity, as occurs with prolonged casting and immobilization following surgery, worsens osteoporosis and leads to fracture in these children.[171,172]

Patterns of fracture differ between ambulatory and non-ambulatory children. Ambulatory children tend to get physioepiphyseal injuries because of repetitive trauma to an anesthetic ankle or knee joint. Those who are ambulatory but have anesthesia above S1 need to be advised to avoid activities involving repetitive trauma such as running and jumping. Nonambulatory children tend to get injuries to metaphyses or diaphyses during passive manipulation, after removal of casts, from falls that seem minor, and occasionally from such insignificant events as having a foot trapped in a bed railing or clothing.

Children with myelomeningocele may show an increased systemic response to these fractures with fever, hypotension, and tachycardia in addition to redness and swelling of the involved area. Sedimentation rate may be elevated. The clinical picture may initially be difficult to differentiate from cellulitis, osteomyelitis, or pyoarthritis. Because the extremity lacks feeling, fractures are frequently painless despite significant swelling due to hematoma formation.[173,174]

To protect children from fractures, it is important to handle the child carefully, especially after a cast has been removed. Use of splints or casts that allow weight bearing, early mobilization, and use of orthoses as appropriate help to lessen the risk of pathological fractures.

Orthotic principles

Bracing is performed to increase function and prevent deformities. It will allow successful ambulation for many, but significant effort and energy expenditure is required. The level of lesion, weight and body mass, other physical limitations, and motivation are all factors that contribute to the success or failure of bracing efforts.[175-177] It is important to avoid limiting active muscle groups and to monitor the child for skin breakdown. Light weight, adjustability for growth, and ease in getting braces on and off are essential for successful orthotic management. Advances in brace manufacture over the past 40 years have been dramatic and have revolutionized our expectations for children using them.

Children with lesions at S1 and L5 generally require ankle-foot orthoses (AFO) and occasionally a walker or crutches. Children with lesions at L4 will usually require ankle-knee orthoses (AKO) but may need knee-ankle-foot orthoses (KAFO) as well as crutches or walkers. Children with lesions above L3 will also require hip support or reciprocating gait hip-knee-ankle-foot orthoses (HKAFO). Braces such as the reciprocating gait orthosis (RGO) may result in a greater number of children with spina bifida who are ambulatory.[178,179] RGO, however, is very expensive, and successful use requires great motivation on the part of individuals with spina bifida and their families as well as a coordinated team effort. Without this type of comprehensive effort, success with the RGO will be low.

PRIMARY AND GENERAL HEALTH CARE CONSIDERATIONS
Nutrition

Obesity and excessive weight gain occur frequently in individuals with myelomeningocele. These conditions have been attributed to low caloric expenditure because of limitations of mobility. Weight reduction, consequently, has been difficult to achieve for similar reasons. Excessive weight makes ambulation difficult, affects pulmonary function, causes problems with brace fittings, and can lead to skin breakdown from poorly fitting braces, inadequate local hygiene, and rubbing in anesthetic regions. Anthropometric techniques and routine inspection are unreliable in assessment of body composition and obesity in children with spina bifida. The indirect technique of underwater weighing is highly accurate but technically difficult. It does, however, correlate well with skinfold thickness in estimation of body fat composition. Increased body fat is found in those with higher level lesions and limited ambulatory status and frequently (50%) in those above age 6 years.[180,181] Programs to prevent development of obesity need to be started in the earliest years.

Obesity has received the most attention but other nutrition-related problems or risk factors (NRF), including feeding disorders, inadequate dietary intake, poor growth, and effects secondary to lack of ambulation and nutrient-drug interactions, have also been reported. These NRF include those who are underweight (16%), overweight (18%) and those who have dental problems (17%), chronic constipation (37%), feeding difficulties (18%), anemia (4%), poor eating behaviors (21%), and those who chronically use medications that affect nutritional status (37%). Two or more NRF were present in 50% of the children; 30% had three or more. Underweight status was of concern in 21% of those under age 3 years, dropped in incidence with age, but remained a problem in 9% by age 6 to 12 years. This is of concern and may be related to the excessive short stature seen in some children with myelomeningocele. Overweight increased from 13% of those under age 3 years to 27% by age 6 to 12 years. The presence of secondary conditions, particularly asthma/pulmonary conditions and seizures, raised the prevalence of nutritional problems even higher. Nutritional problems have significant effect on frequency of UTI, bowel regimens, linear growth, bone demineralization, and the risk of pathological fractures. Early and specific attention to problems of weight and other NRF is important to overall management.[182,183]

Growth and development

Children with myelomeningocele are reported to be short in stature. This has been attributed to contractures of the lower extremities; decreased truncal length from scoliosis, kyphosis, and vertebral anomalies; decreased lower extremity length from factors related to the paralysis; and early physeal closure before achievement of optimal growth.[184] These children have an increased arm-span relative to supine body length, and growth failure appears most marked in the legs. These findings are more common in those with higher level lesions.[185] Accurate anthropometric measurements are difficult to obtain in these children, and great care must be taken in their acquisition.

Precocious puberty is reported in 16% of girls with MMC and hydrocephalus.[186] It is thought to be of central origin with activation of the hypothalamic-pituitary-gonadal axis at an abnormally young age. Recent shunt malfunction prior to onset of sexual development was noted in several of the children. This phenomenon in boys has not been extensively studied, but the authors had the clinical impression of early development.

Menarche occurs at an earlier age (10.25 years with SD 1.68) than published United States means (12.76 years with SD 1.41).[187] Some mothers reported early menarche following a major surgical procedure, but shunt dysfunction did not appear to be related to age of menarche onset. Once established, menses were regular. Severity of menstrual cramps appeared related to neurological level, with individuals with higher lesions reporting minimal problems. Personal hygiene during menses was reported to be difficult because of physical disability, high bracing, and wheelchair use.

Immunizations

Children with chronic illness and neurodevelopmental disabilities are at particular risk for lack of attention or access to primary care. Over the past 10 years many communities in the United States have experienced pertussis and measles epidemics. Pertussis, measles, polio, and hemophilus infections may further complicate the primary neurodevelopmental problems of children with myelomeningocele or pose serious threats when secondary conditions of central hypoventilation, pulmonary hypertension, cor pulmonale, restrictive pulmonary disease, or congenital heart disease exist.

Pertussis immunization has been controversial for many years because of concern about the possibility of vaccine-related reactions, particularly in those with neurological conditions. At present, there does not appear to be any significant risk to children with spina bifida from pertussis immunization. Similarly, risks from other immunizations are not reported to be any greater in children with spina bifida. Of great concern, however, are the large number of children with spina bifida whose immunizations are incomplete. A Massachusetts center[188] reported only 58% of those aged 2 years and 55% of those aged 7 years had successfully completed their immunizations as recommended in guidelines from the American Academy of Pediatrics (AAP). This compared to a reported statewide rate of 97% at school entry. Most children in the spina bifida clinic studied had either private or Medicaid insurance and an identified primary care provider. Acute illnesses, hospitalizations for surgery, emphasis on specialty care, and concerns by both health providers and parents about increased trauma and the risks associated with immunizations were thought to account for the low compliance rate.

Cognitive function

The potential for cognitive function of those born with open spina bifida has been of great concern to parents, health care providers, educators, and policymakers. Observations of poor intellectual development in association with severe physical disability in a significant number of patients led to the development of selection criteria for initial treatment.[189] Since that time, improvement in treatment modalities has decreased mortality and many forms of morbidity, including those adversely effecting cognitive function.[189,190]

On long-term follow-up, 43 of 61 (70%) survivors born 1963 to 1970 in Cambridge (UK) had IQ scores ≥80.[190] Other studies have also reported improvement in the prognosis for intellectual development, particularly for those with low-level lesions and the absence of hydrocephalus. Verbal IQ scores have been reported to be higher than scores on performance IQ. Superficial "cocktail party chatter" has been described as common to children with MMC. However, problems with arithmetic, visual-motor integration, and specific memory impairment have been reported to be common in those with MMC. It has been suggested that these problems may represent a developmental difference in visual-perceptual-organizational cognitive function.[191-194] Verbal and language skills, memory, general intelligence, abstract thinking, and visual organization are especially important to adolescents and young adults with MMC if they are to succeed academically, obtain employment, achieve automobile licensure, and be successful in residential independence.[195-197]

Ventriculitis in infancy has been found to be a significant risk factor with great importance for those with poor intellectual and neurological outcome,[198] although not all studies concur in this.[189] Neonatal complications, including massive hydrocephalus, microcephaly, severe prematurity, or very low birth weight, intraventricular hemorrhage, and other associated major congenital anomalies, are also important for their adverse effect on developmental and cognitive outcome. Additionally, the effects of poverty and poor social conditions have in our experience been significant and must be considered in predicting outcomes. Optimistic predictions on developmental outcome must be tempered when generalized to socially vulnerable populations.

Dental care

Children with myelomeningocele have the same routine dental needs as other children, including the need for fluoride administration, regular toothbrushing, routine dental visits, and good oral hygiene. Those with significant cognitive impairment, cerebral palsy, or seizures, especially if using Dilantin therapy, have particular need for good oral hygiene. In the dental office, attention to adequate seating and positioning in the dental chair is important in view of skin anesthesia. Oral secretions may be increased or decreased, depending on neurological status and specific medication regimens. Precautions for those with latex sensitivity must also be taken. Rubber gloves, bites, and latex in other equipment can be life threatening to some. Those with hydrocephalus may have altered facial bone structure with increased orthodontic needs. Poverty may, in addition, accentuate needs for dental prophylaxis and treatment.

Although bacteremia, in general, is reported to be 28% following dental prophylaxis and 63% in those undergoing extraction, little is known about the risk for shunt infection in those with hydrocephalus undergoing dental procedures. Pediatric dentists and neurosurgeons frequently recommend antibiotic prophylaxis following dental procedures for children with both VA and VP shunts and believe infection risk greater for those with VA shunts.[93] Published reports relating dental procedures to shunt infections, however, do not exist, and prophylaxis, although reasonable for those with VA shunts, seems to have less rationale and justification for those with VP shunts.[94]

Sex and sexuality

Women with spina bifida are fully capable of experiencing and enjoying sexual intercourse with 70% successfully conceiving and having a relatively uneventful pregnancy and delivery. Urinary incontinence may be increased late in pregnancy and C-section is commonly required.[120] Both men and women may engage in sexual activity although natural lubrication is decreased in women. Water-soluble lubricants are recommended during sexual intercourse to protect the vagina and penis, both of which frequently have diminished sensation.[199]

Problems with erection and ejaculation are common. Men with spina bifida, however, have been able to father children. Psychogenic and reflex erections depend on the level of lesion. Those with a defect at or above L2 will usually not have psychogenic erections; those with lesions between T11 and L2 usually lack both types of erection. Ejaculation is possible, particularly for those with sacral level lesions. For those with thoracic and lumbar lesions, retrograde ejaculation is common. Problems of ejaculation, history of high fevers from infection, and occurence of undescended testicles may frequently result in male infertility.[120,199]

The likelihood of orgasm from stimulation of the genital area is diminished in both men and women with spina bifida. Orgasm from stimulation elsewhere, and erotic sensation, stimulation, and sexual pleasure is, however, possible and achievable.[199]

Significant sex education is available, but material specifically for those with disabilities will be increasingly required in the future. Sexual thoughts, behaviors, and desires are certainly as common to adolescents and young adults with spina bifida as others. Health providers and parents need to be sensitive to the fact that the desire to marry and have meaningful relationships is normally present in those with spina bifida.[200-202] Contraception counseling is important to avoid unplanned pregnancy. Condom use is limited in those with latex (rubber) allergy, and such individuals need to be aware that non-latex condoms provide inadequate protection from AIDS and other sexually transmitted diseases.

In the past individuals with spina bifida have reported being socially isolated and sexually inactive. Limitations in mobility, embarassment because of urine and fecal incontinence, low self-esteem, and concerns about fertility were given as reasons for early and continued isolation. This does not need to be the case in the future as more effective interventions for individuals, families, and society are developed.

Skin integrity

Anesthetic skin is best managed by preventive measures. Paraplegia, orthopedic deformity, bowel and urine incontinence, and orthosis use raise the risk of skin breakdown and decubiti. Skin breakdown, once it occurs, is difficult to correct. In a longitudinal study (1960 to 1980) of 524 persons with MMC, 43% had skin breakdown. There were multiple reasons for the 468 observed lesions, including excessive pressure (42%), cast or orthosis use (23%), incontinence (23%), excessive activity (10%), burns (1%), and other causes (1%).[203] Use of a pressure scanner has shown that unbalanced scoliosis, pelvic obliquity, and loss of lordosis following spinal fusion results in abnormally high pressures over a single ischium and/or sacrococcygeal area.[204] Skin breakdown is most frequent in the perineal area and over a kyphotic deformity; it occurs less frequently in the lower extremities. Problems with seating because of poor fitting and asymmetrical weight bearing and soiling from urine and feces lead to skin breakdown over the ischial tuberosity and/or the coccyx. A kyphotic spine has poor protective coverage, and the skin over it is easily damaged by a poor sitting position and other rubbing. These problems are more common in those with L2 or above lesions. Skin breakdown in the lower extremities, however, is more common in those who are active and have motor level L4 to L5 or below.[203] Foot lesions in active individuals, as frequently found in those with sacral lesions, can be difficult to heal and can lead to serious infection, including cellulitis and chronic osteomyelitis, with the necessity for amputation.[205]

Those with high paraplegia, high sensory deficit, mental retardation, macrocephaly, kyphosis, upper extremity impairment, incontinence, and/or poor compliance with medical recommendations and follow-up are at the greatest risk for development of decubiti and other forms of skin breakdown.[203] Hospitalization for skin breakdown and the complications of wound infection, cellulitis, and osteomyelitis are infrequent but costly when they occur. A study of 650 patients (1973 to 1986) reported 75 persons aged 2 to 31 years who required 202 admissions with an average length of stay of 31 days. Individuals with thoracic level lesions accounted for 51% of those affected. The number of bed days per admission steadily decreased over time because of earlier identification and more aggressive management, including surgery.[206]

Treatment of decubiti in the hospital includes cleaning and debridement as needed, hydrotherapy, and antibiotics when infection is present. Myocutaneous rotation flaps with intact vasculature and innervation may provide protective covering and restore sensation[206,207] as well as shortening the length of hospitalization and reducing the risk of readmission. Optimal treatment includes education to make everybody aware of the importance of maintaining skin integrity, improvements in adaptive equipment and custom seating, and early training of parents regarding the importance of skin hygiene. It is important to teach children how to use a mirror for self-inspection and how to apply pressure release techniques to provide elevation of the body and improve blood flow to the area.[206] Additionally, in view of the lack of sensation, careful attention should be paid to avoiding excessive sun exposure and severe sunburn, preventing accidental burns from hot water or caustic agents, and treating diaper dermatitis.

Operative risks

Those with spina bifida will experience multiple surgeries during their lifetime. It is important that they receive care from qualified pediatric specialty surgeons and anesthesiologists. Routine anesthesia precautions for those with MMC appropriate to age are essential.

In the neonate, particular attention is directed to avoidance of hypothermia and intubation in the decubitus position or with the back supported on a "head ring" to minimize danger to the back lesion. Adequate support of the chest and pelvis to avoid pressure on the abdomen with resultant obstruction of the inferior vena cava or pressure on the diaphragm is also important.[208] The anesthesiologist and neonatal team must also be aware of the increased incidence of necrotizing enterocolitis (NEC) in these infants.[209]

Neurosurgical procedures related to the shunt are usually brief but do require specific attention to cardiopulmonary stability and complications of increased ICP. Pulmonary function is frequently impaired in those with significant scoliosis, and restrictive lung disease frequently results from decreased trunk height, decreased flexibility of the thoracic cage, and thoracic lordosis. Preoperative assessment with pulmonary function tests, coagulation panel, and cardiovascular evaluation is required before spinal fusion.

Anesthesiologists and surgeons need to be alert to the risk of intraoperative catastrophe from blood or blood products, anesthetic agents, and anaphylactic reaction to latex.[210,211] Careful preoperative review of the medical history is important to minimize these risks. Intubation may be difficult because 36% of those with spina bifida are reported to have a short trachea, with reduction in the number of cartilage rings from normal 17 to 15 or fewer. A short trachea changes the expected position of tracheal bifurcation with the resultant risk of accidental endobronchial intubation.[212] Malignant hyperthermia has also been reported to be increased with a 1.5% incidence.[213] This may be catastrophic in those with brainstem dysfunction and prolonged seizures. The anesthesiologist must be prepared to deal with this life-threatening emergency.

Latex (rubber) allergy

Latex allergy has been reported to be common in individuals with spina bifida and anomalies of the genitourinary system. The Food and Drug Administration (FDA) *Medical Bulletin* in 1991 reported that 18% to 40% of individuals with spina bifida and up to 6% of medical personnel are latex sensitive.[214] Reactions range from (1) chemical contact dermatitis of the skin with erythema, urticaria, rhinitis, conjunctivitis, and/or swelling of the lips; (2) systemic IgE-mediated reaction with hives, tachycardia, wheezing, angioneurotic edema of the lips and face, hypotension, shock, and anaphylaxis[215]; and (3) intraoperative anaphylactic reactions with hemodynamic instability, including hypotension, increased airway resistance, and circulatory collapse.[216] This latter complication may be difficult to differentiate from other intraoperative catastrophe.[210,211,215]

Latex comes from the sap of the plant *Hevea brasiliensis*, which grows in tropical climates. Reactions are thought to result from the 2% to 3% of residual proteins that remain after the commercial purification process. Significant variation in reaction rates have been reported in rubber products of varying purity. Many products contain rubber components of which we are unaware and environmental exposure to rubber products in both the community and hospital is widespread. Children with spina bifida are exposed to latex in toys including balloons and squash balls, rubber catheters used in bladder continence programs, urinary tubes, enema catheters, latex adhesive tapes and bandages, gloves, components of intravenous infusion sets (particularly sites for medication injection), anesthetic equipment (rubber bellows, diaphragm, and tubing), and dental bite blocks.[216,217]

RAST, skin-prick, and intradermal tests may be used in evaluation for possible latex allergy. Skin-prick tests are highly accurate, but reports of reactions including anaphylaxis have limited their use. RAST testing has significant variation (53% to 100%) in sensitivity reported. Latex specific IgE has been detected by ELISA at 92.3% and RAST at 93.8%.[218] Although useful, these tests do not replace a careful medical and environmental history and recognition by parents, school personnel, and health care providers that latex exposure is to be minimized and avoided whenever possible.

Serious reaction results from a combination of individual sensitivity, route of antigen challenge, and the rate and magnitude of the challenge. Antigen may be delivered by contact with mucous membrane surfaces, aerosolization, and/or intravenous routes.[214,218] Reactions may occur in those as young as 2 years, but are more likely in those who have undergone multiple hospitalizations, particularly surgical procedures. Lengthy procedures such as anterior spinal fusion with significant serosal membrane exposure from which antigen may be absorbed into the bloodstream probably produce a higher risk of intraoperative anaphylaxis. It is, therefore, important to use nonlatex gloves and catheters; wash powder off rubber gloves; avoid rubber face masks, bellows, diaphragms, and tubing in anesthesia equipment; and eliminate rubber portals in intravenous equipment through which medication and fluids are administered.

Prevention is the best approach. Some medical centers have attempted to create a latex-free environment for those with known sensitivity, and, when feasible, for all spina bifida patients. Prophylactic presurgical management with diphenhydramine, cimetidine or ranitidine, and corticosteroids has been advocated and is used in many centers for those with known latex sensitivity. Families and school and community health providers need to be made aware of the hazards of latex exposure, and the latex-sensitive individual needs to be provided with a medical alert bracelet and autoinjectable epinephrine.[218]

Survival

Significant progress has been made over the past 40 years in the care provided to individuals with spina bifida. Before this, less than 5% to 10% of these infants survived the first year of life.[189] The greatest number of deaths now result from brainstem dysfunction in infancy and early childhood years. ESRD, CNS infection, and hydrocephalus continue as additional common causes of death in those with MMC.

The median age of survival for a group of individuals with MMC born in 1963 to 1970 was recently reported to be approximately 30 years.[190] Survival curves become flatter after age 5 years with survival expectations significantly improved after this.[190,219,220] As a result of continued advances in treatment modalities, accurate predictions of expected survival are difficult to provide to families. It is expected, however, that both the life expectancy and quality of life will continue to improve for those born with spina bifida today.

Grateful acknowledgment is given to Liz Dennon and Connie Nicholson of the USC University Affiliated Program at Childrens Hospital Los Angeles for their assistance and patience in the preparation of this manuscript, for the assistance and guidance of Doreen Keough of the Childrens Hospital Los Angeles Medical Library, and for the review and valuable advice of Dr. Barbara Korsch. Preparation of this paper was partially supported by grant funding from the Maternal and Child Health Bureau (MCHB) #MCJ-069145 and the Administration on Developmental Disabilities (ADD) #90DD0318.

REFERENCES

1. Wolraich ML: *The needs of children with spina bifida: a comprehensive view (monograph)*, University of Iowa, 1983, The Division of Developmental Disabilities, Department of Pediatrics.

2. Perrin JM: Children with special health needs: a United States perspective, *Pediatrics Suppl*, 86:1120-1123, 1990.

3. Newacheck PW, Hughes DC, Stoddard JJ, Halfon N: Children with chronic illness and Medicaid managed care, *Pediatr Comment* 93:497-500, 1994.

4. Hughes DC, Newacheck PW, Stoddard JJ, Halfon N: Medicaid managed care: can it work for children? *Pediatrics* 95(4):591-594, 1995.

5. Fox HB, Wicks LB, Newacheck PW: Health maintenance organizations and children with special health needs, *AJDC* 147:546-552, 1993.

6. Kaufman BA, Terbrock A, Winters N, Ito J, Klosterman A, Park TS: Disbanding a multidisciplinary clinic: effects on the health care of myelomeningocele patients, *Pediatr Neurosurg* 21(1):36-44, 1994.

7. Blum FW, Garell D, Hodgman CH, Jorissen TW, Okinow NA, Orr DP, Slap GB: Transition from child-centered to adult health care systems for adolescents with chronic conditions, *J Adolescent Health* 14:570-576, 1993.

8. McComb JG: A practical classification of spinal neural tube defects *(abstract)*, Proceedings of the Society for Research into Hydrocephalus and Spina Bifida, Bristol, *Eur J Pediatr Surg* 5(Suppl I):49, 1995.

9. Dahl M, Ahlsten G, Carlson H, Ronne-Engstrom E, Lagerkvist B, Magnusson G, Norrlin S, Olsen L, Stromberg B, Thuomas K-A: Neurological dysfunction above cele level in children with spina bifida cystica: a prospective study to 3 years, *Dev Med Child Neurol* 37:30-40, 1995.

10. Seller MJ: Risks in spina bifida, *Dev Med Child Neurol* 36:1021-1025, 1994.

11. Strassburg MA, Greenland S, Portigal LD, et al: A population-based case-control study of anencephalus and spina bifida in a low-risk area, *Dev Med Child Neurol* 25:632-641, 1983.

12. Ferguson-Smith MA: The reduction of anencephalic and spina bifida births by maternal serum and a-fetoprotein screening, *Br Med Bull* 39:365-372, 1983.

13. Laurence KM: Short report: a declining incidence of neural tube defects in the UK, *Z Kinderchir* 44(Suppl I):51, 1989.

14. Yen IH, Khoury MJ, Erickson JD, James LM, Waters GD, Berry RJ: The changing epidemiology of neural tube defects, *AJDC* 146:857-861, 1992.

15. Greene WB, Terry RC, DeMasi RA, Herrington RT: Effect of race and gender on neurological level in myelomeningocele, *Dev Med Child Neurol* 33:110-117, 1991.

16. Shaw GM, Schaffer D, Velie EM, Morland K, Harris JA: Periconceptional vitamin use, dietary folate, and the occurrence of neural tube defects, *Epidemiology* 6(3):219-226, 1995.

17. Carter CO: Clues to the aetiology of neural tube malformations, *Dev Med Child Neurol* 16(Suppl 32):3-14, 1974.

18. Milunsky A: Methotrexate-induced congenital malformation, *Pediatrics* 42:790-795, 1968.

19. Jacobsen CB, Berlin CM: Possible reproductive detriment in LSD users, *JAMA* 222:1367-1373, 1972.

20. Taussig HB: A study of the German outbreak of phocomelia, *JAMA* 180:1106, 1962.

21. Nichols MM: Fetal anomalies following maternal trimethadione ingestion, *J Pediatr* 82:885-886, 1973.

22. Robert E, Guibaud P: Maternal valproic acid and congenital NTD, *Lancet* 2:937, 1982.

23. Kallen AJ: Maternal carbamazepine and infant spina bifida, *Reproduc Toxicol* 8(3):203-205, 1994.

24. The California Expanded Alpha-Fetoprotein Screening Program: *Prenatal care provider handbook*, Berkeley, 1994, Department of Health Services, Genetic Disease Branch.

25. Soler NG, Walsh CH, Malins JH: Congenital malformation in infants of diabetic mothers, *Q J Med* 45:303, 1976.

26. Passarge E, True CW, Sueoka WT: Malformation of the CNS in trisomy 18 syndrome, *J Pediatr* 69:771-778, 1966.

27. Creary MR, Alberman ED: Congenital malformations of the central nervous system in spontaneous abortion, *J Med Genet* 13:9-16, 1976.

28. Lese G, Jacobs RA, McComb JG: The incidence of craniosynostosis in a pediatric population with spina bifida (abstract), Proceedings of the Society for Research into Hydrocephalus and Spina Bifida, Bristol, *Eur J Pediatr Surg*, 5(Suppl I):49, 1995.

29. Fraser FC, Czeizel A, Hanson C: Increased frequency of neural tube defects in siblings of children with other malformations, *Lancet II:*144-145, 1982.

30. Nickel RE, Pillers DAM, Merkens M, Magenis RE, Driscoll DA, Emanuel BS, Zonana J: Velo-cardio-facial syndrome and DiGeorge sequence with meningomyelocele and deletions of the 22q11 region, *Am J Med Gen* 52:445-449, 1994.

31. Jacobs RA, Hohn A: Short report—cardiovascular pathology in myelomeningocele care, *Eur J Pediatr Surg* 2 (Suppl I):42, 1992.

32. Chance PF, Smith DW: Hyperthermia and meningomyelocele and anencephaly, *Lancet* 1:769-770, 1978.

33. Zimmerman AW, Rowe DW: Cellular zinc accumulation in anencephaly and spina bifida, *Z Kinderchir* 38(Suppl II):65-67, 1983.

34. Zimmerman AW, Lozzio CB: Interaction between selenium and zinc in the pathogenesis of anencephaly and spina bifida, *Z Kinderchir* 44(Suppl I):48-50, 1989.

35. Smithells RW, Sheppard S, Schorah CJ: Vitamin deficiencies and neural tube defects, *Arch Dis Child* 51:944-950, 1976.

36. Wynn V: Vitamins and oral contraceptive use, *Lancet I:*561-564, 1975.

37. Kasan PN, Andrews J: Oral contraception and congenital anomalies, *Br J Obstet Gynacol* 87:545-551, 1980.

38. Smithells RW, et al: Further experience of vitamin supplementation for prevention of neural tube defect recurrences, *Lancet* 1027-1031, 1983.

39. Laurence KM, James N, Miller M, et al: Double-blind randomized controlled trial of folate treatment before conception to prevent recurrence of neural tube defects, *Br Med J* 282:1509-1511, 1981.

40. MRC Vitamin Study Research Group: Prevention of neural tube defects: results of the Medical Research Council Vitamin Study, *Lancet* 338:131-137, 1991.

41. Czeizel AE, Dudas I: Prevention of the first occurrence of neural tube defects by periconceptional vitamin supplementation, *N Engl J Med* 327:1832-1835, 1992.

42. Vergel RG, Sanchez LR, Heredero BL, et al: Primary prevention of neural tube defects with folic acid supplementation: Cuban experience, *Prenat Diag* 10:149-152, 1990.

43. Centers for Disease Control: Use of folic acid for prevention of spina bifida and other neural tube defects, 1983-1991, *MMWR* 40:513-516, 1991.

44. Milunsky A, Jick H, Jick SS, et al: Multivitamin/folic acid supplementation in early pregnancy reduces the prevalence of neural tube defects, *JAMA* 262:2847-2852, 1989.

45. Centers for Disease Control: Recommendations for the use of folic acid to reduce the number of cases of spina bifida and other neural tube defects, *MMWR* 41:RR-14, 1992.

46. Mills, JL, McPartlin JM, Kirke PN, Lee YJ, Conley MR, Weir DG, Scott JM: Homocysteine metabolism in pregnancies complicated by neural-tube defects, *Lancet* 345:149-151, 1995.

47. Donnai D: What's new in the genetics of hydrocephalus and spina bifida? *Eur J Pediatr Surg* 3(Suppl I):5-7, 1993.

48. Nickel RE: Disorders of brain development, *Inf Young Child* 5(1):1-11, 1992.

49. Golden JA, Chernoff GF: Intermittent pattern of neural tube closure in two strains of mice, *Teratology* 27:73-80, 1993.

50. Van Allen MI, Kalousek DK, Chernoff GF, Hall JG: Evidence for multisite closure of the neural tube in humans, *Am J Med Gen* 47:723-743, 1993.

51. Golden JA, Chernoff GF: Multiple sites of anterior neural tube closure in humans: evidence from anterior neural tube defects (anencephaly), *Pediatrics* 95(4):506-510, 1995.

52. Seller MJ: An essay on research into the causation and prevention of spina bifida, *Z Kinderchir* 34:306-314, 1981.

53. McLone DG, Knepper PA: The cause of Chiari II malformation: a unified theory, *Pediatric Neurosci* 15:1-12, 1989.

54. Wald NJ, Cuckle H: Report of UK Collaborative Study on Alpha-Fetoprotein in Relation to Neural-Tube Defects: maternal serum-alpha-fetoprotein measurement in antenatal screening for anencephaly and spina bifida in early pregnancy, *Lancet I:*1323-1332, 1977.

55. Shurtleff DB: Meningomyelocele: a new or a vanishing disease? *Z Kinderchir* 41(Suppl I):5-9, 1986.

56. Shurtleff DB, editor: *Myelodysplasias and exstrophies: significance, prevention, and treatment*, Orlando, 1986, Grune & Stratton.

57. Nadel AS, Green JK, Holmes LB, Frigoletto FD, Benacerraf BR: Absence of need for amniocentesis in patients with elevated levels of maternal serum alpha-fetoprotein and normal ultrasonographic examinations, *New Engl J Med* 323(9):557-561, 1990.

58. Platt LD, Feuchtbamm L, Filly R, Lustig L, Simon M, Cunningham GC: The California Maternal Serum Alpha-Fetoprotein Screening Program: the role of ultrasonography in the detection of spina bifida, *Am J Obstet Gynecol* 166:1328-1329, 1992.

59. Wald NJ, et al: Sensitivity of ultrasound in detecting spina bifida, correspondence, *New Engl J Med* 324(11):769-770, 1991.

60. Thornton JG, et al: Sensitivity of ultrasound in detecting spina bifida, correspondence, *New Engl J Med* 324(11):771-772, 1991.

61. The California AFP Screening Program: *AFP update for prenatal care providers*, Berkeley, 1994.

62. Shurtleff DB, Luthy DA, Benedetti TJ, Hickok DE, Stuntz T, Kropp RJ: The outcome of pregnancies diagnosed as having a fetus with meningomyelocele, *Z Kinderchir* 42(I):50-52, 1987.

63. Hill AE, Beattie F: Does caesarean section delivery improve neurological outcome in open spina bifida? *Eur J Pediatr Surg* 4(Suppl I):32-34, 1994.

64. Shurtleff DB, Luthy DA, Nyberg DA, Mack LA: The outcome of fetal myelomeningocele brought to term, *Eur J Pediatr Surg* 4(Suppl I):25-28, 1994.

65. Luthy DA, Wardinsky T, Shurtleff DB, et al: Cesarean section before onset of labour and subsequent motor function in infants with myelomeningocele diagnosed antenatally, *N Engl J Med* 324:662-666, 1991.

66. Fost N: Ethical issues in the treatment of critically ill newborns, *Pediatr Ann* 10:16-22, 1981.

67. Laurence KM, Evans RC, Weeks RD, et al: The reliability of prediction of outcome in spina bifida, *Dev Med Child Neurol* 18(Suppl 37):150, 1976.

68. McCullough DC, Balzer-Martin LA: Current prognosis in overt neonatal hydrocephalus, *J Neurosurg* 57:378-383, 1982.

69. Guiney EJ, Surana R: Presidential address to the Society for Research into Spina Bifida and Hydrocephalus at Hartford, Conn, *Eur J Pediatr Surg*, Suppl I:5-9, 1994.

70. Bax M: Disclosure—editorial, *Dev Med Child Neurol* 37:471-472, 1995.

71. Charney EB, Sutton LN, Bruce DA, Schut LB: Myelomeningocele newborn management: time for parental decision, *Z Kinderchir* 38(Suppl II):90-93, 1983.

72. Mezue WC, Eze CB: Social circumstances affecting the initial management of children with myelomeningocele in Nigeria, *Dev Med Child Neurol* 34:338-341, 1992.

73. Lorber J, Salfield SAW: Results of selective treatment of spina bifida cystica, *Arch Dis Child* 56:822-830, 1981.

74. Lorber J: Spina bifida cystica: results of treatment of 270 consecutive cases, with criteria for selection for the future, *Arch Dis Child* 47:854-873, 1972.

75. Surana RH, Quinn FMJ, Guiney EJ, Fitzgerald RJ: Are the selection criteria for the conservative management in spina bifida still applicable? *Eur J Pediatr Surg* 1(Suppl I):35-37, 1991.

76. Blum RW, Resnick MD, Nelson R, St Germaine A: Family and peer issues among adolescents with spina bifida and cerebral palsy, *Pediatrics* 88(2):280-285, 1991.

77. Appleton PL, Minchom PE, Ellis NC, Elliott CE, Boll V, Jones P: The self-concept of young people with spina bifida: a population-based study, *Dev Med Child Neurol* 36:198-215, 1994.

78. Breslaw N, Weitzman M, Messenger K: Psychological functioning of siblings of disabled children, *Pediatrics* 67:344-353, 1981.

79. Cappelli M, McGrath PJ, McDaniels T, Manion I, Schillinger J: Marital quality of parents of children with spina bifida: a case-comparison study, *Dev Behavior Pediatr* 15:320-326, 1994.

80. Jacobs RA, Negrete V, Johnson M, Korsch BM: Parental opinions on treatment decisions for myelomeningocele infants: a descriptive study, *Z Kinderchir* 44(Suppl I):11-13, 1989.

81. Charney EB: Parental attitudes toward management of newborns with myelomeningocele, *Dev Med Child Neurol* 32:14-19, 1990.

82. Guthkelch AN, Pang D, Vries JK: Influence of closure technique on results in meningomyelocele, *Childs Brain* 8:350-355, 1981.

83. Parent AD, McMillan T: Contemporaneous shunting with repair of myelomeningocele, *Pediatric Neurosurg* 22(3):132-135, 1995.

84. Vaishnav A, MacKinnon AE: Progressive hydrocephalus in teenage spina bifida patients, *Z Kinderchir* 41(Suppl I):36-37, 1986.

85. Sperling DR, Patrick JR, Anderson RM, Fyler DC: Cor pulmonale secondary to ventriculoauriculostomy, *Am J Dis Child* 107:308-315, 1964.

86. Emery JL, Hilton HB: Lung and heart complications of the treatment of hydrocephalus by ventriculoauriculostomy, *Surgery* 50:309-314, 1961.

87. Sleigh G, Dawson A, Penny WJ: Cor pulmonale as a complication of ventriculo-atrial shunts reviewed, *Dev Med Child Neurol* 35:65-78, 1993.

88. Sainte-Rose C, Piatt JH, Renier D, Pierre-Kahn A, Hirsch JF, Hoffman HJ, Humphreys RP: Mechanical complications in shunts, *Pediatr Neurosurg* 17:2-9, 1991-1992.

89. Pople IK, Quinn MW, Bayston R: Morbidity and outcome of shunted hydrocephalus, *Z Kinderchir* 45(Suppl I):29-31, 1990.

90. Forrest DM, Tabara ZB, Towu E, Said AJ: Management of the colonised shunt, *Z Kinderchir* 42(Suppl I):21-22, 1987.

91. Charney EB, Melchionni JB, Antonucci DL: Ventriculitis in newborns with myelomeningocele, *AJDC* 145:287-290, 1991.

92. Connolly B, Guiney EJ, Fitzgerald RJ: CSF/shunt infections—the bane of our lives! *Z Kinderchir* 42(Suppl I):13-14, 1987.

93. Acs G, Cozzi E: Antibiotic prophylaxis for patients with hydrocephalus shunts: a survey of pediatric dentistry and neurosurgery program directors, *Pediatr Dent* 14(4):246-250, 1992.

94. Bayston R: *Hydrocephalus shunt infections*, London, 1989, Chapman and Hall.

95. Hesz N, Wolraich M: Vocal cord paralysis and brainstem dysfunction in children with spina bifida, *Dev Med Child Neurol* 27:522-531, 1985.

96. Thompson J, Jacobs RA: Endoscopic vocal cord evaluation in myelomeningocele children, *Eur J Pediatr Surg* 2(Suppl I):41-42, 1992.

97. Park TS, Hoffman JJ, Hendrick EB, et al: Experience with surgical decompression of the Arnold-Chiari malformation in young infants with myelomeningocele, *Neurosurgery* 13:147-152, 1983.

98. Bell WO, Charney EB, Schut L, Sutton L, Bruce D: Symptomatic Arnold-Chiari malformation: review of experience with 22 cases, *J Neurosurg* 66:812-816, 1987.

99. Charney EB, Rorke LB, Sutton LN, Schut L: Management of Chiari II complication in infants with myelomeningocele, *J Pediatr* 3:364-371, 1987.

100. Davidson Ward SL, Jacobs RA, Gates EP, Hart LD, Keens TG: Abnormal ventilatory patterns during sleep in infants with myelomeningocele, *J Pediatr* 109:631-634, 1986.

101. Davidson Ward SL, Nickerson BG, van der Hal AL, Rodriguez AM, Jacobs RA, Keens TG: Absent hypoxic and hypercarbic arousal responses in children with myelomeningocele and apnea, *Pediatrics* 78:44-50, 1986.

102. Ortega M, Davidson Ward SL, Swaminathan W, Jacobs R, Keens TG: Abnormal hypoxic arousal responses in myelomeningocele infants with apnea, *Pediatr Res* 23:324A, 1988.

103. Swaminathan S, Paton JY, Ward SLD, Sargent CW, Jacobs RA, Keens TG: Abnormal control of ventilation in adolescents with myelomeningocele, *J Pediatr* 115:898-903, 1989.

104. Worley G, Oakes WJ, Spock A: The CO_2 response test in children with spina bifida (abstract), *Am Acad Cerebr Palsy Dev Med*, 1240A, 1985.

105. Gozal D, Arens R, Omlin KJ, Jacobs RA, Keens TG: Peripheral chemoreceptor function in children with myelomeningocele and Arnold-Chiari malformation, *Chest* 108:425-431, 1995.

106. Petersen MC, Wolraich M, Sherbondy A, Wagener J: Abnormalities in control of ventilation in newborn infants with myelomeningocele, *J Pediatr* 126(6):1011-1015, 1995.

107. Barnet AB, Weiss IP, Shaer C: Evoked potentials in infant brainstem syndrome associated with Arnold-Chiari malformation, *Dev Med Child Neurol* 35:42-48, 1993.

108. Worley G, Erwin CW, Schuster JM, Park Y, Boyko OB, Griebel ML, Weidman ER, Radtke RA, Oakes WJ: BAEPs in infants with myelomeningocele and later development of Chiari II malformation–related brainstem dysfunction, *Dev Med Child Neurol* 36:707-715, 1994.

109. Worley F, Schuster JM, Oakes WJ: The influence on survival of cervical laminectomy for children with meningomyelocele who have potentially lethal brainstem dysfunction due to the Chiari II malformation, *Dev Med Child Neurol* 33(Suppl 64):19, 1991.

110. Banta JV: The tethered cord in myelomeningocele: should it be untethered? *Dev Med Child Neurol* 33:173-176, 1991.

111. Petersen MC: Tethered cord syndrome in myelodysplasia: correlation between level of lesion and height at time of presentation, *Dev Med Child Neurol* 34:604-610, 1992.

112. McEnery G, Borzyskowski M, Cox TCS, Nevill BGR: The spinal cord in neurologically stable spina bifida: a clinical and MRI study, *Dev Med Child Neurol* 34:342-347, 1992.

113. Vogl D, Ring-Mrozik E, Baierl P, Vogl Th, Zimmermann K: Magnetic resonance imaging in children suffering from spina bifida, *Z Kinderchir* 42(Suppl I):60-64, 1987.

114. Begeer JH, Wiertsema GPA, Breukers SME, Mooy JJA, Ter Weeme CA: Tethered cord syndrome: clinical signs and results of operation in 42 patients with spina bifida aperta and occulta, *Z Kinderchir* 44(Suppl I):5-7, 1989.

115. Begeer JH, Meihuizen de Regt MJ, HogenEsch I, Ter Weeme CA, Mooij JJA, Vencken LM: Progressive neurological deficit in children with spina bifida aperta, *Z Kinderchir* 41(Suppl I):13-15, 1986.

116. Stellman GR, Bannister CM, Hillier V: The incidence of seizure disorder in children with acquired and congenital hydrocephalus, *Z Kinderchir* 41(Suppl I):38-41, 1986.

117. Hack CH, Enrile BG, Donat JF, Kosnik E: Seizures in relation to shunt dysfunction in children with meningomyelocele, *J Pediatr* 116(1):57-60, 1990.

118. Noetzel MJ, Blake JN: Prognosis for seizure control and remission in children with my-elomeningocele, *Dev Med Child Neurol* 33:803-810, 1991.

119. Lewis MA, Webb NJA, Stellman-Ward GR, Bannister CM: Investigative techniques and renal parenchymal damage in children with spina bifida, *Eur J Pediatr Surg* 4(Suppl I):29-31, 1994.

120. Bauer SB: Neurogenic vesical dysfunction in children. In Walsh PC, et al, editors: *Campbell's urology,* ed 6, Philadelphia, 1992, WB Saunders, pp 1634-1668.

121. Brem AS, Martin D, Callaghan J, Maynard J: Long-term renal risk factors in children with meningomyelocele, *J Pediatr* 110(1):51-55, 1987.

122. Lais A, Kasabian NG, Dyro FM, Scott RM, Kelly MD, Bauer SB: The neurosurgical implications of continuous neurourological surveillance of children with myelodysplasia, *J Urol* 150:1879-1883, 1993.

123. Dator DP, Hatchett L, Dyro FM, Shefner JM, Bauer SB: Urodynamic dysfunction in walking myelodysplastic children, *J Urol* 148:362-365, 1992.

124. Hernandez RD, Hurwitz RS, Foote JE, Zimmern PE, Leach GE: Nonsurgical management of threatened upper urinary tracts and incontinence in children with myelomeningocele, *J Urol* 152:1582-1585, 1994.

125. Krahn CG, Johnson HW: Cutaneous vesicostomy in the young child: indications and results, *Urology* 41(6):558-563, 1993.

126. Connolly B, Fitzgerald RJ, Guiney EJ: Has vesicostomy a role in the neuropathic bladder? *Z Kinderchir* 43(Suppl II):17-18, 1988.

127. Lie HR, Lagergren J, Rasmussen F, Lagerkvist B, Hagelsteen J, Borjeson MC, Mutti-lainen M, Taudorf K: Bowel and bladder control of children with myelomeningocele: a nordic study, *Dev Med Child Neurol* 33:1053-1061, 1991.

128. Crooks KK, Ennle BG: Comparison of the ileal conduit and clean intermittent catheterization for meningomyelocele, *Pediatrics* 72:203-205, 1983.

129. Ehrlich O, Brem AS: A prospective comparison of UTI in patients treated with either clean intermittent catheterization or urinary diversion, *Pediatrics* 70:665-669, 1982.

130. Lin-Dyken DC, Wolraich ML, Hawtrey CE, Doja MS: Follow-up of clean intermittent catheterization for children with neurogenic bladders, *Urology* 40(6):525-529, 1992.

131. Lindehall B, Moller A, Hjalmas K, Jodal U: Long-term intermittent catheterization: the experience of teenagers and young adults with myelomeningocele, *J Urol* 152:187-198, 1994.

132. Wolraich ML, Hawtrey C, Mapel J, et al: Results of clean intermittent catheterization for children with neurogenic bladders, *Urology* 22:479-482, 1983.

133. Mulchy JJ, James HE, McRoberts JW: Oxybutynin chloride combined with intermittent clean catheterization in the treatment of meningomyelocele patients, *J Urol* 118:95-96, 1977.

134. Hunt GM: Short report—recent advances in intermittent catheterisation, *Z Kinderchir* 44(Suppl I):50, 1989.

135. Kaplan WE: Intravesical transurethral bladder stimulation, *Z Kinderchir* 41(Suppl I):25-27, 1986.

136. Kaplan WE, Richards TW, Richards I: Intravesical bladder stimulation to increase bladder capacity, *J Urol* 142(Pt 2):600-602, 1989.

137. Sumfest JM, Burns MW, Mitchell ME: The Mitrofanoff principle in urinary reconstruction, *J Urol* 150:1875-1878, 1993.

138. Stellman GR, Gilmore M, Bannister CM: A survey of the problems of bowel manage-

ment experienced by families of spina bifida children, *Z Kinderchir* 38(Suppl II):96-97, 1983.

139. Leibold S: Achieving and maintaining body systems integrity and function: personal care skills. In *Preventing secondary conditions associated with spina bifida or cerebral palsy: proceedings and recommendations of a symposium,* Washington, DC, 1994, Spina Bifida Association of America, pp 78-86.

140. Agnarsson U, Warde C, McCarthy G, Clayden GS, Evans N: Anorectal function of children with neurological problems, *Dev Med Child Neurol* 35:893-902, 1993.

141. Smith KA: Bowel and bladder management of the child with myelomeningocele in the school setting, *J Pediatr Health Care* 4:175-180, 1990.

142. Smith KA: Myelomeningocele: managing bowel and bladder dysfunction in the school-aged child, *Progressions* 3(2):3-11, 1991.

143. Lozes MH: Bladder and bowel management for children with myelomeningocele, *Inf Young Child* 1(1):52-62, 1988.

144. Leibold S: A systematic approach to bowel continence for children with spina bifida, *Eur J Pediatr Surg* 1(Suppl I):23-24, 1991.

145. Willis RA: Faecal incontinence—Willis home bowel washout programme, *Z Kinderchir* 44(Suppl I):46-47, 1989.

146. Walker J, Webster P: Successful management of faecal incontinence using the enema continence catheter, *Z Kinderchir* 44(Suppl I):44-45, 1989.

147. Pompino A, Pompino HJ, Waidmann B: Simple help for spina bifida children with anal incontinence, *Z Kinderchir* 42(Suppl 1):43-45, 1987.

148. Loening-Baucke V, Desch L, Wolraich M: Biofeedback training for patients with myelomeningocele and fecal incontinence, *Dev Med Child Neurol* 30:781-790, 1988.

149. Pappo I, Meyer S, Winter S, Nissan S: Treatment of faecal incontinence in children with spina bifida by biofeedback and behavioural modification, *Z Kinderchir* 43(Suppl II):36-37, 1988.

150. Squire R, Kiely EM, Carr B, Ransley PG, Duffy PG: The clinical application of the Malone antegrade colonic enema, *J Pediatr Surg* 28(8):1012-1015, 1993.

151. Koyle MA, Kaji DM, Duque M, Wild J, Galansky SH: The Malone antegrade continence enema for neurogenic and structural fecal incontinence and constipation, *J Urol* 154:759-761, 1995.

152. Schopler SA, Menelaus MB: Significance of the strength of the quadriceps muscles in children with myelomeningocele, *J Pediatr Orthop* 7:507-512, 1987.

153. McDonald CM, Jaffe KM, Mosca VS, Shurtleff DB: Ambulatory outcome of children with myelomeningocele: effect of lower extremity muscle strength, *Dev Med Child Neurol* 33:482-490, 1991.

154. Mazur JM, Stillwell A, Menelaus MB: The significance of spacticity in the upper and lower limbs in myelomeningocele, *J Bone Joint Surg* 68B:213-217, 1986.

155. Jacobs RA, Wolfe G, Rasmuson M: Upper extremity dysfunction in children with myelomeningocele, *Z Kinderchir* 43(Suppl II):19-21, 1988.

156. Taylor A, McNamara A: Ambulation status of adults with myelomeningocele, *Z Kinderchir* 45(Suppl I):32-33, 1990.

157. Crenshaw AH: *Campbell's operative orthopaedics,* ed 8, St Louis, 1992, Mosby–Year Book, 2433-2462.

158. Mazur JM: Orthopaedic complications of myelomeningocele. In Epps CH, Bowen JR, editors: *Complications in pediatric orthopaedic surgery,* Philadelphia, 1995, Lippincott, 545-563.

159. Sherk HH, Uppal GS, Lane G, Melchionni J: Treatment versus non-treatment of hip dislocations in ambulatory patients with myelomeningocele, *Dev Med Child Neurol* 33:491-494, 1991.

160. Sherk HH, Melchionne J, Smith R: The natural history of hip dislocations in ambulatory myelomeningoceles, *Z Kinderchir* 42(Suppl I):48-49, 1987.

161. Keggi JM, Banta JV, Walton C: The myelodysplastic hip and scoliosis, *Dev Med Child Neurol* 34:240-246, 1992.

162. Williams JJ, Graham GP, Dunne KB, Menelaus MB: Late knee problems in myelomeningocele, *J Pediatr Orthop* 13:701-703, 1993.

163. Banta JV: The evolution of surgical treatment of spinal deformity in myelomeningocele, *Z Kinderchir* 42(Suppl I):10-12, 1987.

164. Koop SE: Myelomeningocele. In Bradford DS, et al, editors: *Moe's textbook of scoliosis and other spinal deformities*, ed 3, 1995, WB Saunders, pp 323-335.

165. Carstens C, Paul K, Niethard FU, Pfeil J: Effect of scoliosis surgery on pulmonary function in patients with myelomeningocele, *J Pediatr Orthop* 11:459-464, 1991.

166. Banta JV, Park SM: Improvement in pulmonary function in patients having combined anterior and posterior spine fusion for myelomeningocele scoliosis, *Spine* 8:765-770, 1983.

167. Mazur JM, Menelaus MB, Dickens DRV, Doing WG: Efficacy of surgical management for scioliosis in myelomeningocele: correction of deformity and alteration of functional status, *J Pediatr Orthop* 6:568-575, 1986.

168. Ward WT, Wenger DE, Roach JW: Surgical correction of myelomeningocele: a critical appraisal of various spinal instrumentation systems, *J Pediatr Orthop* 9:262-268, 1989.

169. Mintz LJ, Sarwark JF, Dias LS, Schafer MF: The natural history of congenital kyphosis in myelomeningocele: a review of 51 children, *Spine* 16:348-350, 1991.

170. McMaster MJ: The long-term results of kyphectomy and spinal stabilization in children with myelomeningocele, *Spine* 13:417-424, 1988.

171. Korhonen BJ: Fractures in myelodysplasia, *Clin Orthop* 79:145-155, 1971.

172. Kumar JS, Cowell HR, Townsend P: Physeal, metaphyseal, and diaphyseal injuries of the lower extremity in children with meningomyelocele, *J Pediatr Orthop* 4:25-27, 1984.

173. Lock TR, Aronson DD: Fractures in patients who have myelomeningocele, *J Bone Joint Surg* 71A:1153, 1989.

174. Anschuetz RH, Freehafer AA, Shaffer JW, et al: Severe fracture complications in myelodysplasia, *J Pediatr Orthop* 4:22-24, 1984.

175. Ogilvie C, Messenger P, Bowker D, Rowley I: Orthotic compensation for non-functioning hip extensors, *Z Kinderchir* 42(Suppl II):33-35, 1988.

176. Findley TW, Birkebak RR, McNally MC: Ambulation in the adolescent with myelomeningocele, *Arch Phys Med Rehab* 68:518-522, 1987.

177. Findley TW, Agre JC: Ambulation in the adolescent with spina bifida. II. Oxygen cost of mobility, *Arch Phys Med Rehab* 69:855-861, 1988.

178. Mazur JM, Sienko-Thomas S, Wright N, Cummings RJ: Swing-through vs. reciprocating gait patterns in patients with thoracic-level spina bifida, *Z Kinderchir* 45(Suppl I):23-25, 1990.

179. McCall RE, Schmidt WT: Clinical experience with the reciprocal gait orthosis in myelodysplasia, *J Pediatr Orthop* 6:157-161, 1986.

180. Shepherd K, Roberts D, Golding S, Thomas BJ, Shepherd RW: Body composition in myelomeningocele, *Am J Clin Nutr* 53:1-6, 1991.

181. Mita K, Akataki K, Iroh K, Ono Y, Ishida N, Oki T: Assessment of obesity of children with spina bifida, *Dev Med Child Neurol* 35:305-311, 1993.

182. Jacobs RA, Blyler E, Baer MT: Nutrition risk factors in children with myelomeningocele, *Eur J Pediatr Surg* 1(Suppl I):22, 1991.

183. Baer MT, Harris AB, Jacobs RA: Comparison of nutritional risk factors in infants/toddlers (0-3) and school-aged (6-12) children with myelomeningocele to a normal paediatric outpatient population, *Eur J Pediatr Surg* 3(Suppl I):37, 1993.

184. Kalen V, Harding CR: Skeletal maturity in myelodysplasia, *Dev Med Child Neurol* 36:528-532, 1994.

185. Duval-Beaupere G, Kaci M, Lougovoy J, Caponi MF, Touzeau C: Growth of trunk and legs of children with myelomeningocele, *Dev Med Child Neurol* 29:225-231, 1987.

186. Elias ER, Sadeghi-Nejad A: Precocious puberty in girls with myelodysplasia, *Pediatrics* 93:521-522, 1994.

187. Furman L, Mortimer JC: Menarche and menstrual function in patients with myelomeningocele, *Dev Med Child Neurol* 36:910-917, 1994.

188. Raddish M, Goldmann DA, Kaplan LC, Perrin JM: The immunization status of children with spina bifida, *AJDC* 147:849-853, 1993.

189. Tew B, Evans R, Thomas M, Ford J: The results of a selective surgical policy on the cognitive abilities of children with spina bifida, *Dev Med Child Neurol* 27:606-614, 1985.

190. Hunt GM, Poulton A: Open spina bifida: a complete cohort reviewed 25 years after closure, *Dev Med Child Neurol* 37:19-29, 1995.

191. Friedrich WN, Lovejoy MC, Shaffer J, Shurtleff DB, Beilke RL: Cognitive abilities and achievement status of children with myelomeningocele: a contemporary sample, *J Pediatr Psychol* 16(4):421-428, 1991.

192. Wills KE, Holmbeck GN, Dillon K, McLone DG: Intelligence and achievement in children with myelomeningocele, *J Pediatr Psychol* 15(2):161-176, 1990.

193. Cull C, Wyke MA: Memory function of children with spina bifida and shunted hydrocephalus, *Dev Med Child Neurol* 26:177-183, 1984.

194. Morrow JD, Wachs TD: Infants with myelomeningocele: visual recognition memory and sensorimotor abilities, *Dev Med Child Neurol* 34:488-498, 1992.

195. Loomis JW, Lindsey A, Javornisky JG, Monahan JJ: Short report—measures of cognition and adaptive behavior as predictors of adjustment outcomes in young adults with spina bifida, *J Pediatr Surg* 4(Suppl I):35-40, 1994.

196. Simms B: Driver education: the needs of the learner driver with spina bifida and hydrocephalus, *Z Kinderchir* 44(Suppl I):35-37, 1989.

197. Hurley AD, Bell S: Educational and vocational outcome of adults with spina bifida in relationship to neuropsychological testing, *Eur J Pediatr Surg* 4(Suppl I):17-18, 1994.

198. McLone DG, Czyzewski D, Raimondi AJ, et al: Central nervous system infections as a limiting factor in the intelligence of children with meningomyelocele, *Pediatrics* 70:338-342, 1982.

199. Sloan SL, Leibold SR, Henry-Atkinson J, editors: *Sexuality and the person with spina bifida*, Washington, DC, 1994, Spina Bifida Association of America, pp 1-25.

200. Blackburn M, Bax MCO, Strehlow CD: Short report—sexuality and disability, *Eur J Pediatr Surg* 1(Suppl I):37, 1991.

201. Sandler AD, Worley G, Leroy EC, Stanley SD, Kalman S: Sexual knowledge and experience among young men with spina bifida, *Eur J Pediatr Surg* 4(Suppl I):36-37, 1994.

202. Cromer BA, Enrile B, McCoy K, Gerhardstein MJ, Fitzpatrick M, Judis J: Knowledge, attitudes, and behavior related to sexuality in adolescents with chronic disability, *Dev Med Child Neurol* 32:602-610, 1990.

203. Okamoto GA, Lamers JV, Shurtleff DB: Skin breakdown in patients with myelomeningocele, *Arch Phys Med Rehab* 64:20-23, 1983.

204. Drummond D, Breed AL, Narechania R: Relationship of spine deformity and pelvic obliquity on sitting pressure distributions and decubitus ulceration, *J Pediatr Orthop* 5:396-402, 1985.

205. Brinker MR, Rosenfeld SR, Feiwell E, Granger SP, Mitchell DC, Rice JC: Myelomeningocele at the sacral level: long-term outcomes in adults, *J Bone Joint Surg* 76(9):1293-1300, 1994.

206. Harris MB, Banta JV: Cost of skin care in the myelomeningocele population, *J Pediatr Orthop* 10:355-361, 1990.

207. Dibbell DG, McCraw JB, Edstrom LE: Providing useful and protective sensibility to

the sitting area in patients with myelomeningocele, *Plast Reconstr Surg* 64:796-799, 1979.

208. Hatch D, Sumner E, Hellmann J: *The surgical neonate: anaesthesia and intensive care*, Boston, 1995, Little, Brown.

209. Costello S, Hellmann J, Lui K: Myelomeningocele: a risk factor for necrotizing enterocolitis in term infants, *J Pediatr* 113:1041-1044, 1988.

210. Karol LA, Richards BS, Prejean E, Safavi F: Hemodynamic instability of myelomeningocele patients during anterior spinal surgery, *Dev Med Child Neurol* 35:258-274, 1993.

211. Hamid RKA: Latex allergy and the anesthesiologist, *Semin Anesth* 12(3):187-191, 1993.

212. Wells TR, Jacobs RA, Senac MO, Landing BH: Incidence of short trachea in patients with myelomeningocele, *Pediatr Neurol* 6:109-111, 1990.

213. Anderson TE, Drummond DS, Breed AL, Taylor CA: Malignant hyperthermia in myelomeningocele: a previously unreported association, *J Pediatr Orthop* 1(4):401-403, 1981.

214. Banta JV, Bonanni C, Prebluda J: Latex anaphylaxis during spinal surgery in chilldren with myelomeningocele, *Dev Med Child Neurol* 35:540-548, 1993.

215. Slater JE, Mostello LA, Shaer C: Rubber specific IgE in children with spina bifida, *J Urol* 146:578-579, 1991.

216. Emans JB: Allergy to latex in patients who have myelodysplasia, *J Bone Joint Surg* 74(A):1103-1109, 1992.

217. Slater JE: Rubber anaphylaxis, *N Engl J Med* 320:1126-1130, 1989.

218. Kwittken PL, Sweinberg SK, Campbell DE, Pawlowski NA: Latex hypersensitivity in children: clinical presentation and detection of latex-specific immunoglobulin E, *Pediatrics* 95:693-699, 1995.

219. McLaughlin JF, Shurtleff DB, Lamers JY, Stunts JT, Hayden PW, Kropp RJ: Influence of prognosis on decisions retarding the care of newborns with spina bifida cystica, *N Eng J Med* 312:1589-1594, 1985.

220. Hunt GM: A study of deaths and handicap in a consecutive series of spina bifida treated unselectively from birth, *Z Kinderchir* 38(Suppl II):100-102, 1983.

CHAPTER 8

Disorders of speech and language development

JAMES C. HARDY
J. BRUCE TOMBLIN

Acquisition of speech and language skills, and thus the ability to communicate orally, comes so naturally to most children that the development of this miraculous, uniquely human behavior is usually taken for granted. However, it has long been recognized that disorders of speech and language development are the most prevalent of handicapping conditions that affect school-aged children.[1] These conditions are heterogeneous with respect to their characteristics, causes, and preferred methods of management. The social and educational development of children who have speech and language disorders may suffer significantly, even in those cases in which the problem appears to be relatively mild. Consequently, early recognition and management should be of high priority to offset such undesirable, and many times preventable, effects on the children who have these problems.

DEFINITION

To meaningfully review the heterogeneous array of problems referred to by the term *disorders of speech and language development,* one must make a distinction between speech disorders and language disorders.[2] The common result of these disorders is that the child will have difficulty, compared with his or her peers, in communicating orally. Also, as will be discussed in regard to some of the disorders, the term "development" should not lead to the assumption that the child will, in time, develop normal oral communication ability. That is particularly the case if the child is not provided timely and appropriate management. Furthermore, depending on the cause and characteristics of the disorder, and even with appropriate management, achievement of normal oral communication ability may not be possible.

The phenomenon referred to as speech is the production of an acoustic signal. It results from an exceedingly complex physiological interaction of the musculatures of the respiratory, laryngeal, and oral structures. Moreover, the signal is made up of a series of sound patterns that are also exceedingly complex. These patterns of sound are grouped in ways to form acoustic symbols that convey meaning, according to the rules of the listener's language. These symbols must conform to the "language code," or there will be a breakdown in the speaker's ability to convey meaning.

The characteristics of the speech signal may vary dramatically and still be accepted as "normal speech" by a listener. The acoustics of children's speech differ from those of adults, and the speech signals of males and females typically differ with respect to vocal pitch. Also, each speaker tends to have a unique pattern of vocal pitch, intonation of his or her speech pattern, quality of the sound of the voice, and so on.

Even though there are differences in the characteristics of the speech signal of each speaker, the signal also contains distinctive patterns of sound production that form symbols of the language code. To the extent that these symbols correspond to the listener's language code, they can be decoded by the listener as meaningful oral communication.

The speech of individuals may be pleasant or unpleasant to the listener. For example, the resonance of a speaker's voice may be unpleasant. Or an individual's speech may be so distinctive that he or she sounds "different." When these differences are severe enough that they detract the listener from interacting appropriately with the speaker, it is likely that the speaker should be designated as having a speech disorder. A hoarse-sounding voice caused by a pathological condition of the vocal folds is an example. Another example is an interruption of the fluency of speech, in which case the speaker may be said to "stutter." Also, of course, if the speaker has difficulty in producing the appropriate signals to form the symbols of the language code, a speech disorder exists. A child with cerebral palsy who has reduced function of the oral structures and therefore cannot accurately produce speech sounds is an example.

The study of language has resulted in identification of a number of its dimensions. Phonology (the order in which speech sounds form the language symbols, or words), the lexicon (the meaningful words, or vocabulary, available to the speaker), semantics (the meaning of messages), and syntax (the order of words) are examples. Pragmatics of language refers to meanings of messages in various contexts. Children who have a reduced vocabulary available for communicating relative to their peers, those who have difficulty generating complete and meaningful messages, and/or those who do not appreciate the subtleties of language, which alter meaning in different social contexts, exemplify those who may be said to have a language disorder.

SPEECH AND LANGUAGE DEVELOPMENT

Children develop both speech and language skills through learning. The skills for producing the various acoustic patterns of speech begin to develop in infancy and continue through the seventh or eighth year. By that age, the distinctive characteristics of the signal that is used to form the symbols of language conform to those of adults, and selected deviations in the developmental process until then may be considered normal. However, children's speech signals will not correspond exactly to those of adults until adolescence, when the laryngeal structures complete their growth, a process that results in a lower pitch of the vocal tone. That change is a well-known developmental process in males, but a similar, more subtle, change occurs in females.

There is no doubt that development of knowledge of language also begins in infancy, when children begin to acquire language skills as they learn to produce speech. Their knowledge increases extremely rapidly through the first few years of life, and this learning process, in a real sense, can continue throughout a person's life.

Production of the speech signal involves intricate and complex physiological processes. Children must learn to produce an ongoing pattern of synchronous muscle activity with their respiratory, laryngeal, and oral mechanisms. This activity must result in sequences of acoustic events that take place within fractions of seconds and that are linked into a continuous signal. For an example, the production of the consonant "b" in a rather simple word such as "book" will take place in a half-second, or less. The production requires at least the following sequence: (1) the respiratory system begins generating an expiratory airstream of a rather specific force, (2) the vocal folds close in the midline, (3) the palatal port closes to keep the speech-producing airstream trapped in the oral cavity, (4) the lips close as the tongue begins to move into a posture necessary for producing the vowel of the word, (5) the muscles of the pharynx and oral cavity make adjustments to permit the airflow through the vocal folds, even though the vocal tract is occluded by the closed lips, (6) the airflow sets the vocal folds into vibration, creating a vocal tone, and (7) that vibration is followed almost immediately by the lips' opening. The result is an acoustic event that combines the plosive noise associated with the release of the airstream, in combination with the voiced vocal tone, through the lips. Even before the production of that "voiced plosive" and as indicated in (3) above, the vocal tract is moving into the postures necessary to form the resonance cavities needed for generation of the word's vowel.

For other classes of speech sounds, the vocal folds are open, so that the sound is generated primarily by the airstream's interacting with the oral structures but without the vocal folds vibrating. The production of "p," a "voiceless plosive," is an example. It is generated similarly to "b" but with the vocal folds open as the lips trap the airstream and then open with the released intraoral air pressure, creating the plosive sound. For other classes of sounds, the airstream acts on an oral structure to create a noise, either in conjunction with, or without, the vocal folds vibrating. For three sounds, "m," "n," and "ng" (as in "ring"), the palatal port opens to acoustically couple the nasal and oral cavities for those "nasal" sounds. For vowels, the vocal tract is open and the tongue is positioned to create resonance chambers of certain relative sizes in the vocal tract, and the different vowels are distinguished by the harmonics of the vocal tone, which are selectively amplified by these chambers.

The normal speech signal contains more attributes that contribute to communication than just speech sounds strung together to form words and sentences. An adequate speech signal also contains stress and intonation patterns, which include changes in emphasis of syllables and/or words. These "complex attributes" result from rapid variations in the pitch and intensity of the signal and the timing with which the units of speech are produced. These changes also, of course, result from rapid and intricate changes in muscle activity throughout the vocal tract.

Children learn to produce the speech signal by listening to the speech of others. Infants are ordinarily capable, very early, of making the perceptual differentiations that permit them to distinguish among certain classes of speech sounds. Therefore they are capable of at least roughly comparing the output of their vocal tracts with the speech signals of others. That comparison leads to their modifying what seems to be random sound making (babbling) into sequenced sounds that will become meaningful acoustic patterns. This process of comparing the speech of those in their environment with the output of their own vocal tract and making modifications until their output acceptably matches the speech of others is expedited by the maturation of their neuromotor systems and the natural rewards that they receive from producing an adequate speech signal.

Children ordinarily begin achieving a knowledge of their language as they learn to produce speech. Although a baby's utterance of a "first word" may be in imitation to an adult model (e.g., "dada") and have no intrinsic meaning to the infant, the formation of phonological rules is being learned. In the case of "dada," the rule is that voiced-plosive consonants may be linked to precede vowels in spoken English.

From such early imitations, the child begins producing an increasing number of single syllables that match meaningful words in his or her language environment. The use of a first word that is meaningful is considered a developmental milestone that, on average, takes place at around 13 months.[3] However, there is great variability of the age at which children develop use of their first meaningful words and other milestones of language acquisition (e.g., first two-word combinations). Specifying the ages of such developmental milestones are confounded by such factors as whether the child is using a word form to mean what a mature language user means, whether the word form is used in only a naming activity, and whether the word form has social meaning. For an example, a child may say "bow-wow" after seeing a picture of a dog but also do so on seeing pictures of other four-legged animals. For another example, appropriate use of "bye-bye" certainly represents a more sophisticated language knowledge than naming pictures of animals.

In the early stages of language learning, the child faces the task of beginning to categorize classes of objects, events, patterns of interaction, and concepts in forming the oral language code. Words spoken in the child's environment must be perceived and associated with what is taking place. Learning to produce word forms depends on development of perceptual systems that enable the child to differentiate characteristics of the speech signal and what the word forms represent, as well as using a speech-producing mechanism that is incomplete in the development of its control.

As the child progresses in his or her use of single meaningful words, the lexicon, or vocabulary, of the language is being learned, and, as exemplified previously, the phonological rules are being acquired. That is, the child is developing the ability to produce more speech sounds and link them appropriately, according to the phonological rules of the language code. Also, the component of phonology that was described as intonation and stress patterns, which may modify meaning of messages, is being learned (e.g., "no" produced at a high intensity carries a stronger message).

When the child enters into the stage of development of linking word forms together, the learning of appropriate ordering of words, or syntax of the language, begins. Words in phrases and sentences are related in certain specified ways that permit a listener to decode a message, and deviations from syntactic rules may lead to misunderstanding. In addition, insertions of certain elements that cannot stand independently in a language may be used to modify the message. Adding an "s" sound to many nouns will change their meaning from singular to plural, and, for more advanced language usage, adding "ed" to verbs indicates something having happened in the past. These uses of sound elements that are not otherwise meaningful units are components of the morphology of the language, and morphological rules must be learned.

The specific meanings of word forms may be altered by the phrases and contexts in which they are used. These alterations also follow certain rules that make up the semantics of the language code. Therefore the content or meaning of a message may differ significantly and be more abstract than the specific definitions of the words (the lexicon) that it contains. Moreover, the semantics of language may be dictated by the societal environment. The dimension of language that varies meanings, according to an accepted use of certain strings of word forms by a community or society of speakers, is referred to as the pragmatics of the language.

Although some of these known rules of language have yet to be shown to have clinical utility in analysis and treatment of language disorders in children, it is clear that competent speakers must adhere to them. As will be discussed later, however, analysis of a child's use of some of the rules has now been demonstrated to be useful in identifying the specific nature of selected developmental language disorders.

This brief review of the processes of speech and language development should provide a basis for recognition of a number of the factors that may contribute to developmental disorders of oral communication. For example, the development of speech depends on the ability of the child to hear the speech of others, a well-functioning neuromotor system, and anatomical and physiological integrity of the respiratory, laryngeal, and oral structures. Moreover, the strategies that the child employs to learn speech must be appropriate for acquiring normal production of the speech signal and for learning the language code that is appropriate for the environment.

For optimal learning of both speech and language, the child's environment, therefore, should be conducive to learning. As will be reviewed in later discussions, the variables that have an impact on language acquisition are a combination of sociological, experiential, and cognitive factors that influence the acquisition of the language code.

DEVELOPMENTAL SPEECH DISORDERS

Disorders of speech are mostly classified on the basis of the characteristics of speech signal that are abnormal. In some instances, however, the terms by which the disorder is designated refer to the cause of the problem.

Articulation disorders

The process by which the speech signal is formed by the movements of the oral structures is referred to as speech articulation. Inability to produce the sounds that make up that signal can be said to be an articulation disorder. These disorders can be the result of a child's having a hearing impairment, a neuromotor disorder that interferes with movement of the oral structures, or an anomaly of an orofacial structure, such as a cleft palate. However, there are children who have difficulty in developing the ability to produce speech sounds accurately or according to the usual developmental sequence for no identifiable reason.

Functional articulation disorders. The term *functional articulation problem* is usually used in reference to that group of children who do not develop speech articulation skills in the manner of their chronological peers for no apparent reason. This group makes up the largest of the types of developmental speech disorders. The use of "functional" in reference to this group came very early in the study of speech disorders to convey that these children have no identifiable psychological or physiological basis for their difficulty in learning to produce speech.

The ability to produce the numerous sounds of spoken English follows a developmental sequence that is variable but, nonetheless, somewhat predictable.[4,5] Infants usually come to generate a number of identifiable vowel sounds. Production of consonants for which the primary articulatory gesture is made by the lips (e.g., "p" and "b") usually precedes the ability to use consonants for which the articulatory gestures are physiologically more complicated (e.g., grooving the tongue through which a jet of air is forced to produce "s"). The difficulty in perceptually detecting the difference among sounds is also likely to be a variable. For example, it is more difficult to perceive the difference between an "f" and "th" than between "p" and "b." Numerous four-year-old children can be heard to substitute the "f" for "th" and, thus, say "fumb" for "thumb." Such children would be considered slow in their development of articulation skills if they used that substitution at 7 to 8 years of age, when acquisition of all speech sounds should be complete.

Some children may show a misarticulation pattern that suggests that they are delayed in their progressing along the continuum of speech sound development. In other cases, there is an actual mislearning of the production of selected sounds. Detailed analysis of the speech patterns of still other children will show problems in learning the phonological rules of the language. Most children use intelligible speech by the age of 4 years. Children with articulation disorders may be exceedingly difficult to understand at much later ages.

As implied by the term "functional," these articulation disorders frequently have no identifiable cause. There is no predictable relationship between level of learning ability and these disorders for children who are in the normal or above-normal ranges of measured intelligence. A larger percentage of these problems are found in children from families of low socioeconomic status, but that variable is nonpredictive. It has been suggested that chronic middle ear infections in infancy and early childhood may contribute to these disorders. It has been shown that some children with functional articulation disorders tend to have difficulty in auditorily discriminating among speech sounds, even though they have normal hearing acuity (see the later discussion of central auditory processing disorders), but this problem may not be routinely identifiable clinically.

Once it is determined that a child's articulatory pattern is delayed or deviant, the assessment process should eliminate a variety of possible contributing factors that are discussed below. These functional articulation disorders of unknown cause in young children are often diagnosed through a process of eliminating the contributing, or etiological, factors. Although that is an unsatisfactory state of affairs, after years of research with this group of speech disorders, it remains the most efficacious approach to differential diagnosis.

In addition to the lack of identifiable etiological factors, one of the better diagnostic indicators of the presence of a functional articulation disorder is likely to be the child's response to a management program. There are highly effective speech learning paradigms that are used with even very young children who have articulation disorders. These paradigms are usually designed to be indirect with preschool children, and they are progressively more direct with older children. If a child's articulation disorder is indeed due primarily to simple mislearning of speech sound production, such management paradigms usually bring these children to a level of speech production competence relatively quickly, and the detrimental social and educational effects of their articulation disorders may be offset.

Developmental disorders of articulation due to known causes. One group of children who manifest developmental disorders of articulation are those with bilateral, high-frequency hearing losses. These children may respond to sound in ways that seem appropriate, but they lack the ability to make precise auditory discriminations among the high-frequency components of the speech signal. Therefore any child who is having difficulty developing articulation skills should have a hearing test that determines his or her threshold throughout the frequency range. That is, gross tests of audition will not suffice to identify these children.

Once it is determined that a child has a bilateral, high-frequency hearing loss, a hearing aid may be indicated that will help the child monitor and improve his or her speech production. A paradigm that teaches these children to learn and monitor their deviant speech sounds by other than auditory cues (e.g., tactile) may also assist them. Furthermore, other management may be indicated, as discussed in Chapter 11, which deals with hearing impairments.

Although the adequacy of the anatomical relationships of the oral structures should be assessed in any child who has an articulation disorder, caution should be used in assuming that minor deviations in these relationships contribute to the disorder. Such deviations usually do not contribute to a speech production learning problem. To the extent that they do, the patterns of misarticulation will likely correspond to those speech sounds for which the deviant structures are involved. In cases in which anatomical deviations of the oral structures do result in an articulation disorder, it may be possible to teach the child to use compensatory movements of the speech mechanism to improve his or her speech.

One frequently overlooked anatomical deviation and/or physiological dysfunction of the oral structures that results in an articulation disorder is deviation of the velopharyngeal port. The effect on the resonance of speech of a child's port not closing appropriately during speech production is reviewed following in the discussion of such disorders; perception that a child's speech is hypernasal may be assumed to be the primary effect of an open port during speech. However, such dysfunction may also cause the child to have difficulty in generating the needed intraoral air pressure that interacts with the oral structures to generate numerous consonant sounds. That is so because, rather than the air pressure being impounded in the oral cavity, the air flows through the path of least resistance, namely the open velopharyngeal port, and out through the nose. Consequently, the child will have significant problems learning to produce those sounds which require the impounding of intraoral air pressure.

Problems of anatomically short, malformed, and absent soft palates are discussed later in the review of problems of clefts of the palate. However, there are children who manifest dysfunctioning velopharyngeal ports at a young age for whom no anatomical nor neurological basis for the problem can be found. These children will not likely respond to the paradigms of speech learning that assist children with functional articulation disorders, and methods of surgical or prosthetic management discussed in the review of problems associated with clefts of the palate should be pursued.

Children with developmental neuromotor problems (e.g., cerebral palsy, which is discussed in Chapter 7A) frequently have articulation disorders. However, children with developmental dysarthria (a disorder that is reviewed briefly later in this chapter) usually manifest other deviations of speech development, in addition to problems with speech articulation. Also, they typically have problems of motor function, in addition to dysfunction of the speech musculature.

There are very infrequent cases in which there is only neuromotor dysfunction of the speech-producing musculature. Indeed, the impairment of the musculature may be relatively mild, and the child with neuromotor disorder may not be diagnosed until his or her speech disorder comes to the attention of professionals. One relatively firm indicator of these infrequently seen cases is that development of aspects of the speech signal other than articulation will be affected; the reduction of function of the speech-producing musculature will also hinder the flexibility of the vocal tract needed for intonation and stress patterns. Management of these types of problems is described briefly in the later discussion of developmental dysarthria.

Developmental apraxia of speech. In the early study of developmental disorders of oral communication, there was a tendency to assume that many of these disorders of both speech and language result from vague, ill-defined prenatal damage to the child's brain.[6] As mentioned in the later discussion of developmental language disorders, this assumption is no longer tenable as a generally applicable explanation for specific language impairments in children.

There has been identified, however, a group of children with developmental speech articulation disorders who appear to have difficulty in developing controlled movements of their oral structures. Also, a number of these children manifest subtle signs of neurological dysfunction.[7] The disordered speech of these children sometimes includes a diminution of intonation and stress patterns. Velopharyngeal dysfunction has also been observed in some. However, whether such dysfunction results from the oropharyngeal mechanism having not "learned" to function for speech production or from a neuromotor dysfunction is unknown.[8]

This group of children has drawn considerable attention and study. There is lack of uniform agreement about the basis of the disorder. However, it is certain that these children are distinguished by their speech disorder's being extremely resistant to modification. Indeed, in contrast to most children with functional articulation disorders, these children require prolonged speech remediation programs over a number of years before they achieve optimal speech production skills.[9]

Voice disorders

The term *voice disorder* refers to an habitually inappropriate vocal tone. It may be used in reference to both deviations in the use of the voice (e.g., a voice that is inordinately soft or loud and/or voice usage in which the pitch is too high or too low) and conditions in which the vibratory patterns of the vocal folds are abnormal (e.g., hoarseness). The latter conditions will be manifested by a perceived aberrant quality of the vocal tone or voice.

The loudness, pitch, and quality of the voice is the result of the force by which the vocal folds are held together in the midline of the larynx, the length and tension of the folds themselves, the magnitude of the air pressure that maintains them in vibration, and the characteristics of their vibratory cycle. In general, soft phonation results from lesser degrees of tension of the vocal folds and force by which they are held together, which, in turn, requires less sublaryngeal air pressure to maintain the vibration of the folds. For louder phonation, or increased vocal intensity, the vocal folds are more tense and held together with more force against greater subglottal air pressure; these changes result in a more violent mode of vocal fold vibration. Elevations of pitch are associated with decreased vocal fold length, increased vocal fold tension, a thinning of the folds, and greater subglottal air pressures; the result is more rapid vibration of the folds.

The quality of the voice, or phonatory signal, depends on the characteristics of the vibratory cycle of the vocal folds. These cycles set the molecules of air above the level of the larynx in the vocal tract into vibration. The shape of the vocal tract selectively amplifies the harmonics of the resulting tone from the larynx, and the result is what is perceived as the vocal tone.

Normal speech production requires constant adjustments of laryngeal muscles, which, with their complex cartilaginous attachments, are capable of very rapid adjustments that can change the position, stiffness, and length of the vocal folds. The phenomenon of vocal stress, mentioned earlier, results from such rapid adjustments. A speaker can form a question with the statement, "John is going uptown?" by elevating the pitch of the last two syllables and increasing their intensity and duration. When pitch, loudness, and/or duration changes are used as a differentiating characteristic to convey meaning, the change in vocal pitch can be as much as an octave of the musical scale. The intonation patterns and stress characteristics of normal discourse require continuous, rapid alterations of laryngeal function and control of the airstream.

Children sometimes use their voices abnormally, which is frequently attributed to personality characteristics. Use of an habitually weak voice in children may be said to result from shyness. Such uses of the voice may not deserve clinical attention. However, there are characteristics in children's use of their voices that may be clinically significant.

Habitually loud voice use and/or certain patterns of voice onset may lead to vocal abuse, which will be discussed later. In rare instances, habitual abnormal vocal intensity and instances in which the child is dysphonic (routinely whispers) may indicate a serious psychological or psychiatric disorder. There are also rare cases in which children's vocal pitch is perceived as being too high. If working with the child indicates an inability to modify that usage, an abnormally small larynx may be present. This problem will become most evident in males if lowering of the vocal pitch does not occur in association with puberty, when normally the vocal folds become longer. In such cases, growth and/or endocrinological disorders should be investigated, if the family history indicates that an abnormally high-pitched voice is not a family characteristic. The quality of the vocal tone is a sensitive indicator of disruption of the normal phonatory cycle. Therefore any chronic abnormal-sounding vocal tone may indicate a clinically significant problem.

The laryngeal mechanism is relatively delicate, and its tissues are subject to pathological changes if the interaction between the muscle activity and vibratory-producing airstream is inappropriate. A usual view is that each laryngeal mechanism has its particular range of vocal pitch at which it can function most efficiently, with minimal stress on its tissues. Most speakers come to adopt a pitch range for conversational speech that is within that efficient range. For increased loudness, the appropriate changes in the sublaryngeal air pressure, in combination with the needed laryngeal muscle adjustments, are critical to avoid abuse of the tissues. An opera singer represents an example of a voice that has been trained so that the vocal mechanism repeatedly generates vocal tones at extreme ranges of pitch and loudness without stressing the laryngeal tissues.

A number of childhood voice disorders result from stress on the laryngeal tissues, or what may be called vocal abuse. A child may adopt a style of voice use that stresses the tissues to the point that some pathological condition results. As indicated previously, habitual loud voice usage and frequent shouting may lead to such problems. The young boy who attempts to habitually use a low-pitched voice in imitation of adult males is another example. The pattern of contraindicated vocal behavior may be as subtle as habitual abrupt, coughlike initiations of phonation, which may be referred to as a glottal initiation of phonation.

Vocal abuse may initially result in only a chronic edema and inflammation of the vocal folds, producing a hoarse voice, as can result from laryngitis. Or the pathological condition may result in polyps. These conditions may develop gradually, or, with the undesirable style of voice usage having been established, they may become manifest after an episode of extreme voice usage and/or infection of the laryngeal tissues. Extreme vocal abuse during episodes of even very mild laryngitis by a speaker with otherwise good vocal habits may result in a persistent problem that requires management.

Even slight edema, very small growths, or subtle changes in the tissues of the larynx are likely to alter the vibratory characteristics of the vocal folds. Such alterations result in changes in the vocal tone that may be perceived as breathy, husky, or hoarse. Any child who experiences such changes may have a vocal pathological condition that may or may not be associated with vocal abuse. Vocal nodes, viral-induced polyps, and laryngeal tumors are potential causes of these voice disorders. Whether the vocal abuse can be identified, a change to an abnormal voice quality that persists for even a few weeks, when no upper respiratory tract infection is present, is an indication for a referral to an otolaryngologist.

Subsequent to any indicated medical treatment, it may be desirable to have the child's voice usage evaluated by a speech-language pathologist who has experience with voice disorders. If abusive patterns are present, therapy may be required to eliminate those patterns. Otherwise the pathological condition may return.

Fluency and stuttering disorders

A number of conditions may result in an interruption of the ongoing flow of the speech signal, with the result that the speaker can be said to be dysfluent. Neuromotor involvement of the speech mechanism may cause a child to prolong the vowels of utterances and to pause inappropriately within phrases. Sequelae of brain damage may include a halting speech pattern and/or rapid repetitions of units of speech. The rhythm and flow of speech of some persons with psychiatric disorders may be severely disrupted. In some children who are diagnosed as autistic, the dysfluency of their speech attempts is one component that contributes to their communication disorder.

The most frequently seen problem of speech fluency in children, however, is "stuttering." This fluency disorder may be manifested by the speaker's interjecting inappropriate sounds into the speech signal, repeating syllables, prolonging syllables, and/or pausing inappropriately before initiating an utterance or during an utterance. In addition, the disorder may include a variety of inappropriate facial gestures (e.g., pursing the lips in an exaggerated fashion) and other mannerisms that are distracting to the listener. Most important, routine problems of self-evaluation and self-esteem by children who stutter frequently have a negative effect on their adjustment in our highly verbal society. The reactions of others to those who stutter and the social stigma associated with the disorder exacerbate these internalized reactions to the problem.

The problem of stuttering has been recognized for centuries. Currently, estimates of incidence usually indicate that 1% of children have this disorder. Because of this incidence and its known dehabilitating effects, the phenomenon of stuttering has drawn significant attention from researchers and clinicians in a number of professions for decades. This attention has led to differing theories of causation and regimens of management based on these theories. These include the theory that people who stutter lack the development of dominance of their cerebral hemispheres to control the speech-producing mechanism. Another belief is that some underlying personality problem leads to the disorder. One of the current emphases is on the concept that the disorder results from a breakdown in motor control of the speech mechanism, without the inference that cerebral dominance is a factor.[10] However, there has been no conclusive evidence that persons designated as stutterers differ from those who are not, with respect to anatomy, physiology, and/or personality characteristics, but there is a large body of evidence, some of which is long standing, that stuttering is a learned behavior.[11,12]

It is important to recognize that there is a significant difference between dysfluencies in speech and stuttering. Some speakers who are considered to have no problem are dysfluent to a distracting degree. Numerous speakers who speak in public as a part of their occupation may pause, seem to search for words, repeat words, and/or interject sounds into their flow of speech. Yet, these dysfluent speakers may neither consider themselves, nor are they considered by others, to stutter. Conversely, there are speakers who, by all standards, speak quite fluently but who consider themselves to be "stutterers." Therefore an element of the stuttering problem is the attitude of the speaker about his or her speaking ability.

Most children are noticeably dysfluent from 3 to 5 years of age. This behavior is believed to result from the child's attempts to participate orally in the environment without yet having the speech and language skills to do so. The dysfluencies are likely to increase in circumstances in which children are uncertain of the language forms to express themselves, are competing with others to communicate, and are communicating in a context of interpersonal conflict. As mentioned previously, approximately 1% of these children will at some time be designated as stutters.

A large proportion of these designated children will retain their highly dysfluent speech behavior into later years, and many will develop a number of the previously-described mannerisms in association with speaking, which suggests that they are having difficulty talking. Most will develop a strong negative attitude about their ability to speak and will anticipate that they are going to have difficulty speaking in specific situations (e.g., talking to selected adults). However, in other situations (e.g., talking to their pet), they will not anticipate problems in speaking, and their speech will be fluent. One of the more consistent behaviors of persons who stutter is that their speech will be fluent in circumstances in which their responsibility for communicating is diminished (e.g., reading aloud in unison with another speaker). Typically, even persons who stutter very severely will be able to speak quite fluently in certain circumstances. Therefore the very puzzling aspects of the disorder's characteristics makes the adjustment to it even more difficult.

One of the more satisfactory explanations of the disorder includes the concept that if a young child's normal dysfluent speech is identified as stuttering and adults begin reacting to the behavior, the problem exists. Such reactions may be subtle or overt, such as instructing the child to modify his or her speaking behavior. These reactions set in motion a sequence of events in which the children, through uncertainty about their speaking behavior, make attempts to change their manner of speaking. These changes (e.g., breath holding) frequently further disrupt fluency. As these children increasingly believe that they have a speaking problem, they continue the vicious circle of incorporating more counterproductive mannerisms into the speaking behavior, and they may adopt the belief that these mannerisms assist them in speaking.

When there is intervention before the child's self-evaluations begin to crystalize, the outcome can be very satisfactory. Parents may be able to grasp intellectually an explanation of the problem from a professional (e.g., their pediatrician), and they may recognize the need for modifying their reactions—and those of others—to the child's speaking behavior. Nevertheless, the parents' level of concern may require they receive supportive counseling and being referred to a speech-language pathologist for that counseling may be indicated. It may be necessary to involve other family members whose reactions are aggravating the problem. Also, some aspects of the child's life may need to be modified to reduce the stress related to his or her communicating. These steps may result in resolution of the problem.

When intervention begins later in a child's life, the speech-language pathologist may need to involve the child's teachers and other adult associates in the program. At some stage, direct work with the child may be indicated, depending on the child's age and the particular facets of that child's situation. For older children, assisting them directly in dealing with their reactions to the communicative process is usually indicated.

Outcomes of management range from resolution of the problem in young children (before it takes the form of the adult problem) to reduced dysfluency and, it is hoped, better adjustment on the part of the child or adult to the problem. As mentioned earlier, some fluent speakers believe that they continue to have the disorder. On the other hand, a number of older children and young adults overcome their problem, with or without professional help, to the degree that they believe that they no longer have a disorder.

There are a few programs that "guarantee" resolution of the problem. These programs should be thoroughly investigated before referrals are made to them.

Disorders of nasal resonance

Normally spoken English contains a component of nasal resonance that results from acoustic coupling of the nasal cavity to that of the oral tract. Through even a very small opening of the velopharyngeal port during speech, the air in the nasal cavity is set into vibration and mingled with the resonance in the oral cavity. This additional resonance is usually most prominent in association with the nasal consonants mentioned earlier, "m," "n," and "ng," because the velopharyngeal port must be open to couple with the nasal cavity for their production. Also, as a result of the positioning of the tongue, muscular connections between the tongue and soft palate, and acoustic characteristics of the vocal tract, a small opening of the velopharyngeal port may be present and accompanied by perceived nasality during productions of some vowels by many speakers. Some regional dialects are characterized by considerable "nasality," and this learned characteristic of speech by persons in that region may be referred to as a "nasal twang."

Hyponasality. When a speaker's nasal cavity is congested, as when there is an upper respiratory tract infection or allergy, the speech may be perceived as void of nasality, or as being hyponasal. Chronic hyponasality in children suggests malformations of the nasal cavities or hypertrophy of the adenoid tissues. Hence, most cases of hyponasality in children, if they are judged to be clinically significant, can be resolved by surgery.

Hypernasality. Chronic hypernasality in children's speech can result for a number of reasons, and, even though it is the only deviation of speech that is present, if the perceived nasal quality is offensive to listeners, clinical management is indicated.

The term *functional hypernasality* may be applied to those cases in which a child has learned to produce speech with too much coupling of the nasal to the oral cavity, as a result of the velopharyngeal port's being open to an undesirable extent. Such children may be unaware that their speech sounds different from others in their environment, and their problem usually can be remedied through training by a speech-language pathologist.

However, when children do not respond to such training, dysfunction of their velopharyngeal port should be suspected. As mentioned in the earlier discussion of articulation disorders, the velopharyngeal mechanism of a few children may be dysfunctional, even though no anatomical nor physiological deviation of their oralpharyngeal mechanism can be found.[13] Significantly hypernasal speech may also be the result of an undetected anatomical malformation of that mechanism. An anatomically short soft palate may be the cause of the problem, and, as will be discussed following, malformation of the hard palate posteriorly may be present, even though the tissue of the soft palate appears to be adequate. This condition, referred to as a submucous cleft of the palate, may result in a problem of velopharyngeal port closure. Also, children with developmental neuromotor disorders may be perceived as having hypernasal speech if their motor dysfunction includes musculatures of the velopharyngeal mechanism.

Children's speech may become hypernasal after they have had an adenoidectomy, and it is usually assumed that the abnormal coupling of the nasal cavity results from the soft palate's not adapting immediately to the larger opening of the velopharyngeal port. Usually, the hypernasality of these children's speech resolves in a relatively short time as their mechanism adapts. It should be noted, however, that for a few of these children, their hypernasality remains, and the management discussed following for nonfunctional cases of hypernasality may be indicated. For any child who shows signs of borderline velopharyngeal closure problems, such as some children with neuromotor deficits, adenoidectomies may be contraindicated, unless the child's health is an issue.

As is also mentioned in the previous discussion of articulation disorders, adequate function of the velopharyngeal port is critical for speech learning. A routinely open port can result in difficulty in impounding the intraoral air pressure necessary for the production of numerous consonants. It appears that children with functional hypernasality have learned to close their velopharyngeal mechanism for production of consonants. However, if a child is having difficulty developing articulation skills in addition to sounding hypernasal, some basis for the problem other than learning must be considered.

For children whose hypernasality is other than functional, those procedures appropriate for clefts of the palate are usually indicated. The procedures include surgical and/or prosthetic management. However, as discussed following, determination of the procedure of choice should be made by an interdisciplinary team that specializes in management of these disorders.

Clefts of the lip and palate

Clefts of the lip and palate are the most frequently seen anomalies of the orofacial complex. It is estimated that some type of cleft occurs once in 600 births. Genetic factors may contribute to this problem, but it is generally agreed that there are a variety of causes that result in this group of malformations.

Onset occurs at some point through the twelfth or thirteenth week of embryonic development, and these malformations occur as three groups: (1) clefts of the lip only, (2) clefts of the palate only, and (3) clefts of both the lip and palate. The manifestation is the lack of midline fusion of the soft tissue and/or bony structures, either partial or complete. There frequently is inadequate presence of the tissues involved. Another group of smaller incidence includes those children with submucous clefts of the palate.

Any child with a dysfunctional velopharyngeal port or absence of tissue of the velopharyngeal mechanism is susceptible to chronic middle ear infections because of patency of the eustachian tubes. Of course, malformations of the dental arch are frequent among children with clefts. Some of these children may also have other malformations, such as heart defects, eye problems, extra fingers and/or toes, and other malformations of the head. This is especially true for children with relatively complete clefts of the palate.

Management of the cleft problem from birth requires a highly-specialized interdisciplinary team composed, ideally, of psychologists, social workers, speech-language pathologists, audiologists, prosthodontists, orthodontists, pediatricians, otolaryngologists, and oral and/or plastic surgeons. Such teams are usually found in tertiary medical centers.

Most of these teams' approach to the problem will include following the child at least through early childhood and, in some cases, longer. Determination of the child's intellectual ability, counselling of the family regarding the stigma of the cleft, management of frequent eating problems, and assessment of the child's hearing are needed components of the management program. Crucial, however, is the surgical intervention that must be designed according to the characteristics of the cleft and timed with known growth factors. Intraoral prosthodontic devices may be needed when surgery is contraindicated or cannot establish appropriate anatomical relationships and function.

The ability of children with clefts to develop speech production skills will, of course, depend on the results of the surgical and/or prosthodontic management and the extent to which other variables associated with speech learning exist. Generally, the primary basis of speech learning disorders in children with cleft palate is the inability to generate the intraoral air pressure needed for production of numerous consonant sounds. One of the primary goals of surgical and/or prosthetic management is to establish competence of the velopharyngeal mechanisms to offset this speech physiology deficit.

A comprehensive review of the cleft palate problem and its management is presented by Morris.[14] As a result of the increasing knowledge that has been obtained regarding cleft palate disorders, children with these conditions do not, in general, face nearly the problems existing in this population a few decades ago.

Developmental and acquired dysarthrias

The term *dysarthria* refers to any speech-production disorder that results from neuromotor dysfunction of the speech-producing musculatures. The specific characteristics of a dysarthria will depend on those musculatures which are affected, and differential degrees of involvement among these muscle groups are frequently seen. For example, the function of the velopharyngeal mechanism may, or may not, be affected.

Acquired dysarthrias in children may result from any injury to the head and/or neck that damages the cortiobulbar system, other motor pathways to the cranial nerve system, the brainstem, or the peripheral cranial nerves.

Developmental dysarthrias are the primary speech-production problems associated with cerebral palsy. Cerebral palsy very frequently includes a number of disorders that have an impact on development of communication skills (e.g., intellectual ability). However, reduction in the function of the speech-producing musculature is the most consistent basis of this group's communication disorder.

As mentioned earlier, a normal speech signal depends on activity of the respiratory musculature and rapid, intricate adjustments of the muscles of the larynx and oral structures. The effects of neuromotor dysfunction are, in general, reduction of the rate of muscular adjustment and range of movement. Consequently, it usually is unrealistic to expect that a child with dysarthria will be able to develop normal speech production. For example, a child with mild involvement throughout his or her musculature may develop speech that is usually intelligible; however, there is likely to be absence of normal rhythm, stress, and intonation patterns. It is not surprising that this characteristic—called *dysprosody*—is a usual component of dysarthria, and it should not be expected that the child will develop the rapid, intricate muscle activity underlying the subtle characteristics of speech.

The characteristics of a dysarthria may vary from a mild dysprosody to inability to produce more than gutteral, strained-sounding, vowel-like grunts. However, for that large percentage of children with dysarthria who can produce some speech, it is a grave disservice to assume that they cannot improve their oral communication.[15] It is frequently possible to teach these children to alter the manner in which they produce the speech signal to best accommodate their speech physiology deficits. For example, teaching the child to speak slowly in short phrases, with inhalations between each phrase, may bring about surprising improvement in intelligibility. First, speaking slowly permits time for the speech-producing structures to reach their target positions, and, second, frequent inhalations throughout utterances compensates for an involved respiratory system that has limited ability to produce a speech-generating airstream.

It is not surprising that the frequently found velopharyngeal port dysfunction may be the most dehabilitating of the speech physiology deficits associated with dysarthria. After all, that deficit alone results in severe speech-learning difficulties in children with only clefts of the palate. For the child with developmental dysarthria whose other speech-producing musculatures also do not function well, velopharyngeal port dysfunction is a very strong indicator of inability to improve speech. However, intraoral prostheses known as palatal lifts have been shown to be successful in resolving the velopharyngeal incompetence in many dysarthric speakers.

Through interaction with a speech-language pathologist who is experienced in working with speakers who have dysarthria, many individuals can develop speech that is usually intelligible. For those who have such severe, generalized involvement of their speech-producing musculature that achieving functional oral communication is impossible, there are now available an array of augmentative communication systems that serve as alternative means to oral communication.[16] These systems range from picture boards for young children to highly sophisticated computer-run devices that produce messages, in the form of speech, that the user programs. Therefore approaches that teach some dysarthric speakers to produce the speech signal within the limitations of their speech physiology mechanisms and augmentative communication systems for children with very severe developmental dysarthria offer the opportunity for many to become reasonably adequate communicators.

DEVELOPMENTAL LANGUAGE DISORDERS

When a clinician diagnoses a child as having a developmental language disorder, this diagnosis expresses a judgment that the child's language is insufficient for the successful accomplishment of important life functions. Thus it can be stated that developmental language disorders exist for children when such children present deficits in the acquisition of their native language to such an extent that undesirable social, educational, and occupational consequences are likely. Clinical management of language disorders is intended to minimize these undesirable consequences.

Children who are identified as having developmental language disorders will often be found to have other conditions. The most commonly associated conditions are those of hearing loss, mental retardation, infantile autism, and problems of social and affective function. These associations demonstrate the close relationship between sensory, cognitive, social/affective abilities, and language development. However, there are many children with a developmental language disorder who appear to have intact sensory, cognitive, and social/affective abilities. For these children, their developmental difficulties seem to be limited to language learning. These children are often referred to as having specific language impairment (SLI). SLI is frequently associated with problems of school achievement, especially in reading.[17,18] It appears that children with SLI during preschool years and children with histories of typically normal spoken language form a group of children diagnosed as learning disabled or dyslexic, a condition which is discussed in Chapter 10A on learning disorders.

Clearly, children with developmental language impairments are a diverse population, and it should not be surprising to find that considerable variation in language characteristics of these children can be found. In recent years, it has been shown that characteristic patterns of language usage can be found in those with certain types of developmental disabilities. As will be discussed further, children with autism often demonstrate much greater difficulties with respect to the pragmatic aspect of language than with grammar or speech sound production.[19] In contrast, those with SLI have more difficulty with certain aspects of grammar than with vocabulary development or pragmatics.[20,21] Recently, it has been shown that those with Williams syndrome are more skilled in grammar and speech sound development than they are in vocabulary development.[22]

Despite the evidence of different patterns of developmental language disorder, there is also considerable evidence of constraint on the variety of these patterns. These different patterns of language impairment usually involve differences in the rates of development of different subsystems of language, thus yielding different characteristic profiles of relative linguistic strength and weakness.

However, within each of these subsystems a slow but typical pattern of language development is usually found. Thus, as children build a knowledge of their language, they seem to have few alternatives in the manner in which they do so, and typical language learners and children with language disorders go about this process in the same fashion. They differ primarily in regard to their rate and thus efficiency in language development. However, the fact that developmental language disorder can be described as a pattern of delay does not mean that, given time, these children will attain fully mature language skills. In many instances, the progress these children make is arrested at less-than-mature levels of language.[23,24] In the remarks following, emphasis will be placed on the common language characteristics of children with developmental language disorders, even though at times aspects of language that may be associated with one particular group will be mentioned.

The fact that developmental language impairments are associated with many other developmental disabilities and problems of child development allows us to predict that, taken as a whole, developmental language disorders are not rare. The actual percentage of individuals with some form of developmental language disorder is difficult to obtain, because data on the occurrence is obtained from studies of each of the particular associated conditions mentioned previously. Thus information must be combined from various sources.

Assuming that most mentally retarded individuals and all autistic individuals show some degree of language impairment, these two groups constitute more than three percent of the population. To this number, children can be added who have had significant hearing loss during infancy and childhood that may have led to a language disorder. Two percent of the population may fall into this category. Tomblin[25] concludes that SLI appears to compose approximately 50% to 80% of those children with developmental language impairments. As a result, the prevalence of SLI could be as small as 1.5% or as large as 10.3%, and the best estimate may be 5%. Thus, if all these conditions are added together, about 10% of the population is likely to have some form of developmental communication disorder. A large proportion of these people are only mildly impaired and probably find their difficulties with communication restricted to early childhood and pre-adolescent years.

Nature of the communication problems

There are various ways in which developmental language disorders can be classified. However, the most common approach used in clinical settings is to describe and treat the problem based on the status of the various components of language described.

Vocabulary. Vocabulary usage entails the ability to derive the appropriate meanings from words that are heard, as well as the ability to retrieve from memory the appropriate word to express intended meaning. Many, though not all, children with developmental language disorders will show deficits in receptive vocabulary, as measured by such tasks as the Peabody Picture Vocabulary Test-R.[26] The most common pattern of vocabulary deficit is one of a reduced level of vocabulary development. In this case, the child seems to be learning the meanings of words in the same manner as most normal children but doing so at older age levels.

In contrast, some children seem to have more spotty vocabulary development. In these cases, the child may not know the meaning of a word that is learned earlier by the normal child, but he or she does know the meanings of words associated with older ages of acquisition. In such cases of "spotty" vocabulary development, the child may not have had a typical exposure to English. In particular, this occurs with children with hearing impairments who are often learning English in formal classroom settings. Also, children who are learning a different variant of English than that represented in the test will show such a pattern. Finally, some children may exhibit apparently normal receptive vocabulary, even though they do have difficulties with the development of other areas of language learning.

In addition to deficits in receptive vocabulary level, many children with a developmental language disorder will also show deficits in expressive vocabulary skills. Often, this limitation in expressive vocabulary parallels the child's receptive difficulties and reveals a basic limitation in word learning. Some children, however, exhibit a problem of vocabulary usage often referred to as a word-finding deficit.[27] Nearly all individuals, at one time or another, fail to recall a name, or some other word, even though the word is known. This exemplifies a normal breakdown in word finding. Those individuals whose frequent word-finding difficulties restrict communication ability may be considered as having a language problem. Children with severe word-finding problems may show numerous hesitations during speaking; they may also make excessive use of nonspecific words, such as "thing" and "guy." Such difficulties with word finding are identified first by the clinician's listening for such breakdowns in spontaneous speech. If the child does show signs of possible word-finding problems, these can be further substantiated through the use of tests that require the child to name pictures and otherwise come up with a particular word.

Sentence usage. Recall that the sentence is the device through which the meaning, ranging from simple actor-action statements to complex propositions, is expressed. Meanings such as these are expressed through the language systems of syntax and morphology.

It would be reasonable to predict that children with language impairment might show considerably different patterns of sentence development than that found in the normal child. While in some instances this may be true, research to date indicates that for the most part children with language impairment seem to follow the same general course of sentence development as that found in normal children.[28]

Discourse. Much of the meaning of stories and conversation comes through the arrangement of sentences in some longer unit, such as a story or explanation in a conversation. In these larger communication units, events expressed in sentences may be given the attribute of causation, result, personal reaction, and so forth. Further, much of this meaning is not explicitly expressed but rather is obtained through inference. As a result, in conversation, as well as in stories, meaning builds on a base of prior utterances and the organization of this prior information. In recent years, speech-language pathologists have become increasingly aware of the difficulties that children with language impairments may have with this domain of language.[29]

Discourse capability is often studied within the context of a narration task. Research in this area has shown that the acquisition of discourse skills in children with language impairments proceeds in a manner that is, again, similar to that found in normal children; however, as in the domain of sentence development, the rate is slower.[30] In many casual communicative situations that require simple utterances, discourse problems may not be too apparent nor may they create substantial communication problems. On the other hand, in the classroom, the child is frequently drawing on these skills to comprehend instruction and understand material that is read, as well as using these skills in various composition activities.

Pragmatics. The ultimate test of an individual's communication abilities comes when that person must express messages and understand the messages of others in various physical and social contexts. As a clinician begins to observe a client with respect to pragmatics, he or she will often begin by observing what kinds of communicative functions the child employs as the child engages in play and conversation. During this time, the clinician notes the extent to which the child contributes to communicative exchanges, how talkative the child is, and, in particular, the extent to which the child initiates comments, makes requests, and responds appropriately to requests directed to him or her. In addition to noting the amount of communicative activities and their different types, the appropriateness of these various types of communicative acts are of concern. A child might inappropriately ask for information that has already been provided, statements may be made that are irrelevant to the activity and conversational topic, or the form or content of the utterance may be inappropriate, given the role relationship of the child and the communicative partner. In addition to a description of the extent and appropriateness of communication act usage, there also is interest in the child's ability to participate in a conversation appropriately by initiating a topic of conversation, taking turns, staying on topic, and going back and repairing information breakdowns when the listener indicates that he or she has not understood.

A large proportion of children with developmental language disorders do not appear to have notable difficulties in the acquisition of the basic principles of pragmatics. Although these children have difficulties in the successful accomplishment of communication, their failures are usually a product of problems with the form and content domains.[31] In some instances, however, these children do develop some atypical pragmatic characteristics simply because of their extensive experience with communication failure. Thus a child with a long history of unintelligibility may not ask for help (request), even though such a request would be expected. In this case, however, it is very likely that the child has not failed to learn about the pragmatics of requesting, but rather, has a reduced willingness to engage in this activity because of frequent failure.

There are some children, however, who do seem to have particular difficulties in the acquisition of pragmatics. One group of children who are noted for their difficulties with pragmatics are those children diagnosed as being autistic.[32] In brief, these children have considerable difficulties in their development of appropriate social skills and the establishment of adequate social relationships. Given that pragmatics is particularly concerned with the social principles governing communication, it should not be surprising that these children will often exhibit pragmatic difficulties.

The areas of difficulties and the extent of severity will vary. Severely affected individuals may be very limited in the amount of communicative activity in which they engage, even to the point that some may be virtually noncommunicative. For the most severely impaired autistic population, words and short phrases that have been heard are often reproduced to accomplish some communicative intent. This repetition of utterances has been termed *echolalia*. An autistic child might use such a phrase as, "Now it's your turn" to signify that he wants a drink, having associated this statement with waiting in line at the drinking fountain. In another instance, if this child were asked the question, "Do you want a cookie?" he might repeat the question in the form, "Do you want a cookie!" as an affirmative answer meaning, "Yes, I want a cookie." In many instances, it is difficult for the unfamiliar adult to determine what the child is intending through echolalic utterances, and it is easy to assume that the child has no communicative intent behind these repetitions. However, this assumption often leads to an underestimation of the child's communication performance. Higher-functioning autistic persons may show few, or no, echolalic behaviors, but they may exhibit problems in pragmatics by failing to consider what the listener knows and needs to know about a certain conversational topic. Thus this individual may talk to a listener who is unfamiliar with a topic as though the listener was very familiar with the topic. In all of these instances, however, there is a common pattern of the autistic individual's having difficulty adapting content and form to suit the particular social and physical properties of the communicative setting. As a result, he or she has substantial communication problems.

Another group of children who display difficulty with pragmatics are those children who have attention deficit hyperactivity disorder (ADHD). In addition to this group's being at considerable risk for the development of language problems involving language structure and content, the problems of self-regulation and impulsivity that characterize this condition influence the child's ability to use language appropriately in social interactions. Westby and Cutler[33] noted that the DSM-IV criteria for ADHS include such behaviors as "difficulty awaiting turns" and "talking excessively," which suggest inappropriate pragmatic behavior. These authors also note that these children often fail to adjust their talking according to the conversational situation. Certainly, many of the behaviors that create problems for these children involve inappropriate communication practices.

Causal factors and language disorders

Up to this point, this discussion of developmental language disorders has been limited to descriptions of the nature of language problems of children. The following is a discussion of factors that cause these problems.

Inadequate language input. An obvious prerequisite for language acquisition is that children must be exposed to the language of their linguistic community. There are a few rare and tragic cases of children who were reared with almost no contact with other language users. Such drastic deprivation leads to very severe language deficits. Lesser degrees of language deprivation have also been found in some residential institutions for developmentally disabled or emotionally disturbed children. In these instances, the children's contacts with proficient language users were very limited as were the opportunities to use language in a purposeful manner. As might be expected, this type of environment provides children with fewer opportunities to experience language than would be the case in most family homes, and studies have shown that there is a resulting restriction of language development.

Fortunately, extreme forms of deprivation such as these do not occur often; however, lack of sufficient language stimulation is sometimes offered as a cause for language deficits in children. In these cases, it is believed that, although the child is receiving an adequate *amount* of language input, the *quality* of the input is insufficient. Adults often adjust the manner in which they speak to young children, and many believe that at least some of these adjustments promote language growth in children. In particular, the use of simplified language forms and the tendency to follow and build on the child's topic have been stressed.

There is some evidence that some parents of children with language impairments do not demonstrate as much of these typical adjustments while speaking to their children as parents of normal children do. Although such results may indicate that these parents have not provided the child with a needed form of language stimulation, it is just as likely that what is being observed are ways in which parents respond to a child who is having difficulty with language development. Their failure to adjust then may be caused by the child's language difficulties, not vice versa.[34] In these cases, however, it is important to help the parent to develop and maintain the patterns of interaction that are thought to be helpful.

Deficits in hearing acuity. The most adequately documented causal factor related to language disorders is hearing loss. As noted previously, exposure to language usage is absolutely necessary for language to develop. Hearing loss can be seen as a biologically determined reduction in the child's exposure to auditory language usage. The nature of hearing loss can vary in several ways, and not all types of hearing deficit have equal bearing on the child's language development. In general, it can be said that the more the hearing loss restricts the child's opportunity to hear language during that time of life when language skills would normally be acquired, the greater the language deficit is likely to be. Admittedly, this rule of thumb overlooks individual differences that may exist in terms of the amount of experience a given child will need to develop language.

The essential role of hearing acuity in language acquisition emphasizes the importance of accurate audiological assessment for any child with a language disorder. When a hearing loss is present, a number of procedures—such as fitting a hearing aid—can be done to minimize the impact of the loss on language learning.

Deficits of cognition, perception, and information processing. The cognitive basis of language acquisition is far from settled. Some have made strong claims that language acquisition is the product of very special mental systems that are dedicated to the language learning process.[35] In contrast, others have proposed that language acquisition and its use build on general-purpose cognition mechanisms.[36] Those subscribing to the latter view have proposed that the basis of many children's language-learning difficulties is some form of a limitation in the cognitive resources needed for language learning.[37]

There is no uniform consensus concerning the nature of the cognitive resources that impair language learning. Gathercole and Baddeley[38] have proposed a very specific limitation in phonological encoding in short-term memory for children with SLI, and others have proposed a similar problem in children with Down syndrome. In contrast, Kail[39] has proposed that this information-processing difficulty is due to a generalized slowing of cognitive operations. Finally, Tallal[40] has proposed that children with SLI have a perceptual limitation in the ability to process rapidly changing visual or auditory events. It remains unclear which of these views correctly accounts for language-learning problems, and it is possible that different groups of children may have different types of cognitive deficits.

Central auditory processing disorders. One concept that has drawn considerable attention as a possible cause of some language development disorders relates to the children who appear to have difficulty in dealing with auditory stimuli, even though their hearing threshold is normal. That is, they may have more difficulty than do their peers in both discriminating among auditory stimuli that contain subtle differences in the signal and recognizing auditory patterns. Because language learning depends on discrimination among and recognition of the auditory patterns that make up the language code, to the extent that a child is having such problems, it might be expected that he or she will manifest a developmental language problem.

The concept has evolved that a central auditory processing disorder could be a possible basis for some developmental language disorders. That is, it is believed that some of the numerous neural mechanisms in the brain may be dysfunctional; the specific mechanisms are those which are responsible for analyzing the physical structure of auditory stimuli, encoding these stimuli, arousing perceptions from the stimuli, and activating responses to these perceptions. There has been documentation of a very few children who have demonstrated severe difficulty in understanding speech and corresponding difficulty in developing language, who also have neurological signs but normal hearing.[41]

However, the concept of a central auditory processing disorder, whether it is believed to result from a neural developmental problem or some type of lesion to the central auditory mechanisms, has been very controversial. The American Speech-Language-Hearing Association has recently adapted a consensus statement that was drafted by a group of knowledgeable audiologists and speech-language pathologists.[42] That statement specifies the need for a series of diagnostic tests, both audiometric and behavioral, that must show positive signs to suggest a central auditory processing deficit. Although it is agreed that such a disorder may be the basis for language-learning problems and/or learning disabilities, it is specifically noted that it should not be assumed that a child who is having difficulty developing language skills has such an auditory processing deficit.

Central nervous system dysfunction. For well over 100 years, it has been known that damage to the brain can result in deficits in language use. For many years, it was believed that many children, particularly those we now describe as having SLI, exhibited these problems because of subtle damage to regions of the brain that are important to language function.

This explanation has been tested rather thoroughly in recent years in children with SLI and has been found to be incorrect. Jerigan, Hesselink, Sowell, and Tallal[43] and Plante[44] have employed brain-imaging techniques to examine the brain structure of children with SLI. In these studies, there was no evidence of brain damage in any of the children who participated. These authors did find evidence that was consistent with studies of individuals with dyslexia that suggested differences in the relative size of certain cortical areas. Thus there may be differences in brain development and function in these children, but these differences are not due to damage to a normally developing brain. Rather, it is likely that various factors contribute to subtle differences in the growth and development of cortical and subcortical structures during fetal development.

Summary. Although it is desirable to be able to explain to parents and children why the language disorder is present, it should be apparent that it is often not possible to do so. In the case of the child with a language disorder and hearing impairment, it may be possible to attribute some or most of the language difficulty to the hearing impairment. On the other hand, for many of the children seen, it is impossible to determine the cause. In spite of this inability, it is possible to provide the child with a program of language therapy because the most common approaches to therapy do not attempt to modify causal factors. Rather, they focus on optimizing the child's learning, regardless of what caused the problem.

Language therapy

Approaches to the treatment of language disorders are almost as varied as the theories concerning language and language disorders. The particular approach adopted by a clinician will depend on that person's knowledge and beliefs about language and language usage, including, of course, the nature of language acquisition and language disorders. However, in spite of the variety of approaches used in therapy, the goal of language therapy is generally agreed on—namely, to establish the language skills necessary for the child to achieve functional and, it is hoped, socially acceptable communication abilities. Although there are diverse approaches to reaching this goal, it is possible to outline the more common methods employed.

One of the prominent approaches to language therapy, and the one that will be described here, begins by approaching language therapy as a process of promoting language learning by creating an optimal learning environment. Remember that much of what is known about the nature of the language deficit in most children with language impairment indicates that they are slower and essentially less efficient language learners. This approach attempts to compensate by adjusting the child's language-learning environment. With this approach, it is assumed that the syntactic, semantic, and pragmatic principles that the child needs to acquire are tacit, unconscious principles that should be discovered by the child rather than being formally taught. Thus the clinician is a facilitator of learning but does not directly tell the child what is to be learned. Rather, the clinician engages the child in activities that will optimally lead to this type of learning.

A variety of activities are used to facilitate this learning. In each case, the child is placed in a situation in which he or she is expected to do something with language and thus will have the opportunity to learn. One common activity used by clinicians is some form of a comprehension activity. Often, this task is very similar to that used in the assessment of comprehension—that is, the child is presented with utterances consisting of words, sentences, or even sets of sentences, along with pictures that either depict the meaning of the utterance or contrast with this meaning in some way. Just as is done in the assessment of comprehension, the child is asked to point to the picture to which the utterance refers. Unlike the assessment of comprehension, however, the clinician provides the child with feedback concerning the accuracy of the response.

Another procedure that emphasizes the child's learning by listening involves modeling. With this method, the clinician selects a particular aspect of language to be learned, such as a morphological rule for the comparative relationship (e.g., "big" contrasted to "bigger"). Unlike procedures to improve comprehension, the child is not asked to do anything in response to hearing the rule that is modeled. Thus the key aspect of this approach is its emphasis on the frequency of exposure as the basis of learning. Modeling can be particularly useful for the development of some aspects of pragmatics, such as taking turns in a conversation. In this case, the child may observe a pair of speakers in which one person frequently interrupts and is corrected or reprimanded. Then the child observes the speaker engaging in a conversation using acceptable turn taking. In this application, the child observes a contrast of acceptable and unacceptable behavior, along with the social consequences of the behavior.

No doubt, the most frequently used method for improving language learning has been the imitation task. In this task, the type of language form is presented to the child, and the child is expected to repeat it. If correct, the child is given positive feedback. If the imitation is in error, the child is given negative feedback. Often, imitation training has been used to promote syntactic development. In these instances, the child is initially asked to imitate only a few words of the sentence; if he or she is successful, additional words are added. In this manner, the child is gradually brought to the point of being able to imitate the full form of the sentences. After this level of success, the child is then shifted to using the sentence as an answer to a question, and, in this manner, the child learns to use the sentence form in a communicative fashion.

The instructional methods described thus far do not require a conversational interaction between the child and the clinician. In fact, these methods are often employed in a fairly drill-like environment. In recent years, some clinicians have attempted to create language-learning environments that maintain basic properties of natural conversations and, in particular, create conversational interactions that contain those interactions that seem to promote language learning in the normal child. One such interaction is the use of conversational continuation. Very simply, the clinician observes and listens to what the child does and says; then the clinician adds new verbal information. Thus, in a manner similar to modeling, the child's learning comes from hearing the meaning expressed by the clinician. In this case, however, the meaning is linked to what the child has said and done. Within the same conversation, the clinician may also employ a technique of expansion, in which selected utterances of the child are repeated by the clinician in a more complete or adult form. The conversationally based approach lends itself very nicely to training programs directed toward parents of young children because it encourages them to interact in very natural ways on an ongoing basis with the child.

The outcome of language therapy as described previously will vary. Some children are able to take advantage of the additional language experience and show considerable progress, whereas others show more limited rates of growth. Unfortunately, the factors have not been identified that differentiate those children who will respond well to therapy programs and those who are less likely to do so. In general, as might be expected, children with less severe problems show greater rates of improvement than those with more severe problems. Unfortunately, it is those with the most severe problems that most need improvement. To optimally help these children, one must determine how to match the particular strategies for enhancing language growth with the particular learning pattern of the child. However, insufficient knowledge regarding language acquisition is available to permit doing so.

Conclusion

Developmental language disorders may consist of a restriction in the acquisition of the sound system of a child's language, or they may extend to include deficits in the acquisition of the semantic (content) and grammatic (form) aspects of the language. On occasion, the language-learning deficit may involve a restriction in the acquisition of knowledge necessary for the appropriate use of language. The clinical management of these disorders begins with a systematic description of the child's communication abilities in each of these areas. This information is then used to identify those aspects of language that may be targeted for a program of therapy. These programs of therapy are, in most instances, concerned with providing the child with experiences that will lead the child to learn more advanced aspects of language. The goal throughout this process is to provide the child with a communication system that will be functional and, whenever possible, will allow the child to function in society unemcumbered by limitations in his or her communication ability.

REFERENCES

1. National Advisory Council on Neurological Diseases and Stroke Council Report: *Human communication and its disorders: an overview*, Bethesda, Md, 1969, National Institutes of Health, Public Health Service.
2. Bernstein DK, Tiegerman E: *Language and communication disorders in children*, ed 3, New York, 1993, Merrill Publishing.
3. Leonard L: Language disorders in preschool children. In Shames GH, Wiig EH, Secord WA, eds: *Human communication disorders: an introduction*, ed 4, New York, 1994, MacMillan Publishing.
4. Tomblin JB: Basic concepts: language. In Curtis JF, ed: *Processes and disorders of human communication*, New York, 1978, Harper & Row.
5. Owens RB: Development of communication, language, and speech. In Shames GH, Wiig EH, Secord WA, eds: *Human communication disorders: an introduction*, ed 4, New York, 1994, MacMillan Publishing.
6. Orton ST: *Reading, writing, and speech problems in children*, New York, 1937, WW Norton & Co.
7. Yoss KA, Darley FL: Developmental apraxia of speech in children with defective articulation, *J Speech Hear Res* 17:399-416, 1974.
8. Hall PK, Hardy JC, LaVelle W: A child with signs of developmental apraxia of speech with whom a palatal lift prosthesis was used to manage palatal dysfunction, *J Speech Hear Disord* 55:454-460, 1990.
9. Hall PK, Jordan LS, Robin DA: *Developmental speech apraxia*, Austin, TX, 1993, Pro-Ed.
10. Prins D: Fluency and stuttering. In Minifie FD, ed: *Communication sciences and disorders*, San Diego, 1994, Singular Publishing Group.
11. Williams DE: Stuttering. In Curtis JF, ed: *Processes and disorders of human communication*, New York, 1978, Harper & Row.
12. Shames GH, Ramig PR: Stuttering and other disorders of fluency. In Shames GH, Wiig EH, Secord WA, eds: *Human communication disorders: an introduction*, ed 4, New York, 1994, MacMillan Publishing.

13. LaVelle WE, Hardy JC: Palatal lift prosthesis for treatment of palatopharyngeal incompetence, *J Prosthet Dent* 42:35-44, 1979.

14. Morris H: *The needs of children with cleft lip and palate: a comprehensive view*, Iowa City, 1983, University of Iowa.

15. Hardy JC: *Cerebral palsy*, Englewood Cliffs, NJ, 1983, Prentice-Hall.

16. Beukelman DR, Mirenda P: *Augmentative and alternative communication: management of severe communication disorders in children and adults*, Baltimore, 1992, Paul H Brooks.

17. Bishop DV, Adams C: A prospective study of the relationship between specific language impairment, phonological disorders and reading retardation, *J Child Psychol Psychiatry* 31:1027-1050, 1990.

18. Stark RE: *Language, speech, and reading disorders in children: neuropsychological studies*, Boston, 1988, Little Brown.

19. Tager-Flusberg H: Dissociations in form and function in the acquisition of language by autistic children. In Tager-Flusberg H, ed: *Constraints on language acquisition: studies of atypical children*, Hillsdale, NJ, 1994, Lawrence Erlbaum Associates.

20. Lahey M: *Language disorders and language development*, New York, 1988, MacMillan Publishing.

21. Leonard LB: Language learnability and specific language impairment in children, *App Psychol* 10:179-202, 1989.

22. Mervis C, Bertrand J: Early lexical development of children with Williams syndrome, *Gen Couns* 6:134-135, 1995.

23. Fowler A, Gelman R, Gleitman L: The course of language learning in children with Down syndrome: longitudinal and language level comparisons with young, normally developing children. In Tager-Flusberg H, ed: *Constraints on language acquisition: studies of atypical children*, Hillsdale, NJ, 1994, Lawrence Erlbaum Associates.

24. Tomblin JB, Freese PR, Records NL: Diagnosing specific language impairment in adults for the purpose of pedigree analysis, *J Speech Hear Res* 35:832-843, 1992.

25. Tomblin JB, Freese PR, Records NL: Diagnosing specific language impairment in adults for the purpose of pedigree analysis, *J Speech Hear Res* 35:832-843, 1992.

26. Dunn L, Dunn L: *The Peabody picture vocabulary test—revised*, Circle Pines, MN, 1981, American Guidance Service.

27. German DJ: Spontaneous language profiles of children with word-finding problems, *Lang Speech Hear Serv Schools* 18:217-230, 1987.

28. Leonard LB: Language learnability and specific language impairment in children, *App Psychol* 10:179-202, 1989.

29. Baltaxe CA, D'Angiola N: Cohesion in the discourse interaction of autistic, specifically language-impaired, and normal children, *J Autism Dev Disord* 22:1-21, 1992.

30. Crais ER, Chapman RS: Story recall and inferencing skills in language/learning-disabled and nondisabled children, *J Speech Hear Disord* 52:50-55, 1987.

31. Lahey M: *Language disorders and language development*, New York, 1988, MacMillan Publishing.

32. Tager-Flusberg H: Dissociations in form and function in the acquisition of language by autistic children. In Tager-Flusberg H, ed: *Constraints on language acquisition: studies of atypical children*, Hillsdale, NJ, 1994, Lawrence Erlbaum Associates.

33. Westby CE, Cutler SK: Language and ADHS: understanding the bases and treatment of self-regulatory deficits, *Topic Lang Disord* 14:58-76, 1994.

34. Paul R, Elwood T: Maternal linguistic input to toddlers with slow expressive language development, *J Speech Hear Res* 1991; 34:982-988.

35. Pinker S: *The language instinct*, New York, 1994, William Morrow & Co.

36. Bates E, Bretherton I, Snyder L: *From first words to grammar*, New York, 1988, Cambridge University Press.

37. Johnston J: Cognitive abilities of children with language impairment. In Watkins R, Kail R, eds: *Specific language impairments in children,* Baltimore, 1994, Paul Brooks.

38. Gathercole SE, Baddeley AD: Phonological memory deficits in language disordered children: is there a causal connection? *J Memory Lang* 29:336-360, 1990.

39. Kail R: A method for studying the generalized slowing hypothesis in children with specific language impairment, *J Speech Hear Res* 37:418-421, 1994.

40. Tallal P: Developmental language disorders. In Kavanaugh JF, Truss TJ, eds: *Learning disabilities: proceedings of the national conference,* Baltimore, 1988, York Press.

41. Stein LK, Curry FKW: Developmental auditory agnosia, *J Speech Hear Disord* 33:361-370, 1968.

42. Task Force on Central Auditory Processing Consensus Development: *Central auditory processing: current status of research and implications for clinical practice,* Rockville, MD, 1995, American Speech-Language-Hearing Association.

43. Jerigan TL, Hessel JR, Sowell R, Tallal P: Cerebral structure on magnetic resonance imaging in language- and learning-impaired children, *Arch Neurol* 48:539-545, 1991.

44. Plante E: MRI findings in the parents and siblings of specifically language-impaired boys, *Brain Lang* 41:67-80, 1991.

CHAPTER 9

Disorders of mental development

General Issues

MARK L. WOLRAICH
DAVID SCHOR

Mental retardation is the diagnosis used to indicate significantly below average abilities in cognition and adaptive functioning. As such it encompasses a broad heterogeneous range of individuals including some individuals who require complete and continuous care as well as others with mild deficits, not easily detectable outside of an educational context. The prevalence of mental retardation varies according to the severity of retardation, with the highest rates at the mild end of the spectrum. For example, the prevalence of severe-to-profound retardation is about 3 to 4 per 1000,[1] while mild retardation is found at a rate of 25 to 30 per 1000.[2] Prevalence rates can also be affected by diagnostic criteria.

The practice of routinely providing care for large numbers of mentally retarded individuals in large state institutions began to change in the 1960s, following the publicizing of inadequate care being given to residents in some of these facilities.[3] This led to the deinstitutionalization of individuals, the encouragement of families to care for their children at home, and to the development of services for children and adults in the community. In the 1970s several federal laws were passed enumerating rights of individuals with mental retardation as well as the rights of those with other developmental disabilities. Laws such as the Education of All Handicapped Children Act of 1974 (Public Law 94-42), now called the Individual with Disability Education Act (IDEA), outlined procedures for evaluation and program planning for children with developmental disabilities as well as confirmed a societal duty to provide education and treatment services appropriate to their special needs. The Civil Rights of Institutionalized Persons Act (CRIPA) of 1980 required states to upgrade their programs and to move individuals out of institutions. In addition to responding to these efforts at the federal level, many states passed laws focusing on community and state-wide responsibilities and needs. Today few individuals with mental retardation are isolated from the community in institutions. In many communities a variety of programs and placements now exist that can be appropriately matched to children and adults having a wide range of mental disabilities. Concurrent with these improved options, the physician's role on behalf of patients with mental retardation has now increased to encompass four distinct functions: identification, treatment, prevention, and advocacy.

IDENTIFICATION

Prompt identification of cognitive impairment opens the way to early intervention. This in turn may reduce some effects of the cognitive impairment, facilitate the early recognition and treatment of specific medical conditions that accompany some types of mental retardation, or minimize the consequences of otherwise minor illnesses having significant handicapping potential to individuals with retardation.[4] Early intervention, as discussed elsewhere in this text, can also help parents develop appropriate coping mechanisms and facilitate their interactions with service providers. Interventions directed at cognitive limitations specifically will involve services from the public school system. Preschool children may receive educational and other services within the home or at preschool developmental centers. Children of traditional school age (5 through 18 years) may obtain specialized educational services provided by the school system. Recognition of mild degrees of retardation are difficult to detect (see chapter on developmental screening) and sometimes are not identified until around the time of school (or preschool) entry.

For the school child whose condition has been previously undiagnosed, the teacher or other school officials may suggest evaluation. The physician should be involved in order to assist in identifying an underlying cause for the mental disability or any secondary medical condition that could contribute to impaired learning or development.

TREATMENT

Treatment of conditions that may be associated with mental retardation, such as seizure disorders, can have a direct impact on the child's mental development and overall health. Some individuals with mental retardation have associated conditions requiring close monitoring. Some of the most common conditions, Down syndrome, fragile X syndrome and fetal alcohol syndrome are described in more detail in separate chapters. Associated conditions commonly seen in individuals with mental retardation include visual and auditory impairments, seizure disorders, constipation, and feeding problems. Physicians may also need to contribute to the management of children with mental retardation who have severe behavior problems for whom behavior management techniques alone have been ineffective. Underlying medical problems, such as dental carries, constipation, or otitis media, need to be ruled out in consideration of the treatment plan and certainly before psychotropic medications are considered.

The physician can rarely provide a treatment that has a positive direct effect on cognitive functioning, although medical management sometimes does influence cognitive performance. In some circumstances, treatments necessary to control accompanying medical problems, such as anticonvulsants and psychotropic agents, will have an adverse consequence on cognition.

PREVENTION

Many activities of primary care clinicians can be viewed as preventive in nature, with immunizations to prevent infectious disease being an obvious example. Prevention of possible mental retardation is widely practiced also; for example, the nearly universal testing of newborn blood samples for evidence of phenylketonuria or hypothyroidism has, as an underlying motivation, the prevention of nearly certain retardation if these generally asymptomatic conditions are not diagnosed and treated during the first few weeks of life. Prevention in mental retardation can be *primary* (designed to prevent the occurrence of the disorder causing retardation); *secondary* (designated to prevent the processes leading to retardation); or *tertiary* (designed to minimize the complications associated with the disorder producing retardation). Examples of activities at each level are given in the box on p. 300.[5]

ADVOCACY

The primary care clinician is in a position to be an effective advocate for the rights of children with mental retardation. Building on prior knowledge, training, and experience, the clinician can use his or her community prominence to speak out in public forums regarding issues of prevention

EXAMPLES OF ACTIVITIES TO PREVENT MENTAL RETARDATION AND ITS COMPLICATIONS

Primary prevention: eliminate the condition producing retardation

Immunizations (rubella, hemophilus, influenza)
Genetic counseling before conception
Prenatal and perinatal services
Programs designed to reduce the teen pregnancy rate
Seatbelt and bike helmet programs to reduce head trauma
Programs in schools to teach child development
Anticipatory guidance of problems likely to face families
Research and training

Secondary prevention: eliminate the retardation through early detection and treatment

Metabolic screening for newborns
Lead level screening
Early detection of child abuse and neglect

Tertiary prevention: minimize complications and associated disabilities

Periodic developmental assessment
Coordination of services for disabled children

Data from Crocker AC: Current strategies in prevention of mental retardation, *Pediatr Ann* 11:450-457, 1982.

and treatment. In addition, the clinician's influence in the community is often very effective in counteracting inaccurate stereotypes of individuals with mental retardation. For example, many clinicians have spoken out against zoning regulations designed to block supervised living programs in residential neighborhoods. In general, the factual information provided by clinicians can act to calm unreasoned fears as well as to provide civic leaders with knowledge that will enable them to act in the best interests of the whole community.

Perhaps more frequently, the clinician will be in the position to become an effective advocate for individual patients with mental retardation. This requires the clinician to become familiar with existing community services as well as current legislation in order to be aware of available services or those services that should be available to patients. Often the clinician is most effective when acting as a member of a team of professionals coordinating efforts on behalf of children with special needs. This team membership may be an unfamiliar role for the primary care clinician, but it is one that, when undertaken, can be effective and is much appreciated by parents. While the clinician most of the time cannot cure retardation, reducing the burden on the family and community can generally be more effectively and efficiently accomplished with the involvement of the medical professional in the team setting.

DEFINITION

The public's perception of mental retardation, rather than any particular numerical or statistical definition, is the primary shaper of both professional and lay attitudes and practices. A well-designed identification and intervention program will include efforts to combat inaccurate stereotypes. The criteria actually used to define mental retardation have varied over the years, resulting in shifting proportions of the population being covered by the label. A trend toward broadening the definition was apparent in the 1960s, when many professionals viewed most children's problems in school as being caused by mental retardation. More recently, the tendency has been to place increasing numbers of children with school problems into programs having no direct connection with retardation. These placements usually provide specialized educational services tailored to the children's needs. An example of this trend is the increased prevalence of classroom programs for children with learning disabilities.

A widely accepted definition of mental retardation has been "significant sub-average general intellectual functioning concurrent with deficits in adaptive behavior manifested during the developmental period."[6] This definition has undergone change in how it is operationalized. As originally formulated by the American Association on Mental Deficiency (AAMD), it did not incorporate specific measurements or methods. Both "general intellectual functioning" and "adaptive behavior" can be thought of as attributes that show complex variations within the population. Most recently, the renamed American Association on Mental Retardation (AAMR) has attempted to further emphasize the concept of adaptive behaviors as central to the diagnoses.[7] The usual cognitive testing (intelligence quotient less than 70 to 75) is required to establish a necessary but not sufficient criteria. However, to establish the diagnoses, the person must have deficits in at least 2 of 10 adaptive behavior domains. The extent of limitation is also used to define severity as mild or severe. These new criteria have been criticized as creating difficulties by identifying too many people with the necessary criteria and not having good formalized measures of adaptive behaviors.[8]

Standardized tests

A component of the previous definition and the core of the general public's understanding of mental retardation is the concept of impaired intellectual functioning. This concept is operationalized through the use of standardized tests such as the Stanford-Binet Intelligence Scale or the Wechsler Intelligence Scale series. These and other measures of general intellectual functioning are discussed in the chapter on measures of cognitive functioning. The measurement derived from these instruments is called an Intelligence Quotient, or IQ score. The term "significantly sub-average performance" has been usually defined in the past by scores on standardized tests.

An IQ score used to be considered the ratio (hence "quotient") between a person's mental age and chronological age, converted to an implied percentage, with a score of 100 being average. Classifications are now calculated based on assumptions regarding normal distribution of scores instead of strict age ratios, as discussed in the chapter on psychometric assessments. In the general population, the distribution of scores does approximate a normal distribution ("bell-shaped curve") (Fig. 9-1). Thus the average score is also the most likely score. Such a distribution is the expected consequence when an outcome variable (in this case, measure of IQ) is the result of multiple interacting factors (such as various hereditary and environmental influences).

Classification of an IQ score as "significantly sub-average" usually occurs when the score is more than 2 SD below that of the population average. For the Wechsler Scales, with an average of 100 and a standard deviation of 15, this implies a score under 70; for the Stanford-Binet, which also has an average of 100 but a standard deviation of 16, the corresponding score would be 68 (Table 9-1). Almost by definition, therefore, about 3% of the population would earn the label of "significantly sub-average general intellectual functioning" if such tests were given to everyone; this is about the proportion of the curve more than 2 SD below the mean. How-

Table 9-1 Defining severity of impairment of intellectual function

Degree of impairment	Standard deviation (SD) scores	Wechsler scales (SD = 15)	Stanford-Binet score (SD = 16)
Mild	−3.00 to −2.01	55 to 69	52 to 67
Moderate	−4.00 to −3.01	40 to 54	36 to 51
Severe	−5.00 to −4.01	25 to 39	20 to 35
Profound	Below −5.00	Under 25	Under 20

ever, not all would be said to have mental retardation. According to the present definition, only those with impaired adaptive functioning in addition to low scores would be considered to have mental retardation.

The majority of school districts use IQ scores as the major determinant in designing program options for students with poor cognitive skills. Children with IQ scores between about 70 and 80 are generally categorized as having borderline intellectual abilities and may be referred to as slow learners. They are not considered to have mental retardation although they are likely to require special help with their academic work.

Most children receiving special education services because of mental retardation are classified by the schools as educable mentally retarded or handicapped (EMR or EMH). They have IQ scores ranging from about 50 to 75; with a slower-paced curriculum, they often attain academic skills

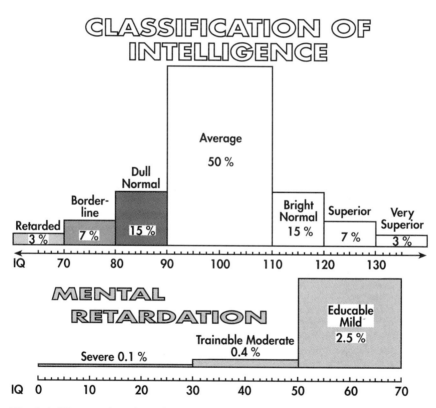

Fig. 9-1 IQ scores based on the normal distribution. *(From Solomons G, Solomons HC: The physician and psychological appraisal, Dev Med Child Neurol 15:95-103, 1973.)*

at the third- to sixth-grade level by mid-adolescence. Children classified by school systems as being trainable mentally retarded or handicapped (TMR or TMH) have IQ scores of about 25 to 50; the educator's primary goal for these children is the attainment of a degree of independence in self-care by the mid-teen years as well as social skills sufficient to function adequately in a predictable and controlled environment. Traditionally, individuals with severe or profound intellectual impairment were considered not suitable for an educational program. This is no longer the case. School systems now do provide specialized programs, and, with intensive individualized approaches to their training, many such individuals are able to acquire and maintain a degree of self-care and interaction.[9] With the changes in the definition of mental retardation by the AAMR, it is possible that the school systems may change the names and criteria of the severity levels.

Distribution of IQ scores

The distribution of IQ scores is presented in Fig. 9-1. Individuals with mild impairment of intellectual functioning comprise nearly 90% of individuals with retardation. Their rate of intellectual development during childhood is at roughly one half to three fourths the rate of children with average intelligence. The child with moderate retardation has a rate of development about one third to one half that of the average child. They comprise about 5% of the population of individuals with mental retardation. Individuals with severe or profound retardation, whose rate of cognitive development is less than one third that of the average child, make up the remaining 5% of individuals with retardation, with more children in the "severe" rather than "profound" category.

Although by strictly statistical definition about 3% of children would, if tested, score low enough to place them in the category of mental retardation, population studies demonstrate a higher than expected proportion of individuals with subaverage cognitive performance. The "excess" is largest among those with the lowest scores. (However, this subgroup still makes up the smallest proportion of those with intellectual impairments). This variation suggests that there are additional and relatively independent pathological factors capable of exerting a significant negative effect on IQ.

Test scores of IQ, like other "lab tests" available to the clinician, can be misused if not understood. A single score may seriously misrepresent the capabilities of the individual, and not all children with an identical score have the same needs or responses to teaching efforts. In addition, day-to-day variations in the child's performance, the skill and experience of the examiner, patterns of interaction between the child and examiner, and inherent measurement error of the test itself all combine to reduce the value of such a score in creating an understanding of a child's capacities. Clinical judgment must therefore always be incorporated into the interpretation of a particular test score.

ETIOLOGY AND PATHOPHYSIOLOGY

The known biological causes of mental retardation can be classified according to the time of their maximum impact on mental development: prenatal, perinatal, and postnatal (see the box below). Other classification schemes focus on anatomical causes or biochemical and physiological mechanisms.

In an individual with mild mental retardation, it is often difficult to identify a single biological or environmental event that can be implicated as *the* cause for his or her slower learning rate. For the individual with mild retardation, it is usually the interaction of multiple hereditary and environmental factors in combination that produces the end result. In an individual with severe or profound mental retardation, however, there is a greater chance of detecting specific biological causes.

Mental retardation can be associated with any disorder that includes central nervous system anomalies or damage. Thus mental retardation is a prominent secondary finding in such disabilities as cerebral palsy or meningomyelocele. Mental retardation is also found in individuals with other easily observed medical conditions (e.g., Down syndrome) and in individuals with conditions having no distinguishing physical

---

FACTORS CONTRIBUTING TO MENTAL RETARDATION

Prenatal	Interactions: genetics, prenatal and
Inherited	postnatal environment
Single gene abnormalities	Perinatal
Inborn errors of metabolism	Prematurity
Other single gene abnormalities	Asphyxia
Chromosomal: translocations	Trauma
Polygenetic	Postnatal
Acquired	Trauma, especially to the brain
Fetal malnutrition	Central nervous system infections
Teratogenic effects	Toxins
Prenatally acquired infections	Family circumstances
Chromosomal: trisomies, "fragile X"	Interactions
	Unknown cause

characteristics (e.g., phenylketonuria). In some circumstances there are subtle physical features in association with mental retardation that can be diagnostic of a syndrome. The child with mental retardation who does not particularly resemble either parent may well have a syndrome accounting for both the mental retardation and the unusual physical features. Standard reference works can assist the primary care clinician in the search for a definable cause of retardation.[10-13] A brief listing of some syndromes involving mental retardation is presented in the box on pp. 307-308.

Other causes of mental retardation include fetal malnutrition; perinatal trauma, with and without prematurity; childhood central nervous system infections; trauma; toxin exposure, with lead being the most prominent example; and environmental factors, such as deprivation and severe intrafamilial stresses. The child with autism or other psychiatric disturbance may also manifest signs of mental retardation. Finally, there are many children with retardation for whom no underlying factor likely to have caused the retardation can be identified.

Mild mental retardation is more commonly related to environmental-familial factors without other underlying causes; therefore, because those mildly affected make up the majority of individuals with mental retardation, for most no specific cause can be found. Furthermore, if a cause is found, it is rare that any intervention would significantly improve future cognitive or adaptive functioning for the affected individual. However, because certain medical conditions are associated with mild mental retardation, such as neurofibromatosis, it is useful to evaluate all children with the diagnosis. In addition, the discovery of such retardation may help prevent its occurrence in other children in the family if etiological factors are identified. Recognition of a defined cause for a child's retardation may permit more precise predictions about the child's future functioning or allow anticipation of medical or developmental problems in the future. The detection of retardation will also alert the clinician to be watchful for those common childhood problems that can be particularly severe for mentally retarded individuals. For example, a finding of poor vision or intermittent hearing loss may be detected and is important to remediate, to prevent it from further hampering a child's progress. Undetected seizure disorder, hypothyroidism, and psychiatric dysfunctions are some of the other possible but less common medical conditions that may be detected during such examinations. Finally, parents are generally relieved to know the cause, even if it is untreatable.

EXAMPLES OF SYNDROMES ACCOMPANIED BY MENTAL RETARDATION*

Chromosomal

XXY syndrome (Klinefelter)
Long limbs
Small testes, incomplete virilization
Trisomy 21 (Down syndrome)
Upward-slanting palpebral fissures, flat facies
Short hands, fifth finger clinodactyly
Hypotonia
Trisomy 18
Small mouth, malformed and low-set ears
Clenched hand, second finger over third
Short sternum
Trisomy 13
Holoprosencephaly (eye, nose, forebrain defects)
Polydactyly, narrow hyperconvex fingernails
Posterior scalp skin defects
Fragile X; listed under "Mendelian"

Mendelian

Acrocephalosyndactyly (Apert syndrome) (dominant†)
Craniosynostosis, midfacial hypoplasia, hypertelorism
Syndactyly, broad distal thumb and toe
Neurofibromatosis (von Recklinghausen disease) (dominant†)
Bone lesions (+/−)
Neurofibromas, cafe-au-lait spots
Tuberous sclerosis (adenoma sebaceum) (dominant†)
Facial skin nodules (hamartoma, pink-to-brown color)
Bone lesions (+/−)
Seizures
Mucopolysaccharidosis type 1 (Hurler) (autosomal recessive)
Coarse facies, cloudy cornea
Stiff joints by 1 yr, kyphosis by 2 yr
Growth deficiency
Fragile X syndrome (X-linked recessive)
Increased head circumference (in some)
"Long" face, prominent chin, midface hypoplasia
Macro-orchidism

Note: the degree of retardation is variable, and retardation is not an essential ingredient in some of these syndromes.
†In over half the cases, the disorder represents a *spontaneous mutation* from the unaffected to the dominantly inherited condition: therefore, there may be no evidence for prior intrafamilial occurrence.

Continued.

Mendelian—cont'd

Mucopolysaccharidosis type II (Hunter) (X-linked recessive)
Coarse facies
Stiff joints by 4 yr
Growth deficiency

Prenatal exposure

Fetal alcohol syndrome
Short palpebral fissure, mild maxillary hypoplasia
Microcephaly, prenatal onset of growth deficiency
Cardiac defect

Fetal hydantoin syndrome
Mild hypertelorism, short nose, low nasal bridge
Hypoplastic distal digits and nails

Rubella syndrome
Cataract, deafness
Patent ductus arteriosus

Unknown or multiple genetic factors

De Lange
Synophrys, thin down-turned lips
Small or malformed hands and feet
Prenatal onset of short stature, early hypertonicity

Noonan
Webbed neck
Pectus excavatum, cryptorchidism, pulmonic stenosis

Prader-Willi (many with chromosome 15 abnormality)
Small hands and feet, hypogonadism
Hypotonia in infancy, obesity after infancy

Rubinstein-Taybi
Microcephaly, slanting palpebral fissures
Broad thumbs and great toes

Williams
Prominent lips, stellate iris, hoarse voice
Supravalvular aortic stenosis
Early feeding problems, later outgoing personality

ASSESSMENT

The clinician's effectiveness in facilitating appropriate diagnostic and treatment services for children with mental retardation depends in part on a willingness to attend to items in the history and physical examination that can suggest this diagnosis. The clinician may be uncertain of a child's cognitive abilities, especially the infant or young preschooler who may be mildly retarded, but can facilitate the diagnostic and referral process by attending to clues. Among the most common signs of mental retardation the physician can observe are parental concerns that a child is "slow" compared to siblings or to expected standards or that a child fails to attain "developmental milestones" (especially language milestones) at appropriate ages. In such circumstances the use of screening instruments that cover a broad range of the child's developmental skills and patterns will increase the probability that individuals with mental retardation will receive an appropriate full assessment before school entry. Issues of developmental screening and early detection have been discussed in a separate chapter.

Much of the history obtained for children with suspected mental retardation and other developmental disabilities can be efficiently collected through the use of a questionnaire filled out by the parents before the office visit.[14] Especially in circumstances in which parents are asked to return a detailed questionnaire before the office visit, such information will help the clinician focus on specific areas of parental and professional concern during the face-to-face history takings.

In the interview itself the clinician and parents should have adequate time together to discuss concerns about the child. In reviewing developmental milestones, the clinician may wish to see if the history suggests a generalized delay in a variety of developmental skills or if noted delays were more evident in certain areas than in others. Parents should be encouraged to consult or bring along their child's baby book so more accurate information may be obtained. The clinician will likely review birth records as well as ask parents to recall events occurring during pregnancy, labor, and delivery, as well as postnatally. Questions regarding family history may be answered more candidly during the history taking than on the questionnaire. Similarly, parents are generally more at ease discussing their fears and concerns about their child directly with the clinician in an unhurried atmosphere.

The examination itself builds on the classic pediatric physical examination. Additional observations and assessments that may contribute to an understanding of a child's developmental delay might include assessment for minor dysmorphic anomalies, especially those involving the head; informal assessment of communication skills; impression of activity type and level; and observation of parent/child interactions. The clinician may wish to keep in mind the conditions and circumstances listed in the boxes on pp. 307-308 while performing the examination. In addition, plotting height, weight, and head circumference on standardized growth charts can be of diagnostic significance, especially in combination with previously obtained measurements.

It is essential that the child undergo a more extensive psychological assessment to confirm the diagnoses and characterize his or her strengths and weaknesses. These assessments are required in order to develop an appropriate intervention program. Frequently a speech and language assessment is required as well as an assessment of the child's fine and gross motor skills. The clinician may find a specific problem that could interfere with cognitive or academic gains, even if the child proves to have appropriate cognitive skills. For example, poor vision or intermittent hearing loss, undetected seizure disorder, hypothyroidism, or psychiatric dysfunctions are some of the medical conditions that may be detected during an examination of the child in the screening follow-up. Regardless of the outcome of further developmental tests, recognition of the diagnoses and appropriate treatment will be beneficial to the child.

MANAGEMENT

Clinicians' attitudes toward individuals with mental retardation can influence their management decisions. Physicians have been found to have lower expectations for mentally retarded individuals than do other service professionals, such as educators and social workers.[15] The problem of physician attitudes affecting patient care appears particularly serious for families with severely and profoundly mentally retarded children. Some of these families stopped bringing their children in for primary care needs because physicians appeared uninterested in the children or made the parents feel abnormal for wishing to keep their children at home.

It would be a mistake for the primary care practitioner to let the severity of mental retardation control treatment decisions for other medical conditions. Most children will make gains if secondary problems such as hearing loss are detected and treated in a timely fashion. Improvements will not necessarily be dramatic, but they may have a significant impact on the child's quality of life and interactions with parents and instructors. For example, a child who becomes a self-feeder has not closed a large developmental gap but has improved his or her chances for receiving adequate nutrition while decreasing the demand on the care providers.

It is rare for direct medical treatment to alter the child's rate of mental development significantly. More commonly, the clinician is called on to manage medical conditions associated with the retardation, such as cerebral palsy and myelomeningocele. The clinician's management role for the child with mental retardation may include prescribing and monitoring the effects of medication such as anticonvulsants for the child with seizures or psychotropic medication for the child with a behavior disorder. Generally, medical interventions are most beneficial when done in consultation and coordination with school officials or other professionals providing diagnostic or treatment services to the child.[16] For example, most of the psychotropic medications will impair cognitive performance, so it is important to try alternative approaches such as skillful behavior modification before attempting to employ pharmacological approaches. It is generally to the child's and family's benefit in complex cases that one member of the group assume a "case-manager" role, coordinating the treatment efforts of a team composed of the health clinician and the other professionals and ensuring clear communication among schools, health clinicians and other treatment agencies, and families.

Educational management

The appropriate educational experiences for retarded children follow along a continuum that ranges from the self-contained program, in which the entirety of instruction is apart from regular classrooms, to programs that integrate the child into the regular curriculum. Many children will have a combination program where they spend part of the school day in a specialized setting and part in regular classes. In a well-designed and well-supported system, the "special education" classroom is small, with a high proportion of instruction in small groups or one-on-one. The level, pacing format, and sequence of instruction are tailored to the child's own needs and behavioral style.[17] There is regular assessment of the child's progress and program, using a multidisciplinary approach in order to understand the child's individual pattern of strengths and weaknesses in the educational setting. Results of such assessments are shared with the parents and with others providing services to the family.

Academic skills developed in the EMR classroom are designed to meet the student's basic survival needs. The program focuses on promoting basic literacy (enabling the student to eventually read want ads, take a written driving test, fill out a job application) and simple arithmetic skills, as well as other functional abilities such as telling time and interpreting bus schedules. The program generally takes place within school buildings housing regular classrooms.

The children in TMR programs usually have more limited contact with children in typical school settings. The more severe cognitive and adaptive limitations found in these children generally result in their placement in more self-contained programs. The goals devised by TMR educators focus on basic self-help, communication, work habits, and social skills. These include goals such as the ability to recognize words like "DANGER" and "REST-ROOM" or how to dial the operator from a pay phone in an emergency. Recent educational interest in inclusion has resulted in a greater integrating of children with more significant limitations in regular classroom settings.

Programs for children with severe and profound retardation have more limited goals that may nevertheless have great impact on the child's quality of life and place of residence if successfully attained. Such goals generally include self-help skills in eating, dressing, and toiletry. In addition, many of these individuals can be instructed in vocational skills that are organized into small steps for acquisition.

Megavitamin and patterning therapies in mental retardation

There is as yet no credible evidence that the use of vitamins, or trace minerals, in large doses is effective in the treatment of mental retardation. However, for some of the rare inborn errors of metabolism characterized by a relative lack of, or inability to utilize, specific compounds, specific treatments have shown some promise. The administration of increased folic acid and vitamin D is indicated for individuals receiving diphenylhydantoin for prolonged periods. Excessive vitamin administration can have harmful effects. When nicotinic acid and nicotinamide were given in unsuccessful efforts to treat schizophrenia, the consequences included liver damage, pruritus, hyperuricemia, and other effects without measurable benefits. The fat-soluble vitamins, especially vitamin A and D, are especially likely to cause harm if used in megadoses. The National Academy of Sciences[18] cautions against administering more than five times the recommended daily allowance for these two substances.

Patterning, or the passive movement of an individual's limbs or head by another person, is based on the hypothesis that induced sensory-motor experiences produce "neurological organization," leading to improved sensory, motor, and cognitive abilities. The program often involves the near continuous application of these movements by teams of parents and volunteers on individuals with profound brain damage acquired as a result of childhood accident or meningitis. This theory is unsupported by animal studies or clinical trials.[19] In addition to being of no established benefit, the treatment has produced stresses and feelings of guilt in families since some advocates of this approach have taken the stance that the failure of treatment to improve children's abilities is due to the inadequacy of efforts expended by the parents and others providing the stimuli.

Both patterning and megavitamin therapies have been tried by parents seeking a solution to their children's disabilities. In an era when many new advances in medicine seem magical, it becomes an important role for the clinician to provide accurate information to families on both old and new proposed therapies.

OUTCOME

Young children with mild impairments in specific areas have the best prognosis, especially if their problems are identified and managed appropriately. The prognosis is also favorable for most children being managed for mild generalized delays identified in the preschool period. Often the most effective intervention for this group involves working with the parents, helping them to be more effective in optimizing the development of their children.

Studies tracking children with borderline intellectual functioning or mild mental retardation into adulthood have demonstrated that a high proportion grow up to become productive, responsible, and relatively independent members of their communities.[20,21] Many have come from lower socioeconomic groups as children and remain there as adults, seemingly indistinguishable from their neighbors. They report as adults that for them the most difficult time of their lives was during their school years, when the nearly constant demand for competent language and cognitive performance placed them under strain. Following a period of adjustment after leaving school, a process that may have been quite difficult and prone to derailments, they frequently manage to fully adapt to their environments. These adults, even those who may have IQ scores in the range of mild mental retardation, would not be included in the AAMR definition of mentally retarded individuals, which require deficits in adaptive functioning.

Bailer and colleagues in a series of studies[20] identified a group of children as retarded or slow learners, then tracked them for 30 years along with higher functioning children. The original cohort was divided into two groups: the low group had IQ scores less than 70, the middle group had IQs up to 85; the higher functioning children had IQs of 100 to 120. About half of each group was located for the follow-up studies. In the low group only about one in six was receiving public assistance, with nearly 80% employed most of the time. Employment in the middle and high groups was in the mid-90% range. The death rate among the low group was about double that expected, with the excess largely due to accidents.

Most adults with retardation will attain some degree of success in employment, ranging from a part-time job in a sheltered workshop to a career-oriented sequence of jobs. When these positive outcomes do occur, explicit activities developing these areas have generally been part of their school curriculum. Although adults who were taught in EMR placements during their school years frequently forget many of their hard earned academic skills, they are more likely to have retained positive work habits and attitudes: persistence at a task, cooperative behavior, friendliness, and self-esteem. However, when these relatively good outcomes do occur, explicit activities developing these areas have generally been part of their prior curriculum.

Although most mildly retarded citizens can function independently as adults, most moderately retarded adults and many with mild mental retardation will find more success in supervised living circumstances. These arrangements offer various amounts of independence and supervision to the young adult. In these settings or in intermediate care facilities or cooperative apartment living arrangements, it is possible to organize programs to encourage appropriate degrees of independence, self-reliance, and self-worth. The concept of the sheltered workshop continues to have merit, with such programs providing supervised work experiences, promoting good work habits, and giving the individual an introduction to the work setting. Usually such tasks often involve repetitive operations in a factory-like setting within a segregated environment; some provide a transition to regular work situations through on the job training and other preparations for gainful employment.

An additional activity in which professional as well as community attitudes play a major role is in recreation. Opportunities to participate in Special Olympics and related programs are growing. The degree of success for any of these community programs varies from region to region and appears to reflect in part the degree of professional commitment to the concepts previously discussed.

REFERENCES

1. Abramowicz HK, Richardson SA: Epidemiology of severe mental retardation in children: community studies, *Am J Ment Defic* 80:18-39, 1973.
2. Rutter M, Tizard J, Whitmore K: *Education, health and behaviour,* London, 1970, Longmans.
3. Rothman DJ, Rothman SM: *The Willowbrook wars,* Baltimore, 1984, Harper & Row.
4. Tjossem TD: *Intervention strategies for high risk infants and children,* Baltimore, 1976, University Park Press.
5. Crocker AC: Current strategies in prevention of mental retardation, *Pediatr Ann* 11:450-457, 1982.

6. Grossman HJ, editor: *Classification in mental retardation,* Washington, DC, 1983, American Association on Mental Deficiency.
7. Luckasson R, Coulter DL, Polloway E, Reiss A, Schalock RS, Snell ME, Spitalnik DM, Stark JA: *Mental retardation: definition, classification, and systems of supports,* ed 9, Washington, DC, 1992, American Association on Mental Retardation.
8. MacMillan DL, Gresham FM, Siperstein GN: Conceptual and psychometric concerns about the 1992 AAMR definition on mental retardation, *Am J Mental Retard* 98:325-335, 1993.
9. Wacker DP: Training moderately and severely mentally handicapped children to use adaptive social skills, *School Psychol Rev* 13:324-330, 1984.
10. Jones KL: *Smith's recognizable patterns of human malformation,* ed 4, Philadelphia, 1988, WB Saunders.
11. Warkany J, Lemire RJ, Cohen MM: *Mental retardation and congenital malformations of the central nervous system,* Chicago, 1981, Year Book Medical Publishers.
12. Bergsma D, editor: *Birth defects compendium,* ed 2, New York, 1976, Alan R Liss, The National Foundation—March of Dimes.
13. McKusick V: *Mendelian inheritance in man: catalogs of autosomal dominant, autosomal recessive, and X-linked phenotypes,* ed 6, Baltimore, 1983, The Johns Hopkins Press.
14. Frankenberg W: *Pediatric developmental diagnosis,* New York, 1981, Thieme-Stratton.
15. Wolraich M, Siperstein G: The prognostications of physicians about mentally retarded individuals, *Ad Dev Behavior Pediatr* 10:109-130, 1992.
16. Wright GF, Vanderpool N: Schools and the pediatrician, *Pediatr Clin North Am* 28:643-662, 1981.
17. Chess S, Korn S: The influence of temperament on the education of mentally retarded children, *J Special Educ* 4:13-27, 1970.
18. American Academy of Pediatrics: *Megavitamins and mental retardation,* Elk Grove Village, IL, 1981, American Academy of Pediatrics.
19. American Academy of Pediatrics: *Doman-Delacato treatment of neurologically handicapped children,* Elk Grove Village, IL, 1982, American Academy of Pediatrics.
20. Bailer WR, Charles DC, Miller EL: Mid-life attainment of the mentally retarded, *Gen Psychol Monogr* 75:235-329, 1967.
21. Tarjan G, Wright SW, Eyman RK, et al: Natural history of mental retardation: some aspects of epidemiology, *Am J Ment Defic* 77:369-379, 1973.

CHAPTER 9B _____
Down syndrome

DIANNE M. MCBRIEN
PHILIP J. MATTHEIS
DON C. VAN DYKE

*If you treat an individual as he is, he will stay as he is;
but if you treat him as if he were what he ought to be
and could be, he will become what he ought to be and
could be.*

GOETHE

In 1866, the medical superintendent of London's Earlswood Asylum for Idiots published a paper describing several of the asylum's inmates, in whom he had observed "a mongolian type of idiocy." Dr. John Langdon Down attributed the condition to parental tuberculosis, and theorized that his subjects' flat features and slanted eyes constituted a regression to an earlier and—to his thinking—more primitive racial type.

Although Doctor Down's theory was mistaken and seems frankly racist to modern minds, he was the first to describe the syndrome that today bears his name. Decades later, his clinical observations would be linked to the presence of extra chromosomal material, and his racial regression theory abandoned. Yet much of the fear and ignorance of his era have continued to constrain the lives of people with Down syndrome. Only in the last three decades have most individuals with Down syndrome or with other mental disabilities been raised and educated in the community; as late as the 1960s, physicians recommended the local version of the Earlswood Asylum to parents of newborns with Down syndrome. The 1981 Baby Doe case, in which surgery was withheld from a newborn girl with Down syndrome and gastrointestinal obstruction, was a highly publicized instance of a commonly held belief for many medical professionals: aggressive intervention is not warranted in this population, who cannot expect a high quality of life.

As public attitudes toward disabled individuals have changed, and as legislation has protected the growing educational opportunities and support services available to them, people with Down syndrome have moved into the community for active participation in school, work, and home. Many children and adolescents are fully included in regular classrooms. After graduation, many young people can look forward to jobs, further education, and independent or supervised living arrangements.

Improved health care has also empowered this population. The advancement of cardiac diagnostic procedures and surgical techniques, for example, has added enormously to the length and quality of life for those with Down syndrome. As knowledge of Down syndrome–associated health problems has grown, preventive medical care has become important in optimizing cognitive and developmental status as well as quality of life.

It is important that primary care providers for children be familiar with the elements of preventive medicine in Down syndrome as well as with the common health problems of this group. The incidence of Down syndrome is estimated to be 1 in 770 live births; thus any care provider is likely to have patients with Down syndrome in his or her practice.[1-3] Individuals with Down syndrome benefit from the care of an interdisciplinary team— the physician must work closely with speech pathology, social work, psychology, nutrition, and educational services as needed to provide a comprehensive plan of care for the child and family. Local, state, and national parent networks and support groups are often an invaluable resource for care providers as well as parents.

The following is a review, by system, of medical problems associated with Down syndrome. Psychological and cognitive abnormalities are reviewed, as well as issues of educational and community adaptation. Where applicable, current guidelines for preventive screening are given.

DIAGNOSIS

The diagnosis of Down syndrome is usually made on a clinical basis and is then confirmed by karyotype. Several resources address combinations of possible findings.[1-4] Clinical experience with affected infants may increase the practitioner's confidence level in making the diagnosis. Since most primary physicians may see a very limited number of newborns with this diagnosis, it may be helpful to identify a local specialist who can assist with questions.

More than 300 physical features have been associated with Down syndrome; however, most individuals demonstrate only a few of these.[5] Many reported features occur infrequently and are of little diagnostic use. Some of the findings, while quite common, are not specific to Down syndrome—for example, palmar creases—while other more infrequent findings, such as Brushfield spots, are more indicative of the syndrome. One of the most recognizable and common findings in Down syndrome is the combination of changes caused by midfacial hypoplasia. The resulting flat nasal bridge, angled palpebral fissures, and epicanthal folds often create a distinctive and suggestive "gestalt." Table 9-2 lists a number of selected features that may be of use in supporting the diagnosis. Some physical findings associated with Down syndrome represent significant potential morbidity and deserve further investigation. Congenital heart disease is the best known example; others will be discussed in the following sections.

A karyotype not only confirms the clinical impression but also defines the specific chromosomal defect. Genetic counseling depends, in part, on this information. There is sometimes an advantage in waiting for laboratory results; some families seem to benefit from a brief delay in diagnostic certainty as they come to terms with their new reality. However, the adjustment process is never easy and should not be unnecessarily prolonged.

Table 9-2   Selected physical features of increased frequency in Down syndrome

Characteristic	Reported range of occurrence
Brachycephaly	63%-98%
Oblique palpebral fissures	70%-98%
Epicanthal folds	28%-79%
Brushfield spots	35%-78%
Flat nasal bridge	57%-87%
Ear abnormalities	28%-91%
Protruding tongue	32%-89%
High arched palate	59%-74%
Loose skin on nape of neck	17%-94%
Short broad hands	38%-75%
Single palmar crease	42%-64%
Short fifth finger	51%-77%
Incurved fifth finger	43%-77%
Gap between first and second toes	44%-97%
Hyperflexibility	47%-92%
Muscular hypotonia	21%-85%
Congenital cardiac defect	40%-50%
Duodenal atresia	5%-8%

Data from Pueschel SM, appearing in Mattheis PJ: Diagnosing Down syndrome. In Redfern DE, editor: *Caring for individuals with Down syndrome and their families: report of the Third Ross Round Table on Critical Issues in Family Medicine*, 1995 (in press).

Most laboratories are capable of a quick—3 to 4 days—turnaround on karyotypes; if the return will take longer the physician should attempt to finalize the diagnosis on clinical grounds.[6]

Much has been written recently about the process of breaking the news of a child's disability to parents.[6-8] The nature of the interview may set the stage for at least the initial phases of coping. The pattern of credibility established by medical personnel in these early contacts may become a model for future interactions. Success in this aspect of patient care requires the same careful planning and attention to detail as the more technical parts of the treatment plan.

Before nursery discharge, the physician should provide the family with telephone numbers of supportive contacts, including other parents of children with Down syndrome, family support groups, and parent networks. Other families are often an excellent source of emotional support and of practical information. Parental networks exist on local, state, national, and international levels; they can help guide families through the maze of educational and social services while serving as clearinghouses for medical information.

Prenatal diagnosis of Down syndrome and of other congenital conditions is becoming available and may sometimes involve the local practitioner. Even when appropriately presented, the prospect of prenatal diagnosis may raise many questions for the family. Family physicians involved in obstetric care need to be able to provide accurate and unbiased answers to assist the family in their decisions. When a prenatal diagnosis of Down syndrome is made and the mother elects to continue her pregnancy, issues regarding the care and prognosis for the new baby will require the same accuracy and objectivity. At such times, a prenatal visit with the baby's anticipated physician can help everyone to prepare for the event.

Family reaction to a new diagnosis of Down syndrome may vary depending on whether the news was delivered before or after birth.[9] In one study, parental comments were often more positive after the delivery than during pregnancy when termination was an option. Careful attention to providing objective and nondirective guidance is the standard maintained by most genetic counselors[10-12] and should be the goal of all who interact with families of children with disabilities.[14,15]

INCIDENCE AND ETIOLOGY

Most individuals with Down syndrome—94% to 95%—have complete trisomy with 95% caused by maternal nondisjunction and 5% by paternal nondisjunction.[1,16] About 3% to 4% are translocations, with the most common abnormalities being 14/21, 15/21, 21/21, and 21/22 translocations.[1,16] There are reported rare translocations involving other chromosomes.[17] Approximately 2% of the cases are the result of mosaicism of normal cells with trisomy 21 cells and of trisomy 21 cells with other abnormal cell populations such as XO or Turner syndrome cells.[1,16] Even in those individuals who are not mosaic, the germ cell line has occasionally been demonstrated to be mosaic.[18,19] This is most clearly demonstrated by individuals with Down syndrome producing children without Down syndrome.[18,19] Partial trisomies due to the duplication of the distal segment of 21q22 result in the classical phenotype of Down syndrome.[20] The recurrence risk of a translocation can be as low as 2% to 3% or as high as 100% depending on which chromosome is involved and which parent carries the translocation.[1,20] Individuals who have had one child with Down syndrome carry a statistical risk estimated to be 1% of bearing a second affected child. The exact risk is not known.

MEDICAL ISSUES

From the perspective of anticipatory health management, potential medical problems can be divided into two types. The first group includes conditions that require anticipatory screening and that usually improve with treatment. Included in this category are cardiac defects, visual and hearing deficits, thyroid dysfunction, and cervical spine instability; thus anticipatory management may include referrals to cardiology, ophthalmology, audiology, otolaryngology, endocrinology, radiology, and possibly neurology or neurosurgery. The second group of conditions do not usually require preventive screening and include problems such as skin lesions, gastroenterologic problems, or hematologic abnormalities. The Down Syndrome Preventive Medicine Checklist is an excellent and complete guide to anticipatory health care.[99]

NEUROLOGY ISSUES

The predominant neurological consequence of Down syndrome is cognitive impairment.[3,4] Speech and language deficits are particularly common and affect expressive communication. Specific learning disorders are also described[21]; when combined with communication problems, they may make effective cognitive evaluation difficult. The presumption that all individuals with Down syndrome are mentally retarded is probably overly simplistic and is being challenged anecdotally by the improved function seen in individuals given optimal support in school and community.

Seizures

The incidence of seizure disorders is increased in individuals with Down syndrome compared to the general population but is reduced relative to other conditions associated with mental retardation.[22] Children with cardiac or pulmonary disease may be at increased risk from cerebral insults related to hypoxia or surgical complications. There does appear to be an additional, intrinsic risk of seizures in children with Down syndrome beyond that explained by medical events. Infantile spasms occur more often in young children with Down syndrome[22] than in normal children; in this population, however, infantile spasms typically respond well to medical therapy and tend to resolve over time.[23] The risk of seizures may increase with age, which has been attributed to the development of central neuropathological changes in the brain similar to those seen in Alzheimer's disease. Usually control of seizures is fairly easily achieved by standard pharmaceutical agents. Any individual with Down syndrome who has seizures should be thoroughly evaluated to determine the etiology, especially when anticonvulsant therapy is planned.

Hypotonia

Most individuals with Down syndrome have some degree of hypotonia; in newborns, this finding often prompts diagnostic workup for Down syndrome.[1] There is considerable variability to the expression of this finding, which is complicated by the lack of any clinically useful and reliable scale to define and describe low tone. The etiology is central, and the course for each person may vary with time. As the child grows, tone generally seems to improve.

Low tone probably has a number of functional consequences, although the absence of measurable criteria makes verification of impact difficult. Ambulation is probably delayed in children with very low tone, particularly when combined with laxity around large weight-bearing joints. Speech output may also be affected by poor tone as the child attempts to organize oral and pharyngeal muscles to produce words. Bulbopharyngeal hypotonia also may affect speech and may necessitate the use of signing or augmentative communication devices to supplement, support, or augment oral speech. Many young children with Down syndrome with delayed verbal expression are able to use adapted sign language as a transient communication method until verbal output emerges.

Attention deficit hyperactivity disorder

Children with Down syndrome often demonstrate behavior and attention problems in school. Much of the time, these issues can be resolved with close attention to appropriate educational programming. As mentioned previously, communication skills and specific learning disorders are common in this group of children; when ignored, attention and behavior problems are frequent clues to the oversight. An underlying medical problem as well as undiagnosed hearing or visual deficits may contribute to behavior and attention problems. Thyroid dysfunction can also produce behavioral and cognitive consequences. Children with Down syndrome also have a high incidence of sleep disturbances, with an elevated risk of significant sleep apnea. A current unpublished study suggests that at least some children with sleep apnea and behavior or attention problems have functional improvement after treatment of the apnea by either surgery or nasal CPAP.

The social environment may drive behavior and attention problems as well. Families with disabled children have greater stress and increased demands on their resources, hampering their adaptive capacities. Expectations directed at the individual with Down syndrome are often unreasonably low and based more upon general stereotypes than on individual evaluation. A child's behavior pattern may be a response to a difficult environment, rather than a sign of a primary attention disorder.

Even though appropriate evaluations may address any relevant social, cognitive, and medical factors, some children with Down syndrome continue to exhibit attentional problems. For these individuals, standard treatment with stimulant therapy seems to hold the same potential for efficacy as in the general population.

Alzheimer's disease

Multiple reports in recent literature have identified an association between Down syndrome and Alzheimer's disease.[24,25] The most compelling evidence comes from autopsies of the brains of individuals with Down syndrome. Neuropathological changes are frequently seen that are similar and occasionally identical to those seen in the brains of individuals diagnosed in life with Alzheimer's disease.[26,27]

Studies that have attempted to correlate these pathological findings to clinical outcomes have been less successful. Studies of institutionalized populations have suggested that earlier onset of dementia may occur with Down syndrome,[28] but current longitudinal follow-up of adults living in their home communities has not documented that trend.[29,30]

Any clinical evaluation of an adult with Down syndrome who demonstrates a loss of functional ability should include Alzheimer's disease within the differential diagnosis. It should be recognized, however, that Alzheimer's disease is a diagnosis of exclusion. Most of the time, the symptoms in a patient with Down syndrome have another explanation.[31] Much more frequent diagnoses include depression, thyroid disease, unrepaired or evolving cardiac disease, or other medical conditions. As many of these conditions are at least partially treatable, a complete workup is essential before a diagnosis of Alzheimer's disease.

MUSCULOSKELETAL PROBLEMS

The combination of joint hyperextensibility, connective tissue hyperelasticity, muscular hypotonia, and structural joint abnormalities predisposes the individual with Down syndrome to significant musculoskeletal problems.[32,33] The most common of these are atlantoaxial subluxation, genu valgus, hip instability, metatarsus primus varus, patellar femoral instability, pes planus, and scoliosis.[33-36]

The management of C1-C2 subluxation, or atlantoaxial instability, presents perhaps the most controversial orthopedic problem in Down syndrome. Subluxation has been reported by a number of authors with an incidence from 9% to 31%.[35-38] Common signs and symptoms of C1-C2 instability are neck pain, torticollis, increased ankle tone, and gait abnormalities including leg weakness and decreased coordination.[36] Most individuals with radiographic evidence of C1-C2 instability are asymptomatic.[36] The American Academy of Pediatrics has recommended obtaining initial cervical spine films at the earliest age at which a child can cooperate with the procedure, usually between 4 to 7 years of age.[33] Films adequate for diagnostic purposes must be obtained without the use of sedation and must demonstrate satisfactory flexion and extension. Classification is based on the interval in millimeters between C1-C2 and the clinical presentation. Treatment ranges, depending on symptomatology and interval length, from continued screening to surgical stabilization.[36]

Thoracolumbar scoliosis has been reported to occur in about 50% of individuals with Down syndrome.[32,33] The curves are rarely progressive.[32,36] Hip problems in Down syndrome generally present in childhood and include congenital hip dislocation, epiphyseal dysplasia, and hip instability.[36] Adolescents and adults may develop slipped capital femoral epiphysis, avascular necrosis of the hip, and degenerative arthritis.[36] The major knee abnormality is patellar instability.[36] Ankle and foot abnormalities are commonly seen in individuals with Down syndrome.[32-34,36] These problems include flat feet, widened forefoot, lax ankles, and related problems such as corns, calluses and bunions.[32,36] The majority of back, knee, and foot/ankle problems are managed conservatively and rarely require surgery. The key issues in management are prevention and monitoring. Degenerative joint and bony changes are frequent findings on x-rays with degenerative osteoarthritis being a major problem for adults with Down syndrome.[32,40]

SKIN PROBLEMS

While a number of skin conditions can be identified in Down syndrome, there are no dermatological disorders unique to this population.[41] Morphological changes, abnormalities in vascular patterning, accelerated skin aging, and changes secondary to drying and infection have been reported in individuals with Down syndrome.[41,42] The most common morphological changes seen are redundant neck skin (80%), fissured tongue, and changes in coloration, particularly due to the acrocyanosis frequently seen in newborn infants.[41] Accelerated aging of the skin, coarseness, and dryness are frequently reported.[41] Other frequently reported skin disorders are dermatophytic infection and bacterial infections, particularly folliculitis, seborrhea, dermatitis vulgaris, and dry skin.[31,41,42] In one study of Down syndrome, 39% of individuals questioned had severe dry skin.[42] Other less common skin conditions seen in individuals with Down syndrome are alopecia areata, vitiligo, Norwegian scabies, syringoma, ichthyosis vulgaris, and seborrheic dermatitis.[41,43]

SLEEP PROBLEMS

Several factors may predispose the individual with Down syndrome to sleep apnea. Bulbopharyngeal hypotonia may promote upper airway collapse, particularly in the supine position. While the Down syndrome tongue is not, as was previously thought, abnormally large, it is outsized for the hypoplastic maxilla and oral cavity and thus may help to occlude the airway.

Tonsillectomy and adenoidectomy performed for indications of sleep apnea must be approached cautiously in this population. Cleft palate occurs more frequently in people with Down syndrome than in the general population; Schendel and Gorlin estimated a frequency of 4.6%.[3,44] The frequency of submucous cleft was 0.78%.[3,44] Hypernasality in Down syndrome individuals who do not have palatal defects is also common.[45] Thus, removal of hypertrophied lymphoid tissue may exacerbate any existing velopharyngeal insufficiency and create related speech problems in these individuals. Therefore, individuals with suspected sleep apnea must be closely managed in conjunction with an otolaryngologist and speech pathologist. Sleep studies, including polysomnogram, may be useful in distinguishing sleep apnea from behavioral sleep disorders, parasomnias, or nocturnal seizures.[45]

Studies have suggested that individuals with Down syndrome have an unusually high incidence of increased pulmonary vascular resistance and an increased propensity for the development of pulmonary hypertension.[46-48] The development of pulmonary hypertension has been documented in individuals with Down syndrome both with and without congenital heart disease, suggesting that noncardiac factors may be involved.[46,47] In a recent study by Marcus et al, overnight sleep studies in individuals with Down syndrome demonstrated pulmonary or airway abnormalities, including obstructive sleep apnea in 63%, hypoventilation in 81%, and O_2 desaturation in 56%.[49] Age, obesity, and the presence of heart disease do not appear to affect the incidence of obstructive sleep apnea, desaturation, or hypoventilation.[49]

HEMATOLOGY AND ONCOLOGY PROBLEMS

Individuals with Down syndrome are 20 times more likely to develop leukemia than are individuals in the general population.[50,51] Acute lymphocytic leukemia (ALL) is the most common leukemia in the child or adult with Down syndrome.[50,51] Acute myelocytic leukemia (AML) is the most common type of leukemia in infants with Down syndrome.[51] Children with Down syndrome have a predisposition to a specific type of AML—M7-megakaryocytic leukemia.[51]

Some neonates with Down syndrome also manifest a transient leukemoid reaction with marked leukocytosis.[50-53] Infants recover from this disorder spontaneously, but 20% eventually develop some form of leukemia.[52]

Polycythemia independent of cyanotic congenital heart disease is well known among neonates with Down syndrome.[54] Therapy includes supportive care including partial exchange transfusion when necessary. Various hematological abnormalities, unassociated with clinical illness, include dysmorphic platelets and mild-to-moderate self-limited thrombocytopenia in infancy unassociated with congenital leukemia or infection.

Marked progress in management of leukemia in Down syndrome has been made.[51] This is in part due to recent advances in medical management, pharmacotherapy, and bone marrow transplantation.[51] Today, 70% of children with Down syndrome who have ALL have a prolonged remission/cure.[51,55] Eight percent of children with Down syndrome with

AML have a prolonged remission/cure.[51,56] This is in marked contrast to a 45% remission rate in typical children.[51] Despite the increased risk of hematological abnormalities in Down syndrome, pathology remains relatively rare. No specific general screening is indicated beyond a heightened awareness of potential morbidity.

INFECTIONS, IMMUNITY, AND IMMUNIZATIONS

Many individuals with Down syndrome have demonstrable immunological abnormalities associated with recurrent infections. A subset of children with Down syndrome have been documented to have a wide range of immune system problems that predispose them to chronic infections.[42] Reported abnormalities include poor lymphocyte proliferation, T-cell defects, abnormal interferon receptor function, and abnormal cell surface receptors.[57-62] In addition, individuals with Down syndrome have an increased tendency to develop autoantibodies that can result in damage to pancreatic, thyroid, and parathyroid tissue,[59,63] with the most common presentation being thyroid dysfunction.[58,59] Individuals with Down syndrome have also been identified as having several IgG subclass deficiencies, with about 70% of individuals having increased susceptibility to infection.[60] The most common subclass deficiency is G4; however, G1, G2, and G3 deficiencies have also been reported.[60,63]

Most individuals should receive all routine childhood immunizations. The rare child with cell-mediated immune dysfunction should avoid immunization with live viral vaccine.[63] Because individuals with Down syndrome may have a history of recurrent infections, they have a relatively high risk of developing chronic active hepatitis, recurrent upper respiratory infection, and pneumonia. Pneumococcal vaccine, influenza vaccine, and hepatitis B vaccine should, therefore, be considered as part of the routine immunization schedule.[63]

EAR, NOSE, AND THROAT PROBLEMS

The primary care provider for individuals with Down syndrome must be able to anticipate and treat a broad spectrum of diseases related to obstruction or infection of the ears, sinuses, nares, and throat. Because of the frequency and severity of ENT disease in this population, close coordination of care with an otorhinolaryngologist is often necessary. Periodic evaluation and follow-up are critical in order to prevent hearing loss and to promote language development.

Multiple anatomical factors predispose the ear of a child with Down syndrome to infection, effusion, and hearing loss. Although the pinnae may be small, low-set, and prone to lop ear deformity, this represents a minor concern when compared with malformations of deeper otic structures.[64]

The external auditory canal is typically narrow and may make full otoscopic examination difficult. Meatal diameter may be more than two standard deviations below that of age-matched controls[64]; in one study, 39% of individuals with Down syndrome had some degree of stenosis.[65] Not surprisingly, a tiny auditory meatus poses two related problems: cerumen impaction and subsequent poor visualization of the tympanic membrane. Not only can wax obscure ear disease, but it also can affect hearing: impacted cerumen has been associated with a mean 24 db hearing loss in subjects with Down syndrome.[66] Regular use of cerumenolytic otic preparations is recommended, particularly for the patient with recurrent middle ear disease who needs frequent examination. For the meatus that cannot be visualized after cleaning—as in some stenotic canals or in neonates—specialized operatory microscopes are available at some tertiary centers or otology clinics.

Several potential anatomical abnormalities promote obstruction and infection in the middle ear. Bulbopharyngeal hypotonia and brachycephaly can produce abnormal vector forces on the tensor veli palatini muscle, contributing to eustachian tube dysfunction and middle ear effusions.[67] Ossicular malformations have also been documented and may represent congenital deformity or acquired damage related to recurrent infection. Balkany and Mischke's 1979 study suggested that many stapedial malformations are congenital, while deformities of the incus and malleus tend to occur in association with chronic inflammation.[68] Inner ear abnormalities include shortened cochlear spirals, which may help to distort auditory input,[69,70] vestibular system deformities with associated endolymphatic hydrops, and fibrous replacement of the round window.[71,72]

Ear infection and effusion are common among children with Down syndrome.[42,73] Schwartz and Schwartz found a 59% prevalence of unilateral middle ear effusion in institutionalized subjects with Down syndrome.[71] Among subjects with stenotic ear canals, the proportion rose to 80%.[74] Of 138 patients studied in 1980 by Samuelson and Nguyen, 39% had ear disease; 63% of these had middle ear effusion.[72] The neonate with Down syndrome may exhibit middle ear effusion on examination and requires careful otoscopic examination before discharge from the nursery.

Appropriate and prompt antibiotic therapy is the mainstay of treatment and of preserving hearing. Myringotomies with ventilation tube insertion may resolve recurrent disease in many. However, despite aggressive surgical intervention, 14% of subjects in one study had recurrent disease.[73] Strome reported that adenoidectomy had little apparent effect on recurrent ear disease in the individuals studied.[65]

Purulent rhinorrhea frequently associated with sinus infection is common in the Down syndrome population. Strome noted purulent rhinorrhea in 40% of his subjects that seemed unrelated to allergy.[65] Adenoidectomy had little or no effect on nasal symptoms. He observed a positive response—resolution of 9 cases out of 10—to empiric treatment with low dose ampicillin: 250 mg twice a day for subjects over 2 years of age, and 125 mg twice a day for those under 2 years of age.[65] Nasal cultures obtained before initiation of antibiotic therapy demonstrated no predominant pathogen.[65] In most cases, good symptomatic control was achieved by beginning antibiotics at the onset of symptoms—often in the early fall—and discontinuing treatment in May.[65]

A hearing loss with mean threshold above 15 db is generally accepted by most clinicians as significant.[73-75] By this definition, significant hearing loss is common in children and adults with Down syndrome. Balkany et al and Downs found significant hearing loss in 78% of individuals studied, with 83% of the losses termed conductive.[68,73] Bilateral hearing loss was noted in 64% of subjects. Fulton et al. described an institutionalized Down syndrome population with a high prevalence of conductive hearing loss.[76] Individuals with effusion-related conductive loss need to be retested after resolution of middle ear disease to make sure that underlying sensorineural loss has not been missed.

Baseline audiometric evaluation is generally recommended during the first year of life[73,99] followed by periodic retesting. The frequency of retesting depends on the individual history of speech deficit, middle ear disease, and the type of hearing loss. Brain stem auditory-evoked response (ABR) is the diagnostic gold standard for those children who may not be able to cooperate with or to respond reliably to impedance and sound field testing.[73,77] It must be emphasized that hearing loss for a child with Down syndrome is not necessarily associated with a history of ear infections. Van Dyke et al. documented flat tympanograms in 25% of individuals studied; these patients had no history of otitis media.[78] Flat tympanograms were closely associated with hearing loss in this study.[78]

EYE PROBLEMS

As the outlook for an active, community-oriented life continues to brighten for the individual with Down syndrome, care providers must adopt an optimistic and aggressive approach to visual health care. Most visual loss in Down syndrome is preventable, can be attributed to syndrome-related eye abnormalities, and is not an inevitable sequela of the trisomic condition. Ophthalmological evaluation is recommended during the first year of life and annually thereafter until 6 years of age.

Ocular malformations are often the first phenotypical clues leading to a diagnosis of Down syndrome.[79] The eye findings typically noted at diagnosis include slanted palpebral fissures, epicanthal folds, and Brushfield spots. Other ocular abnormalities have been documented, including retinal hypopigmentation, increased central retinal vasculature, and optic nerve hypoplasia.[79]

White and yellow nodules of dense stromal tissue circling the iris were first noted in 1902 by Wolfflin; not until 1924 did Brushfield describe their association with Down syndrome.[80] Fierson found Brushfield spots in 30% of his subjects with Down syndrome.[79] Other studies have cited incidences up to 90%.[81,82] While the lesions are strongly associated with Down syndrome, they have been documented in unaffected individuals and so cannot be termed pathognomic.[82] As detected by slit-lamp microscopy, Brushfield spots are more frequently present in light-colored than in dark irides.[82]

Blepharoconjunctivitis

Fierson noted clinical findings of blepharitis, including eyelid margin scaling, conjunctival injection, and exudate in 13% of subjects.[79] Overall incidence in Down syndrome is higher than in the general population and has been estimated to range from 2% to 70%,[79] which probably reflects the lack of firm diagnostic criteria for this condition. Left untreated, blepharitis can lead to conjunctivitis and, rarely, keratitis and secondary corneal scarring.[79]

Blepharitis may be an incidental finding of the clinician who spots redness and crusting on the eyelid margins. It may present with ocular itching and irritation, or, in the later stages, with discharge, crusting, and frank photophobia. Treatment consists of cleansing the eyelid margins with a 1:5 baby shampoo and warm water solution followed by application of Erythromycin or Bacitracin ophthalmic ointment to the involved areas twice a day for 3 to 4 weeks until the condition is under control.[79] Since blepharitis tends to recur, this treatment should probably be repeated monthly in affected patients.

Cataract or lens opacity

The association of lens opacity with Down syndrome has been well known since 1910 when Ormond described "dot-like" opacities in a lamellar distribution throughout the lens.[81] Incidence of lens opacity measured since then ranges between 12% to 46%.[81,82] In 1949, Lowe described what he termed the typical cataract of Down syndrome as consisting of thin "flake-like" opacities, up to 0.25 mm in diameter,[83] in the midperiphery of the lens. These opacities were often so thin that they were missed on direct illumination. Sutural opacities were also frequently observed. Many authors note a progression of the lesions with age.[79]

While Lowe's "typical" lesions are usually asymptomatic in early life, the flake opacities may increase in number and in central location; careful follow-up of any opacity is clearly necessary.[83] Of course, cataracts that involve the central lens axis may compromise vision. Current therapy consists of lensectomy followed by optical replacement with intraocular lens implantation, contact lenses, or glasses.[79] The optical replacement method employed must be implemented with the patient's cognitive and behavioral status in mind; in many cases, lens implantation may simplify management in those patients who cannot comply with glasses or contact lenses.

Keratoconus

Progressive stretching and thinning of corneal stromal tissue resulting in a conical corneal silhouette—rather than the normal spherical outline—is termed keratoconus.[79] The irregular conical shape may promote disordered refraction of incoming light rays and result in poor retinal image composition. The etiology is unknown. Previous workers suggested that a structural defect of corneal collagen was responsible or that the corneal lesion represented acquired damage from chronic rubbing of blepharitic eyes;[79] however, corneal biopsies obtained from keratoplasties demonstrate normal tissue.[79] Incidence of keratoconus is estimated at 10% or less by several authors,[79,80,82] and is generally noted to increase with age. Keratoconus is occasionally complicated by acute hydrops related to rupture of overstretched corneal basement membrane epithelium and subsequent rush of aqueous humor into the corneal stroma. The resultant disruption of corneal lamellar tissue results in a central milky opacity that may cause severe visual impairment.[79] Complications of keratoconus, including uncorrectable astigmatism and hydrops, may be successfully treated with penetrating keratoplasty (corneal transplantation) to help restore visual acuity.[79]

Optic nerve hypoplasia

Fierson found optic nerve hypoplasia in 16 (10.1 %) of his subjects with Down syndrome.[79] Of these cases, 14 exhibited bilateral involvement. Visual acuity may vary considerably; however, significant visual loss is unusual in the absence of coexisting visual disease such as refractive error or strabismus.[79,84]

Nystagmus

While nystagmus has been documented in Down syndrome since 1989,[42,79] it is not common, especially in the absence of other visual defects. Fierson noted the condition in 10% of subjects, the majority of whom exhibited jerk-type nystagmus.[79] Five cases were associated with strabismus.[79] In no case was nystagmus associated with optic nerve hypoplasia.[79]

Refractive error

Most visual loss in Down syndrome is related to refractive error and is thus largely preventable. Caputo et al. noted a 22.5% incidence of myopia in a home-reared population; 38% of these exhibited moderate to severe impairment of greater than 5 diopters.[82] Hyperopia was also noted to be common at 20.9%; most of these cases, however, were termed mild. Astigmatism is common and has been noted by several authors. As in the general population, appropriate prescription glasses are the therapy of choice.[82]

Strabismus

The incidence of strabismus may be overestimated in this population; as previously discussed, epicanthal folds in combination with the flat nasal bridge of Down syndrome may create the impression of "pseudostrabismus." Nevertheless, true strabismus is still relatively common in this population. Most authors note that strabismus tends to be of early onset and to be of the esotropia type. As in the non-Down syndrome population, strabismus requires prompt treatment and careful follow-up to preserve binocular fusion and depth perception and to prevent visual loss. Treatment modalities include patching, glasses to correct existing refractive error, and surgery.[79,83]

DENTAL PROBLEMS

As in the general population, most dental disease in people with Down syndrome is related to poor oral hygiene and is largely preventable. Inattention to oral hygiene in disabled patients is historically quite common among care providers and parents, which may reflect underestimation of the importance of good dental health to adequate nutrition and socialization.

Various dental anomalies occur with greater frequency in Down syndrome than in the general population. Common tooth abnormalities include retained deciduous teeth, delayed eruption of secondary teeth, tooth agenesis, and enamel hypoplasia.[44,85] Tooth shape and size may be atypical; in particular, peg-shaped incisors and unusually slender cuspids have been observed.[44,85] In a 1963 study, Shafer et al. concluded that microdontia is typical of permanent teeth.[44]

Orthodontic studies report a significant (40%) incidence of malocclusion, with mesial, open-bite, and cross-bite malocclusions representing the most typical occlusal relationships.[85] The tongue is often outsized relative to the hypoplastic maxilla and oral cavity; it may promote malocclusion by pushing against the teeth or by preventing mouth closure.[85] Certain oral habits common to this population promote dental disease. Mouth breathing may cause fissured lips and dry mouth. Bruxism is occasionally noted—11% in Lowe's study[85]—and may contribute to dental erosion.

Gingivitis and periodontitis probably pose the most significant threat to the teeth of individuals with Down syndrome.[55] Oral hypotonia may promote inefficient chewing and may predispose an individual to a mechanically soft—and plaque-promoting—diet.[85] Cognitive and neuromotor impairments may make the scrupulous practice of oral hygiene difficult for the individual with Down syndrome.

Thus it is crucial to initiate a good oral hygiene program with individualized and realistic goals and responsibilities delineated for the patient and for the parents or caregivers. Assistive technical devices such as the Water-Pik or battery-operated toothbrush may make daily hygiene easier in this population.[85] Frequent dental recalls for fluoride prophylaxis and scaling may be necessary to prevent chronic, erosive dental disease.

CARDIAC PROBLEMS

It is estimated that 40% to 50% of infants with Down syndrome have a congenital cardiac lesion.[86,87] Cardiac disease in adults is still being studied, but clinical experience suggests an increase in mitral valve disease with valvular prolapse and insufficiency as well as aortic insufficiency. The most common defect in children is complete or partial atrioventricular (AV) canal defect, and the second most common is ventricular septal defect.[86] Other common cardiac defects are ostium secundum atrial septal defect and tetralogy of Fallot.[86] The most common associated lesions are patent ductus arteriosus and pulmonary stenosis.[86] Mitral and aortic valve deformities have also been reported.[86]

Diagnosis

Early diagnosis and treatment of cardiac disease are critical to survival and to optimal growth and development. Cardiac-associated morbidity and mortality are significant in the Down syndrome population. In Greenwood and Nadas' 1973 Boston study, mortality in ventricular septal defect was 20%; in endocardial cushion defect, 38%; in tetralogy of Fallot, 42%; and in complete AV canal, 52%.[86] The most common cause of death in this series of patients was pulmonary vascular obstructive disease, which tended to develop more commonly in AV canal, endocardial cushion defect, and tetralogy of Fallot.[88] Congestive heart failure, hypoxic spells, aspiration and infective pneumonias, and pulmonary hypertension are cited as the most common nonsurgical causes of death in children with Down syndrome and coexisting cardiac disease.[89]

Because of elevated pulmonary artery pressures in the first few weeks of life, the newborn with a shunting lesion may initially be asymptomatic. In light of the high incidence of congenital lesions and the relatively rapid decompensation associated with even moderate shunting lesions in this population, baseline two-dimensional echocardiogram, hematocrit, chest x-ray, ECG, and pediatric cardiac consultation are recommended for all neonates with Down syndrome.[88,89]

The child with a cardiac lesion may experience significant respiratory symptoms related to pulmonary arterial hypertension and subsequent pulmonary vascular obstructive disease.[89] It is well known that vasoocclusive pulmonary disease has an earlier onset in cardiac patients with Down syndrome than in typical patients with congenital heart lesions.[65] Abnormal lung tissue has been documented as well in patients with Down syndrome who do not have cardiac compromise. Conney and Thurlbeck described pulmonary hypoplasia in Down syndrome lung tissue; specifically, they observed relatively few alveoli with underdevelopment of terminal lung units distal to the respiratory bronchioles.[88] The resulting reduced net alveolar surface may promote hypoventilation, hypercarbia, hypoxemia, and acidemia,[88] all of which may contribute to pulmonary arterial hypertension. Sleep apnea and cor pulmonale are potential sequelae of these respiratory and metabolic changes.

For individuals with cardiac lesions, penicillin prophylaxis for subacute bacterial endocarditis is warranted before dental and surgical procedures.[89] A standard prophylaxis schedule includes Penicillin VK, 1 g PO or IM 1 hour before the procedure, followed by 500 mg 6 hours after the procedure, with double doses for patients heavier than 27 kg. Alternatives for penicillin-allergic patients include vancomycin or erythromycin.

Surgical management

Postoperative mortality is greatly reduced over the past two decades but remains significant, as noted in Wells and Lindesmith's 1986 series of AV canal repair, which had a documented mortality rate of 13.5%.[90,91] Postoperative morbidity is high and commonly includes such complications as pulmonary atelectasis and infiltrates, persistent pulmonary hypertension, pneumonia, pleural effusions, arrhythmias and full cardiac arrest, severe bleeding, and residual cardiac disease. On long-term follow-up, residual mitral valve insufficiency was noted as the most common sequela.

The prognosis for untreated congenital lesions, especially AV canal, may be poor. Berger et al. determined by actuarial analysis that only 54% of infants with uncorrected AV canal survive to 6 months of age, 35% to 12 months of age, 15% to 24 months of age, and 4% to 5 years of age.[90] Kirklin and Barratt-Boyes report a 50% chance of surviving to the age of 6 months with uncorrected AV canal.[91] Sondheimer et al. noted that patients referred after the age of 1 year for AV canal surgery fared significantly worse clinically than did those referred earlier in infancy; 5 out of 10 late-referred patients were actually termed inoperable because of advanced pulmonary hypertension.[92] The small proportion of uncorrected patients who achieve long-term survival are severely debilitated—dyspneic and cyanotic, with varying other symptoms of chronic hypoxemia.[92] Quality of life may be significantly impaired.

GYNECOLOGICAL AND REPRODUCTIVE HEALTH PROBLEMS

The disabled individual's right to an emotionally satisfying and culturally appropriate sexual life can no longer be ignored. Over the past two decades, adolescents and young adults with Down syndrome have made their way out of the institutional setting and into the community, where they have formed lasting relationships and possibly may have become part of a family group through marriage or parenting. Reproductive health concerns for both sexes, then, should be given close attention by the primary care provider with an eye toward preventing sexually transmitted disease, sexual abuse, and pregnancy. Early, consistent, and individualized sex education must be provided to these individuals not only to educate them about their bodies but also to counsel them regarding socially appropriate behavior and informed sexual choices.

Gynecology

Menstruation in females with Down syndrome is generally similar to that in typical females with regard to menarchal timing and cycle length.[93,94] Both precocious and delayed puberty have been reported in girls with Down syndrome, but these are clearly not normative.[95] Significant aberrations in pubertal onset must be investigated as in the typical girl but with special attention to thyroid, cardiac, and gastrointestinal function. There may be some decrease in fertility relative to the general female population.[93] Hsiang et al. have reported elevated mean LH and FSH in a group of postpubertal girls, which may suggest a degree of primary ovarian dysfunction.[94] Nevertheless, several live births of both trisomic and normal infants to women with Down syndrome have been reported; therefore, women should be presumed fertile.[95]

The potential need for a contraceptive method should be discussed with the family early in the patient's puberty.[95] Discussions should be honest, nonjudgmental, and structured to allow considerable input from the patient and family.[95] As many people feel uncomfortable discussing sexual concerns in a professional setting, the physician or care provider must anticipate questions and concerns that the family may be hesitant to raise.[95,96] No contraceptive method is totally contraindicated in Down syndrome; however, the method must be chosen with the patient's cognitive and functional status in mind as well as any coexisting chronic illness.[95,97] Contraindications to oral contraceptive use are similar to that in the general population and include a history of thromboembolic disease, hepatic disease, breast cancer, smoking, and a history of dysfunctional uterine bleeding during pregnancy.[95] Barrier methods, including male and female condoms, diaphragm, and cervical cap, may not be practical for individuals with significant cognitive and/or motor impairment as they require application at each coitus.[96,97] Quarterly medroxyprogesterone intramuscular injections (DMPA, Depo-Provera) may be an attractive option for women in whom daily oral contraceptive therapy is not realistic. This method is effective—after one injection, 50% of subjects are amenorrheic—and relatively inexpensive at about $200 per year.[96] It may simplify menstrual hygiene considerably. No protection against sexually transmitted disease is offered, however.[95] Norplant may present another reasonable choice. A progestin-impregnated plastic implant is inserted under local anesthesia into upper arm subcutaneous tissue. It is effective for approximately 5 years but can be removed sooner. Cost ranges between $300 to $400.[95] Irregular vaginal bleeding is occasionally reported.

Surgical sterilization, including laparascopic tubal ligation as well as total abdominal hysterectomy, may also be used for contraceptive purposes.[95,97] These procedures are clearly controversial; if possible, informed consent is usually obtained.[98] The patient should be as involved as possible in decisions concerning surgery. Proceeding with surgery usually requires a Human Subjects' Committee Review; long and complex paperwork is typically required.[95,98] In 1988, the American College of Obstetrics and Gynecological Committee on Ethics issued a statement to guide physicians involved in sterilization decisions.[98] A significant factor in the decision-making process is the patient's health status; coexisting medical problems in Down syndrome can increase anesthetic risk.[95,97]

Guidelines for routine gynecological evaluation are similar to that in the general female population and include an initial pelvic examination and Pap smear at 17 to 18 years of age or earlier if the patient may be sexually active.[99] Recommended frequency of follow-up examinations varies somewhat and depends in part on whether the patient is sexually active, in which case annual evaluation is indicated. A pelvic examination and Pap smear every 2 to 3 years is sufficient in most sexually inactive patients.[99]

Some patients may be able to learn the technique of breast self-examination. Baseline mammogram should be performed between 35 and 40 years of age. As in the general population, the frequency of follow-up is determined by family history and presence of cystic or other abnormal lesions.[97]

Male reproductive issues

Most males with Down syndrome are sterile.[95] The etiology of the sterility is unclear; findings from sperm studies have alternately suggested low sperm counts, abnormal sperm maturation, and spermatogenetic arrest.[95,100-102] Sheridan's 1989 report of a chromosomally normal infant fathered by a man with Down syndrome demonstrates the germ cell mosaicism commonly found in gonadal tissue.[19,95] Pubertal development parallels that of the general male population.[95] Pueschel et al. found no significant difference in genital size between males with Down syndrome and normal controls.[95,103] Mean FSH and LH levels parallel those of normal adolescent males throughout sexual maturation.[95,103] Urogenital anomalies, including hypospadias and double urethral orifice, have been reported.[104,105] An increased incidence of cryptorchidism has been reported by Smith and Berg.[104]

GASTROINTESTINAL AND NUTRITIONAL PROBLEMS

Approximately 12% of infants with Down syndrome have an anomaly of the gastrointestinal tract; these deformities can occur anywhere along its length.[42,104] Duodenal atresia, typically manifested by feeding intolerance, bilious vomiting, and the classic "double-bubble" sign on abdominal plain film, is the most common lesion.[104,106] Tracheoesophageal (TE) fistula, Meckel's diverticulum, Hirschprung's disease, and imperforate anus all occur with increased frequency relative to the general population.[42,106] Duodenal and esophageal atresia as well as TE fistula can present prenatally with polyhydramnios or abnormal ultrasound findings.[42,106]

Clinical issues

Feeding difficulties are common in the infant with Down syndrome.[107] Decreased oral tone and poorly coordinated oral-motor skills tend to promote a weak suck. In particular, breastfeeding may be hard to establish in this population.[107] Infants with congestive heart failure may tire easily while feeding.[89] Infants who have had long postoperative recuperations in the neonatal ICU may be especially slow to feed and may require nasogastric supplementation. The transition to solid food may be difficult and marked by food refusal, gagging, and choking; inefficient chewing and oral skills play a role, as well as a relatively small oral cavity, midface hypoplasia, and any coexisting tonsillar hypertrophy.[107]

Constipation is quite common; hypotonia is probably a significant causal factor, as may be decreased mobility.[42,106] The syndrome-associated conditions of hypothyroidism and Hirschprung's disease should be considered in refractory cases. Treatment typically consists of dietary manipulation to increase fiber and fluid intake; stool softeners and glycerine suppositories may be required in severe constipation. Mineral oil should probably be avoided in this population as some patients may have risk factors for aspiration. The interval between stools should be no longer than 3 days in order to prevent fecal impaction and to preserve anal sphincter tone, rectal sensation, and bowel continence.

Nutritional issues

Obesity can be a significant problem in the individual with Down syndrome.[108] Hypotonia and poor gross motor skills promote a sedentary lifestyle and decreased energy needs. Nutritional counseling emphasizing low-fat food choices, regular physical activity, and careful attention to weight changes at each office visit are recommended to help prevent obesity.

Weight should be plotted on a standardized Down syndrome growth chart.[108]

The question of increased vitamin and mineral requirements in this population is currently being debated. Abnormally low erythrocyte and plasma levels of zinc have been reported;[109,110] zinc supplementation in one study group appeared to reduce the incidence of upper respiratory, ear, and skin infections over several months.[109,110] Vitamin A metabolism has been studied extensively; a 1978 study found a decreased incidence of infections with monthly supplementation.[111] A 1980 study found that Vitamin A serum absorption curves paralleled those of normal controls for 3 hours following Vitamin A loading; at 6 hours post loading, however, serum levels declined faster than in normal controls.[111]

ENDOCRINE PROBLEMS

Thyroid disease occurs in approximately 15% of individuals;[42,112,113] most cases are hypothyroid, but hyperthyroid (Graves') disease and euthyroid thyroiditis occur more commonly than in the general population as well.[42,112,113] The most common etiology of hypothyroidism is chronic lymphocytic (Hashimoto's) thyroiditis.[42] An increased incidence of congenital hypothyroidism is noted in infants with Down syndrome.[42] In addition to routine neonatal screening for congenital hypothyroidism, current Preventive Checklist recommendations indicate annual measurement of T4, T3, and TSH, even in the absence of symptoms.[99] This screening is recommended to allow for the difficulty in distinguishing some hypothyroid symptoms from typical Down syndrome clinical findings.[42] Measurement of anti-thyroid antibodies may be appropriate in the setting of a palpable thyroid mass, hypothyroid clinical state poorly responsive to L-thyroxine replacement, and in the setting of other forms of autoimmune disease such as alopecia areata or insulin-dependent diabetes mellitus.[42] Mildly elevated TSH concentrations have been documented in many subjects without clinical or laboratory symptoms of thyroid dysfunction.[115] Progressive elevations in TSH with normal T4 levels also occur; many care providers treat these patients with L-thyroxine replacement and note improvement of poorly attributable symptoms such as lethargy and constipation.[115]

Short stature is strongly associated with Down syndrome. Males and females have been found to be consistently shorter than their peers throughout the linear growth period.[108] Standardized growth charts are available for boys and girls with Down syndrome; recording parameters on these provides a more realistic picture of growth adequacy than on National Center for Health Statistics (NCHS) charts.[108,116]

True GH deficiency has been reported but seems to be rare.[115] Acceleration in linear growth has been noted in some children with Down syndrome treated with GH.[117] There are many potential causes for growth failure in Down syndrome, and workup should be directed towards ruling out thyroid, cardiac, or gastrointestinal disease—as well as inquiring about feeding problems and recurrent infections—before investigating GH secretion.

ALTERNATIVE THERAPIES

A number of alternative interventions have emerged over time as proposed therapies to improve cognitive and motor function in children and adults with Down syndrome. Most have not undergone formal trials to explore efficacy or safety. When these methods have been tested, the results are often unconvincing or strongly supportive of a placebo effect.

Medical and other professionals tend to promote low functional expectations of individuals with Down syndrome. Consequently, families may find their child doing things that they had been told not to expect. When that occurs, the credibility of the care provider may be called into question, and the family may generalize their mistrust to include all traditional health care providers.

Many families who turn to alternative therapies do so in part from their perception that traditional medicine has no answers, at a time when the proponents of the therapies may be promising a "cure." The lure of anecdotal evidence is tremendous for most families, and guilt is often an important factor in pursuing such treatment. The absence of controlled trials to prove value may mean little to a family driven to "do everything possible" for their child. While alternative therapies may occasionally pose real health risks, wasted time, money, and energy are the most typical adverse consequences. The most dangerous potential consequence of these treatments is the loss of appropriate care when families substitute the alternative therapy for traditional health care. A child who receives "neurodevelopment patterning" or "sensory integration training" in lieu of repair of a worsening cardiac defect, for example, is obviously endangered by alternative therapy. Families often will consult with their local physician regarding the advisability and potential for alternative treatments and will balance that input against the claims of the treatment proponents, as well as opinions of relative and friends. In such an equation, the physician's input is only one voice and often may be seen as peripheral. In many cases, the decision appears to have been made before the physician is approached; the goal of the clinical encounter should then be the preservation of the child's welfare and the avoidance of judgmental statements that may drive the family to abandon traditional medical care.

It must be stressed, however, that some proposed alternative therapies may well provide some benefit. For example, a medication that significantly improved muscle tone could have dramatic impact on function for some individuals. Such effects have been claimed for several substances, but proponents have not undertaken adequate studies. Care providers should encourage families as they investigate their options but should emphasize the importance of double-blinded, controlled trials in proving a treatment's efficacy and safety.

DISCUSSION

The patient with Down syndrome presents a unique challenge to the primary care provider. Many associated medical problems are possible; with appropriate preventive care, however, long-term morbidity and secondary disability can be minimized.

In today's health care market, economic factors will play a crucial role in determining the delivery of health care to this population. The economic advantage of preventive health care will need continued emphasis not only for the benefit of this population but also for that of families, health care providers, and society.

REFERENCES

1. Jones KL: *Recognizable patterns of human malformations*, Philadelphia, 1988, WB Saunders.
2. Pueschel SM: Down syndrome. In Parker S, Zuckerman B, editors: *Behavioral and developmental pediatrics*, New York, 1994, Little Brown.
3. Rogers PT, Coleman M: *Medical care in Down syndrome*, New York, 1992, Marcel Decker.
4. Cooley WC, Graham JM: Down syndrome—an update and review for the primary physician, *Clin Pediatr* 30(4):233-253, 1991.
5. Pueschel SM: Phenotypic characteristics. In Pueschel SM, Pueschel JK, editors: *Biomedical concerns in persons with Down syndrome*. Baltimore, 1992, Paul H. Brookes.
6. Mattheis PJ: Diagnosing Down syndrome. In Redfern DE, editor: *Caring for individuals with Down syndrome and their families*, Report of the Third Ross Round Table on Critical Issues in Family Medicine, 1995 (in press).
7. Sharp MC, Strauss RP, Lorch SC: Communicating medical bad news: parents experiences and preferences, *J Pediatr* 121:539-546, 1992.
8. Cunningham CC, Morgan PA, McGucken RB: Down's syndrome: is dissatisfaction with disclosure of diagnosis inevitable? *Dev Med Child Neurol* 26:33-39, 1984.

9. Lippman A, Wilfond BS: Twice-told tales: stories about genetic disorders, *Am J Hum Genet* 51:936-937, 1992.

10. D'Alton ME, DeCherney AH: Prenatal diagnosis, *NEJM* 328(2):114-120, 1993.

11. Davis JG: Reproductive technologies for prenatal diagnosis, *Fetal Diagn Ther* 8(suppl 1):28-38, 1993.

12. Cowan RS: Aspects of the history of prenatal diagnosis, *Fetal Diagn Ther* 8(suppl 1):10-17, 1993.

13. Elkins TE, Brown D: The cost of choice: a price too high in the triple screen for Down syndrome, *Clin Ob Gyn* 36(3):532-540, 1993.

14. Marteau TM, Slack J, Kidd J, Shaw RW: Presenting a routine screening test in antenatal care: practice observed, *Public Health* 106:131-141, 1992.

15. Marteau TM: Training obstetricians and midwives to offer serum screening for Down syndrome. In Grudzinskas JG, Chard T, Chapman M, Cuckle H, editors: *Screening for Down's syndrome*, New York, 1994, University of Cambridge Press.

16. Peterson MB, Frantzen M, Antonarakis SE, Warren AC, Van Broeckhoven C, Chakatvarti A, Cox TK, Lund C, Olsen B, Poulsen H et al: Comparative study of microsatellite and cytogenetic markers for detecting the origin of the non-disjoined chromosome 21 in Down syndrome, *Am J Hum Genet* 51(3):516-525, 1992.

17. Shaffer LG, Jackson-Cook CK, Meyer J, Brown JA, Spence JE: Molecular genetic approach to the identification of isochromosome of chromosome 21, *Hum Genet* 86:375-382, 1991.

18. Rani AS, Joythi A, Reedy PP, Reedy OS: Reproduction in Down syndrome, *Intern J Gyn Ob* 31:81-86, 1990.

19. Sheridan R, Lierena J, Natkins S, Debenham P: Fertility in a male with trisomy 21, *J Med Genet* 28:294-298, 1989.

20. de Grouchy J, Turleau C: *Clinical atlas of human chromosome,* New York, 1994, John Wiley.

21. Buckley, S: The development of the child with Down syndrome: implications for effective education. In Pueschel SM, Pueschel JK, editors: *Biomedical concerns in persons with Down syndrome,* Baltimore, 1992. Paul H. Brookes.

22. Stafstrom CE, Patxot OF, Gilmore HE, Wisniewski KE: Seizures in children with Down syndrome: etiology, characteristics, and outcome, *Dev Med Child Neurol* 33:191-200, 1991.

23. Stafstrom CE, Konkol RJ: Infantile spasms in children with Down syndrome, *Dev Med Child Neurol* 36:576-585, 1994.

24. Dalton AJ, Wisniewski H: Down's syndrome and the dementia of Alzheimer Disease, *Intern Rev Psychiatr* 2:43-52, 1990.

25. Wisniewski H, Silverman WP, Wegiel J: Aging, Alzheimer disease and mental retardation, *J Intell Disab Res* 38(3)233-239, 1994.

26. Hyman BT: Alzheimer pathology in Down syndrome. In Lott IT, editor: *Down syndrome and Alzheimer disease,* New York, 1992, Wiley-Liss.

27. Cole G, Neal JW, Fraser WI, Cowie VA: Autopsy findings in patients with mental handicap, *J Intell Disab Res* 38:9-26, 1994.

28. Lai F, Williams RS: A prospective study of Alzheimer's disease in Down syndrome, *Arch Neuro* 46:849-853, 1989.

29. Devenny DA, Hill AL, Patxot O, Silverman WP, Wisniewski KE: Aging in higher functioning adults with Down's syndrome: an interim report in a longitudinal study, *J Intell Dis Res* 36(3):241-250, 1992.

30. Carr, J: Annotation: long term outcome for people with Down's syndrome, *J Child Psycho Psychiatry* 35:3:425-439, 1994.

31. Chicoine B, McGuire D, Hebein S, Gilly D: Development of a clinic for adults with Down syndrome, *Ment Retard* 32(2):100-104, 1994.

32. Gahagen CA, Van Dyke DC: Foot and other musculoskeletal problems. In Van Dyke DC, Lang DJ, Heide F, van Duyne S, Soucek MJ, editors: *Clinical perspectives in the management of Down syndrome*, New York, 1990, Springer-Verlag.

33. Diamond LS, Lyme D, Sigman B: Orthopedic disorders in patients with Down syndrome, *Orthop Clinics North Am* 12(1):57-71, 1981.

34. Goldberg MJ, Ampola NG: Birth defect syndromes in which orthopedic problems may be overlooked, *Orthop Clinics North Am* 7(2):285, 1976.

35. Van Dyke DC, Gahagan CA: Cervical spine abnormalities and problems in individuals with Down syndrome, *Clin Pediatr* 27(9):415-418, 1988.

36. Lawhon SM: Orthopedic issues affecting children with Down syndrome. In Van Dyke DC, Eberly SS, Mattheis P, Williams J, editors: *Medical and surgical care for children with Down syndrome*, Rockville, MD, 1995, Woodbine Publishing.

37. Pueschel SM: Atlantoaxial instability in Down syndrome, *Pediatrics* 81(6):879-880, 1988.

38. Pueschel SM, Scola FH: Epidemiologic radiographic and clinical studies of atlantoaxial instability in individuals with Down syndrome, *Pediatr* 80:555-560, 1987.

39. American Academy of Pediatrics Committee on Sports Medicine: Atlantoaxial instability in Down syndrome, *Pediatr* 74:152-154, 1984.

40. Fidone GS: Degenerative cervical arthritis in Down syndrome, *NEJM* 312(5):320, 1986.

41. Sigfreid EM: Skin conditions. In Van Dyke DC, Mattheis P, Eberly S, Williams J, editors: *Medical and surgical care of children with Down syndrome*, Rockville, MD, 1995, Woodbine Publishing.

42. Van Dyke DC, Lang DJ, Miller JD, Heide F, van Duyne S, Chang H: Common medical problems. In Dyke DC, Lang DJ, Heide F, van Dynne S, Soucek MJ, editors: *Clinical perspectives in the management of Down syndrome*, New York, 1990, Springer-Verlag.

43. Du Vivier A, Munro DD: Alopecia areata: auto-immunity in Down syndrome, *Br Med J* 1:191-192, 1975.

44. Shafer WG, Hine MK, Levy BM: *A textbook of oral pathology*, ed 2, Philadelphia, 1963. WB Saunders.

45. Kavanagh, KT: Ear, nose, throat, and sinus conditions of children with Down syndrome. In Van Dyke DC, Eberly SS, Mattheis P, Williams J, editors: *Medical and surgical care for children with Down syndrome*, Rockville, MD, 1995, Woodbine Publishing.

46. Soudon P, Stijns M: Precocity of pulmonary vascular obstruction in Down syndrome, *Europ J Cardiol* 2(4):473-476, 1975.

47. Rowland TW, Nordstrom LG, Bean MS, Burkhardt H: Chronic upper airway obstruction and pulmonary hypertension in Down syndrome, *Am J Dis Child* 135(11):1050-1052, 1981.

48. Loughlin GM, Wynne JW, Victorica BE: Sleep apnea as a possible cause of pulmonary hypertension in Down syndrome, *J Pediatr* 98(3):435-437, 1981.

49. Marcus CL, Keens TG, Bautista DB, von Pechmann WS, Ward SL: Obstructive sleep apnea in children with Down syndrome, *Pediatr* 88:132-139, 1991.

50. Krance RA, Lang DJ: Down syndrome and leukemia. In Van Dyke DC, Lang DJ, Heide F, van Dynne S, Soucek MJ, editors: *Clinical perspectives in the management of Down syndrome*, New York, 1990. Springer-Verlag.

51. de Alarcon P: Children with Down syndrome and cancer. In Van Dyke DC, Eberly SS, Mattheis P, Williams J, editors: *Medical and surgical care for children with Down syndrome*, Rockville, MD, 1995, Woodbine Publishing.

52. Lin HP, Menaka H, Lim KH, Yong HS: Congenital leukemoid reaction followed by fatal leukemia, *Am J Dis Child* 134:939-941, 1980.

53. Barak Y, Mogilner BM, Karov Y, Nir E, Schesinger N, Levine S: Transient acute leukemia in newborns with Down syndrome, *Acta Paediatr Scand* 71:699-701, 1982.

54. McGuiness G: Neonatal polycythemia and hyperviscosity, *Iowa Perinatal Letter* 6(4):15-16, 1985.

55. Regab AH, Abdel-Mageed A, Shuster JJ, Frankel LS, Pullen J, Van Eys J, Sullivan MP, Bovett J, Borowitz J, Crist WM: Clincal characteristics and treatment outcomes of children with acute lymphocytic leukemia in Down syndrome, *Cancer* 67:1057-1063, 1991.

56. Zipursky A , Peeters N, Poon A: Megakaroblastic leukemia : a review of oncology and immunology in Down syndrome, *Prog Clin Bio Res* 246:33-56, 1987.

57. Burgio GR, Uazio A, Nespoli L, Maccario R: Down syndrome: a model of immune deficiency, *Birth Defects* 19(3):325-237, 1983.

58. Fekete G, Kulcsar G, Dann P, Nasz I, Schuler D, Dobos M: Immunological and viriological investigations in Down syndrome, *Europ J Pediatr* 138:59-62, 1982.

59. Fort P, Lifschitz F, Bellisario R, Davis J, Lanes R, Pugliess M, Richman R, Post EM, David R: Abnormalities of thyroid functions in infants with Down syndrome, *J Pediatr* 104:545-549, 1984.

60. Loh RKS, Harth SC, Thong YH, Perraute A: Immunoglobulin subclass deficiency and predisposition to infection in Down syndrome, *Pediatr Infect Dis J* 9(8):547-551, 1990.

61. O'Mahoney D, Whelton MS, Hogan J: Down syndrome and autoimmune chronic active hepatitis: satisfactory outome with therapy, *Irish J Med Sci* 159(1):21-22, 1990.

62. Rabinowe SL, Rubine IL, Seorge KL, Ardri MNS, Eisenbaryh GS: Trisomy 21 (Down syndrome): autoimmunity aging and monoclonal antibody define T-cell abnormalities, *J Autoimmun* 2(1):25-30, 1989.

63. Smith CS: Immune system concerns for children with Down syndrome: Recurrent infections: associated immune conditions and immunizations. In Van Dyke DC, Eberly SS, Mattheis P, Williams J, editors: *Medical and surgical care for children with Down Syndrome*, Rockville, MD, 1995, Woodbine Publishing.

64. Aase JM. Wilson AC, Smith DW: Small ears in Down's syndrome: a helpful diagnostic aid, *J Pediatr* 82(5):845-847, 1973.

65. Strome M: Down's syndrome: A modern otorhinolaryngologal perspective, *Laryngoscope* 91:1581-1594, 1981.

66. Dahle AJ, McCollister FP: Hearing and otologic disorders in children with Down syndrome, *Am J Ment Def* 90:636-642, 1986.

67. Downs MP, Balkany TJ: Otologic problems and hearing impairment in Down syndrome. In Dmitriev V, Oelwein P, editors: *Advances in Down syndrome*, Seattle, 1988, Special Child Publications.

68. Balkany TJ, Mischke RE, Downs MP, Jafek BW: Ossicular abnormalities in Down syndrome, *Otolaryngol Head Neck Surg* 87:372-384, 1979.

69. Walby AP, Schutknecht HF: Concomitant occurrence of cochleosaccular dysplasia in Down syndrome, *Arch Otolaryngol* 110:447-449, 1984.

70. Harada T, Sando I: Temporal bone histopathologic findings in Down syndrome, *Arch Otolaryngol* 107: 96-103, 1981.

71. Schwartz DM, Schwartz RH: Acoustic impedance and otoscopic findings in children with Down syndrome, *Arch Otolaryngol* 104:652-656, 1978.

72. Samuelson ME, Nguyen VT : Middle ear effusion in Down syndrome patients, *Nebraska Med J* 65(4):83-84, 1980.

73. Downs MP: The expanding imperatus of early identification. In Bess FH, editor: *Childhood deafness: causation, assessment, and management*, New York, 1977, Grune & Stratton.

74. Holm V, Kunze L: Effect of chronic otitis media on language and speech development, *Pediatrics* 43:883, 1969.

75. Kessner DM, Snow C, Singer J: Assessment of medical care for children. In *Contrasts in health status*, vol III, Washington, DC, 1974, National Academy of Science

76. Fulton R, Lloyd L: Hearing impairment in a population of children with Down syndrome, *Am J Ment Def* 73:298-307, 1978.

77. Paludetti G, Maurizi M, Altissimi G, Frenguelli A, Ottaviani F, Rosignolli M: L'audiometria del tronco de l'encephalo in alcumi tipi di impoacusie perifericche, *Nuovo Arch It Otol* 7:519-542, 1979.

78. Van Dyke DC, Popejoy ME, Hemenway WG: Ear, nose and throat problems and hearing abnormalities. In Van Dyke DC, Lang DJ, Heide F, van Duyne S, Soucek MJ, editors: *Clinical perspectives in the management of Down syndrome*, New York, 1990, Springer-Verlag.

79. Fierson W: Ophthalmological aspects. In Van Dyke DC, Lang DJ, Heide F, van Duyne S, Soucek JM, editors: *Cllnical perspectives in the management of Down syndrome*, New York, 1990, Springer-Verlag.

80. Wolfflin E: Ein klinischer Beitrag zur kenntnis stinktur der Iris, *Arch Augenheilk* 45:1-4, 1902.

81. Ormond AW: Notes on the ophthalmic conditions of forty-two mongolian imbeciles, *Trans Ophthalm Soc United Kingdom* 2:69, 1910.

82. Caputo AR, Wagner RS, Reynolds DR, Guo S, Goel AK: Down syndrome: clinical review of ocular features, *Clin Pediatr* 28(8):356-357, 1989.

83. Lowe RF: *The eyes of mongolism, Br J Ophthalmol* 33:131-154, 1949.

84. Lambert SR, Hoyt CS, Narahara MH: Optic nerve hypoplasia, *Surv Ophthalmol* 32:1-9, 1987.

85. Lowe O: Dental problems. In Van Dyke DC, Lang DJ, Heide F, van Duyne S, Soucek MJ, editors: *Clinical perspectives in the management of Down syndrome*, New York, 1990, Springer-Verlag

86. Greenwood RD, Nadas AS.: The clinical course of cardiac disease in Down syndrome, *Pediatrics* 58:893-897, 1976.

87. Spicer RL: Cardiovascular disease in Down syndrome, *Pediatr Clin North Am* 31(6):1331-1343, 1984.

88. Conney TP, Thurlbeck WM: Pulmonary hypoplasia in Down syndrome, *NEJM* 307:1170-1173, 1982.

89. Gordon LS: Cardiac conditions. In Van Dyke DC, Lang DJ, Heide F, van Duyne S, Soucek MJ, editors: *Clinical perspectives in the management of Down syndrome*, New York, 1990, Springer-Verlag.

90. Berger TJ, Blackstone EH, Kirklin JW, Bargeron LM, Hazelring JB, Turner ME: Survival and probability of cure without and with operation in complete atrioventricular canal, *Ann Thorac Surg* 27: 104-111, 1978.

91. Kirklin JW, Barratt-Boyes BG: *Cardiac surgery*, New York, 1986, John Wiley.

92. Soundheimer HM, Byrum CJ, Blackman MS: Unequal cardiac care for children with Down syndrome, *Am J Dis Child* 139:68-70, 1985.

93. Goldstein H: Menarche, menstruation, sexual relations and contraception of adolescent females with Down syndrome, *Europ J Ob Reprod Biol* 27:343-349, 1988.

94. Hsiang YH, Berkovitz GD, Bland GL, Migeon CJ, Warren AC Gonadal function in patients with Down syndrome, *Am J Med Genet* 27:449-458, 1987.

95. Van Dyke DC, McBrien DM, Mattheis PJ: *Psychosexual behavior, sexuality, and management issues in individuals with Down syndrome*, Presentation, European Down Syndrome Symposium, Mallorca, Spain, 1995.

96. Laros A: *Adolescent gynecology*, Presentation, Department of Pediatrics, University of Iowa, 1993.

97. Elkins TE: Gynecologic care. In Pueschel SM, Pueschel JK, editors: *Biomedical concerns in persons with Down syndrome*. Baltimore, MD, 1990, Paul H Brookes.

98. American College of Obstetrics and Gynecology Committee on Ethics: *Committee opinion: sterilization of women who are mentally handicapped*, Washington, DC, 1988, ACOG.

99. Ohio-Western Pennsylvania Down Syndrome Network: Down Syndrome Preventive Medical Checklist, *Down Syndrome Paper Abstracts Professional* 15:1, 1992.

100. Stearns PE, Droulard KE, Schhar FH: Studies bearing on fertility of male and female mongoloids, *Am J Ment Def* 65:37-41, 1960.

101. Benda CE: *Down syndrome: mongolism and its management*, New York, 1969, Grune & Stratton.

102. McCoy EE: Endocinre function in Down syndrome. In Lott IT, McCoy EE, editors: *Down syndrome advances in medical care*, New York, 1991, Wiley-Liss.

103. Pueschel SM, Bier JAB : Endocrinologic aspects. In Pueschel SM, Pueschel JM, editors: *Biomedical concerns in persons with Down syndrome*, Baltimore, MD, 1992, Paul H Brookes.

104. Smith GR, Berg JM: *Down's anomaly*, ed 2, New York, 1976, Churchill-Livingston.

105. Lang DJ, Van Dyke DC, Heide F, Lowe PL: Hypospadias and urethral abnormalities in Down snydrome, *Clin Pediatr* 26(1):40-42, 1987.

106. Buie TM, Sandoval AFF: Down Syndrome and the gastrointestinal tract. In Van Dyke DC, Eberly SS, Mattheis P, Williams J, editors: *Medical and surgical care for children with Down syndrome*, Rockville, MD, 1995, Woodbine Publishing.

107. Van Dyke DC, Perterson LL, Hoffman MN: Problems in feeding. In Van Dyke DC, Lang DJ, Heide F, van Duyne S, Soucek MJ, editors: *Clinical perspectives in the management of Down syndrome*, New York, 1990, Springer-Verlag.

108. Baer, MT, Waldron J, Gumm H, Van Dyke DC, Chang H: Nutrition assessment of the child with Down syndrome. In Van Dyke DC, Lang DJ, Heide F, van Duyne S, Soucek MJ, editors: *Clinical perspectives in the management of Down syndrome*, New York, 1990, Springer-Verlag.

109. Franchesci C, Chiricolo M, Licastro F, Zonott M, Masi M, Mocchegiarti R, Fabri SN: Oral zinc supplementation in Down syndrome: restoration of thymic endocrine activity and some immune defects, *Am J Ment Def* 32:169, 1988.

110. Bjorksten B, Back O, Gustavson KH, Hallmans B, Haggloff B, Tariuv KA: Zinc and immune function in Down syndrome, *Acta Paed Scand* 69:183-187, 1980.

111. Palmer S: Influence of vitamin A on the immune response: findings in children with Down syndrome, *Internat J Vitamin Nutrition Res* 48:189, 1980.

112. Pueschel SM: Growth, thyroid function, and sexual maturation in Down syndrome, *Growth, Genetics Hormones* 6:1-5, 1990.

113. Cutler AT, Bemezfa-Obeiter R, Brink SJ: Thyroid function in young children, *Am J Dis Child* 140: 479-483, 1986.

114. Pueschel SM, Pezzullo JC: Thyroid dysfunction in Down syndrome, *Am J Dis Child* 139:636-639, 1985.

115. Foley TP: Thyroid conditions and other endocrine concerns in children with Down syndrome. In Van Dyke DC, Eberly SS, Mattheis P, Williams J, editors: *Medical and surgical care for children with Down syndrome*, Rockville, MD, 1995, Woodbine Publishing.

116. Pipes PL: Nutrition and children with Down syndrome. In Van Dyke DC, Eberly SS, Mattheis P, Williams J, editors: *Medical and surgical care for children with Down syndrome*, Rockville, MD, 1995, Woodbine Publishing.

117. Castels S, Wisniewski KE: *Growth hormone treatment in Down's syndrome*, New York, 1993, John Wiley.

CHAPTER 9C ————————————————————

Fragile X syndrome

RANDI J. HAGERMAN

The fragile X syndrome is the most common known inherited cause of mental retardation. It is caused by a mutation in the fragile X mental retardation gene (FMR1), which is located at the bottom end of the X chromosome at the Xq27.3 location. It is also characterized by a fragile site at this location in cytogenetic studies.

The fragile X syndrome is characterized by a spectrum of developmental problems ranging from learning disabilities and/or emotional problems in mildly affected individuals through all levels of mental retardation.[1] The prevalence of mental retardation caused by fragile X is approximately 1 per 1250 in males and 1 per 2500 in females in the general population.[2] The prevalence of carrier females in the general population is much higher, approximately 1 in 260.[3] Fragile X syndrome represents approximately 30% of all causes of X-linked mental retardation, and it occurs in approximately 2% to 3% of retarded individuals who are cytogenetically tested.[4,5] Although the FMR1 gene is located on the X chromosome, females are also affected by this disorder. They usually have less severe cognitive deficits and behavioral problems than the males, although shyness, social anxiety, math deficits and other learning problems are common among affected females.[6]

HISTORICAL PERSPECTIVE

The first description of the fragile X chromosome was reported by Lubs in 1969 in the evaluation of two retarded brothers.[7] It was not until the 1980s, however, that cytogenetic testing was used routinely to diagnose fragile X syndrome. The work of Sutherland[8] was critical to clarify the tissue culture requirements, including the use of folate deficient media, to elicit the expression of the fragile X chromosome. The decade of the 1980s was important in characterizing the phenotypic involvement in males and females. In addition, it became apparent that both males and females could be unaffected carriers, but the frequency of mental retardation increased through the generations in each family with fragile X syndrome.[9] This phenomenon is known as *anticipation*.

The reason for increased involvement in subsequent generations was not understood until the gene was sequenced in 1991.[10] A unique form of mutation was identified, a trinucleotide repeat expansion $(CGG)_n$ was discovered at the 5' end of the FMR1 gene.[10,11] In normal individuals this expansion includes 5 to 50 repeats of CGG, and it is stable from generation to generation, perhaps because an AGG anchor occurs after every 10 CGG repeats.[12] However, if the repeat number increases beyond 50 or if AGG anchors are lost, the repeat number becomes unstable and the number may increase in the next generation. Individuals with >50 but <200 repeats are said to have the premutation and are usually unaffected themselves but they are at risk to have retarded children when the premutation is passed on by a female. Individuals with >200 repeats have a full mutation and they are usually affected by fragile X syndrome.[11] The full mutation is usually methylated, a process of adding CH_3 groups to the DNA helix, preventing transcription and translation. Therefore the FMR1 protein (FMRP) is not produced, and it is the absence of FMRP that causes the fragile X syndrome. Since females have two X chromosomes, the normal X is producing protein, depending on the X inactivation status in each cell, so that females have less phenotypic involvement than males.

PHYSICAL AND BEHAVIORAL PHENOTYPE
Males

The classical triad of features in males are large and prominent ears, a long face, and large testicles or macroorchidism. These features are seen in approximately 80% of adolescent and adult males, but they are a less common triad in young children.[1] The prominent ears alone are usually the most common feature in the physical examination (Fig. 9-2). Head circumference is often large in childhood because the brain is bigger than in normal individuals, and certain areas of the brain are noticeably larger, including the caudate, hippocampus, and ventricles, whereas the posterior cerebellar vermis is smaller in fragile X patients compared to controls.[13] It is hypothesized that FMRP is important in the paring down of neuronal connections, a normal part of brain development in late gestation and in infancy. The absence of FMRP, therefore, is linked to the absence of normal modifications of neuronal connections. This may explain the enhanced sensitivity fragile X children experience with all sensory input. They often

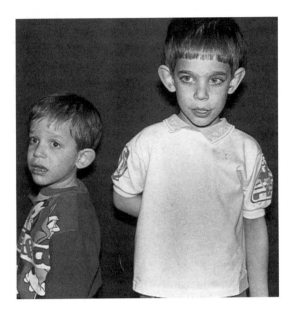

Fig. 9-2 Prominent ears are usually the most common feature in the physical examination.

react adversely to normally pleasant smells, they have poor eye contact, hyperacute hearing, and tactile defensiveness.[1]

A number of physical features appear to be related to a connective tissue disorder associated with fragile X syndrome.[1] Individuals with fragile X have soft and velvet-like skin in addition to sometimes having excessive wrinkles on the palms. Joints are hyperextensible, especially finger joints, and the metacarpal phalangeal (MP) extension is usually 90 degrees or greater in the young child. The feet are flat in most individuals with fragile X syndrome, and 25% have a pectus excavatum. Mitral valve prolapse (MVP) is more common with age and approximately 50% of adult fragile X males have MVP. The large and prominent ears, which often demonstrate cupping of the pinnae, are probably also related to loose connective tissue.[1] Waldstein et al.[14,15] reported histological findings of abnormal elastin fibers, which were thin, broken, and less frequently seen in fragile X males compared to controls. In addition, medical complications associated with fragile X syndrome, such as recurrent otitis media, recurrent sinusitis, hernias, and rare joint dislocations or joint instability, are probably related to this connective tissue disorder.[1]

Macroorchidism is probably not related to connective tissue problems but instead may be caused by hypothalamic dysfunction in fragile X syndrome. The enlarged testes may be present to a very limited degree in early childhood, but in most males with fragile X syndrome the enlargement of the testicle begins at age 9 years. The testicular size will increase throughout puberty reaching an average volume of 50 to 60 ml, although volumes as large as 100 ml have been reported.[16] Macroorchidism is identified when the testicular volume is >30 ml in adolescence and adulthood, and it is present in approximately 80% of mature males with fragile X syndrome. You can measure the testicular volume with an orchidometer or you can calculate the volume *(v)* after measuring the length and width *(w)* with the following formula: $v = \pi/6(1w^2)$.

The enlarged testicles do not cause a medical problem, and several males have been reported to reproduce, so fertility appears to be normal. The sperm carries the premutation even though the rest of the tissues in an affected male have the full mutation. This has led Reyniers et al.[17] and others to hypothesize that the expansion of the CGG repeat number occurs early in embryogenesis, after the cells that are destined to become the gametes have separated. Therefore, in the embryo of an affected male the progenitor cells for the sperm are protected from expansion while the rest of the cells expand to a full mutation.

Females

The physical phenotype, including prominent or large ears, a long face, high palate, hyperextensible finger joints, double-jointed thumbs, and flat feet, are commonly seen in females with the full mutation.[1] Fryns[18] reported that females who are affected cognitively are more likely to have typical physical features of fragile X syndrome. A female's degree of involvement physically is probably reflective of the level of FMRP that is present in her tissues. For females with the full mutation, this is probably related to the pattern X-inactivation or the percentage of cells that have the normal X chromosome as the active X chromosome. The higher this percentage is, the more normal the phenotype should be.[19]

Approximately one third of females affected by fragile X syndrome have behavioral features that are similar to males. Hand flapping, hand biting, and nail biting are seen in 20% to 35% of full mutation females.[1,20] Attention deficit hyperactivity disorder (ADHD) is seen in one third of affected females, although the hyperactivity is not as severe as that commonly seen in males.[6,20] Instead, shyness and social anxiety often causing an avoidant disorder of childhood is seen in the majority of girls affected by fragile X syndrome.[20] If the ADHD symptoms are severe, ADHD can overshadow the shyness and the patient will be more outgoing, although impulsive and hyperactive.[21] Shyness, however, in young girls with the full mutation is generally seen.

A subgroup of females with the premutation may be mildly affected by the fragile X mutation. More prominent ears have been documented in females who carry the premutation compared to controls.[22] In addition, Schwartz et al.[23] have shown that premature menopause is more common in females with the premutation compared to controls or women with the full mutation. A high rate of dizygous twinning is seen in females with the premutation, which is three times the rate seen in controls or in females with the full mutation.[24] These findings suggest a mild phenotypic effect in some individuals with the premutation, although the molecular mechnisms for such an effect have not been clarified.

COGNITIVE DEFICITS

In females with the full mutation, approximately 50% have significant cognitive deficits ranging from borderline intellectual disabilities to mental retardation.[6,25,26] Although an occasional severely retarded or autistic female has been reported, most mentally retarded girls are in the mild range.[27] In females with the full mutation and a normal IQ, learning disabilities are common. Mazzocco et al.[28] have reported frontal or executive function deficits and visual-spatial perceptual problems in normal IQ full mutation females. Therefore, tangential speech, poor organization skills, concentration difficulties, impulsivity, and a tendency to deny emotional problems, perhaps related to a difficulty in integrating past emotional experiences, are often difficulties observed in females with the full mutation.[28,29] Math difficulties are consistently seen in all individuals with the full mutation and are also commonly reported in individuals with the premutation.[1,22]

In males affected by fragile X syndrome, the majority present with mental retardation; however, approximately 13% have an IQ in the non-retarded (IQ >70) range.[30] This presentation is most common in early childhood, but approximately one third of males with the full mutation will experience a significant decline in IQ throughout childhood.[31,32] Male individuals who maintain their IQ in the non-retarded range have been shown to often have a variation in molecular findings, typically an incompletely methylated full mutation, such that a limited amount of FMRP is produced.[30,32,33] Even a small amount of FMRP (10% to 35% of normal levels) appears to improve the cognitive outcome of males with the full mutation. However, the high functioning males with fragile X syndrome usually have significant social deficits and often carry the diagnosis of Asperger syndrome[1] or schizotypal personality disorder.[33]

Recently three males with the premutation have been reported who are mildly affected with fragile X syndrome and have only ADHD symptoms, shyness, and typical physical features. All three were shown to demonstrate a mild deficit of FMRP levels in lymphoblastoid studies.[34] It appears that a spectrum of FMRP deficits translate into a range of disabilities. Emotional problems, such as anxiety, shyness, or avoidant disorder, present in the mildly deficient range of FMRP along with learning disabilities in math and executive function deficits. With increasingly severe deficits of FMRP levels, more severe learning problems ensue until global cognitive deficits are seen with mental retardation and an absence of FMRP. As better methodology becomes available to measure FMRP levels, this spectrum of involvement will become delineated.

DIAGNOSIS

Cytogenetic testing on a peripheral blood sample has been used throughout the 1980s to diagnose fragile X syndrome. In individuals with the full mutation, a fragile site at Xq27.3 will be seen in 1% up to 50% of lymphocytes when folate-deficient tissue culture media is used or when antimetabolites, such as FudR, are added to the media to elicit the fragile site.[35] The problems associated with using cytogenetic testing include the expense ($500 to $800 per study) and time involved to carry out the analysis. Cytogenetic testing does not identify carriers or high-functioning individuals with variant methylation patterns because they may not demonstrate the fragile site. The benefits of cytogenetic testing include the ability to diagnose other chromosomal abnormalities and two mutations distal to FMR1, which also have fragile sites—FRAXE and FRAXF. They both have a variable association with mental retardation and a trinucleotide repeat mutation, but they are far more infrequent than the mutation at FMR1.[36]

The DNA testing for fragile X syndrome involves a Southern blot analysis with a labeled probe for FMR1 or the use of PCR testing.[4,25,26] This testing is less expensive (approximately $200) than cytogenetic testing and is more time efficient. DNA testing gives more information regarding the mutation, including the CGG number and the methylation status of the gene, which is important for prognosis. For research purposes even the X inactivation ratio can be measured from Southern blot testing.[37] All family studies should be carried out using DNA testing because carriers will be accurately identified. High-functioning or learning-disabled individuals who have features of fragile X should be studied with DNA testing. On the other hand, cytogenetic studies should be done when testing individuals who present with mental retardation or autism and dysmorphic features. These individuals may have any number of cytogenetic abnormalities, and these can be assessed by chromosome studies, which include a fragile X analysis. Often laboratories will combine the diagnostic tests and carry out PCR DNA testing first before progressing with the full karyotype.

Recently Willemsen et al.[38] reported a new methodology to detect fragile X syndrome using fluorescent-labeled antibodies to FMRP poured over lymphocytes. In normal individuals the lymphocytes will fluoresce with the presence of FMRP, but in males with fragile X syndrome, there is no fluorescence. This methodology is relatively inexpensive and will be useful in screening mentally retarded males. If the test is positive with no fluorescence, DNA testing should be carried out to confirm the mutation at FMR1. The accuracy of this testing is excellent in males but poor in females because of the additional normal X chromosome, which produces FMRP depending on the X-inactivation status.

It is possible to have fragile X syndrome with an absence of FMRP without the CGG amplification. Several patients have been reported with a deletion of the FMR1 region, and a clinical phenotype typical of fragile X syndrome. Deletions can be detected by DNA testing.

MANAGEMENT
Genetic counseling

At the time of initial diagnosis of the individual, the immediate and extended family members should be offered genetic counseling, preferably by a genetic counselor. The mother is always the carrier when the individual is a male; therefore, she may have multiple siblings who are affected themselves or are carriers. If the mother has a retarded brother, or if she has the full mutation herself, the gene carrier is the mother's mother because the CGG repeat only expands to the full mutation when it is passed on by a female. If the mother's father is the carrier, then all of his daughters are obligate carriers and they are at high risk to have retarded children.

It is helpful to find a motivated family member, such as the individual's mother or aunt, who can contact other family members regarding the diagnosis of fragile X syndrome. The extended family members may contact the genetic counselor or the health care provider to obtain more information about the diagnosis and their risk of involvement. Often if a family member makes the first contact, it is less intrusive than if a stranger (the genetic counselor) contacts the family initially. A general letter describing the diagnosis, the risk to other family members, and the molecular testing that is needed to clarify the carrier status and identify affected individuals is usually helpful to families to distribute among their relatives.

In the counseling of women with the premutation, it is important to clarify the increasing risk of expansion to the full mutation when the premutation CGG repeat number increases. For women with a premutation >90 to 100 repeats, there is 100% risk of expansion to the full mutation when the fragile X chromosome is passed on to the next generation.[39] The differences in the degree of involvement of males and females with the full mutation must also be explained.

Prenatal diagnosis is available for fragile X and can be carried out in CVS samples and from amniocentesis. DNA analysis has remarkably improved the accuracy of prenatal diagnosis, and the findings of a premutation or a full mutation are important for predicting the degree of involvement of the fetus. However, methylation studies are inaccurate in prenatal testing and cannot be used for prognostic purposes because methylation may be delayed until the end of gestation. Therefore complete methylation that is present at birth may not be present at the time of prenatal diagnosis.[40]

Infancy

Newborns with fragile X syndrome may or may not demonstrate typical physical features. An occasional infant has been described with macroorchidism, but this is not typical of babies with fragile X syndrome. A rare patient may have congenital hip dislocation or an inguinal hernia related to the connective tissue abnormalities in fragile X syndrome. Recurrent vomiting is relatively common secondary to gastroesophageal reflux (GER), which may be related to the connective tissue problems. Treatment of GER includes positioning upright after meals and thickening the feeds with rice cereal. On occasion, medication is necessary for treatment of GER, particularly if aspiration, pulmonary symptoms, or failure to thrive occur.[41] Infants at greatest risk for failure to thrive are those who have an affected mother who herself is retarded. These mothers may be overwhelmed by the demands of caring for a difficult infant or child with fragile X syndrome. They need support and guidance from either the close relatives or from social services.

Hypotonia is noticeable from birth in affected infants, and it is related to the neurological abnormalities of fragile X syndrome.[1] Coordination deficits may be noticeable even in learning how to suck and feed. Although most infants do well with sucking and thrive, there is an increased incidence of sudden infant death (SIDS) in fragile X syndrome. In addition, Tirosh and Borochowitz[43] have reported obstructive sleep apnea in 2 of 7 patients with fragile X syndrome evaluated by a sleep study.[43] Prolonged expiratory apnea associated with 60%-70% O_2 saturation was documented in these children. The authors hypothesized obstruction secondary to large adenoids or tonsils, narrow facial structure or hypotonic oropharyngeal muscles in fragile X syndrome. Sleep apnea appears to be responsible for the increase in SIDS in fragile X syndrome. Even though sleep apnea appears to be an infrequent complication of fragile X syndrome, the medical history should always include questions regarding sleeping difficulties, wakefulness, snoring, and pauses in the breathing rate. Individuals who have significant difficulty with snoring and obstructive symptoms should be evaluated by an ENT physician and undergo a sleep study to evaluate episodes of desaturation. An adenoidectomy is often successful in eliminating the snoring and obstructive episodes.

Childhood

Recurrent otitis media is the most common medical problem experienced by children with fragile X syndrome and perhaps for all children in a pediatric practice.[44] Otitis commonly begins in the first or second year of life, and it is recurrent for 60% of children with fragile X syndrome. Repeated ear infections cause a fluctuating hearing loss that interferes with language development. Language delays are a problem for most children with fragile X syndrome, and recurrent otitis can compound the language difficulties. Therefore these children need to be treated vigorously for recurrent otitis with placement of PE tubes early, rather than later, or the use of prophylactic antibiotics. Perhaps the loose connective tissue or the changes in facial structure cause difficulty with drainage of middle ear fluid or cause collapse of the eustachian tubes.

Recurrent sinusitis is also a concern for approximately 10% of children with fragile X syndrome and may be related to facial structural changes that interfere with normal drainage. A handful of children with fragile X syndrome have been noted to have low gamma globulin levels, and they have responded well to monthly gamma globulin injections. Immune abnormalities, however, have never been thoroughly studied in fragile X syndrome. In general, other than otitis media, recurrent infections are not a consistent problem in fragile X syndrome.

Hyperactivity. The most consistent behavioral problem in children with fragile X syndrome is a short attention span, usually accompanied by hyperactivity. All boys with fragile X syndrome have deficits in attention, and approximately 70% to 80% are hyperactive, whereas only 35% of girls with fragile X syndrome have ADHD and severe hyperactivity is far less frequent.[1] By history, problems with hyperactivity sometimes begin in utero and are more overtly manifested when the child begins to walk. Children in their second and third year often begin to have tantrums, particularly when they are overstimulated, overtired, or when they make transitions. They usually do not self-calm well and simply giving them time outs may not be sufficient. Aggression involving kicking or biting is common and appears to be related to impulsivity and tantrum behavior. Hand flapping and hand biting also begins in the toddler years for the majority of boys with fragile X syndrome.[1]

These behavioral problems can be severe and overwhelming for many parents. The treatment for these difficulties includes the efforts of the occupational therapist to use sensory integration techniques to calm the child, and efforts of the behavioral psychologist to teach the family to recognize escalating behavior problems, to use positive reinforcement, to facilitate transitions, and to avoid overstimulation.[45,46] In addition medication can often be helpful for these difficulties.[47]

The treatment of hyperactivity and attention problems in fragile X syndrome usually includes the use of a stimulant medication, such as methylphenidate, dextroamphetamine, or pemoline. Methylphenidate is most commonly used, and a double-blind crossover study found methylphenidate to be most helpful with the fewest side effects, compared to dextroamphetamine and placebo in 15 children with fragile X syndrome.[48] However, some children did better on dextroamphetamine, and anecdotal evidence suggests that dextroamphetamine may be better tolerated in the child under 5 years of age. Children with fragile X syndrome are often very sensitive to the dose of stimulants, and irritability with an increase in tantrum behavior is common when the dose is high (i.e., methylphenidate >0.6 mg/kg/dose), particularly in young children.

Irritability with stimulants has often lead to alternative medications, particularly for the child under 5 years of age. Since tantrums, overstimulation, and hyperactivity are common in the 3- to 5-year-old child, clonidine has been frequently used for its calming effect.[49] Clonidine is an alpha$_2$ presynaptic agonist that lowers overall norepinephrine levels. Clonidine usually calms the child, decreases hyperactivity, improves attention, and decreases aggression. In a survey of over 30 children with fragile X syndrome, clonidine was helpful in 80%.[49] The main side effect is sedation, which can last for 2 weeks or longer. Clonidine will also lower blood pressure, and it generally should not be given to children under 3 years old. In the 3-to 5-year-old age group, it should be given in low doses such as one fourth of a 0.1 mg tablet twice a day to start and a gradual increase as sedation improves. Clonidine also comes in a patch form (Catapres TTS1, 2 and 3 sizes), which is changed every 5 to 7 days as needed. The patch is placed in the mid-back area, hopefully where the child can't reach it. The TTS1 patch can be cut so that a quarter or a half of a patch can be used in the preschool child. Clonidine usually helps with sleeping difficulties, which are common in children with fragile X syndrome. Clonidine can also be used in addition to stimulant medication. Clonidine is most helpful in the afternoon and evening for its calming effect, whereas methylphenidate is most helpful for improving attention and concentration at school.

For the child under 3 years of age who is diagnosed with fragile X syndrome, there are no routinely used medications for behavior problems. Folic acid is controversial, with some reports suggesting that it is helpful for ADHD symptoms and others showing that it is not helpful.[47,51] In my experience, approximately 50% of mothers feel that folate therapy is helpful for their child's behavior or language development, so routinely the child or infant is given a trial of folic acid for a 3-month period.[47,51] The dose is 1 mg/kg/d up to a maximum of 10 mg/d divided bid. The pharmacy can make a liquid solution of 5 mg/cc and this is given as 1 cc orally twice a day. If folic acid seems beneficial after a 3-month trial, it is continued; otherwise it is discontinued. It is recommended that a multiple vitamin with B_6 is used daily because folate therapy may lower B_6 levels and less commonly serum zinc levels.[47] These blood levels should be checked at least yearly while the child is on folate therapy. Folate appears to act like a weak stimulant medication, so when the child is old enough to tolerate other more effective stimulants, the folate can usually be discontinued without negative effects.

Other medications that can be used in fragile X syndrome to improve hyperactivity and attention include imipramine,[52] desipramine, amantadine,[47] bupropion, and thioridazine,[47] but controlled studies have not been carried out to evaluate efficacy.

Seizures. Seizures occur in approximately 20% of children with fragile X syndrome, and they usually begin in early childhood.[1] They may be subtle with just staring spells or arm jerking, or they may be grand mal episodes. They are usually treated with carbamazepine, which also has a beneficial effect on behavior.[47] Carbamazepine and valproic acid are helpful in stabilizing mood, which leads to less aggression and fewer mood swings. An EEG should be done if seizures are suspected. Rolandic spikes are common, and usually seizures are well controlled on anticonvulsants.[53,54]

Eye abnormalities. Eye abnormalities are common in fragile X syndrome, including refraction errors, strabismus, and nystagmus.[1] Strabismus is present in 30% to 40% of males with fragile X syndrome, and whenever this problem is seen the child should be referred to an ophthalmologist. Even if no problems are present on a general examination, every child with fragile X syndrome should have an examination by an optometrist or ophthalmologist before age 4 or 5 years because occult problems, such as refraction errors, are common.

Heart murmur. If a heart murmur or click is present on examination, concern for mitral valve prolapse (MVP) increases, and the patient should be referred to cardiology for an echocardiogram. If significant MVP is present, then SBE prophylaxis is recommended.[1,47]

Throughout childhood, children with fragile X syndrome should be seen at least yearly by their physicians to monitor behavior problems and to examine for complications regarding loose connective tissue. Recurrent otitis media usually decreases in severity after age 5 or 6 years. Scoliosis occurs in less than 20%, and hernias are only occasionally seen. Joint dislocations are rare, but they require orthopedic referral. Precocious puberty has been described in a few young females with fragile X syndrome,[1] and it requires endocrine consultation. More frequent visits are required for children on medications so that growth parameters and side effects can be monitored.

Adolescence

Usually hyperactivity improves by adolescence, but aggression may be an increasing problem in males as testosterone increases in puberty. Approximately 30% of patients have difficulty with episodic dyscontrol or intermittent outbursts of aggression. The aggression usually occurs when the patient becomes overstimulated by environmental situations, such as transitions and noisy or crowded circumstances. Sometimes they misinterpret an action or become angry, and then their behavior often escalates to a verbal or physical outburst. The patient's mood can fluctuate easily to anger, and he can have difficulty inhibiting impulsive behavior. Counseling can be beneficial to help the patient recognize situations that lead to an outburst and to give the patient concrete calming techniques that can be self-initiated, such as counting, calming statements, walking away, and visualization techniques.[55]

Medications may also be helpful for aggression. Both the stimulants and clonidine help the inhibitory system to decrease impulsive behavior, and this often helps with aggression. The selective serotonin-reuptake inhibitors (SSRIs), such as fluoxetine (Prozac) or sertraline (Zoloft), can be helpful in decreasing aggression, probably because they help to stabilize mood. Although SSRIs are used as antidepressants in the general population, they are used more frequently for decreasing aggression, decreasing obsessive/compulsive behavior, and decreasing anxiety in the developmentally disabled population. In a survey of fluoxetine's efficacy in patients affected with fragile X syndrome, it was found to be helpful in approximately 70%.[50] In males the most common indication for use was aggression manifested by verbal or physical outbursts, and, in females, many of whom were carriers, the most common reason for use was depression. Fluoxetine is a relatively safe medication that does not cause cardiac problems or liver dysfunction, and blood levels do not have to be followed. It can be used with most other medications; however, it can enhance the metabolism of many, including anticonvulsants, which will require more frequent monitoring. Fluoxetine has a mild activation effect, and sleeping difficulties may be seen in the first few weeks of treatment. In an occasional patient, the activation can lead to an increase in outbursts or mania. In general, however, the activation effect improves socialization and sometimes verbalizations.[56] Mild gastrointestinal symptoms, such as nausea, appetite changes, and diarrhea, are seen in less than 20% and are more of a problem with fluoxetine than with sertraline. A rare patient may have an increase in obsessive/compulsive (OCD) symptoms or suicidal ideation so that therapy is usually recommended for close follow up when these medications are prescribed.

In females with the full mutation, adolescence can be a difficult time because of increasing demands on socialization. Shyness and avoidant behavior are seen in the majority of females.[6,20] If ADHD symptoms are significant, impulsive outgoing behavior predominates.[21] Stimulants can be helpful for the ADHD symptoms even in adolescence. More commonly, mood lability, verbal outbursts, OCD symptoms, depression, or anxiety are problems in adolescence, and the SSRIs are usually helpful for all of these problems. Again, weekly counseling can be helpful to monitor the medication effects in addition to building social skills, improving self-image, and treating anxiety or depression.[29]

In males enlarged testicles or macroorchidism are noticeable throughout puberty. The size of the testicle usually stabilizes at a mean of 50 ml in volume by the end of puberty, which is approximately twice normal size.

Although males with fragile X syndrome are fertile, most males with mental retardation do not reproduce because of difficulties with social interactions and intimacy.

Adulthood

The transition to adulthood is usually difficult for those with mental retardation because social and financial independence from parents is more difficult to attain compared to the normal population. Appropriate vocational training is important for success in a job. Usually public high school programs focus on vocational training from ages 17 to 21 years. Placement in a community job may also require a job coach for the first several sessions. Most adult males with fragile X syndrome do well in an adult living program that involves limited supervision in an apartment living situation or a group home program. Often medication for outburst behavior is necessary for young adults. The same medications discussed in the adolescence section can be used in adulthood. Stimulants are usually not helpful, although on occasion they can be beneficial if hyperactivity persists in males or females. SSRIs may also be helpful. On occasion SSRIs can induce manic symptoms that respond either to elimination of the medication or use of a mood stabilizer, such as lithium, carbamazepine, or valproic acid.

On occasion, psychotic ideation, including delusions, hallucinations, or enhanced paranoia, may cause a deterioration in functioning that requires treatment with antipsychotic medication. Consultation with a psychiatrist who has had experience in working with developmentally disabled patients is helpful in sorting out psychosis from typical fragile X symptoms and in finding an appropriate antipsychotic medication. Often risperidone is tried first since it is the least likely, compared to other antipsychotics, to cause tardive dyskinesia.[47] Clozaril (Clozapine) is a relatively new antipsychotic that has a novel mechanism of action that does not lead to tardive dyskinesia. Although it has been anecdotally helpful for a few psychotic patients with fragile X syndrome, it has significant side effects, including bone marrow suppression, requiring mandatory monitoring of CBC and other studies.[57]

Medical follow-up of the adult patients with fragile X syndrome include monitoring for connective tissue complications, such as hernias and joint problems. Mitral valve prolapse is more common in adulthood although it usually does not lead to long-term cardiac complications. The life span for adult patients with fragile X syndrome is considered to be normal.

ACKNOWLEDGMENTS

The support of the staff of the Child Development Unit and the Fragile X Research and Treatment Center of the Children's Hospital in Denver, Colorado, has been invaluable to me. Mrs. Barbara Wheeler's exceptional secretarial support has made this manuscript possible, and I am very grateful to her. The Children's Research Institute of the Developmental Psychobiology Research Group (DPRG) of the Department of Psychiatry, University of Colorado Health Sciences Center, has supported much of the research reported here, in addition to grants from NIMH #MH45916 and grant #5 M01 RR00069 of the general Clinical Research Centers Program, National Center for Research Resources, NIH.

REFERENCES

1. Hagerman RJ: Physical and behavioral phenotype. In Hagerman RJ, Silverman AC, editors: *The fragile X syndrome: diagnosis, treatment and research*, Baltimore, 1991, Johns Hopkins University Press.
2. Webb TP, Bundey S, Thake A, et al: The frequency of the fragile X chromosome among school children in Coventry, *J Med Gen* 23:396-399, 1986.
3. Rousseau F: *The prevalence of the premutation of FMR1 in females.* Presented at the Fourth International Conference of Fragile X and X-linked Mental Retardation, National Fragile X Foundation, Albuquerque, New Mexico, June 8-12, 1994.
4. Brown WT, Houck GE Jr, Jeziorwska A et al: Rapid fragile X carrier screening and prenatal diagnosis using a nonradioactive PCR test, *JAMA* 270:1569-1575, 1993.
5. Hagerman R, Berry R, Jackson AW et al: Institutional screening for the fragile X syndrome, *Am J Dis Child* 142:1216-1221, 1988.
6. Hagerman RJ, Jackson C, Amiri K et al: Fragile X girls: physical and neurocognitive status and outcome, *Pediatrics* 89:395-400, 1992.
7. Lubs HA: A marker X chromosome, *Am J Hum Gen* 21:231-244, 1969.
8. Sutherland GR: Heritable fragile sites on human chromosomes. I. Factors affecting expression in lymphocyte culture, *Am J Hum Gen* 31:125-135, 1979.
9. Sherman SL, Jacobs, PA, Morton, NE et al: Further segregation analysis of the fragile X syndrome with special reference to transmitting males, *Hum Gen* 69:289-299, 1985.
10. Verkerk AJ, Pieretti M, Sutcliffe JS et al: Identification of a gene (FMR1) containing a CGG repeat coincident with a breakpoint cluster region exhibiting length variation in fragile X syndrome, *Cell* 65:905-914, 1991.
11. Fu Y-H, Kuhl DPA, Pizzuti A et al: Variation of the CGG repeat at the fragile X site results in genetic instability: resolution of the Sherman paradox, *Cell* 67:1047-1058, 1991.
12. Snow K, Tester DJ, Kruckeberg KE et al: Sequence analysis of the fragile X trinucleotide repeat: implications for the origin of the fragile X mutation, *Hum Molec Gen* 3:1543-1551, 1994.
13. Reiss AL, Abrams MI, Greenlau R et al: Neurodevelopmental effects of the FMR1 full mutation in humans, *Nature Med* 1:159-167, 1995.
14. Waldstein G, Mierau G, Ahmad R et al: Fragile X syndrome: skin elastin abnormalities. In Gilbert EF, Opitz JM, editors: *Genetic aspects of developmental pathology,* New York, 1987, March of Dimes, OAS, Vol 23, No 1, Alan R Liss.
15. Waldstein G, Hagerman RJ: Aortic hypoplasia and cardiac valvular abnormalities in a young male with fragile X syndrome, *Am J Med Gen* 30:83-98, 1988.
16. Butler MG, Brunschwig A, Miller LK et al: Standards for selected anthropometric measurements in males with the fragile X syndrome, *Pediatrics* 89(6):1059-1062, 1992.

17. Reyniers E, Vits L, DeBoulle K et al: The full mutation in the FMR-1 gene of male fragile X patients is absent in their sperm, *Nature Gen* 4:143-146, 1993.

18. Fryns JP: The female and the fragile X: a study of 144 obligate female carriers, *Am J Med Gen* 23:157-169, 1986.

19. Abrams MT, Reiss AL, Freund LS et al: Molecular-neurobehavioral associations in females with the fragile X full mutation, *Am J Med Gen* 51:317-327, 1994.

20. Freund LS, Reiss AL, Abrams M: Psychiatric disorders associated with fragile X in the young female, *Pediatrics* 91:321-329, 1993.

21. Sobesky W, Porter D, Pennington BF et al: Dimensions of shyness in fragile X females, *Dev Brain Dysfunction* 8:282-292, 1995.

22. Hull CE, Hagerman RJ: A study of the physical, behavioral, and medical phenotype, including anthropometric measures of females with fragile X syndrome, *AJDC* 147:1236-1241, 1993.

23. Schwartz C, Dean J, Howard-Peebles P et al: Obstetrical and gynecological complications in fragile X carriers: a multicenter study, *Am J Med Gen* 51:400-402, 1994.

24. Turner G, Robinson H, Wake S et al: Dizygous twinning and premature menopause in fragile X syndrome, *Lancet* 344:1500, 1994.

25. Rousseau F, Heitz D, Tarleton J et al: A multicenter study on genotype-phenotype correlations in the fragile X syndrome using direct diagnosis with probe StB12.3: the first 2253 cases, *Am J Hum Gen* 55:225-237, 1994.

26. Rousseau F, Heitz D, Biancalana V et al: Direct diagnosis by DNA analysis of the fragile X syndrome of mental retardation, *New Engl J Med* 325:1673-1681, 1991.

27. Pennington B, O'Connor R, Sudhalter V: Toward a neuropsychological understanding of fragile X syndrome. In Hagerman RJ, Silverman AC, editors: *The fragile X syndrome: diagnosis, treatment and research*, Baltimore, 1991, Johns Hopkins University Press.

28. Mazzocco M, Pennington B, Hagerman R: The neurocognitive phenotype of female carriers of fragile X: further evidence for specificity, *J Dev Behav Pediatr* 14:328-335, 1993.

29. Sobesky WE, Hull CE, Hagerman RJ: The emotional phenotype in mildly affected carriers. In Hagerman RJ, McKenzie P, editors: *International Fragile X Conference Proceedings (1992)*, Denver, 1992, Spectra Publishing and the National Fragile X Foundation.

30. Hagerman RJ, Hull CE, Carpenter I et al: High functioning fragile X males: demonstration of an unmethylated fully expanded FMR1 mutation associated with protein expression, *Am J Med Gen* 51:298-308, 1994.

31. Lachiewicz AM, Gullion CM, Spiridigliozzi GA et al: Declining IQs of young males with the fragile X syndrome, *Am J Mental Retard* 92:272-278, 1987.

32. Wright-Talamante C, Cheema A, Riddle JE et al: A controlled study of longitudinal IQ changes in females and males with fragile X syndrome, *Am J Med Gen* (in press, 1996).

33. Merenstein SA, Shyu V, Sobesky WE et al: Fragile X syndrome in a normal IQ male with learning and emotional problems, *J Am Acad Child Adoles Psychiatr* 33:1316-1321, 1994.

34. Hagerman RJ, Staley LW, O'Connor R et al: Mildly affected males with a fragile X CGG expansion in the upper premutation size range, *Pediatrics* 97:8-12, 1996.

35. Jacky P: Cytogenetics. In Hagerman RJ, Silverman AC, editors: *The fragile X syndrome: diagnosis, treatment and research*, Baltimore, 1991, Johns Hopkins University Press.

36. Willems PJ: Dynamic mutations hit double figures, *Nature Gen* 8:213-215, 1994.

37. Rousseau F, Heitz D, Oberle et al: Selection in blood cells from female carriers of the fragile X syndrome: inverse correlation between age and proportion of active X carrying the full mutation, *J Am Gen* 28:830-836, 1991.

38. Willemsen R, Mohkemsing S, DeVries B et al: Rapid antibody test for fragile X syndrome, *Lancet* 345:1147-1148, 1995.

39. Snow K, Doud LK, Hagerman RJ et al: Analysis of a CGG sequence at the FMR1 locus in fragile X families in the general population, *Am J Hum Gen* 53:1217-1228, 1993.

40. Sutcliffe JS, Nelson DL, Zheng F et al: DNA methylation represses FMR1 transcription in fragile X syndrome, *Hum Molecul Gen* 1:397-400, 1992.

41. Goldson E, Hagerman R: Fragile X syndrome and failure to thrive, *AJDC* 147:605-607, 1993.

42. Fryns JP, Moerman P, Gillis F et al: Suggestively increased incidence of infant death in children of fragile X positive mothers, *Am J Med Gen* 30:73-75, 1988.

43. Tirosh E, Borochowitz Z: Sleep apnea in fragile X syndrome, *Am J Med Gen* 43:124-127, 1992.

44. Hagerman RJ, Altshul Stark D, McBogg P: Recurrent otitis media in fragile X syndrome, *Am J Dis Child* 141:184-187, 1987.

45. Scharfenaker S, Hickman L, Braden M et al: An integrated approach to intervention. In Hagerman RJ, Cronister A, editors: *The fragile X syndrome: diagnosis, treatment, and research*, ed 2, Baltimore, 1996, Johns Hopkins University Press.

46. Brown J, Braden M, Sobesky W: The treatment of behavioral and emotional problems. In Hagerman RJ, Silverman AC, editors: *Fragile X syndrome: diagnosis, treatment, and research*, Baltimore, 1991, Johns Hopkins University Press.

47. Hagerman RJ: Medical follow up and psychopharmacology. In Hagerman RJ, Silverman AC, editors: *The fragile X syndrome: diagnosis, treatment, and research*, Baltimore, 1991, Johns Hopkins University Press.

48. Hagerman RJ, Murphy MA, Wittenberger M: A controlled trial of stimulant medication in children with fragile X syndrome, *Am J Med Gen* 30:377-392, 1988.

49. Hagerman RJ, Riddle JE, Robert LS et al: A survey of the efficacy of clonidine in fragile X syndrome, *Dev Brain Dysfunction* 8:336-344, 1995.

50. Hagerman R, Bregman JD, Tirosh E: Clonidine. In Aman M, Reiss S, editors: *Handbook of psychopharmacology* (in press).

51. Hagerman RJ, Jackson AW, Levitas A et al: Oral folic acid versus placebo in the treatment of males with fragile X syndrome, *Am J Med Gen* 23:241-262, 1986.

52. Hilton DK, Martin CA, Heffron WM et al: Imipramine treatment of ADHD in a fragile X child, *J Am Acad Child Adolesc Psychiatr* 30(5):831-834, 1991.

53. Musemeci SA, Colognola RM, Ferri R et al: Fragile X syndrome: a particular epileptogenic EEG pattern, *Epilepsia* 29:41-47, 1988.

54. Wisniewski KE, Segan SM, Miezejeski CM et al: The fragile X syndrome: neurological, electrophysiological, and neuropathological abnormalities, *Am J Med Gen* 38:476-480, 1991.

55. Brown J, Braden M, Sobesky W: The treatment of behavioral and emotional problems. In Hagerman RJ, Silverman AC, editors: *The fragile X syndrome: diagnosis, treatment, and research*, Baltimore, 1991, Johns Hopkins University Press.

56. Hagerman RJ, Fulton MJ, Leaman A: Fluoxetine therapy in fragile X syndrome, *Dev Brain Dysfunction* 7:155-164, 1994.

57. Levitas A: Psychosis in fragile X syndrome. In Hagerman RJ, McKenzie P, editors: *International Fragile X Conference Proceedings (1992)*, Denver, 1992, Spectra Publishing and the National Fragile X Association.

CHAPTER 9D _____

Fetal alcohol syndrome

J. WADE WHITE

In the last two decades, there has been an increased awareness of maternal substance abuse and its adverse effects on the fetus. Alcohol consumption is more readily accepted in our society than is the use of illicit drugs, but it has far more effect on public health and safety. Some phenotypical syndromes have been associated with maternal exposure to pharmacological agents. The fetal hydantoin syndrome, resulting from phenytoin exposure, and phocomelia associated with thalidomide have been described. However, the most common dysmorphical condition is that termed *fetal alcohol syndrome (FAS)*.

Despite the prevalence of alcoholism and alcohol consumption, FAS was only alluded to until recently. In antiquity, Aristotle stated that "foolish, drunk, and hare-brained women for the most part bring forth children like unto themselves, difficult and listless."[1] In this century, the features of FAS, first described in the 1970s are now well recognized as associated with excessive maternal alcohol consumption.[2] Short-term cognitive and developmental effects have been described, and long-term effects are only recently being defined.

The effects of alcohol on the fetus in the prenatal period and beyond, when the syndrome is not present, have not been well established. The dysmorphological, behavioral, and neurological effects of alcohol may exist along a spectrum. When children possess only some characteristics of FAS but have had antenatal alcohol exposure, the term *fetal alcohol effect (FAE)* has been used.[3,71] Sokol and Clarren[71] have suggested the term *alcohol-related birth defects (ARBD)* rather than FAE in an attempt to avoid confusion. The long-term behavioral and developmental effects of maternal alcohol consumption have been difficult to ascertain because of such antenatal variables as maternal smoking or other substance abuse. Frequently, poor social and family situations may also contribute to poor developmental or behavioral outcome. Also the difficulties inherent in accurately assessing maternal alcohol consumption further hamper researchers' abilities to assess the threshold exposure at which damage to the fetus may occur. In this chapter, the features of FAS are reviewed, and the potential short- and long-term effects on development are discussed. The serious long-term consequences to children with FAS make prevention and early identification and intervention for the child and family imperative.

PATTERN OF MALFORMATION

There is currently no reliable test for antenatal diagnosis of FAS and making the diagnosis in the neonatal period depends on knowledge of the dysmorphical features of the syndrome. Because they may be difficult to recognize, the features of FAS may be commonly missed in the infant period. In one retrospective study series, all affected children were not diagnosed in early infancy, despite medical record documentation of maternal alcohol consumption.[11] Nevertheless, the facial features associated with fetal alcohol exposure are readily identifiable, and recognition problems need not be a major obstruction in the diagnosis of FAS.[6]

The specific malformations associated with FAS were first described by Jones and Smith et al. in 1973.[29] In this study and one subsequent companion study, a total of 11 children were described. A pattern of craniofacial, limb, and cardiovascular defects with prenatal-onset growth retardation and developmental delay was identified. Although none of the features are pathognomonic, the combination of typical features and alcohol exposure should leave little doubt as to the diagnosis. A child suspected of having the features of FAS must have effects in three separate areas:

- Prenatal or postnatal growth retardation
- Evidence of central nervous system involvement (developmental delay, mental retardation, attention deficit hyperactivity disorder)
- Characteristic facies, including at least two of the following:
  Microcephaly
  Short palpebral fissures
  Diminutive philtrum
  Thin upper lip
  Blurring of the vermillion border
  Maxillary hypoplasia

Other associated physical findings include atrial or ventricular septal defects, bilateral clinodactyly, abnormal palmar crease pattern, hypoplasia of the fingernails, dental malalignments, malocclusions, and eustachian tube dysfunction.[7,8,9] Clarren and Smith[10] recorded the major features observed in 245 patients with FAS. From 50% to 80% of patients had microcephaly, short palpebral fissures, short upturned nose, diminutive philtrum, maxillary hypoplasia, thin upper lip, and micrognathia.[10] Radiological manifestations seen in FAS consist of epiphyseal calcifications, which are more likely to be seen in the lower limbs.[69] FAS involves various neural crest structures, corneal endothelial anomalies, and auditory dysfunction.[12] Mattson and colleagues[5] documented abnormalities of the corpus callosum and reduction in size of the basal ganglia and thalamus in individuals with FAS. There has also been a case report of septooptic dysplasia concomitant with other major cerebral deformities.[13] Children with FAS often have associated ocular abnormalities, including strabismus, blepharoptosis, and epicanthus, as well as cataracts, glaucoma, and retinal and optic nerve anomalies. Rats exposed to alcohol in utero developed similar ocular defects.[73]

As individuals mature, short stature and microcephaly may persist. Relatively short palpebral fissures, smooth philtrum, and thin upper lip usually are important discriminating features in the older patient. In some instances, the facies of the adult patient may become normalized to the point of requiring childhood photographs to confirm the diagnosis.[14] Practitioners will need to make themselves familiar with the features of FAS to make early diagnoses and to provide anticipatory guidance. Involved professionals need to be knowledgeable and sensitive regarding the diagnosis. Many alcoholic mothers feel guilt about their child's situation. Treatment plans must include rehabilitation for the mother, which may be presented to her as part of the plan for the well-being of her child.

PREVALENCE

The established pattern of malformation associated with maternal alcohol consumption occurs in 5 to 9 per 10,000 alcoholic mothers. FAS is the most commonly recognized cause of mental retardation and has a worldwide incidence of 1.9 per 1000 live births. Incidence in the United States is higher at 2.2 per 1000 live births.[15,16] The true incidence may be higher, because the characteristics of FAS may be underdiagnosed.[11] The NIDA Household Survey on Drug Abuse estimated that 75% of fertile women aged 15 to 44 years consumed alcohol in the previous year.[9] It is estimated that as many as 65% of mothers in the United States expose their unborn children to alcohol.[17] Tragically, as much as 5% of congenital anomalies in general may be attributed to preventable prenatal alcohol exposure.[63,74] The potential cost to society of FAS has been estimated to be close to $1.4 million for the lifetime of a single child.[14] Significant maternal alcohol consumption, even in the absence of dysmorphology, may have an adverse physiological effect on the infant postnatally. Little et al.[11] were able to show that neonatal exposure to alcohol through breast milk affected infants by decreasing their milk consumption. Long-term effects of alcohol from neonatal exposure are unknown. The impact of public awareness and community health programs on the incidence of FAS needs continued evaluation to assess their effectiveness.

PATHOPHYSIOLOGY

The pathophysiological mechanism by which alcohol exerts its adverse effects has not been well established. It is possible that there are direct toxic effects on the fetus from ethanol or its metabolite acetaldehyde.[18] There may be other contributing substances in the beverages that women consume as well. The effect of other abused substances, including marijuana and cigarette smoking, cannot be ignored and may be additive.[19,20-23]

Studies of maternal alcohol consumption have shown that a woman whose child has FAS has typically consumed about 14 drinks per day. Alcohol appears to exert a dose-response effect on the fetus in human and animal studies.[8,24,25] Animal studies have shown that fetal exposure to alcohol results in chronic fetal hypoxia, expressed as decreased brain weight, suppression of mitosis, lower cell number, and malformation of the brain.[8,26] A dose response has been shown between the amount of ethanol consumed during pregnancy and the presence of craniofacial deformity in humans.[27] The features of FAS have been noted to dramatically increase up to four-fold when exposure increased from 1 or 2 oz daily to more than 5 oz per day of absolute alcohol.[28] It may, however, be that there is no safe dose of ethanol in pregnancy.[30] This aspect remains controversial.[1] There may be other metabolical factors that make one fetus more susceptible, compared to others with the same exposure. This is sometimes observed in the same family, such as in an unpublished case report by White and Butler (1994) of four children born to an intact family, all with similar exposure. The 12-year-old boy showed all major features of FAS, but the remaining children showed only minimal features or none at all. Indeed Jones and his colleagues[29] observed this variable effect within the families of the original cohort of FAS children. Such reports suggest that there may be individual biological factors that put an infant at increased risk. Low ethanol consumption of two or three drinks per day has not shown to affect birth weight, but more subtle, long-term CNS effects may exist in these children. Just how much alcohol consumption increases a child's risk of developing FAS has not been determined. One prospective study has shown that at 8 months of age, infants antenatally exposed to eight or more drinks per day attained lower Bayley scores of infant development than controls exposed to one drink or less per day.[31] One study found a linear relationship between fine and gross motor function and antenatal alcohol exposure at 4 years of age and distractibility at age 7 years.[32,33] Children with minimal exposure (0.5 oz of ethanol [one drink]) had poorer fine and gross motor performance.[32] These effects were small, and the presence of confounding variables—such as low birth weight and poor mother-child interaction—make interpretation of these findings difficult. Although some data suggest that moderate alcohol abuse may result in FAS, some long-term effects—especially inattention, overactivity, and motor incoordination—may result from minimal antenatal exposure. The effect of binge drinking vs. continuous high- or low-dose exposure needs further clarification as well. Data to date support that the developing fetus is damaged from either binge drinking or continuous exposure.[1,35] The present understanding, therefore, of antenatal alcohol exposure does not include an absolute threshold for adverse effects.

The mechanisms of neurological damage and developmental or genetic insult on the fetus are unknown. All infants exposed to high ethanol levels in utero do not develop FAS. Autti et al.[18,36,37] reported an increased number of minor congenital anomalies in infants exposed to alcohol, which were not associated with binge drinking but were correlated with moderate pervasive exposure. Sokol and colleagues[37] studied 8331 pregnancies, in which they compared FAS and unaffected groups. They noted significant risk factors for development of FAS. These were pervasiveness of drinking during pregnancy, positive Michigan Alcoholism Screening Test, African-American race, and high parity.[37] The general risk of developing FAS with ethanol exposure is about 3%. If all four of the risk factors are present, this risk rises to 85.2%.[37] No clear evidence exists for adverse effects from fewer than two drinks per day.[1] However, Mills et al.[28] did observe an increase in genitourinary malformations in groups who had low exposure—that is, one or two drinks per day. It is difficult to separate the influence of environment on behavior dysfunction in children with FAS; however, mounting evidence exists for a peculiar role of alcohol related to brain damage affecting cognitive functioning. In the study by Day et al.,[38a] children who were exposed to alcohol prenatally were significantly smaller in weight, height, head circumference, and palpebral fissure width at 6 years of age.

There were no effects of prenatal marijuana or tobacco exposure on growth at the same age. There were also no significant relationships between prenatal exposure to alcohol, marijuana, or tobacco and the rate of morphological anomalies, including the features of the FAS in this low-exposure cohort.[38a] Neurodysfunction is an expected part of FAS. Alcohol may have adverse effects in infants and children in the absence of dysmorphology. In a study of prenatally exposed infants, Autti-Ramo et al.[18,36] reported that 76% of moderate to highly exposed infants showed some degree of neurodysfunction, whereas low to moderate alcohol intake had no significant effect on newborn neurological status in a cohort reported by Walpole et al.[75] Jacobsen[40] found adverse effects of moderate to heavy prenatal alcohol exposure in the third trimester on Bayley Scale performance were as strong or stronger than those of drinking at conception. Autti-Ramo et al.[18] reported that psychomotor developmental delay increased toward the end of the first year after birth in infants exposed to alcohol. The longer the exposure, the more common and severe was the developmental delay. The beneficial effect of reducing maternal alcohol consumption before the last trimester of the child's development was clear.[18]

Twin studies further the argument that individual genetic factors increase the risk of adverse effects of alcohol exposure. Despite equivalent alcohol exposure within twin pairs, alcohol teratogenesis appears to be more uniformly expressed in monozygotic twins than in dizygotic twins. These data are interpreted as reflecting the modulating influence of genes in the expression of the teratogenic effects of alcohol.[7,66] Intrauterine growth retardation is a hallmark of FAS. A contributing factor may be altered placental function, which could affect fetal growth and development. Alcohol exposure of cultured human placental trophoblasts was shown to significantly affect hormonal and cyclical AMP production.[2] The significance of these effects is not yet known, but they do show a potential wide-ranging effect on the fetus.[42]

ASSESSMENT

The practitioner needs to be aware of the possibility of FAS. This is especially true if the population served has a higher prevalence of alcohol-related illness or alcohol abuse. Diagnosis in the newborn period can be difficult but should be suspected when there is a combination of low birth weight and maternal alcohol consumption. Physical features may be difficult to determine in mild cases. Some children may not be identified until a pattern of delayed development is discovered. Children considered to be at risk for the syndrome by history of maternal alcohol consumption should have focused screens of their development as part of their well child care. This may be done by the primary practitioner, or the child may be followed by developmental specialists. A formal developmental evaluation is warranted at about 18 months of age to assess language, cognitive, and adaptive skills. Developmental delays are nonspecific and may be early indicators of eventual impaired cognitive ability in the mentally retarded range. These children should be followed closely from a developmental standpoint at least until age 3, when it is possible to determine whether they have serious developmental anomalies. As the children mature, they continue to be at risk for cognitive delays and learning disabilities. There is insufficient evidence for specific cognitive difficulties unique to children with FAS. However, inattention and impulse control are fairly pervasive. There is some evidence that reading and especially mathematical skills are more impaired, relative to other cognitive abilities. School-aged children with below-average academic performance should have comprehensive cognitive and achievement testing to determine whether specific learning disabilities are present. As more children with FAS are tested for learning disabilities, a specific pattern of cognitive difficulty may become apparent. It appears that the cognitive anomalies resulting from maternal alcohol exposure are diffuse and nonspecific, thereby requiring a comprehensive review of each child, rather than a focused evaluation.

OUTCOME

Adult outcome of children with FAE has not been well studied. Streissguth et al.[41] found a dismal outcome at the 10-year follow-up of the originally described cohort of children. Two of the eleven had died, and all the children had serious cognitive deficiency. Half of the children required complete supervision outside of the home. The severity of the dysmorphic features of the condition correlated well with lower IQ scores. Three of the children's natural mothers had died by the time the children were 6 years old.[41] Children with FAS may be expected to require extensive special education and vocational training, and many may require some degree of supervision as adults because of mental retardation.[25,42] Adults who had milder ethanol exposure may have milder cognitive effects and have a better prognosis for independence. The literature characterizes short- and long-term outcomes for individuals with FAS.

Short-term developmental outcome

Maternal alcohol abuse is related to an increased incidence of second trimester spontaneous abortion of up to four times the expected rate.[43]

Infants with FAS have a three-fold increase in premature birth, as well as increased risk of abruptio placentae and breech delivery.[44] Infants with FAS have an average birth weight that is 700 g less than other children. Neurobehavioral dysfunction has been reported in some infants. Although some of these infants have had behavioral characteristics described as consistent with withdrawal from alcohol, multiple confounding variables were present, including being small for gestational age and premature, as well as being subjected to the influence of other substances.[40] Symptoms of alcohol withdrawal that may be seen in the neonatal period include abdominal distension, apnea, cyanosis, tremor, agitation, opisthotonos, and convulsions. These symptoms typically appear in the first hours after birth and resolve after a few days.[10,47] Infants may also have disturbances of sleep, including diminished REM and quiet sleep durations.[45] Other studies have found impaired arousal and poor habituation.[46] Additional investigations have not found a connection between maternal alcohol consumption and neurobehavioral function in the neonate.[47] These complications may be related to several factors, including fetal damage, poor maternal nutrition, other substance abuse, poor prenatal care, and poor maternal health. To date, there has been no specific study of the impact of a dysfunctional family environment on the development and behavior of children with FAS.[64,65] Maternal caretaking is adversely affected by substance abuse in general, which may be an important confounding variable in assessing the neurological impact of alcohol on the developing fetus.[72] Mothers who abuse substances may engage in more adverse parenting, including verbal abuse, physical abuse, and neglect. Dysfunctional parent-child interactions may influence the child's ability to recover from the physiological insult of antenatal drug exposure. The ability to modulate changes of state and arousal is impaired in infants exposed to drugs in utero.[67] This has been extensively described in infants exposed to cocaine. Mothers whose interactions with their children are overstimulating or intrusive appear to be at higher risk of having children who are hyperactive. Also, mothers who abuse alcohol may not be as responsive to their infants' needs, leading to neglect and the infants' failure to thrive. Maternal depression is often present, and this leads to additional mother-child interaction problems, injuries, school problems, attention deficit hyperactivity disorder, and childhood depression. Families in which one or both parents abuse alcohol are at higher risk of family violence. Post-traumatic stress disorder and the behaviors associated with it may develop.[70] These behaviors include impaired impulse control, thrill seeking, or emotional withdrawal. Follow-up examination of the original cohort suggests that social factors are less important than teratogenicity and toxicity of ethanol. Children in stable, long-term foster homes still had major neuro-dysfunction.[41]

Long-term outcome

It is now well recognized that there are long-term detrimental effects on behavior and neurological function from significant prenatal ethanol exposure. FAS has surpassed trisomy 21 and neural tube defects as the most common cause of mental retardation.[15] Characteristics described include diffuse developmental delay, hyperactivity, and impaired motor development. Growth retardation expressed initially as low birth weight tends to persist with only partial catch-up growth typically seen in other infants who are small for gestational age.[43] Length and head circumference are more affected than weight.[50] Heavier alcohol intake in pregnancy correlates with slower linear and head circumference growth and increased dysmorphology in 6-year-old children exposed to alcohol prenatally.[49]

Specific signs of neuromotor dysfunction include tremors, motor incoordination, poor grip strength, and impaired eye-hand coordination.[52] Attention deficit hyperactivity disorder has been the only consistently identified long-term sequela.[55] One study indicated that as affected children aged, their cognition and mental health improved, but symptoms of attention deficit hyperactivity disorder did not. Other studies have described comorbid conditions with FAS, including autism, disciplinary problems, and learning disabilities.[53,55] Most children with FAS have been found to have delay in mental, motor, and social functioning.[24,31,34,55-57] It is unclear whether these deficits persist; however, one group noted adversely affected cognitive scores up to the age of 6 years.[22,23,58] Low-level ethanol exposure appeared to have no measurable influence after 48 months of age.[59] Streissguth and colleagues[57] reported severely-impaired to low-normal cognitive function in their series of children with FAS.[57] The long-term effects of mild to moderate maternal alcohol consumption on the child without FAS are still unclear.[60]

The facial features of FAS may disappear with maturity. The long philtrum and microcephaly may persist. Cognitive studies on adolescents and adults revealed average performance between second and fourth grade academic levels with average IQ of 68.[14] Adults tended to continue to exhibit behavioral disturbances and attention deficit hyperactivity disorder.[14] Affected individuals tend to remain short and microcephalic, with normalization of weight parameters. Verbal cognitive performance lags behind performance scores. Mathematical deficits are reported as most characteristic of learning disabilities associated with FAS. Specific language deficits may exist independent of cognitive skills in older children with FAS who possess syntactic deficits, whereas younger FAS children exhibit more global language deficits.[61] More specific cognitive deficits have been elucidated. Reading and, particularly, mathematical skills, were adversely affected and were linearly related to severity of binge drinking.[54] In addition, prenatal alcohol exposure was significantly related to attention/memory deficits in a dose-dependent fashion. The number of drinks per occasion was the strongest predictor of poor attention and short-term memory performance. Not all exposed offspring showed deficits.[25,57] Compounding the characteristics of inattention is the observation that many of these individuals have chronic otitis media, which may result in partial hearing impairment. Social and adaptive skill deficits have been observed in most children with FAS. One study found serious impairment of adaptive functioning, with particular difficulty in considering consequences of action, lack of appropriate initiative, unresponsiveness to subtle social cues, and lack of reciprocal friendships, even in patients who were technically not retarded. Also 62% of patients exhibit significant levels of maladaptive behaviors, with an additional 38% having intermediate dysfunction. Maladaptive behaviors include poor concentration and attention, dependency, stubbornness or sullenness, social withdrawal, teasing or bullying, crying or laughing too easily, impulsivity, and periods of high anxiety. Striking is the fact that none of the individuals in this series were receiving any resources to help deal with mental health problems.[14] These behavior problems appear to be more severe than those observed in other mentally retarded individuals, such as those with Down syndrome. Psychopathology is reported to be related to the degree of morphological damage and IQ in FAS children.[62] Other cognitive comorbid conditions may be present—for example, six children with autism were reported by Nanson et al.[53,55]

Although impaired intellectually, attentional difficulties present in children with FAS or FAE are similar to those of children with attention deficit hyperactivity disorder; thus they may also benefit from the same interventions.[56] The cornerstone of intervention for attention difficulties in children has been essentially the same as for any children with attention deficit hyperactivity disorder.

Grip strength was the only positive neuropsychological measure shown in children with FAE. Thus neuropsychological testing has not yet been shown to be a helpful tool in determining the cognitive effects of alcohol exposure in utero.[68]

TREATMENT

The best intervention method for FAS remains that of prevention. Pregnant women need to continue to be warned of the effects of ethanol on the developing fetus. Prevention must begin with the mother to include early treatment of alcohol abuse and alcoholism. Women at risk should be offered effective birth control, just as are women who are taking other teratogenic drugs. It is doubtful that the Surgeon General's warning to pregnant women on labels of alcoholic beverages will be effective in significantly decreasing alcohol abuse. Easily accessible, low-cost prenatal care may be able to significantly influence maternal alcohol consumption if comprehensive rehabilitative services can be offered. However, the presence of the syndrome in children of parents of high socioeconomic status questions even this approach. When preventive measures fail, there is no currently available in utero treatment. Teratogenic and cognitive effects are permanent. Other contributing factors—such as continued maternal alcohol abuse, family dysfunction, divorce, physical abuse, neglect, and low socioeconomic status—may be addressed by community resources and rehabilitation programs. Although currently unproved specifically for this population, involvement of the children in early intervention programs to address developmental delays and family needs is likely to improve short- and long-term outcomes, as it does for children who are developmentally delayed and at risk for such delays. Special education curricula to address cognitive impairments and to provide vocational training should be offered. Specific intervention for attention deficits and behavior disorders may also improve ultimate outcome. Children with FAS who have the characteristics of attention deficit hyperactivity disorder typically respond to standard management, consisting of curriculum and environment manipulation in the classroom, behavior management, and stimulant medication.[55] Stimulant medication—such as methylphenidate or dextroamphetamine—may be used, but the relative effectiveness of any particular medication for the purpose of improving attention and tempering hyperactivity and impulsivity has not been studied in this population.[53,54,57] The addition of psychological counseling to the treatment plan for these children needs serious consideration, because they may be at more risk for low self-esteem and behavior disturbance related to poor social interaction and family dysfunction. The comprehensive treatment of attention deficit hyperactivity disorder is discussed elsewhere in this text.

SUMMARY

FAS is the most common cause of mental retardation. Short- and long-term adverse effects on development and behavior of the exposed child are documented. Although there are significant adverse environmental factors present affecting the development of the child, clear evidence for neurobiological damage exists. Children identified with significant FAE should be directed to adequate community resources to assist in preventing further sequelae from adverse environmental factors, including poor socioeconomic condition, family violence, and maternal depression. Developmental follow-up and early intervention, as well as special education, may improve the ultimate outcome for these children. The major effort should continue to focus on prevention because the syndrome is entirely preventable. Maternal education will likely not be sufficient because chronic alcoholic mothers may continue to drink as part of their own disease process. Efforts by communities will need to focus on the circumstances that increase the likelihood of substance abuse in general. Because alcohol is often not thought of by the general public as a potentially dangerous drug, warning labels on beverages containing ethanol—as recommended by the Surgeon General—is not sufficient education. The 10-year follow-up of the original cohort of FAS children poignantly emphasizes the need for prevention. Two of the eleven have died, and all of the children have had serious adaptive or behavior difficulties.

Treatment must be family based, providing developmental services and comprehensive treatment planning for alcoholic mothers. Minimal evidence exists for FAE in infants of mothers who consume fewer than two drinks per day. However, the presence of genitourinary deformity with even mild alcohol exposure dictates caution. Although dose-related response is now generally accepted, pregnant women should continue to be informed of the risk from any alcohol consumption throughout their pregnancy. Additional research is needed to identify the specific mechanisms of injury in FAS and possibly ascertain populations at particular risk of developing long-term effects from even low-level antenatal alcohol exposure.

REFERENCES

1. Alpert J, Zuckerman B: Alcohol use during pregnancy: what is the risk? *Pediatr Rev,* 12(12), June, 1991.
2. Karl P, Fisher S: Ethanol alters hormone production in cultured human placental trophoblasts, *Alcohol Clin Exp Res* 17(4):816-821, 1993.
3. Ernhart CB, Wolf AW, Linn PL, et al: Alcohol-related birth defects: syndromal anomalies, intrauterine growth retardation, and neonatal behavioral assessment, *Alcoholism* 9:447-453, 1985.
4. Spohr H, Wills J, Steinhausen H: Prenatal alcohol exposure and long term developmental consequences, *Lancet* 10:341(885):907-910, 1993.

5. Mattson S, Riley EP, Jernigan T, Ehlers C, Delis D, Jones K, Stern C, Johnson K, Hesselink J, Bellugi U: Fetal alcohol syndrome: a case report of neuropsychological, MRI and EEG assessment of two children, *Alcohol Clin Exp Res* 16(5):1001-1003, 1992.

6. Abel EL, Martier S, Kruger M, Ager J, Sokol R: Ratings of fetal alcohol syndrome facial feature by medical providers and bomedical scientists, *Alcohol Clin Exp Res* 17(3):717-721, 1993.

7. Streissguth A, Dehaene P: Fetal alcohol syndrome in twins of alcoholic mothers: concordance of diagnosis and IQ, *Am J Med Gen* 47(6):857-861, 1993.

8. Streissguth AP, Landesman-Dwyer S, Martin JC, et al: Teratogenic effects of alcohol in humans and laboratory animals, *Science* 209:353-361, 1980.

9. US Department of Health and Human Services: *National household survey of drug abuse,* 1994.

10. Clarren SK, Smith DW: The fetal alcohol syndrome, *N Engl J Med* 298(19):1063-1067, 1978.

11. Little B, Snell L, Rosenfeld C, Gilstrap L, Gat N: Failure to recognize fetal alcohol syndrome in newborn infants, *Am J Dis Child* 144:1142-1146, 1990.

12. Carones F, Brancato R, Venturi E, Bianchi S, Magni R: Corneal endothelial anomalies in the fetal alcohol syndrome, *Arch Ophthalmol* 110(8):1228-31, 1992.

13. Coulter C, Leech R, Schaefer G, Scheithauer B, Brumback R: Midline cerebral dysgenesis, dysfunction of the hypothalamic pituitary axis, and fetal alcohol effects, *Arch Neurol* 50(7):771-775, 1993.

14. Streissguth AP, Aase JM, Sterling K, et al: Fetal alcohol syndrome in adolescents and adults, *JAMA* 265:1961-1967, 1991.

15. Abel EL, Sokol RJ: Fetal alcohol syndrome is now the leading cause of mental retardation, *Lancet* 2:1222, 1986.

16. Abel EL, Sokol RJ: Incidence of fetal alcohol syndrome and economic impact of FAS-related anomalies, *Drug Alcohol Depend* 19(1):51-70, 1987.

17. Pietrantoni M, Krnuppel R: Alcohol use in pregnancy, *Clin Perinatol* 18(1):93-111, 1991.

18. Autti-Ramo I, Granstrom M: The psychomotor development during the first year of life of infants exposed to intrauterine alcohol of various duration: fetal alcohol exposure and development, *Neuropediatrics* 22(2):59-64, 1991.

19. Day N, Cornelius M, Goldschmidt L: The effects of prenatal tobacco and marijuana use on offspring growth from birth through 3 years of age, *Neurotoxicol Teratol* 14(6):407-414, 1992.

20. Feng T: Substance abuse in pregnancy, *Obstet Gynecol* 5:16-23, 1993.

21. Fried PA, Makin JE: Neonatal behavioral correlates of prenatal exposure to marijuana, cigarettes and alcohol in a low risk population, *Neurotoxicol Teratol* 9(1):1-7, 1987.

22. Fried PA, O'Connell CM, et al: A comparison of the effects of prenatal exposure to tobacco, alcohol, cannabis on birth size and subsequent growth, *Neurotoxicol Teratol* 9(2):79-85, 1987.

23. Fried PA, O'Connell CM, Watkinson B: 60 and 72 month follow-up of children prenatally exposed to marijuana, cigarettes and alcohol: cognitive and language assessment, *J Dev Behav Pediatr* 13:383, 1992.

24. Streissguth AP, Martin DC, Martin JC, et al: The Seattle longitudinal prospective study on alcohol and pregnancy, *Neurobehav Toxicol Teratol* 3(2):223-233, 1981.

25. Streissguth AP, Sampson PD, Barr HM: Neurobehavioral dose-response effects of prenatal alcohol exposure in humans from infancy to adulthood, *Ann NY Acad Sci* 562:145-158, 1989.

26. Sulik KK, Johnston MC: Sequence of developmental alterations following acute ethanol exposure in mice: craniofacial features of the fetal alcohol syndrome, *Am J Anat* 166(3):257-269, 1983.

27. Hanson JW, Streissguth AP, Smith DW: The effects of moderate alcohol consumption during pregnancy on fetal growth and morphogenesis, *J Pediatr* 92(3):457-460, 1978.

28. Mills J, Graubard M: Is moderate drinking during pregnancy associated with an increased risk for malformations? *Pediatrics* 80(3):309-314, 1987.

29. Jones KL, Smith DW, Ulleland CN, et al: Pattern of malformation in offspring of chronic alcoholic women, *Lancet* 1:1267-1271, 1973.

30. Streissguth AP, Barr H, Martin DC, et al: Effects of maternal alcohol, nicotine, and caffeine use during pregnancy on infant mental and motor development at eight months, *Alcoholism* 4:132, 1980.

31. Abel EL, Sokol RJ: Is occasional light drinking during pregnancy harmful? Controversies in the addiction field. In Engs RC, ed: Dubuque, IA, 1990, Kendall-Hunt Publishing.

32. Barr HM, Darbv BL, Streissguth AP, et al: Prenatal exposure to alcohol, caffeine, tobacco, and aspirin: effects on fine and gross motor performance in 4-year-old children, *Dev Psychol* 26:339-348, 1990.

33. Streissguth AP, Barr HI, Sampson PD, et al: Attention, distraction and reaction time at age 7 years and prenatal alcohol exposure, *Neurobehav Toxicol Teratol* 8:717-725, 1986.

34. Behrman RE: The effects of moderate alcohol consumption during pregnancy on fetal growth and morphogenesis, *J Pediatr* 92(3):457-460, 1978.

35. Autti-Ramo I, Granstrom M: The effect of intrauterine alcohol exposition in various durations on early cognitive development, *Neuropediatrics* 22(4):203-10, 1991.

36. Autti-Ramo I, Korkman M, Hilakivi-Clarke L, Lehtonen M, Halmesmaki E, Granstrom M: Mental development of 2-year-old children exposed to alcohol in utero, *J Pediatr* 120(5):740-746, 1992.

37. Sokol RJ, Ager J, Martier S, et al: Significant determinants of susceptibility to alcohol teratogenicity, *Ann NY Acad Sci* 477:87-102, 1986.

38. Day NL, Jasperse D, Richardson G, et al: Prenatal exposure to alcohol: effect on infant growth and morphologic characteristics, *Pediatrics* 84(3):536-541, 1989.

38a. Day N, Richardson G, Geva D, Robles N: Alcohol, marijuana, and tobacco: effects of prenatal exposure on offspring growth and morphology at age six, *Alcohol Clin Exp Res* 18(4):786-794, 1994.

39. Zuckerman B, Breshahan K: Developmental and behavioral consequences of prenatal drug and alcohol exposure, *Pediatr Clin North Am* 38(6):1387-1406, 1991.

40. Jacobson SW, Fein GG, Jacobson JL, et al: Neonatal correlates of prenatal exposure to smoking, caffeine, and alcohol, *Infant Behav Dev* 7:253-265, 1984.

41. Streissguth AP, Clarren SK, Jones KL: Natural history of fetal alcohol syndrome: a 10-year follow-up of eleven patients, *Lancet* 13:85-91, 1985.

42. Streissguth AP, Herman CS, Smith DW, et al: Intelligence, behavior, and dysmorphogenesis in the fetal alcohol syndrome: a report on 20 patients, *J Pediatr* 92(3):363-367, 1978.

43. Harlap S, Shiono PH: Alcohol, smoking, and incidence of spontaneous abortions in the first and second trimester, *Lancet* 26:173-176, 1980.

44. Halliday HL, Reid MM, McClure G: Results of heavy drinking in pregnancy, *Br J Obstet Gynaecol* 89:892-895, 1982.

45. Pierog S, Chandavasu O, Wexler I: Withdrawal symptoms in infants with the fetal alcohol syndrome, *J Pediatr* 90(4):630-633, 1977.

46. Streissguth AP, Barr HM, Martin DC: Maternal alcohol use and neonatal habituation assessed with the Brazelton scale, *Child Dev* 54(5):1109-1118, 1983.

47. Coles CD, Smith IE, Fernhoff PM, et al: Neonatal neurobehavioral characteristics as correlates of maternal alcohol use during gestation, *Alcohol Clin Exp Res* 9(5):454-460, 1985.

48. Geva D, Goldschmidt L, Stoffer D, Day N: A longitudinal analysis of the effect of prenatal alcohol exposure on growth, *Alcohol Clin Exp Res* 17(6):1124-1129, 1993.

49. Russell M, Cxarnecki D, Cowan R, McPherson E, Mudar P: Measures of maternal alcohol use as predictors of development in early childhood, *Alcohol Clin Exp Res* 15(6):991-1000, 1991.

50. Aronson M, Kyllerman M, Sabel KG, et al: Children of alcoholic mothers: developmental, perceptual and behavioral characteristics as compared to matched controls, *Acta Paediatr Scand* 74:27-35, 1985.

51. Shaywitz SE, Cohen DJ, Shaywitz B: Behavior and learning difficulties in children of normal intelligence born to alcoholic mothers, *J Pediatr* 96:978-982, 1980.

52. Streissguth AP, Barr HM, Martin DC: Alcohol exposure in utero and functional deficits in children during the first four years of life, *Ciba Found Symp* 105:176-196, 1984.

53. Nanson J: Autism in fetal alcohol syndrome: a report of six cases, *Alcohol Clin Exp Res* 16(3):558-565, 1992.

54. Streissguth A, Barr H, Olson H, Sampson P, Bookstein F, Burgesss D: Drinking during pregnancy decreases word attack and arithmetic scores on standardized tests: adolescent data from a population based prospective study, *Alcohol Clin Exp Res* 18(2):248-254, 1994.

55. Nanson J, Hissock M: Attention deficits in children exposed to alcohol prenatally, *Alcohol Clin Exp Res* 14(5):656-662, 1990.

56. Streissguth AP, Barr HM, Sampson PD, et al: IQ at age 4 in relation to maternal alcohol use and smoking during pregnancy, *Dev Psychol* 25(1):3-11, 1989.

57. Streissguth AP, Barr HM, Sampson PD: Moderate prenatal alcohol exposure: effects on child IQ and learning problems at age 7½ years, *Alcohol Clin Exp Res* 14(5):662-669, 1990.

58. Fried PA, Watkinson B: 36 and 48 month neurobehavioral follow-up of children prenatally exposed to marijuana, cigarettes and alcohol, *J Dev Behav Pediatr* 11:4958, 1990.

59. Fried PA, Watkinson B: 36 and 48 month neurobehavioral follow-up of children prenatally exposed to marijuana, cigarettes and alcohol, *J Dev Behav Pediatr* 11:4958, 1990.

60. Green T, Ernhart CB, Ager J, et al: Prenatal alcohol exposure and cognitive development in the preschool years, *Neurotoxicol Teratol* 13(1):57-68, 1991.

61. Carney L, Chermak G: Performance of American Indian children with fetal alcohol syndrome on the test of language development, *J Commun Disord* 24(2):123-34, 1991.

62. Steinhausen H, Willms J, Spohr H: Correlates of psychopathology and intelligence in children with fetal alcohol syndrome, *J Child Psychol Psychiatry* 35(2):323-331, 1994.

63. Autti-Ramo I, Gaily E, Granstrom M: Dysmorphic features in offspring of alcoholic mothers, *Arch Dis Child* 67(6):712-716, 1992.

64. Bays J: Substance abuse and child abuse: impact of addiction on the child, *Pediatr Clin North Am* 37:881, 1990.

65. Black R, Mayer J: Parents with special problems: alcoholism and opiate addiction, *Child Abuse Negl* 4:45, 1980.

66. Christoffel KK, Salabsk NT: Fetal alcohol syndrome in dizygotic twins, *J Pediatr* 84:963-965, 1975.

67. Coles CD, Smith IE, Femhoff PM, et al: Neonatal ethanol withdrawal: characteristics in clinically normal, nondysmorphic neonates, *J Pediatr* 105:445-451, 1984.

68. Conry J: Neuropsychological deficits in fetal alcohol syndrome and fetal alcohol effects, *Alcohol Clin Exp Res* 14(5):650-655, 1990.

69. Leicher-Duber A, Schumacher R, Spranger J: Stippled epiphyses in fetal alcohol syndrome, *Pediatr Radiol* 20(5):369-370, 1990.

70. Pynoss RS: Post-traumatic stress disorder in children and adolescents. In Garfinkle BD, Carlson GA, Weller EB, editors: *Psychiatric disorders in children and adolescents*, Philadelphia, 1987, WB Saunders, pp 48-63.

71. Sokol RJ, Clarren SK: Guidelines for use of terminology describing the impact of prenatal alcohol on the offspring, *Alcohol Clin Exp Res* 13(4):597-598, 1989.

72. Streissguth AP, Barr HM, Martin DC: Effects of maternal alcohol, nicotine, and caffeine use during pregnancy on infant mental and motor development at eight months, *Alcohol Clin Exp Res* 4(2):152-164, 1980.

73. Stromland K, Pinazo D: Optic nerve hypoplasia: comparative effects in children and rats exposed to alcohol during pregnancy, *Teratology* 50(2):100-111, 1994.

74. Tillner I, Majewski I: Furrow and dermal ridges of the hand in patients with alcohol embryopathy, *Hum Gen* 42:307-314, 1978.
75. Walpole I, Zubrick S, Pontre J, Lawrene C: Low to moderate maternal alcohol use before and during pregnancy, and neurobehavioral outcome in the newborn infant, *Dev Med Child Neurol* 33(10):875-883, 1991.

CHAPTER 9E _____

Pervasive Developmental Disorders: Autism

WENDY L. STONE
OPAL Y. OUSLEY

DEFINITION

Autism is a developmental disorder characterized by a triad of symptoms: impaired social relating and reciprocity, abnormal language and communication development, and a restricted behavioral repertoire that includes repetitive activities and routines. The term was coined in 1943 by Dr. Leo Kanner,[1] who provided detailed case studies of 11 children demonstrating a similar pattern of unusual development. Although certain aspects of the conceptualization of autism have changed over the years, many of Kanner's original observations have been retained in current diagnostic formulations.

Since 1980, the standard for diagnosis has been provided by the American Psychiatric Association's *Diagnostic and Statistical Manual*. In the most recent edition (i.e., *DSM-IV*), autistic disorder is one of five conditions classified within the category of pervasive developmental disorders (PDD).[2] The category of PDD is used to describe children who exhibit qualitative impairments in social interaction, qualitative impairments in verbal and nonverbal communication, or the presence of restricted or repetitive interests or behaviors. A diagnosis of autistic disorder is used for children who show significant impairments in all three areas and an onset of symptoms before 3 years. Consistent with current formulations of autism as a spectrum disorder,[3-5] the other pervasive developmental disorders are differentiated from autistic disorder on the basis of their severity, age of onset, and/or progression of symptomatology (Table 9-3).

The four other conditions included within the PDD category are Asperger's disorder, Rett's disorder, childhood disintegrative disorder, and pervasive developmental disorder not otherwise specified (PDD-NOS).[2] Asperger's disorder describes children who exhibit impairments in social

Table 9-3   Required characteristics for diagnosing pervasive developmental disorders

Characteristic	Autistic disorder	Asperger's disorder	Rett's syndrome	Childhood disintegrative disorder	PDD-NOS
Social impairment	+	+	+	+[a]	+[b]
Language/ communication impairment	+		+	+[a]	+[b]
Restricted/repetitive interests and activities	+	+	+	+[a]	+[b]
Period of normal development			+	+	
Loss of skills in several areas			+	+	
Development of stereotyped hand movements			+		
Onset before 36 months	+				
Average intelligence		+			

[a]At least two of the three characteristics must be present.
[b]At least one of the three characteristics must be present.

interaction and restricted, repetitive interests but who do not exhibit general delays in language. Although only a minority of children with autistic disorder function intellectually within the average range, all children with Asperger's disorder have normal cognitive development. Rett's disorder and childhood disintegrative disorder describe children who have experienced significant developmental regression. Rett's disorder is a progressive condition with an onset before 4 years of age. It has been diagnosed only in females and is characterized by a deceleration of head growth, a loss of purposeful hand skills, and the subsequent development of stereotyped hand movements. Social, language, and gross motor skills are also affected. Childhood disintegrative disorder describes children who exhibit normal development for at least 2 years and then experience significant regression in at least two of the following areas before age 10: social or adaptive behavior, play skills, language skills, motor skills, and bowel or bladder control. A diagnosis of PDD-NOS is used for children with symptoms in the areas of social relating, communication, or restricted activities and interests who do not meet the criteria for any other PDD. This diagnosis includes children with atypical, late onset, or subthreshold forms of autistic disorder.

Although the diagnostic criteria for autism have become increasingly refined in light of empirical research, accurate diagnosis can be complicated by several factors. First, there are no biological markers or medical tests that can detect the presence of autism. As a result, the diagnosis is behaviorally based. Because of its low prevalence, many professionals receive little exposure to individuals with autism in the course of their training and thus are unfamiliar with its behavioral expression. Second, the characteristics and behavioral manifestations of autism often vary as a function of age or developmental level.[6] Diagnostic features prominent during the preschool years may not be the same as those seen in middle childhood or adolescence.[7-9] For example, recent research suggests that very young children may not have developed the language abnormalities or repetitive behaviors and routines that characterize older children.[10-12] A third factor complicating diagnosis is the overlap of symptoms between autism and other disabilities, most notably mental retardation and language disorders.[13-15] Fourth, changes in the conceptualization of autism since its first description in 1943 have contributed to the prevalence of outdated and erroneous beliefs among many professional groups.[16,17]

These diagnostic difficulties may result in unfortunate delays in the identification of autism and in referral to appropriate intervention programs. Although the average age of symptom onset reported by parents is 18 months,[15,18] most children do not receive a definitive diagnosis of autism until the age of 4 to 4½ years.[15,17] This time lag can have negative consequences for the child as well as his or her family.[19] A definitive diagnosis can alleviate family stress by helping parents and siblings understand the child's puzzling behaviors and begin the process of adaptation.[20] Moreover, the diagnostic label often provides the "ticket" that allows access to specialized intervention services. A delay in diagnosis can postpone or prevent participation in specialized early intervention programs, which have resulted in marked improvements for many young children with autism (see following discussion).

INCIDENCE

Autism is a relatively rare disorder. A review of eight epidemiological studies of autism conducted through 1985 found a fairly consistent prevalence rate of 4 to 5 children with autism or autistic-like conditions per 10,000.[21] However, more recent population-based studies have found substantially higher prevalence rates, ranging from 10 to 13 children out of 10,000.[22-24] These higher rates suggest that autism may be more common than previously thought. Rather than indicating an increased incidence of autism, these higher prevalence estimates may reflect an increased level of awareness of autism among parents and professionals that has resulted in a greater likelihood of detection.

Autism occurs more commonly in males than females, with reported sex ratios ranging from 2.3:1 to 3.7:1.[22,23,25-27] Several studies have found sex ratios to differ as a function of intellectual status, with higher proportions of females found at lower intellectual levels.[22,23,27,28] For example, Ritvo[27] found a male:female ratio of 6.3:1 for children with IQs above 70, and a corresponding ratio of 2.7:1 for children with IQs below 50. Other studies have found that females, as a group, score lower on measures of IQ than males,[29-31] and show more evidence of neurological impairment.[32] Observations that females are less commonly but more severely affected have been used to support a multifactorial model of genetic transmission.[31]

Autism appears to be distributed equally among all social classes. Although early studies suggested an upper socioeconomic status (SES) bias,[33,34] more recent investigations have failed to find evidence that autism occurs more commonly at higher SES levels.[27,35-38] Several authors have proposed that certain selection factors, such as access to services, accounted for the earlier association of autism with higher SES. For example, when the diagnosis and availability of specialized programs were less common than they are presently, upper class families were probably more likely to have the resources that enabled them to find these programs. Conversely, recent trends toward increased recognition of autism and wider availability of public funding for services have led to greater access for families at lower SES levels.[36,37]

ETIOLOGY AND PATHOPHYSIOLOGY

Some of the early views of autism placed an emphasis on psychogenic, rather than organic, causes of the disorder. Autism was thought to result from early environmental stress or trauma, deficient parent-child interaction, or parental psychopathology, such as emotional coldness or rejection of the child.[39] Empirical research over the past several decades has failed to support these views. For example, children with autism do not have a stronger history of early stressors than children with other language disorders.[41] Moreover, parents of children with autism do not differ from parents of other disabled or nondisabled children in early child care practices, nurturance or acceptance of their child,[42] history of psychiatric disorder,[41] or personality traits, including warmth or obsessiveness.[41,43,44]

Early views of autism as an emotional disorder have given way to the more contemporary conceptualization of autism as a biological disorder with diverse organic causes. Increasing evidence of brain dysfunction and association of autism with neurological conditions has emerged as a result of advances in medical technology and diagnostic techniques. Major organic, neurobiological conditions have been reported in 28%[26] to 49%[23] of individuals with autism (see the box below for a summary.) Seizure disorders have been found in 11% to 42% of autistic individuals,[45] with an increased incidence in those functioning at lower cognitive levels.[45-47] A distinctive pattern of seizure onset has been reported, with a peak of onset occurring during early childhood and another in adolescence.[46-49] In addition, several studies have found an increased incidence of prenatal and perinatal complications, relative to controls, in the birth histories of children with autism,[48,50,51] lending further support to an underlying organic etiology.

Neurobiological investigations of the etiology of autism have examined genetic influences, structural abnormalities, and neurophysiological and neurochemical factors. Recent neuropsychological studies have also provided interesting data pertinent to etiology. However, the general conclusion from these studies is that there is no single neurobiological factor that is uniquely and universally associated with autism. Rather, there are a variety of organic causes that may contribute to the development of autism in individual cases.[52,53] A summary of the biological factors that have been investigated as etiological agents is presented following.

There is strong evidence that genetic factors play a role in the etiology of autism. This evidence derives from family and twin studies as well as the association of autism with disorders of known genetic etiology. First, the prevalence of autism in siblings of autistic children is 2% to 3%, which is about 50 times higher than that expected by chance.[54] Second, concordance rates for autism are higher for monozygotic twins than for dizygotic twins. Although the observed rates vary from study to study (i.e., monozygotic concordance ranging from 36% to 96% and dizygotic concordance

MAJOR NEUROBIOLOGICAL CONDITIONS ASSOCIATED WITH AUTISM

Fragile X syndrome	Congenital rubella
Tuberous sclerosis	Herpes encephalitis
Neurofibromatosis	Cytomegalovirus
Phenylketonuria	Rett's syndrome
Moebius syndrome	Epilepsy

ranging from 0% to 24%), the pattern of higher concordance rates for monozygotic twins has been consistent.[55] Third, high rates of cognitive, language, and social impairments have been found in the families of individuals with autism.[54] Finally, autism appears to be associated with several known genetic disorders, including fragile X syndrome, phenylketonuria, tuberous sclerosis, and neurofibromatosis.[56] Although several different models of genetic transmission have been proposed, none has received conclusive support.[57,58]

The search for structural abnormalities in the brains of autistic individuals has involved postmortem studies as well as radiological techniques, such as pneumoencephalogram, CT, and MRI studies. In general, although structural abnormalities have been found in many autistic subjects, the abnormalities are not uniform across subjects and the findings tend to vary from one laboratory to another.[59,60] Specific structural abnormalities that have been reported include ventricular enlargement, especially in the left temporal horn;[61,62] cerebellar abnormalities (i.e., loss of Purkinje cells and hypoplasia of vermal lobules);[63,64] decreased brainstem size, especially the pons,[65,66] and forebrain abnormalities.[67,68]

Neurophysiological investigations of individuals with autism have found evidence of dysfunction at the cortical and subcortical levels. Support for cortical dysfunction has been obtained through EEG studies and event-related potentials (ERPs). Abnormal EEGs have been reported for 32% to 43% of autistic children,[69] and atypical patterns of hemispheric lateralization have also been found.[70,71] In addition, reduction in the P3 component of event-related potentials (i.e., the component associated with detection of novel, unpredictable stimuli) has been demonstrated in autistic samples.[70,72] Evidence for subcortical dysfunction is derived from studies demonstrating abnormal vestibular and autonomic responses in autistic subjects, as well as prolonged brainstem transmission times for a subgroup of autistic subjects participating in brainstem auditory-evoked potential (BAER) studies.[70,71]

A variety of neurochemical studies have been performed, with the bulk of research focused on monoamine neurotransmitters (i.e., serotonin, dopamine, norepinephrine), their precursors and metabolites, and associated enzymes. Studies of neuroendocrine functioning (e.g., cortical secretion), psychoactive amines (e.g., bufotenin), and neuropeptides (e.g., β-endorphin) have also been conducted.[73,74] The most consistent finding in autistic populations has been increased levels of serotonin, which is thought to modulate a number of different behavioral processes, including pain and sensory perception, motor function, and learning and memory.

However, the implications of this finding are unclear, as hyperserotonemia is found in only about a third of autistic samples, and elevated serotonin levels are also common in nonautistic samples with mental retardation.[74,75] Abnormal levels of endogenous opioids (e.g., β-endorphin), which are thought to be associated with disturbances in social and emotional behavior, decreased response to pain, and stereotypic and self-abusive behavior, have also been reported in autistic individuals.[73,76]

Results from recent neuropsychological studies have implicated frontal lobe dysfunction. Autistic individuals have consistently been found to perform more poorly than controls on executive function tasks, which measure frontal lobe functions such as cognitive flexibility and response inhibition.[77-79,81] Moreover, a relationship between executive function skills and social-communicative skills has been demonstrated in this population.[78] Several different neuropsychological models linking brain function with behavior in autism have been proposed, some emphasizing frontal areas,[82,83] and others implicating other areas of the brain.[70,71] Although highly speculative at this point, this line of research shows much promise for fostering an understanding of the causes of autism.

In summary, there is considerable evidence that central nervous system abnormalities play a role in the etiology of autism, although no specific biological markers have been identified. Moreover, it is equally clear that no single etiological agent is likely to account for all cases of autism. We must look toward future technological advances and methodological improvements to aid in the identification of distinct etiological subgroups as well as establish closer links between biology and behavior in individuals with autism.

ASSESSMENT AND FINDINGS

Because autism is a complex disorder affecting many areas of development, formal assessment and diagnosis are often provided by multidisciplinary centers with a specialization in autism. Diagnostic teams commonly include a developmental pediatrician, psychologist, speech-language pathologist, educational specialist, and occupational therapist. Because the diagnosis of autism is behaviorally based, information about the child's behavior should be gathered from multiple sources and across multiple settings.[84] A comprehensive diagnostic assessment should include information obtained through detailed interviews with parents and other care providers (e.g., teachers) as well as observation of the child in structured situations (such as developmental testing) and unstructured situations (such as play). Recent research suggests that multiple sources of information are necessary for obtaining a comprehensive view of a child's behavioral patterns. For example, parents may be better able to provide details regarding low frequency or context-specific behaviors, such as the quality of peer relationships and the presence of imaginative play and stereotyped body movements, whereas clinicians may be more likely to detect some of the more subtle aspects of abnormal social behavior and communication.[85]

A number of specialized instruments have been developed for the purpose of gathering diagnostically relevant information through observations or parental report and are presented in the box below. One or more of these instruments will most likely be used during the course of a comprehensive diagnostic evaluation. The interested reader is referred to reviews by Morgan[86] and Sevin et al.[87] for more detailed discussions of these instruments.

Cognitive and behavioral features

The overall severity of autism, as well as the expression of each characteristic, may vary widely across individuals. In addition, the behavioral expression of these characteristics may vary within an individual throughout the course of development. Unfortunately, little empirical research has examined symptom expression as a function of age or developmental level.

Cognitive ability. Kanner[1] originally believed that children with autism have the capacity for normal intellectual functioning. However, empirical

---

DIAGNOSTIC ASSESSMENT INSTRUMENTS FOR AUTISM

Observational scales

Autism Behavior Checklist (ABC)[88]
Autism Diagnostic Observation Schedule (ADOS)[89]
Behavior Rating Instrument for Autistic and Atypical Children (BRIAAC)[90]
Childhood Autism Rating Scale (CARS)[91]
Diagnostic Checklist for Behavior-Disturbed Children (Form E-2)[92]
Ritvo-Freeman Real Life Rating Scale (RLRS)[93]

Parental interviews

Autism Diagnostic Interview—Revised (ADI-R)[94]
Parent Interview for Autism (PIA)[12]

research has consistently revealed that there is great variability in the cognitive capabilities of individuals with autism, with the majority (i.e., 70% to 80%) functioning intellectually within the range of mental retardation.[22,23,95] Moreover, there is evidence that IQ scores are as valid and stable in children with autism as they are in other children.[95-97] Given the pattern of cognitive and behavioral deficits in children with autism, the use of nonverbal tests and specialized assessment techniques is often necessary to provide the best estimate of cognitive functioning and learning potential.[98]

Social deficits. Deficits in social relating and reciprocity are currently viewed by many researchers as the core characteristics of autism.[99-101] Social difficulties usually are first apparent in the autistic child's interactions with his or her parents, with peer interaction difficulties (i.e., lack of interest in peers, inability to play cooperatively, failure to develop friendships) becoming more evident in the preschool years. A number of social behaviors have been investigated in an attempt to quantify the somewhat elusive construct of reciprocity; these behaviors include eye gaze, imitation, attachment, affect, and perspective-taking.

One of the earliest social deficits to appear is in the area of motor imitation. Children with autism have consistently been found to have more difficulty imitating body movements and the use of objects relative to developmentally matched controls.[102-106] Moreover, their performance on motor imitation tasks is inferior to their performance on other sensorimotor tasks (e.g., object permanence).[107] Motor imitation skills appear to have great potential for use in the early screening for autism. There is evidence that these skills improve with age,[108] although certain deficits in the imitation of body movements have been found even in high-functioning adolescents with autism.[109]

Deficits in the use of eye gaze represent another early developing social behavior that has historically been associated with autism. Recent research suggests that children with autism do not differ from developmentally matched peers in the amount of eye contact they use, although they do differ in the ways it is used.[110-112] For instance, autistic children demonstrate more eye contact toward quiet, inactive adults and toward adults following a tickle game but less frequent use of eye contact to establish joint attention with adults[112] or to seek information from their caregiver in an ambiguous situation.[113]

A variety of deficits in the recognition and use of affect also are associated with autism. Young children with autism have been found to display less positive affect,[114] more neutral affect,[115] and more incongruent combinations of affect[115] relative to controls. Positive affect has also been found to occur more often in conjunction with self-absorbed activity rather than directed toward interactional partners in autistic samples.[114] In addition, children with autism have been found to smile less often in response to their mothers' smiles[110] and to pay less attention to an adult simulating distress.[116] Unusual affective expressions[116] and difficulty with affective understanding and empathy[118,119] have also been documented in older, high-functioning individuals with autism.

A related area of research has been the social-cognitive, or perspective-taking, skills of individuals with autism. Numerous studies have revealed that high-functioning autistic individuals are impaired in their understanding of the thoughts and beliefs of others.[120,121] This difficulty in attributing mental states to others has been referred to as an impaired "theory of mind." A theory of mind enables one to impute internal states to others and to predict other people's behavior on the basis of these inferences. Theory of mind deficits have been hypothesized to be specific to autism and to underlie many of its characteristic features.[122]

In contrast to the social deficits described previously, research on attachment behavior has revealed that children with autism are similar to other groups in attachment security. For example, they exhibit different behaviors with their mothers compared with strangers and they show increased approach behavior upon reunion with their mothers in experimental situations. [123-126] However, the specific behavioral and affective expressions of attachment they demonstrate may be different from those of other children.[124]

Language and communication deficits. Individuals with autism exhibit a wide range of language and communication difficulties. About 50% of autistic individuals fail to develop functional use of speech.[8] Those who do acquire speech often evidence delayed milestones[127] as well as a disordered pattern of development.[128] A number of unusual language features are exhibited by individuals with autism; these include immediate and delayed echolalia, pronoun reversal, repetitive language, neologisms, and idiosyncratic use of words and phrases.[129,130] Abnormal prosody, which includes the pitch, stress, rate, and rhythm of language, is also present in individuals with autism.[131-133]

Deficits have also been documented in pragmatics, or the social use of language. Examples of pragmatic language deficits are using pedantic speech, failing to consider another person's perspective, asking embarrassing questions, perseverating on topics, engaging in one-sided conversations, and failing to engage in conversational turn-taking.[134]

Communication deficits are also present in autistic children who have not acquired speech. At a young age, one of the most salient aspects of abnormal communication development in autism is the failure to coordinate one's attention between another person and an object or event of interest. Several studies have revealed that children with autism are less likely than other developmentally delayed children to engage in joint attention behaviors, such as showing a toy to another person, pointing toward an object of interest, or alternating gaze between a person and an object.[112,135-137] It is interesting to note that children with autism may use pointing to request objects but are less likely to point as a means of engaging in joint attention relative to children matched on language ability.[138,139] In addition, when joint attention does occur in children with autism, it is less likely to be accompanied by positive affect.[140]

Restricted activities and interests. This category comprises a number of diverse behaviors—ranging from stereotyped movements to sensory abnormalities to insistence on complex routines—that are all thought to serve the function of attempting to impose some degree of invariance onto the environment.[14] Although the literature is replete with rich examples of these very interesting and often unusual behaviors, there has been a relative paucity of empirical studies examining the nature of these behaviors in autistic and developmentally comparable samples.

On the basis of parental report, Wing[141] found that abnormal body movements occurred more commonly in children with autism than in those with mental retardation and language disorders but with equal frequency in children with sensory impairments (i.e., visual and hearing deficits). The most common stereotypies reported by parents of autistic children are arm, hand, or finger flapping; head or body rocking; and spinning.[17,142]

Three types of sensory abnormalities in autism have been described: hyporeactivity, heightened awareness, and heightened sensitivity.[143] Wing[141] found sensory abnormalities in vision and the proximal senses (i.e., touch, pain, taste, and smell) occur more commonly in children with autism than in those with other handicaps, with the exception of children with sensory impairments.

Another characteristic that can be observed in young children with autism is the use of restricted and repetitive forms of play. Autistic children have been found to demonstrate less appropriate, less diverse, and more repetitive play (e.g., spinning, shaking, or twirling toys) than control children.[115,144,145] They also exhibit less functional play, less play with dolls, and less pretend play relative to comparison groups.[104,105,112]

The specific form of repetitive activities exhibited by children with autism appears to be related to a child's developmental level. For example, lower functioning children with autism are more likely to demonstrate stereotyped movements, while higher functioning individuals are more likely to engage in complex routines and to exhibit perseverative interests.[146] In addition, young children are less likely than older children to exhibit unusual habits or routines.[7,10,11,147]

Early identification

In recent years there has been increased recognition of the importance of early identification of autism. At a practical level, improved understanding of the characteristics of young children with autism can enhance early identification and intervention efforts; at a theoretical level, this information can help differentiate between the primary features of autism and later emerging, secondary sequelae.[148,149] Although the symptoms of autism are thought to be present from early in life, only three studies have compared the behaviors of autistic children under 3 years old with those seen in developmentally comparable peers.[7,147,150] A summary of the behaviors that have been found to differentiate very young children with autism from developmentally matched controls is presented in the box below. As the box illustrates, a number of characteristics in the areas of social and communicative development, as well as repetitive activities, can be observed in very young children. In contrast, behaviors indicative of disordered peer

---

SYMPTOMS OF AUTISM IN CHILDREN UNDER 36 MONTHS

Social interactions and reciprocity

Poor imitation of actions and gestures
Failure to use eye contact in a social or communicative manner
Lack of response to the social bids of others
Little interest in social games such as pat-a-cake or peek-a-boo
Preference for playing alone instead of with others
Bland or flat facial expression

Communication

Delayed acquisition of speech
Little use of gestures such as pointing or waving
Failure to attract attention to his/her own activities, such as holding up or showing objects

Restricted and repetitive activities

Repetitive motor behaviors, such as spinning or finger posturing
Repetitive play activities, such as arranging objects into lines or patterns
Attachment to unusual objects
Failure to respond to sounds or his/her name being called
Unusual visual interests, such as staring at lights or spinning objects

relationships, abnormal language features, and a need for sameness do not differentiate children with autism under 3 years old from their developmentally delayed peers.[11,12] Despite the fact that all diagnostic features may not be present, there is evidence that the diagnosis of autism can be made reliably below the age of 3 years.[4,10,151]

A recent development in the area of early diagnosis has been the compilation of a screening instrument designed to detect autism in 18-month-old children.[152] The Checklist for Autism in Toddlers (CHAT) assesses five behaviors deficient in autism: social interest, social play, pretend play, joint attention, and pointing for the purpose of communicating interest in an object or event. In a prospective study of 41 younger siblings of children with autism and 50 normal children (mean ages = 19 months and 18 months, respectively), four children in the former group missed two or more of the five diagnostically relevant items, whereas no control children missed more than one item. Follow-up at the age of 30 months revealed that these four children received an independent diagnosis of autism. These results suggest that screening for autism may be performed effectively as young as 18 months.

In summary, there is strong evidence that the diagnosis of autism can be made reliably below the age of 3 years. Behaviors most likely to be observed are those indicative of social and communicative deficits as well as repetitive activities. However, it is important to emphasize that the nature of the social and communicative impairments in young children are subtle, in that they often represent the *absence* of normative behaviors (e.g., not imitating, not using gestures) rather than the *presence* of noticeably unusual behaviors (e.g., peculiar language use).

MANAGEMENT

There is no cure for autism at the present time. The primary goals of treatment are to promote the development of social, communicative, and adaptive living skills; to reduce maladaptive behaviors such as rigidity and stereotypies; and to alleviate family stress.[153,154]

Child-oriented approaches

The most well-established and efficacious treatment approaches for children with autism are those employing educational and behavioral interventions. Several characteristics of educational intervention have been found to be effective in promoting the learning and development of autistic students. One characteristic is the provision of structure, or external organization and direction. Classroom structure includes the physical organization of the classroom, the provision of visual cues, and the use of schedules, individual work systems, and routines.[155] Structured settings have been associated with higher levels of on-task behavior,[156-158] more appropriate eye contact and social relating,[157-159] fewer stereotypic behaviors; and greater educational achievement[156] in autistic individuals.

A second important component of educational intervention is the provision of individualized programming that is developmental in nature and focuses on the specific deficit areas of autism.[153,160,161] Third, the use of nondisabled peers as agents of change has led to beneficial effects for children with autism[162-166] as well as the peer models.[166,167] A fourth characteristic is the use of behavioral techniques to foster the acquisition of new skills and behaviors, reduce disruptive or self-stimulatory behavior, and enhance attention and motivation.[168,169] Finally, parental involvement in the teaching of their children with autism has also been demonstrated to be efficacious.[168,170,171] Significant increases in positive social and play behaviors and reductions in negative behaviors have been observed as a result of parents' active participation in the teaching of their children.[172,173]

There is also compelling evidence that educational intervention should begin at young ages. A number of studies have reported dramatic cognitive and behavioral improvements for autistic children participating in specialized early intervention programs.[161,163,166,168,174,175] Several characteristics of successful early intervention programs for children with autism have been delineated: structured behavioral treatment, parental involvement, treatment at an early age, intensive treatment, and emphasis on generalization of skills.[176]

Medication can be a useful adjunct to educational and behavioral intervention in some individuals with autism. The purpose of medication in this population is not to correct or reverse the underlying disorder but to ameliorate some of the problematic behavioral symptoms. Although a number of pharmacological agents have been investigated for use in children with autism, their effectiveness has proven to be modest at best, and medication is generally not a routine component of treatment.[177] Several medications are reviewed following and recommended daily dosage levels are presented in Table 9-4.

The most well-investigated drug in autism has been haloperidol, a dopamine antagonist that has been found to decrease symptoms of agitation, hyperactivity, aggression, stereotyped behavior, and affective lability.[178,179] However, like other neuroleptics, haloperidol is associated with a number of side effects, the most severe being tardive dyskinesia. For this reason,

Table 9-4   Daily dosages of drugs used clinically or experimentally in the treatment of behavioral symptoms associated with autism

Drug	Daily dosage
Haloperidol (Haldol)	.04-0.2 mg/kg
Fenfluramine (Pondimin)	1.1-1.8 mg/kg
Naltrexone (Trexan)	0.5-2.0 mg/kg
Clomipramine (Anafranil)	25-75 mg
Methylphenidate (Ritalin)	0.3-0.7 mg/kg
Dextroamphetamine (Dexedrine)	.15-0.5 mg/kg
Clonidine (Catapres)	0.1-0.4 mg
Buspirone (BuSpar)	0.2-0.6 mg/kg
Carbamazepine (Tegretol)	15-30 mg/kg
Propranolol (Inderal)	40-960 mg
Valproic acid (Depakote)	10-60 mg/kg

haloperidol is recommended only for short-term use and only for the control of severe behavior problems.[179,180] Fenfluramine is a drug with antiserotonergic properties that also has been well studied in this population. Despite initial reports of improvements in IQ, hyperactivity, withdrawal, and stereotypies, more recent studies have suggested limited efficacy,[181,182] diminished effectiveness over time,[178] and concerns about potential neurotoxicity.[178,179] Another drug that has shown recent promise in the treatment of autism is naltrexone, which is an opioid antagonist. Reduction of self-injurious behavior, stereotypies, aggression, and social withdrawal have been reported for this drug; however, the long-term effects of naltrexone are not yet known.[178-180]

Several other drugs have been evaluated for their ability to reduce specific behavioral symptoms seen in autism. Clomipramine, a tricyclic antidepressant used in the treatment of obsessive-compulsive disorder, has been effective in treating the compulsive and repetitive behaviors of some children with autism.[183,184] Stimulants, such as methylphenidate and dextroamphetamine, have been used in autistic populations to decrease inattention and hyperactivity. However, these medications have been associated with side effects that include increased stereotypic and self-injurious behaviors.[179,180] It has been suggested that the use of stimulants may be more effective for autistic children functioning at higher intellectual levels than for those with concomitant mental retardation.[177,180] A number of medications are also in the process of being investigated for their utility in controlling aggressive behavior; these medications include carbamazepine, propranolol, valproic acid, buspirone, and clonidine.[180]

Family-oriented approaches

The presence of a child with autism can stress a family system in a number of different ways. Increased expenses for health care, child care, and respite care may create a financial burden.[185] Certain characteristics of the child, such as communication difficulties, sleep difficulties, and unpredictable behaviors can place an emotional strain on the family as well as interfere with daily activities.[186] The specific causes of stress to the family may change with the child's developmental stage. For example, with a younger child, families must adjust to the shock of the initial diagnosis, learn to manage noncompliant and/or unusual behaviors, and locate appropriate early intervention and educational services. As the child enters adolescence, new challenges faced by families may include the onset of seizures, the emergence of sexuality, management difficulties caused by increased physical size and strength, and the need to plan for their child's future.[187,188]

Families experiencing stress may benefit from the use of community respite services and from individual or family counseling. Goals of individual therapy may include promoting greater understanding of the child's disorder, fostering acceptance of the diagnosis, and learning to cope with chronic stress.[187] Goals of family therapy may include helping parents learn to rely on each other for emotional support, discussing issues of marital satisfaction, teaching parenting skills, facilitating access to community resources, and helping parents to develop advocacy skills.[188]

Some siblings of children with autism may experience stress that is expressed in emotional or behavioral difficulties.[189-191] For this subgroup of children, individual or group counseling that emphasizes the following goals may be beneficial: enhancing knowledge of autism, identifying and coping with the emotions related to having a sibling with autism, learning to deal with the difficult behaviors associated with autism, and achieving an equitable share of attention and resources from their parents.[187]

In summary, the most important interventions for children with autism at the present time are educational and behavioral in nature. Participation in specialized early intervention programs appears to be especially beneficial for improving the behavior and learning of children with autism. Parental and sibling stress should be monitored, and the need for intervention addressed if necessary.

OUTCOME

The first review of outcome studies of individuals with autism was published by Lotter[192] in 1978. This review focused on eight follow-up studies conducted through the mid 1970s and portrayed a rather gloomy prognostic picture. Although the outcome for children with autism was found to be quite variable, for the majority of children (i.e., 61% to 73%) the outcome was described as "poor" (i.e., severe handicap, no independent social progress) or "very poor" (i.e., unable to lead any kind of independent existence). A small minority of children (5% to 17%) was reported to have a "good" outcome (i.e., normal or near normal social life and satisfactory functioning at school or work). Institutionalization rates for adolescents and adults with autism ranged from 39% to 74%, while employment rates ranged from 0% to 13%. The most potent predictors of outcome across the studies were IQ and the presence of useful speech by the age of five.[192]

Six follow-up studies have been published since Lotter's review,[192] four consisting of samples heterogeneous with respect to cognitive level and two focusing exclusively on "high-functioning" individuals with autism (Table 9-5). The studies employing heterogeneous samples found a more favorable prognosis than that found in previous studies; good outcomes were reported for 4% to 32% of children with autism, and poor-to-very poor outcomes for 20% to 48%.[49,193-195] Although independent living and college attendance were rare in these samples,[49,195] one study reported a competitive employment rate of 21%.[194]

The outcome for high-functioning individuals with autism (i.e., children obtaining early IQ scores above 60 or 65) appears to be even more promising. At the time of follow-up, 9% to 31% of the samples studied were living independently, 27% to 38% were working competitively, and 11% to 50% had attended at least some college.[196,197] In addition, Szatmari et al.[196] reported that 25% of their sample was married or dating regularly at follow-up.

In summary, recent follow-up studies suggest that the outcome for children diagnosed with autism continues to be variable. However, relative to earlier outcome studies, the proportion of children obtaining good outcomes appears to have increased, while the proportion of children obtaining poor outcomes has decreased. This positive trend is most likely a reflection of advances in education and community-based services that have occurred over the past 20 years. Independent living, competitive employment, and college attendance should be considered potential outcomes for high-functioning individuals with autism.

Table 9-5. Outcome reported in follow-up studies conducted since 1986

Authors	Subjects	Initial IQ	Length of follow-up (yrs)	Age at follow-up (yrs)	Classification (%)[a]	Outcome Status
Chung, et al.[193]	58 M 8 F	<50: 32%[b] 50-70: 47% >70: 21%	2-10	<12: 86% >12: 14%	G-32 F-48 P-17 VP-3	
Gillberg and Steffenburg[49]	17 M 6 F	<50: 39% 50-70: 35% >70: 26%	6-11	16-23	G-4 F-13 I-35 P-39 VP-9	4% living independently
Kobayashi et al.[194]	166 M 31 F	<50: 49% 50-69: 28% ≥70: 24%	5-28	18-33	G-27 F-27 P-23 VP-23	21% employed 6% attending college
Szatmari et al.[196]	12 M 4 F	All > 65 (M = 89)	11-27	17-34	G-25	31% living independently 38% employed 50% attending college
Venter et al.[197]	35 M 23 F	All > 60 (M = 80)	M = 8	10-37		9% living independently[c] 27% employed[c] 11% attending college[d]
Wolf and Goldberg[195]	64 M & F (combined)	<55: 68% 55-70: 19% >70: 11%	8-24	<20: 31% 20-29: 61% >30: 7%	G-12 F-30 VP-47	5% living independently 6% employed

[a]G = good; F = fair; I = intermediate; P = poor; VP = very poor.
[b]N = 38.
[c]Based on 22 subjects > 18 years old.
[d]Based on 18 subjects > 25 years old.

REFERENCES

1. Kanner L: Autistic disturbances of affective contact, *Nerv Child* 2:217-250, 1943.
2. American Psychiatric Association: *Diagnostic and statistical manual of mental disorders*, ed 4, Washington, DC, 1994, American Psychiatric Association.
3. Allen DA: Autism spectrum disorders: clinical presentation in preschool children, *J Child Neurol* 3(suppl):48-56, 1988.
4. Lord C: Methods and measures of behavior in the diagnosis of autism and related disorders, *Psychiatr Clin North Am* 14:69-80, 1991.
5. Provence S, Dahl EK: Disorders of atypical development: diagnostic issues raised by a spectrum disorder. In Cohen DJ, Donnellan AM, editors: *Handbook of autism and pervasive developmental disorders*, Silver Spring, MD, 1987, VH Winston & Sons, 677-689.
6. Siegel B: Toward DSM-IV: a developmental approach to autistic disorder, *Psychiatr Clin North Am* 14:53-68, 1991.
7. Ohta M, Nagai Y, Hara H, Sasaki M: Parental perception of behavioral symptoms in Japanese autistic children, *J Autism Dev Disord* 17:549-563, 1987.
8. Rutter M: Diagnosis and definition of childhood autism, *J Autism Dev Disord* 8:139-161, 1978.
9. Wing L, Attwood A: Syndromes of autism and atypical development. In Cohen DJ, Donnellan AM, editors: *Handbook of autism and pervasive developmental disorders*, Silver Spring, MD, 1987, VH Winston & Sons, 3-19.
10. Gillberg C, Ehlers S, Schaumann H, et al: Autism under age 3 years: a clinical study of 28 cases referred for autistic symptoms in infancy, *J Child Psychol Psychiatr* 31:921-934, 1990.
11. Lord C: *Follow-ups of two-years-olds referred for possible autism.* Paper presented at the Meeting of the Society for Research in Child Development, Seattle, WA, April, 1991.
12. Stone WL, Hogan KL: A structured parent interview for identifying young children with autism, *J Autism Dev Disord* 23:639-652, 1993.
13. Paul R, Cohen DJ, Caparulo BK: A longitudinal study of patients with severe developmental disorders of language learning, *J Am Acad Child Psychiat* 22:525-534, 1983.
14. Rutter M, Schopler E: Autism and pervasive developmental disorders: concepts and diagnostic issues, *J Autism Dev Disord* 17:159-186, 1987.
15. Siegel B, Pliner C, Eschler J, Elliott GR: How children with autism are diagnosed: difficulties in identification of children with multiple developmental delays, *Dev Behav Peds* 9:199-204, 1988.
16. Stone WL: Cross-disciplinary perspectives on autism, *J Ped Psychol* 12:615-630, 1987.
17. Stone WL, Rosenbaum JL: A comparison of teacher and parent views of autism, *J Autism Dev Disord* 18:403-414, 1988.
18. Volkmar FR, Cohen DJ, Paul R: An evaluation of DSM-III criteria for infantile autism, *J Am Acad Child Psychiat* 25:190-197, 1986.
19. Akerley M: What's in a name? In Schopler E, Mesibov GB, editors: *Diagnosis and assessment in autism*, New York, 1988, Plenum, 59-67.
20. Marcus LM, Stone WL: Assessment of the young autistic child. In Schopler E, Van Bourgondien ME, Bristol MM, editors: *Preschool issues in autism*, New York, 1993, Plenum, 149-173.
21. Zahner GEP, Pauls DL: Epidemiological surveys of infantile autism. In Cohen DJ, Donnellan AM, editors: *Handbook of autism and pervasive developmental disorders*, Silver Spring, MD, 1987, VH Winston & Sons, 199-207.
22. Bryson SE, Clark BS, Smith IM: First report of a Canadian epidemiological study of autistic syndromes, *J Child Psychol Psychiatr* 29:433-445, 1988.
23. Gillberg C, Steffenburg S, Schaumann H: Is autism more common now than ten years ago? *Br J Psychiatr* 158:403-409, 1991.

24. Sugiyama T, Abe T: The prevalence of autism in Nagoya, Japan: a total population study, *J Autism Dev Disord* 19:87-96, 1989.

25. Burd L, Fisher W, Kerbeshian J: A prevalence study of pervasive developmental disorders in North Dakota, *J Am Acad Child Adolesc Psychiatr* 26:700-703, 1987.

26. Cialdella P, Mamelle N: An epidemiological study of infantile autism in a French department (Rhone): a research note, *J Child Psychol Psychiatr* 30:165-175, 1989.

27. Ritvo ER, Freeman BJ, Pingree C, et al: The UCLA–University of Utah epidemiological survey of autism: prevalence, *Am J Psychiatr* 146:194-199, 1989.

28. Wing L: Language, social, and cognitive impairments in autism and severe mental retardation, *J Autism Dev Disord* 11:31-44, 1981.

29. Konstantareas MM, Homatidis S, Busch J: Cognitive, communication, and social differences between autistic boys and girls, *J Applied Dev Psychol* 10:411-424, 1989.

30. Lord C, Schopler E, Revicki D: Sex differences in autism, *J Autism Dev Disord* 12:317-330, 1982.

31. Tsai LY, Beisler JM: The development of sex differences in infantile autism, *Br J Psychiatr* 142:373-378, 1983.

32. Tsai LY, Stewart MA, August G: Implication of sex differences in the familial transmission of infantile autism, *J Autism Dev Disord* 11:165-173, 1981.

33. Lotter V: Epidemiology of autistic conditions in young children. II. Some characteristics of parents and children, *Social Psychiatr* 1:163-173, 1967.

34. Treffert DA: Epidemiology of infantile autism, *Arch Gen Psychiatr* 22:431-438, 1970.

35. Gillberg C, Schaumann H: Social class and infantile autism, *J Autism Dev Disord* 12:223-228, 1982.

36. Schopler E, Andrews CE, Strupp K: Do autistic children come from upper-middle-class parents? *J Autism Dev Disord* 9:139-152, 1979.

37. Tsai LY, Stewart MA, Faust M, Shook S: Social class distribution of fathers of children enrolled in the Iowa Autism Program, *J Autism Dev Disord* 12:211-221, 1982.

38. Wing L: Childhood autism and social class: a question of selection? *Br J Psychiatr* 137:410-417, 1980.

39. Bristol MM: Designing programs for young developmentally disabled children: a family systems approach to autism, *RASE* 6:46-53, 1985.

40. Cantwell DP, Baker L, Rutter M: Family factors. In Rutter M, Schopler E, editors: *Autism: a reappraisal of concepts and treatment*, New York, 1978, Plenum, 1978, 269-296.

41. Cox A, Rutter M, Newman S, Bartak L: A comparative study of infantile autism and specific developmental receptive language disorder. II. Parental characteristics, *Br J Psychiatr* 126:146-159, 1975.

42. DeMyer MK, Pontius W, Norton JA, et al: Parental practices and innate activity in normal, autistic, and brain-damaged infants, *J Autism Child Schizophr* 2:49-66, 1972.

43. Koegel RL, Schreibman L, O'Neill RE, Burke JC: The personality and family-interaction characteristics of parents of autistic children, *J Consult Clin Psychol* 5:683-692, 1983.

44. McAdoo WG, DeMyer MK: Personality characteristics of parents. In Rutter M, Schopler E, editors: *Autism: a reappraisal of concepts and treatment*, New York, 1978, Plenum, 251-267.

45. Tuchman RF, Rapin I, Shinnar S: Autistic and dysphasic children. II. Epilepsy, *Pediatrics* 88:1219-1225, 1991.

46. Rutter M: Autistic children growing up, *Dev Med Child Neurol* 26:122-129, 1984.

47. Volkmar FR, Nelson DS: Seizure disorders in autism, *J Am Acad Child Adolesc Psychiatr* 29:127-129, 1990.

48. Deykin EY, MacMahon B: The incidence of seizures among children with autistic symptoms, *Am J Psychiatr* 136:1310-1312, 1979.

49. Gillberg C, Steffenburg S: Outcome and prognostic factors in infantile autism and similar conditions: a population-based study of 46 cases followed through puberty, *J Autism Dev Disord* 17:273-287, 1987.

50. Bryson SE, Smith IM, Eastwood D: Obstetrical suboptimality in autistic children, *J Am Acad Child Adolesc Psychiatr* 27:418-422, 1988.

51. Gillberg C, Gillberg IC: Infantile autism: a total population study of reduced optimality in the pre-, peri-, and neonatal period, *J Autism Dev Disord* 13:153-166, 1983.

52. Coleman M: The search for neurological subgroups in autism. In Schopler E, Mesibov GB, editors: *Neurobiological issues in autism*, New York, 1987, Plenum, 163-178.

53. Gillberg C: Autism and pervasive developmental disorders, *J Child Psychol Psychiatr* 31:99-119, 1990.

54. Folstein SE, Piven J: Etiology of autism: genetic influences, *Pediatrics* 87(suppl):767-773, 1991.

55. Smalley SL, Asarnow RF, Spence MA: Autism and genetics, *Arch Gen Psychiatr* 45:953-961, 1988.

56. Folstein SE, Rutter ML: Autism: family aggregation and genetic implications, *J Autism Dev Disord* 18:3-30, 1988.

57. Smalley SL: Genetic influences in autism, *Psychiatr Clin North Am* 14:125-139, 1991.

58. Szatmari P, Jones MB: IQ and the genetics of autism, *J Child Psychol Psychiatr* 32:897-908, 1991.

59. Lotspeich LJ, Ciaranello RD: The neurobiology and genetics of infantile autism, *Int Rev Neurobiol* 35:87-129, 1993.

60. Tsai LY: Recent neurobiological findings in autism. In Gillberg C, editor: *Diagnosis and treatment of autism*, New York, 1989, Plenum, 83-104.

61. DeLong GR, Bauman ML: Brain lesions in autism. In Schopler E, Mesibov GB, editors: *Neurobiological issues in autism*, New York, 1987, Plenum, 229-242.

62. Golden GS: Neurological functioning. In Cohen DJ, Donnellan AM, editors: *Handbook of autism and developmental disorders*, Silver Spring, MD, 1987, VH Winston & Sons, 133-147.

63. Courchesne E: Neuroanatomic imaging in autism, *Pediatrics Suppl* 781-790, 1991.

64. Ritvo ER, Freeman BJ, Schiebel AB, et al: Lower Purkinje cell counts in the cerebella of four autistic subjects: initial findings of the UCLA-NSAC autopsy research report, *Am J Psychiatr* 143:862-866, 1986.

65. Gaffney GR, Kuperman S, Tsai LY, Minchin S: Morphological evidence for brainstem involvement in infantile autism, *Biol Psychiatr* 24:578-586, 1988.

66. Hashimoto T, Tayama M, Miyazaki M, et al: Brainstem and cerebellar vermis involvement in autistic children, *J Child Neurol* 8:149-153, 1993.

67. Bauman ML: Microscopic neuroanatomic abnormalities in autism, *Pediatrics Suppl* 791-796, 1991.

68. Gaffney GR, Kuperman S, Tsai LY, Minchin S: Forebrain structure in infantile autism, *J Am Acad Child Adolesc Psychiatr* 28:534-537, 1989.

69. Minshew NJ: Indices of neural functions in autism: clinical and biologic implications, *Pediatrics Suppl* 774-780, 1991.

70. Dawson G, Lewy A: Reciprocal subcortical-cortical influences in autism: the role of attentional mechanisms. In Dawson G, editor: *Autism: nature, diagnosis, and treatment*, New York, 1989, Guilford, 144-173.

71. Ornitz EM: Autism at the interface between sensory and information processing. In Dawson G, editor: *Autism: nature, diagnosis, and treatment*, New York, 1989, Guilford, 174-207.

72. Courchesne E: A neurophysiological view of autism. In Schopler E, Mesibov GB, editors: *Neurobiological issues in autism*, New York, 1987, Plenum, 285-324.

73. Cook EH: Autism: review of neurochemical investigation, *Synapse* 6:292-308, 1990.

74. Volkmar FR, Anderson GM: Neurochemical perspectives on infantile autism. In Dawson G, editor: *Autism: nature, diagnosis, and treatment,* New York, 1989, Guilford, 208-224.

75. Yuwiler A, Freedman DX: Neurotransmitter research in autism. In Schopler E, Mesibov GB, editors: *Neurobiological issues in autism,* New York, 1987, Plenum, 263-284.

76. Panksepp J, Sahley TL: Possible brain opioid involvement in disrupted social intent and language development in autism. In Schopler E, Mesibov GB, editors: *Neurobiological issues in autism,* New York, 1987, Plenum.

77. Bishop DVM: Annotation: autism, executive functions and theory of mind: a neuropsychological perspective, *J Child Psychol Psychiatr* 34:279-293, 1993.

78. McEvoy RE, Rogers SJ, Pennington BF: Executive function and social communication deficits in young autistic children, *J Child Psychol Psychiatr* 34:563-578, 1993.

79. Ozonoff S, Pennington BF, Rogers SJ: Executive function deficits in high-functioning autistic individuals: relationship to theory of mind, *J Child Psychol Psychiatr* 32:1081-1105, 1991.

80. Prior MR, Hoffman W: Brief report: neuropsychological testing of autistic children through an exploration with frontal lobe tests, *J Autism Dev Disord* 20:581-590, 1990.

81. Rumsey J, Hamburger S: Neuropsychological divergence of high-functioning autism and severe dyslexia, *J Autism Dev Disord* 20:155-168, 1988.

82. Damasio AR, Maurer RG: A neurological model for childhood autism, *Arch Neurol* 35:777-786, 1978.

83. Rogers SJ, Pennington BF: A theoretical approach to the deficits in infantile autism, *Dev Psychopathol* 3:137-162, 1991.

84. Lord C: Early social development in autism. In Schopler E, Van Bourgondien ME, Bristol MM, editors: *Preschool issues in autism,* New York, 1993, Plenum, 61-94.

85. Stone WL, Hoffman EL, Lewis SL, Ousley OY: Early recognition of autism: parental report vs. clinical observation, *Am J Dis Child* (in press).

86. Morgan S: Diagnostic assessment of autism: a review of objective scales, *J Psychoed Assess* 6:139-151, 1988.

87. Sevin JA, Matson JL, Coe DA, et al: A comparison of three commonly used autism scales, *J Autism Dev Disord* 21:417-432, 1991.

88. Krug DA, Arick JR, Almond PJ: Behavior checklist for identifying severely handicapped individuals with high levels of autistic behavior, *J Child Psychol Psychiatr* 21:221-229, 1980.

89. Lord C, Rutter M, Goode S, et al: Autism diagnostic observation schedule: a standardized observation of communicative and social behavior, *J Autism Dev Disord* 19:185-212, 1989.

90. Ruttenberg BA, Kalish BI, Wenar C, Wolf E: *The behavior rating instrument for autistic and other atypical children,* Chicago, Stoelting Co., 1977.

91. Schopler E, Reichler RJ, Renner BR: *The childhood autism rating scale,* Los Angeles, 1988, Western Psychological Services.

92. Rimland B: The differentiation of childhood psychoses: an analysis of checklists for 2,218 psychotic children, *J Aut Childhood Schizophr* 1:161-174, 1971.

93. Freeman BJ, Ritvo ER, Yokota A, Ritvo A: A scale for rating symptoms of patients with the syndrome of autism in real life settings, *J Am Acad Child Psychiatr* 25:130-136, 1986.

94. Lord C, Rutter M, Le Couteur A: Autism diagnostic interview—revised: a revised version of a diagnostic interview for caregivers of individuals with possible pervasive developmental disorders, *J Autism Dev Disord* 24:659-685, 1994.

95. Freeman BJ, Ritvo ER, Needleman R, Yokota A: The stability of cognitive and linguistic parameters in autism: a five-year prospective study, *J Am Acad Child Psychiatr* 24:459-464, 1985.

96. DeMyer MK, Barton S, Alpern GD, et al: The measured intelligence of autistic children, *J Autism Child Schizophr* 4:42-60, 1974.

97. Lord C, Schopler E: Stability of assessment results of autistic and non-autistic language-impaired children from preschool years to early school age, *J Child Psychol Psychiatr* 30:575-590, 1989.

98. Marcus L, Baker A: Assessment of autistic children. In Simeonsson RJ, editor: *Psychological and developmental assessment of special children,* Boston, 1986, Allyn & Bacon, 279-304.

99. Fein D, Pennington B, Markowitz P, et al: Toward a neuropsychological model of infantile autism: are the social deficits primary? *J Am Acad Child Psychiatr* 25:198-212, 1986.

100. Mundy P, Sigman M: Specifying the nature of the social impairment in autism. In Dawson G, editor: *Autism: nature, diagnosis, and treatment,* New York, 1989, Guilford, 3-21.

101. Volkmar FR, Sparrow SS, Goudreau D, et al: Social deficits in autism: an operational approach using the Vineland Adaptive Behavior Scales, *J Am Acad Child Adolesc Psychiatr* 26:156-161, 1987.

102. DeMyer MK, Alpern GD, Barton S, et al: Imitation in autistic, early schizophrenic, and nonpsychotic subnormal children, *J Autism Child Schizophr* 2a:264-287, 1972.

103. Jones V, Prior M: Motor imitation abilities and neurological signs in autistic children, *J Autism Dev Disord* 15:37-46, 1985.

104. Sigman M, Ungerer JA: Cognitive and language skills in autistic, mentally retarded, and normal children, *Dev Psychol* 20:293-302, 1984a.

105. Stone WL, Lemanek KL, Fishel PT, et al: Play and imitation skills in the diagnosis of autism in young children, *Pediatrics* 86:267-272, 1990.

106. Stone WL, Ousley OY, Littleford C: *A comparison of elicited imitation in young children with autism and developmental delay,* Poster session presented at the Annual Gatlinburg Conference on Research and Theory in Mental Retardation and Developmental Disabilities, Gatlinburg, TN, March, 1995.

107. Dawson G, Adams A: Imitation and social responsiveness in autistic children, *J Abnorm Child Psychol* 12:209-226, 1984.

108. Garfin DG, McCallon D, Cox R: Validity and reliability of the Childhood Autism Rating Scale with autistic adolescents, *J Autism Dev Disord* 18:367-378, 1988.

109. Rogers SJ, McEvoy RE: *Praxis in high-functioning persons with autism,* Paper presented at the Meeting of the Society for Research in Child Development, New Orleans, April, 1993.

110. Dawson G, Hill D, Spencer A, Galpert L, Watson L: Affective exchanges between young autistic children and their mothers, *J Abnorm Child Psychol* 18:335-345, 1990.

111. Mirenda PL, Donnellan AM, Yoder DE: Gaze behavior: a new look at an old problem, *J Autism Dev Disord* 13:397-409, 1983.

112. Mundy P, Sigman M, Ungerer J, Sherman T: Defining the social deficits of autism: the contribution of non-verbal communication measures, *J Child Psychol Psychiatr* 27:657-669, 1986.

113. Phillips W, Baron-Cohen S, Rutter M: The role of eye contact in goal detection: evidence from normal infants and children with autism or mental handicap, *Dev Psychopathol* 4:375-383, 1992.

114. Snow ME, Hertzig ME, Shapiro T: Expression of emotion in young autistic children, *J Am Acad Child Adolesc Psychiatr* 26:836-838, 1987.

115. Yirmiya N, Kasari C, Sigman M, Mundy P: Facial expressions of affect in autistic mentally retarded and normal children, *J Child Psychol Psychiatr* 30:725-735, 1989.

116. Sigman MD, Kasari C, Kwon JH, Yirmiya N: Responses to the negative emotions of others by autistic, mentally retarded, and normal children, *Child Dev* 63:796-807, 1992.

117. Macdonald H, Rutter M, Howlin P, et al: Recognition and expression of emotional cues by autistic and normal adults, *J Child Psychol Psychiatr* 30:865-877, 1989.

118. Hobson RP, Ousten J, Lee A: What's in a face? the case of autism, *Br J Psychol* 79:441-453, 1988.

119. Yirmiya N, Sigman MD, Kasari C, Mundy P: Empathy and cognition in high-functioning children with autism, *Child Dev* 63:150-160, 1992.

120. Baron-Cohen S: Do people with autism understand what causes emotion? *Child Dev* 62:385-395, 1991.

121. Leslie AM, Frith U: Autistic children's understanding of seeing, knowing, and believing, *Br J Dev Psychol* 6:315-324, 1988.

122. Baron-Cohen S, Leslie AM, Frith U: Does the autistic child have a "theory of mind?" *Cognition* 21:37-46, 1985.

123. Rogers SJ, Ozonoff S, Maslin-Cole C: A comparative study of attachment behavior in young children with autism or other psychiatric disorders, *J Am Acad Child Adolesc Psychiatr* 30:483-488, 1991.

124. Rogers SJ, Ozonoff S, Maslin-Cole C: Developmental aspects of attachment behavior in young children with pervasive developmental disorders, *J Am Acad Child Adolesc Psychiatr* 32:1274-1282, 1993.

125. Shapiro T, Sherman M, Calamari G, Koch D: Attachment in autism and other developmental disorders, *J Am Acad Child Adolesc Psychiatr* 26:480-484, 1987.

126. Sigman M, Ungerer J: Attachment behaviors in autistic children, *J Autism Dev Disord* 14:231-244, 1984b.

127. Paul R: Communication. In Cohen DJ, Donnellan AM, editors: *Handbook of autism and developmental disorders,* Silver Spring, MD, 1987, Winston & Sons, 61-84.

128. Tager-Flusberg H: A psycholinguistic perspective on language development in the autistic child. In Dawson G, editor: *Perspectives on the nature of autism: social, cognitive, and language development of individuals with autism,* New York, 1989, Guilford Press, 92-115.

129. Frith U: A new look at language and communication in autism, *Br J Disord Commun* 24:123-150, 1989.

130. Volden J, Lord C: Neologisms and ideosyncratic language in autistic speakers, *J Autism Dev Disord* 21:109-130, 1991.

131. Baltaxe CAM: Use of contrastive stress in normal, aphasic, and autistic children, *J Speech Hear Res* 27:97-105, 1984.

132. Baltaxe CAM, Guthrie D: The use of primary sentence stress by normal, aphasic, and autistic children, *J Autism Dev Disord* 17:255-271, 1987.

133. Fine J, Bartolucci G, Ginsberg G, Szatsmari P: The use of intonation to communicate in pervasive developmental disorders, *J Child Psychol Psychiatr* 32:771-782, 1991.

134. Baron-Cohen S: Social and pragmatic deficits in autism: cognitive or affective? *J Autism Dev Disord* 18:379-402, 1988.

135. Landry SH, Loveland KA: Communication behaviors in autism and developmental language delay, *J Child Psychol Psychiatr* 29:621-634, 1988.

136. Loveland KA, Landry SH: Joint attention and language in autism and developmental language delay, *J Autism Dev Disord* 16:335-349, 1986.

137. Mundy P, Sigman M, Kasari C: A longitudinal study of joint attention and language development in autistic children, *J Autism Dev Disord* 20:115-128, 1990.

138. Baron-Cohen S: The autistic child's theory of mind: a case of specific developmental delay, *J Child Psychol Psychiatr* 30:285-297, 1989.

139. Curcio F: Sensorimotor functioning and communication in mute autistic children, *J Autism Child Schizophr* 8:281-292, 1978.

140. Kasari C, Sigman M, Mundy P, Yirmiya N: Affective sharing in the context of joint attention interactions of normal, autistic, and mentally retarded children, *J Autism Dev Disord* 20:87-100, 1990.

141. Wing L: The handicaps of autistic children: a comparative study, *J Child Psychol Psychiatr* 10:1-40, 1969.

142. DeMyer MK, Mann NA, Tilton JR, Loew LH: Toy-play behavior and use of body by autistic and normal children as reported by mothers, *Psychol Rep* 21:973-981, 1967.

143. Ornitz EM, Guthrie D, Farley AJ: The early symptoms of childhood autism. In Serban, editor: *Cognitive defects in the development of mental illness,* New York, 1978, Brunner/Mazel, 24-42.

144. Sherman M, Shapiro T, Glassman M: Play and language in developmentally disordered preschoolers: a new approach to classification, *J Am Acad Child Psychiatr* 22:511-524, 1983.

145. Tilton JR, Ottinger DR: Comparison of the toy play behavior of autistic, retarded, and normal children, *Psychol Rep* 15:967-975, 1964.

146. Wing L: Social, behavioral, and cognitive characteristics: an epidemiological approach. In Rutter M, Schopler E, editors: *Autism: a reappraisal of concepts and treatment,* New York, 1978, Plenum, 1-25.

147. Dahlgren SO, Gillberg C: Symptoms in the first two years of life, *Eur Arch Psychiatr Neurol Sci* 238:169-174, 1989.

148. Rapin I: Searching for the cause of autism: a neurologic perspective. In Cohen DJ, Donnellan AM, editors: *Handbook of autism and pervasive developmental disorders,* Silver Spring, MD, 1987, VH Winston & Sons, 710-717.

149. Ungerer JA: The early development of autistic children: Implications for defining primary deficits. In Dawson G, editor: *Autism: nature, diagnosis, and treatment,* New York, 1989, Guilford, 75-91.

150. Hoshino Y, Kumashiro H, Yashima Y, et al: Early symptoms of autistic children and its diagnostic significance, *Folia Psychiatr Neurol Jpn* 36:367-374, 1982.

151. Adrien JL, Barthelemy C, Perrot A, et al: Validity and reliability of the infant behavioral summarized evaluation (IBSE): a rating scale for the assessment of young children with autism and developmental disorders, *J Autism Dev Disord* 22:375-394, 1992.

152. Baron-Cohen S, Allen J, Gillberg C: Can autism be detected at 18 months? the needle, the haystack, and the CHAT, *Br J Psychiatr* 161:839-843, 1992.

153. Lansing MD, Schopler E: Individualized education: a public school model. In Rutter M, Schopler E, editors: *Autism: a reappraisal of concepts and treatment,* New York, 1978, Plenum, 439-452.

154. Rutter M: The treatment of autistic children, *J Child Psychol Psychiatr* 26:193-214, 1985.

155. Mesibov GB, Schopler E, Hearsey K: Structured teaching. In Schopler E, Mesibov GB, editors: *Assessment and treatment of behaviors problems in autism,* New York, Plenum Press (in press).

156. Bartak L: Educational approaches. In Rutter M, Schopler E, editors: *Autism: a reappraisal of concepts and treatment,* New York, 1978, Plenum, 423-438.

157. Clark P, Rutter M: Autistic children's responses to structure and interpersonal demands, *J Autism Dev Disord* 11:201-217, 1981.

158. Volkmar FR, Hoder EL, Cohen DJ: Compliance, "negativism," and the effects of treatment structure in autism: a naturalistic, behavioral, study, *J Child Psychol Psychiatr* 26:865-877, 1985.

159. Schopler E, Brehm SS, Kinsbourne M, Reichler RJ: Effect of treatment structure on development in autistic children, *Arch Gen Psychiatr* 24:415-421, 1971.

160. Dawson G, Galpert L: A developmental model for facilitating the social behavior of autistic children. In Schopler E, Mesibov GB, editors: *Social behavior in autism,* New York, 1986, Plenum, 237-261.

161. Rogers SJ, Lewis H: An effective day treatment model for young children with pervasive developmental disorders, *J Am Acad Child Adolesc Psychiatr* 28:207-214, 1989.

162. Goldstein H, Kaczmarek L, Pennington R, Shafer K: Peer-mediated intervention: attending to, commenting on, and acknowledging the behavior of preschoolers with autism, *J Appl Behav Anal* 25:289-305, 1992.

163. Hoyson M, Jamieson B, Strain PS: Individualized group instruction of normally devel-

oping and autistic-like children: the LEAP curriculum model, *J Div Early Childhood,* Summer, 1984, 157-172.

164. Lord C: The development of peer relations in children with autism, *Applied Dev Psychol* 1:165-230, 1984.

165. Mchale S: Changes in autistic children's behavior as a function of interaction with non-handicapped children, *Am J Orthopsychiatr* 53:81-91, 1983.

166. Strain PS, Hoyson M, Jamieson B: Normally developing preschoolers as intervention agents for autistic-like children: effects on class deportment and social interaction, *J Div Early Childhood,* Spring, 1985, 105-115.

167. Odom SL, Mcevoy MA: Integration of young children with handicaps and normally developing children. In Odom SL, Karnes MB, editors: *Early intervention for infants and children with handicaps,* Baltimore, 1988, Paul H Brooks, 241-267.

168. Lovaas OI: Behavioral treatment and normal educational and intellectual functioning in young autistic children, *J Consult Clin Psychol* 55:3-9, 1987.

169. Schreibman L, Koegel RL, Charlop MH, Egel AL: Infantile autism. In Bellack AS, Hersen M, Kazdin AE, editors: *International handbook of behavior modification and therapy,* New York, 1990, Plenum, 763-789.

170. McClannahan LE, Krantz PJ, McGee GG: Parents as therapists for autistic children: a model for effective parent training, *Anal Interven Dev Disabil* 2:223-252, 1982.

171. Short AB: Short-term treatment outcome using parents as co-therapists for their own autistic children, *J Child Psychol Psychiatr* 25:443-458, 1984.

172. Dunlap G, Robbins FR, Darrow MA: Parent's reports of their children's challenging behaviors: results of a statewide survey, *Ment Retard* 32:206-212, 1994.

173. Moran DR, Whitman TL: Developing generalized teaching skills in mothers of autistic children, *Child Family Behav Ther* 13:13-37, 1991.

174. Harris SL, Handleman JS, Gordon R, et al: Changes in cognitive and language functioning of preschool children with autism, *J Autism Dev Disord* 21:281-290, 1991.

175. McEachin JJ, Smith T, Lovaas OI: Long-term outcome for children with autism who received early intensive behavioral treatment, *Am J Ment Retard* 97:359-372, 1993.

176. Simeonsson RJ, Olley JG, Rosenthal SL: Early intervention for children with autism. In Guralnick MJ, Bennett FC, editors: *The effectiveness of early intervention for at-risk and handicapped children,* Orlando, FL, 1987, Academic Press, 275-296.

177. Lord C, Rutter M: Autism and pervasive developmental disorder. In Rutter M, Taylor E, Hersov L, editors: *Child and adolescent psychiatry,* London, 1994, Blackwell Science, 569-593.

178. Holm VA, Varley CK: Pharmacological treatment of autistic children. In Dawson G, editor: *Autism: nature, diagnosis, and treatment,* New York, 1989, Guilford, 386-404.

179. Sloman L: Use of medication in pervasive developmental disorders, *Psychiatr Clin North Am* 14:165-182, 1991.

180. Gillman JT, Tuchman RS: Autism and associated behavioral disorders: pharmacotherapeutic intervention, *Ann Pharmacother* 29:47-56, 1995.

181. Duker PC, Welles K, Seys D, et al: Brief report: effects of fenfluramine on communicative, stereotypic, and inappropriate behaviors of autistic-type mentally handicapped individuals, *J Autism Dev Disord* 21:355-363, 1991.

182. Leventhal BL, Cook EH, Morford M, et al: Clinical and neurochemical effects of fenfluramine in children with autism, *J Neuropsychiatr Clin Neurosci* 5:307-315, 1993.

183. Gordon CT, State RC, Nelson JE, et al: A double-blind comparison of clomipramine, desipramine, and placebo in the treatment of autistic disorder, *Arch Gen Psychiatr* 50:441-447, 1993.

184. McDougle CJ, Price LH, Volkmar FR et al: Clomipramine in autism: preliminary evidence of efficacy, *J Am Acad Child Psychiatr* 31:746-750, 1992.

185. Birenbaum A, Cohen HJ: Mini-symposium: helping families, *Ment Retard* 31:67-74, 1993.
186. Norton P, Drew C: Autism and potential family stressors, *Am J Family Ther* 22:67-76, 1994.
187. Bristol M, Schopler E: The family in the treatment of autism. In American Psychiatric Association: *Treatment of psychiatric disorders*, vol 1, Washington, DC, 1989, American Psychiatric Association.
188. Powers MD, Bruey CT: Treating the family system. In Powers MD, editor: *Expanding systems of service delivery for persons with developmental disabilities*, Baltimore, MD, 1988, Paul H. Brookes, 17-41.
189. Bagenholm A, Gillberg C: Psychosocial effects on siblings of children with autism and mental retardation: a population-based study, *J Ment Defic Res* 35:291-307, 1991.
190. Gold N: Depression and social adjustment in siblings of boys with autism, *J Autism Dev Disord* 23:147-163, 1993.
191. Rodrigue JR, Geffken GR, Morgan SB: Perceived competence and behavioral adjustment of siblings of children with autism, *J Autism Dev Disord* 23:665-674, 1993.
192. Lotter V: Follow-up studies. In Rutter M, Schopler E, editors: *Autism: a reappraisal of concepts and treatment*, New York, 1978, Plenum, 475-495.
193. Chung SY, Luk SL, Lee PWH: A follow-up study of infantile autism in Hong Kong, *J Autism Dev Disord* 20:221-232, 1990.
194. Kobayashi R, Murata T, Yoshinaga K: A follow-up study of 201 children with autism in Kyushu and Yamaguchi areas, Japan, *J Autism Dev Disord* 22:395-411, 1992.
195. Wolf L, Goldberg B: Autistic children grown up: an eight to twenty-four year follow-up study, *Can J Psychiatr* 31:550-556, 1986.
196. Szatmari P, Bartolucci G, Bremner R, et al: A follow-up study of high-functioning autistic children, *J Autism Dev Disord* 19:213-225, 1989.
197. Venter A, Lord C, Schopler E: A follow-up study of high-functioning autistic children, *J Child Psychol Psychiatr* 33:489-507, 1992.

CHAPTER **10** _____

Academic disorders

CHAPTER **10A** _____

Learning Disabilities

DONALD K. ROUTH

The term *learning disabilities* refers for the most part to difficulties in basic academic skills, such as reading, spelling, and arithmetic. These skills are necessary in themselves in daily adult life in a modern industrialized country. They also provide a foundation for later mastery of more advanced school subjects, vocational skills, and activities of daily living, such as using computers. We ordinarily expect children attending elementary school to progress at a certain rate in developing these abilities. If they fall too far behind the expected rate, the possibility of a learning disability should be considered.

At any time in history or at any place in the world, a 3-year-old child who could not walk, could not speak, or could not distinguish the difference between a single object and a pair of them would be considered to have a disability. However, learning disabilities are not that absolute. They cannot be defined simply as a deficit in skill in comparison to some general standard of performance. First, learning disabilities must been seen in relation to cultural expectations. Symbolic "tools," such as the Roman alphabet, Chinese characters, or Arabic numerals, that are used in reading, writing, and calculation are relatively recent inventions in human history and are still not in universal use among adults throughout the world. The Industrial Revolution in places such as western Europe, the United States, and Japan created the need for an educated, literate, and numerate work force and provided the social setting that was historically necessary for the development of the public schools. Even today, a child from some third-

406

world country whose parents are illiterate or a child who had never been to school could not be considered to suffer from a learning disability but rather should be viewed within the framework of a different set of local societal expectations.

Second, learning disorders are to some extent relative to the individual's overall developmental level. If one observed the activities of members of the general population, a number of individuals would be discovered who could not read, spell, or do correct mathematical calculations. However, some of these academic nonachievers would be discovered to have difficulty with all kinds of other cognitively demanding tasks as well. For example, such a person might have difficulty with language in general or with many everyday problem-solving situations, with adult functioning at approximately the mental level of a preschool age child. If a person has such a grossly apparent cognitive difficulty, it makes more sense to describe it as severe mental retardation or a severe general language impairment than as a learning disability.

ETIOLOGY

It would perhaps be a satisfying state of affairs if the clinician could examine a child with a learning disability and give the child, the parents, and the school an unequivocal explanation for a particular area of academic failure. It makes one somewhat envious of those working in a field such as alexia (acquired neurological reading disorders sometimes seen in adults), in which the clinician can at least occasionally make a clear statement of etiology, based on an established model of the brain-behavior relationships involved. For example, in the rare syndrome of pure alexia without agraphia,[1] the patient has normal visual perception, including the ability to distinguish the different letters of the alphabet from each other as visual displays. Similarly, the patient's spoken language and written language are intact. Before the present illness, the individual had been able to read normally but now suddenly can no longer do so. Proper examination of the brain by a neuroradiologist will often demonstrate in such cases that while the left hemisphere language areas and the right hemisphere visual-perceptual areas are intact, there is some kind of lesion, perhaps affecting an area in the splenium of the corpus callosum, that has disconnected the perception and language areas and that also affects the left occipital lobe, impeding the processing of visual information on that side of the brain.

In studying the case of a child with a learning disability, the clinician will rarely find any such gross evidence of neurologic dysfunction. The other etiological possibility that immediately comes to mind is that the child has not had proper instruction in the academic skill area(s) in question. In a somewhat trivial sense, deficient education as an etiological factor has been ruled out by definition. In other words, as stated previously, if a child has never been to school or has never received instruction in the relevant skills, poor performance would be expected and would not be considered evidence of a "disability." But, in actuality, instruction is the area of etiology that deserves a much more thorough investigation than it usually gets. The fact that a child may have been in a conventional instructional program (i.e., one or several years in a public elementary school) does not mean that adequate teaching *for that child* has gone on. All children do not respond to academic instruction in the same way or at the same rate. If a remedial approach exists that can overcome a particular child's difficulty, then we must conclude that—until that approach has been tried—the child has not had a proper academic experience. This is the logic that underlies the view sometimes expressed that there are not really learning disabilities, only teaching disabilities.

Correlates

Various *correlates* of academic difficulty have been found, although both their existence and their significance is unclear. One common finding has been that reading and spelling difficulties are much more common in boys than in girls. However, some influential recent research[2] has suggested that this finding is partly an artifact caused by the referral of more boys to special education or to clinics—in the community, it seems that almost as many girls as boys have reading and spelling difficulties.

On the other hand, at least in junior high school and after, females are more likely than males to have specific difficulty in mathematics. The relative roles of biological and cultural factors in these sex differences are not clearly established; however—especially in the case of the difficulty females have with mathematics—a cultural origin is suspected (adolescent girls may just generally fail to enroll in additional mathematics courses after a certain age). For whatever reason, the excess at present of males over females at the highest levels of mathematical achievment is unquestionable.[3]

A second, widespread generalization is that learning disabilities (reading difficulties in particular) often run in families. Thus the clinician should inquire carefully concerning a child's background and not be surprised to find that parents, aunts and uncles, or grandparents had similar problems in school. The current weight of professional opinion is that the familial distribution of reading and spelling difficulties is evidence for some kind of genetic transmission, but the details of how this operates are only partly known. There are some specific genetic syndromes involving patterns of academic difficulty. For example, patients with Turner's syndrome (females with only a single X chromosome) typically have difficulty with spatial perception, which entails certain deficits in mathematics achievement.[4] With the rapid pace of current research in genetics, there are likely to be an increasing number of syndromes discovered where learning disabilities are part of a more complex picture. Even if a child is known to suffer from a particular genetic syndrome involving learning disabilities, the psychological mechanisms by which these disabilities occur will often be unknown, and one should not despair of finding appropriate educational remedial strategies.

Other correlates of learning disabilities are conduct problems (e.g., involving aggression against peers) and attention deficit hyperactivity disorder (ADHD).[5] Children with learning disabilities are also more often neglected or rejected by their peers.[6] Both conduct disorder and ADHD are more commonly seen in boys than in girls. It is not proper, however, to consider such behavioral problems necessarily to be "etiological factors" in a learning disability. A child with conduct problems might, it is true, also defy the teacher's instructions in class or fail to do homework assignments, and this could be part of the explanation for slow academic progress. Similarly, a child with ADHD might be off-task quite a bit in class with the same results. Nevertheless, it has not generally been shown that remediation of such conduct or attention problems by means of behavior management or pharmacological treatment has long-term beneficial effects on cognitive ability or academic achievement. (However, medication can clearly improve classroom performance in the short term.) If anything, the case is stronger for the reverse direction of effect (e.g., that improving a child's academic performance tends to reduce classroom misbehavior). Therefore it is better to regard behavior problems in children as simply coexisting difficulties rather than somehow being explanations of a child's learning disabilities.

ASSESSMENT

The most common test in the clinical appraisal of learning disabilities at present is probably the Wechsler Individual Achievement Test (WIAT). Another commonly used test is the Woodcock-Johnson Psycho-Educational Battery—Revised (WJ-R).[7] Both of these tests have the advantage that they are individually administered, so that one can be relatively sure that the child understands what is required. The disadvantage of such individual tests is that administration is more expensive than with group procedures. However, with group administration the clinician can never be sure that a particular child understood the instructions or paid proper attention to the task. Although a high score on a group achievement test suggests competence, a low score may merely indicate disinterest or confusion rather than a specific problem with the particular academic skills assessed. A child referred for evaluation in part because of poor performance in group testing needs further individual evaluation to confirm or discount its results.

In regular academic achievement testing, there is generally a certain domain of skill about which the examiner wishes to make a statement. For example, one may be interested in a child's ability to add two-digit numbers. The universe of content, in this case all possible pairs of two-digit numbers, is known, and in principle it is only necessary to sample randomly from it to create tests that will give us an accurate measure of the child's ability to perform the particular skill. This is what is known as *criterion-referenced testing*, in that there is a defined criterion against which the child's performance may be compared. The child's scores on a series of such achievement tests indicate which skills have been mastered and which have not and suggest, therefore, where additional instruction should begin (see Lesiak and Bradley-Johnson[8] for specific examples of criterion-referenced tests).

However, the approach that is more familiar to clinicians, which is exemplified by the WIAT and the Woodcock-Johnson, is called *norm-referenced testing*. Instead of indicating where the child is in terms of mastery of a domain of content, this kind of test indicates how the child's performance compares to that of some normative group (i.e., the percentile rank of this child's score relative to the scores of other 7-year-old children, other second graders, and so on). There is no technical reason that a test cannot be both "criterion referenced" and "norm referenced," but there are at present no such tests on the market.

Norm-referenced tests are easy for the clinician to interpret to the parents and to the child because they indicate where the child's academic performance is in relation to the child's age. However, they are less useful to the teacher since they are not closely coordinated to the curriculum materials that are available and do not lend themselves to planning specific educational strategies. In order to communicate meaningfully with the child's teacher, the examination of the child needs to be truly "diagnostic" in the educational sense. Such detailed and educationally helpful appraisals of learning disabilities are unfortunately beyond the capability of many clinics today and ideally are carried out by examiners who work in close collaboration with the child's teachers.

Let us now discuss assessment of more specific categories of learning problems.

Assessment of reading

The main point of reading is comprehending the meaning of written materials. This should therefore be the first area of inquiry in evaluating a child's reading ability. Fortunately, both the WIAT and the Woodcock-Johnson include procedures for evaluating reading comprehension—e.g., the Passage Comprehension subtest of the WJ-R. Another crucial aspect of the assessment of reading is the child's ability to decode individual words to speech. Again, both the WIAT and the WJ-R include such procedures—e.g., the Letter-Word Identification subtest of the WJ-R.

In early research the conventional way to define reading disability was reading performance 2 years below the child's grade level in school, assuming at least average intellectual status. Later, it became conventional to define specific reading disability by a discrepancy between a child's reading score and an intelligence test of some kind. The research most often cited in support of this practice was a study[9] indicating that there were major differences between children with "specific" reading retardation (as defined by the preceding type of discrepancy) and those who were generally "backward" readers who had both low reading and relatively low IQ scores. In this research, these two groups of poor readers seemed to form discontinuous distributions.

Now some influential current researchers[10] argue for a simpler definition of reading disability, using achievement test scores only, and disregarding the IQ (at least, presumably, for children whose mental status is no lower than borderline ability or mild mental retardation). As Fletcher[11] says:

> What is not generally emphasized is that Rutter and Yule (1975) applied no exclusionary criteria to the sample, so that the [General Reading Backwardness] group had a higher incidence of acquired neurological disorders, including epilepsy and cerebral palsy. The downward exclusion of the IQ-reading distribution in Rutter and Yule may reflect, in part, the influence of specific cognitive deficits secondary to brain injury on IQ scores . . .

The writer finds this argument persuasive. It seems to be true the problems of the "garden variety" poor readers are much more similar to those of children with so-called "specific" reading disability than they are different. For example, children in both groups typically have problems with phonological awareness. Of course, it may take some time for this more straightforward new definition of reading disability to prevail in the field. Meanwhile, clinicians will have to cope with the fact that official handbooks such as DSM-IV as well as federal and state laws and school regulations still use one variety or another of "discrepancy" definition, requiring the use of IQ tests as well as achievement measures.

Further testing. Given that the child has difficulty comprehending written text, further testing should elaborate the nature of the problem in order to help the teacher with the task of planning appropriate remediation. The first question to be asked in this exploration is whether the problem is specific to reading or reflects general verbal comprehension difficulty. Young children who are just learning to read generally understand spoken language far better than written language. It is for this reason children like to have read to them stories that may be at a far higher level than those they can read to themselves. Mature readers, in contrast, appear to comprehend written text and spoken language about equally well. For these reasons, some researchers have recommended that reading disability be defined as a discrepancy between listening comprehension and reading comprehension.[12,13] So far, however, this idea has not had widespread acceptance.

If reading comprehension is impaired relative to age in a child who is not grossly mentally retarded or language impaired, remedial reading should be recommended. Now the question for the examiner becomes how well the child does at various skills that are components of reading. Logically, one of the first questions would seem to be whether the child can distinguish the various letters of the alphabet and name them. Ordinarily this is not a problem, even in children with severe reading disorders. In fact, controlled research has found that training in letter names and letter sounds was not beneficial to the early reading skills of kindergarten children, in contrast to training that also included phoneme awareness.[14]

A second component skill in reading is "word-attack"—i.e., using phonological skills, such as segmentation and blending and knowledge of letter-sound relationships, to "sound out" and pronounce unfamiliar words. This skill is assessed by the Word Attack subtest of the WJ-R, in which the child is asked to read out loud a list of pseudo-words that conform to the conventions of English orthography. Several decades of research now exist demonstrating the importance of phonological skills involved in word-attack to reading and reading disability.[5-18] The phonological awareness deficits underlying word attack difficulties are seen not only in children who read poorly but persist in adult dyslexics.[19]

A third component skill that is important is sight-word recognition, which relies on the child's memory for familiar words as well as the use of phonological and morphological information. Both the WIAT and WJ-R have well-standardized lists of sight words for the child to read. An inadequate sight-word vocabulary means that the child will be slow in reading individual words and thus have trouble comprehending the sentences of which the words are a part. Skilled reading is characterized by sight-word reading that is not only accurate but also rapid and "automatic," freeing up attentional processes for sentence comprehension and the use of higher order strategies.[20]

A further method of evaluating reading skills that is intermediate between comprehension and sight word lists is one in which the child is asked to read connected passages aloud. The graded paragraphs of the Gray Oral Reading Tests[21] are often used for this purpose. By means of this kind of battery of reading tests, a skilled educational diagnostician can arrive at a statement that includes not only the child's overall level of reading skill but also specific recommendations for remediation. The statement of skill level is often expressed in three parts: the child's independent reading level, instructional level, and "frustration" level. The independent level of difficulty characterizes a text the child can read without help, as in doing homework for other classes such as literature, science, or social studies. The instructional level (as the term implies) specifies the grade level appropriate for materials to be used in the teaching of reading itself. Although the child can to some extent process reading materials at the "frustration" level, their continued use will likely lead to discouragement in learning to read. A practical scheme for identifying the difficulty level of texts for any reader[22] is as follows: out of every 5 words of text, one is deleted at random, with a blank being substituted for the missing word. If the reader can guess 60% or more of the missing words, the text is at the "independent" level. If 40% to 60% of the missing words can be guessed, the text is at the "instructional level." If fewer than 40% of the missing words can be guessed, the text is at the "frustration" level.

Assessment of spelling

The time-honored method of assessing spelling involves the oral dictation to the child of a graded list of words for the child to write. The WIAT and the WJ-R include such spelling tests with up-to-date norms in terms of age and grade level. This method is more useful than a multiple-choice spelling test in that it provides more information about the nature of the spelling errors made and thus to some extent about the underlying processes involved.

Spelling is admittedly not nearly as important as reading or arithmetic as an area of academic achievement. Many adults who are highly competent in other areas of their lives are poor spellers.[23] One reason why it is nevertheless important to evaluate spelling as a part of the appraisal of learning disabilities is that reading and spelling difficulties may be linked. It is often true that poor readers are even worse in spelling than they are in reading. On the other hand, there are some individuals whose reading is quite adequate but who have specific difficulties in spelling, sometimes referred to as "dysgraphia." Knowing that a child has a problem in reading only, in reading plus spelling, or in spelling only tells us something important about the nature of the disability.

The development of spelling skills in English has been shown to go through different stages, each characterized by somewhat different strategies in the task. Young children who cannot yet read nevertheless often try to spell out words using their knowledge of letter names to do so.[24] Thus a child might spell the word "while" with the letters *YL*, the names of which do combine to make the appropriate sound. Similarly, a preliterate child might try to spell the word "chicken" as *HKN*, using the "ch" sound in the name of the letter *H* for the purpose. This kind of strategy, in principle, can be spotted in a dictated spelling test, which is one reason this type of test is viewed as preferable to a multiple-choice one.

In the second stage of the development of spelling skills in English, children generally discover a phonetic strategy. This requires that they analyze spoken words into their component sounds, remember the letters that might correspond to these sounds, and put these together to try to spell the word. This works only moderately well because there are so many alternative letter-sound combinations used in English to represent the same sounds and because the orthography of so many words violates phonetic principles.

The most advanced stage in children's learning of spelling skills in English is the use of a morphemic strategy. In this stage, the child learns to use the various orthographic transformations, prefixes, and suffixes. For example, -*s* is often used in English orthography to represent the plural form and -*ed* to represent the past tense form of words, regardless of variations in pronunciation. Thus the plural of dog is pronounced as if it were "dogz" but spelled "dogs," while that of "cats" is spelled and pronounced with a terminal /s/ sound. Once more, it is often possible to see from a child's written spelling in response to dictation whether a morphemic strategy is being used. Perhaps in the future more use will be made of formal quantitative measures of a child's spelling strategies, perhaps using nonsense words to overcome what is otherwise the unavoidable confounding of strategy with the child's memory of how certain particular actual words are spelled.[25]

Assessment of mathematical skills

Learning disabilities involving mathematics do not seem to be as common as those involving reading and spelling and are certainly not as thoroughly studied. Some children have trouble in all three areas, but there is also a group whose problem is specific to mathematics and does not include reading or spelling.[3] A number of the interventions that have been shown to promote better reading and spelling skills (e.g., Bryant and Bradley[15]) have no effect on children's performance in mathematics.

The WIAT includes assessment of children's ability to carry out numerical operations and of mathematical reasoning (these skills seem to be somewhat independent of each other). Similarly, the WJ-R includes separate subtests on Basic Mathematics Skills and Mathematics Reasoning as well as a more general Broad Mathematics subtest. Thus the formal assessment of learning disabilities in mathematics is not difficult. As is the case with reading, there is much to be said for the value of the informal assessment of children's mathematical skills by a skilled teacher. Thus, in addition to noting whether a child gets the correct answer on an addition problem, the child's strategies could be observed. For example, when adding the numbers 5 and 3 on a pair of dice some children count on their fingers and some count verbally. And some count all the dots, while others note the larger number at a glance and count up from there. Children who are even more sophisticated note each number at a glance and automatically retrieve the sum from memory.

Researchers[3] who have studied the development of children's skills in mathematics, have identified a definite sequence in which these skills develop. It appears that even infants as well as many nonhuman species of animals have some built-in sensitivity to numbers, at least of the differences among, for example, 1, 2, and 3. Even without special instruction, young children learn to count, perhaps using their fingers, according to schemas that differ somewhat from one culture to another. Piaget's[26] work on the development of number conservation is well known, as is his viewpoint that children are not simply taught certain mathematical principles but in a sense have to rediscover them for themselves through experience and dialogue with peers.

Research has been reviewed[3] documenting significant differences in mathematics achievement in different countries and not just between those in industrialized vs. third-world countries. The writer was shocked (but convinced) by this reviewer's summary statement that "American children are among the most poorly educated children in mathematics in the industrialized world." There are at least some reasons for this phenomenon that are embedded in cultural and linguistic differences. To quote the same reviewer further:

> For English-speaking children and for children speaking most European-derived languages, learning the words for numbers greater than 10 is particularly difficult. . . . This is so because the number words for values up to the hundreds are irregular in these languages; that is, the names of these words do not map onto the underlying base-10 structure of the number system. In contrast, in most Asian languages there is a direct one-to-one relationship between the number words greater than *ten* and the underlying base-10 values represented by these words. . . . For instance, the Chinese, Japanese, and Korean words for 11 are translated as *ten one*.

Aside from such built-in advantages, children in other industrialized countries spend more time on mathematics in class than U.S. children do, do more math homework, and receive superior instruction. Clinicians, as they become aware of the deficiencies in our own educational system compared to others, should be in a position to act as effective advocates for positive change in their communities.

Assessment of written expression

As children move toward mastery of basic reading and spelling skills, they are expected to do more assignments that involve writing. The focus of such instruction may be the writing process itself or writing papers in other subject matter areas, such as personal or business correspondence, imaginative writing, science, or social studies. Each successive academic level from middle school to graduate school makes increasingly higher demands on skills in written expression. However, there is not much agreement as to how written instruction should be evaluated. Perhaps for this reason it would be best to depend on judgments by experienced teachers of specific samples of the child's written work.

Assessment of related speech and language problems

It is beyond the scope of this chapter to discuss more general problems of speech and language, such as articulation disorders or general language delay. Nevertheless, it is well known that learning disabilities often co-occur with speech and language problems. The clinician, therefore, needs to be aware of this fact and to be ready to refer the child for evaluation and treatment by specialists in speech and language pathology and audiology.

MANAGEMENT

In the past, the educational management of learning disabilities has been chaotic and subject to many fads. Children with academic skill deficits have been subjected to a great variety of activities that, at least to the casual observer, seem to have little relationship to learning to read, spell, or calculate. Thus, in various remedial or therapeutic programs, children with learning disabilities have been asked to go back and learn how to crawl correctly, to walk balance beams, to engage in training in proper eye movements, to draw geometric shapes, or to deal with their emotional conflicts in play therapy sessions. There is little evidence, however, that any of these approaches have had the intended effects on academic skill acquisition.

The public schools throughout the country clearly have the legal mandate to remediate learning disabilities. This includes identification and educational diagnosis, the use of resource rooms where children with learning disabilities can spend part of their time each week, or even self-contained classes for those with the most severe difficulties. The child can be helped to progress in other academic areas despite, for example, reading problems, by the use of peer readers or peer scribes in science, social studies, etc. Private schools also would seem to be accountable to those who pay children's tuition to see that effective remedial teaching is put into place.

It seems to the writer that there has been a striking contrast between medicine and education regarding any consensus that can exist on appropriate interventions in a problem area and on the degree of linkage between research and practice. In medicine, when some new discovery is made by researchers, there is often a fairly rapid transmission of the new information to practitioners by means of professional journals, continuing education presentations, drug detail personnel, and so on. Although the prevailing consensus is by no means always correct (when evaluated in retrospect), there does seem to be relatively good agreement at a given time as to what procedures are appropriate for particular clinical conditions. In education, this has not been the case. Plenty of research gets done in education, educational psychology, and in the basic study of the development of language and cognitive processes. However, the research seems to move forward with little transmission of its current findings to educational practitioners. Unlike physicians, elementary school teachers, including special educators, rarely feel obliged to read professional journals. The continuing education programs available are not well linked to the forefront of research, and there is little activity on the part of the private sector to transmit current research to the classroom teacher.

Until fairly recently, even the established approaches to direct remedial instruction were best characterized as schools of thought or philosophies of special education. For example, Grace Fernald,[27] working in Los Angeles, advocated a method of teaching children who were reading disabled that involved a combination of what is now called the "language experience" method and tactile stimulation. Children would be allowed to dictate their own spontaneous stories to be at first written down by the teacher. In this way, they were in effect choosing the written words they wanted to learn. Each unknown written word would then be written down for the child, who would manually trace its letters over and over until it could be written down from memory, without referring to the model. As each word was mastered in this way, it could be deposited in the child's file of words. This method was very slow and laborious at first, but it was anecdotally reported that it could resolve some of the most refractory reading problems encountered. Variants of this approach are still in use. For example, it was used in the remedial reading classrooms of the Fernald School at UCLA and in the generations of teachers who learned it. It has *not*, however, to the writer's knowledge, ever been subjected to a proper controlled study of its efficacy. Is it not time that the advocates of this venerable approach be asked either to carry out proper controlled research on its efficacy or stop spending the taxpayers' money to use it in the public schools?

In New York, another approach to the remediation of reading problems was developed by Anna Gillingham and her colleague, Bessie Stillman,[28] under the sponsorship of the well-known psychiatrist (and neuropathologist) Samuel T. Orton, who had developed a distinctive theory of childhood dyslexia. The Orton-Gillingham-Stillman (OGS) approach was equally laborious and also multisensory, but it began with letters and sounds rather than whole words and encouraged the child through systematic drill to master phonics and the sounding out of unknown written words. Like the Fernald method, the Orton approach has been taught to generations of teachers. It seems to be especially favored in private preparatory schools in New England and on the East Coast. Once more, to the writer's knowledge, the Orton-based methods have not ever been subject to a proper controlled study of efficacy. There are several prominent academic physicians and scientists on the governing body of the Orton Dyslexia Society, who in their own scientific work are certainly familiar with the concept of "clinical trials." It is curious that they do not press for the same kind of rigorous type of evaluation of the OGS approach to the remediation of dyslexia.

New approaches. In the last several decades, a number of researchers have been interested in the child's phonemic awareness or ability to segment, blend, and otherwise manipulate the sounds of spoken language as one important cognitive prerequisite (and outcome) of reading. Earlier research developed various measures of phonological awareness and investigated their correlation with reading and reading disability. Subsequently, a number of controlled intervention studies have grown out of these approaches. In one of the first studies of this kind,[29] researchers established the efficacy of training in phonological awareness in helping African-American, kindergarten-age inner-city children derive maximum benefit from their later first-grade reading instruction. In the early 1980s two separate well-controlled studies[30,31] demonstrated the efficacy of similar types of training involving phonemic awareness components, in remediating the reading performance of learning disabled children who were elementary school aged. Subsequent controlled intervention research[15] showed that training young children in phonological skills, especially rhyming, using plastic letters to symbolize the sounds had a significantly more positive effect on their subsequent reading skills than training in phonological skills alone and that both of these were better than a control condition. A controlled study of phoneme awareness training vs. letter-sound training[14] mentioned earlier in this chapter, also found phoneme awareness training more effective. Most recently, researchers[32] worked with 124 poor readers in Yorkshire who were 7 years old. The children were divided into four matched groups and assigned to 20 weeks of training of one of the following kinds of instruction: phonological skills alone, reading plus phonological skills, and a control group. The group trained in both reading and phonological skills made the most progress in reading and spelling. The phonological skills alone group did the best in the phonological skills themselves but not as well in reading as the joint group. As expected, the interventions had no effect on the children's performance in arithmetic.

In summary, recent educational research on reading disability has clearly moved into the stage where its own type of "clinical trials" are becoming almost routine. So far the controlled studies that have been reported are unanimous in supporting the efficacy of some kind of training in phonological skills for either the prevention or treatment of reading and spelling disabilities in children. It is thus time for clinicians, as advocates for children with these types of learning disabilities, to begin to insist that the schools pay attention to these research results.

It is to be hoped that eventually intervention research on mathematics disabilities in children will reach a similar state of maturity. So far there seems to be little work of this kind.

OUTCOME

One of the safest axioms in psychology is that the best predictor of future behavior of any kind is the same behavior as assessed in the past. Thus one should not be surprised to find that children with disorders of reading, spelling, and arithmetic commonly grow up to be adults who still have the same sorts of problems. However, it is somewhat reassuring to know that such learning disabilities clearly do not have such serious prognostic implications as, say, mental retardation or general language disability. This is one more aspect of learning disabilities that is relative rather than absolute. After all, most humans throughout history got along quite acceptably without being able to read, write, and spell. The rest of the world somehow survived for years before the zero was introduced by the Arabs for use in mathematics. Medieval European kings did not find it necessary to learn to read when they could command scribes to do so for them. In ancient Greece, Socrates criticized the use of written language because he believed it would lead to a deterioration of people's capacity to memorize (this was probably true—e.g., how many performers are there today who can chant an entire epic poem as Homer did?).[33]

A follow-up study that perhaps bears out the nonessential nature of reading skills was Margaret Rawson's[34] work with the students of an Eastern private school. In her study one group of students was described as having dyslexia, which generally meant relatively severe problems in reading, spelling, and related aspects of language. These boys were given what must have been very careful remedial attention by teachers trained in the Orton-Gillingham-Stillman tradition. The control group was comprised of other boys from the same school who had similar intellectual ability but who were not dyslexic and who therefore received only the curriculum that was usual in the school. On following up these students in adulthood many years later, Rawson made the interesting discovery that there were no differences in occupational attainment between the former dyslexics and the control group. In fact, if anything, the dyslexic group had achieved more vocationally than the controls.

Rawson herself and many of her colleagues in the Orton Dyslexia Society seem to view her study as one of the prime pieces of evidence for the efficacy of the OGS remedial strategies. In fact, Rawson[35] has recently published another follow-up of the same subjects more than 50 years after they left the school. However, the study has been criticized as unrepresentative of the outcomes of learning disabled children because its subjects had so many advantages. Their mean IQ was about 130, and their families were often wealthy and influential people. The follow-up report says a lot more about their educational and vocational attainments than it does about their actual adult skills in reading and spelling. There are at least hints in the book that many of these very successful "ex-dyslexic" adults still had difficulties with the printed word. Perhaps they compensated for this by their strong general cognitive skills, using conversations with colleagues as a substitute for a lot of reading and good secretaries as editors of their writing. Finally, because Rawson did not have any control group of dyslexics who did not receive remedial instruction, one cannot be sure from her data of the efficacy of this instruction itself. After all, it is possible that children who are that bright may be able to remediate their own academic problems to a greater extent than others would be able to do.

As already noted, a recent researcher[19] reported that dyslexics' phonological awareness problems (which were presumably part of the basis of their difficulties in reading and spelling to start with) were highly persistent upon subsequent follow-up. Other researchers[36] found that "compensated" adult dyslexics were still not very fluent in reading and made numerous spelling errors. A recent review of the literature on the postschool adjustment of persons with learning disabilities,[37] found that the learning disabilities tended to persist into adulthood. Spelling was the academic skill most frequently mentioned as being a problem, and there was also concern with the fact that reading and arithmetic skills were not sufficiently "automatic." However, the adults themselves were much less worried about their academic skills as such and listed their greatest need for assistance as being in the area of social skills.

In conclusion, one might say that the specific prognosis (i.e., in terms of future skills at reading, spelling, or arithmetic) for learning disabilities may be poor, but the general prognosis is somewhat better. In other words, a child with a learning disability is likely to have problems with the same skills as an adult. However, many persons discover ways of getting along well in adulthood despite these continuing academic difficulties.

Counselors of the family (including physicians) can thus encourage parents to keep up the child's self-esteem by emphasizing areas of strength (whether these be sports, music, or whatever) in addition to seeking remedial help of established efficacy for the learning disabilities.

Research related to the field of special education has made excellent progress although its translation into practice is still too slow. It should be our goal in the future to help special education imitate more mature sciences in fostering a close linkage of research findings and the activities of the practitioner.

REFERENCES

1. Dejerine J: Contribution a l'etude anatomopathologique et cliniques des differentes varietes de cecite verbale, *Comptes Rendus Hebdomadaires des Seances et Memoires de la Society de Biologie* 4:61-90, 1892.
2. Shaywitz SE, Shaywitz BA, Fletcher JM, Escobar MD: Prevalence of reading disability in boys and girls: results of the Connecticut Longitudinal Study, *JAMA* 264:998-1002, 1990.
3. Geary DC: *Children's mathematical development*, Washington, DC, 1994, American Psychological Association.
4. Downey J, Elkin EJ, Ehrhardt AA, Meyer-Bahlburg HFL, Bell JJ, Morishima A: Cognitive ability and everyday functioning in women with Turner syndrome, *J Learning Disabil* 24:32-39, 1991.
5. Bender WN, Smith JK: Classroom behavior of children and adolescents with learning disabilities: a meta-analysis, *J Learning Disabil* 23:298-305, 1990.
6. Stone WL, La Greca AM: The social status of children with learning disabilities: a reexamination, *J Learn Disabil* 23:32-37, 1990.
7. Woodcock R, Johnson M: *Woodcock-Johnson Psycho-Educational Battery—Revised*, Allen, TX, 1989, DLM Teaching Resources.
8. Lesiak J, Bradley-Johnson S: *Reading assessment for placement and programming*, Springfield, IL, 1983, Charles C Thomas.
9. Rutter M, Yule W: The concept of specific reading retardation, *J Child Psychol Psychiatr* 16:181-197, 1975.
10. Shaywitz SE, Escobar MD, Shaywitz BA, Fletcher JM, Makuch R: Evidence that dyslexia may represent the lower tail of a normal distribution of reading ability, *N Engl J Med* 326:145-150, 1992.
11. Fletcher JM: The validity of distinguishing children with language and learning disabilities according to discrepancies with IQ, *J Learning Disabil* 25:546-548, 1992.
12. Stanovich K: Has the learning disabilities field lost its intelligence? *J Learn Disabil* 22:487-492, 1989.
13. Stanovich K: Discrepancy definitions of reading disability: has intelligence led us astray? *Read Res Quart* 26:7-29, 1991.
14. Ball EW, Blachman BA: Does phoneme awareness training in kindergarten make a difference in early word recognition and developmental spelling? *Read Res Quart* 26:49-66, 1991.
15. Bryant PE, Bradley L: *Children's reading problems*, Oxford, 1985, Basil Blackwell.
16. Fox B, Routh DK: Phonemic analysis and synthesis as word-attack skills, *J Educa Psychol* 68:70-74, 1976.
17. Fox B, Routh DK: Phonemic analysis and synthesis as word-attack skills: revisited, *J Educa Psychol* 76:1059-1064, 1984.

18. Wagner RK, Torgesen JK: The nature of phonological processing and its causal role in the acquisition of reading, *Psychol Bull* 101:192-212, 1987.

19. Bruck M: Persistence of dyslexics' phonological awareness deficits, *Dev Psychol* 28:874-886, 1992.

20. Spear-Swerling L, Sternberg RJ: The road not taken: an integrative theoretical model of reading disability, *J Learning Disabil* 27:91-103, 1994.

21. Gray W: *Gray oral reading tests,* Indianapolis, IN, 1967, Bobbs-Merrill.

22. Rye J: *Cloze procedure and the teaching of reading,* London, 1982, Heinemann Educational.

23. Frith U, editor: *Cognitive processes in spelling,* London, 1980, Academic Press.

24. Bissex GL: *GNYS AT WRK: A child learns to write and read,* Cambridge, MA, 1980, Harvard University Press.

25. Campbell R: Writing nonwords to dictation, *Brain Lang* 19:153-178, 1983.

26. Piaget J: *The child's conception of number,* New York, 1965, Norton.

27. Fernald G: *Remedial techniques in basic school subjects,* New York, 1943, McGraw-Hill.

28. Gillingham A, Stillman BE: *Remedial training for children with specific disability in reading, spelling, and penmanship,* Cambridge, MA, 1969, Educators Publishing Service.

29. Wallach MA, Wallach L: *Teaching all children to read,* Chicago, 1976, University of Chicago Press.

30. Gittelman R, Feingold I: Children with reading disorders. I. Efficacy of reading remediation, *J Child Psychol Psychiatr* 24:167-191, 1981.

31. Williams JP: Teaching decoding with an emphasis on phoneme analysis and phoneme blending, *J Educa Psychol* 72:1-15, 1980.

32. Hatcher PJ, Hulme C, Ellis AW: Ameliorating early reading failure by integrating the teaching of reading and phonological skills: the phonological linkage hypothesis, *Child Dev* 65:41-57, 1994.

33. Postman N: Illiteracy in America: position papers: the politics of reading, *Harvard Educ Rev* 40:244-251, 1970.

34. Rawson MB: *Developmental language disability: adult accomplishment of dyslexic boys,* Baltimore, 1968, Johns Hopkins University Press.

35. Rawson MB: *Dyslexia over the lifespan: a fifty-five-year longitudinal study,* Cambridge, MA, 1995, Educators Publishing Service.

36. Lefly D, Pennington B: Spelling errors and reading fluency in compensated adult dyslexics, *Ann Dyslex* 41:143-162, 1991.

37. White WJ: The postschool adjustment of persons with learning disabilities, *J Learn Disabil* 25:448-456, 1992.

CHAPTER 10B ————————————————————

Attention deficit hyperactivity disorder

ANNA BAUMGAERTEL
LINDA COPELAND
MARK L. WOLRAICH

The particular symptom complex this chapter addresses has had a long list of diagnostic names applied to it, such as *minimal brain dysfunction, hyperkinetic syndrome,* and *attention deficit disorder.* The history of how the various terminologies developed is an interesting one. The encephalitis epidemic after World War I resulted in a variety of postencephalitic behavior disorders in children that led to the eventual popularization of the idea of "brain injury" as the explanation for certain behavioral and perceptual dysfunctions in children. These dysfunctions were brought together under the concept of minimal brain dysfunction (MBD). Clements[1] described 99 separate symptoms of MBD, the most frequently cited of which was hyperactivity. Empirical studies attempting to confirm the existence of an MBD syndrome were, however, unsuccessful.[2] There are two main problems with the concept of MBD. The first is the lack of evidence for any clustering of the behaviors defined by the concept, and the second is that there is only indirect evidence that brain dysfunction is necessarily an etiological factor.[2,3]

DSM, the classification system for mental disorders most commonly used in the United States, has moved away from an etiologically based definition to a symptom-based classification and shifted the focus from hyperactivity to problems of attention and cognitive disorganization.[4] DSM II[5] described a "hyperkinetic reaction of childhood," which was revised in DSM III[6] to an attention deficit disorder with hyperactivity (ADDH) and without hyperactivity (ADD) and in DSM III-R[7] to an attention deficit hyperactivity disorder (ADHD). The most recent revision, DSM IV,[8] is based on extensive re-analysis of previous data and on field trials testing the earlier DSM criteria, as well as other symptoms commonly associated with ADHD.[9] Factor analysis of these data consistently identified two independent behavioral dimensions, one expressing hyperactivity and impulsivity and the other expressing inattention and cognitive disorganization.[10,11] These dimensions may occur alone or in combination. Accordingly, the current DSM classification of ADHDs includes three subtypes: (1) a predominantly inattentive type, (2) a predominantly hyperactive-impulsive type, and (3) a combined type.

Whether these subtypes actually represent etiologically distinct disorders or different manifestations of the same pathological condition is a topic of much debate and research and remains unresolved.[12-15] The clinical validity and reliability of the "new" DSM IV subtypes remain to be established. However, recent screenings of large, nonreferred populations of students in different school settings substantiate previous research findings implying that there are distinct cognitive, as well as behavioral, differences in the predominantly inattentive and the predominantly hyperactive-impulsive subtypes.[16] These studies found that the majority of students meeting criteria for ADHD (predominantly inattentive type) had academic problems and low comorbidity with oppositional defiant disorder (ODD), whereas students who were predominantly hyperactive-impulsive tended to be at least average academically, had somewhat higher rates of ODD, and had a high degree of teacher-perceived behavior problems. Children with the combined type had the "worst of both worlds," showing high rates of academic and behavioral problems and a 50% comorbidity with ODD.[17,18] As more is learned about the causes of ADHD, the definitions and classifications are likely to undergo further revision.

SYMPTOMATOLOGY AND DIAGNOSTIC CRITERIA

Despite the conceptual fluidity, there is reasonable consensus on the behavioral manifestations of ADHD formulated in the DSM IV criteria presented in the box on pp. 426-427. The most frequently cited primary or core symptoms include developmentally inappropriate degrees of inattention, cognitive disorganization, distractibility, impulsivity, and hyperactivity, all of which are likely to show variability in different situations and across time.[19] Commonly seen secondary symptoms are perceptual and emotional immaturity, poor social skills, disruptive behaviors, and academic problems.[20,21] Because the symptoms of ADHD are developmental in their manifestations, their constellations may shift with age, with younger children tending to show more hyperactivity and impulsivity, which tend to become less apparent as the children get older and attentional and cognitive problems move into the foreground.[12,22] Low

DIAGNOSTIC CRITERIA FOR ATTENTION DEFICIT HYPERACTIVITY DISORDER (ADHD)[8]

I. Either (A) or (B):

A. Six (or more) of the following symptoms of **inattention** have persisted for at least 6 months to a degree that is maladaptive and inconsistent with developmental level:

Inattention

1. Often fails to give close attention to details or makes careless mistakes in schoolwork, work, or other activities
2. Often has difficulty sustaining attention in tasks or play activities
3. Often does not seem to listen when spoken to directly
4. Often does not follow through on instructions and fails to finish schoolwork, chores, or duties in the workplace (not due to oppositional behavior or failure to understand instructions)
5. Often has difficulty organizing tasks and activities
6. Often avoids, dislikes, or is reluctant to engage in tasks that require sustained mental effort (e.g., schoolwork or homework)
7. Often loses things necessary for tasks or activities (e.g., toys, school assignments, pencils, books, or tools)
8. Is often easily distracted by extraneous stimuli
9. Is often forgetful in daily activities

B. Six (or more) of the following symptoms of **hyperactivity-impulsivity** have persisted for at least 6 months to a degree that is maladaptive and inconsistent with developmental level:

Hyperactivity

1. Often fidgets with hands or feet or squirms in seat
2. Often leaves seat in classroom or in other situations in which remaining seated is expected
3. Often runs about or climbs excessively in situations in which it is inappropriate (in adolescents or adults, may be limited to subjective feelings of restlessness)
4. Often has difficulty playing or engaging in leisure activities quietly
5. Is often "on the go" or often acts as if "driven by a motor"
6. Often talks excessively

Impulsivity

7. Often blurts out answers before questions have been completed
8. Often has difficulty awaiting turn
9. Often interrupts or intrudes on others (e.g., butts into conversations or games)

II. Some hyperactive-impulsive or inattentive symptoms that caused impairment were present before 7 years of age.

III. Some impairment from the symptoms is present in two or more settings (e.g., at school [or work] and at home).

IV. There must be clear evidence of clinically significant impairment in social, academic, or occupational functioning.

DIAGNOSTIC CRITERIA FOR ATTENTION DEFICIT HYPERACTIVITY DISORDER (ADHD)—cont'd

V. The symptoms do not occur exclusively during the course of a pervasive developmental disorder, schizophrenia, or other psychotic disorder and are not better accounted for by another mental disorder (e.g., mood disorder, anxiety disorder, dissociate disorder, or a personality disorder).

Code based on type:

314.01 Attention Deficit Hyperactivity Disorder, Combined Type: If both criteria IA and IB are met for the past 6 months

314.01 Attention Deficit Hyperactivity Disorder, Predominantly Inattentive Type: If criterion IA is met, but criterion IB is not met for the past 6 months

314.01 Attention Deficit Hyperactivity Disorder, Predominantly Hyperactive-Impulsive Type: If criterion IB is met, but criterion IA is not met for the past 6 months

Coding note: For individuals (especially adolescents and adults) who currently have symptoms that no longer meet full criteria, "in partial remission" should be specified.

---

self-esteem and emotional and social complications frequently are the dominating features by adolescence, whether or not the core symptoms persist.[23]

An ADHD diagnosis is indicated only for children whose behavior problems are severe enough to impair academic or social function and are manifest in several situations over more than a 6-month period.[8] Because the symptoms are typically variable, they may not be observed directly by the clinician; behavioral observations by caretakers and other consistently involved persons are indispensable to the diagnostic process. Primary consideration should be given to the teacher reports because of teachers' familiarity with age-appropriate norms and their opportunity to observe the children in demanding situations.[24] Onset should be before the age of 7, but symptoms may not become obvious until after the child starts school. The symptoms should not be due to schizophrenia and other psychoses, severe-to-profound mental retardation, other neurological disease (e.g., absence seizures), or severe sensory deficits, such as a significant hearing impairment.

COMORBIDITY

The disorder rarely occurs alone and is frequently comorbid with other neurodevelopmental and mental disorders, although the etiological relationships are complex and poorly elucidated. The severity and type of comorbidities are powerful factors in determining interventions and outcome.

Between 10% and 30% of children with ADHD have specific learning disabilities (LDs),[15,19,25,26] and about 30% to 50% have language disorders.[27] Central auditory processing dysfunction (CAPD) may represent a common etiological element in some forms of ADHD and language disorders,[28,29] and, because of the high comorbidity of ADHD with LD and speech-language disorders, common neuropathological mechanisms have been hypothesized but not identified. Persons diagnosed with Asperger's syndrome (see chapter on pervasive developmental disorders) may have associated ADHD symptoms.[30] Hyperactivity, distractibility, and inattention can frequently occur in children with mental retardation. However, the core symptoms need to be discrepant with the developmental age of the child in order to consider a diagnosis of ADHD, and, in more severely mentally retarded children, the behaviors may differ markedly in cause, symptomatology, and treatment response.

Between 30% and 80% of children with ADHD are also reported to have a diagnosis of oppositional defiant or conduct disorder,[25,31] but each has been shown to represent a distinctly separate disorder.[25,31,32,33] Conduct disorder (CD) may be associated with abnormal serotonin metabolism[34] and is also thought to develop on the basis of familial risk factors, including severe psychosocial adversity.[33,35] ADHD with CD is considered a true hybrid disorder.[33] ADHD co-occurs to a significant degree with obsessive-compulsive disorder (OCD), tic disorders, anxiety disorders, post-traumatic stress disorder (PTSD), and major affective disorders.[36,37] ADHD symptoms may precede the onset of major affective disorders by several years.[38] The differential diagnosis between ADHD and other psychiatric disorders may be quite complex. On the one hand, anxiety disorders, PTSD, OCD, and major depressive disorders may superficially mimic ADHD in their symptomatology; on the other hand, these psychiatric disorders may occur with ADHD, requiring independent diagnostic and therapeutic consideration. Comorbidity rates will vary somewhat, depending on the source of the sample—that is, whether it was obtained in epidemiological, pediatric, or psychiatric settings.[39]

PREVALENCE

ADHD is the single most frequent chronic behavior disorder in pre-adolescent children.[40] Like most childhood behavior disorders, ADHD is more common in boys than in girls, with gender ratios ranging from 5:1 for the predominantly hyperactive-impulsive type to 2:1 for the predominantly inattentive type.[17,18]

Reported rates vary widely, depending on methodology and population that is studied, and there has been much debate about the ability to arrive at a "true" rate.[41] The most frequently reported rates occur between 3% and 5%[19] with much higher rates found in American inner city populations. A recent epidemiological survey[18] of children in a semirural county in Tennessee found prevalence rates of about 7% using DSM III-R criteria on teacher questionnaires, which matched those found in a large Iowa school population in an earlier study.[42] Using DSM IV criteria increased the total rate in the Tennessee county to 11% to 12%, with an even distribution between the three subtypes. The predominantly inattentive type was about 4%; the hyperactive impulsive type, 3.3%; and the combined type, also about 4%. The difference reflects the broadening of ADHD criteria to include the predominantly inattentive children. However, these studies included only teacher information. The actual prevalence is probably lower.

The symptoms of ADHD are not unique to American culture. They have been reported in other western countries, as well as in some rapidly developing third world countries. However, there have been some gross discrepancies in the frequency with which ADHD is diagnosed in the United States, as compared with, for example, Great Britain. Rutter[2] found only 1:1000 children to be hyperactive in a general population survey on the Isle of Wight, considerably lower than any reported prevalence rates in the United States. This discrepancy probably stems from the more restrictive concept of hyperactivity defined by the International Classification of Diseases (ICD) at the time of that survey (1970), but it may also result from cultural differences of a more complex nature.[43]

ETIOLOGY AND PATHOPHYSIOLOGY

The diversity of descriptors for ADHD reflects the existing uncertainty about the cause. In the earlier literature, hyperactivity was generally attributed to innate and acquired organic pathological conditions. This view fell into disfavor for awhile but has recently been rehabilitated by newer research resurrecting many of the concepts formulated in the earlier part of this century (see Barkley's book, *Attention Deficit Hyperactivity Disorder: A Handbook for Diagnosis and Treatment*, for a review of this fascinating history).[19] Evidence of a causative relationship of brain dysfunction to ADHD is given by the increased incidence of ADHD (as well as learning disabilities and language problems) in children with biodevelopmental risk factors. Such prenatal factors as prematurity with low and very low birth weight,[44,45] intrauterine exposure to alcohol,[46-48] drugs, and maternal smoking,[49,50] as well as postnatal insults to the developing brain through malnutrition,[51] lead exposure,[52] and CNS infections[53] are all independently associated with ADHD. However, in the majority of diagnosed cases, no such antecedents can be identified. Evidence is accumulating that familial, including genetic factors, play a dominant role in the cause, with a high incidence of ADHD reported in the first-degree relatives of persons diagnosed with ADHD.[54] In addition, an increase of specific neuropsychopathology—such as anxiety disorders, learning and language disorders, major depression, and antisocial personality disorders—is found in the relatives of children with ADHD.[55-57]

Dietary factors—such as sugar and food additives and allergies—have been implicated as causes for ADHD,[58,59] but such claims are not consistently supported by scientific evidence.[59] There has been some debate regarding the relationship of traumatic brain injury (TBI) to ADHD and other neurocognitive and neurobehavioral sequelae.[2] Symptoms of inattention, impulsivity, and hyperactivity may occur together with major cognitive dysfunction in the subacute post-traumatic phase of severe head injuries[3] but may remain as significant independent morbidity after other CNS symptoms have resolved.[61,62] There is isolated evidence that even mild TBIs may result in hyperactivity as a long-term sequela.[63] ADHD symptomatology appears to represent a final common pathway of many varied mechanisms affecting CNS functioning.[64]

Currently the focus of etiological research has shifted from a monocausal to a transactional model, in which individual factors (i.e., biological risk factors, intelligence, and temperament) interact within a familial and social environmental context, which in turn directly affects neuronal and synaptic differentiation of the developing brain. The preexisting vulnerability and degree of symptom expression may therefore be beneficially or adversely modulated by the immediate environment, especially in the early years of development.[65,66] Significant environmental factors include parental psychopathological conditions, parenting styles, education, and general family functioning.[19] Such a model, which integrates biological and environmental variables, appears most useful in considering the development of ADHD and its comorbidities and eliminates the need for the age-old nature-nurture dichotomy, which so frequently confuses etiological and therapeutic considerations.

There are several hypothetical models for the pathophysiology of ADHD, based on neurometabolical, neuroanatomical, and neurophysiological approaches.[56,67] Evidence for any specific mechanisms or structural abnormalities remains indirect, and it appears likely that no single model will suffice to explain the multiple manifestations of this disorder. Nonetheless, recent research has identified metabolical and perfusion differences in the CNS of ADHD patients that may relate causally to ADD. Lou et al.[68] found hypoperfusion in the white matter of the frontal lobes and in the caudate nuclei of patients with ADD on positron emission tomography (PET). Perfusion in the mesencephalon and basal ganglia of these ADD patients was increased with methylphenidate therapy, while perfusion of motor and primary sensory cortical areas was decreased. Lou's findings have been supported by Zametkin et al.,[69] with neurometabolic (PET) studies showing decreased cerebral glucose metabolism in frontal, parietal, and occipital cortical areas of previously untreated adults with ADD who were parents of children with ADD. However, these findings could not be reproduced in children or adolescents. In studies demonstrating metabolic differences between ADHD and control subjects, the administration of stimulants did not significantly affect either the global metabolism or regional metabolism in those regions found to have reduced glucose metabolism at baseline although there was clearly a clinical response to stimulants.[70] Recent studies of brain metabolism comparing adolescent boys and girls have found that an association of ADHD symptoms with altered metabolism appears stronger in females than in males, and there is speculation that this may be due to a greater severity of the disorder in girls.[71]

Anatomically speaking, dysfunction of the frontal and prefrontal cortex in those with ADHD is directly and indirectly implicated in multiple studies of neuropsychological test performance, as well as in neuroimaging studies of subjects with ADHD.[67] Zametkin et al.[72] showed decreased frontal lobe activity on PET, which corresponds to the increased hyperactive behavior of children with frontal lobe lesions, as well as to specific deficits on neuropsychological testing, such as in measures of response inhibition, a central neuropsychological frontal lobe feature impaired in ADHD.[73] Other neuroanatomical areas that may be involved are the corpus callosum[74] and the striatum,[75] structures vital to interhemispheric connection and cortical-limbic integration, respectively.

A further pathogenetic model hypothesizes neurotransmitter abnormalities, mainly involving central monoaminergic and specifically dopaminergic and noradrenergic systems. Animal models show that early developmental dopamine depletion is related to hyperactivity in young experimental animals and persistent deficits in avoidance learning as they mature.[76] It is hypothesized that dopamine and norepinephrine may be selectively deficient in the frontal-prefrontal-limbic system in those with ADHD. This hypothesis is supported by the responsiveness of ADHD symptoms to stimulant medications (amphetamines and their derivatives, such as methylphenidate), which derive their pharmacological effect from the release of dopamine from dopaminergic receptors and inhibition of reuptake.[77] Similarly, noradrenergic receptors of the prefrontal cortex have been shown to play a crucial role in the control of distractibility, with decreased norepinephrine associated with increased distractibility,[78] which corresponds to the therapeutic effect of the alpha-adrenergic agonists clonidine and guanfacine. In summary, current research indicates that neurotransmitter, perfusion and neurometabolical dysfunction in the prefrontal-frontal-limbic system and its integrative structures are all involved in as yet unspecified ways in the symptomatology of ADHD.

ASSESSMENT

There are no definitive tests or unequivocally positive markers that will diagnose ADHD. The child's history, observation of the child's immediate behavior, and reports of the child's behavior by adults in the child's environment form the basis for the diagnosis. However, formal psychological testing, speech and language assessment, and educational evaluation are, in almost all cases, standard requirements to identify coexisting cognitive, language, or learning impairments and to establish appropriate interventions. It is important to note that the child with ADHD may not demonstrate symptomatic behaviors while in the physician's office or even in a one-on-one testing situation. Sleator and Ullman,[79] found that only 21% of hyperactive children referred to a physician exhibited obviously hyperactive behaviors during the evaluation. Despite this, the hyperactive children who did not demonstrate symptomatic behaviors in the office differed in no respect from those who did in terms of classroom behavior, academic achievement, and medication parameters (need for, dosage, and duration of medication). For many of these children, a novel environment, interesting stimuli, or the undivided attention of an adult helps them to focus their attention and decrease their motor activity. Similarly, the intense stimuli of television viewing or video game playing may mask the inattentive behaviors. Therefore information about the child's behavior in multiple settings is important in clarifying the diagnosis.

History

A history of infant and early childhood behavior frequently shows unusual feeding, sleeping, or crying patterns or unusual sociability (aloof or excessively demanding); restless moving in their cribs; and increased activity, such as excessive running and climbing. In the school-aged child, it is important to obtain the educational history, including peer relationships. In addition to the behavioral and school history, a detailed medical history—with special considerations regarding the prenatal, neurodevelopmental, and family history—may provide important clues about risk factors and possible underlying associated medical conditions. Distinguishing inattention from absence seizures is a further consideration in the differential diagnosis, as well as possible behavioral effects of medications that the child is taking regularly.

A detailed social history is salient in light of the fact that parents of children with ADHD have an increased rate of psychopathological conditions and marital discord. A large percentage of mothers of children diagnosed with ADHD have been found to be depressed whereas fathers show increased problems with antisocial behavior and job instability, when compared with controls.[23,66,80] This information is important not only for its implications as to cause,[66] but also because it can affect the choice of interventions. Information about family functioning, including the status of siblings, is important. Children with ADHD frequently place a great deal of stress on the family, and family dynamics themselves may improve when specific interventions for ADHD are implemented.[81]

Physical examination

The physical examination does not generally contribute to the diagnosis of ADHD. However, a detailed physical, and especially neurologic, examination is essential because it may give clues to potential organic disease associated with disturbances in behavior. ADHD-type symptoms may be presenting complaints in children with nutritional deficiencies; anemia; lead intoxication; neurocutaneous syndromes, such as neurofibromatosis and tuberous sclerosis; autoimmune disorders, such as systemic lupus with CNS involvement; neuromuscular disorders; chromosonal abnormalities; and cerebral palsy.[53]

Despite the fact that there is an increased frequency of certain minor congenital anomalies—such as inner canthal folds and clinodactaly—in children with behavior difficulties, mental retardation, or other neurological disease, these anomalies are nonspecific and can occur in otherwise normal children.[82] Children with ADHD often show increased abnormalities of "soft" neurologic signs as indicators of delayed neurological maturation, although these signs are nonspecific and by themselves do not indicate functional deficits. The "soft signs" consist of such manifestations as mixed hand preference, impaired balance, stereognosis and graphesthesia problems, poor thumb-finger mobility, poor finger localization, and dysdiadochokinesis.[82] However, children with other conditions—such as MR, LD, or developmental coordination disorder—or otherwise completely normal children may have soft neurological signs. Assessing "soft" neurological signs will help detect children who may have problems in competitive sports and, in cases of marked fine-motor skill deficits, problems with handwriting clarity and with completing written work in a timely fashion.

Behavioral assessments

It is important to document the child's current (i.e., over the last 6 months) behavior in a familiar environment, primarily through parents' and teachers' reports. Teacher observations are considered by many clinicians and researchers to be the most reliable sources of information about a child's behavior. This is not only because of the assumption that teachers are more experienced in their evaluation and judgment of children but also because ADHD behaviors are often most clearly and consistently observed in the school and classroom environment. Obviously, the school situations depend on the teacher's personality, teaching style, and expectations; on class size; and on the classroom environment (e.g., excessive extraneous sensory stimuli and disruptive classmates). Teacher and parent observations can be systematized and semiquantified by use of behavior rating scales. They are inexpensive, simple to use, and particularly appropriate for parents, teachers, and others having long-term contact with the child.[24] Lahey et al.[83] compared validity and agreement of parent and teacher rating scales with comprehensive clinical evaluations of children with ADD with hyperactivity and found that rating scales accurately classified 70% to 75% of children. In addition, DuPaul[84] found the teacher rating scale to be a highly reliable measure of classroom performance.

The Conner's Rating Scale and its versions was one of the first scales to be used extensively for children with ADHD.[24] The Conner's Scale, however, does not appear to adequately separate aggressive from hyperactive and inattentive behaviors and has been supplanted by a multitude of other rating scales.[19] However, the Conner's Abbreviated Symptom Questionnaire (ASQ)[19] is still used frequently as a sensitive assessment tool for medication effects. Rating scales are somewhat idiosyncratic to the institutions and individuals who are using them. It is desirable to use a broadband behavior rating scale, such as the Child Behavior Checklist,[85] to screen for a broad range of behaviors and then augment this with more specifically focused diagnostic scales that use DSM criteria, such as the ADHD Diagnostic Teacher Rating Scale[86] or the SNAP-IV.[87] Rating scales alone should not be the basis for making a diagnosis. It is important to review the behaviors characteristic of ADHD with at least the parents by direct interviews. Behavioral assessments need validation by obtaining information about the teacher's and parent's behavioral expectations, the home environment, and the nature of the child's activities within and outside the home. This is especially important in the case of those children who are considered to be "hyperactive" by parents or teachers who are not well informed about normal developmental and behavioral issues, where there is family discord and dysfunction, and where there are poor parenting or teaching practices. In some areas, schools may provide information on direct observation of the child in the classroom by a trained observer.

In addition to assessing behavior, one should assess the child's intellectual abilities and achievement skills.[88] This can frequently be obtained through the school psychological services at no cost to the family. An undiagnosed learning disability or inappropriate class placement can be a significant source of disruptive behavior and inattention. It is also important to obtain information about the child's strengths and interests because knowledge of these are of vital importance to successful intervention. Last, it is important to interview the child directly, particularly to assess possible mood or anxiety states.

Laboratory measures. Direct measures of activity in children are generally not clinically useful because norms for activity levels among children at various ages have not been established. Some measures of attention are available in the form of laboratory tasks that emphasize components of attention, such as stimulus selection and vigilance. The most popular of these are various forms of continuous performance tests (CPTs), which also allow measures of impulsivity. Commercial computer programs for CPT tasks are available but do not replace clinical diagnostic evaluations. They are used primarily for research purposes and may aid in monitoring of medication.[89] However, the degree of clinical medication response is not reflected quantitatively in such laboratory tasks, and there are varying results as to how well CPT measures correlate with actual naturalistic behavior.[19] As with the other assessment tools, conventional laboratory measures do not provide a definitive diagnosis but may be used to complement overall clinical assessment.

EEGs are generally not helpful in an ADHD evaluation. No specific EEG abnormalities are generally recognized as pathognomic for ADHD children, but EEG variance has been found in some investigations. While one cross-national study[90] of a large sample of children in Japan, China, and Korea with ADHD and non-ADHD types of behavioral problems found that the hyperactive children showed "immaturity" of their EEGs, a U.S. study of routine EEG screenings of children hospitalized for behavior problems—including ADD—showed that 91% of the tracings were of normal variance.[91] Unless there is reason to exclude a seizure disorder, EEGs are not indicated in the assessment of ADHD.

Observational procedures, on the other hand, have been successfully used with hyperactive children and can, in blinded conditions, detect behavioral changes caused by stimulant medication. They allow recording of ongoing behavior in the child's natural or in selected environments. Examples include parental diaries and "time sampling" procedures by trained professionals—most commonly, of performance in the school setting. A strong advantage of such procedures is that they have direct relevance to the child's problems. Direct observation of behavior by the experienced clinician is desirable, but it is a luxury few diagnostic centers can afford. However, increasing coordination of services between clinical and school settings may allow for increased behavioral observations, and some school systems already require direct observations by the school psychologist as part of the assessment for ADHD.

The clinician in many areas can be aided in his or her diagnostic efforts by the school system. Federal legislation, PL101-476, called the Individuals With Disabilities Education Act (IDEA), defines ADHD as a disability under the category of "health impaired." This federal law is elaborated by state laws that establish the criteria, the assessment procedures, and the professionals who provide diagnostic certification. Evaluation procedures need to include an appropriate medical evaluation as well as evaluations of social and physical adaptive behaviors relating to the impairment. These mandatory evaluation components may necessitate formal psychological, educational, and speech and language assessments, in addition to the medical evaluation. Some school systems are providing service to children with ADHD under 504 legislation, rather than IDEA. This path allows less extensive evaluation procedures and does not require input from physicians in establishing the diagnosis. Most school systems have developed or are developing diagnostic and treatment procedures to address this condition. It is important for the primary care clinician to be aware of the services in the community and how to access them.

MANAGEMENT

Documented efficacious interventions for children with ADHD fall into three broad categories of treatment approaches that can, and often should, be used together: behavior modification, educational modification, and stimulant medication. Mention will be made of other therapies that are less substantiated as useful in the management of this disorder.

General considerations

Treatment of ADHD is comparable to treatment of other chronic disorders and must be seen as taking place in a socioenvironmental, as well as individual biological, context. An analogy to diabetes is very useful in explaining the multimodal approach to ADHD treatment: insulin is likely to be required as the basis of treatment, but diet, exercise, control of coexisting pathological conditions, as well as psychosocial management, are essential components of maintaining a well-controlled state and also help to keep the insulin requirements to a minimum. Similarly, pharmacological treatment of ADHD may be necessary for a particular child as the cornerstone of adequate management, but it is also highly interactive with and affected by the way in which home, school, and extracurricular environments are managed. It is crucial that the individual requirements and context for each child be considered in developing a therapeutic plan.[92,93] It is also crucial that the frequently present comorbid disorders be given equal therapeutic consideration in pharmacological and psychotherapeutic management decisions. This "holistic" approach reflects the attitudes of most clinicians working with children diagnosed with ADHD but runs counter to the preliminary results of the multicenter multimodal treatment studies[94] currently under way, which show no added benefit from multimodal interventions, as compared with pharmacological treatment alone.[95] Other studies have found therapy with stimulant medication and behavioral interventions to be equivalant[96] and the combination of both to decrease the dose of medication required.[97] Long-term outcomes of individualized multimodal interventions need to be studied to resolve these apparently conflicting results.

Psychostimulants are the most popular form of psychotropic medication prescribed for children in the United States[98] and are by far the drugs of choice for ADHD. Tricyclic antidepressants and alpha-adrenergic agonists, primarily represented by clonidine, are second-line drugs for this indication and much less frequently prescribed. Antipsychotic drugs were used in the past but have fallen into disuse because of their significant potential for serious side effects.

Stimulant medications

Methylphenidate (Ritalin) is the most popular and extensively researched stimulant, with dextroamphetamine (Dexedrine) and pemoline (Cylert) much less frequently used. Amphetamines had been dramatically successful since first introduced in 1937[99] in the treatment of institutionalized, severely behaviorally disturbed children and became increasingly used as less potent derivatives (methylphenidate, dextroamphetamine) were developed. Unfortunately, by the late 1960s, stimulants were rather indiscriminately prescribed for children whose diagnosis had not been solidly established. This led to a campaign to discredit them as addictive and mind-altering drugs. Allegations of dangerous side effects—such as brain damage, psychosis, and addiction—still periodically recur in the popular press. However, despite this emotional and public debate, use of stimulants has almost tripled in the recent past, and it is estimated that about 90% of children with a clinical diagnosis of ADHD will have stimulant treatment at some point in their childhood.[77]

The popularity of the stimulants is based on their safety, effectiveness, and low cost. The characteristic rapid onset of action, short half-life, and easily observable effects and side effects have also made stimulants the most extensively researched psychopharmacological agents in use. Nonetheless, and despite the vast clinical use and scientific study, a certain mystique about stimulants still prevails. In a recent "review of reviews," Swanson et al.[100] examined the popular and research literature for commonly held opinions and expectations of stimulant medications. This metaanalysis indicated that stimulants improve the core behaviors of inattention, impulsivity, and hyperactivity for the duration of action of the medication, as well as provide temporary improvement of associated features, including aggression, social interaction, and academic productivity. Contrary to expectation, stimulants do not have a paradoxical and therefore "pathognomonic" response in children with ADHD but produce the same effects as in normal children and adults; the response to stimulants cannot be predicted by other physical signs. More significant side effects—such as the appearance or increase in tics—are infrequent, but effects on appetite and sleeping are relatively common. The analysis also noted less improvement in learning and achievement than in behavior and no major effects on physical skills or higher order processes. Improvement in long-term adjustment, as measured by academic achievement or reduction in antisocial behavior, was not demonstrated, although there is more recent evidence that stimulants may improve specific cognitive performance.[101,102] Unresolved issues include the effects of long-term treatment, the differential effects on behavior and learning,[103,104] the role of stimulants in multimodal interventions, and the outcome of treatment relating to comorbid diagnoses. For a comprehensive review, the reader is referred to Wilens and Biederman.[77]

Generally, improvement is found in about 75% of children. In fact, a recent study demonstrated that even among children considered to be "nonresponders," high effectiveness was seen for both dextroamphetamine and methylphenidate when trials with both stimulants in a wide range of doses were given.[105] Dose-response relationships for behavior and attention usually parallel those for academic achievement; however, there are subgroups of children whose academic achievement shows no response at all or less response than their classroom behavior and attention as their dose is increased.[104,106] The response does not appear to be affected by the presence of comorbid disorders,[107] with the exception that stimulants have been shown to have less of a beneficial effect and produce more adverse effects in children with ADHD with internalizing symptoms.[108] There is some concern about the development of tolerance to stimulants, which on careful examination does not seem to be justified.[77] While response to stimulant medication among the new subtypes has not been studied, earlier studies comparing ADD with and without hyperactivity (ADD wo) found that 75% of children with ADD wo responded to methylphenidate—generally at a lower (5 mg bid) dose—and 95% of those with hyperactivity responded at moderate-to-high doses.[13]

Most of the research on stimulant treatment of ADHD has been on elementary school children. Some but much less data is available on preschoolers, adolescents, and adults. Recent reports about stimulant treatment in hyperactive preschoolers indicate that this age-group shows good clinical response, with markedly positive effects on maternal-child interaction, improved cognitive play, and social behavior[109] and few short-term side effects noted. Although predictability of response is less consistent than in older children, the weight of the evidence indicates that stimulant medication can be beneficial for preschool children with ADHD.[77] However, the preference is to remain conservative in the use of stimulants for this age-group, first intervening with the parents to improve their behavior management skills before relying on intervention with stimulant medication.

While about 50% to 80% of children diagnosed with ADHD during childhood continue to have significant symptoms and treatment requirements into adolescence,[23,110] there are only a few studies systematically evaluating the drug response in this age-group. However, this research literature has found effects in adolescents to be similar to those in younger children.[77] In addition, despite concerns, adolescents with ADHD but not CD as a co-morbid condition and who are receiving stimulants for therapeutic reasons do not appear to be at greater risk for drug abuse than their peers.[23] A significant number of children with ADHD will continue to show symptoms into adulthood, where stimulants continue to be the drugs of choice.[111] Because the risk of addiction is higher in adults, pemoline—which has much less abuse potential—may be a better first choice.

About 50% of patients diagnosed with Tourette's syndrome (TS) have a codiagnosis of ADHD, with ADHD symptoms usually preceding the onset of Tourette's.[112] Stimulant effects on tic severity are very variable and unpredictable, ranging from no change to worsening or improvement.[113] Isolated studies imply that short-term use of stimulants does not confer significant risk toward TS deterioration and, in fact, may be beneficial for both the tic symptomatology, as well as the comorbid ADHD.[114] In contrast, Riddle et al.[115] demonstrated that tic frequency decreased in TS-ADHD children receiving long-term stimulants when stimulants were temporarily withdrawn. However, there is little other systematic information on the long-term effects of long-term stimulant treatment in children with tic disorders. Gadow et al.[113] point out that ADHD patients with TS face only a 1 in 50 or even only 1 in 50,000 chance of protracted or irreversible tic worsening with ADHD treatment. If alternative medications for ADHD—such as tricyclic antidepressants or alpha-adrenergic agents—are contraindicated or ineffective, it is worthwhile to cautiously use stimulants—even in the presence of tics—unless significant worsening of the tics occurs.[116,112]

While in the past stimulant therapy has been thought to decrease the seizure threshold in children with seizure disorders and concurrent ADHD, more recent evidence supports the safety and efficacy of stimulants in this group.[77,117] There is also increasing evidence that stimulant medications are effective in children with lesser degrees of mental retardation and ADHD[118] but that they also may be associated with more pronounced adverse effects.[119] Stimulants have so far been shown to be effective in only a minority of children with autism.

Methylphenidate (Ritalin) is by far the most widely used and researched of the three stimulants. The generic form is pharmacologically equivalent to Ritalin, but there are some recent anecdotal reports that they are not entirely interchangeable. In 1973, Sprague and Sleator[103] showed that on a laboratory test of learning, methylphenidate is somewhat more than half as potent as dextroamphetamine on a weight basis. The peak behavioral effects of methylphenidate occur 1 to 2 hr after administration and decline within 3 to 5 hr. Dextroamphetamine has a somewhat longer effect, with a half-life of 4 to 6 hr and peak plasma levels after 2 to 3 hr.[77] These pharmacokinetic properties have the advantage of creating easily observable therapeutic and side effects but can also lead to rebound or withdrawal symptoms in some children. Methylphenidate and dextroamphetamine are available in sustained release forms and have been shown to be clinically as effective as the regular formulations,[120] although there are conflicting reports about their equivalency on a dose-by-dose comparison. Methylphenidate-SR has a half-life of between 4 and 6 hr and behavioral effects are observed for 2 to 8 hr after ingestion; dextroamphetamine spansules have a somewhat longer duration. Methylphenidate-SR appears to have a lower absorption curve than regular methylphenidate and does not appear to reach the same maximal serum concentrations.[121] However, it is important to note that responses to methylphenidate are highly individual.[92] Pemoline (Cylert) is a relatively mild CNS stimulant, being less potent than methylphenidate (by approximately 6 to 1), but it has a prolonged action enabling once-a-day dosage. Behavioral effects are observable within 2 days after treatment inception and within 2 hr on maintenance therapy. There is a linear dose-response relationship, and peak plasma levels are found at about 2 hr. It is therapeutically comparable to methylphenidate on measures of classroom functioning,[122] and behavioral side effects are similar to the other stimulants. Rare (1 to 3:1000) liver enzyme elevations and isolated reports of death caused by acute hepatic failure have been reported. This requires monitoring of liver function every 6 months. Because of pemoline's potential liver toxicity and because it does not show greater benefit than methylphenidate and dextroamphetamine, pemoline has been much less widely used and studied and is usually the choice in cases where methylphenidate or dextroamphetamine have been unsuccessful or when once-a-day dosage is necessary. An additional benefit of pemoline is that it has less abuse potential and is therefore licensed as a class II drug by the DEA. It may be more appropriate in cases in which there appears to be an increased risk for abuse and with adolescents and adults (Table 10-1).

Current recommendations for methylphenidate are between 0.3 and 0.6 to 1 mg/kg per dose; starting doses may be as low as 2.5 mg per dose and can then be gradually increased by 2.5 to 5 mg per dose per week. Dosage and frequency requirements are highly individualistic and depend only in part on the size and age of the child. Medication can be given for school

Table 10-1　Psychostimulants in ADHD

Psychostimulant	Onset	Maximal effect	Duration	Half-life	mg/dose (average)	mg/kg
Short-acting						
Methylphenidate (Ritalin)	20″-30″	1-2 hr	3-5 hr	2-3 hr	2.5-25 (10 bid)	0.2-1.0
Dextroamphetamine (Dexedrine)	20″-60″	1-2 hr	4-5 hr	4-6 hr	1.21-10 (5 bid)	0.1-0.5
Sustained release						
Methylphenidate-SR (Ritalin-SR 20)	1-3 hr	2 hr	8 hr	2-6 hr	20 mg	Variable
Dextrovariable amphetamine-SR (Dexedrine SR)	1+ hr	2+ hr	9+ hr	6+ hr	10 mg	
Pemoline (Cylert)	2 hr (at maintenance)	2+ hr	7+ hr	7-8 hr	56.25 (18.5-112.5[122])	Good

days, with a morning dose just before school (after breakfast) and a dose after lunch if the primary problems are school related. An additional dose may be required when children have severe difficulties in completing their homework after school; in participating in afterschool activities, such as organized sports in which increased behavioral and attentional control is required; when the parents have problems with their behavior at home; or when rebound is an identified and significant problem. If needed, medication can be given 7 days a week. Children who do not respond at lower dosages generally show behavioral improvement at higher doses, although academic improvement is not predictably coupled to behavioral improvement.[104] Dextroamphetamine has very similar properties to methylphenidate and can follow the same treatment plan but at half the dose. Because the site of action is slightly different, children who do not respond to methylphenidate may respond to dextroamphetamine. Sustained-release methylphenidate and dextroamphetamine spansules given alone or in addition to the regular form can be used when once-a-day dosage is desirable or when the "roller coaster" effect some patients experience on the regular form alone is to be avoided. The initial recommended dose of pemoline is 18.75 or 37.5 mg once a day in the morning and gradually increased by 18.75- or 37.5-mg increments to a maximum of 112.5 mg or 1.8 mg/kg/ dose, and an average dose of 56.5 mg/day.[122] Absorption is not significantly affected by prandial state, but stimulants should be given after meals to avoid appetite suppression. The effects can be monitored with behavior (e.g., ACTeRS)[123] and side effect (e.g., Barkley Side Effects Questionnaire)[124] rating scales completed by parents and teachers. Decisions about the dosage and duration of treatment depend on patient variables, as well as on the availability and committedness of continued academic and familial support. Greenhill[98] recommends planning the direction of medication administration year-by-year, including individualizing drug-free observation periods.

The side effects of the stimulants are due mostly to their CNS actions, although there are some cardiovascular effects that may become significant with overdosage. In therapeutic doses, systolic and diastolic blood pressures may both be slightly increased and heart rate progressively slowed. Cardiac output, however, is not enhanced, and thus the blood flow is little changed.[125] Psychotic reactions have been found in very rare instances in children receiving chronic therapeutic doses of stimulants, a response thought to be an unmasking of an underlying psychotic predisposition.[98] With the exception of the rare severe side effects, a major reason for the popularity of the stimulant medications is their wide therapeutic-to-toxic ratio with a margin of safety of 100 to 1, making it one of the safest drugs used in the treatment of children.[98] Evidence of the low incidence of side effects comes from a long-term study of 1056 treated children, in which the mean duration of contact was 30 months.[126] Only four instances of side effects severe enough to warrant discontinuation of medication occurred in children treated with methylphenidate (N=377), and only 16 incidences occurred in those treated with dextroamphetamine (N=371). Several other more recent placebo-controlled drug trials have reported similar results.[124,127,128] Interestingly, these studies showed significant occurrence of "side effects" on the placebo condition, indicating that behaviors attributed to stimulants were actually caused by ADHD.

The most common reported side effects are insomnia, decreased appetite, weight loss, irritability, abdominal pain, headaches, drowsiness, sadness, and proneness to crying. Tics are a much less frequent side effect than generally feared. A recent study of a large cohort of children treated with stimulant medication found that only 9% developed transient tics and less than 1% actually developed Tourette's syndrome.[129] All three stimulants can affect growth adversely during active treatment, but most studies report catch-up growth during prolonged cessation of drug treatment or in adolescence after treatment cessation. However, Spencer and Biederman[77] have reported a small percentage of children on methylphenidate with highly significant growth suppression. From these studies, one can conclude that in the vast majority of cases, treatment before adolescence does not affect final height in adolescents, even when it does retard growth in the treatment phase. Another potential concern has been the abuse potential of dextroamphetamine and methylphenidate, but stimulant treatment itself does not appear to confer a higher rate for drug abuse in ADHD children.[23] Contrary to rumor, methylphenidate does not impair flexibility of thinking in children with ADHD, even in higher doses,[130] nor do increasingly high doses impair cognitive performance.[131]

In terms of significant pharmacological interactions of stimulant drugs with other medications, methylphenidate appears to inhibit certain drug-metabolizing enzymes of the liver, causing prolongation of the half-lives of such drugs as phenobarbital, phenytoin (Dilantin), primidone (Mysoline), and imipramine. Interactions of stimulants with oral bronchodilators may enhance cardiac side effects and increase CNS stimulation. Combinations with MAO inhibitor antidepressants are also contraindicated because of possibly dangerously increased blood pressure. Further, stimulants should not be given with serotonin reuptake blockers, such as fluoxetine (Prozac) because it increases the side effects of agitation.[98]

Alternative medications

Alternative psychopharmacological medications may be required if children develop significant side effects, if they show no therapeutic response, or if comorbid disorders require a broader spectrum of psychopharmacological interventions. It is important to note that a child should receive an adequate trial of all three stimulant medications before trying alternative medications.

Tricyclic antidepressants. Tricyclic antidepressants are second-line drugs for those with ADHD. Desipramine and nortriptyline have become the tricyclic antidepressants of choice because of their high efficacy in non-responders to stimulant therapy, as well as their decreased sedative and anticholinergic side effects relative to impramine.[132,133] Reports of response rates vary; with cautious treatment initiation, it may take 3 weeks to see an effect. Side effects primarily result from anticholinergic properties (e.g., dry mouth, sedation, weight gain, and constipation), but cardiovascular side effects can also occur, which at therapeutic doses consist of increases in heart rate, blood pressure, and an increase in ECG conduction parameters.[77] Since 1990, sudden death has been reported in a very small number of children receiving desipramine[134] who previously had normal ECGs. These occurrences have led to a sharp debate on the safety, effectiveness, and indications for tricyclics[135] and increased caution in their application. Current treatment guidelines recommend excluding children with a family history of sudden cardiac death and children with ECG abnormalities. Dosage should not exceed 5 mg/kg/day, beginning with 10 to 25 mg (0.5/1.5 mg/kg per day) in divided doses and raised by 1 mg/kg per week. Treatment effectiveness should be assessed every two weeks. ECG monitoring is recommended at baseline and at 1 mg/3 mg/5 mg/kg and should be repeated at 3-month intervals.[77,98] The combination of tricyclics with stimulants increases both anticholinergic and cardiovascular side effects.[136] Other nontricyclic antidepressants are still in the experimental stage in their application to children.[137]

Alpha-adrenergic agonists (**clonidine and guanfacine**). Clonidine—an alpha-adrenergic agonist that inhibits the release of norepinephrine at the synapse, thereby decreasing sympathetic responses—was shown to be effective in children with ADHD in one study.[138] Despite its growing popularity in clinical settings, clonidine has not been validated as a treatment for ADHD by larger double-blind, placebo-controlled drug trials,[139] and its use for ADHD remains unapproved by the FDA. Recently guanfacine (Tenex), a second alpha-adrenergic agonist with less sedative and hypotensive effects, has been introduced as an alternative to clonidine,[140] with preliminary investigations documenting therapeutic responses on tic behavior as well as on attention and impulse control. [141] There is the suggestion that children with ADHD who are hyperaroused and more aggressive may show a better response to alpha-adrenergic agonists than to stimulants. Steingard et al.[142] was able to show that children with ADHD and comorbid tic disorders had a more frequent positive behavioral response to clonidine than did children with ADHD alone. The recommended clonidine dose begins at 0.05 mg once a day before bedtime and with increases of 0.05 mg weekly as needed to be in a range of 0.1 to 0.3 mg a day, corresponding to 3 to 4 µg/kg/day. It must be taken daily and may be given in four doses a day. Transdermal patches are also available and are effective for 5 to 7 days. Side effects are dry mouth, sedation, and slowing of the heart rate, which usually improve after approximately 2 weeks. Clonidine should not be stopped suddenly because this may cause depression, hypertension, and cardiac arrhythmias.[125] Rare but potentially lethal cardiovascular side effects have been reported for clonidine alone or in combination with methylphenidate.[143] No information regarding such effects of guanfacine are available to date.

Unorthodox treatments: diet and vitamin therapies and EEG biofeedback. It is worthwhile to note the established requirements for valid studies of drug efficacy. Sprague and Werry[144] defined six such requirements.

These are (1) placebo control, (2) random assignment of subjects, (3) double-blind method, (4) standardized dosage, (5) standardized evaluations, and (6) appropriate statistical analyses. These same requirements should be applied to other forms of treatment as well. Dietary interventions have been based on observations by parents and occasionally clinicians that the children or patients appeared to show hyperactive behavior in response to certain foods, especially sugar, chocolate, food dyes, and other additives.[58] Various restriction diets based on these assumptions have been used, with variable clinical success. The best known of these is the Feingold diet, based on salicylate and food dye restriction and named after its proponent Dr. Benjamin Feingold.[145] There are several methodologically stringent studies of the Feingold diet that have failed to support its effects, except in possibly a very small percentage of children with ADHD.[59] The effects of other specific foods, such as sugar and aspartame,[60] have not been substantiated. However, recent studies have shown behavioral responses to a restriction diet and hyposensitization with foods indicated by parents to produce disruptive behavior in their children.[146] Currently these studies are few in number and need further replication to be substantiated. In regard to megavitamin therapy, Haslam et al.[147] found that megavitamins are ineffective in the management of hyperactivity and should not be used because of their potential toxicity. More recently, EEG-biofeedback training has been promoted by a small group of therapists as being successful in improving behavior, as well as cognitive functioning, in children with ADHD.[148] No objective studies have been executed to date supporting these claims.

Nonpharmacological management

There is a need for adjunctive and alternative modalities (1) because management strategies are needed when children are off medication, such as in the evenings, and on drug holidays; (2) because the concurrent use of other interventions can reduce the dose of medication required[97]; and (3) because it is not clear that long-term use of stimulant medication alone actually improves the prognosis of children with ADHD.[149] Behavioral interventions in children may be likened to pharmacological interventions in that their effects are essentially symptomatic, as well as effective, only as long as they are being applied. For a review of behavior modification approaches and their effectiveness in those with ADHD, see Pelham and Sams.[150] Clinical behavioral therapy, as applied in a direct contingency management program, was found to show behavioral improvement but not to the extent that "normal-level" functioning in important parameters was achieved. Improvement was rarely global but highly differential and individual as assessed by means of parent and teacher ratings, peer nominations, and classroom observation. A further behavioral approach is by cognitive behavioral therapy, in which a therapist teaches the individual child cognitive techniques that can help the child control his or her impulsive and inattentive behavior outside of the therapeutic setting. However, it has been shown that such methods—which are based primarily on self-instruction—are generally not effective in children with ADHD, although they may be of great benefit in children with other childhood disorders.[151]

Social skills training[152]—preferably in peer groups and within the school setting—and parent behavior management training[19,153] are interventions that appear to be promising, but their generalizability has not been well established. In addition to the behavioral intervention, modifications of the classroom environment and academic tasks and goals are significant aspects of the treatment plan.[154,155] Since the implementation of Public Law 101-476, the effect of ADHD on academic and cognitive performance has been acknowledged and classroom modifications should be specified in an Individual Education Plan (IEP) for children certified as ADHD. Modifications include behavior management, structuring of the classroom environment, and adaptation of the actual pedagogical presentation of academic work to the child's cognitive style through teacher modeling, guided practice, and feedback. Some issues to be considered are alternating active and quiet periods and play and academic activities in a reasonable manner; giving specific attention to materials, work space, and transitional times, depending on individual requirements; and enhancing communication between teacher and student by seating the child close to the teacher, making direct eye contact, and using physical cues when possible. The procedures must be structured, allow the child a high degree of active involvement, and provide immediate feedback. This includes reviewing all rules and expectations frequently and implementing consequences, positive or negative, immediately. Identification and development of nonacademic talents and aptitudes, such as sports or arts, should be encouraged to provide alternative sources of competency and self-esteem.

The most promising approach seems to be one in which there is a combination of behavioral, educational, and pharmacological treatments. This approach is more likely to reach "normalization" of academic and psychosocial functioning than if each modality is used in isolation. There is evidence that the effects of behavioral and pharmacological treatment are complementary and synergistic[156] but that the form and "dosage" of each modality needs to be individualized. Regardless of what form of treatment or combinations of treatments are used, there is strong intra-individual and individual variations in response to the interventions, which again points to the hetrogenity of the disorder. For a discussion of the various treatment modalities see Whalen and Henker.[157]

Outcome

The outcome depends on continuation of ADHD symptomatology, type and degree of comorbidity, intelligence, and psychosocial factors, including parental discord and psychopathological conditions.[80] Longitudinal studies have included mostly male subjects with core symptoms that include hyperactivity, whereas little is known about the natural course in girls and subjects who are predominantly inattentive. Hyperactive preschoolers followed into adolescence showed that only one fourth had met recovery criteria; generally, these subjects had poorer academic, cognitive, and social skills and increased family discord[158] and antisocial behavior.[23] In adolescence, children with hyperactivity and concomitant CD were at greater risk for substance abuse than those with hyperactivity alone,[23] whereas hyperactivity was the determining factor for academic performance, with concomitant CD greatly increasing the drop-out, expulsion, and suspension rate from school.[159] At least 50% of children with ADHD continue to maintain dysfunctional symptoms into adulthood.[110] Longitudinal studies show relatively poorer occupational and educational outcomes, regardless of current psychiatric status; greater psychiatric comorbidity than in controls; and significantly higher rates of socialization disorders and substance use disorders when ADHD symptoms persisted.[110]

These outcome findings may not be specific for ADHD, as it may be that children with any psychiatric pathological condition have a worse outcome than do normal children. The cited outcome studies are also based on psychiatric clinic populations that are generally considered to have more severe pathology. Few studies have been done in which the natural history of the disorder is not confounded by multiple aggravating variables, and there are none to date that examine the outcome when long-term comprehensive management has been implemented in an environmentally benign context. There is, however, a large body of anecdotal evidence describing productive, creative, and fulfilling lives for many individuals with ADHD who manage to find a personal and occupational place in life that allows an integration of their temperamental and behavioral style.

REFERENCES

1. Clements SD: *Minimal brain dysfunction in children: terminology and identification,* Washington, DC, 1966, US Dept of Health, Education, and Welfare.
2. Rutter M: Syndromes attributed to "minimal brain dysfunction" in childhood, *Am J Psychiatr,* 139:1, 21-31, 1982.
3. Tramontana M, Hooper S: Neuropsychology of child psychopathology. In Reynolds CR, Fletcher-Jansen E, editors: *Handbook of clinical neuropsychology,* New York, 1989, Plenum.
4. Douglas VI, Peters KG: Toward a clearer definition of the attentional deficit of hyperactive children. In Hale GA, Lewis M, editors: *Attention and the development of cognitive skills,* New York, 1979, Plenum.
5. American Psychiatric Association Committee on Nomenclature: *Diagnostic and statistical manual (DSM) II,* Chicago, 1968, The Association.
6. American Psychiatric Association: *Diagnostic and statistical manual of mental disorders, third edition,* Washington, DC, 1980, The Association.
7. American Psychiatric Association: *Diagnostic and statistical manual of mental disorders, third edition—revised,* Washington, DC, 1987, The Association.
8. American Psychiatric Association: *Diagnostic and statistical manual of mental disorders, fourth edition,* Washington, DC, 1994, The Association.
9. McBurnett F, Lahey B, Pfiffner L: Diagnosis of attention deficit disorders in DSM-IV: scientific basis and implications for education, *Except Child* 60(2):108-117, 1993.
10. Lahey BB, Applegate B, McBurnett K, Biederman J, Greenhill L, Hynd GW, Barkley RA, Newcorn J, Jensen P, Richters J, et al: DSM-IV field trials for attention deficit hyperactivity disorder in children and adolescents, *Am J Psychiatr* 151(11):1673-1685, 1994.
11. Pelham W, Gnagy E, Greenslade K, Milich R: Teacher ratings of DSM III-R symptoms for the disruptive behavior disorders, *J Am Acad Child Adolesc Psychiatr* 31(2):210-218, 1992.
12. Barkley RA: A critique of current diagnostic criteria for attention deficit hyperactivity disorder: clinical and research implications, *J Dev Behav Pediatr* 11(6):343-352, 1990.
13. Barkley RA, DuPaul GJ, McMurray MB: Attention deficit disorder with and without hyperactivity: clinical response to three dose levels of methylphenidate, *Pediatrics* 87:519-531, 1994.
14. Lahey B, Pelham W, Schaughency E, Atkins M, Murphy H, Hynd G, Russo M, Hartdagen S, Lorys A: Dimensions and types of attention deficit disorders, *J Am Acad Child Adolesc Psychiatr* 27(3):330-335, 1988.
15. Shaywitz BA, Fletcher JM, Shaywitz SE: Defining and classifying learning disabilities and attention-deficit hyperactivity disorder, *J Child Neurol* 10(1):550-557, 1995.
16. Lahey B: Attention deficit disorder without hyperactivity: a review of research relevant to DSM-IV. In Widinger AJ, Frances HA, Pincus W, Davis M: *DSM-IV source book,* vol 1, Washington, DC, 1994, American Psychiatric Press.
17. Baumgaertel A, Wolraich ML, Dietrich M: Comparison of diagnostic criteria for attention deficit disorders in a German elementary school sample, *J Am Child Adolesc Psychiatr* 34(5):629-638, 1995.
18. Wolraich ML, Hannah JN, Baumgaertel A, Pinnock TP, Brown J: Comparison of diagnostic criteria for attention-deficit hyperactivity disorder in a county-wide sample, *J Am Acad Child Adolesc Psychiatr* 35(3):319-324, 1996.
19. Barkley R: *Attention deficit hyperactivity disorder: a handbook for diagnosis and treatment,* New York, 1990, Guilford Press.
20. Frick P, Lahey B, Kamphaus R, Loeber R, Christ MAG, Hart EL, Tannenbaum LE: Academic underachievement and the disruptive behavior disorders, *J Consult Clin Psych* 59(2):289-294, 1991.

21. Faraone SV, Biederman J, Lehman BK, Spencer T, Norman D, Seidman LJ, Kraus I, Perrin J, Chen WJ, Tsuang MT: Intellectual performance and school failure in children with ADHD and in their siblings, *J Abnorm Child Psychol* 102(4):616-623, 1993.

22. Nussbaum NL, Grant ML, Roman MJ, Poole JH, Bigler ED: Attention deficit disorder and the mediating effect of age on academic and behavioral variables, *J Dev Behav Pediatr* 11(1):22-26, 1990.

23. Barkley RA, Fischer M, Edelbrock CS, Smallish L: The adolescent outcome of hyperactive children diagnosed by research criteria: 1. An 8-year prospective follow-up study, *J Am Acad Child Adolesc Psychiatr* 29(4):546-557, 1990.

24. Conners CK: A teacher rating scale for use in drug studies with children, *Am J Psychiatr* 126:152-156, 1969.

25. Shaywitz BA, Shaywitz SE: Comorbidity: a critical issue in attention deficit disorder, *J Child Neurol (suppl)* 6:S13-S20, 1991.

26. Dykman RA, Ackerman PT: Attention deficit disorder and specific reading disability: separate but often overlapping disorders, *J Learn Disabil* 24(2):96-103, 1991.

27. Cantwell DP, Baker L: *Psychiatric and developmental disorders in children with communication disorders*, Washington, DC, 1991, American Psychiatric Press.

28. Riccio CA, Hynd GW, Cohen MJ, Hall J, Molt L: Comorbidity of central auditory processing disorder and attention-deficit hyperactivity disorder, *J Am Acad Child Adolesc Psychiatr* 33(6):849-857, 1994.

29. Cook JR, Mausbach T, Burd L, Gascon GG, Slotnick HB, Patterson B, Johnson RD, Hankey B, Reynolds BW: A preliminary study of the relationship between central auditory processing disorder and attention deficit disorder, *J Psychiatr Neurosci* 18(3):130-137, 1993.

30. Szatmari P, Bremner R, Nagy J: Asperger's syndrome: a review of clinical features, *Can J Psychiatr* 34:539-560, 1992.

31. Biederman J, Munir K, Knee D: Conduct and oppositional disorders in clinically referred children with attention deficit disorder: a controlled family study, *J Am Child Adolecs Psychiatr* 26(5):724-727, 1987.

32. Szatmari P, Boyle M, Offord D: ADDH and conduct disorder: degree of diagnostic overlap and differences among correlates, *J Am Acad Child Adolesc Psychiatr* 28(6):865-872, 1989.

33. Schachar R, Tannock R: Test of four hypotheses for the comorbidity of attention deficit disorder and conduct disorder, *J Am Acad Child Adolesc Psychiatr* 34(5):639, 1995.

34. McKay KE, Newcorn JH, Schulz K, Kopstien I, Schwartz ST, Halperin JM: *Serotonin, aggression and family psychopathology in ADHD boys*, Proceedings of the Annual Meeting of the American Academy of Child and Adolescent Psychiatry, New Orleans, 1995.

35. Lewis DO, Pincus JH, Lovely R, Spitzer E, Moy E: Biopsychosocial characteristics of matched samples of delinquents and nondelinquents, *J Am Acad Child Adolesc Psychiatr* 26:744-752, 1987.

36. Biederman J, Newcorn J, Sprich S: Comorbidity of ADHD with conduct, depressive, anxiety, and other disorders, *Am J Psychiatr* 148(5):564-577, 1991.

37. Angold A, Costello EJ: Depressive comorbidity in children and adolescents: empirical, theoretical, and methodological issues, *Am J Psychiatr* 150:1779-1791, 1993.

38. Biederman J, Faraone S, Mick E, Lelon E: Psychiatric comorbidity among referred juveniles with major depression: fact or artifact? *J Am Acad Child Adolesc Psychiatr* 34(5):579-590, 1995.

39. Verhulst FC, Van der Emde J: Comorbidity in an epidemiological sample: a longitudinal perspective, *J Child Psychol Psychiatr* 34(5):767-783, 1993.

40. Shaywitz BA, Fletcher J, Shaywitz SE: Issues in the definition and classification of attention deficit disorders, *Top Lang Disord* 14:1-25, 1994.

41. Szatmari P, Offord D, Boyle M: Ontario child health study: prevalence of attention deficit disorder with hyperactivity, *J Child Psych Psychiatr* 30:219-230, 1989.

42. Lindgren S, Wolraich M, Stromquist A, Davis C, Milich R, Watson D: *Re-examining attention deficit hyperactive disorder,* Presentation at the 8th Annual Meeting of the Society for Behavioral Pediatrics, Denver, 1990.

43. Weisz JR, Weiss B, Walter BR, Suwanlert S, Chaiyasit W, Anderson WW: Thai and American perspectives on over- and undercontrolled child behavior problems: exploring the threshold model among parents, teachers, and psychologists, *J Consult Clin Psychol* 56(4):601-609, 1988.

44. Ross G, Lipper EG, Auld P: Social competence and behavior problems in premature children at school age, *Pediatrics* 86:391-397, 1990.

45. Klebanov PK, Brooks-Gunn J, McCormick MC: Classroom behavior of very low birth weight elementary school children, *Pediatrics* 94:700-708, 1991.

46. Streissguth A, Barr H, Martin D, et al: The fetal alcohol syndrome as a model for the study of behavioral teratology of alcohol. In Krasnegor N, Gray D, Thompson T: *Developmental behavioral pharmacology,* Hillsdale NJ, 1986, Erlbaum.

47. Azuma SD, Cheshoff IJ: Outcome of children prenatally exposed to cocaine and other drugs: a pathanalysis of three-year data, *Pediatrics* 92:396-402, 1993.

48. Berlin CM: Effects of drugs on the fetus, *Pediatr Rev* 12:282-287, 1991.

49. Ferguson D, Horwood J, Lynsky M: Maternal smoking before and after pregnancy: effects on behavioral outcomes in middle childhood, *Pediatrics* 92:815-822, 1993.

50. Milberger S, Biederman J, Faraone SV, Chen L, Jones J: *Maternal smoking during pregnancy as a risk factor for ADHD,* Proceedings of the Annual Meeting of the American Academy of Child and Adolescent Psychiatry, New Orleans, 1995.

51. Galler JR, Ramsey F, Solimano G, et al: The influence of early malnutrition on subsequent behavioral development. II. Classroom behavior, *J Am Acad Child Psychiatr* 22:16-22, 1983.

52. Needleman HL, Gunnoc C, Leviton A, et al: Deficits in psychological and classroom performance in children with elevated dentine lead levels, *N Engl J Med* 300:689-695, 1979.

53. Shaywitz BA, Shaywitz SE: Learning disabilities and attention disorders. In Swaiman KF, ed: *Pediatric neurology: principles and practice,* St Louis, 1989, Mosby.

54. Biederman J, Faraone SV, Spencer T, Wilens T, Norman D, Lapey KA, Mick E, Lehman BK, Doyle A: Patterns of psychiatric comorbidity, cognition, and psychosocial functioning in adults with attention deficit hyperactivity disorder, *Am J Psychiatr* 150:1792-1798, 1992.

55. Biederman J, Faraone SV, Keenan K, Benjamin J, Krifcher B, Moore C, Sprich-Buckminster S, Ugaglia K, Jellinek MS, Steingard R, et al: Further evidence for family genetic risk factors in attention deficit hyperactivity disorder. Patterns of comorbidity in probands and relatives psychiatrically and pediatrically referred samples, *Arch Gen Psychiatr* 49(9):728-738, 1992.

56. Hechtman L: Genetic and neurobiological aspects of attention deficit hyperactive disorder: a review, *J Psychol Neurosci* 19(3):192-210, 1994.

57. Faraone SV, Biederman J, Lehman BK, Keenan K, Norman D, Seidman LJ, Kolodmy R, Kraus I, Perrin J, Chen WJ: Evidence for the independent familial transmissions of attention deficit hyperactivity disorder and learning disabilities: results from a family genetic study, *Am J Psychiatr* 150(6):891-895, 1993.

58. Conners CK, Blouin AB: Nutritional effects on behavior of children, *J Psychiatr Res* 17:193-201, 1982-83.

59. Wender EH: The food additive–free diet in the treatment of behavior disorders: a review, *J Dev Behav Pediatr* 7:35-42, 1986.

60. Wolraich ML, Lindgren SD, Stumbo PJ, Stegink LD, Appelbaum MI, Kristy MC: Effects of diets high in sucrose or aspartame on the behavior and cognitive performance of children, *New Engl J Med* 330(5):301-307, 1994.

61. Nelson VS: Pediatric head injury, *Traum Brain Injury* 3(2):461-474, 1992.

62. Murray R, Shum D, McFarland K: Attentional deficits in head injured children: an information processing analysis, *Brain Cognition* 18:99-115, 1992.

63. Bijur PE, Haslum M, Goldring J: Cognitive and behavioral sequelae of mild head injury in children, *Pediatrics* 86:337-344, 1990.

64. Weiss G: Hyperactivity in childhood, *N Engl J Med* 323:1443-1445, 1990.

65. Anastasiow NJ: Implications of the neurobiological model for early intervention. In Meisels SJ, Shonkoff JP, eds: *Handbook of early childhood intervention*, New York, 1990, Cambridge University Press.

66. Biederman J, Milberger S, Faraone SV, Kiely K, Guite J, Mich BA, Ablon JS, Warburton R, Reed E, Davis SG: Impact of adversity on functioning and comorbidity in children with attention-deficit hyperactivity disorder, *J Am Acad Child Adolesc Psychiatr* 34(11):1495-1503, 1995.

67. Riccio CA, Hynd GW, Choen MJ, Gonzales JJ: Neurological basis of attention deficit hyperactivity disorder, *Excep Child* 60:118-124, 1993.

68. Lou H, Henriksen L, Bruhn P: Focal cerebral hypoperfusion in children with dysphasia and/or attention deficit disorder, *Arch Neurol* 41:825-829, 1984.

69. Zametkin AJ, Nordahl TE, Gross M, King AC, Semple WE, Rumsey J, Hamburger S, Cohen M: Cerebral glucose metabolism in adults with hyperactivity of childhood onset, *New Engl J Med* 323:1361-1366, 1990.

70. Matuchik JA, Liebenauer LL, King AC, Szymanski HV, Cohen RM, Zametkin AJ: Cerebral glucose metabolism in adults with attention deficit hyperactivity disorder after chronic stimulant treatment, *Am J Psychiatr* 151(5):658-664, 1994.

71. Ernst M, Liebenauer LL, King C, Fitzgerald GA, Cohen RM, Zametkin AJ: Reduced brain metabolism in hyperactive girls, *J Am Acad Child Adolesc Psychiatr* 33(6):858-868, 1994.

72. Zametkin AJ, Liebenauer LL, Fitzgerald GA: Brain metabolism in teenagers with attention deficit hyperactivity disorder, *Arch Gen Psychiatr* 50:333-340, 1993.

73. Barkley RA, Grodzonski G, DuPaul GJ: Frontal lobe functions in attention deficit disorder with and without hyperactivity: a review and research report, *J Am Acad Child Psychiatr* 20:163-188, 1992.

74. Semrud-Clikeman M, Filipek PA, Biederman J, Steingard R, Kennedy D, Renshaw P, Bekken K: ADHD: magnetic resonance imaging morphometric analysis of the corpus callosum, *J Am Acad Child Adolesc Psychiatr* 33(6):875-881, 1994.

75. Lou H, Henriksen L, Bruhn P, Bower H, Nielsen J: Striatal dysfunctions in attention deficit and hyperactivity disorders, *Arch Neurol* 46:48-52, 1989.

76. Shaywitz SE, Shaywitz BA, Cohen DJ, Young JG: Monoaminergic mechanisms in hyperactivity. In Rutter M, editor: *Developmental neuropsychiatry*, London, 1983, Guilford Press.

77. Wilens TE, Biederman J: The stimulants, *Psychiatr Clin North Am* 15(1):191-222, 1992.

78. Coull JT: Pharmacological manipulations of the alpha 2-noradrenergic system. Effects on cognition, *Drugs Aging* 5(2):116-26, 1994.

79. Sleator EK, Ullman RK: Can the physician diagnose hyperactivity in the office? *Pediatrics* 67:13-17, 1981.

80. Fischer M, Barkley RA, Fletcher KE, Smallish L: The adolescent outcome of hyperactive children: predictors of psychiatric, academic, social, and emotional adjustment, *J Am Acad Child Adolesc Psychiatr* 32(2):324-332, 1993.

81. Schachar R, Taylor E, Wieselberg MB, Ghorley G, Rutter M: Changes in family function and relationships in children who respond to methylphenidate, *J Am Acad Child Adolesc Psychiatr* 26(5):728-732, 1987.

82. Touwen B: *Examination of the child with minor neurological dysfunction*, Philadelphia, 1979, Lippincott.

83. Lahey B, McBurnett K, Piacentinit J, Hartdagen S, Walker J, Frick P, Hynd G: Agreement of parent and teacher rating scales with comprehensive clinical assessments of attention deficit disorder with hyperactivity, *J Psychol Behav Assess* 9(4):429-439, 1987.

84. DuPaul GJ: Parent and teacher ratings of ADHD symptoms: psychometric properties in a community-based sample, *J Clin Child Psychiatr* 20(3):245-253, 1991.

85. Achenbach T, Edelbrock L: *Manual for the child behavior checklist and revised child behavior profile*, Burlington, 1983, University of Vermont.

86. Wolraich ML, Hannah JN, Baumgaertel A, Pinnock TP, Law D: Further examination of diagnostic criteria for attention deficit/hyperactivity disorder (DSM-IV) in a county wide sample (unpublished manuscript).

87. Swanson JM: *School based assessments and intervention for ADD students*, Irvine, CA, 1992, KC Publishing.

88. Atkins MS, Pelham WE: School-based assessment of attention deficit-hyperactivity disorder, *J Learn Disabil* 24(4):197-204, 1991.

89. Corkum PV, Siegel LS: Is the continuous performance task a valuable research tool for use with children with attention-deficit hyperactivity disorder? *J Child Psychol Psychiatr* 34(7):1217-1239, 1993.

90. Matsuura M, Okubo Y, Toru M, Kojima T, He Y, Hou Y, Shen Y, Lee CK: A cross-national EEG study of children with emotional and behavioral problems: a WHO collaborative study in the Western Pacific Region, *Biol Psychiatr* 34(1-2):59-65, 1993.

91. Phillips BB, Drake ME Jr, Hietter SA, Andrews JE, Bogner JE: Electroencephalography in childhood conduct and behavior disorders, *Clin Electroencephalogr* 24(1):25-30, 1993.

92. Pelham WE, Milich R: Individual differences in response to Ritalin in classwork and social behavior. In Greenhill L, Swan BPO, editors: *Ritalin theory and patient management*, New York, 1991, Mary Ann Liebert, Inc.

93. Nathan WA: Integrated multimodal therapy of children with attention-deficit hyperactivity disorder, *Bull Menninger Clin* 56(3):283-312, 1992.

94. Richters JE, Arnold LE, Jensen PS, Abikoff H, et al: NIMH collaborative multisite multimodal treatment study of children with ADHD. 1. Background and rationale, *J Am Acad Child Adolesc Psychiatr* 34(8):987-1000, 1995.

95. Hechtman L, Abikoff H: *Multi-modal treatment plus stimulants vs stimulant treatment for ADHD Children*, Proceedings of the Annual Meeting of the American Academy of Child and Adolescent Psychiatry, New Orleans, 1995.

96. Pelham WE, Carlson C, Sams SE, Vallano G, Dison MJ, Hoza B: Separate and combined effects of methylphenidate and behavior modification on boys with attention deficit hyperactivity disorder in the classroom, *J Consult Clin Psychol* 61(3):506-515, 1993.

97. Pelham WE, Schnedler RW, Bologna NC, Conteras JA: Behavioral and stimulant treatment of hyperactive children: a therapy study with methylphenidate probes in a within-subject design, *J Appl Behav Anal* 13:221-236, 1980.

98. Greenhill LL: Pharmacologic treatment of attention deficit hyperactivity disorder, *Psychiatr Clin North Am* 15(1):109-129, 1992.

99. Bradley W: The behavior of children receiving benzedrine, *Am J Psychiatr* 94:577-585, 1937.

100. Swanson JM, McBurnett K, Wigal T, Pfiffner LJ, Lerner MA, et al: Effect of stimulant medication on children with ADD: a "review of reviews," *Except Child* 60(2):154-162, 1993.

101. Rapport MD, Carlson GA, Kelly KL, Pataki C: Methylphenidate and desipramine in hospitalized children. 1. Separate and combined effects on cognitive function, *J Am Acad Child Adolesc Psychiatr* 32(2):333-342, 1993.

102. Sunohara G, Malone MA, Taylor MJ, Kershner JR, Roberts W, Humphries T: *Methylphenidate effects on sustained and selective attention processing in ADHD children*, Proceedings of the Annual Meeting of the American Academy of Child and Adolescent Psychiatry, New Orleans, 1995.

103. Sprague RL, Sleator EK: Effects of psychopharmacologic agents on learning disorders, *Pediatr Clin North Am* 20:719-735, 1973.

104. Rapport MD, Denney C, DuPaul GJ, Gardner MJ: Attention deficit disorder and methylphenidate: normalization rates, clinical effectiveness, and response prediction in 76 children, *J Am Acad Child Adolesc Psychiatr* 33(6):882-893, 1994.

105. Elia J, Borcherding BG, Rapoport JL, Keysor CS: Methylphenidate and dextroamphetamine treatment of hyperactivity: are there true nonresponders? *Psychiatr Res* 36(2):141-155, 1991.

106. Tannock R, Schachar RJ, Carr RP, Logan GD: Dose response effects of methylphenidate on academic performance and overt behavior in hyperactive children, *Pediatrics* 84:648-657, 1989.

107. Biederman J, Baldessarini RJ, Wright V, Kennan K, Faraone S: A double-blind placebo controlled study of desipramine in the treatment of ADD. III. Lack of impact of comorbidity and family history factors on clinical response, *J Am Acad Child Adolesc Psychiatr* 32(1):199-204, 1993.

108. DuPaul GJ, Barkley RA, McMurray MB: Response of children with ADHD to methylphenidate: interaction with internalizing symptoms, *J Am Acad Child Adolesc Psychiatr* 33(6):894-903, 1994.

109. Alessandri SM, Schramm K: Effects of dextroamphetamine on the cognitive and social play of a preschooler with ADHD, *J Am Acad Child Adolesc Psychiatr* 30(5):768-772, 1991.

110. Weiss G, Hechtman L, Milroy T, Perlman T: Psychiatric status of hyperactives as adults: a controlled prospective 15-year follow-up of 63 hyperactive children, *J Am Acad Child Psychiatr* 24(2):211-220, 1985.

111. Fargason RE, Ford CF: Attention deficit hyperactivity disorder in adults: diagnosis, treatment, and prognosis, *South Med J* 87(3):302-309, 1994.

112. Singer HS: Tic disorders, *Pediatr Ann* 22(1):22-29, 1993.

113. Gadow KD, Sverd Y: Stimulants for ADHD in child patients with Tourette's syndrome: the issue of relative risk, *J Dev Behav Pediatr* 11(5):269-275, 1990.

114. Sverd J, Gadow KD, Paolicelli LM: Methylphenidate treatment of ADHD in boys with Tourette's syndrome, *J Am Acad Child Adolesc Psychiatr* 28(4):574-579, 1989.

115. Riddle MA, Lynch K, Seahill L, deVries A, Cohen DJ, Leckman JF: *Methylphenidate discontinuation and re-initiation during long-term treatment of boys with Tourette's disorder and with attention deficit disorder (ADHD)*, Presented at the 40th Annual Meeting of the American Academy of Child and Adolescent Psychiatry, San Antonio, Tex, 1993.

116. Cohen CJ, Riddle M, Leckman J: Pharmacotherapy of Tourette's syndrome and associated disorders, *Psychiatr Clin North Am* 15(1):109-130, 1992.

117. Feldman H, Crumrine P, Handen BL, Alvin R, Teodori J: Methylphenidate in children with seizures and attention deficit disorder, *Am J Dis Child* 143(9):1081-1086, 1989.

118. Johnson CR, Handen BL, Lubetsky MJ, Sacco KA: Efficacy of methylphenidate and behavioral intervention on classroom behavior in children with ADHD and mental retardation, *Behav Mod* 18(4):470-487, 1994.

119. Handen BL, Feldman H, Gosling A, Breaux AM, McAuliffe S: Adverse side effects of methylphenidate among mentally retarded children with ADHD, *J Am Acad Child Adolesc Psychiatr* 31(2):241-245, 1991.

120. Pelham WE, Greenslade KE, Vodde-Hamilton M, et al: Relative efficacy of long-acting stimulants on children with ADHD: a comparison of standard methylphenidate, sustained-release methylphenidate, sustained-release dextroamphetamine, and pemoline, *Pediatrics* 86:226-237, 1990.

121. Birmaher B, Greenhill LL, Cooper TB, Fried J, Maminski B: Sustained release methylphenidate: pharmacokinetic studies in ADDH males, *J Am Acad Child Adolesc Psychiatr* 28(5):768-772, 1989.

122. Pelham WE, Swanson J, Ferman M, Schmidt H: Pemoline effects on children with ADHD: a time-response by dose-response analysis on classroom measures, *J Am Acad Child Adolesc Psychiatr* 34(11):1504-1513, 1995.

123. Ullman R, Sleator E, Sprague R: *ADD-H comprehensive teacher rating scale ACTeRS*, Champaign, IL, 1984, Metn'Tech.

124. Barkley RA, McMurray MB, Edelbrock CS, Robbins K: Side effects of methylphenidate in children with ADHD: a systemic, placebo-controlled evaluation, *Pediatrics* 86:184-192, 1990.

125. Goodman AB, Rall TW, Nies AS, Taylor P, *Goodman and Gilman's the pharmacological basis of therapeutics*, ed 5, New York, 1990, Pergamon Press.

126. Gross MD, Wilson WC: *Minimal brain dysfunction*, New York, 1974, Brunner/Mazel.

127. Fine S, Johnston C: Drug and placebo side effects in methylphenidate-placebo trials for attention deficit hyperactivity disorder, *Child Psychiatr Hum Dev* 24(1):25-30, 1993.

128. Ahmann PA, Waltonen SJ, Olson KA: Placebo-controlled evaluation of Ritalin side effects, *Pediatrics* 91(6):1101-1106, 1993.

129. Lipkin PH, Goldstein IJ, Adesman AR: Tics and dyskinesias associated with stimulant treatment in attention-deficit hyperactivity disorder, *Arch Pediatr Adolesc Med* 148(8): 859-861, 1994.

130. Douglas VI, Barr RG, Desilets J, Sherman E: Do high doses of stimulants impair flexible thinking in attention-deficit hyperactivity disorder? *J Am Acad Child Adolesc Psychiatr* 34(7):877-885, 1995.

131. Klein RG: Effects of high mehtylphenidate doses on the cognitive performance of hyperactive children, *Bratisl Lek Listy* 92:534-539, 1991.

132. Wilens TE, Biederman J, Geist D, Steingard R, Spencer T: Nortriptyline in the treatment of ADHD: a chart review of 58 cases, *J Am Acad Child Adolesc Psychiatr* 32(2):343-349, 1993.

133. Spencer T, Biederman J, Kerman K, Steingard R, Wilent T: Desipramine treatment of children with attention-deficit hyperactivity disorder and tic disorder or Tourette's syndrome, *J Am Acad Child Adolesc Psychiatr* 32(2):354-360, 1993.

134. Riddle MA, Nelson JC, Kleinman CS, Rasmusson A, Leckman JF, King RA, Cohen DJ: Sudden death in children receiving Norpramin: a review of three reported cases and commentary, *J Am Acad Child Adolesc Psychiatr* 30(1):104-108, 1991.

135. Werry JS, Biederman J, Thisted R, Greenhill L, Ryan N: Resolved: cardiac arrhythmias make desipramine an unacceptable choice in children, *J Am Acad Child Adolesc Psychiatr* 34:1239-1248, 1995.

136. Pataki CS, Carlson GA, Kelly KL, Rapport MD, Biancaniello TM: Side effects of methylphenidate and desipramine alone and in combination in children, *J Am Acad Child Adolesc Psychiatr* 32(5):1065-1072, 1993.

137. Biederman LL, Perry PJ, Allen AJ, Kuperman S, Arndt SV, Herrmann KJ, Schumacher E: Buprion versus methylphenidate in the treatment of attention deficit hyperactivity disorder, *J Am Acad Child Adolesc Psychiatr* 34:649-657, 1995.

138. Hunt RD, Minderaa RB, Cohen DJ: Clonidine benefits children with ADHD: report of a double-blind placebo-crossover therapeutic trial, *J Am Acad Child Adolesc Psychiatr* 24(5):617-629, 1985.

139. Hart-Santoury D, Hart L: Clonidine in attention deficit hyperactivity disorder, *Ann Pharmacother* 26:37-39, 1992.

140. Hunt RD, Arnsten AF, Asbell MD: An open trial of guanfacine in the treatment of attention-deficit hyperactivity disorder, *J Am Acad Child Adolesc Psychiatr* 34:50-54, 1995.

141. Chapell PB, Riddle MA, Scahill L, Lynch KA, Scultz R, et al: Gratification treatment of comorbid attention-deficit hyperactivity disorder and Tourette's syndrome: preliminary clinical experience, *J Am Acad Child Adolesc Psychiatr* 39:1140-1146, 1995.

142. Steingard R, Biederman J, Spencer T, Wilens T, Gonzalez A: Comparison of clonidine response in the treatment of attention-deficit hyperactivity disorder with and without comorbid tic disorders, *J Am Acad Child Adolesc Psychiatr* 32(2):350-353, 1993.

143. Chandran KS: ECG and clonidine, *J Am Acad Child Adolesc Psychiatr* 33:1351-1352, 1994.

144. Sprague RL, Werry JS: Methodology of psychopharmacoilogical studies with the retarded, *Int Rev Res Ment Retard* 5:147, 1971.

145. Feingold B: *Why your child is hyperactive,* New York, 1975, Random House.

146. Egger J, Stella A, McEwen L: Controlled trial of hyposensitification with food-induced hyperkinetic syndrome, *Lancet* 334:1150-1153, 1992.

147. Haslam R, Dalby J, Rademaker A: Effects of megavitamin therapy on children with attention deficit disorders, *Pediatrics* 74:103-111, 1984.

148. Lubar JF: Discourse on the development of EEG diagnostics and biofeedback for attention-deficit/hyperactivity disorders, *Biofeedback Self Regul* 16(3):201-225, 1991.

149. Hechtman L, Weiss RE, Pedman T: Young adult outcome of hyperactive children who received long-term stimulant treatment, *J Am Acad Child Psychiatr* 23:261-269, 1984.

150. Pelham WE, Sams SE: Behavior modification, *Child Adolesc Psychiatr Clin North Am* 1(2):505-517, 1992.

151. Abikoff H: Cognitive training in ADHD children: less to it than meets the eye, *J Learn Disabil* 24(4):205-209, 1991.

152. Cousins LS, Weiss G: Parent training and social skills training for children with ADHD: how can they be combined for greater effectiveness? *Can J Psychiatr* 38:449-457, 1993.

153. Anastopoulos AD, Shelton TL, DuPaul GJ, Guervremont DC: Parent training for attention-deficit hyperactivity disorder: its impact on parent functioning, *J Abnorm Child Psychol* 21(5):581-596, 1993.

154. Fiore TA, Becker EA, Nero RC: Educational interventions for students with ADD, *Except Child* 60(2):163-173, 1993.

155. Zentall SS: Research on the educational implications of ADHD, *Except Child* 60(2):143-153, 1993.

156. Hozar B, Pelham W, Sam S, Carlson C: An examination of the "dosage" effects of both behavior therapy and methylphenidate on the classroom performance of two ADHD children, *Behav Mod* 16:164-192, 1992.

157. Whalen CK, Henker B: Therapies for hyperactive children: comparisons, combinations, and compromises, *J Consult Clin Psychol* 59(1):126-137, 1991.

158. McGee R, Partridge F, Williams S, Silva PA: A twelve-year follow-up of preschool hyperactive children, *J Am Acad Child Adolesc Psychiatr* 30(2):244-232, 1991.

159. Mannuza S, Klein RG, Bessler A, et al: Adult outcome of hyperactive boys: educational achievement, occupational rank, and psychiatric status, *Arch Gen Psychiatr* 50:565, 1993.

CHAPTER 11

Disorders of sensation: hearing and visual impairment

DESMOND P. KELLY
STUART W. TEPLIN

Hearing and vision are primary conduits of information, and even mild limitations of these senses can have far-reaching effects on development. Early detection of such problems is vital, and a comprehensive approach to medical management and habilitation, with support and advocacy for the child and family, will assist children with hearing or visual impairments in reaching their full potential.

HEARING IMPAIRMENT

Hearing plays a central role in the development of language and social skills. Hearing impairment too often remains undetected during critical early developmental stages.[1] The median age of diagnosis for severe or profound hearing loss is 2 to 2.5 years, by which time the child will have been denied many opportunities for language development.[2] Infants and young children are also vulnerable to the detrimental effects of milder degrees of hearing loss, such as can be associated with persistent otitis media with middle ear effusion.[3] C. Everett Koop, while Surgeon General, set a goal of diagnosing hearing loss in all affected children before the age of 12 months, and health professionals should be alert to risk factors and knowledgeable regarding the causes and consequences of hearing impairment.[2]

Definitions and terminology

Hearing impairment can be classified by a variety of dimensions, based on degree, type, cause, and age of onset.[4] Hearing loss can occur at differ-

457

ing frequencies. The frequency (or pitch) of speech sounds ranges from about 500 hertz (Hz)(vowel sounds and certain consonant sounds such as "m" and "b" are of lower frequency) to 4000 Hz (consonants such as "s" and "f").[5] Degrees of hearing loss are usually categorized by an average across these frequencies. The loudness or intensity of sound is measured in decibels (dB). While the threshold for mild hearing impairment has been defined as 25 dB, any loss above 15 dB can potentially influence speech perception in young children.

Categorizations of degree of hearing loss have been developed and published by various organizations. The box below outlines the range from mild through moderate to severe and profound hearing loss and summarizes the attendant functional impairment.[5] Those with hearing loss up to 70 dB are sometimes referred to as "hard of hearing" and in the 70 to 90 dB range as having "partial hearing." Deafness[11] denotes a hearing loss of greater than 90 dB (profound), resulting in an inability to distinguish elements of spoken language. Hearing loss can also be categorized in the following way:

1. *Conductive hearing loss* follows an interruption of the mechanical elements required for the transduction of sound waves in air into hydraulic waves in the inner ear. These elements include the pinna, external ear canal, tympanic membrane, and the middle ear ossicles connecting to the oval window. Accumulation of fluid in the middle ear secondary to otitis media is the most common cause of conduc-

---

DEGREES OF HEARING LOSS, ASSOCIATED FUNCTIONAL IMPAIRMENT, AND INTERVENTIONS

- *Mild (26 to 40 dB):* Difficulty with soft spoken speech. Preferential seating in class, amplification.
- *Moderate (41 to 55 dB):* Able to understand speech only when short distance (3 to 5 feet) from source. Hearing aids.
- *Moderate to severe (56 to 70 dB):* Only able to hear loud speech a short distance from source. Hearing aids, language therapy, and educational interventions.
- *Severe (71 to 90 dB):* May hear loud speech or a shout at 1 foot and may distinguish vowels, but have trouble, even with hearing aids, distinguishing consonants. Hearing aids, auditory training, individualized language and educational interventions.
- *Profound (greater than 90 dB):* Auditory channel cannot serve as primary mode of communication. Primarily reliant on visual perception for communication; potential benefit from cochlear implant.

tive hearing loss, and the impairment is more marked in the lower frequency ranges. Conductive hearing loss is usually limited to 50 dB, as sounds louder than this are conducted directly via bone to the cochlea.

2. *Sensorineural hearing loss* denotes involvement of the cochlea or the neural connections to the auditory cortex via the eighth cranial nerve and central pathways. Severe or profound hearing loss is always sensorineural, and higher frequency sounds are usually most affected. Frequently, there is a combination of several types of hearing loss, termed a *mixed* hearing loss. Rarely, hearing impairment can occur centrally at the cortical level with difficulty related to auditory perception or discrimination.

3. *Congenital* hearing loss is present at birth.

4. Hearing loss can be *hereditary* (as an isolated condition or part of a syndrome) or *acquired* (such as secondary to congenital infection). Hearing loss of postnatal onset is usually acquired although some forms of hereditary deafness have delayed onset and can be associated with progressive loss.

5. *Prelingual* deafness refers to hearing impairment with onset before acquisition of expressive language (2 to 3 years). Other terms used include *prevocational* (before the onset of work experience) and *late-onset* (in adulthood) deafness.

Severe-to-profound hearing loss afflicts 1 to 2 per 1000 children at birth in developed countries and probably twice that number in developing nations. A further 2 to 3 per 1000 subsequently acquire severe loss.[4] Many more young children experience some degree of conductive hearing loss secondary to otitis media. All clinicians in practice, therefore, will likely have contact with children who have some degree of hearing impairment.

Etiology and pathogenesis

Prenatal. Deafness can be inherited as an autosomally dominant or recessive or X-linked condition and can be an isolated trait or constitute one component of a recognizable syndrome. Malformation syndromes can also be associated with hearing impairment.[6] Table 11-1 outlines some of the more common causes of deafness. Prenatal acquired causes include the congenital infections. Congenital rubella, previously one of the most common causes of congenital deafness, is now rare, but other infections such as congenital cytomegalovirus (CMV) and toxoplasmosis remain signifi-

Table 11-1   Some causes of hearing loss and potential associated health problems

Mode of acquisition	Condition	Potential associated problems
Conductive hearing loss		
Autosomal-dominant in-heritance	Mandibulofacial dyosto-sis (Treacher-Collins)	Cleft palate Coloboma Respiratory problems
Autosomal-recessive in-heritance	Cryptophthalmos syn-drome	Mental retardation
X-linked inheritance	Otopalatodigital syn-drome	Mental deficiency Small stature
Malformation/ deformation conditions	Goldenhar syndrome (hemifacial microsomia)	Microtia
Acquired	Otitis media Tympanic membrane dis-ruption Ossicular dislocation	Vertebral anomalies
Sensorineural hearing loss		
Autosomal-dominant in-heritance	Clinically undifferenti-ated deafness	
	Syndromes:Waardenburg, Alport	Pigmentary anomalies Nephritis
Autosomal-recessive in-heritance	Clinically undifferenti-ated deafness	
	Syndromes: Usher Pendred Jervell and Lange-Nielsen	Retinitis pigmentosa Goiter Cardiac conduction problems (prolonged Q-T interval)
X-linked inheritance	Hunter syndrome	Mental deficiency, slowed growth
Malformation/ deformation conditions	Klippel-Feil syndrome (Wildervanck)	Fusion of cervical verte-brae Congenital heart defects
Acquired prenatal	Maternal infection: ru-bella, cytomegalovirus, toxoplasmosis, syphilis	Cataracts Retinitis Hepatic involvement Cognitive impairment
	Maternal diabetes	
Acquired postnatal	Ototoxins Bacterial meningitis Acoustic injury Tumor	

cant factors. These infections can be asymptomatic apart from the hearing loss or can involve multiple organ systems. The hearing loss can be progressive.

Perinatal. Extremely premature infants are at increased risk of hearing loss because of a variety of factors, including hypoxia, acidosis, hypoglycemia, hyperbilirubinemia, high levels of ambient noise, and ototoxic drugs such as aminoglycosides. It is likely that these influences are additive. Kernicterus is now a much less common condition, but there is still uncertainty as to what levels of bilirubin are harmful in sick premature infants. Neonatal infections, including meningitis, carry a relatively high risk of associated hearing loss.

Postnatal. Bacterial meningitis has been a relatively common cause of sensorineural hearing loss, with this sequela occurring in up to 10% of cases.[7] The introduction of *Haemophilus influenzae* type B immunization has decreased the overall incidence of this infection. However, pneumococcal meningitis, now the more prevalent etiological agent, has a higher incidence of associated neurological complications. Prolonged exposure to loud noise, either environmental or recreational (audio headphones), can damage cochlear hair cells and result in a predominantly high-frequency loss. Certain conditions, such as Down syndrome and cleft palate, are associated with a higher risk of conductive hearing loss.

Clinical manifestations

The obvious manifestations of hearing loss in infants include failure to startle to loud noises or to turn to localize a sound. Toddlers might not respond to requests or instructions or might position themselves closer to sound sources. In most cases, however, hearing impairment is subtle and can quite easily elude detection. Even infants with a profound hearing loss will begin to vocalize before 6 months of age, with delays in further language development only becoming apparent later. Recent investigations have demonstrated that children with severe-to-profound hearing loss do not develop "canonical babbling" (use of discrete syllables such as "ba" "da" "na") by 11 months as is the case in children with normal hearing.[8] Delayed development of speech is a universal symptom of hearing impairment but is unfortunately a late manifestation. Behavioral problems and/or impaired social interactions secondary to hearing problems might be incorrectly ascribed to disorders such as autism, oppositional defiant disorder, or mental retardation.

Developmental impact

There are many determinants of developmental outcome in addition to the most obvious factor—degree of hearing loss.[9] These include the etiology of the hearing impairment, quality of early communication, and the diversity of social experience among others.[9] Children who have had the opportunity to acquire language before losing their hearing are more likely to be able to communicate orally than those with deafness of prelingual onset. Deaf children born into families with other deaf members benefit from earlier adaptation and effort to promote communication.[10] Other developmental problems associated with hearing impairment can include visual impairment, neuromotor difficulties, seizure disorders, and learning disabilities. These have been reported in up to 30% of children with deafness, especially those with acquired causes such as congenital infections or extreme prematurity, which reflect more diffuse damage to the central nervous system. Although the overall prevalence of attention deficits does not appear to be increased in hearing-impaired children, certain subgroups such as those with acquired deafness do appear to be at increased risk.[11]

Motor development. While motor milestones are generally reached within the expected age ranges, some deaf children will experience difficulties with balance and gross motor coordination secondary to vestibular dysfunction.[12] These difficulties can usually be traced to the causes of deafness, such as meningitis with labyrinthal injury. Fine motor skills are well practiced in children using sign language.

Language development. Even profoundly deaf children will coo and babble during the first year of life. Depending on the degree of hearing loss, subsequent spoken language skill development will be impeded to a greater or lesser degree. Early diagnosis is crucial to enable development of alternate forms of communication, including sign language. In general, deaf children of deaf parents show earlier, more normal language development than deaf children whose parents do not have hearing impairment.[9] American Sign Language (ASL) is viewed by the deaf Americans who use it as a primary language, which is equal to English as a natural language.[13]

Cognitive development. Measuring intelligence in deaf children is challenging and prone to inaccuracy because of the heavy emphasis on reading and language abilities in the majority of standarized intelligence tests. In general, the performance of deaf children on nonverbal measures of intelligence falls in the average range.[9,13] Academic achievement levels are much lower, however. As a group, deaf high school graduates at 18 years of age are only reading at a third to fourth grade level.[9] Math skills are somewhat better, at an average 7th grade level. Debate continues on the role of standard language in fixing ideas and facilitating abstract thought. Deaf children, while often being described as concrete and rigid in their thinking, are reported to have creative abilities equal to hearing children.[13]

Social and emotional development. Reports of the social skill development of deaf children are also prone to bias because of the influence of language limitations and the tendency of parents to be overprotective. Deaf children have been described as socially immature with a tendency to be egocentric. An increased frequency of impulsivity has also been described, although this might also reflect acquired patterns of social interaction and response (such as somtimes having to touch people to get their attention) rather than specific deficits in internal controls.[13]

Evaluation

The key to an optimal outcome for the child with a hearing impairment is early diagnosis and intervention. There have been recent recommendations promoting universal screening of all newborns for hearing loss.[2] The use of a "high-risk register" was previously promoted to identify those children at most significant risk for hearing loss. The factors recommended by the Joint Committee on Infant Hearing in 1990 have been revised and expanded in a 1994 position statement.[2] These "risk factors" are:

1. *Neonates (birth through 28 days):* Family history of hereditary childhood sensorineural hearing loss; in utero infection associated with hearing loss; presence of craniofacial anomalies; birth weight <1500 g; neonatal jaundice at a serum level requiring exchange transfusion; ototoxic medications; bacterial meningitis; evidence of severely depressed physiological status at birth (e.g., Apgar score 0 to 4 at 1 minute or 0 to 6 at 5 minutes); mechanical ventilation lasting 5 days or longer; physical findings of syndrome known to be associated with hearing loss.

2. *Infants (age 29 days through 2 years) with certain health conditions that require re-screening of hearing:* Parent/caregiver concern regarding hearing, speech, language, and/or developmental delay; bacterial meningitis and other infections associated with hearing loss; head trauma associated with loss of consciousness or skull fracture; stigmata of a syndrome associated with sensorineural and/or conductive hearing loss; ototoxic medications; recurrent or persistent otitis media with effusion for at least 3 months.

3. *Infants (age 29 days through 3 years) who require periodic monitoring of hearing:* Those with a family history of hereditary childhood hearing loss; in utero infections such as cytomegalovirus, rubella, syphilis, herpes, or toxoplasmosis; neurofibromatosis, type II; recurrent or persistent otitis media with effusion; anatomical deformities and other disorders that affect eustachian tube function; neurodegenerative disorders.

Because only 50% of infants or young children with profound hearing loss will manifest one of the risk factors at birth, there have been renewed efforts to promote universal screening of newborns for hearing loss. A National Institutes of Health Consensus panel made this recommendation in a 1993 statement, and in 1994 the concept was endorsed by the Joint Committee on Infant Hearing.[2,14] It is recognized that there are many hurdles to overcome in implementing the ideal of universal screening, and such recommendations have evoked some controversy. In the meantime, clinicians must be alert to parental concerns regarding a child's hearing, delays in language development, or significant articulation deficits. Language development can be monitored by instruments such as the Early Language Milestone Scale or the Clinical Linguistic Milestone Scale.[15,16] The second edition of the Denver Developmental Scale incorporates an expanded language section, which is also helpful in this regard.[17] In children with otitis media with persistent middle ear effusion, the level of hearing loss should be documented and monitored closely. Perfunctory assessments of hearing in a clinic setting can be misleading. Response to a bell, hand clap, or other loud sound does not rule out milder levels of hearing loss and does not distinguish hearing at various frequencies. If there is any question of hearing impairment, the child should be referred for formal audiological evaluation.

Hearing can be assessed accurately in children at any age. For younger infants and those who cannot or will not cooperate, auditory brainstem-evoked response (ABR) testing is accurate and reliable and can also detect unilateral loss. A click is introduced at the external canal and the transmission of the low energy–evoked potential through the brainstem pathways to the auditory cortex is recorded by means of scalp electrodes. This test does not measure how the sound is being interpreted and processed. Automated ABR tests (where responses are interpreted by computer and reported as "pass" or "fail") are being used more frequently, especially in newborn intensive care nurseries.

A relatively new method of screening for hearing loss in neonates and infants is the technique of evoked otoacoustic emissions (EOAE). EOAE are a form of acoustic energy produced by active movements of the outer hair cells of the cochlea in response to sound. EOAE testing entails the introduction of a click via a probe in the ear canal with measurement of the emissions from the inner ear by a microphone. This technique is relatively simple and highly sensitive but is less specific than ABR testing. Therefore ABR testing has been recommended as a second-stage test for babies failing EOAE screening.[2]

By 6 months, behavioral audiometry is possible using conditioned responses to speech or tones from speakers in a soundproof booth. This method relies heavily on the experience, skill, and patience of the audiologist. More accurate measurement of response to pure tones or speech in each ear becomes possible as older children accept headphones and are able to respond to instructions.

Tympanometry measures acoustic energy passed through the middle ear system (admittance) or reflected back (impedance). Mobility of the tympanic membrane and middle ear pressure can be gauged. This technique is very helpful in the assessment of middle ear effusions. The presence of the acoustic reflex (contraction of the stapedius muscle in response to sounds of greater than 70 dB) confirms the presence of hearing but is not sensitive to lesser degrees of hearing loss.

When hearing loss has been identified, further medical assessment is necessary.[18] In children with sensorineural hearing loss, it is essential to rule out any associated conductive component that could be treated relatively easily but which could exaggerate the loss. A detailed general physical examination should include pneumatic otoscopy and tests of vestibular function. Comprehensive evaluation is important to look for associated disabilities. For example, unexplained fainting spells in a deaf child might signal a cardiac conduction defect (long Q-T interval) of Jervell and Lange-Nielsen syndrome. Other associated findings are listed in Table 11-1. Ophthalmological evaluation is also essential to rule out conditions such as retinitis pigmentosa with progressive loss of vision, that occurs in children with Usher syndrome. Chorioretinitis accompanies some of the congenital infections, and this finding might help establish an etiological diagnosis. Routine evaluation for refractive errors is important to ensure optimal vision for children who are reliant on visual input for communication and learning.

Special investigations should be dictated by the specific clinical characteristics of each case and might include tests of renal function or metabolic function, immunological testing, or an electrocardiogram (ECG). A computed tomographic (CT) scan of the temporal bone can help to identify any anatomical abnormalities of the inner ear, and a brain scan might also reveal calcifications, indicating congenital infection. It is important to recognize that certain forms of hearing loss can be progressive, and the level of hearing loss should be re-evaluated routinely on an annual basis.

Management

Treatment of hearing impairment should incorporate prevention activities. These should occur at a primary level (genetic counseling, limiting and monitoring use of ototoxic medications, etc.), a secondary level (alleviating complications of prematurity), and a tertiary level (early diagnosis to limit secondary disabilities). Comprehensive management should include attention to medical treatment, language and educational interventions, use of assistive devices, and support and advocacy. The primary care clinician is in an excellent position to facilitate and coordinate many of these interventions. Referral to an audiologist is necessary for formal audiological testing as well as recommendations and follow-up for amplification devices. Otolaryngologists will be able to assess middle ear function and to evaluate for any surgically correctable causes of hearing loss.

Management of persistent middle ear effusions gives rise to controversy. In general, the presence of bilateral effusions with documented bilateral hearing loss for a total of 4 to 6 months is an indication for the insertion of tympanostomy tubes.[19] Although this treatment improves hearing in the short term, long-term benefits are less well established.

When a significant hearing loss has been discovered, the child should be fitted with a *hearing aid* as soon as possible. A variety of forms of amplification are available. Traditional body-worn receivers are used primarily by younger children and have generally been replaced by behind-the-ear aids or units that are self-contained in a mold within the pinna and external canal. Technological advances have resulted in devices that amplify sounds differentially in the frequency spectra most affected in the individual. Bone conduction devices are used for children with malformations of the external canal. A newer form of hearing augmentation for children with profound loss is the cochlear implant.[20] This consists of an external microphone and amplifier with an induction coil set in the temporal bone and connected to a multichannel electrode placed within the cochlea. While this treatment is of well-established benefit in adults with postlingual hearing loss, there is a need for careful screening of which children with congenital deafness will benefit. Implants do not necessarily enable discrimination of speech sounds but can facilitate the appreciation of environmental sounds and have been reported to improve language skills in certain children.[20] Children who use any form of amplification device need auditory training to help them understand the meaning of the newly amplified sounds.

Vibrotactile devices that present auditory stimuli as patterns on the skin are also being developed. Additional assistive devices include telecommunication devices for the deaf (TDD), closed captioning of television, and adapted warning devices, such as flickering lights to indicate a ringing alarm or telephone.[5]

The key to successful outcome is early intervention to promote language development. The child with profound hearing loss, his or her parents, and other caregivers should receive professional assistance in establishing a functional system of communication as soon as possible. There are many differing opinions regarding the most appropriate communication and instructional techniques. Options include sign language (manual communication), lip reading and use of speech (oral communication), or a combination (total communication). Children with profound hearing loss usually experience great difficulty learning to read lips and to speak fluently and are best served by early exposure to visual and manual forms of communication such as sign language. However, children with milder degrees of loss may be better able to communicate with those of normal hearing by development of their oral language skills. Educational interventions should be tailored to the individual needs of each child. Options range from use of interpreters in a regular school and classroom to special programs in a regular school or enrollment in a school for the deaf.[21] Children with hearing impairment must have the opportunity for full participation in academic and social activities. The optimal school setting to achieve this goal depends on individual characteristics of the child and the educational system in that geographical region. The clinician should be familiar with local educational resources, including institutions of higher learning for the deaf such as Gallaudet University and the National Technical Institute for the Deaf.

The primary care clinician is a vital source of information and support for families of children with severe hearing impairment. There are often a number of specialists involved, and parents may receive conflicting advice regarding both medical and educational interventions deemed necessary for the child. They face numerous stresses, including adjustment to the diagnosis and the need to learn new forms of communication. There are many ways in which they can be helped. The role of the clinician in promoting optimal development in hearing impaired children is discussed at the end of the section on visual impairment.

VISUAL IMPAIRMENT

In sighted children, vision is a powerful organizer of important information about the environment. Unlike hearing, which operates primarily through discontinuous, sequential bits of information, visual information is both continuous and simultaneous. This allows the child to integrate information from multiple sensory inputs almost instantaneously. Sighted infants' early incidental and sensorimotor learning about their world occurs largely through this automatic and constant visual channel as they first passively, and then more actively, interact with nearby people and objects. For children who are significantly visually impaired, reliance on any residual vision—as well as hearing, touch, and, to a lesser degree, smell—can still provide essential information about the environment. Often the blindness itself is not as handicapping as the uninformed or negative attitudes of others and the experiential deprivation that often inadvertently occurs.

Definitions and terminology

Legal blindness refers to a central visual acuity of 20/200 or less in the better eye with corrective lenses or a restriction in the visual field of 20 degrees or less in the better eye. However, the term *"blindness"* is often a misnomer because roughly 75% of legally blind individuals have some residual, useful visual function. Roughly 50% of legally blind adults have sufficient vision to read large print.[22] Students are often classified as *educationally visually impaired* if their central acuity is 20/70 or worse; they usually require and are eligible for at least some modification of educational materials in the classroom. For children with extremely limited vision (below about 20/400), some ophthalmologists use more functional designations—e.g., *hand motion* or *object perception* (child can detect presence and motion of nearby large objects), *light projection* (child can determine the direction of a light source), *light perception* (child can notice whether or not there is light present), and *no light perception* (total blindness). Children who have some residual vision are sometimes also said to have *low vision*. *Functional vision* refers to qualities of vision which, in addition to acuity, are important in determining how efficiently residual vision is used. For example, two children may have identical distance visual acuities (e.g., 20/400), but, because of other aspects of functional vision, one child may be able to read large print, while for the other, Braille may be the most efficient mode of reading.

Prevalence, etiologies, and pathogenesis

Lack of uniform classification criteria, ascertainment biases (underestimates of visually impaired children who are multiply handicapped), and variability in reporting systems have limited the validity of prevalence data. Estimates of the prevalence of blindness and severe visual impairment range from 2 to 10 per 10,000 children.[23,24] If lesser degrees of visual impairment are included, significantly more children are affected.

In North America and Europe, approximately half of all congenital and late-onset blindness is of genetic origin, including many types of cataracts, albinism, and a variety of retinal dystrophies.[23] Other congenital causes include intrauterine infections (rubella, CMV, and toxoplasmosis) and malformations and/or atrophy of the eye (coloboma, micro- or anophthalmia), the optic nerve (optic nerve hypoplasia, optic atrophy), and the brain. Sometimes such malformations are associated with chromosomal abnormalities (e.g., trisomy 13, trisomy 21) or other syndromes (CHARGE association, see p. 476). Major perinatal causes of visual impairment include hypoxic-ischemic damage to cortical visual pathways and the retinopathy of prematurity (ROP). Following the epidemic of blindness caused by ROP in the early 1950s, there was an initial dramatic decrease in its prevalence for nearly two decades. But with technological advances permitting the survival of increasingly immature preterm infants, the prevalence of ROP has increased again in recent years, accounting for approximately 400 to 500 significantly visually impaired infants each year.[25] Major causes of acquired or later-onset visual impairment include tumors such as retinoblastoma, genetic conditions such as retinitis pigmentosa, central nervous system infections including bacterial meningitis, accidental head and eye trauma, and child abuse (particularly shaking injuries). Amblyopia resulting from prolonged strabismus (ocular misalignment) or anisometropia (a significant difference in the refractive error between the two eyes) is another important and often preventable cause of acquired visual impairment.

Approximately 30% to 70% of children with severe visual impairment also have other disabilities, including cerebral palsy, mental retardation, autism, hearing impairment, and epilepsy.[24,26] The clinician needs to systematically check visual function in children who have other disabilities and to remember to consider the possibility of multiple handicaps in a child with obvious visual impairment. Table 11-2 shows the range of developmental disabilities that can accompany major causes of childhood visual impairment.

Clinical manifestations

In contrast to most children with hearing impairments who elude detection until well after their first birthday, many children with significant visual impairment are brought to the clinician's attention during the first year of life. By the time the infant is 3 to 6 months, parents are usually

Table 11-2   Some conditions often associated with both severe visual impairment and other developmental disabilities

Conditions/causes	Possible eye problems	Associated disabilities
Primary abnormal prenatal development of brain (e.g., congenital hydrocephalus, absence of corpus callosum, congenital microcephaly, etc.)	Cortical visual impairment Optic atrophy Nystagmus Anophthalmia Microphthalmia	Mental retardation Cerebral palsy Behavioral problems Epilepsy
Prenatal exposure to maternal viral infections (e.g., rubella, cytomegalovirus [CMV], toxoplasmosis, herpes)	Cataracts Retinopathy Microphthalmia Glaucoma Chorioretinitis	Hearing impairment Mental retardation Behavioral problems Epilepsy
Genetic and other multisystem syndromes (e.g., Hurler, Tay Sachs, Marfan, Lowe, Zellweger, Refsum, Usher syndromes, CHARGE association, etc.)	Cataracts Glaucoma Ectopic lens Corneal clouding Optic atrophy Retinitis pigmentosa Coloboma	Hearing impairment Mental retardation Behavioral problems Epilepsy Renal problems Poor growth
Chromosomal abnormalities (e.g., Down syndrome [trisomy 21], trisomy 13, cri-du-chat syndrome [partial absence of short arm of chromosome 5])	Coloboma Microphthalmia Cataracts Corneal clouding Strabismus	Mental retardation Behavioral problems Epilepsy Heart problems Cleft palate Poor growth
Other congenital opthalmological syndromes of uncertain etiology (e.g., Leber's, optic nerve hypoplasia, etc.)	Retinal dysfunction Optic nerve hypoplasia Coloboma Corneal abnormalities	Mental retardation Poor growth Hormone problems
	Retinopathy of prematurity (ROP, RLF) Secondary glaucoma Strabismus Cortical visual impairment	Mental retardation Cerebral palsy Hydrocephalus Respiratory problems Poor growth
Bacterial meningitis (e.g., *Haemophilus influenzae*, group B strep, meningococcal, pneumococcal)	Cortical visual impairment Strabismus Optic atrophy	Mental retardation Cerebral palsy Hydrocephalus Epilepsy Behavioral problems Hearing impairment
Head trauma (e.g., child abuse, auto accident, near-drowning)	Cortical visual impairment Strabismus Optic atrophy Retinal hemorrhage	Mental retardation Cerebral palsy Behavioral problems Epilepsy

From Teplin SW: Visual impairment in infants and young children, *Infants Young Child* 8:18-51, 1995, Aspen Publishers.

quick to notice their infant's poor visual attention to objects or people and may readily detect such important opthalmological signs as nystagmus, "lazy eye" (strabismus), and excessive tearing in the absence of crying. The presence of sensory nystagmus in a visually impaired child is a fairly reliable sign that the visual impairment was of very early onset, and the etiology is ocular and not cortical.[27] Other signs of potentially significant visual impairment include lack of accurate reaching for objects by 6 months, haziness of the cornea, persisting photophobia, persistent conjunctival erythema, asymmetry of pupillary size, and abnormalities of pupillary shape ("keyhole" defect indicating a coloboma of the iris).

A variety of behavioral manifestations of children with severe visual impairments may also be apparent to parents and clinicians. Common behaviors include stereotyped movements, such as rocking, hand-flapping, rhythmic head or body swaying, and prolongation of echolalic speech patterns. A long-term follow-up study of severely impaired children showed that many of these stereotypical behaviors had been spontaneously abandoned by the time of adulthood.[28] Light-gazing and brief, sideways-glancing at objects and people seem to be more characteristic of children with cortical visual impairment.[28] Eye-pressing, on the other hand, is more typical of children with retinal disorders.[29] Tactile defensiveness (an excessive sensitivity and resistance to touching certain textures) is sometimes a problem, posing the threat of further sensory deprivation. This can also affect feeding practices, as many blind children go through a prolonged phase of tolerating only soft foods, rejecting many harder textured foods that require chewing.

Developmental impact

Because of the extreme heterogeneity of the population of children with severe visual impairment, particularly when such a large proportion have additional developmental disabilities, generalizations about developmental sequences may have very little application to the individual child. Factors influencing development are similar to those related to children with hearing loss and include specific etiology of the visual impairment, severity of the visual impairment, age of onset (congenital vs. acquired after several years of age), presence of additional disabilities and/or chronic illness, individual temperamental characteristics, and the psychosocial milieu in which the child is raised. With the aid of parents and other caregivers who actively introduce the child to many facets of his or her environment, using any intact sensory modalities, young blind children can often progress through the same developmental phases and often on similar timetables as their sighted peers. However, some important qualitative and sequential differences between developmental patterns of blind and sighted children are often apparent.

Motor development. In the absence of specific motoric disabilities, such as cerebral palsy, many severely visually impaired young children can achieve postural milestones, such as sitting and standing, on roughly the same timetable as sighted infants. Skills involving movement through space, such as crawling and walking, are often delayed. The visually impaired young child must first "figure out" through repeated experience that the sounds he or she hears represent objects that can be touched if he or she moves toward that sound. Mild hypotonia and the element of insecurity—having to move through "unknown" space—may also impede motivation to move.[30] Even after walking is achieved, many severely visually impaired children without other disabilities have continuing motor difficulties related to low muscle tone and decreased balance, poor posture, and a broad-based, toe-out gait. Early intervention and ongoing feedback about posture from parents, physical therapists, and orientation and mobility teachers can minimize these habitual motor patterns.

Cognitive development. Acquisition of concepts and knowledge about the environment is often "delayed" compared to norms for sighted children, but several studies have documented a wide variability in the mastery, for example, of such cognitive achievements as understanding object permanence. There tends to be more concreteness and less abstractness in visually impaired children's description of objects, but even this reveals wide variability among samples of visually impaired children.[31] In the absence of associated learning problems and given the appropriate learning opportunities, severely visually impaired children can eventually master the same general concepts as do their sighted peers.

Language development. Language serves as a critical interface between the severely visually impaired child and his or her environment. Early acquisition of vocabulary tends to be on a timetable similar to that of sighted infants, but, during the second year, some qualitative differences often emerge. The types of words most frequently used focus more on objects and people and less on actions. Some children succeed in rote-learning and using many words, but experiential limitations may render these words with little if any true meaning for the child (so called "verbalism").[32] Similarly, there may also be a prolonged phase of echolalia or parroting of what the child has heard and confusion at younger ages about "I" vs. "you." By providing meaningful experience to match the child's words, caretakers can facilitate stronger cognitive connections between words and their meanings.

Social and emotional development. Several classic signs of emotional attachment for the visually impaired generally emerge on a similar timetable as those for sighted peers. For example, recognition of a parent's voice and demonstration of anxiety when held by a stranger are strong indicators of a visually impaired infant's attachment. Nevertheless, babies with visual handicaps may be at increased risk for attachment disorders. Smiling in visually impaired infants is often less easily elicited and more fleeting than for sighted babies. This, in addition to their lack of eye contact, delayed reaching out, and tendency to be passive may falsely connote emotional distance or cognitive slowness to parents who are already emotionally vulnerable themselves. Parents' feelings of guilt, stress, and inadequacy may lead to lowered expectations for their infant's development. For some parents who lack adequate social supports or information, this combination of miscues between parent and child can lead to inadvertent parental emotional withdrawal or overprotectiveness.

Another aspect of social development is the child's ability to engage in social and representational play. Blind preschool children tend to be more passive in their play and less likely to initiate social interactions during play than their sighted peers. Often a visually impaired child is the only one in his or her school to have such special needs. In addition to the importance of learning how to interact with his or her sighted peers in a "sighted world," the visually impaired child's self-esteem can be enhanced by opportunities to meet other children with similar disabilities.

Evaluation

Although it will be important for an ophthalmologist to do the detailed assessment of a child's eyes and visual function, the American Academy of Pediatrics (AAP) recommends that the primary care clinician, as part of routine continuing care of children, perform screening for visual acuity and to detect significant eye diseases and problems of ocular alignment.[33] Despite this recommendation, many problems exist with vision and eye screening programs in primary care settings.[34]

Soliciting parents' descriptions of and concerns about a child's visual behavior is a critical part of the assessment. Physical examination techniques further define the existence and nature of any visual problem. In the newborn period, checking for symmetrical red reflexes and pupillary shape and response to light are important. Most newborns with normal vision are capable of limited visual tracking of slow-moving, high-contrast targets about 8 to 12 inches from their faces during alert periods. By the time an infant is 2 to 4 months of age, parental reports of social smiling and nearly automatic visual tracking of people and bright objects should be elicited as well as observations of persistent in- or out-turning of one or both eyes. Examination should include elicitation of a social smile, visual tracking of the examiner's face and/or a bright toy across the infant's visual field, observations of pupillary light reactions, checking for red reflexes, and at least brief glimpses of the fundi. By 6 to 8 months, observations of an infant's reaching for and attempted grasping of nearby small objects (1-mm cake sprinkle, 6-mm candy bead, 1-cm Cheerio, 1-inch red cube, etc.) as well as obvious reactions to more distant people or large objects can further document visual function. Visually searching for a silently dropped object (the red yarn in the Denver Developmental Screening Test kit) is also notable after about 5 to 6 months. Screening for visual acuity, alignment of the eyes (using the cover-uncover test), and ocular diseases at 4 to 6 months is critical for timely detection of conditions such as strabismus and cataracts, which, if left untreated, can eventually lead to amblyopic visual loss.[35]

It is important for each primary care clinician to have a close working relationship with an ophthalmologist who is comfortable in examining infants and children and is knowledgeable regarding their eye problems. However, many ophthalmologists have little or no training in children's development and should not necessarily be expected to know how to guide or support parents of severely visually impaired children regarding interventions to promote optimal development.

A child with severe visual impairment, just like one with any other type of developmental disability, needs to have an initial interdisciplinary evaluation as the foundation of an intervention plan, as specified by the Individuals with Disabilities Education Act (IDEA). Knowledge of the ophthalmologist's diagnosis and visual acuity data are critical for such an evaluation but may be insufficient to adequately describe important qualitative aspects of the child's day-to-day visual functioning, such as the extent to which sounds are distracting, whether the child's medications affect visual function, and how the ambient lighting and contrast of the toys or written materials affect the child's performance. Having on the assessment team a person with expertise and experience in working with children with severe visual impairments will help ensure that cognitive and other types of testing are done in a way that takes advantage of the child's best use of any residual vision and does not unfairly bias the results on the basis of the visual impairment.

Management

Following the initial ophthalmological and developmental evaluations, intervention strategies can be planned, with professionals and parents collaborating on goals, priorities, and the optimal use of community and educational resources. Early intervention service systems vary from state to state; therefore, clinicians need to be aware of how and to whom to make referrals and how they can participate in the planning and monitoring process.

As the child passes from preschool to school age, families, eye-care specialists, and child educators must usually face a series of educational decisions.[36] What will be the most appropriate classroom setting (residential school vs. self-contained class vs. resource class vs. "inclusion" in the regular classroom)? What visual and/or technological aids are most helpful and most acceptable to the child (large print, closed circuit TV, hand-held magnifier, stand-magnifier, magic marker rather than pencil, etc.)?

Role of the clinician in promoting optimal development in hearing and/or visually impaired children. In addition to the factors unique to the individual, there are a number of ways in which the clinician can promote optimal development.[37] The child should be treated as an average child as much as possible, avoiding overprotection. The clinician can provide emotional support for the parents, encourage discussion of their child's development, and explore the impact on siblings. The clinician should become knowledgeable about, and refer to, community resources (developmental preschools, interdisciplinary evaluation centers, state agencies, and early intervention programs for infants). Communication should be maintained with the programs in which the patient participates, and the clinician should be available to clarify to teachers and parents the practical, functional implications of the child's impairment(s). The clinician can help the family prepare for the child's enrollment in school and should encourage parents' early exploration of the availability of special classrooms, teachers, and materials. The clinician can also help put families in contact with relevant parent support groups and can refer them to written materials, books, and pamphlets that will provide further information and ideas for home activities and adapted toys. The clinician can thus be a knowledgeable "consumer guide" as well as an advocate for the child and family.

Deaf-blindness (combined hearing and visual impairments)

A child who is deaf-blind has a combination of visual and auditory impairment that results in multi-sensory deprivation and renders inadequate the traditional approaches to child-rearing used to alleviate the handicaps of blindness, deafness, or retardation.[38]

In the United States, an estimated 10,000 deaf-blind children, from birth to 21 years of age, received special education services in schools during 1994, and about 85% had additional disabilities, most commonly mental retardation, speech impairments, and orthopedic handicaps.[39]

The primary causes of deaf-blindness include conditions related to prematurity and/or perinatal hypoxic-ischemic injury (retinopathy of prematurity combined with central nervous system damage), exposure to intrauterine infections (rubella, CMV), syndromes of uncertain etiology (CHARGE association*), postnatal infections (meningitis), head injuries (both accidental and those due to child abuse), and genetic conditions such as Cockayne, Stickler, Usher, and Laurence-Moon-Biedl syndromes.

The usual external stimuli that serve as motivators for mobility, communication, and learning about the environment are beyond access or are distorted for these children, limiting their initial awareness to the confines of their "random reach."[40]

Because traditional tests of vision, hearing, and cognitive abilities are frequently inappropriate in the evaluation of such children, medical and educational specialists who are trained and experienced with this population need to be involved early on in the diagnostic and intervention-planning phases of care. When a child has a combination of impairments of both the auditory and visual channels, appropriate interventions need to address the important areas of communication, socialization, concept formation, and mobility.[41]

Recently, the use of mechanical or electrical vibrotactile devices has been shown to be a feasible type of assistive technology for children who are deaf-blind.[41]

For the child who loses the second sensory function adventitiously (the child with Usher syndrome who is deaf from birth but only gradually loses vision from retinitis pigmentosa as adolescence approaches), helping the child and family cope with the emotional adjustments to this loss will be critical.

The clinician also needs to guard against an unfounded bias in assuming that the child with deaf-blindness must be "profoundly retarded" and/or "unable to learn."

---

*CHARGE association—*C*oloboma, *H*eart disease, *A*tresia choanae, *R*etarded growth, *G*enital anomalies, *E*ar anomalies.

REFERENCES

1. Coplan J: Deafness: ever heard of it? Delayed recognition of permanent hearing loss, *Pediatrics* 79:206, 1987.
2. Joint Committee on Infant Hearing 1994: Position statement, *Pediatrics* 95(1):152-156, 1994.
3. Roberts JE, Burchinal MR, Medley LP, Zeisel SA, et al: Otitis media, hearing sensitivity, and maternal responsiveness in relation to language during infancy, *J Pediatr* 126:481-489, 1995.
4. Davidson J, Hyde ML, Alberti PW: Epidemiologic patterns in childhood hearing loss, *Int J Ped Otorhinolaryngol* 17(3):239, 1989.
5. Kelly DP: Hearing impairment. In Levine MD, Carey WB, Crocker AC, editors: *Developmental-behavioral pediatrics*, ed 2, Philadelphia, 1992, WB Saunders.
6. Fraser GR: *The causes of profound deafness in childhood*, London, 1976, Bailliere Tindall.
7. Dodge P, Davis H, Feigin R, et al: Prospective evaluation of hearing loss as a sequela of acute bacterial meningitis, *N Engl J Med* 311:869-874, 1984.
8. Eilers RE, Kimbrough Oller D: Infant vocalizations and the early diagnosis of severe hearing impairment, *J Pediatr* 124:199-203, 1994.
9. Marschak M: *Psychological development of deaf children*, New York, 1993, Oxford University Press.
10. Meadow KP: *Deafness and child development*, Berkeley, CA, 1980, University of California Press.
11. Kelly DP, Kelly BJ, Jones ML, Moulton NJ, et al: Attention deficits in children and adolescents with hearing loss: a survey, *Am J Dis Child* 147:737-741, 1993.
12. Butterfield SA, Erving WF: Influence of age, sex, etiology, and hearing loss on balance performance by deaf children, *Percept Motor Skill* 62:653-659, 1986.
13. Lane H: Is there a "psychology of the deaf"? *Except Child* 55(1):7-19, 1988.
14. National Institutes of Health: *Early identification of hearing loss in infants and young children: Consensus Development Conference on Early Identification of Hearing Loss in Infants and Young Children*, Bethesda, MD, 1993, National Institutes of Health.
15. Coplan J: *The Early Language Milestone Scale*, Tulsa, OK, 1987, Modern Education.
16. Capute AJ, Shapiro BK, Wachtel RC, et al: The Clinical Linguistic and Auditory Milestone Scale (CLAMS) identification of cognitive deficits in motor-delayed children, *Am J Dis Child* 140:694, 1986.
17. Frankenberg WK, Dodds JB: *Denver Developmental Screening Test II*, Denver, 1990, Denver Developmental Materials.
18. Rapin I: Hearing disorders, *Pediatr Rev* 14:43, 1993.
19. The Otitis Media Guideline Panel: Managing otitis media with effusion in young children, *Pediatrics* 94(5):766-773, 1994.
20. Waltzman SB, Cohen NL, Shapiro WH: Use of a multichannel cochlear implant in the congenitally and prelingually deaf population, *Laryngoscope* 102:395-399, 1992.
21. Moores DF: *Educating the Deaf*, ed 3, Boston, 1987, Houghton Mifflin.
22. Buncic JR: The blind child, *Pediatr Clin North Am* 34:1403-1414, 1987.
23. Baird G, Moore AT: Epidemiology. In Fielder AR, Best AB, Bax MCO, editors: *The management of visual impairment in childhood*, London, 1993, MacKeith Press.
24. Robinson CG: Causes, ocular disorders, associated handicaps, and incidence and prevalence of blindness in childhood. In Jan J, Freeman R, Scott E, editors: *Visual impairment in children and adolescents*, New York, NY, 1977, Grune & Stratton, pp 27-47.
25. Phelps D: Retinopathy of prematurity, *Pediatr Rev* 16:50-56, 1995.
26. Ferrell K, Trief E, Dietz, et al: The Visually Impaired Infants Research Consortium: first year results, *J Vis Impair Blind* 84:404-410, 1990.

27. Jan JE, Groenveld M: Visual behaviors and adaptations associated with cortical and ocular impairment in children, *J Vis Impair Blind* 87:101-105, 1993.

28. Freeman R, Goetz E, Richards D, et al: Defiers of negative prediction: a 14-year follow-up study of legally blind children, *J Vis Impair Blind* 85:365-370, 1991.

29. Jan JE, McCormick AQ, Scott EP, et al: Eye pressing by visually impaired children, *Dev Med Child Neurol* 25:755-762, 1983.

30. Warren DH: *Blindness in children—an individual differences approach*, Cambridge, 1994, Cambridge University Press, pp 30-55.

31. Warren DH: *Blindness in children—an individual differences approach*, Cambridge, 1994, Cambridge University Press, pp 152-153.

32. Andersen ES, Dunlea A, Kekelis LS: Blind children's language: resolving some differences, *J Child Lang* 11:645-664, 1984.

33. Committee on Practice and Ambulatory Medicine, American Academy of Pediatrics: Vision screening and eye examination in children, *Pediatrics* 77:918-919, 1986.

34. Wasserman RC: Screening for vision problems in pediatric practice, *Pediatr Rev* 1992;13:4-5.

35. Magramm I: Amblyopia: etiology, detection, and treatment, *Pediatr Rev* 13:7-14, 1992.

36. Teplin SW: Developmental issues in the care of visually impaired infants and children, *Pediatr Rounds Growth Nutri Dev* 3(2):1-6, 1994.

37. Teplin SW: Developmental issues in blind infants and children. In Silverman WA, Flynn JT, editors: *Retinopathy of prematurity*, Oxford, 1985, Blackwell, p 286.

38. McInnes JM, Treffry JA: The deaf-blind child. In Jan JE, Freeman RD, Scott EP, editors: *Visual impairment in children and adolescents*, New York, 1977, Grune & Stratton, pp 337-364.

39. Demographics Update: The number of deaf-blind children in the United States, *J Vis Impair Blind News Serv* 89(3):13, 1995.

40. McInnes JM, Treffry JA: *Deaf-blind infants and children—a developmental guide*, Toronto, 1982, University of Toronto Press.

41. MacFarland SZC: Teaching strategies or the van Dijk curricular approach, *J Vis Impair Blind* 89(3):222-228, 1995.

42. Franklin B: Tactile sensory aids for children who are deaf-blind, *Traces (Teaching Research Assistance to Children and Youth Experiencing Sensory Impairments)*, Summer, 1(3):2-3, 1991.

Appendix I

Information and Service Organizations for Those with Hearing Impairment

Alexander Graham Bell Association for the Deaf
3417 Volta Place NW
Washington, DC 20007

American Speech and Hearing Association
10801 Rockville Pike
Rockville, MD 20852

Conference of Executives of American Schools for the Deaf and Convention of American Instructors of the Deaf
5034 Wisconsin Avenue NW
Washington, DC 20016

Council on Education of the Deaf
Clark School for the Deaf
Northampton, MA 01060

Council for Exceptional Children
1920 Association Drive
Reston, VA 22091

Council of Organizations Serving the Deaf
4201 Connecticut Avenue NW
Suite 210
Washington, DC 20008

Deafness Research Foundation
9 East 38th Street
New York, NY 10017

International Association of Parents of the Deaf
814 Thayer Avenue
Silver Spring, MD 20910

National Association of the Deaf
814 Thayer Avenue
Silver Spring, MD 20910

National Association of Hearing and Speech Agencies
919 18th Street NW
Washington, DC 20006

National Committee for Multi-Handicapped Children
239 14th Street
Niagara Falls, NY 14303

National Information Center on Deafness
Gallaudet University
800 Florida Avenue NE
Washington, DC 20002

National Technical Institue for the Deaf
Rochester Institute of Technology
Rochester, New York 14623

Western Institute for the Deaf
215 East 18th Avenue
Vancouver 10, British Columbia
Canada

SUGGESTED READING

Sacks O: *Seeing voices: a journey into the world of the deaf,* Berkeley, CA, 1989, University of
California Press.

Appendix II

Resources and Publications for Parents and Caregivers of Visually Impaired Young Children

BROCHURES, ARTICLES, AND BOOKS

1. Educational booklets (in English and Spanish) from the **Blind Children's Center** (4120 Marathon Street, PO Box 29159, Los Angeles, CA 90029-0159; Phone: [213] 664-2153; Fax [213] 665-3828). Cost is $1 to $3 for each booklet (except *First Steps*).

   Talk To Me: A language guide for parents of young blind children.

   Talk To Me II: Sequel to *Talk To Me.*

   Heart to Heart: Feelings expressed by parents of blind and visually impaired children.

   Move With Me: A guide (for parents) to movement development for visually impaired infants.

   Learning to Play: Play activities for visually impaired preschool children (English only).

   Dancing Cheek to Cheek: Early social, play, and language interactions for visually impaired young children (English only).

   Reaching, Crawling, Walking. . . Orientation and mobility for preschool children who are visually impaired.

   Selecting a Program: A guide for parents of infants and preschoolers with visual impairments.

   First Steps: A handbook for teaching young children who are visually impaired.

2. Booklets from the **American Foundation for the Blind** (11 Penn Plaza, Suite 300, New York, NY 10001; AFB information line: [800] 232-5463; Publication/Video orders: [718] 852-9873).

   Dominguez B, Dominguez J. *Building blocks: foundations for young blind and visually impaired children,* 1991.

   Ferrell KA: *Parenting preschoolers: suggestions for raising young blind and visually impaired children,* 1984.

   Scholl GT, editor: *Foundations of education for blind and visually handicapped children and youth—theory and practice,* 1986.

   Pogrund R, Fazzi D, Lampert J, editors: *Early focus: working with young blind and visually impaired children and their families,* 1992.

481

3. Scott EP, Jan JE, Freeman RD: *Can't your child see?* Baltimore, MD, 1977, University Park Press.

4. Jan J, Freeman R, Scott E: *Visual impairment in children and adolescents,* New York, NY, 1977, Grune & Stratton.

5. Warren DH: *Blindness and children—an individual differences approach,* Cambridge, 1994, Cambridge University Press.

6. Booklets and materials from **Blind Children's Fund** (2875 Northwind Drive, Suite 211, East Lansing, MI 48823-5040; Phone: [517] 333-1725; Fax: [517] 333-1730).
   VIP Newsletter.
   Get a Wiggle On.
   Move It.
   Videos (Collection #1 and Collection #2).

7. Publications from the **American Printing House for the Blind** (PO Box 6085, Louisville, KY 40206-0085, Phone: [502] 895-2405).
   Moore S: *Beginnings: a practical guide for parents and teachers of visually impaired babies* (Catalogue #7-11710-00).
   Parents and visually impaired infants (Catalogue #7-96150-00).

PARENT ORGANIZATIONS AND CORRESPONDENCE COURSES

1. **National Association for Parents of the Visually Impaired (NAPVI)** (PO Box 317, Watertown, MA 02272).

This is a non-profit organization of, by, and for parents committed to providing support to the parents of children who have visual impairments.

2. **The Hadley School for the Blind** (PO Box 299, Winnetka, IL 60093; Phone: [800] 323-4238).

Offers correspondence courses to parents at no charge. Examples: Child Development, Knowing the System, Hope for Parents of Blind Children, The Human Eye, and Introduction to Microcomputers.

Modified with permission, from Teplin SW: Visual impairment in infants and young children, *Infants Young Child* 8:18-51, 1995, Aspen Publishers.

CHAPTER 12

The developmental consequences of prematurity

EDWARD GOLDSON

Since more and more very low birth weight infants (VLBWI) (<1500 g) survive, their care becomes increasingly important to the primary care pediatrician.[1,2] The pediatrician's skills will not only need to expand to meet these infants' quite complex medical needs, but will also need to become more sophisticated to meet the associated developmental and psychological challenges. Children who were once VLBWIs are now in school! In the past pediatricians have been concerned only with the survival of VLBWIs and the medical and developmental sequelae of their pre-, peri-, and post-natal experiences. These remain pressing issues for the neonatologist and primary care physician. However, the affective and cognitive sequelae of very low birth weight are now emerging as significant issues. The purpose of this chapter is to provide a historical overview of the emergence of neonatal intensive care and to examine the relatively short-term as well as long-term outcome of these infants.

HISTORICAL OVERVIEW

It is noteworthy that even though centers for the care of premature infants were developed in the 1950s, these had very little effect on the outcome of VLBWIs, and a mortality rate of about 75% continued to be reported for the next 10 years.[3] Nevertheless, among those infants who did survive, some did relatively well.[4,5] However, it was not until the 1960s with major advances in basic scientific knowledge and technology and more rigorous neonatal intensive care that survival increased. Indeed, it was in 1960 that Alexander Schaffer coined the term *neonatology* to identify the then newly emerging pediatric subspecialty that was to devote itself to the care of the sick, premature, and low birth weight infant.

Two major factors proved to be critical for the advances made later in the care of these infants. The first was an increase in the understanding of fetal and neonatal physiology, which led to advances in technology. Recognition of the significance of maintaining normal body temperature, providing adequate nutrition, and preventing infection[6] led to the development of the early neonatal intensive care nursery. The understanding of the effect of oxygen and its use in the treatment of respiratory distress was also a significant achievement.[7] It is true that an incomplete understanding of the properties of oxygen and its toxicity led to retrolental fibroplasia (RLF) (now called retinopathy of prematurity [ROP]); nevertheless, the introduction of oxygen resulted in the survival of many small infants who, in the past, would have succumbed. Another example of the new understanding of neonatal physiology was the appreciation of the role of bilirubin in the etiology of kernicterus and athetoid cerebral palsy. The association between blood group incompatibilities and hemolytic anemia of the newborn led to the development of RhoGAM and thus led, through prenatal measures, to a marked diminution in the incidence of severe hyperbilirubinemia and kernicterus. A further example was recognition of the need for prompt feeding of the newborn.[8,9] Consequently, nurseries stopped waiting the customary 24 hours before feeding the infant, thus avoiding hypoglycemia and other metabolic disturbances of delayed feeding.

The technology that was developed as a result of this expanded knowledge of physiology played a major role in the survival of the small infant. Although small babies had been ventilated in the 1950s and 1960s, the greatest impact on the small infant was the development of constant positive airway pressure (CPAP), which evolved in response to an understanding of lung and chest wall mechanics.[10] CPAP stabilizes the alveoli, prevents atelectasis, and facilitates respiration. This technique also led to the development of more efficient and effective ventilators and an increased ability to ventilate the very small baby. The development of more sophisticated monitoring systems, including the capability to noninvasively monitor blood gases,[11-14] allowed for better control of oxygenation with the aim of decreasing the incidence of the complications of oxygen therapy. The discovery of phototherapy for the treatment of hyperbilirubinemia decreased the incidence of athetoid cerebral palsy, resulting from kernicterus. The development of hyperalimentation[15] and its application to the prematurely born infant facilitated the support of infants with significant bowel disturbances and those too small or too sick to feed on their own. With the ability to synthesize surfactant, attempts are now being made to prevent the major pulmonary complications of surfactant deficiency in the VLBW infant by administering surfactant to the infant at birth.[16-20] Finally, with the recent discovery of the multiple properties of nitric oxide (NO), among them its vasodilator effects with potential use in neonatology, there is more hope for the survival of VLBWIs and the avoidance of the complications of neonatal intensive care.[21]

In summary, then, the care of very small infants in the last 25 years has progressed from minimal support to highly aggressive intervention, which has emerged from the expansion of knowledge of neonatal physiology together with significant technological advances. Moreover, infants surviving today are a different group of babies than those surviving 30 years ago. They are smaller and sicker than any other group of infants cared for in the past. Their presence has stimulated a wide range of investigations that monitor mortality and morbidity,[22,23] evaluate long-term outcome, determine the quality of their lives,[24] and question whether these infants should be saved in the first place.[25] These questions continue to be asked as resources in our society become increasingly limited. At the same time, survival of these infants has stimulated questions about mother-infant attachment,[26,27] the nature of the temperament of premature infants,[28,29] and the impact the premature and potentially disabled infant has on the family.

REVIEW OF FOLLOW-UP STUDIES OF VERY LOW BIRTH WEIGHT INFANTS

Over the years considerable information has been gathered about the outcome of VLBWIs and extremely low birth weight infants (ELBWI— those with birth weights ≤ 1000 g). Some data from perinatal programs demonstrate the effectiveness of neonatal intensive care.[30] In early studies, all premature infants were grouped together. As a result, an increase in survival among these infants was demonstrated following the introduction of intensive care. However, it soon became apparent that this group of babies was not homogeneous. There is a big difference between an infant weighing 2000 g at birth and one weighing 1250 g. There is a significant difference between an infant who is appropriately grown for gestational age (AGA) as compared to one who is small-for-gestational age (SGA).[31] Moreover, many of these studies were performed after relatively short periods and tended to focus on gross abnormalities while ignoring more subtle, long-term issues that later confronted many of these babies. As a result, the understanding of these babies was somewhat limited and superficial. Furthermore, there was a tendency to think that the results were better than they really were.

In the late 1970s and early 1980s, workers began to examine different populations of infants more closely and proceeded to more rigorously consider other factors contributing to outcome, including not only birth weight and gestational age but also perinatal and postnatal complications, such as intracranial hemorrhage (ICH) and bronchopulmonary dysplasia (BPD) as well as socioeconomic status (SES), access to care, and place of birth.

Early studies

Among the earlier studies were the works of Douglas[4] and Dann et al.[5] Douglas reported on 163 infants with birth weights of ≤2000 g born in the United Kingdom during a single week in 1946. Some of the babies were delivered at home and some in the hospital. Of those cared for in hospital, 18 received oxygen and 11 were in incubators. None of the <1000 g infants, whether born at home or in the hospital, survived, and only 32% of the 1001 to 1500 g infants lived. Of the heavier babies who did survive, none had handicaps. Of the entire population who were followed, 17% of the low birth weight infants had significant physical, neurological, mental, or behavioral problems. In 1958 Dann et al.[5] described the outcome for 73 of 116 infants born in the New York City area between 1940 and 1952 with birth weights of ≤1000 g or whose weight dropped below 1000 g during their hospitalization. It is noted that the babies were kept in incubators, and most received oxygen and meticulous but nonintrusive medical support. The infants were later evaluated between 1950 and 1957. All 73 of the 116 survivors were found to have generally good physical health with few neurological defects. Most had caught up in height but often not until after 4 years. However, their intelligence quotients (IQ), although in the average range, were below their full-term siblings, and 16% were below 80. Finally, the authors found that after considering variables such as birth weight, gender, race, and socioeconomic status (SES), the infants who had the highest IQs were found among the families with higher SES. It should be noted that both studies are unique in that they preceded, by some two decades, the establishment of modern neonatal intensive care and the follow-up of very small infants.

These two studies are reviewed in some detail because they provide a historical perspective and also demonstrate that even without neonatal intensive care some low birth weight infants did survive and did well. It is apparent, however, that with the introduction of new methods of care, survival increased and outcome improved, although other issues have emerged.[32-34] The remainder of this section will review follow-up studies on the VLBWI and the ELBWI published since 1979.

In reviewing studies published since 1979, the results of the modern age of neonatology emerge. Progress has been made in the evolution of care for the VLBW infant. One can discern the increasing complexity of the follow-up as the authors begin to consider not only the effects but also the complications of premature birth as well as the psychosocial circumstances impinging on the lives of these children and their families. Also brought into relief are the changes that continue to occur in the field and the need for continuous assessment. Moreover, this overview highlights not only the medical aspects and early morbidity and mortality associated with neonatal intensive care but also the neurodevelopmental, educational, and behavioral sequelae.

In 1979 Yu and Hollingsworth[35] reported on 55 infants with birth weights of ≤1000 g born in 1977 and 1978. The overall survival was 60%; 44% of infants weighing 501 to 750 g and 67% of infants weighing 751 to 1000 g survived. The authors reported no major abnormalities and suggested that the prognosis for these very small babies was good. It should be noted, however, that this suggestion was based on only a 1-year follow-up, during which time no formal neurodevelopmental assessments were performed. These authors also did not identify whether or not there were complications of prematurity nor did they compare their results to those of earlier studies. Nevertheless, this work set the stage for researchers in the 1980s who maintained that the chances for the very small infant surviving were improving and the developmental outcomes were also improving.

Studies in the 1970s and 1980s

In 1981 Rothberg et al.[36] reported on the 2-year outcome of 28 infants with birth weights of <1250 g who were born between May 1, 1973 and July 31, 1976 and who had been mechanically ventilated. It is noteworthy that these authors addressed not only survival and early morbidity but also the effect of various complications of prematurity, aspects that had not been examined in earlier studies. These 28 infants were part of a population of 144 infants, 22% of whom were born in their hospital and 78% who were born outside that hospital and then transported to the authors' neonatal intensive care unit. Eighty-four (58%) of the total group of 144 infants survived. The mean birth weight of the survivors was 1041 g (range 775 to 1247 g) with a mean gestational age of 27.5 weeks (range 25 to 31 weeks). Thirteen of the 28 mechanically ventilated infants in the study (46%) had normal neurological and developmental assessments. In the infants identified as having developmental disorders, abnormal neurodevelopmental sequelae were characterized as spastic diplegia, spastic quadriplegia, hydrocephalus with ventriculoperitoneal shunts, hyperactivity, hemiparesis, and speech delay. The one medical result noted was the presence of stage II or greater ROP, which occurred in nine infants (32%). There were eight infants with severe delays; these infants had lower mean birth weights (971 g) and shorter gestations (26.5 weeks) than the rest of the group. For some of these infants there were other confounding variables, such as sepsis, an increased number of maternal and obstetrical risk factors, and the fact that seven of them had been born in a community hospital and transported to the neonatal center. No bronchopulmonary dysplasia (BPD) was reported. Thus, at least from this small sample, despite the numerous advances in neonatal intensive care, the mortality and morbidity for these small infants remained high. It was suggested that, if the best results were to be obtained, these infants should be delivered in perinatal centers; failing this, such VL-BWIs should be expeditiously transferred to a tertiary care nursery.

Ruiz et al.[37] reported the 1-year outcome for 38 infants born between 1976 and 1978 with birth weights <1000 g. These infants were drawn from a cohort of 134 infants, 47 (35%) of whom survived. The 38 infants were evaluated at 8 and 15 months. Twenty of the 38 infants were ventilated[14]; 70% had BPD at the Northway stage of III or IV, which represents the most severe pulmonary changes of atelectasis, hyperinflation, and unequal aeration.[38] It was noted that in infants born outside the center, the incidence of respiratory distress (RDS), seizures, and cardiac arrest was higher for those ventilated than for those not so treated. A higher incidence of intraventricular hemorrhage (IVH) occurred among ventilated babies (8/20) but occurred in only 4 of the 18 unventilated infants. ROP was diagnosed in 13 of 20 ventilated infants but in only two not receiving ventilatory support. With respect to neurodevelopmental functioning, 45% of the entire group showed some delay, and 21% exhibited severe delay (>2 SD below the mean). The ventilated babies seemed to fare worse than the nonventilated infants. Multiple handicaps were common, with overlap between neuromuscular and developmental problems. Of the 38 infants studied, 10 were severely handicapped, 7 had multiple handicaps, 3 had severe neurological or developmental impairment. No problems were seen in 20 infants (53%).

Britton et al.[24] raised the question as to whether intensive care was justified for infants weighing <801 g at birth. They examined a population of 158 infants weighing <801 g born during 1974 to 1977 who were transported to the intensive care unit. From the entire group, 25% survived;

35% survived among those weighing 700 to 800 g. A total of 119 (75%) infants died; 39 with intraventricular hemorrhage (IVH), 26 with respiratory distress syndrome (RDS), and 13 with infection. Thirty-seven of the 39 survivors were followed up to 18 months. Growth failure was common, with weight being most frequently affected; 57% were below the third percentile. Eighteen (49%) had significant neurodevelopmental problems. Five children (14%) had major neurological sequelae, including cerebral palsy. Eighteen (48.6%) fell below the average range on developmental testing. When the group was divided into those infants with birth weights above and below 700 g, it was found that none of the <700 g infants were intact while only 39% of the heavier babies had handicaps. The authors concluded that every effort should be made to care for the >700 g infant. Another report addressing the same weight group, but written 3 years later,[39] noted an 80% mortality. Of those infants who survived, little symptomatic central nervous system disease was present. The infants with birth weights >750 g did somewhat better than those of lower birth weights. They had an overall handicap rate of 19%. This suggested that potentially handicapped infants of extremely low birth weight usually die despite vigorous efforts to sustain them in contrast to heavier infants. However, those who do survive may do relatively well. Hirata et al.[40] had a similar experience with 22 infants with birth weights 501 to 750 g, 36.7% of whom survived. Of these 22 infants, 18 were followed up from 20 months to 7 years. The overall conclusion was that 11% had neurological sequelae, 22% were functional and of borderline or below average intelligence, and 67% were normal. It was suggested that the outcome for these babies was better than hitherto expected and that aggressive therapy will improve the outcome.

In 1982 Orgill et al.[41] published 6- and 12-month follow-up findings on 123 survivors of a cohort of 148 infants born between January, 1979 and July, 1980, with birth weights of ≤1500 g. Twenty-one infants had birth weights of ≤1000 g. At 18 months, 57% were alive. Of this group of infants, 19% were handicapped, which was defined as having a developmental level 2 standard deviations (SD) below the norm, cerebral palsy, visual deficits, or sensorineural deafness. No bronchopulmonary dysplasia (BPD) was reported, but one child had retinopathy of prematurity (ROP). However, the authors did recognize that this was indeed a very short-term follow-up, and the numbers were small.

In a similar study with patients born between 1973 and 1978, Saigal et al.[42] found that among the 294 infants weighing ≤1000 g there was a 31.9% survival rate. Thirty-seven infants in this weight group were discharged and followed for a minimum of 2 years. It was found that 24.3% had some handicap. A functional classification was made when the infants reached 2 years of age. Of the 35 patients evaluated, 60% had some dysfunction, while 40% were determined to be normal. Among the 21 with some dysfunction, nine had neurological handicaps, which included hydrocephalus and cerebral palsy (CP). Factors associated with poor outcome included ventilatory support and intracranial hemorrhage (ICH). As with the previous study, these authors felt they were seeing improvement in the outcome for this population although they conceded that minor handicaps tended to be underestimated in younger infants.

Driscoll et al.[43] reported on a prospective study of 23 infants born in 1977 to 1978 who survived with birth weights of ≤1000 g, one half of whom were born in a center with a NICU. Infants were fed parenterally using glucose, amino acids, and intralipids until they were able to tolerate enteral feedings. When it was not possible to maintain adequate oxygenation using ambient oxygen, continuous distending pressure with nasal prongs was instituted. When necessary, mechanical ventilation was used. None of the infants with birth weights <700 g survived. The 53 survivors were followed from 18 months to 3 years. Seventeen percent had neurological deficits and 16% had intellectual deficits, defined as a Mental Developmental Index (MDI) of < 84 on the Bayley Scales of Infant Development. The neurological deficits included spastic quadriparesis, hydrocephalus, and static encephalopathy. There were other sequelae, including BPD, in 30% of the survivors and ROP in 23%. The authors note that there had been improvement in the survival of these small infants but that there was a high complication rate, including intellectual impairment of 30% of the group. Unfortunately, the authors did not separate the outcome of children with BPD and/or ICH from those without these complications, resulting in a less than complete picture of their population.

Kitchen et al.[44] reported on 351 infants born in one region in Australia with birth weights of 500 to 999 g who were followed for 2 years. Eighty-nine (25.4%) survived, and 83 were evaluated. Overall, 22.5% had severe functional handicaps, 29.2% had moderate-to-mild handicaps, and 48.3% had no handicap. Thirteen and a half percent had CP, 3.4% had bilateral blindness, and 3.4% had severe sensorineural hearing loss. Those born in tertiary care centers did better than those who were born elsewhere, as reflected in a significantly lower incidence of functional handicaps and higher scores on the MDI. Therefore, the authors concluded, in order to optimize their outcome, VLBW infants should be delivered in the setting most capable of responding to their unique needs. This view is similar to that of Rothberg et al.[36] and Lubchenco et al.[45]

Kitchen et al.[46] reported on 54 children with birth weights of 500 to 999 g born during 1977 to 1980 and seen at 2 years corrected age. Fifty of these children were also seen at 5½ years. There was a 39.6% survival rate with a mean birth weight of 864 g. At 2 years, the study children had a mean MDI on the Bayley Scales of Infant Development of 91.1 (SD 16.5) and a mean psychomotor developmental index (PDI) of 87.7 (SD 17.0), both of which are below the population mean. When the children were evaluated at 5½ years corrected age, 60% (30/50) had no impairment, 10% had severe sensorineural hearing loss or intellectual deficits, 10% had mild-to-moderate impairment, and 20% had minor neurological abnormalities. Three children had spastic diplegia. The mean score on the full Wechsler Preschool and Primary Scales of Intelligence (WPPSI) was 101.8. This study suggests that outcome may improve from 2 to 5½ years among VLBW survivors. Nevertheless, even at the later time, 40% of survivors had some difficulty. The authors also noted a small number of patients with sensorineural deficits and blindness.

In another population Kitchen et al.[47] reported on the 5-year outcome for the same weight group (500 to 999 g) born during 1979 and 1980. The survival rate in this group was 25.4%; 83 of 89 were evaluated. Seventy-two percent had no functional impairment, 19% had severe impairment, 5% had moderate impairment, and 4% had mild involvement. The patients who were not born at the tertiary care center in this regional study did worse than those born at the center. Eight children had CP, six were blind, and four had sensorineural or mixed deafness. Once again, the authors found that the outcome at 5 years was better than at 2 years. However, no comment was made as to whether or not these children had been in any kind of therapy or early intervention program. This, unfortunately, is characteristic of many studies, which leaves the reader with an incomplete picture of the population being described.

The studies reporting on the survival and follow-up of children born in the 1970s were by and large optimistic. There was a definite increase in the survival of small infants, including those with birth weights < 800 g. Moreover, those infants who did survive, including those of extremely low birth weight, seemed to do fairly well, at least over the short term. Thus, it was believed that one should provide every support possible for these infants. However, there began to emerge a nagging concern that, although many of these infants survived and did fairly well, they would have problems that would emerge as the children grew up. Furthermore, it began to become apparent that premature infants were not a homogenous group, and many other factors had to be considered in the follow-up of these infants. The means by which these concerns were to be addressed started to become operationalized in the follow-up of infants reported in the 1980s and 1990s.

Recent studies

In 1989 Hack and Fanaroff[1] reported on the outcome of infants with birth weights of less than 750 g born between 1982 and 1988. Ninety-eight infants were born between July 1982 and June 1985 (period 1), and 120 infants were born between July 1985 and June 1988 (period 2). There was some increase in survival among infants with gestational ages between 25 and 27 weeks (52% vs. 71%), but the overall neonatal morbidity was similar between the two groups. The neurodevelopmental outcomes were also similar. Period 1 children had Bayley motor and mental scores of 90 + 17 and 88 + 14, respectively, at 20 months corrected age. The period 2 children were seen at 8 months corrected age and had motor and mental scores of 77 + 25 and 81 + 30. There was more aggressive intervention with the period 2 children who had many complications, including BPD, septicemia, ROP, and IVH, in addition to less than optimal neurodevelopmental functioning.

O'Callaghan et al.[48] reported on the 2-year outcome of children of ELBW born between 1988 and 1990 and cared for in a neonatal intensive care unit. Despite the fact that this was not a large study—63 children—these children had the benefit of the most recent level of intensive care and so provide some insight into how more recent cohorts of ELBW children may be functioning at 2 years of age. The children were compared to matched controls using a cognitive function measure, a neurosensory motor developmental assessment, and a medical assessment. Furthermore, the ELBW group was divided into the total group and a low-risk group, which included children with no intracranial hemorrhage (ICH), periventricular leukomalacia (PVL), or chronic lung disease (i.e., BPD). The findings are quite interesting in that they very much mirror the findings of earlier studies. The ELBW group differed significantly from the control group with respect to cognitive and personal-social functioning although as a group they were in the average range. The low-risk ELBW group did not differ from the controls. There were more striking differences, however, when the neurosensory motor findings were reviewed. The total ELBW group as well as the low-risk ELBW group did less well than the controls on the total score as well as on the gross and fine motor subscales.

In the past there was considerable interest in the cognitive outcome of children born very early. Most studies assessed early neurodevelopmental functioning and found that, as a group, the VLBWIs did less well than the older and heavier premature infants or a matched term control group. However, studies now are able to assess more subtle aspects of CNS function that contribute to cognitive functioning.

Herrgåard et al.[49] carried out a 5-year neurodevelopmental assessment of 60 children born ≤ 32 weeks of age, obtaining neurodevelopmental profiles. These children were matched with 60 term controls. Assessment tools used included a standardized neurological examination, a neuropsychological assessment, an audiological examination, and an ophthalmological examination. Included in the preterm group were children felt to be handicapped (children with cerebral palsy, mental retardation (IQ < 70), bilateral hearing loss, visual impairment, and epilepsy) and those not handicapped. So far as IQ was concerned, there were significant differences between the entire preterm group and the control group as well as significant differences between the handicapped and nonhandicapped preterm groups. The controls had the highest IQs, while the nonhandicapped did less well, and the handicapped group did the least well. The neurodevelopmental profile was composed of eight functional entities: gross motor, fine motor, visual-motor, attention, language, visual-spatial, sensorimotor, and memory skills. Several interesting findings emerged from this study. First, all of the children born preterm had difficulty with gross, fine, and visual-motor skills. They also had difficulty with language, sensorimotor, visual-spatial, and memory skills. Second, the nonhandicapped children with minor neurodevelopmental difficulties had a similar spectrum of difficulties although their IQs were in the average range, some even being in the exceptional range. These findings are similar to those made by Sostek[50] in her study of children of gestational age ≤ 33 weeks and a mean birth weight of 1358 g who were compared to children born at term. None of the premature children had lung disease, ICH, or other medical problems. It was found that, although these children had normal IQs, they were compromised with respect to perceptual-motor integration and recognition, perceptual/performance tasks, quantitative tasks, memory, visual/ motor skills and were found to be more distractible and had poorer attention and less readiness for kindergarten when compared to term controls.

Teplin et al.[51] assessed at 6 years the neurodevelopmental, health, and growth status of 28 children with birth weights < 1001 g. They found the ELBWI, when compared to 26 control children born at term, had significantly more mild or moderate-to-severe neurological problems—61% vs. 23%—which included cerebral palsy, abnormalities of muscle tone, speech and articulation immaturities, and immaturity of balance. When cognitive function was assessed, the controls scored significantly higher than the children of ELBW. Moreover, more than half of the ELBW children with normal IQs had mildly abnormal neurological findings, whereas the controls with normal IQs had normal neurological examinations. When an overall functional status was determined, it was found that, of the ELBW children, 46%, were normal, 36% were mildly disabled, and 18% were moderately to severely disabled. This compares with 75% of the controls being normal, 4% significantly disabled, and the remainder having some mild degree of abnormality. Interestingly, attentional disturbances were not a problem for the preterm groups described in these two papers, which is contrary to what other groups have reported where attentional difficulties have been noted.[52,53]

Another provocative and important study was the one carried out by Halsey et al.[54] on children with ELBW when they were in preschool. They studied 60 white, middle-class ELBW children and compared them to a matched peer group. They used a general developmental scale as well as a scale of visual-motor integration. They found that the ELBW group's mean scores were significantly lower than the controls although they were still within one standard deviation of the mean. Twenty-three percent of the ELBW children were clearly disabled, 51% obtained borderline scores, and 26% were average. The control group had cognitive scores 15 to 18 points higher than the ELBW group and were 2½ times more likely to have normal development. The authors were reluctant to make any predictions on the basis of these data but expressed concern that this pattern of performance placed the ELBW children at risk for later difficulties. As will be shown in a different study to be discussed, these data are indeed predictive of later difficulties. Thus, in considering the studies discussed in this section, VLBW premature infants, despite relatively intact cognitive skills as evidenced by normal IQs, appear to have neuropsychological and neuromotor disturbances that can adversely affect their school performance, self-esteem, and behavior.

The studies of the 1980s, in which children were followed only to preschool, bore out the concerns of the 1970s. It was true, there was an increase in survival and many children did do well. However, when these children were compared to their peers, they were functioning at much lower levels and had a variety of neurodevelopmental problems that had not been identified or appreciated in earlier studies. These problems included deficiencies in their perceptual skills, social skills, and their level of maturity.

Effects of these difficulties

The studies reviewed thus far report on VLBWIs evaluated only after 2 to 6 years. However, among the most important indicators of "successful" outcome are the child's social-emotional adaptation and how well the child does in school. It is acknowledged that many VLBWIs have significant difficulties that persist throughout their lives. However, as has already been noted, although such children may have IQs in the average range, they do not perform as well as controls on measures of fine and gross motor and visual-motor tasks and have what have been called "minor disabilities" that become apparent in school. An important question, then, that emerges from these findings is: what effect do these difficulties have on school performance and peer relationships? Eilers et al.[56] studied a group of children with birth weights of ≤1250 g born between July 1974 and July 1978. There were 43 survivors, 33 of whom were studied at 5 to 8 years of age. Sixteen of these children were functioning at an age-appropriate level; three had major handicaps, and 14 were in regular classes but needed remedial help. The authors noted that 51.5% of this group required more special education efforts, compared to 21.4% of the general school population. Finally, the group without special needs tended to have older mothers and to come from higher SES households.

Vohr and Garcia Coll[57] reported on a 7-year longitudinal study of children with birth weights of ≤1500 g born in 1975. Of their original population 62 (51.2%) survived, and 42 (67%) were followed. The study evaluated patterns of neurological and developmental functioning at 1 year of age and compared them to functioning at age 7. They found that the patterns at 1 year, once the children were classified into three categories— normal, suspect, and abnormal—were significantly related to the 7-year findings. The point to be made is that 54% of the total sample required special education or resource help at 7 years. Furthermore, those who had abnormal findings at 1 year were most likely to have difficulties at 7 years. This was less clear for the suspect and normal groups. The final breakdown for the group, given their 1-year identification was that 27% of the normal children, 50% of the suspect children, and 87% of the abnormal children required special educational services by age 7. Another important finding was that 45% of the normal children, 75% of the suspect group, and 100% of the abnormal group had visual-motor disturbances.

Another study[58] found that even among a relatively normal group of children with birth weights ≤1500 g there was an increased incidence of visual-motor problems. Klein et al.[53], in evaluating the same population at 9 years of age, found that the VLBW infants as a group, compared to full-term controls, scored lower on tests measuring general intelligence, visual or spatial skills, and academic achievement. When they examined a subset of VLBW children with normal IQs, they found these children showed significant deficits in mathematics skills. Crowe et al.[59] reported on 90 children born between 24 and 36 weeks gestation who participated in a longitudinal follow-up program and were evaluated at 4 ½ years corrected age. Children with major neurological impairments, such as cerebral palsy, were excluded. The researchers found that motor development was relatively intact, but that children with birth weights ≤1000 g displayed significantly poorer motor skills. Moreover, those children with symptomatic ICH also had significantly poorer motor performance.

Saigal et al.,[60] who have conducted a longitudinal regionally based study for many years, reported on the cognitive abilities and school abilities at 8 years of a regional cohort of relatively socioeconomically advantaged infants with birth weights 501 to 1000 g born between 1977 and 1981. Intellectual, motor, visual-motor, adaptive capabilities, and teachers' perceptions were compared to a matched group of children born at term. They found that, although the majority of the ELBW children had IQs in the normal range, they were nevertheless significantly lower than those of the controls. This was true even when handicapped children were excluded from the analysis. Moreover, the ELBW group was significantly disadvantaged on every measure. This was also true for neurologically normal children who performed below the normal range on tests of visual-motor and motor abilities. Furthermore, the teachers rated the ELBW group as performing below grade level.

Hack et al.[61] reported the 8-year neurocognitive abilities of a group of 249 VLBWIs born 1977 to 1979 who were compared to 363 randomly normal children born at the same time. A neurological examination and tests of intelligence, language, speech, reading, mathematics, spelling, visual and fine motor abilities, and behavior were administered. Twenty-four (10%) of the VLBW children had a major neurological abnormality. None of the controls had such a finding. With the exception of speech and total behavior scores, the VLBW group scored significantly poorer than the controls on all tests. Even normal IQ, neurologically intact VLBW children had significantly poorer scores than did the controls in expressive language, memory, visual-motor function, fine motor function, and measures of hyperactivity. When social risk, a significant determinant of poor outcome, was controlled for, VLBW still had an adverse affect on functioning. Of interest is the fact that a relationship but not in a negative direction was found between VLBW and social risk only in verbal IQ. That is to say, these children did not do worse in this domain. An explanation may be that prematurity may contribute only minimally to the negative impact of a poor psychosocial environment in this area. For more advantaged children, however, the biological factors may contribute more to the deficits when these children are compared to their peers.

In a more recent study Hille et al.[62] assessed the school performance at 9 years of age of VLBW infants born in the Netherlands. From an almost complete birth cohort they were able to gather data on 84% (n = 813) of the survivors at 9 years. Nineteen percent were in special education programs, half of whom had been placed there at 5 years of age because of identified problems. Of the children with VLBW in mainstream classes, 32% were in a grade below their age level and another 38% required special assistance. Moreover, of those children who had been retained, 60% required special assistance as compared to children in an age-appropriate grade (28%). Finally, the authors identified a number of factors at 5 years of age that predicted school difficulties at 9 years. These included developmental delays, speech/language delay, behavioral problems, and low SES. These findings confirm the work of Hack et al.[61] and Halsey et al.[54]

A final issue to consider with this group of children is the effect VLBW may have on behavior. It has already been noted that from an academic viewpoint many of these children have significant problems with hyperactivity and attention. Weisglas-Kuperus et al.[63] have addressed the issue of behavior problems in this population of children. In a study of 73 VLBW children who were compared to 192 term children at 3½ years of age, the authors found a significant degree of behavioral disturbance in the VLBW group. Problems included depression and internalizing problems.

OTHER COMPLICATIONS

The studies reviewed thus far were published during a time when aggressive and sophisticated neonatal care was provided to extremely small and sick infants. One sees a degree of improvement in survival and perhaps in the 2- to 5-year outcomes. Nevertheless, these reports reveal the presence of impairments in from 20% to 60% of the survivors, depending on the neonatal care center, the year of birth, the infant's birth weight, whether the child was born in a tertiary care center or elsewhere, and the child's socioeconomic status. It must also be noted that among the survivors there is an increase in visual-motor disturbances and an increased need for special education, even among the children who appear to show the least effects of their prematurity and low birth weight. However, in most of the reports described, the infants were evaluated as a homogeneous group, so it is unclear, other than with respect to birth weight, gestational age, and neurological disturbance, which morbidities—such as ICH, BPD, and ROP—were associated with the outcomes. It would seem that in order to get a somewhat clearer picture, these different populations must be examined more closely and grouped not only by birth weight and gestational age, but also by associated morbidities.

Bronchopulmonary dysplasia (BPD)

There is strong evidence that BPD has a significantly adverse effect on the developmental outcome for the VLBWI. Goldson,[64] studying a small group of infants with birth weights of ≤ 1000 g, matched for birth weight and gestational age and without ICH or ROP, found that those infants with severe BPD, according to the Northway classification, did significantly worse on developmental and neuromotor testing than those with mild or no BPD. However, he also found that in the latter group there was a high incidence of neuromotor dysfunction characterized by hypotonia, hyperreflexia, and disorganized motor behavior. Meisels et al.[65] studied the growth and development of 37 infants, 20 of whom had RDS (mean birth weight 1527, SD ± 302) and 17 with BPD (mean birth weight 1291, SD ± 519). The RDS group had scores comparable to those of average, healthy full-term infants, while the infants with BPD performed in the low-average to delayed range. Among the infants with BPD, 35% displayed an MDI < 85, and 45% had a PDI < 85. They also showed more delays in growth than did the RDS group. Nevertheless, a question still remains as to the significance of many of these early findings.

Vohr et al.[66] reported on the neurodevelopmental and medical status of 30 VLBW survivors, 15 with BPD and 15 controls without BPD at 10 to 12 years of age, and compared them to 15 full-term children. A wide range of assessments of neurological function, cognitive ability, and medical status revealed that the BPD survivors weighed less than full-term children and had smaller head circumferences than the full-term children and the non-BPD preterm children. The BPD survivors also had more neurological abnormalites, such as CP, when compared to the full-term and preterm controls. The entire preterm group did less well on arithmetic and visual-motor testing and had a greater need of resources and special education than did the full-term controls.

Robertson et al.[67] assessed the 8-year school performance, neurodevelopmental, and growth outcome of infants with BPD. Three groups of infants were followed to 8 years: group 1 had gestational ages ≤ 31 weeks and received oxygen until 36 weeks gestation, group 2 was of the same gestational age as group 1 but received oxygen only to 28 days, and group 3 had a gestational age ≥ 32 and required oxygen for more than 28 days. Each group was then individually matched to a preterm peer group without BPD and a term peer group. When compared to the preterm peer group, the BPD group showed academic delays. This was true even when the handicapped children in the BPD group were excluded from the analysis. It should be noted that the most severely affected group also had the greatest number of handicapped children, so that the more severe the BPD the worse the outcome. However, even without BPD, prematurity and adverse social circumstances (which were assessed in this study) compromised the outcome of the low birth weight infants. Thus, one can see from these last two studies, that the presence of prematurity not only has adverse affects on intellectual functioning in the older child but that BPD has an especially adverse affect on these children.

Intracranial hemorrhage (ICH)

ICH is also a frequent and significant complication of very premature birth. Not only is there a significant mortality associated with this complication, but there are also long-term neurocognitive sequelae. Palmer et al.[68] found that children with ICH plus ventricular dilatation did significantly worse on neurological and developmental assessments than those without ICH or those with ICH without dilatation. Moreover, the deficits were associated more with the post-hemorrhagic dilatation than with the initial bleed.

Sostek[50] reported on the effect of intraventricular hemorrhage (IVH) in a group of preterm infants at 4½ to 5½ years of age who had mean birth weights < 1250 g and gestational age ≤ 30 weeks. She identified three groups of children: those with no documented IVH after screening, those with minor IVH, and those with major bleeds. The Papile Grading System, which grades IVH on a scale of 1 (subependymal bleed) to 4 (massive bleed),[69] was used. It was found that the major IVH children performed more poorly than the mild or no IVH children on general cognition, recognition/discrimination, alphabet recitation, and kindergarten readiness. However, when compared to the term children, all of the preterm children did poorly on visual-motor integration and on assessments of activity and distractibility.

Unfortunately, more than one complication may be present in an individual low birth weight child. Landry et al[70] examined the differential effect of various complications on 2-year outcome of infants with birth weights of ≤1500 g. She divided her group of infants with ICH and respiratory distress syndrome (RDS) in the following way: children with RDS with no ICH, children with BPD without ICH, children with BPD and ICH, and hydrocephalus (HYD) secondary to ICH. At 2 years of age, she found no difference between the ICH-RDS and ICH-nonRDS groups. Both were in the average range. The BPD and HYD groups performed much more poorly than the others. There was also no significant difference between grades I to II and grades III to IV ICH groups, although a small number of the latter group showed significantly delayed developmental quotients at 6 and 12 months. Finally, duration of hospitalization was directly related to poorer quotients at 24 months; infants with BPD had prolonged hospitalizations. In a later study using the same study design, Landry et al.[71] assessed the longitudinal outcome for these infants. They assessed 78 infants with birth weight < 1600 g at 6, 12, 24, and 36 months of age and found that on the mental scale both grade III and grade IV children did less well and grade IV and BPD groups did the least well at 36 months of age. Moreover, when examined longitudinally the infants with BPD showed little improvement, while the other groups improved but then plateaued at 24 and 36 months. On the motor scales there was gradual improvement in all groups but the most affected children—BPD and Grade IV—did less well than the others.

Similar findings were encountered by Bozynski et al.[72] in an 18-month follow-up of infants weighing ≤1200 g with and without ICH, associated with and without prolonged mechanical ventilation (PMV). In the study the population was divided into four groups: group 1 included infants with ICH and PMV, group 2 included infants without ICH who received PMV, group 3 included infants with ICH and no PMV, and group 4 included infants without ICH and without PMV. First, it was demonstrated that PMV was a powerful predictor of poor development whether or not it was associated with ICH. Second, uncomplicated ICH in the absence of PMV was not associated with adverse cognitive development. Third, over time, the motor scores fell among infants with uncomplicated ICH. Finally, race (nonwhite in this instance) was associated with low SES, which was associated with a poorer outcome. It is noted that the data on ICH are not in agreement with the findings in other studies, which have tended to suggest that the worse the grade of ICH, the worse the outcome. Also, Scott et al.[73] suggested that ICH, even of the lesser grades, may have an adverse effect on outcome. However, none of these studies identified whether or not periventricular leukomalacia (PVL) was present. As will be noted below, PVL is associated with poor outcomes. The discrepancies among some of these early studies may be a reflection of the varying incidence of PVL in the different populations, which was not specifically identified at the time of the study.

Periventricular leukomalacia (PVL)

As noted previously, there is yet another phenomenon to consider, namely the presence of PVL. It has been usually accepted, with reasonably good data to support the belief, that the worse the grade of ICH, the worse the outcome, particularly if there was extension into the parenchyma or associated hydrocephalus. However, clinically, this did not always seem to be true, in that there were many instances in which infants with grade IV bleeds did better than those with grade I hemorrhages.

In 1962 Banker and Larroche[74] documented the presence of periventricular leukomalacia (PVL). It was noted that PVL was an infarction of the white matter that led to demyelination.[75] With the development of more sophisticated imaging techniques, the effect of PVL has been taken more seriously. Fawer et al.[76] found that major neurodevelopmental sequelae were associated with PVL, and, that the more extensive the PVL, particularly that involving the frontal-parietal and frontal-parietal-occipital regions, the worse the outcome both neurologically and developmentally. This was also reported by Nwaesei et al.[77] These authors found that the timing of the ultrasound was critical for predicting those who would have significant later problems. They found that the presence of significant PVL at 40 weeks postconceptional age was highly predictive of later problems. These concerns continue to be borne out. Rogers et al.[78] evaluated the effect of cystic periventricular leukomalacia in 26 of 27 infants born at ≤ 32 weeks gestation. They found that all of the infants had CP (54% quadriplegia, 42% diplegia, and 4% hemiplegia) and that their development at 2 years was compromised; the quadriplegic infants, who had the largest cysts, were the most affected. Unfortunately, many of the children had other perinatal complications, such as BPD and apnea/bradycardia, which were not included in the analysis. Nevertheless, the presence of PVL had a significantly adverse affect on these infants although there was a spectrum of effect. Bennett et al.[79] performed a similar study but also looked at Grade III/IV IVH. They found that the IVH was a better predictor of poor outcome than was the presence of PVL. Although there are differences in the results between these two studies, the major point to bear in mind is that infants with evidence of PVL and/or ICH are at markedly increased risk for later neurological problems, including CP.

Cerebral palsy (CP)

One other issue that needs discussion is the extent of handicapping conditions in the very low birth weight population. There has been an ongoing debate as to whether there has been an improvement in the outcome for these small infants. As has been discussed, there is certainly evidence that many of these children have significant learning and behavioral problems. The other question is—has there been a trend for more significant neurological problems, such as CP? Pharoah et al.[80] noted that among the 6%

to 7% of infants of low birth weight 25% to 40% have CP. In reviewing the CP register of the Mersey region in the United Kingdom they found that the incidence of CP among infants with birth weight > 2500 g has not changed from 1967 to 1984. However, there was a significant increase among low birth weight infants (≤2500 g) and that this is most prominent among the ≤1500 g infants. The marked increase started in 1976 to 1978 at a time when there was an increased survival of the VLBWI. However, it must be noted that this increase is accompanied by an increasing proportion of infants surviving unimpaired. Bhushan et al.[81] reviewing epidemiologic studies from the United States as well as international data, including those from the Mersey region, concluded that there was an increased incidence of CP in industrialized nations and that this was associated with the increased survival of VLBW infants occurring in conjunction with improved obstetric and neonatal care. Focusing on the United States, the authors noted that from 1960 to 1983 the survival of white infants with birth weights 500 to 999 g increased from 6.5/1000 live births to 461.2/1000 live births and from 422.6 to 845.9/1000 live births for those weighing 1000 to 1499 g. On the other hand, during this same period there has been a rising incidence of CP from 1.9 to 2.3/1000 live births. These results, however, should not detract from the achievements of neonatal intensive care in that for every surviving VLBW infant with CP in 1986, 11 VLBW infants who would not have survived in 1960 now survive without CP.

CONCLUSIONS

It is apparent that many changes have taken place with the introduction of neonatal intensive care. Moreover, research continues that will certainly lead to new approaches to management and changes in outcome. For now what conclusions can be drawn from this review?

- It is apparent that enormous strides have been made in the last 30 years with increasing numbers of low birth weight infants being saved. However, there is disagreement as to whether the absolute number of children surviving but with some disability may be increasing. Stewart et al.[33] maintain that the numbers of children with disabilities are not increasing, while Paneth et al.,[23] Pharoah et al.,[80] and Bhushan et al.,[81] suggest the opposite. Considering all of these reports, the current data suggest that the incidence of CP has increased but that more children are surviving without major handicaps than would have been the case in 1960.

- If one looks at 2- and 5-year developmental outcomes, one finds that some advances have occurred in improving the developmental outcomes for these children. Nevertheless, 20% to 60% of the survivors still have some disability, with approximately 10% to 20% having significant adverse sequelae. Moreover, even those who seem to do well initially appear to have more difficulties in school over and above difficulties experienced by the general population.
- It appears that the 2-year outcome for these children is related to birth weight and neonatal morbidities. That is to say, the smaller the infant the higher the incidence of early morbidities, such as RDS and ICH, which often lead to long-term morbidities, such as BPD, HYD, and CP. Thus, the smaller the baby, the greater the risk for pre-and postnatal complications and the less positive the outcome.
- The results of school studies at 6 to 8 years of age report a significant incidence of learning and behavioral disorders among children of ELBW and VLBW, even among those without significant handicapping conditions such as CP, hydrocephalus, and ROP. These may be some of the "sleeper effects" of being born early. The appearance of these disorders needs to monitored rigorously in this high-risk population of children.
- Infants having specific morbidities such as BPD, ICH, severe ROP, and significant sensorineural hearing loss do worse than those without these problems.
- Among the nonmedical contributors to poor outcome are being born outside a perinatal center, low maternal education, and low socioeconomic status.

DISCUSSION

This overview has discussed the longitudinal study of high-risk populations with a focus on the ELBWI and the VLBWI. Earlier studies have not been rigorous in population selection and have tended to include children from different backgrounds, institutions, and with multiple problems, while viewing them as being homogeneous. More recent studies have established stricter criteria for the populations being studied and so have provided more insight into the factors contributing to outcome. Furthermore, an attempt has been made to evaluate, or at least take into consideration, the effects of various medical complications, coming from different socioeconomic strata and being delivered at institutions where varying levels of care were provided. It must be noted that the smaller the infant, the greater will be the number of complications at birth and as a result of neonatal intensive care and the less positive the outcome. Third, it appears that prematurity, *per se,* has a deleterious effect on growth and development and that adverse social factors further contribute to a poor outcome. Finally, there appear to be "sleeper effects" of prematurity that may only emerge when these children enter school, and it is found that they have special needs.

REFERENCES

1. Hack M, Fanaroff AA: Outcomes of extemely low-birth-weight infants between 1982 and 1988, *N Engl J Med* 321:1642-1647, 1989.
2. Allen MC, Donohue PK, Dusman AE: The limit of viability—neonatal outcome of infants born at 22 to 25 weeks' gestation, *N Engl J Med* 329:1597-1601, 1993.
3. Hess JH: Experiences gained in a thirty-year study of prematurely born infants, *Pediatrics* 11:425-434, 1953.
4. Douglas JWB: Premature children at primary school, *Brit Med J* 1:1008-1013, 1960.
5. Dann M, Levine SZ, New EV: The development of prematurely born children with birth weights or minimal postnatal weights of 1,000 grams or less, *Pediatrics* 22:1037-1052, 1958.
6. Gordon HH: Perspectives on neonatology. In Avery GB, editor: *Neonatology,* Philadelphia, 1975, Lippincott.
7. Silverman WA: *Retrolental fibroplasia: a modern parable,* New York, 1980, Grune & Stratton.
8. Davies PA, Russel H: Later progress of 100 infants weighing 1000 to 2000 grams at birth fed immediately with breast milk, *Dev Med Child Neurol* 10:725-735, 1968.
9. Rawlings G, Reynolds EOR, Stewart AL, Strang LB: Changing prognosis for infants of very low birth weight, *Lancet* i:516-519, 1971.
10. Gregory GA, Kitterman JA, Phibbs RH, Tooley WH, Hamilton WK: Treatment of idiopathic respiratory distress syndrome with continuous positive airway pressure, *New Engl J Med* 284:1333-1340, 1971.
11. Huch R, Huch A, Albani M , Gabriel M, Schulte FJ, Wolf H, Rupprath G, Emmrick P, Stechele U, Duc G, Bucher H: Transcutaneous PO_2 monitoring in routine management of infants and children with cardiorespiratory problems, *Pediatrics* 57:681-690, 1976.
12. Conway M, Durbin GM, Ingram D, McIntosh N, Parker D, Reynolds EOR, Soutter LP: Continuous monitoring of arterial oxygen tension using a catheter-tip polarographic electrode in infants, *Pediatrics* 57:244-250, 1976.
13. Aoyagi T, Kishi M, Yamaguchi K, Watanabe S: Improvement of the earpiece oximeter, *Abstrac Japan Society Med Electron Biol Engineer, Tokyo,* Rp 90-91, 1974.
14. Poets CF, Southall DP: Noninvasive monitoring of oxygenation in infants and children: practical considerations and areas of concern, *Pediatrics* 93:737-746, 1994.
15. Heird WC: Nutritional support of the pediatric patient. In Winters RW, Green HL, editors: *Nutritional support of the seriously ill patient,* New York, 1993, Academic Press.
16. Gitlin JD, Soll RF, Parad RB, Horbar JD, Feldman HA, Lucey JF, Taeusch HW: Randomized controlled trial of exogenous surfactant for the treatment of hyaline membrane disease, *Pediatrics* 31:31-37, 1987.
17. Robertson CMT: Surfactant replacement therapy for severe neonatal respiratory distress syndrome: an international randomized clinical trial, *Pediatrics* 82:683-691, 1988.
18. Dunn MS, Shennan AT, Hoskins EM, Enhorning G: Two-year follow-up of infants enrolled in a randomized trial of surfacant replacement therapy for prevention of neonatal respiratory distress syndrome, *Pediatrics* 82:543-547, 1988.

19. Vaucher YE, Merritt TA, Hallman M, Jarvenpaa AL, Telsey AE, Jones BL: Neurodevelopmental and respiratory outcome in early childhood after human surfactant treatment, *Am J Dis Child* 142:927-930, 1988.

20. Survanta Multidose Study Group: Two-year follow-up of infants treated for neonatal respiratory distress syndrome with bovine sufactant, *J Pediatr* 124:962-967, 1991.

21. Abman SH, Kinsella J.P: Nitric oxide in the pathophysiology and treatment of neonatal pulmonary hypertension, *Neonat Respir Dis* 4:1-11, 1994.

22. Kiely J, Paneth N, Stein Z, Susser M: Cerebral palsy and newborn care. II. Mortality and neurological impairment in low-birth weight infants, *Dev Med Child Neurol* 5:650-666, 1981.

23. Paneth N, Kiely L, Stein Z, Susser M: Cerebral palsy and newborn care. III. Estimated prevalence rates of cerebral palsy under differing rates of mortality and impairment of low-birth weight infants, *Dev Med Child Neurol* 23:801-817, 1981.

24. Britton SB, Fitzhardinge PM, Ashby S: Is intensive care justified for infants weighing less than 801 gm at birth? *J Pediatr* 99:937-943, 1981.

25. Shelp EE: *Born to die? Deciding the fate of critically ill newborns*, New York, 1986, The Free Press.

26. Klaus MH, Kennell JH: *Parent-infant bonding*, ed 2, St Louis, 1982, Mosby.

27. Plunkett JW, Meisels SJ, Stiefel GS, Pasick PL, Roloff DW: Patterns of attachment among preterm infants of varying biological risk, *J Am Acad Child Psychiatr* 25:794-800, 1986.

28. Washington J, Minde K, Goldberg S: Temperament in preterm infants: style and stability, *J Am Acad Child Psychiatr* 25:493-502, 1986.

29. Oberklaid F, Prior M, Sanson A: Temperament of preterm versus full-term infants, *Dev Behav Pediatr* 7:159-162, 1986.

30. Cohen RS, Stevenson DK, Malachowski N, Ariagno RL, Kimble KJ, Hopper AO, Johnson JO, Ueland K, Sunshine P: Favorable results of neonatal intensive care for very low-birth-weight infants, *Pediatrics* 69:621-625, 1982.

31. Lubchenco LO, Searls DT, Brazie JV: Neonatal mortality rate: relationship to birth weight and gestational age, *J Pediatr* 1972; 81:814-822, 1972.

32. Koops BL, Harmon RJ: Studies on long-term outcome in newborns with birth weights under 1500, *Adv Behav Pediatr* 1:1-28, 1980.

33. Stewart AL: Follow-up studies. In Robertson, NRC, editor: *Textbook of neonatology*, Edinburgh, 1986, Churchill Livingstone.

34. Goldson E: Follow-up of low birth weight infants: a contemporary review. In Wolraich M, Routh DL, editors: *Advances in developmental and behavioral pediatrics*, vol 9, London, 1992, Jessica Kingsley Publishers, pp 159-179.

35. Yu VYH, Hollingsworth E: Improving prognosis for infants weighing 1000 g or less at birth, *Arch Dis Child* 55:422-426, 1979.

36. Rothberg AD, Maisels MJ, Bagnato S, Murphy S, Gifford K, McKinley K, Parlmer EA, Vannucci RC: Outcome for survivors of mechanical ventilation weighing less than 1250 grams at birth, *J Pediatr* 98:106-111, 1981.

37. Ruiz MPD, LeFever JA, Hakanson DO, Clark DA, Williams ML: Early development of infants of birth weight less than 1000 grams with reference to mechanical ventilation in newborn period, *Pediatrics* 68:330-335, 1981.

38. Northway WH, Rosan RC, Porter DY: Pulmonary disease following respiratory therapy of hyaline membrane disease, *N Engl J Med* 276:357-368, 1967.

39. Bennett FC, Robinson NM, Sells CJ: Growth and development of infants weighing less than 800 grams at birth, *Pediatrics* 71:319-323, 1983.

40. Hirata T, Epcar JT, Walsh A, Mednick J, Harris M, McGinnis MS, Sehring S, Papedo G: Survival and outcome of infants 501-750 grams: a six-year experience, *J Pediatr* 102:741-748, 1983.

41. Orgill AA, Astbury J, Bajuk B, Yu VYH: Early neurodevelopmental outcome of very low birthweight infants, *Aust Paediatr J* 18:193-196, 1982.

42. Saigal S, Rosenbaum P, Stoskopf B, Milner R: Follow-up of infants 501 to 1500 gm weight delivered to residents of a geograpahically defined region with perinatal intensive care facilities, *J Pediatr* 100:606-613, 1982.

43. Driscoll JM, Driscoll YT, Steir ME, Stark RI, Dangman BC, Perez A, Wung J-T, Kritz P: Mortality and morbidity in infants less than 1001 grams birth weight, *Pediatrics* 69:21-26, 1982.

44. Kitchen W, Ford G, Orgill A, Rickards A, Astbury J, Lissenden J, Bajuk B, Yu V, Drew J, Campbell N: Outcome of infants with birth weight 500 to 999 gm: a regional study of 1979 and 1980 births, *J Pediatr* 104:921-927, 1984.

45. Lubchenco LO, Butterfield LJ, Delaney-Black V, Goldson E, Koops BL, Lazotte DC: Outcome of very-low-birth-weight infants: does antepartum versus neonatal referral have a better impact on mortality, morbidity, or long-term outcome? *Am J Obstet Gynecol* 160:539-545, 1989.

46. Kitchen WH, Ford GW, Rickards AL, Lissenden JV, Ryan MM: Children of birthweight < 1000 g: changing outcome between ages 2 and 5 years, *J Pediatr* 110:283-288, 1987.

47. Kitchen W, Ford G, Orgill A, Rickards A, Astbury J, Lissenden J, Bajuk B, Yu V, Drew J, Campbell N: Outcome in infants of birth weight 500 to 999 g: a continuing regional study of 5-year-old survivors, *J Pediatr* 111:761-766, 1987.

48. O'Callaghan MJ, Burns Y, Gray P, Harvey JM, Mohay HI, Rogers Y, Tudehope DI: Extremely low birth weight and control infants at 2 years corrected age: a comparison of intellectual abilities, motor performance, growth and health, *Early Hum Dev* 40:115-125, 1995.

49. Herrgård E, Luoma L, Tuppurainen K, Karjalainen S, Martikainen A: Neurodevelopmental profile at five years of children born at ≤ 32 weeks gestation, *Dev Med Child Neurol* 35:1083-1086, 1993.

50. Sostek AM: Prematurity as well as intraventricular hemorrhage influence developmental outcome at 5 years. In Friedman SL, Sigman MD, editors: *The psychological development of low birthweight children,* New Jersey, 1992, Ablex Publishing, pp 259-274.

51. Teplin SW, Burchinal M, Johnson-Martin N, Humphry RA, Kraybill EN: Neurodevelopmental, health, and growth status at 6 age years of children with birth weights less than 1001 grams, *J Pediatr* 118:768-777, 1991.

52. Saigal S, Szatmari P, Rosenbaum P, Campbell D, King S: Cognitive abilities and school performance of extremely low birth weight children and matched term control children at age 8 years: a regional study, *J Pediatr* 118:751-760, 1991.

53. Klein NK, Hack M, Breslau, N: Children who were very low birth weight: development and academic achievement at nine years of age, *Dev Behav Pediatr* 10:32-37, 1989.

54. Halsey CL, Collin MF, Anderson CL: Extremely low birth weight children and their peers: a comparison of preschool performance, *Pediatrics* 91:807-811, 1993.

55. Crowe TK, Deitz JC, Bennett FC, Tekolste K: Preschool motor skills of children born prematurely and not diagnosed as having cerebral palsy, *Dev Behav Pediatr* 9:189-193, 1988.

56. Eilers BL, Desai NS, Wilson MA, Cunningham MD: Classroom performance and social factors of children with birth weights of 1250 grams or less: follow-up at 5 to 8 years of age, *Pediatrics* 77:203-208, 1986.

57. Vohr BR, Garcia Coll CT: Neurodevelopmental and school performance of very low birth weight infants: a seven-year longitudinal study, *Pediatrics* 76:345-350, 1985.

58. Klein N, Hack M, Gallagher J, Fanaroff AA: Preschool performance of children with normal intelligence who were very low-birth-weight infants, *Pediatrics* 75:531-537, 1985.

59. Crowe TK, Deitz JC, Bennett FC, Tekolste K: Preschool motor skills of children born prematurely and not diagnosed as having cerebral palsy, *Dev Behav Pediatr* 9:189-193, 1988.

60. Saigal S, Szatmari P, Rosenbaum P, Campbell D, King S: Cognitive abilities and school performance of extremely low birth weight children and matched term control children at age 8 years: a regional study, *J Pediatr* 118:751-760, 1991.

61. Hack M, Breslau N, Aram D, Weissman B, Klein N, Borawski-Clark E: The effect of very low birth weight and social risk on neurocognitive abilities at school age, *J Dev Behav* 13:412-420, 1992.

62. Hille ETM, Den Ouden A, Bauer L, van den Oudenrijn C, Brand R, Verloove-Vanhoorick SP: School performance at nine years of age in very premature and very low birth weight infants: perinatal risk factors and predictors at five years of age, *J Pediatr* 125:426-434, 1994.

63. Weisglas-Kuperus N, Koot HM, Baerts W, Fetter WPF, Sauer PJJ: Behaviour problems of very low-birthweight children, *Dev Med Child Neurol* 35:406-416, 1993.

64. Goldson E: Severe bronchopulmonary dysplasia in the very low birth weight infant: its relationship to developmental outcome, *Dev Behav Pediatr* 5:165-168, 1984.

65. Meisels SJ, Plunkett JW, Roloff DW, Pasick PL, Stiefel GS: Growth and development of preterm infants with respiratory distress syndrome and bronchopulmonary dysplasia, *Pediatrics* 77:345-352, 1986.

66. Vohr BR, Garcia Coll CT, Lobato D, Yunis KA, O'Dea C, Oh W: Neurodevelopmental and medical status of low-birthweight survivors of bronchopulmonary dysplasia at 10 to 12 years of age, *Dev Med Child Neurol* 33:690-697, 1991.

67. Robertson CMT, Etches RC, Goldson E, Kyle JM: Eight-year school performance, neurodevelopmental, and growth outcome of neonates with bronchopulmonary dysplasia: a comparative study, *Pediatrics* 89:365-672, 1992.

68. Palmer P, Dubowitz LMS, Levene MI, Dubowitz V: Developmental and neurological progress of preterm infants with intraventricular hemorrhage and ventricular dilatation, *Arch Dis Child* 57:748-753, 1982.

69. Papile LS, Burstein J, Burstein R, Koffler H: Incidence and evolution of the subependymal intraventricular hemorrhage: a study of infants with weights less than 1500 grams, *J Pediatr* 92:529-534, 1978.

70. Landry SH, Fletcher JM, Zarling CL, Chapieski L, Francis DJ: Differential outcomes associated with early medical complications in premature infants, *J Pediatr Psychol* 9:385-401, 1984.

71. Landry SH, Fletcher JM, Denson SE: Longitudinal outcome for low birth weight infants: effects of intraventricular hemorrhage and bronchopulmonary dysplasia, *J Clin Exp Neuropsychol* 15:205-218, 1993.

72. Bozynski MEA, Nelson MN, Matalon TAS, O'Donnell KJ, Naughton PM, Vasan U, Meir WA, Ploughman L: Prolonged mechanical ventilation and intracranial hemorrhage: impact on developmental progress through 18 months in infants weighing 1200 grams or less at birth, *Pediatrics* 79:670-676, 1987.

73. Scott DT, Ehrenkranz RA, Warshaw JB: Evidence for late developmental deficit in very low birth weight infants surviving intraventricular hemorrhage, *Child Brain* 11:261-269, 1984.

74. Banker B, Larroche JC: Periventricular leukomalacia of infancy: a form of neonatal anoxic encephalopathy, *Arch Neurol* 7:386-410, 1962.

75. Larroche JC: *Pathology of the neonate*, New York, 1977, Excepta Medica.

76. Fawer CL, Diebold P, Calme A: Periventricular leucomalacia and neurodevelopmental outcome in preterm infants, *Arch Dis Child* 62:30-36, 1987.

77. Nwaesei CG, Allen AC, Vincer MJ, Brown SJ, Stinson DA, Evans JR, Byrne JM: Effect of timing of cerebral ultrasonography on the prediction of later neurodevelopmental outcome in high-risk preterm infants, *J Pediatr* 112:159-162, 1988.

78. Rogers B, Msall M, Owens T, Guernsey K, Brody A, Buck G, Hudak M: Cystic periventricular leukomalacia and type of cerebral palsy in preterm infants, *J Pediatr* 125:51-58, 1994.

79. Bennett FC, Silver G, Leung EJ, Mack LA: Periventricular echodensities detected by cranial ultrasonography: usefulness in predicting neurodevelopmental outcome in low-birthweight preterm infants, *Pediatrics* 85:400-404, 1990.

80. Pharoah POD, Cooke T, Cooke RW, Rosenbloom L: Birthweight specific trends in cerebral palsy, *Arch Dis Child* 65:602-606, 1990.

81. Bhushan V, Paneth N, Kiely JL: Impact of improved survival of very low birth weight infants on recent secular trends in the prevalence of cerebral palsy, *Pediatrics* 91:1094-1111, 1993.

Index